Digital Design

FRANK VAHID
University of California, Riverside

John Wiley & Sons, Inc.

To my family, Amy, Eric, Kelsi, and Maya;
and to those engineers who apply their skills
to build things that improve the human condition.

VP AND EXECUTIVE PUBLISHER	BRUCE SPATZ
ASSOCIATE PUBLISHER	DAN SAYRE
SENIOR ACQUISITIONS EDITOR AND PRODUCT MANAGER	CATHERINE FIELDS SHULTZ
PROJECT EDITOR	GLADYS SOTO
SENIOR EDITORIAL ASSISTANT	DANA KELLOGG
MEDIA EDITOR	STEVEN CHASEY
SENIOR PRODUCTION EDITOR	VALERIE A. VARGAS
MARKETING MANAGER	PHYLLIS CERYS
COVER ILLUSTRATION	MICHAEL JUNG
COVER DESIGNER	MADELYN LESURE
PRODUCTION SERVICES	INGRAO ASSOCIATES

This book is printed on acid free paper.

To order books or for customer service please call 1-800-CALL WILEY (225-5945).

ISBN   978-0-470-04437-7

Printed in the United States of America

10 9 8 7 6 5 4 3 2

Preface

TO STUDENTS ABOUT TO STUDY DIGITAL DESIGN

Digital circuits, which form the basis of general-purpose computers as well as special-purpose devices like cell phones or video game consoles, are dramatically changing the world. Studying digital design not only gives you the confidence that comes with fundamentally understanding how digital circuits work, but also introduces you to an exciting and useful possible career direction. This statement applies regardless of whether your major is Electrical Engineering, Computer Engineering, or even Computer Science (in fact, the need for digital designers with strong computer science skills continues to increase). I hope you find this subject to be as interesting, exciting, and useful as I do.

Throughout this book, I have tried not only to introduce concepts in the most intuitive and easy to learn manner, but I have also tried to show how those concepts can be applied to real-world systems, such as pacemakers, ultrasound machines, printers, automobiles, and cell phones. Young and capable engineering students (including computer science students) sometimes leave their major, claiming they want a job that is more "people oriented." Yet we need those people-oriented students more than ever, as engineering jobs are increasingly people-oriented, in several ways. First, engineers usually work in *tightly-integrated groups* involving numerous other engineers (rather than "sitting alone in front of a computer all day" as many students believe). Second, engineers often work *directly with customers* (such as business people, doctors, lawyers, government officials, etc.), and must therefore be able to connect with those non-engineer customers. Third, and in my opinion most importantly, *engineers build things that dramatically impact people's lives*. Needed are engineers who combine their enthusiasm, creativity, and innovation with their solid engineering skills to conceive and build new products that improve people's quality of life.

I have included "Designer Profiles" at the end of most chapters. The designers, whose experience levels vary from just a year to several decades, and whose companies range from small to huge, share with you their experiences, insights, and advice. You will notice how commonly they discuss the people aspects of their jobs. You may also notice their enthusiasm and passion for their jobs.

TO INSTRUCTORS OF DIGITAL DESIGN

This book breaks from the 1970s/1980s digital design view emphasizing size-limited design, instead emphasizing the 2000s situation of *register-transfer-level (RTL)* design. By cleanly distinguishing the topic of basic design from optimization, two topics previously inseparably intertwined, the book allows a first course on digital design to reach and even emphasize the topic of RTL design. A student exposed to RTL design in a first course will have a more relevant view of the modern digital design field, leading not only to a better appreciation of modern computers and other digital devices, but a more accurate understanding of careers involving digital design. Such an accurate understanding is critical to attract computing majors to careers involving some amount of digital design, and to create a cadre of engineers with the comfort in both "software" and "hardware" necessary in modern embedded computing system design.

The distinguishing of basic design from optimization should not be interpreted as avoiding a bottom-up approach or glossing over important steps — the book takes a concrete bottom-up approach, starting from transistors, and building incrementally up through gates, flip-flops, registers, controllers, datapath components, etc. Rather, the distinguishing enables the student to initially develop a solid understanding of basic design, before considering the more advanced topic of optimization, akin to how a physics book introduces Newton's laws of motion initially assuming frictionless surfaces and no wind resistance. Furthermore, optimization today involves more than just size minimization, instead requiring a broader understanding of tradeoffs among size, performance, and power, and even of tradeoffs among custom digital circuits and microprocessor software. Again, coverage is kept concrete and appropriate to an introductory digital design course.

Nevertheless, the book distinguishes basic design from optimization in a way that cleanly provides an instructor maximum flexibility to introduce optimization at the times and to the extent desired by the instructor. In particular, the optimization chapter's subsections (Chapter 6) each correspond directly to one earlier chapter, such that Section 6.2 can directly follow Chapter 2, Section 6.3 can follow Chapter 3, 6.4 can follow 4, and 6.5 can follow 5.

Several additional features of the book include:

- *Extensive use of applied examples and figures.* After describing a new concept and providing basic examples, the book provides examples that apply the concept to applications recognizable to a student, like a seat belt unfastened warning system, a computerized checkerboard game, a color printer, or a digital video camera. Furthermore, the end of most chapters include a product profile, intended to give students an even broader view of the applicability of the concepts, and to introduce clever application-specific concepts the students may find very interesting — like the idea of beamforming in an ultrasound machine or of filtering in a cellular phone. The book extensively uses figures to illustrate concepts, containing over 600 figures.

- *Learning through discovery.* The book emphasizes understanding the need for new concepts, which not only helps students learn and remember the concepts, but develops reasoning skills that can apply the concepts to other domains. For example, rather than just defining a carry-lookahead adder, the book shows intuitive but inefficient approaches to building a faster adder, eventually solving the inefficiencies and leading to ("discovering") the carry-lookahead design.

- *Introduction to FPGAs.* The book includes a fully bottom-up introduction to FPGAs, showing students concretely how a circuit can be converted into a bitstream that programs the individual lookup tables, switch matrices, and other programmable components in an FPGA. This concrete introduction eliminates the mystery of the increasingly-common FPGA devices.

- *HDL coverage flexibility.* The book's organization cleanly allows instructors to cover HDLs (hardware description languages) intermixed with the introduction of design concepts, to cover HDLs later, or to not cover HDLs at all. The HDL chapter's subsections (Chapter 9) each correspond to an earlier chapter, such that Section 9.2 can directly follow Chapter 2, 9.3 can follow 3, 9.4 can follow 4, and 9.5 can follow 5. Furthermore, rather than the book choosing just one of the popular languages — VHDL, Verilog, and the relatively new SystemC — the book provides equal coverage of all three of those HDLs. And, we use our extensive experience in synthesis with commercial tools to create HDL descriptions well-suited for synthesis, in addition to being suitable for simulation.

- *Accompanying HDL-introduction books.* Instructors wishing to cover HDLs to an even greater extent can utilize one of our HDL-introduction books specifically designed to accompany this textbook, written by the same author as this textbook. Our HDL-introduction books follow the same chapter structure as, and use examples from, this textbook, eliminating the common situation of students struggling to correlate their distinct, and sometimes contradicting, HDL book and digital design book subjects. Our HDL-introduction books discuss language, simulation, and testing concepts in more depth, providing numerous HDL examples, and are also designed to be usable by themselves for HDL learning or reference. The books emphasize use of the language for real design, clearly distinguishing HDL use for synthesis from HDL use for testing, and include extensive examples and figures throughout to illustrate concepts. Our HDL-introduction books come with complete PowerPoint slides that use graphics and animations to serve as an easy-to-use tutorial on the HDL.

- *Author-created graphical animated PowerPoint slides.* A rich set of PowerPoint slides are available to instructors. The slides were created by the textbook's author, resulting in consistency of perspective and emphasis between the slides and this book. The slides are designed to be a truly effective teaching tool for the instructor. Most slides are graphics based (avoiding slides consisting of just bulleted lists of text). The slides make extensive us of animation where appropriate to gradually unveil concepts or build-up circuits, yet even animated slides can be printout out and understood. Nearly every figure, concept, and example from this book is included in the set of almost 500 slides, from which instructors can choose.

- *Complete solutions manual.* Instructors may obtain a complete solutions manual (about 200 pages) containing solutions to every end-of-chapter exercise in this book. The manual extensively utilizes figures to illustrate solutions.

- *WileyPLUS website.* Digital Design is supported by WileyPLUS — a powerful and highly integrated suite of teaching and learning resources designed to bridge the gap between what happens in the classroom and what happens at home. WileyPLUS includes a complete online version of the text, algorithmically generated problems and guided online exercises. Additional assets include video solutions of selected examples, animations of pertinent concepts (both prepared by Professor Ed Doering of Rose-Hulman Institute), complete solutions manual and author-created animated PowerPoints, plus course and homework management tools, in one easy-to-use website.

To learn how to access these features, go to the Book Companion Site at www.wiley.com/college/vahid, or www.ddvahid.com.

HOW TO USE THIS BOOK

This book was designed to allow flexibility to choose among the most common approaches to material coverage. We describe several approaches below.

RTL-focused approach

An RTL-focused approach would simply cover the first 6 chapters in order:

1. Introduction (Chapter 1)
2. Combinational logic design (Chapter 2)
3. Sequential logic design (Chapter 3)
4. Combinational and sequential component design (Chapter 4)
5. RTL design (Chapter 5)
6. Optimizations and Tradeoffs (Chapter 6), to the extent desired
7. Physical implementation (Chapter 7) and/or Processor design (Chapter 8), to the extent desired.

We think this is a great way to order the material, resulting in students doing interesting RTL designs in about 7 weeks. HDLs can be introduced at the end if time permits, or left for a second course on digital design (as done at UCR), or covered immediately after each chapter — all three approaches appear to be quite common.

Traditional approach with some reordering

This book can be readily used in a traditional approach that introduces optimization along with basic design, with a slight difference from the traditional approach being the swapping of coverage of combinational components and sequential logic, as follows:

1. Introduction (Chapter 1)
2. Combinational logic design (Chapter 2) followed by combinational logic optimization (Section 6.2)
3. Sequential logic design (Chapter 3) followed by sequential logic optimization (Section 6.3)
4. Combinational and sequential component design (Chapter 4) followed by component tradeoffs (Section 6.4)
5. RTL design (Chapter 5) to the extent desired, followed by RTL optimization/ tradeoffs (Section 6.5)
6. Physical implementation (Chapter 7) and/or Processor design (Chapter 8), to the extent desired.

This is a very reasonable and effective approach, completing all discussion of one topic (e.g., FSM design as well as optimization) before moving on to the next topic. The reordering from a traditional approach introduces basic sequential design (FSMs and controllers) before combinational components (e.g., adders, comparators, etc.). Such reordering may lead into RTL design more naturally than a traditional approach, following instead an approach of increasing abstraction rather than the traditional approach that separates combinational and sequential design. HDLs can again be introduced at the end, left for another course, or integrated after each chapter. This approach could also be used as an intermediary step when migrating from a fully-traditional approach to an RTL approach. Migrating might involve gradually postponing the Chapter 6 sections — for example, covering Chapters 2 and 3, and then Sections 6.2 and 6.3, before moving on to Chapter 4.

Completely traditional approach

This book could also be used in a completely traditional approach, as follows:

1. Introduction (Chapter 1)
2. Combinational logic design (Chapter 2) followed by combinational logic optimization (Section 6.2)
3. Combinational component design (Sections 4.1, 4.3, 4.4, 4.5, 4.7, 4.8, 4.9) followed by combinational component tradeoffs (Section 6.4 — Adders)
4. Sequential logic design (Chapter 3) followed by sequential logic optimization (Section 6.3)
5. Sequential component design (Chapter 4, Sections 4.2, 4.6, 4.10) followed by sequential component tradeoffs (Section 6.4 — Multipliers)
6. RTL design (Chapter 5) to the extent desired, followed by RTL optimization/tradeoffs (Section 6.5)
7. Physical implementation (Chapter 7) and/or Processor design (Chapter 8), to the extent desired.

This is the most widespread approach during the past two decades, with the addition of RTL towards the end. Although the emphasized distinction between combinational and sequential design may no longer be relevant in the era of RTL design (where both types of design are intermixed), some people believe that such distinction makes for an easier learning path, which may be true. HDLs can be included at the end, left for a later course, or integrated throughout.

ACKNOWLEDGEMENTS

Many people and organizations contributed to this edition of the book.

- Staff members at John Wiley and Sons Publishers have extensively supported the book's development, including Catherine Shultz, Gladys Soto, Dana Kellogg, and Kelly Boyle. Bill Zobrist supported my earlier "Embedded System Design" book, motivated me to write the present book, and provided great advice throughout development.

- Ryan Mannion contributed many items, including the appendices, numerous examples and exercises, several subsections, the complete exercise solutions manual, fact-checking, extensive proofreading, tremendous assistance during production, help with the slides, plenty of ideas during discussions, and much more.

- Roman Lysecky developed numerous examples and exercises, contributed most of the content of the HDL chapter, and co-authored our accompanying HDL-introduction books. Roman and Susan Lysecky provided much proofreading assistance.

- Numerous reviewers provided outstanding feedback on various versions of the book. Special thanks go to early adopters, such as Nikil Dutt, Shannon Tauro, J. David Gillanders, Sheldon Tan, Travis Doom, Roman Lysecky, and others, who provided excellent feedback from themselves and from their students.

- The importance of the support provided to my research and teaching career by the National Science Foundation cannot be overstated. Additional support from the Semiconductor Research Corporation catalyzed industry collaborations that in turn influenced many of the perspectives in this book.

ABOUT THE COVER

The cover's image of shrinking squares graphically depicts the amazing real-life phenomena of digital circuits ('computer chips') shrinking in size by one half roughly every 18 months, for several decades now, a phenomena often referred to as Moore's Law. Such shrinking has enabled incredibly powerful computing circuits to fit in tiny devices, like modern cell phones, medical devices, and portable video games. See pages 34 and 35 for a discussion of Moore's Law.

ABOUT THE AUTHOR

Frank Vahid is a Professor of Computer Science & Engineering at the University of California, Riverside. He holds Electrical Engineering and Computer Science degrees; has worked/consulted for Hewlett Packard, AMCC, NEC, Motorola, and medical equipment makers; holds 3 U.S. patents; has received several teaching awards; helped setup UCR's Computer Engineering program; has authored two previous textbooks; and has published over 120 papers on digital design topics (automation, architecture, and low-power).

Reviewers and Evaluators

Rehab Abdel-Kader	Georgia Southern University
Otmane Ait Mohamed	Concordia University
Hussain Al-Asaad	University of California, Davis
Rocio Alba-Flores	University of Minnesota, Duluth
Bassem Alhalabi	Florida Atlantic University
Zekeriya Aliyazicioglu	California Polytechnic State University, Pomona
Vishal Anand	SUNY Brockport
Bevan Baas	University of California, Davis
Noni Bohonak	University of South Carolina, Lancaster
Don Bouldin	University of Tennessee
David Bourner	University of Maryland Baltimore County
Elaheh Bozorgzadeh	University of California, Irvine
Frank Candocia	Florida International University
Ralph Carestia	Oregon Institute of Technology
Rajan M. Chandra	California Polytechnic State University, Pomona
Ghulam Chaudhry	University of Missouri, Kansas City
Michael Chelian	California State University, Long Beach
Russell Clark	Saginaw Valley State University
James Conrad	University of North Carolina, Charlotte
Kevan Croteau	Francis Marion University
Sanjoy Das	Kansas State University
James Davis	University of South Carolina
Edward Doering	Rose-Hulman Institute of Technology
Travis Doom	Wright State University
Jim Duckworth	Worcester Polytechnic Institute
Nikil Dutt	University of California, Irvine
Dennis Fairclough	Utah Valley State College
Paul D. Franzon	North Carolina State University
Subra Ganesan	Oakland University
Zane Gastineau	Harding University
J. David Gillanders	Arkansas State University
Clay Gloster	Howard University
Ardian Greca	Georgia Southern University
Eric Hansen	Dartmouth College
Bruce A. Harvey	FAMU-FSU College of Engineering
John P. Hayes	University of Michigan
Michael Helm	Texas Tech University
William Hoff	Colorado School of Mines
Erh-Wen Hu	William Paterson University of New Jersey
Baback Izadi	SUNY New Paltz

Jeff Jackson	University of Alabama
Anura Jayasumana	Colorado State University
Bruce Johnson	University of Nevada, Reno
Richard Johnston	Lawrence Technological University
Rajiv Kapadia	Minnesota State University, Mankato
Bahadir Karuv	Fairleigh Dickinson University
Robert Klenke	Virginia Commonwealth University
Clint Kohl	Cedarville University
Hermann Krompholz	Texas Tech University
Timothy Kurzweg	Drexel University
Jumoke Ladeji-Osias	Morgan State University
Jeffrey Lillie	Rochester Institute of Technology
David Livingston	Virginia Military Institute
Hong Man	Stevens Institute of Technology
Gihan Mandour	Christopher Newport University
Diana Marculescu	Carnegie Mellon University
Miguel Marin	McGill University
Maryam Moussavi	California State University, Long Beach
Olfa Nasraoui	University of Memphis
Patricia Nava	University of Texas, El Paso
John Nestor	Lafayette College
Rogelio Palomera	Garcia University of Puerto Rico, Mayaguez
James Peckol	University of Washington
Witold Pedrycz	University of Alberta
Andrew Perry	Springfield College
Denis Popel	Baker University
Tariq Qayyum	California Polytechnic State University, Pomona
Gang Qu	University of Maryland
Mihaela Radu	Rose-Hulman Institute of Technology
Suresh Rai	Louisiana State University, Baton Rouge
William Reid	Clemson University
Musoke Sendaula	Temple University
Scott Smith	Boise State University
Gary Spivey	George Fox University
Larry Stephens	University of South Carolina
James Stine	Illinois Institute of Technology
Philip Swain	Purdue University
Shannon Tauro	University of California, Irvine
Carlos Tavora	Gonzaga University
Marc Timmerman	Oregon Institute of Technology
Hariharan Vijayaraghavan	University of Kansas
Bin Wang	Wright State University
M. Chris Wernicki	New York Institute of Technology
Shanchieh Yang	Rochester Institute of Technology
Henry Yeh	California State University, Long Beach
Naeem Zaman	San Jaoquin Delta College

Contents

CHAPTER 1

Introduction

▶ 1.1 DIGITAL SYSTEMS IN THE WORLD AROUND US

Meet Arianna. Arianna is a five-year-old girl who lives in California. She's a cheerful, outgoing kid who loves to read, play soccer, dance, and tell jokes that she makes up herself.

One day, Arianna's family was driving home from a soccer game. She was in the middle of excitedly talking about the game when suddenly the van in which she was riding was clipped by a car that had crossed over to the wrong side of the highway. Although the accident wasn't particularly bad, the impact caused a loose item from the rear of the van to project forward inside the van, striking Arianna in the back of the head. She went unconscious.

Arianna was rushed to a hospital. Doctors immediately noticed that her breathing was very weak—a common situation after a severe blow to the head—so they put her onto a ventilator, which is a medical device that assists with breathing. She had sustained brain trauma during the blow to the head, and she remained unconscious for several weeks. All her vital signs were stable, except she continued to require breathing assistance from the ventilator. Patients in such a situation sometimes recover, and sometimes they don't. When they do recover, sometimes that recovery takes many months.

Thanks to the advent of modern portable ventilators, Arianna's parents were given the option of taking her home while they hoped for her recovery, an option they chose. In addition to the remote monitoring of vital signs and the daily at-home visits by a nurse and respiratory therapist, Arianna was surrounded by her parents, brother, sister, cousins, other family, and friends. For the majority of the day, someone was holding her hand, singing to her, whispering in her ear, and encouraging her to recover. Her sister slept nearby. Some studies show that such human interaction can indeed increase the chances of recovery.

And recover she did. One day, several months later, with Arianna's mom sitting at her side, Arianna opened her eyes. Later that day, she was transported back to the hospital. After some time, she was weaned from the ventilator. Then, after a lengthy time of recovery and rehabilitation, Arianna finally went home. Today, six-year-old Arianna shows few signs of the accident that nearly took her life.

What does this story have to do with digital design? Arianna's recovery was aided by a portable ventilator device, which in turn is possible thanks to digital circuits. Over the past three decades, the amount of digital circuitry that can be stored on a single computer chip has increased dramatically—by nearly 100,000 times, believe it or not. Thus, ventilators, along with almost everything else that runs on electricity, can take advantage of incredibly powerful and fast yet inexpensive digital circuits. The ventilator in Arianna's case was the Pulmonetics LTV 1000 ventilator. Whereas a ventilator of the early 1990s might have been the size of a large copy machine and cost perhaps $100,000, the LTV 1000 is not much bigger or heavier than this textbook and costs only a few thousand dollars—small enough, and inexpensive enough, to be carried in medical rescue helicopters and ambulances for life-saving situations, and even to be sent home with a patient. The digital circuits inside continually monitor the patient's breathing, and provide just the right amount of air pressure and volume to the patient. *Every breath* that the device delivers requires *millions* of computations for proper delivery, computations carried out by the digital circuits inside.

Portable ventilator

Photo courtesy of Pulmonetics

Photo courtesy of Pulmonetics

Portable ventilators help not only trauma victims, but even more commonly help patients with debilitating diseases, like multiple sclerosis, to gain mobility. Such people can today move about in a wheelchair, and hence do things like attend school, visit museums, and take part in a family picnic, experiencing a far better quality of life than was feasible just a decade ago when those people would have been confined to a bed connected to a large, heavy, expensive ventilator. For example, the young girl pictured on the left will likely require a ventilator for the rest of her life—but she will be able to move about in her wheelchair quite freely, rather than being mostly confined to her home.

The LTV 1000 ventilator described above was conceived and designed by a small group of people, pictured on the left, who sought to build a portable and reliable ventilator in order to help people like Arianna and thousands of others like her (as well as to make some good money doing so!). Those designers probably started off like you, reading textbooks and taking courses on digital design, programming, electronics, and/or other subjects.

The ventilator is just one of literally *thousands* of useful devices that have come about and continue to be created thanks to the era of digital circuits. If you stop and think about how many devices in the world around you rely on or are made possible because of digital circuits, you may be quite surprised. A few such devices include:

Antilock brakes, airbags, autofocus cameras, automatic teller machines, aircraft controllers and navigators, camcorders, cash registers, cell phones, computer networks, credit card readers, cruise controllers, defibrillators, digital cameras, DVD players, electric card readers, electronic games, electronic pianos, fax machines, fingerprint identifiers, hearing aids, home security systems, modems, pacemakers, pagers, personal computers, personal digital assistants, photocopiers, portable music players, robotic arms, scanners, televisions, thermostat controllers, TV set-top boxes, ventilators, video game consoles—the list goes on.

One indicator of the rate that new inventions are developed is the number of new patents granted— 170,000 per year in the U.S. alone!

Those devices were created by tens of thousands of designers, including computer scientists, computer engineers, electrical engineers, mechanical engineers, and others, working together with scientists, doctors, business people, teachers, etc. One thing that seems clear is that new devices will continue to be invented for the foreseeable future— devices that in another decade will be hundreds of times smaller, cheaper, and more powerful than today's devices, enabling new applications that today we don't even dream of. Already, we are seeing amazing new applications that seem futuristic even though they exist today, like tiny digital-circuit-controlled medicine dispensers implanted under the skin, voice-controlled cell phones and appliances, robotic self-guiding household vacuum cleaners, laser-guided automobile cruise control, and more. What's not clear is what new and exciting applications will be developed in the future, or who those devices will benefit. Future designers, like yourself perhaps, will help determine that.

▶ 1.2 THE WORLD OF DIGITAL SYSTEMS

Digital versus Analog

A *digital* signal is a signal that at any time can have one of a finite set of possible values, and is also known as a discrete signal. In contrast, an *analog* signal can have one of an infinite number of possible values, and is also known as a continuous signal. A signal is just some physical phenomena that has a unique value at every instant of time. An everyday example of an analog signal is the temperature outside, because physical temperature is a continuous value—the temperature may be 92.356666... degrees. An everyday example of a digital signal is the number of fingers you hold up, because the value must be either 0, 1, 2, 3, 4, 5, 6, 7, 8, 9, or 10—a finite set of values. In fact, the term "digital" comes from the Latin word for "digit" (digitus), meaning finger.

In computing systems, the most common digital signals are those that can have one of only two possible values, like on or off (often represented as 1 or 0). Such a two-valued representation is known as a *binary* representation. A *digital system* is a system that takes digital inputs and generates digital outputs. A *digital circuit* is a connection of digital components that together comprise a digital system. In this textbook, the term digital will refer to systems with binary-valued signals. A single binary signal is known as a binary digit, or *bit* for short (*bi*nary dig*it*). Digital electronics became extremely popular in the mid-1900s after the invention of the transistor, an electric switch that can be turned on or off using another electric signal. We'll describe transistors further in the next chapter.

A general-purpose computer

Digital circuits are the basis for computers

The most well-known use of digital circuits in the world around us is probably to build the microprocessors that serve as the brain of general-purpose computers, like the personal computer or laptop computer that you might have at home. General-purpose computers are also used as servers, which operate behind the scenes to implement banking, airline reservation, web search, payroll, and similar such systems. General-purpose computers take digital input data, such as letters and numbers received from files or keyboards, and output new digital data, such as new letters and numbers stored in files or displayed on a monitor. Learning about digital design is therefore useful in understanding how computers work "under the hood," and hence has been required learning for most computing and electrical engineering majors for decades. Based on material in upcoming chapters, we'll design a simple computer in Chapter 8.

Embedded systems

Digital circuits are the basis for much more

Increasingly, digital circuits are being used for much more than implementing general-purpose computers. More and more new applications convert analog signals to digital ones, and run those digital signals through customized digital circuits, to achieve numerous benefits. Such applications include cell phones, automobile engine controllers, TV set-top boxes, music instruments, digital cameras and camcorders, video game consoles, and so on. Digital circuits found inside applications other than general-purpose computers are often called *embedded systems*, because those digital systems are embedded inside another electronic device.

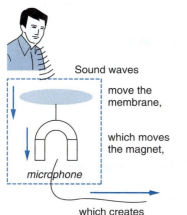

Sound waves

move the membrane,

which moves the magnet,

microphone

which creates current in the nearby wire

The world is mostly analog, and therefore many applications were previously implemented with analog circuits. But many implementations have changed or are changing over to digital implementations. To understand why, we might first notice that although the world is mostly analog, humans often obtain advantages when converting analog signals to digital signals before "processing" that information. For example, a car horn is actually an analog signal—the volume can take on infinite possible values, and the volume varies over time due to variations in the battery strength, temperature, etc. But, we humans neglect those variations, and we "digitize" the sound we hear into one of two values: the car horn is "off," or the car horn is "on" (get out of the way!).

Converting analog phenomena to digital, for use with digital circuits, can also yield many advantages. Let's illustrate this point by considering one example, audio recording, in some detail. Audio is clearly an analog signal, with infinite possible frequencies and volumes. Consider recording an audio signal, like music, through a microphone, so that the music can later be played over speakers in an electronic stereo system. One type of microphone, a dynamic microphone, works based on a principle of electromagnetism—moving a magnet near a wire causes changing current (and hence voltage) in a nearby wire. The more the magnet moves, the higher the voltage on the wire. So a microphone has a small membrane attached to a magnet near a wire—when sound hits the membrane, the magnet moves, causing current in the wire. Likewise, a speaker works on the same principle in reverse—a changing current in a wire will cause a nearby magnet to move, which if attached to a membrane will create sound. (If you get a chance, open up an old speaker—you'll find a strong magnet inside.) If the microphone is attached directly to the speaker (through an amplifier that strengthens the microphone's output current), then no digitization is required. But what if we want to save the sound on some sort of media, so we can record a song now and play the song back later? We can record sound using analog methods or digital methods, but digital methods have many advantages.

One advantage of digital methods is lack of deterioration in quality over time. When I was growing up, the audio cassette tape, an analog method, was the most common method for recording songs. Audio tape contains huge numbers of magnetic particles that can be moved to particular orientations using a magnet and that hold that orientation even after the magnet is removed. Thus, using magnetism, we could change the tape's surface, some parts up, some higher, some down, etc. This is similar to how you can spike your hair, some up, some sideways, some down, using hair gel. The possible orientations of the tape's particles, and your hair, are infinite, so the tape is definitely analog. To record onto a tape, we pass the tape under a "head" that generates a magnetic field based on the electric current over the wire coming from a microphone. The tape's particles would thus be moved to particular orientations. To play a recorded song back, we would pass the tape under the head again, but this time the head operates in reverse, generating current over a wire based on the changing magnetic field of the tape, and that current then gets amplified and sent to the speakers.

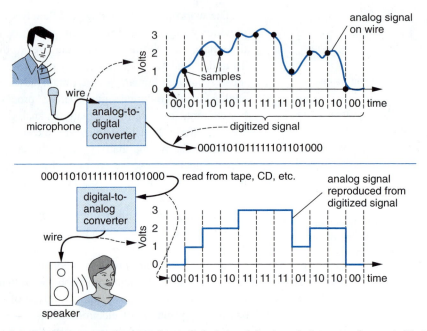

Figure 1.1 Converting an analog signal to a digital signal (top), and vice versa (bottom). Notice some quality loss in the reproduced signal.

A problem with audio tape is that the orientations of the particles on the tape's surface change over time—just like a spiked hairdo in the morning eventually flattens out throughout the day. Thus, audio tape quality deteriorates over time. Such deterioration is a problem with many analog systems.

Digitizing the audio can reduce such deterioration. Digitized audio works as shown in Figure 1.1. The figure shows an analog signal on a wire during a period of time. We *sample* that signal at particular time intervals, shown by the dashed lines. Assuming the analog signal can range from 0 Volts to 3 Volts, and that we plan to store each sample using two bits, then we must round each sample to the nearest Volt (0, 1, 2, or 3), shown as points in the figure. We can store 0 Volts as the two bits 00, 1 Volt as the two bits 01, 2 Volts as the two bits 10, and 3 Volts as the two bits 11. Thus, we would convert the shown analog signal into the following digital signal: 0001101011111101101000.

To record this digital signal, we just need to store 0s and 1s on the recording media. We could use regular audio tape, using a short beep to represent a 1 and no beep to represent a 0, for example. While the audio signal on the tape will deteriorate over time, we can still certainly tell the difference between a beep and no beep, just like we can tell the difference between a car horn being on or off. A slightly quieter beep is still a beep. You've likely heard digitized data communicated using a manner similar to such beeps when you've picked up a phone being used by a computer modem or a fax machine. Even better than audio tape, we can record the digital signal using a media specifically designed to store 0s and 1s. For example, the surface of a CD (compact disk) can be configured to either reflect a laser beam to a sensor strongly or weakly, thus storing 1s and 0s easily. Likewise, computer hard disks in computers use magnetic particle orientation to store 0s and 1s, making such disks similar to audio tape, but enabling faster access to random parts of the disk since the head can move sideways across the top of the spinning disk.

To play back this digitized audio signal, we can simply convert the digital value of each sampling period to an analog signal, as shown at the bottom of Figure 1.1. Notice that the reproduced signal is not an exact replica of the original analog signal. However, the faster we sample the analog signal and the more bits we use for each sample, the closer the reproduced analog signal derived from the digitized signal will be to the original analog signal—at some point, humans can't notice the difference between a pure audio signal and one that has been digitized and then converted back to analog.

Another advantage of digitized audio is compression. Suppose that we'll be storing each sample with ten bits, instead of two bits like above, to achieve much better quality due to less rounding. But that's a lot more bits for the same audio—the signal in Figure 1.1 has eleven samples, and at ten bits per sample, that yields one hundred ten bits to store the audio. If we sample hundreds or thousands of times a second, we end up with huge numbers of bits. Suppose, though, that a particular audio recording has many samples that have the value 0000000000 and the value 1111111111. We could compress the digital file by using the following trick: if the first bit of a sample is 0, the next bit being 0 means the sample is actually supposed to be expanded to 0000000000; the next bit being 1 means the sample is 1111111111. So 00 is shorthand for 0000000000, and 01 is shorthand for 1111111111. If the first bit of a sample is 1, then the next ten bits represent the actual sample. So the digitized signal "0000000000 0000000000 0000001111 1111111111" would be compressed to "00 00 10000001111 01." The receiver, which must know the compression scheme, would decompress that signal into the original digitized signal. There are many other tricks that can be used to compress digitized audio. Perhaps the mostly widely known audio compression scheme is known as *MP3*, which is popular for compressing digitized songs. A typical song might require many tens of megabytes uncompressed, but compressed usually only requires about 3 or 4 megabytes. An audio CD can store about 20 songs uncompressed, but about 200 songs compressed. Thanks to compression (combined with higher-capacity disks), today's portable music players can store thousands of songs—a capability undreamt of by most people in the 1990s.

Digitized audio is widely used not only in music recording, but also in voice communications. For example, digital cellular telephones digitize your voice and then compress the digital signal before transmitting the signal, enabling far more cell phones to operate in a particular region than possible using analog cell phones.

	Satellites		DVD players		Video recorders		Musical instruments
Portable music players		Cell phones		Cameras		TVs	???
1995	1997	1999	2001	2003	2005	2007	

Figure 1.2 More and more analog products are becoming primarily digital.

Pictures and video can be digitized in a manner similar to that described for audio. Digital cameras, for example, store pictures in highly-compressed digital form, and digital video recorders store video onto tapes or disks in compressed form too.

Digitized audio, pictures, and video are just a few of the hundreds of new and future applications that benefit from digitization of analog phenomena. As shown in Figure 1.2, over the past decade, numerous popular products, previously based on analog technology, have converted primarily to digital technology. Portable music players, for example, switched from cassette tapes to CDs in the middle 1990s, and recently to MP3s and other digital formats. Early cell phones used analog communication, but in the late 1990s digital communication, similar in idea to that shown in Figure 1.1, became dominant. In the early 2000s, analog VHS video players gave way to digital DVD players. Video recorders have begun to digitize video before storing the video onto tape, while cameras have eliminated film entirely and instead store photos using digital cards. Musical instruments are increasingly digital-based, with electronic drums and keyboards increasing in popularity, and electric guitars with digital processing appearing recently. Analog TV is also giving way to digital TV. Hundreds of other devices have converted from analog to digital in past decades, such as clocks and watches, household thermostats, human temperature thermometers (which now work in the ear rather than under the tongue or other places), car engine controllers, gasoline pumps, hearing aids, and so on.

Many devices were never analog, instead being introduced in digital form from the very start. For example, video games have been digital since their inception.

Digitization requires that we encode things into 1s and 0s. Computations using digital circuits require that we represent numbers using 1s and 0s. We introduce these aspects of digital circuits now.

▶ THE TELEPHONE.

The telephone, patented by Alexander Graham Bell in the late 1800s (though invented by Antonio Meucci), operates using the electromagnetic principle described earlier—your speech creates sound waves that move a membrane, which moves a magnet, which creates current on a nearby wire. Run that wire to somewhere far away, put a magnet connected to a membrane near that wire, and the membrane will move, producing sound waves that sound like you talking. Much of the telephone system today digitizes the audio to improve quality and quantity of audio transmissions over long distances. A couple of interesting facts about the telephone:
- Believe it or not, Western Union actually turned down Bell's initial proposal to develop the telephone, perhaps thinking that the then-popular telegraph was all people needed.

- Bell and his assistant Watson disagreed on how to answer the phone: Watson wanted "Hello," which won, but Bell wanted "Hoy hoy" instead. (Fans of the TV show "The Simpsons" may have noticed that Homer's boss, Mr. Burns, answers the phone with a "hoy hoy.")

An early-style telephone.

(Source of some of the above material: www.pbs.org, transcript of "The Telephone").

Digital Encodings and Binary Numbers

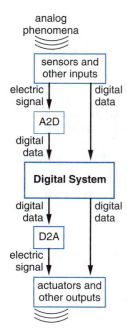

Figure 1.3 A typical digital system.

The previous section showed an example of a digital system, which involved digitizing an audio signal into bits, which we could then process using a digital circuit to achieve several benefits. Those bits *encoded* the data of interest. Encoding data into bits is a central task in digital systems. Some of the data we want to process may already be in digital form, while other data may be in analog form (e.g. audio, video, temperature) and thus require conversion to digital data first, as illustrated at the top of Figure 1.3. A digital system takes digital data as input, and produces digital data as output.

Encoding analog phenomena

Any analog phenomena can be digitized, and hence countless applications have evolved and continue to evolve that digitize analog phenomena. Automobiles digitize information about the engine temperature, car speed, fuel level, etc., so that an on-chip computer can monitor and control the vehicle. The ventilator we introduced earlier digitizes the measure of the air flow into the patient, so that a computer can make calculations on how much additional flow to provide. And so on. Digitizing analog phenomena requires:

* A *sensor* that measures the analog physical phenomena and converts the measured value to an analog electrical signal. One example is the microphone (which measures sound) in Figure 1.1. Other common examples include video capture devices (which measure light), thermometers (which measures temperature), and speedometers (which measure speed).

* An *analog-to-digital converter* that converts the electrical signal into binary encodings. The converter must sample (measure) the electrical signal at a particular rate and convert each sample to some value of bits. Such a converter was featured in Figure 1.1, and shown as the *A2D* component in Figure 1.3.

Likewise, a *digital-to-analog converter* (shown as *D2A* in Figure 1.3) converts bits back to an electrical signal, and an *actuator* converts that electrical signal back to physical phenomena. Sensors and actuators together represent types of devices known as *transducers*—devices that convert one form of energy to another.

In many examples throughout this book, we will utilize idealized sensors that themselves directly output digitized data. For example, we might utilize a temperature sensor that reads the present temperature and sets its 8-bit output to an encoding that represents the temperature as a binary number (see next sections for binary number encodings).

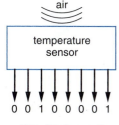

Encoding digital phenomena

Other phenomena are inherently digital. Such phenomena can only assume one value from a finite set of values.

Some digital phenomena can assume only one of two possible values, and thus can be straightforwardly encoded as a single bit. For example, the following types of sensors may output an electrical signal that assumes one of two values:

* Motion sensor: outputs a positive voltage (say +3 V) when motion is sensed, 0 volts when no motion is sensed.

- Light sensor: outputs a positive voltage when light is sensed, 0 V when dark.
- Button (sensor): outputs a positive voltage when the button is pressed, 0 V when not pressed.

We can straightforwardly encode each sensor's output to a bit, with 1 representing the positive voltage and 0 representing 0 V. In examples throughout this book, we will utilize idealized sensors that directly output the encoded bit value.

Other digital phenomena can assume several possible values. For example, a keypad may have four buttons, colored red, blue, green, and black. A designer might create a circuit such that when red is pressed, a three-bit output has the value 001; blue might output 010, green 011, and black 100. If no button is pressed, the output might be 000. Figure 1.4 illustrates such a keypad.

An even more general digital phenomena is the English alphabet. Each character comes from a finite set of characters, so typing on a keyboard results in digital, not analog, data. We can convert the digital data to bits by assigning a bit encoding to each character. A popular encoding of English characters is known as ASCII (standing for American Standard Code for Information Interchange), which encodes each character into seven bits. For example, the ASCII encoding for the uppercase letter 'A' is "1000001," and for 'B' is "1000010." A lowercase 'a' is "1100001," and 'b' is "1100010." Thus, the name "ABBA" would be encoded as "1000001 1000010 1000010 1000001." ASCII defines 7-bit encodings for all 26 letters (upper- and lowercase), the numerical symbols 0 through 9, punctuation marks, and even a number of encodings for nonprintable "control" operations. There are 128 encodings total in ASCII. A subset of ASCII encodings is shown in Figure 1.5. Another encoding, Unicode, is increasing in popularity due to its support of international languages. Unicode uses 16 bits per character, instead of just the 7 bits used in ASCII, and represents characters from a diversity of languages in the world.

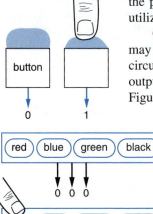

Figure 1.4 Keypad encodings.

Symbol	Encoding	Symbol	Encoding
R	1010010	r	1110010
S	1010011	s	1110011
T	1010100	t	1110100
L	1001100	l	1101100
N	1001110	n	1101110
E	1000101	e	1100101
0	0110000	9	0111001
.	0101110	!	0100001
<tab>	0001001	<space>	0100000

Figure 1.5 Sample ASCII encodings.

Encoding numbers

Perhaps the most important use of digital circuits is to perform arithmetic computations. In fact, a key driver of early digital computer design was the arithmetic computations of ballistic trajectories in World War II. To perform arithmetic computations, we need a way to represent numbers using binary digits—we need binary numbers.

> ► **WHY BASE TEN?**
>
> Humans have ten fingers, so they chose a numbering system where each digit can represent ten possible values. There's nothing magical about base ten. If humans had nine fingers, we'd probably use a base nine numbering system. It turns out that base twelve was used somewhat in the past too, because by using our thumb, we can easily point to twelve different spots on the remaining four fingers on that thumbs's
>
> hand—the four tops of those fingers, the four middle parts of those fingers, and the four bottoms of those fingers. That's likely why the number twelve is common in human counting today, like the use of the term "dozen," and the twelve hours of a clock.
>
> (Source: "Ideas and Information," Arno Penzias, W.W. Norton and Company).

$$\overline{} \quad \overline{} \quad \overline{5}_{10^2} \quad \overline{2}_{10^1} \quad \overline{3}_{10^0}$$

Figure 1.6 Base ten number system.

To understand binary numbers, we might first ensure that we understand decimal numbers. Decimal numbers use a base ten numbering system. The basic definition of base ten is a numbering system where the rightmost digit represents the number of ones (10^0) we have, the next digit represents the number of groups of tens (10^1) we have, the next digit represents the number of groups of ten tens (10^2) we have, and so on, as illustrated in Figure 1.6. So the digits "523" in base 10 represent $5*10^2 + 2*10^1 + 3*10^0$.

*The Web search engine **Google's** name comes from the word "googol" —a 1 followed by 100 zeroes, apparently implying the engine can search a lot of information.*

Because humans have ten fingers, they developed and used a base ten numbering system. They came up with symbols to represent quantities ranging from no fingers (0) to all the fingers but one (9)—these are called "ones" rather than "fingers" though, because we aren't always counting fingers. To represent a larger quantity than nine ones, humans introduced another digit to represent the number of groups of all the fingers, called "ten." Note that we don't need a unique symbol for the quantity ten itself, since that quantity can be represented as one group of ten and no ones. To represent more than nine tens, humans introduced yet another digit, to represent the number of groups of ten tens, which are called "hundreds." To represent ten hundreds, they introduced another digit, called "thousands." English (as spoken in America) doesn't have a name for a group representing ten thousands, nor for the group representing ten ten thousands, which is referred to as hundred thousands. The next group is called millions, and further groups that are multiples of one thousand have names too (billions, trillions, quadrillions, etc.).

$$\overline{} \quad \overline{} \quad \overline{1}_{2^2} \quad \overline{0}_{2^1} \quad \overline{1}_{2^0}$$

Figure 1.7 Base two number system.

Now that we better understand base ten numbers, we can introduce base two numbers, known as **binary numbers**. Since digital circuits work with values that are either "on" or "off," such circuits need only two symbols, rather than ten symbols. Let those two symbols be 0 and 1. If we need to represent a quantity more than 1, we'll use another digit, which will represent the number of groups of 2^1 which we'll call two. So "10" in base two represents 1 two and 0 ones. Be careful not to call "10" ten—instead, you might say "one-two." If we need a bigger quantity, we'll use another digit, which will represent the number of groups of 2^2, which we'll call four. The weights of each digit in base two are shown in Figure 1.7.

I saw the following on a T-shirt, and found it rather funny:

"There are 10 types of people in the world: those who get binary, and those who don't."

For example, the number 101 in base two equals $1*2^2 + 0*2^1 + 1*2^0$, or 5, in base ten. In other words, 101 can be spoken as "one-four zero-two one-one." Most people comfortable with binary might instead just say "one zero one." To be very clear, you might say "one zero one, base two." But you should definitely *not* say "one-hundred one, base two." 101 is one-hundred one in base ten, but the leftmost 1 does not represent one-hundred in base two.

▶ COUNTING "CORRECTLY" IN BASE TEN.

The fact that there are names for some of the groups in base ten, but not others, prevents many people from gaining an intuitive understanding of base ten. Further adding to the confusion are the abbreviated names for groups of tens—the numbers 10, 20, 30, ..., 90 should be called one ten, two ten, three ten, ..., nine ten, but instead use abbreviated names: one ten as just "ten," two ten as "twenty," three ten as "thirty," ..., and nine ten as "ninety." You can see how "ninety" is a shortening of "nine ten." Furthermore, short names are also used for the numbers between 10 and 20. 11 should be "one ten one," but is instead "eleven," while 19 should be "one ten nine" but is instead "nineteen." Table 1.1 indicates how to count "correctly" in base ten (where I boldly define "correctly" as counting the way I think makes more sense). Thus, the number 523 would be spoken as "five-hundred two-ten three" rather than "five-hundred twenty-three." I believe that kids have a harder time learning math because of the confusing number naming—for example, carrying a one from the ones column to the tens column makes more sense if the ones column adds to "one ten seven" rather than to "seventeen"—the result obviously adds one to the tens column. Learning binary is slightly harder for some students due to a lack of a solid understanding of base 10, caused largely by the naming confusion. Perhaps, when a store clerk tells you "that will be ninety-nine cents," you can correct him by saying "you mean nine-ten nine cents." If enough of us do this, perhaps it will catch on?

TABLE 1.1   Counting "correctly" in base ten.

0 to 9	As usual: "zero," "one," "two," etc.
10 to 99	10, 11, 12, ... 19: "one ten," "one ten one," "one ten two," ... "one ten nine" 20, 21, 22, ..., 29: "two ten," "two ten one," "two ten two," ... "two ten nine" 30, 40, ... 90: "three ten," "four ten," ... "nine ten"
100 to 900	As usual: "one hundred," "two hundred," ... "nine hundred." Even better would be to replace the word "hundred" by "ten to the power of 2."
1000 and up	As usual. Even better: replace "thousand" by "ten to the power of 3", "ten thousand" by "ten to the power of 4," etc., eliminating all the names.

When we are writing numbers of different bases and the base of the number is not obvious, we indicate the base with a subscript, as follows: $101_2 = 5_{10}$. We might say this as "one zero one in base two equals five in base ten."

	1	0	1
16	8	4	2	1

Figure 1.8 Base two number system.

Note that since binary isn't as popular as decimal, people haven't created short names for its groups of 2^1, 2^2, and so on, like they have for groups in base ten (hundreds, thousands, millions, etc.). Instead, people just use the equivalent base ten name for the group—a source of some confusion to people just learning binary. Nevertheless, it may still be easier to think of each group in base two using base 10 names, rather than increasing powers of two, as shown in Figure 1.8.

▶ EXAMPLE 1.1   Binary to decimal

Convert the following binary numbers to decimal numbers: 1, 110, 10000, 10000111, and 00110.

1_2 is just $1*2^0$, or 1_{10}.

110_2 is $1*2^2 + 1*2^1 + 0*2^0$, or 6_{10}. We might think of this using the group weights shown in Figure 1.8: $1*4 + 1*2 + 0*1$, or 6.

10000_2 is $1*16 + 0*8 + 0*4 + 0*2 + 0*1$, or 16_{10}.

10000111_2 is $1*128 + 1*4 + 1*2 + 1*1 = 135_{10}$. Notice this time that we didn't bother to write out the groups with a 0 bit.

00110_2 is the same as 110_2 above — the leading 0's don't change the value.   ◀

Knowing powers of two
helps in learning binary:

1	128
2	256
4	512
8	1024
16	2048
32	...
64	

When converting from binary to decimal, people often find it useful to be comfortable knowing the powers of two, since each successive place to the left in a binary number is two times the previous place. In binary, the first, rightmost place is 1, the second place is 2, then 4, then 8, 16, 32, 64, 128, 256, 512, 1024, 2048, and so on. You might stop at this point to practice counting up by powers of two: 1, 2, 4, 8, 16, 32, 64, 128, 256, 512, 1024, 2048, etc., a few times. Now, when you see the number 10000111, you might move along the number from right to left and count up by powers of two for each bit to determine the weight of the leftmost bit: 1, 2, 4, 8, 16, 32, 64, *128*. The next highest 1 has a weight of (counting up again) 1, 2, *4*; adding 4 to 128 gives 132. The next 1 has a weight of 2; adding that to 132 gives 134. The rightmost 1 has a weight of 1; adding that to 134 gives 135. Thus, 10000111 equals 135 in base ten.

▷ **EXAMPLE 1.2** Counting in binary

Counting from 0 to 7 in binary looks as follows: 000, 001, 010, 011, 100, 101, 110, 111. ◀

An interesting fact about binary numbers—you can quickly determine whether a binary number is odd just by checking if the rightmost digit has a 1. If the rightmost digit is a 0, the number must be even, since the number is the sum of even numbers.

Converting between decimal and binary numbers using the subtraction method
As we saw earlier, converting a binary number to decimal is easy—we just add the weights of each digit having a 1. Converting a decimal number to binary takes slightly more effort. One method for converting a decimal number to a binary number that is easy for humans to carry out by hand, which we'll call the ***subtraction method***, is shown in Table 1.2. The method starts with a binary number that is all 0s.

TABLE 1.2 Subtraction method for converting a decimal number to a binary number.

	Step	Description
Step 1	Put 1 in highest place	Put a 1 in the highest binary place whose weight is less than or equal to the decimal number.
Step 2	Update decimal number	Update the decimal number by subtracting the highest binary place's weight from the decimal number. The new decimal number is the remaining quantity to be converted to binary. If the updated decimal number is not zero, return to step 1.

For example, we can convert the decimal number 12 as shown in Figure 1.9.

1. Put 1 in highest place
   Try place 16, too big (16>12)
   Next place, 8, is highest (8<12)
2. Update decimal number
   Decimal not zero, return to Step 1

Decimal: 12, −8, 4

Binary: X̶ 1 0 0 0 (*current value is 8*)
16 8 4 2 1

1. Put 1 highest place
   Next place, 4, is highest (4=4)
2. Update decimal number
   Decimal number is zero, done.

Decimal: −4, 0

Binary: 1 1 0 0 (*current value is 12*)
16 8 4 2 1

Figure 1.9 Converting the decimal number 12 to binary using the subtraction method.

We can check our work by converting 1100 back to decimal: $1*8 + 1*4 + 0*2 + 0*2 = 12$.

As another example, Figure 1.10 illustrates the subtraction method for converting the decimal number 23 to binary. We can check our work by converting the result, 10111, back to decimal: $1*16 + 0*8 + 1*4 + 1*2 + 1*1 = 23$.

	Decimal	Binary	
1. Put 1 in highest place	23	1 0 0 0 0	(current value
Place 32 too big, but 16 works.		16 8 4 2 1	is 16)
2. Update decimal number	-16		
Decimal not zero, return to Step 1	7		
1. Put 1 in highest place		1 0 1 0 0	(current value
Next place is 8, too big (8>7)		16 8 4 2 1	is 20)
4 works (4<7)			
2. Update decimal number	-4		
Decimal number not zero, return	3		
to Step 1			
1. Put 1 in highest place		1 0 1 1 0	(current value
Next place is 2, works (2<3)	-2	16 8 4 2 1	is 22)
2. Update decimal number	1		
Decimal not zero, return to Step 1			
1. Put 1 in highest place		1 0 1 1 1	(current value
Next place is 1, works (1=1)	-1	16 8 4 2 1	is 23)
2. Update decimal number	0		
Decimal number is zero, done			

Figure 1.10 Converting the decimal number 23 to binary using the subtraction method.

▶ **EXAMPLE 1.3**   Decimal to binary

Convert the following decimal numbers to binary using the subtraction method: 8, 14, 99.

To convert 8 to binary, we start by putting a 1 in the 8's place, yielding 1000. Since 8–8=0, we are done—the answer is 1000.

To convert 14 to binary, we start by putting a 1 in the 8's place (16 is too much), yielding 1000. $14-8=6$, so we put a 1 in the 4's place, yielding 1100. $6-4=2$, so we put a 1 in the 2's place, yielding 1110. $2-2=0$, so we are done—the answer is 1110. We can quickly check our work by converting back to decimal: $8 + 4 + 2 = 14$.

To convert 99 to binary, we start by putting a 1 in the 64's place (the next higher place, 128, is too big—notice that being able to count by powers of two is handy in this problem), yielding 1000000. $99-64$ is 35, so we put a 1 in the 32's place, yielding 1100000. $35-32$ is 3, so we put a 1 in the 2's place, yielding 1100010. $3-2$ is 1, so we put a 1 in the 1's place, yielding the final answer of 1100011. We can check our work by converting back to decimal: $64 + 32 + 2 + 1 = 99$.   ◀

Converting between decimal and binary numbers using the divide-by-2 method

An alternative approach for converting a decimal number to binary, perhaps less intuitive than the subtraction method but easier to automate using a computer program, involves repeatedly dividing the decimal number by 2—we'll call this the *divide-by-2 method*. The remainder at each step (either 0 or 1) becomes a bit in the binary number, starting from the least significant (rightmost) digit. For example, the process of converting the decimal number 12 to binary using the divide-by-2 method is shown in Figure 1.11.

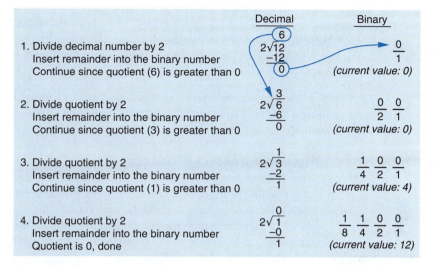

Figure 1.11 Converting the decimal number 12 to binary using the divide-by-2 method.

▶ **EXAMPLE 1.4** Decimal to binary using the divide-by-2 method

Convert the following numbers to binary using the divide-by-2 method: 8, 14, 99.

To convert 8 to binary, we start by dividing 8 by 2: 8/2=4, remainder 0. Then we divide the quotient, 4, by 2: 4/2=2, remainder 0. Then we divide 2 by 2: 2/2=1, remainder 0. Finally, we divide 1 by 2: 1/2=0, remainder 1. We stop dividing because the quotient is now 0. Combining all the remainders, least significant digit first, yields the binary number 1000. We can check this answer by multiplying each binary digit by its weight and adding the terms: $1*2^3 + 0*2^2 + 0*2^1 + 0*2^0 = 8$.

To convert 14 to binary, we follow a similar process: 14/2=7, remainder 0. 7/2=3, remainder 1. 3/2=1, remainder 1. 1/2=0, remainder 1. Combining the remainders gives us the binary number 1110. Checking the answer verifies that 1110 is correct: $1*2^3 + 1*2^2 + 1*2^1 + 0*2^0 = 8 + 4 + 2 + 0 = 14$.

To convert 99 to binary, the process is the same but naturally takes more steps: 99/2=49 remainder 1. 49/2=24, remainder 1. 24/2=12, remainder 0. 12/2=6, remainder 0. 6/2=3, remainder 0. 3/2=1, remainder 1. 1/2=0, remainder 1. Combining the remainders together gives us the binary number 1100011. We know from Example 1.3 that this is the correct answer. ◀

Converting from any base to any other base using the divide-by-*n* method
We have been dividing by 2 in order to convert to base 2, but we can use the same basic method to convert a base 10 number to a number of *any* base. To convert a number from base 10 to base *n*, we simply repeatedly divide the number by *n* and add the remainder to the new base *n* number, starting from the least significant digit.

▶ **EXAMPLE 1.5** Decimal to arbitrary bases using the divide-by-*n* method

Convert the number 3439 to base 10 and to base 7.

We know the number 3439 is 3439 in base 10, but let's use the divide-by-*n* (where *n* is 10) method to illustrate that the method works for any base. We start by dividing 3439 by 10: 3439/10=343, remainder 9. We then divide the quotient by 10: 343/10=34, remainder 3. We do the same with the new quotient: 34/3=3, remainder 4. Finally, we divide 3 by 10: 3/10=0, remainder 3. Combining the remainders, least significant digit first, gives us the base 10 number 3439.

To convert 3439 to base 7, the approach is similar, except we now divide by 7. We begin by dividing 3439 by 7: 3439/7=491, remainder 2. Continuing our calculations, we get: 491/7=70, remainder 1. 70/7=10, remainder 0. 10/7 = 1, remainder 3. 1/7=0, remainder 1. Thus, 3439 in base 7 is 13012. Checking the answer verifies that we have the correct result: $1*7^4 + 3*7^3 + 0*7^2 + 1*7^1 + 2*7^0 = 2401 + 1029 + 7 + 2 = 3439$. ◀

Generally, a number can be converted from one base to another by first converting that number to base ten, then converting the base ten number to the desired base using the divide-by-n method.

Hexadecimal and octal numbers

Base sixteen numbers, known as *hexadecimal numbers* or just *hex*, are also popular in digital design, mainly because one base sixteen digit is equivalent to four base two digits, making hexadecimal numbers a nice shorthand representation for binary numbers. In base sixteen, the first digit represents up to fifteen ones—the sixteen symbols commonly used are 0, 1, 2, ..., 9, A, B, C, D, E, F (so A=ten, B=eleven, C=twelve, D=thirteen, E=fourteen, and F=fifteen). The next digit represents the number of groups of 16^1, the next digit the number of groups of 16^2, etc., as shown in Figure 1.12. So $8AF_{16}$ equals $8*16^2 + 10*16^1 + 15*16^0$, or 2223_{10}. Since one digit in base 16 represents 16 values, and four digits in base two represents 16 values, each digit in base 16 represents four digits in base two, as shown at the bottom of Figure 1.12. Thus, to convert $8AF_{16}$ to binary, we convert 8_{16} to 1000_2, A_{16} to 1010_2, and F_{16} to 1111_2, resulting in $8AF_{16} = 100010101111_2$. You can see why hexadecimal is a popular shorthand for binary: 8AF is a lot easier on the eye than 100010101111.

hex	binary	hex	binary
0	0000	8	1000
1	0001	9	1001
2	0010	A	1010
3	0011	B	1011
4	0100	C	1100
5	0101	D	1101
6	0110	E	1110
7	0111	F	1111

Figure 1.12 Base sixteen number system.

To convert a binary number to hexadecimal, we just substitute every four bits with the corresponding hexadecimal digit. Thus, to convert 101101101_2 to hex, we group the bits into groups of four starting from the right, yielding 1 0110 1101. We then replace each group of four bits with a single hex digit. 1101 is D, 0110 is 6, and 1 is 1, resulting in the hex number $16D_{16}$.

▶ **EXAMPLE 1.6** Hexadecimal to/from binary

Convert the following hexadecimal numbers to binary: FF, 1011, A0000. You may find it useful to refer to Figure 1.12 to expand each hexadecimal digit to four bits.

FF_{16} is 1111 (for the left F) and 1111 (for the right F), or 11111111_2.

1011_{16} is 0001, 0000, 0001, 0001, or 0001000000010001_2. Don't be confused by the fact that 1011 didn't have any symbols but 1 and 0 (which makes the number look like a binary number). We said it was base 16, so it was. If we said it was base 10, then 1011 would equal one thousand and eleven.

$A0000_{16}$ is 1010, 0000, 0000, 0000, 0000, or 10100000000000000000_2.

Convert the following binary numbers to hexadecimal: 0010, 01111110, 111100.

0010_2 is 2_{16}.

01111110_2 is 0111 and 1110, meaning 7 and E, or $7E_{16}$.

111100_2 is 11 and 1100, which is 0011 and 1100, meaning 3 and C, or $3C_{16}$. Notice that we start grouping bits into groups of four from the right, not the left. ◀

The subtraction or divide-by-16 method can also be used to convert decimal to hexadecimal, however, converting directly from decimal to hexadecimal can be a bit unwieldy for humans since we are not used to working with powers of sixteen. Instead, it is often quicker to convert from decimal to binary using the subtraction or divide-by-2 method and then converting from binary to hexadecimal by grouping sets of 4 bits.

► **EXAMPLE 1.7**   Decimal to hexadecimal

Convert 29 base 10 to base 16.

To perform this conversion, we can first convert 29 to binary and then convert the binary result to hexadecimal.

Converting 29 to binary is straightforward using the divide-by-2 method: 29/2=14, remainder 1. 14/2=7, remainder 0. 7/2=3, remainder 1. 3/2=1, remainder 1. 1/2=0, remainder 1. Thus, 29 is 11101 in base 2.

Converting 11101_2 to hexadecimal can be done by grouping sets of four bits, so 11101_2 is 1_2 and 1101_2, meaning 1_{16} and D_{16}, or $1D_{16}$.

Of course, we can use the divide-by-16 method to convert directly from decimal to hexadecimal. Starting with 29, we divide by 16: 29/16=1, remainder 13 (D_{16}). 1/16=0, remainder 1. Combining the remainders together gives us $1D_{16}$. Though this particular conversion was simple, converting larger numbers directly from decimal to hexadecimal can be time-consuming, and the two-step conversion may be preferable.   ◄

Base eight numbers, known as *octal numbers*, are sometimes used as a binary shorthand too, since one base eight digit equals three binary digits. 503_8 equals $5*8^2 + 0*8^1 +3*8^0 = 323_{10}$. We can convert 503_8 directly to binary simply by expanding each digit into three bits, resulting in $503_8 = 101\ 000\ 011$, or 101000011_2. Likewise, we can convert binary to octal by grouping the binary number into groups of three bits starting from the right, and then replacing each group with the corresponding octal digit. Thus, 1011101_2 yields 1 011 101, or 135_8.

Appendix A discusses number representations further.

► 1.3 IMPLEMENTING DIGITAL SYSTEMS: PROGRAMMING MICROPROCESSORS VERSUS DESIGNING DIGITAL CIRCUITS

Designers can implement a digital system for an application using one of two common digital system implementation methods—programming a microprocessor or creating a custom digital circuit (known as digital design).

As a concrete example, consider a simple application that turns on a lamp whenever there is motion in a dark room. Assume a motion detector has an output wire called a that outputs a 1 bit when motion is detected, and a 0 bit otherwise. Assume a light sensor has an output wire b that outputs a 1 bit when light is sensed, and a 0 bit otherwise. And assume a wire F turns on the lamp when F is 1, and turns off the lamp when 0. A drawing of the system is shown in Figure 1.13(a).

The design problem is to determine what goes in the block named *Detector*. The *Detector* block takes wires a and b as inputs, and generates a value on F, such that the light turns on when motion is detected when dark. The *Detector* application is readily implemented as a digital system, as the application's inputs and outputs obviously are digital, having only two possible values each. A designer can implement the *Detector* block by programming a microprocessor (Figure 1.13(b)) or using a custom digital circuit (Figure 1.13(c)).

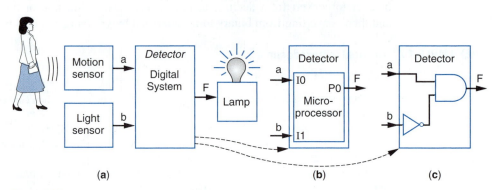

Figure 1.13 Motion-in-the-dark-detector system: (a) system block diagram, (b) implementation using a microprocessor, (c) implementation using a custom digital circuit.

Software on Microprocessors: The Digital Workhorse

Designers that need to work with digital phenomena often buy an off-the-shelf microprocessor and write software for that microprocessor, rather than design a custom digital circuit. Microprocessors are really the "workhorse" of digital systems, handling most digital processing tasks.

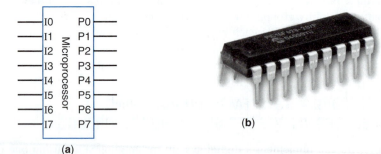

A "processor" processes, or transforms, data. A "microprocessor" is a programmable processor implemented on a single computer chip—the "micro" just means small here. The microprocessor term became popular in the 1980s when processors shrank down from multiple chips to just one. The first single-chip microprocessor was the Intel 4004 chip in 1971.

Figure 1.14 Basic microprocessor's input and output pins.

A **microprocessor** is a programmable digital device that executes a user-specified sequence of instructions, known as a *program* or as *software*. Some of those instructions read the microprocessor's inputs, others write to the microprocessor's outputs, and other instructions perform computations on the input data. Let's assume we have a basic microprocessor with eight input pins named I0, I1, ..., I7, and eight output pins named P0, P1, ..., P7, as shown in Figure 1.14(a). A photograph of a real microprocessor package with such pins is shown in Figure 1.14(b) (the ninth pin on this side is for power, on the other side for ground).

A microprocessor-based solution to the motion-in-the-dark detector application is illustrated in Figure 1.13(b), and a photograph of an actual physical implementation shown in Figure 1.15. The designer connects the a wire to the microprocessor input pin I0, the b wire to input pin I1, and output pin P0 to the F wire. The designer could then specify the instructions for the microprocessor by writing the following C code:

```
void main()
{
    while (1) {
        P0 = I0 && !I1; // F = a and !b,
    }
}
```

C is one of several popular languages for describing the desired instructions to execute on the microprocessor. The above C code works as follows. The microprocessor, after being powered up and reset, executes the instructions within main's curly brackets { }. The first instruction is "while (1)" which simply means to repeat the instructions in the while's curly brackets forever. Inside the while's curly brackets is only one instruction "P0 = I0 && !I1," which assigns the microprocessor's output pin P0 with a 1 if the input pin I0 is 1 *and* (written as &&) the input pin I1 is not 1 (meaning I1 is 0). Thus, the output pin P0, which turns the lamp on or off, forever gets assigned the appropriate value based on the input pin values, which come from the motion and light sensors.

Figure 1.16 shows an example of signals a, b, and F over time, with time proceeding to the right. As time proceeds, each signal may be either 0 or 1, illustrated by each signal's associated line being either low or high. We made

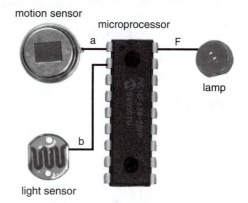

Figure 1.15 Physical motion-in-the-dark detector implementation using a microprocessor.

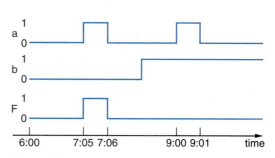

Figure 1.16 Timing diagram of motion-in-the-dark detector system.

a equal to 0 until 7:05, when we made a become 1. We made a stay 1 until 7:06, when we made a return back to 0. We made a stay 0 until 9:00, when we made a become 1 again, and then we made a become 0 at 9:01. On the other hand, we made b start as 0, and then become 1 sometime between 7:06 and 9:00. The diagram shows what the value of F would be given the C program executing on the microprocessor—when a is 1 and b is 0 (from 7:05 to 7:06), F will be 1. A diagram with time proceeding to the right, and the values of digital signals shown by high or low lines, is known as a *timing diagram*. We draw the input lines (a and b) to be whatever values we want, but then the output line (F) must describe the behavior of the digital system.

▶ **EXAMPLE 1.8**   Outdoor motion notifier using a microprocessor

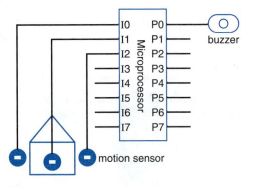

Figure 1.17 Motion sensors connected to microprocessor.

Let's use the basic microprocessor of Figure 1.14 to implement a system that sounds a buzzer when motion is detected at any of three motion sensors outside a house. We connect the motion sensors to microprocessor input pins I0, I1, and I2, and connect output pin P0 to a buzzer (Figure 1.17). (We assume the motion sensors and buzzers have appropriate electronic interfaces to the microprocessor pins.) We can then write the following C program:

```
void main()
{
    while (1) {
        P0 = I0 || I1 || I2;
    }
}
```

The program executes the statement inside the while loop repeatedly. That statement will set P0 to 1 if I0 is 1 *or* (written as || in the C language) I1 is 1 or I2 is 1, otherwise the statement sets P0 to 0. ◀

▶ **EXAMPLE 1.9**   Counting the number of active motion sensors

In this example, we'll use the basic microprocessor of Figure 1.14 to implement a simple digital system that outputs in binary the number of motion sensors that presently detect motion. We'll assume two motion sensors, meaning we'll need to output a two-bit binary number, which can represent the possible counts 0 (00), 1 (01), and 2 (10). We'll connect the motion sensors to microprocessor input pins I0 and I1 and output the binary number onto output pins P1 and P0. We can then write the following C program:

```
void main()
{
    while (1) {
        if (!I0 && !I1) {
            P1 = 0; P0 = 0; // output 00, meaning zero
        }
        else if ( (I0 && !I1) || (!I0 && I1) ) {
            P1 = 0; P0 = 1; // output 01, meaning one
        }
        else if (I0 && I1) {
            P1 = 1; P0 = 0; // output 10, meaning two
        }
    }
}
```
◀

Designers like to use microprocessors in their digital systems because microprocessors are readily available, inexpensive, easy to program, and easy to reprogram. It may surprise you to learn that you can buy certain microprocessor chips for under $1. Such microprocessors are found in places like telephone answering machines, microwave ovens, cars, toys, certain medical devices, and even in shoes with blinking lights. Examples include the 8051 (originally designed by Intel), the 68HC11 (made by Motorola), and the PIC (made by MicroChip). Other microprocessors may cost tens of dollars, found in places like cell phones, portable digital assistants, office automation equipment, and medical equipment. Such processors include the ARM (made by the ARM corporation), the MIPS (made by the MIPS corporation), and others. Other microprocessors, like the well-known Pentium processors from Intel, may cost several hundred dollars and may be found in desktop computers. Some microprocessors may cost several thousand dollars and are found in a mainframe computer running perhaps an airline reservation system. There are literally hundreds, possibly even thousands, of different microprocessor types available, differing in performance, cost, power, and other metrics. And many of the small low-power processors cost under $1.

(a)

(b)

Figure 1.18 Microprocessor chip packages: (a) PIC and 8051 microprocessors, costing about $1 each, (b) a Pentium processor with part of its package cover removed, showing the silicon chip inside.

Intel named their evolving 1980s/ 90s desktop processors using numbers: 80286, 80386, 80486. As PCs became popular, Intel switched to catchier names: the 80586 was called a Pentium ("penta" means 5), followed by the Pentium Pro, the Pentium II, and others. Eventually, the names dominated over the numbers.

Some readers of this book may be familiar with software programming, others may not. Knowledge of programming is not essential to learning the material in this book. We will on occasion compare custom digital circuits with their corresponding software implementations—the ultimate conclusions of those comparisons can be understood without knowledge of programming itself.

Digital Design—When Microprocessors Aren't Good Enough

With microprocessors readily available, why would anyone ever need to design new digital circuits, other than those relatively few people designing microprocessors themselves? The reason is that software running on a microprocessor often isn't good enough for a particular application. In many cases, software may be too slow. Microprocessors only execute one instruction (or at most a few instructions) at a time. But a custom digital circuit can execute dozens, or hundreds, or even thousands of computations in parallel. Many applications, like picture or video compression, fingerprint recognition, voice command detection, or graphics display, require huge numbers of computations to be done in a short period of time in order to be practical—after all, who wants a voice-controlled phone that requires 5 minutes to decode your voice command, or a digital camera that requires 15 minutes to take each picture? In other cases, microprocessors are too big, or consume too much power, or would be too costly, making custom digital circuits preferable.

For the motion-in-the-dark-detector application, an alternative to the microprocessor-based design uses a custom digital circuit inside the *Detector* block. A *circuit* is an interconnection of electric components. We must design a circuit that, for each different combination of inputs a and b, generates the proper value on F. One such circuit is shown in Figure 1.13(c). We'll describe the components in that circuit later. But you've now seen one simple example of designing a digital circuit to solve a design problem. The microprocessor also has a circuit inside, but because that circuit is designed to execute programs rather than just detect motion at night, the microprocessor's circuit may contain about ten thousand components, compared to just two components in our custom digital circuit. Thus, our custom digital circuit may be smaller, cheaper, faster, and consume less power than an implementation on a microprocessor.

Many applications use both microprocessors and custom digital designs to attain a system that achieves just the right balance of performance, cost, power, size, design time, flexibility, etc.

▶ **EXAMPLE 1.10** Deciding among a microprocessor and custom digital circuit

We must design a digital system to control a fighter jet's aircraft wing. In order to properly control the aircraft, the digital system must execute, 100 times per second, a computation task that adjusts the wing's position based on the aircraft's present and desired speeds, pitch, yaw, and other flight factors. Suppose we estimate that software on a microprocessor would require 50 ms (milliseconds) for each execution of the computation task, whereas a custom digital circuit would require 5 ms per execution.

Executing the computation task 100 times on the microprocessor would require 100 * 50 ms = 5000 ms, or 5 seconds. But we require those 100 executions to be done in 1 second, so the microprocessor is not fast enough. Executing the task 100 times with the custom digital circuit would require 100 * 5 ms = 500 ms, or 0.5 seconds. As 0.5 seconds is less than 1 second, the custom digital circuit can satisfy the system's performance constraint. We thus choose to implement the digital system as a custom digital circuit. ◀

▶ **EXAMPLE 1.11** Partitioning tasks in a digital camera

A digital camera captures pictures digitally using several steps. When the shutter button is pressed, a grid of a few million light-sensitive electronic elements capture the image, each element storing a binary number (perhaps 16 bits) representing the intensity of light hitting the element. The camera then performs several tasks: the camera *reads* the bits of each of these elements, *compresses* the tens of millions of bits into perhaps a few million bits, and *stores* the compressed bits as a file in the camera's flash memory, among other tasks. Table 1.3 provides sample task execution times on an inexpensive low-power microprocessor versus a custom digital circuit.

TABLE 1.3 Sample digital camera task execution times (in seconds) on a microprocessor versus a digital circuit.

Task	Microprocessor	Custom digital circuit
Read	5	0.1
Compress	8	0.5
Store	1	0.8

We need to decide which tasks to implement on the microprocessor and which to implement as a custom digital circuit, subject to the constraint that we should strive to minimize the amount of custom digital circuitry in order to reduce chip costs. Such decisions are known as *partitioning*. Three partitioning options are shown in Figure 1.19. If we implement all three tasks on the microprocessor, the camera will require 5 + 8 + 1 = 14 seconds to take a picture—too much time for the camera to be popular with consumers. We could implement all the tasks as custom digital circuits, resulting in 0.1 + 0.5 + 0.8 = 1.4 seconds. We could instead implement the read and compress tasks with custom digital circuits, while leaving the store task to the microprocessor, resulting in 0.1 + 0.5 + 1, or 1.6 seconds. We might decide on this last implementation option, to save cost without much noticeable time overhead. ◀

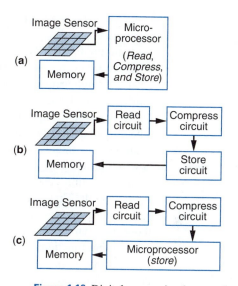

Figure 1.19 Digital camera implemented with: (a) a microprocessor, (b) custom circuits, and (c) a combination of custom circuits and a microprocessor.

▶ 1.4 ABOUT THIS BOOK

Section 1.1 discussed how digital systems now appear everywhere around us and significantly impact the way we live. Section 1.2 highlighted how learning digital design accomplishes two goals: showing us how microprocessors work "under the hood," and enabling us to implement systems using custom digital circuits rather than or alongside microprocessors to achieve better implementations. This latter goal is becoming increasingly significant since so many analog phenomena, like music and video, are becoming digital. That section also introduced a key method of digitizing analog signals, namely binary numbers, and described how to convert among decimal and binary numbers. Section 1.3 described how designers tend to prefer to implement digital systems by writing software that executes on a microprocessor, yet designers often use custom digital circuits to meet an application's performance requirements or other requirements.

In the remainder of this book you will learn about the exciting and challenging field of digital design, wherein we convert desired system functionality into a custom digital circuit. Chapter 2 will introduce the most basic form of digital circuit, combinational circuits, whose outputs are simply a function of the present values on the circuit's inputs. That chapter will show how to use a form of math called Boolean algebra to describe our desired circuit functionality, and will provide clear steps for converting Boolean equations to circuits. Chapter 3 will introduce a more advanced type of circuit, sequential circuits, whose outputs are a function not only of the present input values, but also of previous input values—in other words, sequential circuits have memory. Such circuits are commonly referred to as controllers. That chapter will show us how to use another mathematical abstraction, known as a finite-state machine, to represent desired sequential functionality, and will provide clear steps for converting finite-state machines to circuits. As with any form of design, we often use pre-designed building blocks, or components, to make our design task easier. Chapter 4 describes several such components, known as datapath components, including registers (for storing digital data), adders, comparators, multipliers, and small memories called register files, among other blocks. Chapter 5 introduces the modern approach to digital design, known as register-transfer level design, wherein we design systems consisting of datapath components controlled by controllers, to implement interesting and useful custom digital circuits. In fact, that chapter shows how to convert a C program to a custom digital circuit—clearly demonstrating that any desired function can be implemented as software on a microprocessor or as a custom digital circuit. That chapter also introduces some additional components, including ROM and RAM memories, and queues. Chapters 1 through 5 form the core of this book—after those five chapters, the reader can specify a wide variety of desired functionality and can convert that functionality to a working custom digital circuit.

Chapter 6 introduces methods for designing *better* digital circuits. The chapter describes methods for improving basic combinational circuits, basic sequential circuits, datapath components, and register-transfer level designs. That chapter emphasizes the important notion of *tradeoffs*, wherein we might make one aspect of the design better, but at the expense of worsening another aspect. Tradeoffs are the essence of design.

Chapter 7 describes different physical devices on which we can implement our digital circuits, including application-specific integrated circuits, field-programmable gate-arrays (FPGAs), simple programmable logic devices, and cheap off-the-shelf ICs.

Chapter 8 applies the digital design methods of earlier chapters to build a widely-used type of digital circuit—a programmable microprocessor. This chapter demystifies the workings of a microprocessor, using a very simple microprocessor design to illustrate the concepts.

Chapter 9 introduces hardware description languages, which are widely used in modern digital design for describing desired circuit functionality as well as for representing the final custom digital circuit design. Hardware description languages, looking much like software programming languages but with important extensions and differences, serve as the input to most modern digital design tools.

▶ 1.5 EXERCISES

SECTION 1.2: THE WORLD OF DIGITAL SYSTEMS

1.1 Suppose an analog audio signal comes in over a wire, and the voltage on the wire can range from 0 Volts (V) to 3 V. You want to convert the analog signal to a digital signal. You decide to encode each sample using two bits, such that 0 V would be encoded as 00, 1 V as 01, 2 V as 10, and 3 V as 11. You sample the signal every 1 millisecond and detect the following sequence of voltages: 0V 0V 1V 2V 3V 2V 2V. Show the signal converted to digital as a stream of 0s and 1s.

1.2 Use the mapping of voltages to 2-bit encodings from Exercise 1. for this problem. You are given a digital encoding of an audio signal as follows: 1111101001010000. Plot the re-created signal with time on the *x*-axis and voltage on the *y*-axis. Assume that each encoding's corresponding voltage should be output for 1 millisecond.

1.3 Assume that a signal is encoded using 12 bits. Assume that many of the encodings turn out to be either 000000000000, 000000000001, or 111111111111. We thus decide to create compressed encodings by representing 000000000000 as 00, 000000000001 as 01, and 111111111111 as 10. 11 means that an uncompressed encoding follows. Using this encoding scheme, decompress the following encoded stream:

00 00 01 10 11 010101010101 00 00 10 10

1.4 Using the same encoding scheme as in Exercise 3., compress the following unencoded stream:

000000000000 000000000001 000000000000 100000000000
111111111111

1.5 Encode the following words into bits using the ASCII encoding table in Figure 1.5.
(a) LET
(b) RESET!
(c) T9.Net

1.6 Convert the following binary numbers to decimal numbers:
(a) 100
(b) 1011
(c) 0000000000001
(d) 111111
(e) 101010

1.7 Convert the following binary numbers to decimal numbers:
(a) 1010
(b) 1000000
(c) 11001100
(d) 11111
(e) 10111011001

1.8 Convert the following binary numbers to decimal numbers:
(a) 000111
(b) 1111
(c) 11110
(d) 111100
(e) 0011010

1.9 Convert the following decimal numbers to binary numbers using the subtraction method:
(a) 9
(b) 15
(c) 32
(d) 140

1.10 Convert the following decimal numbers to binary numbers using the subtraction method:
(a) 19
(b) 30
(c) 64
(d) 128

1.11 Convert the following decimal numbers to binary numbers using the subtraction method:
(a) 3
(b) 65
(c) 90
(d) 100

1.12 Convert the following decimal numbers to binary numbers using the divide-by-2 method:
  (a) 9
  (b) 15
  (c) 32
  (d) 140

1.13 Convert the following decimal numbers to binary numbers using the divide-by-2 method:
  (a) 19
  (b) 30
  (c) 64
  (d) 128

1.14 Convert the following decimal numbers to binary numbers using the divide-by-2 method:
  (a) 3
  (b) 65
  (c) 90
  (d) 100

1.15 Convert the following decimal numbers to binary numbers using the divide-by-2 method:
  (a) 23
  (b) 87
  (c) 123
  (d) 101

1.16 Convert the following binary numbers to hexadecimal:
  (a) 11110000
  (b) 11111111
  (c) 01011010
  (d) 1001101101101

1.17 Convert the following binary numbers to hexadecimal:
  (a) 11001101
  (b) 10100101
  (c) 11110001
  (d) 1101101111100

1.18 Convert the following binary numbers to hexadecimal:
  (a) 11100111
  (b) 11001000
  (c) 10100100
  (d) 011001101101101

1.19 Convert the following hexadecimal numbers to binary:
  (a) FF
  (b) F0A2
  (c) 0F100
  (d) 100

1.20 Convert the following hexadecimal numbers to binary:
  (a) 4F5E
  (b) 3FAD
  (c) 3E2A
  (d) DEED

1.21 Convert the following hexadecimal numbers to binary:
   (a) B0C4
   (b) 1EF03
   (c) F002
   (d) BEEF

1.22 Convert the following hexadecimal numbers to decimal:
   (a) FF
   (b) F0A2
   (c) 0F100
   (d) 100

1.23 Convert the following hexadecimal numbers to decimal:
   (a) 10
   (b) 4E3
   (c) FF0
   (d) 200

1.24 Convert the decimal number 128 to the following number systems:
   (a) binary
   (b) hexadecimal
   (c) base three
   (d) base five
   (e) base fifteen

1.25 Compare the number of digits necessary to represent the following decimal numbers in binary, octal, decimal, and hexadecimal representations. You need not determine the actual representations—just the number of required digits. For example, representing the decimal number 12 requires four digits in binary (1100 is the actual representation), two digital in octal (14), two digits in decimal (12), and one digit in hexadecimal (C).
   (a) 8
   (b) 60
   (c) 300
   (d) 1000
   (e) 999,999

1.26 Determine the decimal number ranges that can be represented in binary, octal, decimal, and hexadecimal using the following numbers of digits. For example, 2 digits can represent decimal number range 0 through 3 in binary (00 through 11), 0 through 63 in octal (00 through 77), 0 through 99 in decimal (00 through 99), and 0 through 255 in hexadecimal (00 through FF).
   (a) 1
   (b) 3
   (c) 6
   (d) 8

SECTION 1.3: IMPLEMENTING DIGITAL SYSTEMS: PROGRAMMING MICROPROCESSORS VERSUS DESIGNING DIGITAL CIRCUITS

1.27 Use a microprocessor like that in Figure 1.14 to implement a system that sounds an alarm whenever there is motion detected at the same time in three different rooms. Each room's motion sensor output comes to us on a wire as a bit, 1 meaning motion, 0 meaning no motion. We sound the alarm by setting an output wire "alarm" to 1. Show the connections to and from the microprocessor, and the C code to execute on the microprocessor.

1.28 Use a microprocessor like that in Figure 1.14 to implement a system that counts the number of cars in a parking lot with seven spaces. Each space has a sensor that outputs a 1 if a car is present, and that outputs a 0 otherwise. The output should be written in binary over three wires. Show the connections with the microprocessor and the C code. Hint: use a loop and an integer variable to count the number of cars present, then use an if-else statement or a switch statement to convert the integer to the appropriate 3-bit output.

1.29 Use a microprocessor like that in Figure 1.14 to implement a system that displays the number of people in a waiting room onto an LED display. There are eight LEDs arranged in a row and eight chairs in the waiting room, each equipped with a sensor that will output a 1 when the seat is in use. The number of LEDs lit will correspond to the number of seats being occupied. For instance, if two seats are occupied (regardless of which two seats those are), the first two LEDs will light up; if three seats are occupied, the first three LEDs in the row will light up. Regardless of which particular seats are occupied, the lights will light up incrementally. Show the connections with the microprocessor and the appropriate C code.

1.30 Suppose a particular TV set-top box at a hotel supports encrypted video, and that decrypting each video frame consists of three sub-tasks A, B, and C. The execution times of each task on a microprocessor versus a custom digital circuit are 100 ms versus 1 ms for A, 10 ms versus 2 ms for B, and 15 ms versus 1 ms for C. Partition the tasks among the microprocessor and custom digital circuitry, such that you minimize the amount of custom digital circuitry, while meeting the constraint of decrypting at least 30 frames per second.

1.31 The owner of a baseball stadium wants to eliminate paper tickets for gaining entrance to baseball games. She would like to sell tickets electronically and allow those attending the game to enter by scanning their fingerprint. The owner has two options for installing the fingerprint recognition system. The first option is a system that implements the fingerprint recognition using software executing on a microprocessor. The second option is a custom digital circuit designed specifically for fingerprint recognition. The software system requires 5.5 seconds to recognize an individual's fingerprint and costs $50 per unit, whereas the digital circuit requires 1.3 seconds for recognition and costs $100 per unit. The owner wants to ensure that everyone attending the game will be able to enter the stadium before the game starts, and thus needs to be able to support 100,000 people entering the stadium within 15 minutes. Compare the two alternative systems in terms of how many people per minute each system can support, how many units of each system would be needed to support 100,000 people in 15 minutes, and what the overall cost of installation would be for the two competing systems.

1.32 How many possible partitionings are there of a set of N tasks where each task can be implemented on a microprocessor or as a custom digital circuit?

1.33 *Write a program that automatically partitions a set of 10 tasks among a microprocessor and custom digital circuitry. Assume that each task has two associated execution times, one for the microprocessor and the other for custom digital circuitry. Assume also that each task has an associated size number, representing the amount of digital circuitry required to implement that task. Your program should read in the execution times and sizes from a file. Your program should seek to minimize the amount of digital circuitry while meeting a constraint specified on the sum of the task execution times. Your program should output the partitioning (each task's name and whether the task is mapped to the microprocessor or to custom digital circuitry), the total execution time of the tasks for that partitioning, and the total digital circuit size. Hint: you probably can't try all possible partitionings of the 10 tasks, so use a partitioning approach that makes some educated guesses. Your program likely won't be able to guarantee that it finds the best partitioning, but it should at least find a good partitioning.

Kelly first became interested in engineering while attending a talk about engineering at a career fair in high school. "I was dazzled by the interesting ideas and the cool graphs." While in college, though, she learned that "there was much more to engineering than ideas and graphs. Engineers *apply* their ideas and skills to build things that really make a difference in people's lives, for generations to come."

In her first few years as an engineer, Kelly has worked on a variety of projects "that may help numerous individuals." One project was a ventilator system like the one mentioned earlier in this chapter. "We designed a new control system that may enable people on ventilators to breathe with more comfort while still getting the proper amount of oxygen." In addition, she examined alternative implementations of that control system, including on a microprocessor, as a custom digital circuit, and as a combination of the two. "Today's technologies, like FPGAs, provide so many different options. We examined several options to see what the tradeoffs were among them. Understanding the tradeoffs among the options is quite important if we want to build the best system possible."

She also worked on a project that developed "small self-explanatory electronic blocks that people could connect together to build useful electronic systems involving almost any kind of sensor, like motion or light sensors. Those blocks could be used by kids to learn basic concepts of logic and computers, concepts which are quite important to learn these days. Our hope is that these blocks will be used as teaching tools in schools. The blocks can also be used to help adults set up useful systems in their homes, perhaps to monitor an aging parent, or a child at home sick. The potential for these blocks is great—it will be interesting to see what impact they have."

"My favorite thing about engineering is the variety of skills and creativity involved. We are faced with problems that need to be solved, and we solve them by applying known techniques in creative ways. Engineers must continually learn new technologies, hear new ideas, and track current products, in order to be good designers. It's all very exciting and challenging. Each day at work is different. Each day is exciting and is a learning experience."

"Studying to be an engineer can be a great deal of work but it's worth it. The key is to stay focused, to keep your mind open, and to make good use of available resources. Staying focused means to keep your priorities in order—for example, as a student, studying comes first, recreation second. Keeping your mind open means to always be willing to listen to different ideas and to learn about new technologies. Making good use of resources means to aggressively seek information, from the Internet, from colleagues, from books, and so on. You never know where you are going to get your next important bit of information, and you won't get that information unless you seek it."

CHAPTER 2

Combinational Logic Design

▶ 2.1 INTRODUCTION

A digital circuit whose outputs depend solely on the *present combination of the circuit inputs' values* is called a **combinational circuit**. Combinational circuits are a basic but important class of digital circuits, able to implement some systems, but more importantly serving as the basis for more complex classes of circuits. This chapter introduces the design of basic combinational circuits. Later chapters will deal with more advanced combinational circuits, and with sequential circuits, whose outputs depend on the sequence (history) of values that have appeared at the circuit's inputs. Figure 2.1 illustrates the difference between combinational and sequential circuits.

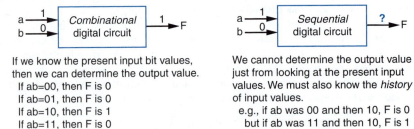

If we know the present input bit values, then we can determine the output value.
If ab=00, then F is 0
If ab=01, then F is 0
If ab=10, then F is 1
If ab=11, then F is 0

We cannot determine the output value just from looking at the present input values. We must also know the *history* of input values.
e.g., if ab was 00 and then 10, F is 0
but if ab was 11 and then 10, F is 1

Figure 2.1 Combinational versus sequential digital circuits.

The chapter will introduce the basic building blocks of combinational circuits, known as logic gates, and will also introduce a form of mathematics, known as Boolean algebra, that is useful for designing combinational circuits.

▶ 2.2 SWITCHES

Electronic switches form the basis of all digital circuits, so they make a good starting point for the discussion of digital circuits. You use a type of switch, a light switch, whenever you turn lights on or off. To understand a switch, it helps to understand some basic electronics.

Electronics 101

You're probably familiar with the idea of electrons, or let's just say charged particles, flowing through wires and causing lights to illuminate or stereos to blast music. An analogous situation is water flowing through pipes and causing sprinklers to pop up or turbines to turn. We now describe three basic electrical terms:

Although understanding the electronics underlying digital logic gates is optional, many people find a basic understanding satisfies much curiosity and also helps in understanding some of the non-ideal digital gate behavior later on.

- **Voltage** is the difference in electric potential between two points. Voltage is measured in volts (V). Convention says that the earth, or *ground*, is 0 V. Informally, voltage tells us how "eager" the charged particles on one side of a wire are to get to ground (or any lower voltage) on the wire's other side. Voltage is analogous to the pressure of water trying to flow through a pipe—water under higher pressure is more eager to flow, even if the water can't actually flow perhaps because of a closed faucet.

- **Current** is a measure of the flow of the charged particles. Informally, current tells us the rate that particles are actually flowing. Current is analogous to water flowing through a pipe. Current is measured in amperes (A), or amps for short.

- **Resistance** is the tendency of a wire (or anything, really) to resist the flow of current. Resistance is analogous to a pipe's diameter—a narrow pipe resists water flow, while a wide pipe lets water flow more freely. Electrical resistance is measured in ohms (Ω).

Consider a battery. The particles at the positive terminal want to flow to the negative terminal. How "eager" are they to flow? That depends on the voltage difference between the terminals—a 9 V battery's particles are more eager to flow than a 1.5 V battery's particles, because the 9 V battery's particles have more potential energy. Now suppose you connect the positive terminal through a light bulb back to the negative terminal as shown in Figure 2.2. The 9 V battery will result in more current flowing, and thus a brighter lit light, than the 1.5 V battery. Precisely how much current will flow is determined using the equation:

$$V = IR \text{ (known as Ohm's Law)}$$

where V is voltage, I is current, and R is resistance (in this case, of the light bulb). So if the resistance were 2 ohms, a 9 V battery would result in 4.5 A (since 9 = I*2) of current, while a 1.5 V battery would result in 0.75 A.

Rewriting the equation as I = V/R might make more intuitive sense—the higher the voltage, the more current; the higher the resistance, the less current. Ohm's Law is perhaps the most fundamental equation in electronics.

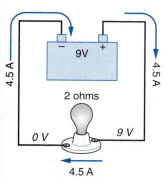

Figure 2.2 9V battery connected to light bulb.

The Amazing Shrinking Switch

Now back to switches. Figure 2.3(b) shows that a switch has three parts—let's call them the source input, the output, and the control input. The source input has higher voltage than the output, so current wants to flow from the source input through the switch to the output. The whole purpose of a switch is to block that current when the control sets the switch "off," and to allow that current to flow when control sets the switch "on." For example, when you flip a light switch up to turn the switch on, the switch causes the source input wire to physically touch the output wire, so current flows. When you flip the switch down to turn the switch off, the switch physically separates the source input from the output. In our water analogy, the control input is like a faucet valve that determines whether water flows through a pipe.

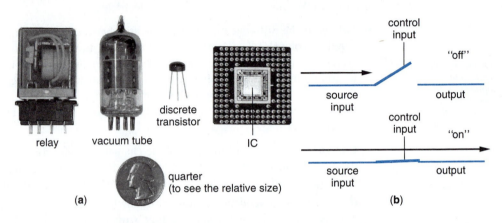

Figure 2.3 (a) The evolution of switches: relays (1930s), vacuum tubes (1940s), discrete transistors (1950s), and integrated circuits (ICs) containing transistors (1960s–present). IC's originally held about ten transistors; now they can hold more than a billion. (b) Simple view of a switch.

Switches are what cause digital circuits to utilize binary numbers made from bits—the on or off nature of a switch corresponds to the 1s and 0s in binary. We now discuss the evolution of switches over the 1900s, leading up to the CMOS transistor switches commonly used today in digital circuits.

1930s—Relays

Engineers in the 1930s tried to devise ways to compute using electronically controlled switches—switches whose control input was another voltage. One such switch, an electro-magnetic relay like that in Figure 2.3(a), was already being used by telephone industry for switching telephone calls. A relay has a control input that is a type of magnet, which becomes magnetized when the control has a positive voltage. In one type of relay, that magnet pulls a piece of metal down, resulting in a connection from the source input to the output—akin to pulling down a drawbridge to connect one road to another. When the control input returns to 0 V, the piece of metal returns up again (perhaps pushed by a small spring), disconnecting the source input from the output. In telephone systems, relays enabled calls to be routed from one phone to another, without the need for those nice human operators that previously would manually connect one phone's line to another.

1940s—Vacuum Tubes

Relays relied on metal parts moving up and down, and thus were rather slow. In the 1940s and 1950s, vacuum tubes, shown in Figure 2.3(a) and originally used to amplify weak electric signals like those in a telegraph, began to replace relays in computers. Vacuum tubes had no moving parts, so the tubes were much faster than relays.

The machine said to be the world's first general-purpose computer, the ENIAC (Electronic Numerical Integrator And Computer), was completed in the U.S. in 1946. ENIAC contained about 18,000 vacuum tubes and 1500 relays, weighed over 30 tons, was 100 feet long and 8 feet high (so it would likely not fit in any room of your house, unless you have an absurdly big house), and consumed 174,000 watts of power. Imagine the heat generated by a room full of 1740 100-watt light bulbs. That's hot. For all that, ENIAC could compute about 5000 operations per second—compare that to the billions of operations per second of today's personal computers, and even the tens of millions of computations per second by a handheld cell phone.

Although vacuum tubes were faster than relays, they consumed a lot of power, generated a lot of heat, and failed frequently.

Vacuum tubes were commonplace in many electronic appliances in the 1960s and 1970s. I remember taking trips to the store with my dad in the early 1970s to buy replacement tubes for our television set. Vacuum tubes still live today in a few electronic devices. One place you might still find tubes is in electric guitar amplifiers, where the tube's unique-sounding audio amplification is still demanded by rock guitar enthusiasts who want their versions of classic rock songs to sound just like the originals.

1950s—Discrete Transistors

The invention of the transistor in 1947, credited to William Shockley, John Bardeen, and Walter Brattain of Bell Laboratories (the research arm of AT&T), resulted in smaller and lower-power computers. A solid-state (discrete) transistor, shown in Figure 2.3(a), uses a small piece of silicon, "doped" with some extra materials, to create a switch. Since these switches used "solid" materials rather than a vacuum or even moving parts in a relay, they were commonly referred to as solid-state transistors. Solid-state transistors were smaller, cheaper, faster, and more reliable than tubes, and became the dominant computer switch in the 1950s and 1960s.

Jack Kilby of Texas Instruments and Robert Noyce of Fairchild Semiconductors are often credited with each having independently invented the IC.

1960s—Integrated Circuits

The invention of the *integrated circuit (IC)* in 1958 really revolutionized computing. An IC, a.k.a. a chip, packs numerous tiny transistors on a fingernail-sized piece of silicon. So instead of 10 transistors requiring 10 discrete electronic components on your board, 10 transistors can be implemented on one component, the chip. Figure 2.3(a) shows a picture of an IC that has a few million transistors. Though early ICs featured only tens of transistors, improvements in IC technology have resulted in nearly ONE BILLION transistors on a chip today. IC technology has shrunk transistors down to a totally different scale. A vacuum tube (about 100 mm long) is to a modern IC transistor (about 100 nm) as a skyscraper (about 0.5 km) is to the thickness of a credit card (about 0.5 mm).

I've been working in this field for two decades, and the amount of transistors on a chip still amazes me. The number 1 billion is bigger than most of us have an intuitive feel for. Think of pennies, and consider the volume that 1 billion pennies would occupy. Would they fit in your bedroom? The answer is probably no (unless you have a really huge bedroom), since a typical bedroom is about 40 cubic meters, while 1 billion pennies would occupy about 400 cubic meters. So you would need about 10 bedrooms, roughly the size of an entire house, packed from wall to wall, floor to ceiling, with pennies, to store all that money. And if we stacked the pennies, they would reach nearly 1000 miles into the sky—for comparison, a jet flies at an altitude of about 5 miles. That's a lot of pennies. But we manage to fit 1 billion transistors onto silicon chips of just a few square centimeters. Truly amazing.

The wires that connect all those transistors on a chip, if straightened into one straight wire, would be several miles long.

IC transistors are much smaller, more reliable, faster, and less power-hungry than discrete transistors. Thus, IC transistors are now by far the most commonly used switch in computing.

ICs of the early 1960s could hold tens of transistors, and are known today as small-scale integration (*SSI*). As transistor sizes shrank, in the late 1960s and early 1970s, ICs could hold hundreds of transistors, known as medium-scale integration (*MSI*). The 1970s saw the development of large-scale integration (*LSI*) ICs with thousands of transistors, while very-large scale integration (*VLSI*) chips evolved in the 1980s. Since then, ICs have continued to increase in their capacity, to around 1 billion transistors. To calibrate your understanding of this number, consider that the first Pentium microprocessor of the early 1990s required only about 3 million transistors, and some popular but relatively small microprocessors require only about 100,000 transistors. Many of today's high-end chips therefore contain dozens of microprocessors, and can conceivably contain hundreds of the relatively small microprocessors (or just one or two big microprocessors).

IC density has been doubling roughly every 18 months since the 1960s. The doubling of IC density every 18 months is widely known as *Moore's Law*, named after Gordon Moore, a co-founder of Intel Corporation, who made predictions back in 1965 that the number of components per IC would double every year or so. At some point, chip makers won't be able to shrink transistors any further. After all, the transistor has to at least be

▶ A SIGNIFICANT INVENTION

We now know that the invention of the transistor was the start of the amazing computation and communication revolutions that occurred in the latter half of the 20th century, enabling us to today do things like see the world on TV, surf the web, and talk on cell phones. But the implications of the transistor were not known by most people at the time of its invention. Newspapers did not headline the news, and most stories that did appear predicted simply that transistors would improve things like radios and hearing aids. One may wonder what recently invented but unnoticed technology might significantly change the world once again.

▶ HOW DO THEY MAKE TRANSISTORS SO SMALL? USING PHOTOGRAPHIC METHODS

If you took a pencil and made the smallest dot that you could on a sheet of paper, that dot's area would hold many thousands of transistors on a modern silicon chip. How can chip makers create such tiny transistors? The key lies in photographic methods. Chip makers lay a special chemical onto the chip, special because the chemical changes when exposed to light. Chip makers then shine light through a lens that focuses the light down to extremely small regions on the chip—similar to how a microscope's lens lets us see tiny things by focusing light, but in reverse. The chemical in the small illuminated region changes, and then a solvent washes away the chemical—but some regions stay because of the light that changed that region. Those remaining regions form parts of transistors. Repeating this process over and over again, with different chemicals at different steps, results not only in transistors, but also wires connecting the transistors, and insulators preventing crossing wires from touching.

Photograph of a Pentium processor's silicon chip having millions of transistors. Actual size is about 1 cm each side.

wide enough to let electrons pass through. People have been predicting the end of Moore's Law for over a decade now, but transistors keep shrinking.

Not only do smaller transistors and wires provide for more functionality in a chip, but they also provide for faster circuits, in part because electrons need not travel as far to get from one transistor to the next. This increased speed is the main reason why personal computer clock speeds have improved so drastically over the past few decades, from kilohertz frequencies in the 1970s to gigahertz frequencies in the early 2000s.

▶ 2.3 THE CMOS TRANSISTOR

The most popular type of IC transistor is the CMOS transistor. Although a detailed explanation of how a CMOS transistor works is beyond the scope of this book, nevertheless, I've found that a simplified explanation seems to satisfy much curiosity.

A chip is made primarily from the element silicon. A chip, also known as an integrated circuit, or IC, is typically about the size of a fingernail. Even if you open up a computer or other chip-based device, you would not actually see the silicon chip, since chips are actually inside a larger, usually black, protective package. But you certainly should be able to see those black packages, mounted on a printed circuit board, inside a variety of household electronic devices.

Figure 2.4 illustrates a cross section of a tiny part of silicon chip, showing the side view of one type of CMOS transistor—an nMOS transistor. The transistor has the three parts of a switch: (1) the **source** input; (2) the output, which is called the **drain**, I suppose because electric particles flow to the drain like water flows to a drain; and (3) the control input, which is called the **gate**, I suppose because the gate blocks the current flow like a gate blocks a dog from escaping the backyard. A chip maker creates the source and drain by injecting certain elements into the silicon. Figure 2.4 also shows the electronic symbol of an nMOS transistor.

Suppose the drain was connected to a small positive voltage (modern technologies use about 1 or 2 V) known as the "power supply," and the source was connected through

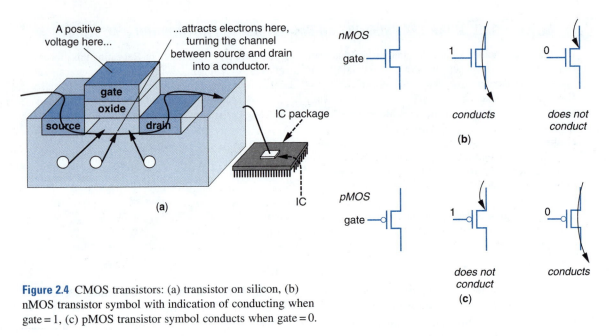

Figure 2.4 CMOS transistors: (a) transistor on silicon, (b) nMOS transistor symbol with indication of conducting when gate = 1, (c) pMOS transistor symbol conducts when gate = 0.

a resistor to ground. Current would thus want to flow from drain to source, and on to ground. (Note: unfortunately, convention is that current flow is defined using positive charge, even though actually negatively charged electrons are flowing—so you may notice that we say current flows from drain to source, even though electrons flow from source to drain.) However, the silicon channel between source and drain is not normally a conductor, or in other words, the channel is normally an insulator. We can think of an insulator as an extremely large resistance. Since I = V/R, then I will essentially be 0. The switch is off.

The really interesting thing about silicon is that we can change the channel from an insulator to a conductor just by applying a small positive voltage to the gate. That gate voltage doesn't result in current flow from the gate to channel, because of the small insulator (oxide) between the gate and the channel. But, that gate voltage does create a positive electric field that attracts electrons, which have a negative charge, from the larger silicon region into the channel region—akin to how you can move paper clips on a tabletop by moving a magnet under the table. When enough electrons gather into the channel, the channel all of a sudden becomes a conductor. A conductor has extremely low resistance, so current flows almost freely between drain and source. The switch is now on. As you can see, silicon is not quite a conductor but not quite an insulator either, rather representing something in between—hence the term *semiconductor*.

An analogy to the current trying to cross the channel is a person trying to cross a river. Normally, the river might not have enough stepping stones for the person to be able to walk across. But if we could attract stones from other parts of the river into one pathway (the channel), the person could easily walk across the river (Figure 2.5).

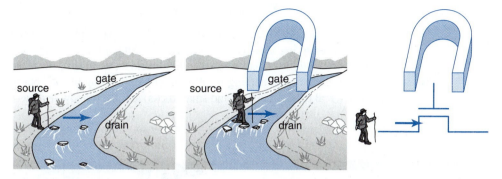

Figure 2.5 CMOS transistor operation analogy—A person may not be able to cross a river until just enough stepping stones are attracted into one pathway. Likewise, electrons can't cross the channel between source and drain until just enough electrons are attracted into the channel.

We mentioned that nMOS was one type of CMOS transistor. The other type is pMOS. A pMOS is similar except that the channel has the opposite functionality—the channel is a conductor normally, and then *doesn't* conduct when the gate has a positive voltage. Figure 2.4 shows the electronic symbol for a pMOS transistors. The use of these two "complementary" types of transistors is where the C comes from in CMOS. The MOS stands for Metal Oxide Semiconductor, but the reasons for that name go beyond the scope of this discussion.

► SILICON VALLEY, AND THE SHAPE OF SILICON

Silicon Valley is not a city, but refers to an area in Northern California, about an hour south of San Francisco, that includes several cities like San Jose, Mountain View, Sunnyvale, Milpitas, Palo Alto, and others. The area is heavily populated by computer and other high-technology companies, and to a large extent is the result of Stanford University's (located in Palo Alto) efforts to attract and create such companies. **What shape is silicon?** Once, as my plane arrived in Silicon Valley, the person next to me (who happened to be a college senior studying Computer Science) asked "What shape is a silicon anyways?" I eventually realized he thought silicon was a type of polygon, like a pentagon or an octagon. Well, the words do sound similar. Silicon is not a shape, but an element, like carbon or aluminum or silver. Silicon has an atomic number of 14, has a chemical symbol of "Si," and is the second most abundant element (next to oxygen) in the earth's crust, found in items like sand and clay. Silicon is used to make mirrors and glass, in addition to chips.

In fact, to the naked eye, a silicon chip actually looks like a small mirror.

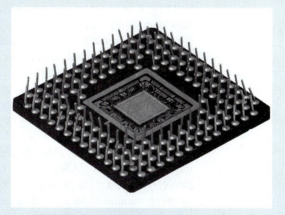

A chip package with its chip cover removed—you can see the mirror-like silicon chip in the center.

▶ 2.4 BOOLEAN LOGIC GATES—BUILDING BLOCKS FOR DIGITAL CIRCUITS

You've seen that CMOS transistors can be used to implement switches on an incredibly tiny scale. However, trying to use switches as our building blocks to build complex digital circuits is akin to trying to use small rocks to build a bridge, as illustrated in Figure 2.6. Sure, you could probably build something from rudimentary building blocks, but the building process would be a real pain. Switches (and small rocks) are just too low-level as building blocks.

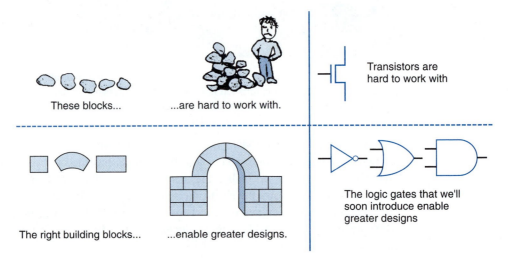

These blocks...   ...are hard to work with.   Transistors are hard to work with

The right building blocks...   ...enable greater designs.   The logic gates that we'll soon introduce enable greater designs

Figure 2.6 Having the right building blocks can make all the difference when building things.

Boolean Algebra and Its Relation to Digital Circuits

Fortunately, Boolean logic gates help us in the design task by representing digital circuit building blocks that are much easier to work with than switches. Boolean logic was developed in the mid-1800s by the mathematician George Boole, not to build digital circuits (which weren't even a glimmer in anyone's eye back then), but rather as a scheme for using algebraic methods to formalize human logic and thought.

An *algebra* is a branch of mathematics that uses letters or symbols to represent numbers or values, where those letters/symbols can be combined according to a set of known rules. **Boolean algebra** uses variables whose values can only be 1 or 0 (representing true or false, respectively) and whose operators, like AND, OR, and NOT, operate on such variables and return 1 or 0. So we might declare variables x, y, and z, and then say that z = x OR y, meaning z is 1 only if at least one of x or y is 1. Likewise, we might say z = x AND NOT(y), meaning z is 1 only if x is 1 and y is 0. Contrast Boolean algebra with the regular algebra you're familiar with from perhaps high school, in which variable values could be integers (for example), and operators could be addition, subtraction, and multiplication.

The basic Boolean operators are AND, OR, and NOT:

- AND returns 1 if *both* its operands are 1. So the result of a AND b is 1 if both a=1 and b=1, otherwise the result is 0.

"ab=01" is shorthand for "a=0, b=1."

- OR returns 1 if *either or both* of its operands are 1. So the result of a OR b is 1 in any of the following cases: ab=01, ab=10, ab=11. Thus, the only time a OR b is 0 is when ab=00.

- NOT returns 1 if its operand is 0. So NOT(a) return 1 if a is 0, and returns 0 if a is 1.

We use Boolean logic operators all the time in everyday thought, such as in the statement "I'll go to lunch if Mary goes OR John goes, AND Sally does not go." To represent this using Boolean concepts, let F represent my going to lunch (F=1 means I'll go to lunch, F=0 means I won't go). Let Boolean variables m, j, and s represent Mary, John, and Sally each going to lunch. Then we can translate the above English sentence into the Boolean equation:

$$F = (m \ OR \ j) \ AND \ NOT(s)$$

So F will equal 1 if either m or j is 1, and s is 0. Now that we've translated the English sentence into a Boolean equation, we can perform several mathematical activities with that equation.

One thing we can do is determine the value of F for different values of m, j, and s:

- m=1, j=0, s=1 → F = (1 OR 0) AND NOT(1) = 1 AND 0 = 0
- m=1, j=1, s=0 → F = (1 OR 1) AND NOT(0) = 1 AND 1 = 1

In the first case, I don't go to lunch; in the second, I do.

A second thing we could do is apply some algebraic rules (which we'll discuss later) to modify the original equation to the equivalent equation:

$$F = (m \ and \ NOT(s)) \ OR \ (j \ and \ NOT(s))$$

In other words, I'll go to lunch if Mary goes AND Sally does not go, OR if John goes AND Sally does not go. That statement, as different as it may look from the earlier one, is equivalent to the earlier one.

A third thing we could do is formally prove properties about the equation. For example, we could prove that if Sally goes to lunch (s=1), then I don't go to lunch (F=0) no matter who else goes, using the equation:

$$F = (m \ OR \ j) \ AND \ NOT(1) = (m \ OR \ j) \ AND \ 0 = 0$$

No matter what the values of m and j, F will equal 0.

Noting all the mathematical activities we can do using Boolean equations, you can start to see what Boole was trying to accomplish in formalizing human reasoning.

▶ **EXAMPLE 2.1** Converting a problem statement to a Boolean equation

Convert the following problem statements to Boolean equations using AND, OR, and NOT operators. F should equal 1 only if:

1. a is 1 and b is 1. *Answer:* F = a AND b

2. either of a or b is 1. *Answer:* F = a OR b

3. both a and b are not 0. *Answer:*

    (a) Option 1: F = NOT(a) AND NOT(b)

    (b) Option 2: F = a OR b

4. a is 1 and b is 0. *Answer:* F = a AND NOT(b)

Convert the following English problem statements to Boolean equations:

1. A fire sprinkler system should spray water if high heat is sensed and the system is set to enabled. *Answer:* Let Boolean variable h represent "high heat is sensed," e represent "enabled," and F represent "spraying water." Then an equation is: F = h AND e.

2. A car alarm should sound if the alarm is enabled, and either the car is shaken or the door is opened. *Answer:* Let a represent "alarm is enabled," s represent "car is shaken," d represent "door is opened," and F represent "alarm sounds." Then an equation is: F = a AND (s OR d).

    (a) Alternatively, assuming that our door sensor d represents "door is closed" instead of open (meaning d=1 when the door is closed, 0 when open), we obtain the following equation: F = a AND (s OR NOT(d)). ◀

▶ **EXAMPLE 2.2** Evaluating Boolean equations

Evaluate the Boolean equation F = (a AND b) OR (c AND d) for the given values of variables a, b, c, and d:

- a=1, b=1, c=1, d=0. *Answer:* F = (1 AND 1) OR (1 AND 0) = 1 OR 0 = 1.
- a=0, b=1, c=0, d=1. *Answer:* F = (0 AND 1) OR (0 AND 1) = 0 OR 0 = 0.
- a=1, b=1, c=1, d=1. *Answer:* F = (1 AND 1) OR (1 AND 1) = 1 OR 1 = 1.

◀

Shannon, by the way, is also considered the father of information theory due to his later work on digital communication.

One might now be wondering what Boolean algebra has to do with building circuits using switches. In 1938, an MIT graduate student named Claude Shannon wrote a paper (based on his Masters thesis) describing how Boolean algebra could be applied to switch-based circuits, by showing that "on" switches could be treated as a 1 (or true), and "off" switches as a 0 (or false), by connecting those switches in a certain way (Figure 2.7). His thesis is widely considered as the seed that developed into modern digital design. Since Boolean algebra comes with a rich set of axioms, theorems, postulates, and rules, we can use all those things to manipulate digital circuits using algebra. In other words:

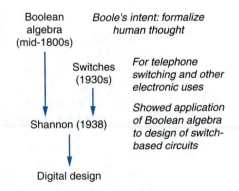

Figure 2.7 Shannon applied Boolean algebra to switch-based circuits, providing a formal basis to digital circuit design.

We can build circuits by doing math.

That's an extremely powerful concept. We'll be building circuits by doing math throughout this chapter.

AND, OR, & NOT Gates

Earlier we said a "gate" was the switch control input of a CMOS transistor, but now we're talking about "logic gates." In an unfortunate naming similarity, the same word (gate) refers to two different things. Don't worry though; after the next section, we'll just be using the word gate to refer to a "logic gate."

To build digital circuits that can be manipulated using Boolean algebra, we first implement the Boolean operators AND, OR, and NOT using small circuits of switches, and we call those circuits Boolean logic gates. Then, *we forget about switches*, and instead use Boolean logic gates as our building blocks. Suddenly, we have the power of Boolean algebra at our fingertips when designing more complex circuits! This is akin to first assembling rocks into three shapes of bricks, and then building structures like a bridge from those bricks, as illustrated in Figure 2.6. Trying to build a bridge from small rocks is much harder than building a bridge from the three basic brick shapes. Likewise, trying to build a motion-in-the-dark circuit (or any digital circuit) from switches is harder than building a circuit from Boolean logic gates.

Let's first implement Boolean logic gates using CMOS transistors, and then later we'll show you how Boolean algebra helps build better circuits. You really don't *have* to understand the underlying transistor implementations of logic gates to learn the digital design methods in the rest of this book, and in fact many textbooks omit the transistor discussion entirely. But an understanding of the underlying transistor implementation can be quite satisfying to a student, leaving no "mysteries." Such an understanding can also help in understanding the nonideal behavior of logic gates that one may later have to learn to deal with in digital design.

We'll start by using "1" to represent the power supply's voltage level, which today is usually around 1 to 2 V for CMOS technology (e.g., 0.7 V, or 1.3 V). Let's use "0" to represent ground. Note that we could have chosen any two symbols or words, rather than "1" and "0," to represent power and ground voltage levels. For example, we could have used "true" and "false," or "H" and "L." Remember that the "1" does not necessarily correspond to 1 V, and the "0" does not necessarily correspond to 0 V. In fact, each usually represents a voltage *range*, like "1" representing any voltage between 1.2 V to 1.4 V.

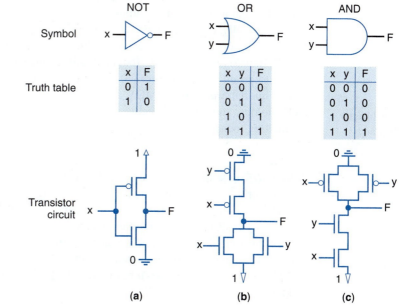

Figure 2.8 Basic logic gates symbols, truth tables, and transistor circuits: (a) NOT (inverter) gate, (b) 2-input OR gate, (c) 2-input AND gate. Warning: real AND and OR gates *aren't* actually built this way, but rather in a more complex manner—see Section 2.8.

NOT Gate

A **NOT gate** has an input x and an output F. F should always be the opposite, or inverse, of x—for this reason, a NOT gate is commonly called an **inverter**. We can build a NOT gate using one pMOS and one nMOS transistor, as shown in Figure 2.8(a). The triangle at the top of the transistor circuit represents the positive voltage of the power supply, which we represent as 1. The series of lines at the bottom of the circuit represents ground, which we represent as 0. When the input x is 0, the pMOS transistor will conduct, but the nMOS will not, as shown in Figure 2.9(a). In that case, we can think of the circuit as a wire from 1 to F, so when x = 0, F = 1. On the other hand, when x is 1, the nMOS will conduct, but the pMOS will not, as shown in Figure 2.9(b). In that case, we can think of the circuit as a wire from 0 to F, so when x=1, F=0. The table in Figure 2.8, called a **truth table**, summarizes the NOT gate's behavior by listing the gate's output for every possible input.

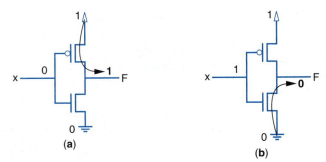

(a)   (b)

Figure 2.9 Inverter conduction paths when: (a) the input is 0, and (b) the input is 1.

Figure 2.10 shows a timing diagram for an inverter—when the input is 0, the output is 1; when the input is 1, the output is 0.

Electrically, combining pMOS and nMOS in this way has the benefit of low-power. Notice in Figure 2.8(a) that for any value of x, either the pMOS or nMOS transistor will be nonconducting. Thus (conceptually), current can never flow from the power source to ground—this feature will also be true for the AND and OR gates we'll define next. This feature makes CMOS circuits consume far less power than other transistor technologies, and partly explains why CMOS is the most popular logic gate transistor technology today.

Figure 2.10 Inverter timing diagram.

OR Gate

A basic **OR gate** has two inputs x and y and an output F. F should be 1 only if at least one of x or y is 1. We can build an OR gate using two pMOS transistors and two nMOS transistors, as shown in Figure 2.8(b) (although we will see in Section 2.8 that OR gates are actually built in a more complex manner). If at least one of x or y is 1, then we get a connection from 1 to F, but no connection from 0 to F, so F is 1, as shown in Figure 2.11(a). If both x and y are 0, then we get a connection from 0 to F, but no connection from 1 to F, so F is 0, as shown in Figure 2.11(b). The truth table for the OR gate appears in Figure 2.8(b).

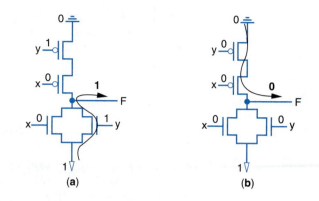

Figure 2.11 OR gate conduction paths when: (a) one input is 1, and (b) both inputs are 0.

(a)   **(b)**

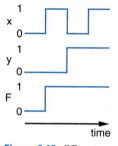

Figure 2.12 OR gate timing diagram.

Figure 2.12 shows a timing diagram for an OR gate. (See Section 1.3 for an introduction to timing diagrams.) We set inputs x and y to each possible combination of values, and show that F will be 1 if either or both inputs is a 1.

Larger OR gates, having more than two inputs, are also possible. If at least one of the OR gate's inputs are 1, the output is 1. For a three-input OR gate, the transistor circuit Figure 2.8(b) would have three pMOS transistors on top and three nMOS transistors on the bottom, instead of two transistors of each kind.

AND Gate

A basic *AND gate* has two inputs x and y and an output F. F should be 1 only if both x and y are 1. We can build an AND gate using two pMOS transistors and two nMOS transistors, as shown in Figure 2.8(c) (again, we will see in Section 2.8 that AND gates are actually built in a more complex manner). If both x and y are 1, then we get a connection from power to F, but no connection from ground to F, so F is 1, as shown in Figure 2.13(a). If at least one of x or y is 0, then we get a connection from ground to F, but no connection from power to F, so F is 0, as shown in Figure 2.13(b). The truth table for the AND gate appears in Figure 2.8(c).

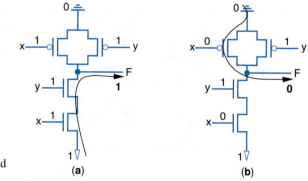

Figure 2.13 AND gate conduction paths when: (a) all inputs are 1, and (b) and input is 0.

(a)   **(b)**

Figure 2.14 AND gate timing diagram.

Figure 2.14 shows a timing diagram for an AND gate. We set inputs x and y to each possible combination of values, and show that F will be 1 only if both inputs are a 1.

Larger AND gates, having more than two inputs, are possible. The output is 1 only if all the inputs are 1. For a three-input AND gate, the transistor circuit Figure 2.8(b) would have three pMOS transistors on top and three nMOS transistors on the bottom, instead of two transistors of each kind.

Building Simple Circuits Using Gates

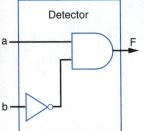

Having built logic gate building blocks from transistors, we now show how to build useful circuits from those building blocks. Recall the digital system example of Figure 1.13, the motion-in-the-dark detector. a=1 meant motion, and b=0 meant dark, so we wanted F = a AND NOT(b). We can connect b through an inverter to get NOT(b), and connect the result along with a into an AND gate, whose output is F. The resulting circuit appears in Figure 1.13(c), shown again to the left for convenience. We now provide more examples.

▶ **EXAMPLE 2.3** Converting a Boolean equation to a circuit with logic gates

Convert the following equation to a circuit:

```
F = a AND NOT( b OR NOT(c) )
```

We start by drawing F on the right, and then working backwards toward the inputs. (We could instead start by drawing the inputs on the left and working toward the output.) The equation for F ANDs two items: a, and the output of a NOT. We thus begin by drawing the circuit of Figure 2.15(a). The NOT's input comes from an OR of two items: b, and NOT(c). We thus complete the drawing in Figure 2.15(b) by including an OR gate and NOT gate as shown. ◀

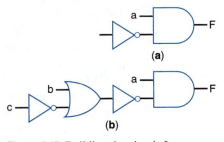

(a)

(b)

Figure 2.15 Building the circuit for F: (a) partial, (b) complete.

▶ **EXAMPLE 2.4** More examples converting Boolean equations to gates

Figure 2.16 provides two more examples of converting Boolean equations to circuits built from logic gates. We again start from the output and work backwards to the inputs. The figure shows the correspondence between equation operators and gates, and the order in which we placed each gate in the circuit.

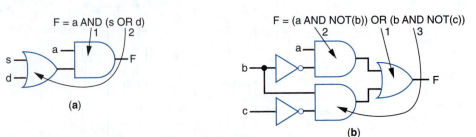

Figure 2.16 Examples of converting Boolean equations to circuits.

▶ **EXAMPLE 2.5** Using AND and OR gates with more than two inputs

Figure 2.17(a) shows an implementation of the equation F = a AND b AND c, using two-input AND gates. However, designers would typically instead implement such an equation using a single three-input AND gate, shown in Figure 2.17(b). The function is the same, but the three-input AND gate uses fewer transistors, 6 rather than 4+4=8 (as well as having less delay—more on delay later). Likewise, F = a AND b AND c AND d would typically be implemented using a four-input AND gate.

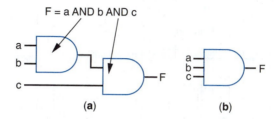

Figure 2.17 Using multiple-input AND gates: (a) using 2-input AND gates, (b) using a 3-input AND gate.

The same approach applies to OR gates. For example, F = a OR b OR c would typically be implemented using a single three-input OR gate. ◀

We now provide examples starting from English problem descriptions, which we convert to Boolean equations, and then finally implement as a circuit.

▶ **EXAMPLE 2.6** Seatbelt warning light

Suppose you want to design a system for an automobile that illuminates a warning light whenever the driver's seatbelt is not fastened and the key is in the ignition. Assume the following sensors:

- a sensor with output s indicates whether the driver's belt is fastened (s = 1 means the belt is fastened), and

- a sensor with output k indicates whether the key is in the ignition (k = 1 means the key is in).

Assume the warning light has a single input w that illuminates the light when w is 1. So the inputs to our digital system are s and k, and the output is w. w should equal 1 when both of the following occur: s is 0 and k is 1.

Let's first write a simple C program executing on a microprocessor to solve this design problem. If we connect s to I0, k to I1, and w to P0, then our C code inside the C program's main() function would be:

```
while (1) {
    P0 = !I0 && I1;
}
```

The code repeatedly checks the sensors and updates the warning light.

Now let's write a Boolean equation describing a circuit implementing the design:

$$w = NOT(s) \text{ AND } k$$

Using the AND and NOT logic gates that we introduced earlier, we can easily complete the design of our first system, by connecting s to a NOT gate, and connecting the resulting NOT(s) and k to the inputs of a 2-input AND gate, as shown in Figure 2.18.

Figure 2.19 provides a timing diagram for the circuit. In a timing diagram, we can set the inputs to whatever values we want, but then we must draw the output line to match the circuit's function. In the figure, we set s and k to 00, then 01, then 10, then 11. The only time that the output w will be 1 is when s is 0 and k is 1, as shown in the figure. ◀

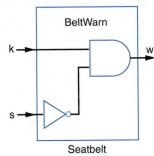

Figure 2.18 Seatbelt warning circuit.

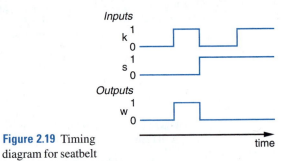

Figure 2.19 Timing diagram for seatbelt warning circuit.

We stated earlier that logic gates are more appropriate than transistors as building blocks for designing digital circuits. Note, however, that the logic gates are ultimately implemented using transistors, as shown in Figure 2.20. For C programmers, an analogy is that writing software in C is easier than writing in assembly, even though the C ultimately gets implemented using assembly. Notice how much less intuitive and less descriptive is the transistor-based circuit in Figure 2.20 than the equivalent logic gate-based circuit in Figure 2.18.

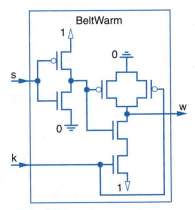

Figure 2.20 Seat belt warning circuit using transistors.

▶ **EXAMPLE 2.7** Seat belt warning light with driver sensor

Let's extend the previous example by adding a sensor, with output p, that detects whether a person is actually sitting in the driver's seat, and by changing the system's behavior to only illuminate the warning when a person is detected in the seat (p=1). So the new circuit equation is:

$$w = p \text{ AND NOT}(s) \text{ AND } k$$

In this case, we need a 3-input AND gate. The circuit is shown in Figure 2.21.

Be aware that the order of the AND gate's inputs does not matter. ◀

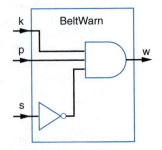

Figure 2.21 Seat belt warning circuit with person sensor.

▶ **EXAMPLE 2.8** Seat belt warning light with initial illumination

Let's further extend the previous example. Automobiles typically light up all their warning lights when you first turn the key, so you can check that all the warning lights are working. Assume that our system receives an input t that is 1 for the first 5 seconds after a key is inserted into the ignition, and 0 afterward (don't worry about who or what sets t in that way). So we want w=1 when p=1 and s=0 and k=1, OR when t=1. Note that when t=1, we illuminate the light, regardless of the values of p, s, and k. The new circuit equation is:

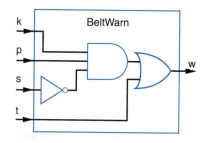

Figure 2.22 Extended seat belt warning circuit.

```
w = (p AND NOT(s) AND k) OR t
```

The circuit is shown in Figure 2.22. ◀

Some circuit drawing rules and conventions

There are some rules and conventions that designers commonly follow when drawing circuits of logic gates:

- Logic gates have one or more inputs and one output, but we typically don't label each gate's inputs or output. Remember that the order of the inputs into a gate doesn't impact the logical behavior of the gate.

- Each wire has an implicit direction, going from one gate's output to another gate's input, but we typically don't draw arrows showing each direction.

- A single wire can be branched out into two (or more) wires going to multiple gate inputs—the branches have the same value as the single wire. But two wires can NOT be merged into one wire—what would be the value of that one wire if the incoming two wires had different values?

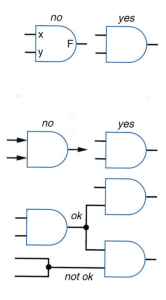

▶ 2.5 BOOLEAN ALGEBRA

Logic gates are useful for implementing circuits, but equations are better for manipulating circuits. The algebraic tools of Boolean algebra enable us to manipulate Boolean equations so we can do things like simplify the equations, check if two equations are equivalent, find the inverse of an equation, prove properties about the equations, etc. Since a Boolean equation consisting of AND, OR, and NOT operations can be straightforwardly transformed into a circuit of AND, OR, and NOT gates, manipulating Boolean equations can be considered as manipulating digital circuits.

We'll informally introduce some of the most useful algebraic tools of Boolean algebra. Appendix A provides a formal definition of Boolean algebra.

Notation and Terminology

We now define some notation and terminology for describing Boolean equations. We'll use these definitions extensively throughout the book.

Operators

Writing out the AND, OR and NOT operators in equations is cumbersome. Thus, Boolean algebra uses simpler notation for those operators:

- "NOT(a)" is typically written as a' or $\overline{a}$. We'll use a', which one speaks of as "a *prime*." a' is also known as the *complement* of a, or the *inverse* of a.

- "a OR b" is typically written as "$a + b$," specifically intended to look similar to the addition operator in regular algebra. "$a + b$" is even referred to as the *sum* of a and b. "$a + b$" is usually spoken of as "a or b."

- "a AND b" is typically written as "$a * b$" or "$a \cdot b$," specifically intended to look similar to the multiplication operator in regular algebra, and even referred to as the *product* of a and b. Just as in regular algebra, we can even write "ab" for the product of a and b, as long as the fact that a and b are separate variables is clear. "$a*b$" is usually spoken of as "a and b" or even just as "a b."

Mathematicians often use other notations for Boolean operators, but the above notations seem to be the most popular among engineers, likely due to the intentional similarity of those operators with regular algebra operators.

Using the simpler notation, our earlier seat belt example of:

$$w = (p\ AND\ NOT(s)\ AND\ k)\ OR\ t$$

could be rewritten more concisely as:

$$w = ps'k + t$$

which would be spoken of as "w equals p s prime k, or t."

▶ **EXAMPLE 2.9**   Speaking Boolean equations

Speak the following equations:

1. $F = a'b' + c$. *Answer:* "F equals a prime b prime or c."

2. $F = a + b * c'$. *Answer:* "F equals a or b and c prime."

Convert the following spoken equations into written equations:

1. "F equals a b prime c prime." Answer: $F = ab'c'$.

2. "F equals a b c or d e prime." Answer: $F = abc + de'$.   ◀

The rules of Boolean algebra require that we evaluate expressions using the precedence rule that $*$ has precedence over $+$, that complementing a variable has precedence over $*$ and $+$, and that we of course compute what's in parentheses first. We can make the earlier equation's order of evaluation explicit using parentheses as follows: $w = (p * (s') * k) + t$.

Table 2.1 summarizes Boolean algebra precedence rules.

2.5 Boolean Algebra ◀ **49**

TABLE 2.1 Boolean algebra precedence, highest precedence first.

Symbol	Name	Description
( )	Parentheses	Evaluate expressions nested in parentheses first
'	NOT	Evaluate from left to right
*	AND	Evaluate from left to right
+	OR	Evaluate from left to right

Conventions

Although we borrowed the multiplication and addition operations from regular algebra and even use the terms sum and product, we *don't* say "times" for AND or "plus" for OR.

Digital design textbooks typically name each variable using a single character, because using a single character makes for concise equations like the equations above. We'll be writing many equations, so conciseness will aid understanding by preventing equations that wrap across multiple lines or pages. Thus, we'll usually follow the convention of using single characters. However, when you describe digital systems using a hardware description language or a programming language like C, you should probably use much more descriptive names so that your code is readable. So instead of using "s" to represent the output of a seat-belt-fastened sensor, you might instead use "SeatBeltFastened."

▶ **EXAMPLE 2.10** Evaluating Boolean equations using precedence rules

Evaluate the following Boolean equations, assuming a=1, b=1, c=0, d=1.

1. F = a * b + c. *Answer:* * has precedence over +, so we evaluate the equation as F = (1 * 1) + 0 = (1) + 0 = 1 + 0 = 1.

2. F = ab + c. *Answer:* the problem is identical to the previous problem, using the shorthand notation for *.

3. F = ab'. *Answer:* we first evaluate b' because NOT has precedence over AND, resulting in F = 1 * (1') = 1 * (0) = 1 * 0 = 0.

4. F = (ac)'. *Answer:* we first evaluate what is inside the parentheses, then we NOT the result, yielding (1*0)' = (0)' = 0' = 1.

5. F = (a + b') * c + d'. *Answer:* The parentheses have highest precedence. Inside the parentheses, NOT has highest precedence. So we evaluate the parentheses part as (1 + (1')) = (1 + (0)) = (1 + 0) = 1. Next, * has precedence over +, yielding (1 * 0) + 1' = (0) + 1'. The NOT has precedence over the OR, giving (0) + (1') = (0) + (0) = 0 + 0 = 0. ◀

Variables, Literals, Terms, and Sum of Products

Let's define a few more concepts, using the example equation: F(a,b,c) = a'bc + abc' + ab + c.

- *Variable:* A variable represents a quantity (0 or 1). The above equation has three variables: a, b, and c. We typically use variables in Boolean equations to represent the inputs of our systems. Sometimes we explicitly list a function's variables as above ("F(a,b,c) = ..."). Other times we omit the explicit list ("F = ...").

- *Literal:* A literal is the appearance of a variable, in either true or complemented form. The above equation has 9 literals: a', b, c, a, b, c', a, b, and c.
- *Product term:* A product term is a product of literals. The above equation has four terms: a'bc, abc', ab, and c.
- *Sum-of-Products:* An equation written as an ORing of product terms is known as being in sum-of-products form. The above example equation for F is in sum-of-products form. The following equations are all in sum-of-products form:

```
abc + abc'
ab + a'c + abc
a + b' + ac  (note that a product term can have just one literal).
```

The following equations are all NOT in sum-of-products form:

```
(a + b)c
(ab + bc)(b + c)
(a')' + b
a(b + c(d + e))
(ab + bc)'
```

Some Properties of Boolean Algebra

We now list some of the key rules of Boolean algebra. Assume a, b, and c are Boolean variables, which each hold either the value of 0 or 1.

Basic Properties

The following properties, known as postulates, are assumed to be true:

- *Commutative*

$$a + b = b + a$$
$$a * b = b * a$$

This property should be obvious. Just try it for different values of a and b.

- *Distributive*

$$a * (b + c) = a * b + a * c$$
$$a + (b * c) = (a + b) * (a + c) \text{ (this one is tricky!)}$$

Careful, the second one may not be obvious. It's different than regular algebra. But you can verify that both of the distributive properties hold simply by evaluating both sides for all possible values of a, b, and c.

- *Associative*

$$(a + b) + c = a + (b + c)$$
$$(a * b) * c = a * (b * c)$$

Again, try it for different values of a and b to see that this holds.

- *Identity*

$$0 + a = a + 0 = a$$
$$1 * a = a * 1 = a$$

Makes intuitive sense, right? ORing a with 0 (a+0) just means that the result will be whatever a is. After all, 1+0 is 1, while 0+0 is 0. Likewise, ANDing a with 1 (a*1) results in a. 1*1 is 1, while 0*1 is 0.

- *Complement*

$$a + a' = 1$$
$$a * a' = 0$$

This also makes intuitive sense. Regardless of the value of a, a' is the opposite, so you get a 0 and a 1, or you get a 1 and a 0. One of (a, a') will always be a 1, so ORing them (a+a') must yield a 1. Likewise, one of (a, a') will always be a 0, so ANDing them (a*a') must yield a 0.

Let's now apply these basic properties to some digital design examples, to see how these properties can help us.

► **EXAMPLE 2.11** Applying the basic properties of Boolean algebra

Use the properties of Boolean algebra for the following problems:

- Show that abc' is equivalent to c'ba.
  The commutative property allows us to swap the operands being ANDed, so a*b*c' = a*c'*b = c'*a*b = c'*b*a = c'ba.

- Show that abc + abc' = ab.
  The first distributive property allows us to factor out the ab term: abc + abc' = ab(c+c'). Then, the complement property allows us to replace the c+c' by 1: ab(c+c') = ab(1). Finally, the identity property allows us to remove the 1 from the AND term: ab(1) = ab*1 = ab.

- Show that the equation x + x'z is equivalent to x + z.
  The second distributive property (the tricky one) allows us to replace x+x'z by (x+x')*(x+z). The complement property allows us to replace (x+x') by 1, and the identity allows us to replace 1*(x+z) by x+z. ◄

► **EXAMPLE 2.12** Simplification of an automatic sliding door system

Suppose you wish to design a system to control an automatic sliding door, like one that might be found at a grocery store's entrance. An input p to our system indicates whether a sensor detects a person in front of the door (p=1 means a person is detected). An input h indicates whether the door should be manually held open (h=1) regardless of whether a person is detected. An input c indicates whether the door should be forced to stay closed (like when the store is closed for business)—c = 1 means the door should stay closed. The latter two would normally be set by a manager with the proper keys. An output f opens the door when f is 1.

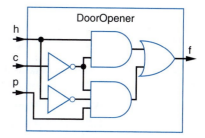

Figure 2.23 Initial door opener circuit.

We want to open the door if the door is set to be manually held open, OR if the door is not set to be manually held open but a person is detected. However, in either case, we only open the door if the door is not set to stay closed. We can translate these requirements into a Boolean equation as:

$$f = hc' + h'pc'$$

We could build a circuit to implement this equation, as in Figure 2.23.

Now let's manipulate the equation using the properties described earlier. Looking at the equation, we believe we can factor out the c'. We might then be able to simplify the remaining "h+h'p" part too. Let's try some transformations, first factoring out c':

f = hc' + h'pc'	
f = c'h + c'h'p	(by the commutative property)
f = c'(h + h'p)	(by the first distributive property)
f = c'((h+h')*(h+p))	(by the 2nd distributive property—tricky one!)
f = c'((1)*(h + p))	(by the complement property)
f = c'(h+p)	(by the identity property)

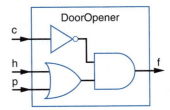

Note that the simpler equation still makes intuitive sense—we open the door only if the door is not set to stay closed (c'), AND either the door is set to be manually held open (h) OR a person is detected (p). A circuit implementing this equation is shown in Figure 2.24. Thus, by applying the algebraic properties, we obtained a simpler circuit. In other words, we used math to simplify the circuit. ◀

Figure 2.24 Simplified door opener circuit.

Simplification of logic circuits will be the focus of Section 2.11.

▶ **EXAMPLE 2.13** Equivalence of two automatic sliding door systems

Suppose you found a really cheap device for automatic sliding door systems. The device had inputs c, h, and p and output f, as in Example 2.12, but the device's documentation said that:

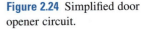

$$f = c'hp + c'hp' + c'h'p$$

Does that device do the same as that in Example 2.12? One way to check is to see if we can manipulate the above equation into the equation in Example 2.12:

f = c'hp + c'hp' + c'h'p	
f = c'h(p + p') + c'h'p	(by the distributive property)
f = c'h(1) + c'h'p	(by the complement property)
f = c'h + c'h'p	(by the identity property)
f = hc' + h'pc'	(by the commutative property)

That's the same as the original equation of Example 2.12, so the device should work for us. ◀

Additional Properties

Let's consider some additional properties, which happen to be known as theorems because they can be proven using the above postulates:

- *Null elements*

$$a + 1 = 1$$
$$a * 0 = 0$$

These should be fairly obvious. 1 OR anything is going to be 1, while 0 AND anything is going to be 0.

- *Idempotent Law*

$$a + a = a$$
$$a * a = a$$

Again, this should be fairly obvious. If a is 1, 1+1=1 and 1*1=1, while if a is 0, 0+0=0 and 0*0=0.

- *Involution Law*

$$(a')' = a$$

Again, fairly obvious. If a is 1, the first negation gives 0, while the second gives 1 again. Likewise, if a is 0, the first negation gives 1, while the second gives 0 again.

- *DeMorgan's Law*

$$(a + b)' = a'b'$$
$$(ab)' = a' + b'$$

These are not as obvious. Their proofs are in Appendix A. Let's consider both equations intuitively here. Consider (a + b)' = a'b'. The left side will only be 1 if (a + b) evaluates to 0, which only occurs when both a AND b are 0, meaning a'b' — the right side. Likewise, consider (ab)' = a' + b'. The left side will only be 1 if (ab) evaluates to 0, meaning at least one of a OR b must be 0, meaning a' + b'— the right side. DeMorgan's Law can be stated in English as follows: The complement of a sum equals the product of the complements; the complement of a product equals the sum of the complements. DeMorgan's Law is widely used, so take the time now to understand it and to remember it.

Let's apply some of these additional properties in more examples.

▶ **EXAMPLE 2.14** Applying the additional properties

- Convert the equation F = ab(c+d) into sum-of-products form.
  The distributive property allows us to "multiply out" the equation to F = abc + abd.

- Convert the equation F = wx(x'y + zy' + xy) into sum-of-products form, and make any obvious simplifications.
  The distributive property allows us to "multiply out" the equation: wx(x'y+zy'+ xy) = wxx'y + wxzy' + wxxy. That equation is in sum-of-products form. The complement property allows us to replace wxx'y by w*0*y, and the null element property means that w*0*y = 0. The idempotent property allows us to replace wxxy by wxy (because xx = x). The resulting equation is 0 + wxzy' + wxy = wxzy' + wxy.

- Prove that x(x' + y(x'+y')) can never evaluate to 1.
  Repeated application of the first distributive property yields: xx'+xy(x'+y') = xx' + xyx' + xyy'. The complement property tells us that xx'=0 and yy'=0, yielding 0 + 0*y + x*0. The null element property leads to 0 + 0 + 0, which equals 0. Thus, the equation always evaluates to 0, regardless of the actual values of x and y.

- Determine the opposite function of F = (ab' + c).
  The desired function is G = F' = (ab'+c)'. DeMorgan's Law yields G = (ab')' * c'. Applying DeMorgan's Law again to the first term yields G = (a'+(b')') * c'. The involution property yields (a' + b) * c'. Finally, the distributive property yields G = a'c' + bc'.

◀

▶ EXAMPLE 2.15 Applying DeMorgan's Law in an aircraft lavatory sign

Commercial aircraft typically have an illuminated sign indicating whether a lavatory (bathroom) is available. Suppose an aircraft has three lavatories. Each lavatory has a sensor outputting 1 if the lavatory door is locked, 0 otherwise. Our circuit will have three inputs, a, b, and c, coming from those sensors, as shown in Figure 2.25. If *any* lavatory door is unlocked (whether one, two, or all three doors are unlocked), we should illuminate the "Available" sign by setting the circuit's output S to 1.

Figure 2.25 Aircraft lavatory sign block.

With this understanding, we recognize that the OR function suits the problem, as OR outputs 1 if any of its inputs are 1, regardless of how many inputs are 1. We begin writing an equation for S. S should be 1 if a is 0 OR b is 0 OR c is 0. Saying a is 0 is the same as saying a'. Thus, the equation for S is:

$$S = a' + b' + c'$$

We translate the equation to the circuit in Figure 2.26.

We can apply DeMorgan's Law (in reverse) to the equation by noting that $(abc)' = a'+b'+c'$, so we can replace the equation by:

$$S = (abc)'$$

The circuit for that equation appears in Figure 2.27. ◀

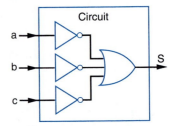

Figure 2.26 Aircraft lavatory sign circuit.

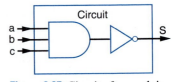

Figure 2.27 Circuit after applying DeMorgan's Law.

▶ EXAMPLE 2.16 Proving a property of the automatic sliding door system

Your boss wants you to *prove* that the automatic sliding door circuit of Example 2.12 ensures that the door will stay closed when the door is supposed to be forced to stay closed, namely, when c=1. If the function $f = c'(h+p)$ describes the sliding door, you can prove the door will stay closed (f=0) using properties of Boolean algebra:

$$f = c'(h+p)$$
Let c = 1 (door forced closed)
$$f = 1'(h+p)$$
$$f = 0(h+p)$$
$$f = 0h + 0p \text{ (by the distributive property)}$$
$$f = 0 + 0 \text{ (by the null elements property)}$$
$$f = 0$$

Therefore, no matter what the values of h and p, if c=1, f will equal 0—the door will stay closed. ◀

▶ EXAMPLE 2.17 Automatic sliding door with opposite polarity

In Example 2.12, we computed the function to open an automatic sliding door as:

$$f = c'(h + p)$$

▶ *YOUR PROBLEM IS MY PROBLEM*

The use of Boolean algebra for digital design is an example of the powerful general concept of mapping one problem to another. By mapping a new problem (digital design) to an old problem (logic representation), the solutions (Boolean algebra) to the old problem can be applied to the new problem. Immediately, the new problem can benefit from perhaps decades of work of solving the old problem. Mapping one problem to another is extremely common in engineering, especially in computing. After all, why reinvent the wheel?

Suppose your automatic door control has an input with the opposite polarity as what we expect: 0 means open the door, while 1 means close. We can compute the function g that opens the door, and simplify that function, as follows:

```
g = f'
g = (c'(h+p))'          (by substituting the equation for f)
g = (c')' + (h+p)'      (by DeMorgan's Law)
g = c + (h+p)'          (by the Involution Law)
g = c + h'p'            (by DeMorgan's Law)
```
◀

▶ 2.6 REPRESENTATIONS OF BOOLEAN FUNCTIONS

A *Boolean function* is a *mapping* of each possible combination of values for the function's variables (the inputs) to either a 0 or 1 (the output). An example of a Boolean function described in regular English is a function F of variables a and b, such that the function outputs 1 when a is 0 and b is 0, or when a is 0 and b is 1. There are several better representations than English for describing a Boolean function, including equations, circuits, and truth tables, as shown in Figure 2.28. Each representation has its own advantages and disadvantages, and each is useful at different times during design. Yet all the representations, as different as they look from one another, represent the very same function. It's like how there are different ways to represent a particular recipe for chocolate chip cookies: written words, pictures, or even a video. But no matter how the recipe is represented, it's the same recipe.

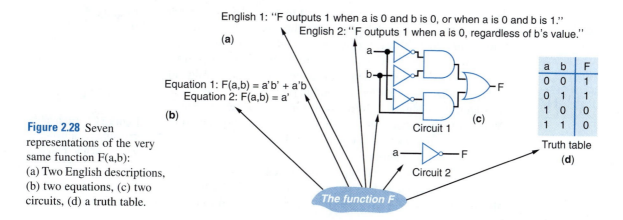

English 1: "F outputs 1 when a is 0 and b is 0, or when a is 0 and b is 1."
English 2: "F outputs 1 when a is 0, regardless of b's value."
(a)

Equation 1: F(a,b) = a'b' + a'b
Equation 2: F(a,b) = a'
(b)

Circuit 1
Circuit 2
(c)

a	b	F
0	0	1
0	1	1
1	0	0
1	1	0

Truth table
(d)

The function F

Figure 2.28 Seven representations of the very same function F(a,b): (a) Two English descriptions, (b) two equations, (c) two circuits, (d) a truth table.

Equations

One way to represent a Boolean function is by using an equation. An *equation* is a mathematical statement equating one expression with another. $F(a,b) = a'b' + a'b$ is an example of an equation. The right-hand side of the equation is often referred to as an *expression*, which evaluates to either 0 or 1.

We've seen that different equations can represent the same function. The equation $F(a,b) = a'b' + a'b$ represents the same function as does the equation $F(a,b) = a'$. Both equations perform exactly the same mapping of the input values to output values—pick any input values (e.g., $a=0$ and $b=0$), and both equations map those input values to the same output value (e.g., $a=0$ and $b=0$ would be mapped to $F=1$ by either equation).

One advantage of an equation as a Boolean function representation compared to other representations is that we can easily manipulate an equation using properties of Boolean algebra, enabling us to simplify an equation, prove that two equations represent the same function, prove properties about a function, and more.

Circuits

A second way to represent a Boolean function is using a circuit of logic gates. A *circuit* is an interconnection of components. Because each logic gate component has a predefined mapping of input values to output values, and because wires just transmit their values unchanged, a circuit describes a function.

We've seen that different circuits can represent the same function. The two circuits in Figure 2.28 both represent the same function F. The bottom circuit uses fewer gates, but the function is exactly the same as the top circuit.

One advantage of a circuit as a Boolean function representation compared to other representations is that a circuit may represent an actual physical implementation of a Boolean function, and ultimately our goal is to implement digital circuits physically. Another advantage is that a circuit drawn graphically can enable quick and easy comprehension of a function by humans.

Truth Table

A third way to represent a Boolean function is using a *truth table*. A truth table's left side lists the input variables, and shows *all possible value combinations of those inputs*, with one row per combination, as shown in Figure 2.29. A truth table's right side would then list the function's output value (1 or 0) for the row's particular combination of input values, as was shown in Figure 2.28(d). Any function of two variables will have those four input combinations on the left side. People usually list the input combinations in order of increasing binary value (00=0, 01=1, 10=2, 11=3), as we've done above, though strictly speaking, we could list the combinations in any order as long as we listed all possible combinations. For any combination of input values (e.g., $a=0$, $b=0$), we merely need to look at the corresponding value in

Inputs		Output
a	b	F
0	0	
0	1	
1	0	
1	1	

Figure 2.29 Truth table structure for a two-input function F(a,b).

the output column (in the case of a=0, b=0, the output shown in Figure 2.28(d) is 1) to determine the function's output.

Figure 2.30 shows the truth table structures for a two-input function, a three-input function, and a four-input function.

a	b	F
0	0	
0	1	
1	0	
1	1	

(a)

a	b	c	F
0	0	0	
0	0	1	
0	1	0	
0	1	1	
1	0	0	
1	0	1	
1	1	0	
1	1	1	

(b)

a	b	c	d	F
0	0	0	0	
0	0	0	1	
0	0	1	0	
0	0	1	1	
0	1	0	0	
0	1	0	1	
0	1	1	0	
0	1	1	1	
1	0	0	0	
1	0	0	1	
1	0	1	0	
1	0	1	1	
1	1	0	0	
1	1	0	1	
1	1	1	0	
1	1	1	1	

(c)

Figure 2.30 Truth table structures for: (a) a two-input function F(a,b), (b) a three-input function F(a,b,c), and (c) a four-input function F(a,b,c,d). Defining a specific function would involve filling in the rightmost column for F with a 0 or a 1 for each row.

Truth tables are not only found in digital design. If you've studied basic biology, you've likely seen a type of truth table describing the outcome of various gene pairs. For example, the table on the right shows outcomes for different eye color genes. Each person has two genes for eye color, one (labeled M) from the

Gene pair		Outcome
M	D	F
blue	blue	blue
blue	brown	brown
brown	blue	brown
brown	brown	brown

mom, one (labeled D) from the dad. Assuming only two possible values for each gene, blue and brown, the table lists all possible combinations of eye color gene pairs that a person may have. For each combination, the table lists the outcome. Only when a person has two blue eye genes will they have blue eyes; having one or two brown eye genes results in brown eyes (due to the brown eye gene being dominant over the blue eye gene.)

Unlike equations and circuits, a Boolean function has only *one* truth table representation.

One advantage of a truth table as a Boolean function representation compared to other representations is the fact that a function has only one truth table representation, so we can convert any other Boolean function representations to truth tables to determine if different representations represent the same function—if they represent the same function, their truth tables will be identical. Truth tables are also quite intuitive to human readers, as a truth table clearly shows the output for every possible input. Thus, notice that we used truth tables in Figure 2.8 to describe in an intuitive manner the behavior of basic logic gates.

A drawback of truth tables is that for a large number of inputs, the number of truth table rows can be extremely large. Given a function with n inputs, the number of input combinations is 2^n. A function with 10 inputs would have $2^{10} = 1024$ possible input combinations—you can't easily see much of anything in a table having 1024 rows. A function with 16 inputs would have 65,536 rows in its truth table.

▶ **EXAMPLE 2.18** Capturing a function as a truth table

TABLE 2.2 Truth table for 5-or-greater function.

a	b	c	F
0	0	0	0
0	0	1	0
0	1	0	0
0	1	1	0
1	0	0	0
1	0	1	1
1	1	0	1
1	1	1	1

Create a truth table describing a function that detects whether a three-bit input's' value, representing a binary number, is 5 or greater. Table 2.2 shows a truth table for the function. We first list all possible combinations of the three input bits, which we've labeled a, b, and c. We then enter a 1 in the output row if the inputs represent 5, 6, or 7 in binary. We enter 0s in all remaining rows.   ◀

Converting among Boolean Function Representations

Given the above representations, we can view combinational logic design as defining the appropriate Boolean function to solve a particular problem, and then creating a circuit representation of that function. Defining the appropriate Boolean function requires not only that we think about what that function should be, but also that we capture that function in some form—typically either as an equation or a truth table. Then, we must convert the captured function representation into a circuit. Thus, combinational logic design requires that we know how to convert from one Boolean function representation to another. For the three representations we have discussed so far (equations, circuits, and truth tables), there are six possible conversions from one representation to another, which we now describe (Figure 2.31).

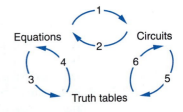

Equations   Circuits

Truth tables

Figure 2.31 Possible conversions from one Boolean function representation to another.

1. Equations to circuits
Converting an equation to a circuit can be done straightforwardly by using an AND gate for every AND operator, an OR gate for every OR operator, and a NOT gate for every NOT operator. We already gave several examples of such conversions in Section 2.4.

2. Circuits to equations
Converting a circuit into an equation can be done by starting from the circuits inputs, and then writing the output of each gate as an expression involving the gate's inputs. The expression of the last gate before the output represents the expression for the circuit's

function. For example, suppose we are given the circuit in Figure 2.32. To convert to an equation, we start with the inverter, whose output will represent `c'`. We continue with the OR gate—note that we can't determine the output for the AND gate yet until we create expressions for all that gate's inputs. The OR gate's output represents `h+p`. Finally, we write the output of the AND as `c'(h+p)`. Thus, the equation `F(c,h,p) = c'(h+p)` represents the same function as the circuit.

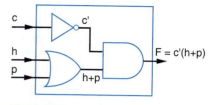

Figure 2.32 Converting a circuit to an equation.

3. Equations to truth tables

Converting an equation to a truth table can be done by first creating a truth table structure appropriate for the number of function input variables, and then evaluating the right-hand side of the equation for each combination of input values. For example, to convert the equation `F(a,b) = a'b' + a'b` to a truth table, we would first create the truth table structure for a two-input function, as shown in Figure 2.30(a). We would then evaluate the right-hand side of the equation for each row's combination of input values, as follows:

Inputs		Output
a	b	F
0	0	1
0	1	1
1	0	0
1	1	0

Figure 2.33 Truth table for F(a,b)=a'b'+a'b.

- `a=0` and `b=0`, `F = 0'*0' + 0'*0 = 1*1 + 1*0 = 1 + 0 = 1`
- `a=0` and `b=1`, `F = 0'*1' + 0'*1 = 1*0 + 1*1 = 0 + 1 = 1`
- `a=1` and `b=0`, `F = 1'*0' + 1'*0 = 0*1 + 0*0 = 0 + 0 = 0`
- `a=1` and `b=1`, `F = 1'*1' + 1'*1 = 0*0 + 0*1 = 0 + 0 = 0`

We would therefore fill in the table's right column as shown in Figure 2.33. Note that we applied properties of Boolean algebra (mostly the identity property and null elements property) to evaluate the equations.

Notice that converting the equation `F(a,b)=a'` to a truth table results in exactly the same truth table as shown in Figure 2.33. In particular, evaluating the right-hand side of the equation for each row's combination of input values yields:

- `a=0` and `b=0`, `F = 0' = 1`
- `a=0` and `b=1`, `F = 0' = 1`
- `a=1` and `b=0`, `F = 1' = 0`
- `a=1` and `b=1`, `F = 1' = 0`

Inputs				Output
a	b	a' b'	a' b	F
0	0	1	0	1
0	1	0	1	1
1	0	0	0	0
1	1	0	0	0

Figure 2.34 Truth table for F(a,b)=a'b'+a'b with intermediate columns.

Some people find it useful to create intermediate columns in the truth table to compute the equation's intermediate values, thus filling each column of the table from left to right, moving to the next column only after filling all rows of the current column. An example for the equation `F(a,b) = a'b' + a'b` is shown in Figure 2.34.

4. Truth tables to equations

To convert a truth table to an equation, we create a product term for each 1 in the output column, and we then OR all the product terms. For the table on the right (Figure 2.35), we get the terms shown in the rightmost column of that table. ORing those terms yields $F = a'b' + a'b$.

Inputs		Outputs	Term
a	b	F	F = sum of
0	0	1	a' b'
0	1	1	a' b
1	0	0	
1	1	0	

Figure 2.35 Converting a truth table to an equation.

5. Circuits to truth tables

We can convert a combinational circuit to a truth table by first converting the circuit to an equation (described earlier), and then converting the equation to a truth table (described earlier).

6. Truth tables to circuits

We can convert a truth table to a circuit by first converting the truth table to an equation (described earlier), and then converting the equation to a circuit (described earlier).

▷ **EXAMPLE 2.19** Parity generator circuit design starting from a truth table

Nothing is perfect, and digital circuits are no exception. Sometimes a bit on a wire changes when it's not supposed to. So a 1 becomes a 0, or a 0 becomes a 1. For example, a 0 may be traveling along a wire, when suddenly some electrical noise comes out of nowhere and changes the 0 to a 1. While we can reduce the likelihood of such errors, perhaps by using well-insulated wires, we can't completely prevent such errors, nor can we detect and correct all of them—but we can detect *some* of them. Designers typically look for situations where errors are likely to occur, such as data being transmitted between two chips over long wires—like from a computer over a printer cable to a printer, or from a computer over a telephone line to another computer. For those situations, designers add circuits that at least try to detect that an error has occurred, in which case the receiving circuit can ask the sending circuit to resend the data.

One common method of detecting an error is called parity. Say we have 7 data bits to transmit. We add an extra bit, called the parity bit, to make 8 bits total. The sender sets the parity bit to a 1 if that would make the total number of 1s even—that's called **even parity**. For example, if the 7 data bits were 0000001, then the parity bit would be 1, making the total number of 1s equal to 2 (an even number). The complete 8 bits would be 00000011. If the 7 data bits were 1011111, then the parity bit would be 0, making the total number of 1s equal to 6 (an even number). The complete 8 bits would be 10111110.

The receiver now can detect if a bit has changed during transmission by checking that there's an even number of 1s in the 8 bits received. If even, the transmission is assumed correct. If not even, an error occurred during transmission. For example, if the receiver receives 00000011, the transmission is assumed to be correct, and the parity bit can be discarded, leaving 0000001. Suppose instead that an error occurred and the receiver receives 10000011. Seeing the odd number of 1s, the receiver knows that an error occurred—note that the receiver does *not* know which bit is erroneous. Likewise, 00000010 would represent an error too. Notice in this case that the error occurred in the parity bit, but the receiver doesn't know where the error occurred.

For this example, starting from a truth table is a more natural choice than an equation.

Let's describe a function that generates an even parity bit P for 3 data bits a, b, and c. Starting from an equation is hard—what's the equation? For this example, starting with a truth table is the natural choice, as shown in Table 2.3. For each configuration of data bits (i.e., for each row in the truth table), we set the parity bit to make the total number of 1s even. From the truth table, we then obtain the following equation for the parity bit:

$$P = a'b'c + a'bc' + ab'c' + abc$$

We could then design the circuit using four AND gates and an OR gate.

Note that even parity doesn't mean for sure that the data is correct (note that we were careful to say earlier that the transmission was "assumed" to be correct if the parity was correct). In particular, if two errors occur on different bits, then the parity will still be even. For example, the sender may send 0110, but the receiver may receive 1111. 1111 has even parity and thus looks correct. More powerful error detection methods are possible to detect multiple errors like this one, but at the price of adding extra bits.

Odd parity is also a common kind of parity—the parity bit value makes the total number of 1s odd. There's no quality difference between even parity and odd parity—the key is simply that the sender and receiver must both use the same kind of parity, even or odd.

A popular representation of letters and numbers is known as ASCII, which encodes each character into 7 bits. ASCII adds 1 bit for parity, for a total of 8 bits per character.   ◀

TABLE 2.3 Even parity for 3-bit data.

a	b	c	P
0	0	0	0
0	0	1	1
0	1	0	1
0	1	1	0
1	0	0	1
1	0	1	0
1	1	0	0
1	1	1	1

▶ **EXAMPLE 2.20**   *Converting a combinational circuit to a truth table*

Convert the circuit depicted in Figure 2.36(a) into a truth table.

We begin by converting the circuit to an equation. Starting from the gates closest to the inputs—the leftmost AND gate and the inverter in this case—we label each gate's output as an expression of the gate's inputs. We label the leftmost AND gate's output, for example, as ab. Likewise, we label the leftmost inverter's output as c'. Continuing through the circuit's gates, we label the rightmost inverter's output as (ab)'. Finally, we label the rightmost AND gate's output as (ab)'c', which corresponds to the Boolean equation for F. The fully labeled circuit is shown in Figure 2.36(b).

From the Boolean equation, we can now construct the truth table for the combinational circuit. Since our circuit has three inputs—a, b, and c—there are $2^3 = 8$ possible combinations of inputs (i.e. abc = 000, 001, 010, 011, 100, 101, 110, 111), so our truth table has the eight rows shown in Figure 2.37. For each input, we compute the value of F and fill in the corresponding entry in the truth table. For example, when a=0, b=0, and c=0, F is (00)'*0' = (0)'*1 = 1*1 = 1. We compute the circuit's output for the remaining combinations of input using a truth table with intermediate values, shown in Figure 2.37.   ◀

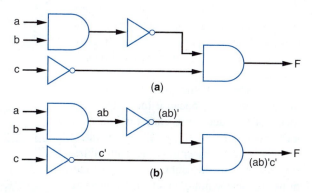

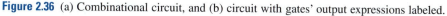

Figure 2.36 (a) Combinational circuit, and (b) circuit with gates' output expressions labeled.

Inputs						Outputs
a	b	c	ab	(ab)'	c'	F
0	0	0	0	1	1	1
0	0	1	0	1	0	0
0	1	0	0	1	1	1
0	1	1	0	1	0	0
1	0	0	0	1	1	1
1	0	1	0	1	0	0
1	1	0	1	0	1	0
1	1	1	1	0	0	0

Figure 2.37 Truth table for the circuit's equation.

Standard Representation and Canonical Form

Truth tables as a Boolean function standard representation

We stated earlier that, although there are many possible equation representations and circuit representations of the same Boolean function, there is only one possible truth table representation of a Boolean function. Truth tables therefore represent a *standard representation* of a function—for any function, there may be many possible equations, and many possible circuits, but there is only *one* truth table. The truth table representation is unique.

One use of a standard representation of a Boolean function is for comparing two functions to see if they are equivalent. Suppose you wanted to check if two Boolean equations were equivalent. One way would be to try to manipulate one equation to be the same as the other equation, like we did in our automatic sliding door example in Example 2.13. But suppose we were not successful in getting them to be the same—is that because they really are not the same, or because we just didn't manipulate the equation enough? How do we really know the two equations are not the same?

A conclusive way to check if two functions are the same is to create a truth table for each, and then check whether the truth tables are identical. So to determine whether $F = ab + a'$ is equivalent to $F = a'b' + a'b + ab$, we could generate truth tables for each, using the method described earlier of evaluating the function for each output row, as shown to the right.

We see that the two functions are indeed equivalent, because the outputs are identical for each input combination. Now let's check if $F = ab + a'$ is equivalent to $F = (a+b)'$ by comparing truth tables.

As seen to the right, those two functions are clearly not equivalent. Comparing truth tables leaves no doubt.

$F = ab + a'$

a	b	F
0	0	1
0	1	1
1	0	0
1	1	1

$F = a'b' + a'b + ab$

a	b	F
0	0	1
0	1	1
1	0	0
1	1	1

$F = ab + a'$

a	b	F
0	0	1
0	1	1
1	0	0
1	1	1

$F = (a+b)'$

a	b	F
0	0	1
0	1	0
1	0	0
1	1	0

While comparing truth tables works fine when a function has only 2 inputs, what if a function has 5 inputs, or 10, or 32? Creating truth tables becomes increasingly cumbersome, and in many cases just plain unrealistic, since a truth table's number of rows equals 2^n, where n is the number of inputs. 2^n grows very quickly. 2^{32} is approximately 4 billion, for example. We can't realistically expect to compare 2 tables of 4 billion rows each.

However, in many cases, the number of output 1s in a truth table may be very small compared to the number of output 0s. For example, consider a function G of 5 variables a, b, c, d, and e: G = abcd + a'bcde. A truth table for this function would have 32 rows, but only three 1s in the output column—one 1 from a'bcde, and two 1s from abcd (which covers rows corresponding to abcde and abcde'). This leads to the question:

Is there a more compact but still *standard* representation of a Boolean function?

Canonical Form—Sum-of-Minterms Equation

The answer to the above question is "yes". The key is to create a standard representation that only describes the situations where the function outputs 1, with the other situations assumed to output 0. An equation, such as G = abcd + a'bcde, is indeed a representation that only describes the situations where G is 1, but that representation is not unique, that is, the representation is not standard. We therefore want to define a standard form of a Boolean equation, known as a *canonical form*.

You've seen canonical forms in regular algebra. For example, the canonical form of a polynomial of degree two is: $ax^2 + bx + c$. To check if the equation $9x^2 + 3x + 2 + 1$ is equivalent to the equation $3*(3x^2 + 1 + x)$, we convert each to canonical form, resulting in $9x^2 + 3x + 3$ for both equations.

One canonical form for a Boolean function is known as a sum-of-minterms. A *minterm* of a function is a product term whose literals include every variable of the function *exactly once*, in either true or complemented form. The function F(a,b,c) = a'bc + abc' + ab + c has four terms. The first two terms, a'bc and abc', are minterms. The third term, ab, is not a minterm since c does not appear. Likewise, the fourth term, c, is not a minterm, since neither a nor b appears in that term. An equation is in *sum-of-minterms form* if the equation is in sum-of-product form, and every product term is a minterm.

Converting any equation to sum-of-minterms canonical form can be done following just a few steps:

1. First, we manipulate the equation until it is in sum-of-products form. Suppose we are given the equation F(a,b,c)=(a+b)(a'+ac)b. We manipulate it as follows:

F = (a+b)(a'+ac)b	
F = (a+b)(a'b+acb)	(by the distributive property)
F = a(a'b+acb) + b(a'b+acb)	(distributive property)
F = aa'b + aacb + ba'b + bacb	(distributive property)
F = 0*b + acb + a'b + acb	(complement, commutative, idempotent)
F = acb + a'b + acb	(null elements)
F = acb + a'b	(idempotent)

2. Second, we expand each term until every term is a minterm:

```
F = acb + a'b
F = acb + a'b*1              (identity)
F = acb + a'b*(c+c')        (complement)
F = acb + a'bc + a'bc'      (distributive)
```

3. (Optional step) For neatness, we can arrange the literals within each term to a consistent order (say alphabetical), and we can also arrange the terms in the order they would appear in a truth table:

```
F = a'bc' + a'bc + abc
```

The equation is now in sum-of-minterms form. The equation is in sum-of-products form, and every product term includes every variable exactly once.

An alternative canonical form is known as product-of-maxterms. A ***maxterm*** is a sum term in which every variable appears exactly once in either true or complemented form, such as (a + b + c') for a function of three variables a, b, and c. An equation is in ***product-of-maxterms form*** if the equation is the product of sum terms, and every sum term is a maxterm. An example of a function (different from that above) in product-of-maxterms form is J(a,b,c) = (a + b + c')(a' + b' + c'). To avoid confusing the reader, we will not discuss the product-of-maxterms form further here, as sum-of-minterms form is more common in practice, and sufficient for our purposes.

▶ **EXAMPLE 2.21**   Comparing two functions using canonical form

Suppose we want to determine whether the functions G(a,b,c,d,e) = abcd + a'bcde and H(a,b,c,d,e) = abcde + abcde' + a'bcde + a'bcde(a' + c) are equivalent. We first convert G to sum-of-minterms form:

```
G = abcd + a'bcde
G = abcd(e+e') + a'bcde
G = abcde + abcde' + a'bcde
G = a'bcde + abcde' + abcde
```

We then convert H to sum-of-minterms form:

```
H = abcde + abcde' + a'bcde + a'bcde(a' + c)
H = abcde + abcde' + a'bcde + a'bcdea' + a'bcdec
H = abcde + abcde' + a'bcde + a'bcde + a'bcde
H = abcde + abcde' + a'bcde
H = a'bcde + abcde' + abcde
```

Clearly, G and H are equivalent.

Note that checking the equivalence using truth tables would have resulted in 2 rather large truth tables having 32 rows each. Using sum of minterms was probably more appropriate here.   ◀

Compact sum-of-minterms representation

A more compact representation of sum-of-minterms form involves listing each minterm as a number, with each minterm's number determined from the binary representation of its variables' values. For example, a'bcde corresponds to 01111, or 15; abcde' corresponds to 11110, or 30; and $abcde$ corresponds to 11111, or 31. Thus, we can say that the function H represented by the equation:

$$H = a'bcde + abcde' + abcde$$

is the sum of the minterms 15, 30, and 31, which can be compactly written as:

$$H = \Sigma m(15,30,31)$$

The summation symbol means the sum, and then the numbers inside the parentheses represent the minterms being summed on the right side of the equation.

Multiple-Output Combinational Circuits

Many combinational circuits not only involve more than one input, but also involve more than one output. The simplest approach to handling a multiple-output circuit is to treat each output separately, leading to a separate circuit for each output. Actually, the circuits need not be completely separate—they could share common gates. We'll show how to handle multiple-output circuits through examples.

▶ **EXAMPLE 2.22** Two-output combinational circuit

Design a circuit to implement the following two equations of three inputs a, b, and c:

$$F = ab + c'$$
$$G = ab + bc$$

We can design the circuit by simply creating two separate circuits, as in Figure 2.38(a).

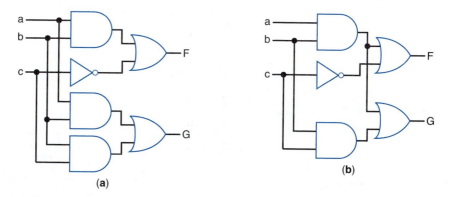

(a)

(b)

Figure 2.38 Multiple-output circuit: (a) treated as two separate circuits, and (b) with gate sharing.

We can instead notice that the term ab is common to both equations. Thus, the two circuits can share the gate that computes ab, as shown in Figure 2.38(b). ◀

▶ **EXAMPLE 2.23** Binary number to seven-segment display converter

Many electronic appliances display a number for us to read. Example appliances include a clock, a microwave oven, and a telephone answering machine. A very popular and simple device for displaying a single digit number is a seven-segment display, illustrated in Figure 2.39.

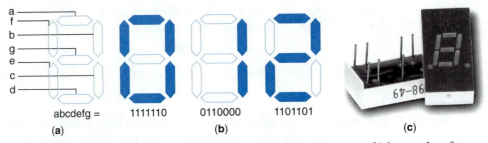

Figure 2.39 Seven-segment display: (a) connections of inputs to segments, (b) input values for numbers 0, 1, and 2, and (c) a pair of real seven-segment display components.

The display consists of seven light segments, each of which can be illuminated independently of the others. We can display the desired digit by setting the signals a, b, c, d, e, f, and g appropriately. So to display the digit 8, we set all seven signals to 1. To display the digit 1, we set b and c to 1.

A useful combinational circuit is one that converts a binary number to the seven-segment display signals a–g that display the number as a decimal digit. We need four bits, say w, x, y, and z, to represent the binary values of the ten possible digits 0 to 9. Table 2.4 describes the conversion of each binary number to the seven-segment display's signals. We decided to activate no segments for the numbers 10 through 15.

For this example, starting from a truth table is a more natural choice than an equation.

TABLE 2-4   4-bit binary number to seven-segment display truth table

w	x	y	z	a	b	c	d	e	f	g
0	0	0	0	1	1	1	1	1	1	0
0	0	0	1	0	1	1	0	0	0	0
0	0	1	0	1	1	0	1	1	0	1
0	0	1	1	1	1	1	1	0	0	1
0	1	0	0	0	1	1	0	0	1	1
0	1	0	1	1	0	1	1	0	1	1
0	1	1	0	1	0	1	1	1	1	1
0	1	1	1	1	1	1	0	0	0	0
1	0	0	0	1	1	1	1	1	1	1
1	0	0	1	1	1	1	1	0	1	1
1	0	1	0	0	0	0	0	0	0	0
1	0	1	1	0	0	0	0	0	0	0
1	1	0	0	0	0	0	0	0	0	0
1	1	0	1	0	0	0	0	0	0	0
1	1	1	0	0	0	0	0	0	0	0
1	1	1	1	0	0	0	0	0	0	0

We can create a custom logic circuit to implement the converter. Note that the above table is in the form of a truth table having multiple outputs (a through g). We can treat each output separately, so we design a circuit for a, then for b, etc. Looking at the 1s in the a column, we obtain the following equation for a:

$$a = w'x'y'z' + w'x'yz' + w'x'yz + w'xy'z + w'xyz' + w'xyz + wx'y'z' + wx'y'z$$

Looking at the 1s in the b column, we obtain the following equation for b:

$$b = w'x'y'z' + w'x'y'z + w'x'yz' + w'x'yz + w'xy'z' + w'xyz + wx'y'z' + wx'y'z$$

We could then proceed to create equations for the remaining outputs c through g. Finally, we would create a circuit for a having 8 4-input AND gates and an 8-input OR gate, another circuit for b having 8 4-input AND gates and an 8-input OR gate, and so on for c through g. We could, of course, have minimized the logic for each equation before creating each of the circuits.

You may notice that the equations for a and b have several terms in common. For example, the term w'x'y'z' appears in both equations. So it would make sense for both outputs to share one AND gate generating that term. Looking at the truth table, we see that the term w'x'y'z' is in fact needed for outputs a, b, c, e, f, and g, and thus the one AND gate generating that term could be shared by all six of those outputs. Likewise, each of the other required terms is shared by several outputs, meaning each gate generating each term could be shared among several outputs. ◀

▶ 2.7 COMBINATIONAL LOGIC DESIGN PROCESS

Based on the previous sections, we can define a straightforward method for designing combinational logic, summarized in Table 2.5

TABLE 2.5 **Combinational logic design process.**

	Step	Description
Step 1	*Capture* the function	Create a truth table or equations, whichever is most natural for the given problem, to describe the desired behavior of the combinational logic.
Step 2	*Convert* to equations	This step is only necessary if you captured the function using a truth table instead of equations. Create an equation for each output by ORing all the minterms for that output. Simplify the equations if desired.
Step 3	*Implement* as a gate-based circuit	For each output, create a circuit corresponding to the output's equation. (Sharing gates among multiple outputs is OK optionally.)

Gate-based circuits designed such that the inputs feed into a column of AND gates that feeds into a single OR gate are known as *two-level logic implementations*.

▶ EXAMPLE 2.24   Three 1s pattern detector

We want to implement a circuit that can detect whether a pattern of at least three adjacent 1s occur anywhere in an 8-bit input, and that outputs a 1 in that case. The inputs are a, b, c, d, e, f, g, and h, and the output is y. So for an input of abcdefgh = 00011101, y should be 1, since there are three 1s in a row (on inputs d, e, and f). For an input of 10101011, the output should be 0, since there are not three 1s in a row anywhere. An input of 11110000 should result in y = 1, since having more than three 1s in a row should still output a 1. Such a circuit is an extremely simple example of a general class of circuits known as pattern detectors. Pattern detectors are widely used, for example, in image processing to detect things, like humans or tanks, in a digitized video image, or to detect specific spoken words in a digitized audio stream.

For this example, starting from an equation is a more natural choice than a truth table.

Step 1: ***Capture the function.*** We could capture the function as a rather large truth table, listing out all 256 combinations of inputs, and entering a 1 for y in each row where at least three 1s occur. However, a simpler method for capturing this particular function is to create an equation that lists the possible occurrences of three 1s in a row. One possibility is that of abc=111. Another is that of bcd=111. Likewise, if cde=111, def=111, efg=111, or fgh=111, we should output a 1. For each possibility, the values of the other inputs don't matter. So if abc=111, we output a 1, regardless of the values of d, e, f, g, and h. Thus, an equation describing y is simply:

$$y = abc + bcd + cde + def + efg + fgh$$

Step 2: ***Convert to equations.*** We can skip this step since we already have an equation.

Step 3: ***Implement as a gate-based circuit.*** No simplification of the equation is possible. The resulting circuit is shown in Figure 2.40.

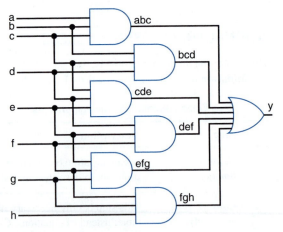

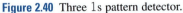

Figure 2.40 Three 1s pattern detector.

▶ **EXAMPLE 2.25** Number-of-1s counter

For this example, starting from a truth table is a more natural choice than an equation.

We want to design a circuit that counts the number of 1s present on 3 inputs a, b, c, and outputs that number in binary using 2 outputs, y and z. An input of 110 has two 1s, so our circuit should output 10. The number of 1s on 3 inputs can range from 0 to 3, so a 2-bit output is sufficient, since 2 bits can represent 0 to 3. A number-of-1s counter circuit is useful in a variety of situations, such as detecting the density of electronic particles hitting a collection of sensors by counting how many sensors are activated. As another example, there are airport parking lots that have sensors above each parking spot, coupled with signs that inform drivers of the number of available parking spots on a particular level of a multilevel parking structure (by counting the number of zeros, but that's the same as counting the number of 1s with all inputs first complemented).

Step 1: **Capture the function.** Capturing the function for this example is most naturally achieved using a truth table. We list all the possible input combinations, and the desired output number, as in Table 2.6.

TABLE 2.6 **Truth table for number-of-1s counter.**

Inputs			(# of 1s)	Outputs	
a	b	c		y	z
0	0	0	(0)	0	0
0	0	1	(1)	0	1
0	1	0	(1)	0	1
0	1	1	(2)	1	0
1	0	0	(1)	0	1
1	0	1	(2)	1	0
1	1	0	(2)	1	0
1	1	1	(3)	1	1

Step 2: **Convert to equations.** We create equations for each output as follows:

$$y = a'bc + ab'c + abc' + abc$$
$$z = a'b'c + a'bc' + ab'c' + abc$$

We can simplify the first equation algebraically:

$$y = a'bc + ab'c + ab(c' + c) = a'bc + ab'c + ab$$

Step 3: **Implement as a gate-based circuit.** We then create the final circuits for the two outputs, as shown in Figure 2.41. ◄

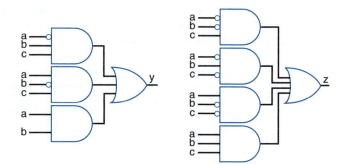

Figure 2.41 Number-of-1s counter gate-based circuit.

Simplifying circuit notations

We used a couple of new simplifying notations in our circuits in the previous example. One simplifying notation is to list the inputs multiple times, to avoid having lines in our drawing crossing one another—an input listed multiple times is assumed to have been branched from the same input.

Another simplifying notation is the use of an inversion bubble at the input of a gate, rather than the use of a NOT gate. An input that is inverted into many gates is assumed to feed through a single inverter that is then branched out to those gates. An alternative simplification is to simply include complemented variables, like b', as inputs.

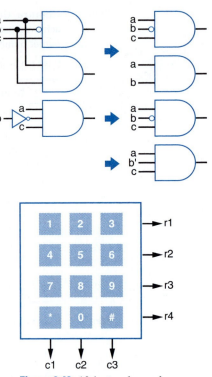

▶ **EXAMPLE 2.26** 12-button keypad to 4-bit code converter

You've probably seen 12-button keypads in many different places, like on a telephone or at an ATM machine as shown in Figure 2.42. The first row has buttons 1, 2, and 3, the second row has 4, 5, and 6, the third row has 7, 8, and 9, and the last row has *, 0, and #. The outputs of such a keypad consist of seven signals—one for each of the four rows (r1, r2, r3, and r4), and one for each of the three columns (c1, c2, and c3). Pushing a particular button causes exactly two outputs to become 1, corresponding to the row and column of that button. So pushing button "1" causes r1=1 and c1=1, while pushing button "#" causes r4=1 and c3=1. We want to design a circuit that converts the seven signals from the keypad into a 4-bit binary number wxyz indicating which button is pressed. We want buttons "0" to "9" to be coded as 0000 through 1001 (0 through 9 in binary), respectively. Let's encode button "*" as 1010, # as 1011, and let's let 1111 mean that no button is pressed. Let's assume for now that only "one" button can ever be pressed at a given time.

For this example, starting from equations is a more natural choice than a truth table, although we used an informal table (not a truth table) to help us determine the equations.

Figure 2.42 12-button keypad.

We could capture the functions for w, x, y, and z using a truth table, with the seven inputs on the left side of the table, and the four outputs on the right side, but that table would have $2^7 = 128$ rows, and most of those rows would correspond merely to multiple buttons being pressed. Let's try instead to capture the functions using equations. The informal Table 2.7 might help us get started.

TABLE 2.7 Informal table for the 12-button keypad to 4-bit code converter.

Button	Signals		4-bit code outputs				Button	Signals		4-bit code outputs			
			W	X	Y	Z				W	X	Y	Z
1	r1	c1	0	0	0	1	8	r3	c2	1	0	0	0
2	r1	c2	0	0	1	0	9	r3	c3	1	0	0	1
3	r1	c3	0	0	1	1	*	r4	c1	1	0	1	0
4	r2	c1	0	1	0	0	0	r4	c2	0	0	0	0
5	r2	c2	0	1	0	1	#	r4	c3	1	0	1	1
6	r2	c3	0	1	1	0	(none)			1	1	1	1
7	r3	c1	0	1	1	1							

Inside a standard computer keyboard is a small micro-processor and a ROM. The microprocessor detects which key is being pressed, looks up the 8-bit code for that key (much like the 12-button keypad in Example 2.26) from the ROM, and sends that code to the computer. There's an interesting story behind the way the keys are arranged in a standard PC keyboard, which is known as a QWERTY keyboard because those are the keys that begin the top left row of letters. The QWERTY arrangement was made in the era of typewriters (shown in the picture below), which, in case you haven't seen one, had each key connected to an arm that would swing up and press an ink ribbon against paper.

Arms stuck!

An annoying problem with typewriters was that arms would often get jammed side-by-side up near the paper if you typed too fast—like too many people getting jammed side-by-side while trying to simultaneously walk through a doorway. So typewriter keys were arranged in the QWERTY arrangement to *slow down* typing by *separating* common letters, since slower typing reduced the occurrences of jammed keys. When PCs were invented, the QWERTY arrangement was the natural choice for PC keyboards, as people were accustomed to that arrangement. Some say the differently-arranged Dvorak keyboard enables faster typing, but that type of keyboard isn't very common, as people are just too accustomed to the QWERTY keyboard.

Keys connected to arms

Using this table, we can derive equations for each of the four outputs, as follows:

```
w = r3c2 + r3c3 + r4c1 + r4c3 + r1'r2'r3'r4'c1'c2'c3'
x = r2c1 + r2c2 + r2c3 + r3c1 + r1'r2'r3'r4'c1'c2'c3'
y = r1c2 + r1c3 + r2c3 + r3c1 + r4c1 + r4c3 +
    r1'r2'r3'r4'c1'c2'c3'
z = r1c1 + r1c3 + r2c2 + r3c1 + r3c3 + r4c3 +
    r1'r2'r3'r4'c1'c2'c3'
```

We could then create a circuit for each output. Obviously, the last term of each equation could be shared by all four outputs. Likewise, other terms could be shared too (like r2c3).

Note that this circuit would not work well if multiple buttons can be pressed simultaneously. Our circuit will output either a valid or invalid code in that situation, depending on which buttons were pressed. A preferable circuit would treat multiple buttons being pressed as no button being pressed. We leave the design of that circuit as an exercise.

Circuits similar to what we designed above exist in computer keyboards, except that there are a lot more rows and columns. ◀

▶ **EXAMPLE 2.27** Sprinkler valve controller

Automatic lawn sprinkler systems use a digital system to control the opening and closing of water valves. A sprinkler system usually supports several different zones, such as the backyard, left side yard, right side yard, front yard, etc. Only one zone's valve can be opened at a time in order to maintain enough water pressure in the sprinklers in that zone. Suppose a sprinkler system supports up to 8 zones. Typically, a sprinkler system is controlled by a small, inexpensive microprocessor executing a program that opens each valve only at specific times of the day and for specific durations. Suppose the microprocessor only has 4 output pins available to control the valves, not 8 outputs as required for the 8 zones. We can instead program the microprocessor to use 1 pin to indicate whether a valve should be opened, and use the 3 other pins to output the active zone (0, 1, ..., 7) in binary. Thus, we need to design a combinational circuit having 4 inputs, e (the enabler) and a, b, c (the binary value of the active zone), and having 8 outputs d7, d6, ..., d0 (the valve controls), as shown in Figure 2.43. When e=1, the circuit should decode the 3-bit binary input by setting exactly one output to 1.

Step 1: **Capture the function.** Valve 0 should be active when abc=000 and e=1. So the equation for d0 is:

$$d0 = a'b'c'e$$

Likewise, valve 1 should be active when abc=001 and e=1, so the equation for d1 is:

$$d1 = a'b'ce$$

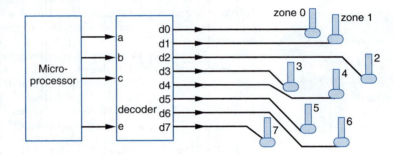

Figure 2.43 Sprinkler valve controller block diagram.

For this example, starting from equations is a more natural choice than a truth table.

The equations for the remaining outputs can be determined similarly:

$$d2 = a'bc'e$$
$$d3 = a'bce$$
$$d4 = ab'c'e$$
$$d5 = ab'ce$$
$$d6 = abc'e$$
$$d7 = abce$$

Step 2: **Convert to equations.** No conversion is needed since we already have equations.

Step 3: **Implement as a gate-based circuit.** The circuit implementing the equations is shown in Figure 2.44. The circuit we've designed is actually a commonly used component known as a *decoder with enable*. We'll introduce decoders as a building block in an upcoming section. ◀

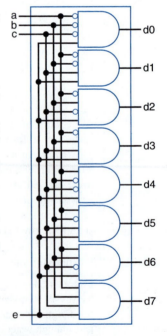

Figure 2.44 Sprinkler valve controller circuit (actually a 3x8 decoder with enable).

▶ 2.8 MORE GATES

We earlier introduced three basic logic gates: AND, OR, and NOT. Designers commonly use several other types of gates too: NAND, NOR, XOR, and XNOR.

NAND & NOR

A *NAND* gate (short for "not AND") has the opposite output as an AND gate, outputting a 0 when all inputs are 1, and outputting a 1 if any input is a 0. A NAND gate has the same behavior as an AND gate followed by a NOT gate. Figure 2.45(a) illustrates a NAND gate.

A *NOR* gate (short for "not OR") has the opposite output as an OR gate, outputting a 0 if at least one input is a 1, and outputting 1 if all inputs are 0. A NOR gate has the same behavior as an OR gate followed by a NOT gate. Figure 2.45(b) illustrates a NOR gate.

We earlier warned you in Section 2.4 that our CMOS transistor implementations of AND and OR gates were not realistic. Here's why. It turns out that pMOS transistors don't actually conduct 0s very well, but they conduct 1s just fine. Likewise, nMOS transistors don't conduct 1s well, but they conduct 0s just fine. The reasons for these asymmetries are beyond this book's scope. But the implications are that the AND and OR gates we built earlier (see Figure 2.8) are not feasible, since they rely on pMOS transistors to conduct 0s (but pMOS conducts 0s poorly) and nMOS transistors to conduct 1s (but nMOS conducts 1s poorly). On the other hand, if we swap power and ground in the AND and OR circuits of Figure 2.8, we obtain the gates shown in Figure 2.45 (a) and (b). Those gates have the behavior of NAND and NOR gates, which makes sense since output 1s become replaced by 0s, and 0s by 1s.

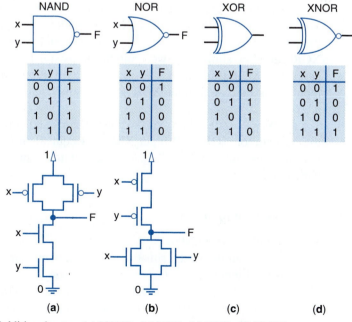

Figure 2.45 Additional gates: (a) NAND, (b) NOR, (c) XOR, (d) XNOR.

We can still implement an AND gate in CMOS, but we would do so by appending a NOT gate at the output of a NAND gate (NAND followed by NOT gives us AND), as shown in Figure 2.46. Likewise, we would implement an OR gate by appending a NOT gate at the output of a NOR gate. But that's obviously slower than a circuit directly implemented as NAND and NOR. Fortunately, we can apply straightforward methods to convert any AND/OR/NOT circuit to a NAND-only circuit, or to a NOR-only circuit. We'll describe those methods in Section 7.2.

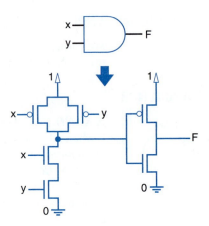

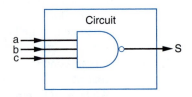

Figure 2.46 AND gate in CMOS.

▶ **EXAMPLE 2.28** Aircraft lavatory sign using a NAND gate

Example 2.15 created a lavatory available sign using the following equation:

$$S = (abc)'$$

Noticing that the term on the right side corresponds to a NAND, we can implement the circuit using a single NAND gate, as shown in Figure 2.47.   ◀

Figure 2.47 Circuit using NAND.

XOR & XNOR

A 2-input XOR gate, short for "exclusive or" and pronounced as "ex or," outputs a 1 if *exactly* one of the two inputs is a 1. So if such a gate has inputs a and b, then the output F is 1 if a=1 and b=0, or if b=1 and a=0. Figure 2.45(c) illustrates an XOR gate (for simplicity, we omit the transistor-level implementation of an XOR gate). For XOR gates with 3 or more inputs, the output is 1 only if the number of input 1s is odd. A 2-input XOR gate is equivalent to the function F = ab' + a'b.

An XNOR gate, short for "exclusive nor" and pronounced "ex nor," is simply the opposite of XOR. A 2-input XNOR is equivalent to F = a'b' + ab. Figure 2.45(d) illustrates an XNOR gate, omitting the transistor-level implementation for simplicity.

Interesting Uses of These Additional Gates

Detecting all 0s using NOR

A NOR gate can detect the situation of a data item equal to 0, since NOR outputs a 1 only when all inputs are 0. For example, suppose a byte (8-bit) input to your system is counting down from 99 to 0, and when the byte reaches 0, you wish to sound an alarm. You can detect the byte being equal to 0 by simply connecting the 8 bits of the byte into an 8-input NOR gate.

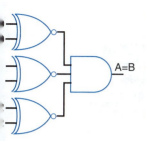

Detecting equality using XNOR

XNOR gates can be used to compare two data items for equality, since a 2-input XNOR outputs a 1 only when the inputs are both 0 or are both 1. For example, suppose a byte input A (a7a6a5...a0) to your system is counting down from 99, and you want to sound an alarm when A has the same value as a second byte input B (b7b6b5...b0). You can detect such equality using eight 2-input XNOR gates, by connecting a7 and b7 to the first XNOR gate, a6 and b6 to the second XNOR gate, etc. Each XNOR gate tells us whether the bits in that particular position are equal. By ANDing all the XNOR outputs, we can tell whether every position is equal.

Generating and detecting parity using XOR

An XOR gate can be used to generate a parity bit for a set of data bits (see Example 2.19). XORing the data bits results in a 1 if there's an odd number of 1s in the data, so XOR computes the correct parity bit for even parity, since the XOR's output 1 would make the total number of 1s even. Notice that the truth table we created for generating an even parity bit in Table 2.3 does in fact represent a 3-bit XOR.

Likewise, an XNOR gate can be used to generate an odd parity bit.

XOR can also be used to detect proper parity. XORing the incoming data bits along with the incoming parity bit will yield 1 if the number of 1s is odd. Thus, for even parity, XOR can be used to indicate that an error has occurred, since the number of 1s is supposed to be even.

XNOR can be used to detect an error when odd parity is used.

Completeness of AND/OR/NOT, AND/NOT, OR/NOT, NAND, NOR

It should be fairly obvious that if you have AND gates, OR gates, and NOT gates, you can implement any Boolean function. This is because a Boolean function can be represented as a sum of products, which consists only of AND, OR, and NOT operations.

What might be slightly less obvious is that if you had only AND and NOT gates, you could still implement any Boolean function. Why? Here's a simple explanation—to obtain an OR, simply put NOT gates at the inputs and outputs of an AND. This works because F = (a'b')' = a'' + b'' (by DeMorgan's Law) = a + b.

Likewise, if you had only OR and NOT gates, you could implement any Boolean function. To obtain an AND, you could simply invert the inputs and outputs of an OR, since F = (a'+b')' = a''*b'' = ab.

It follows that if you *only* had NAND gates available to you, you could still implement any Boolean function. Why? Because we can think of a NOT gate as a 1-input NAND gate, and we can implement an AND gate using a NAND gate followed by a 1-input NAND gate. Since we can implement any Boolean function using NOT and AND, we can therefore implement any Boolean function using just NAND. A NAND gate is thus known as a ***universal*** gate.

Likewise, if you had only NOR gates, you could implement any Boolean function, because we can implement a NOT gate as a 1-input NOR gate, and an OR gate using a NOR following by a 1-input NOR. Since NOT and OR can implement any Boolean function, so can NOR. A NOR gate is thus also known as a universal gate.

Number of Possible Logic Gates

Having seen several different types of basic 2-input logic gates (AND, OR, NAND, NOR, XOR, XNOR), one might wonder how many possible 2-input logic gates exist. That question is the same as asking how many Boolean functions exist for two variables. To answer the question, we first note that a two-variable function's truth table will have $2^2=4$ rows. For each row, the function could output one of two possible values (0 or 1). Thus, as illustrated in Figure 2.48, there are $2 * 2 * 2 * 2 = 2^4 = 16$ possible functions.

a	b	F		
0	0	0 or 1	2 choices	2
0	1	0 or 1	2 choices	* 2
1	0	0 or 1	2 choices	* 2
1	1	0 or 1	2 choices	* 2

$2^4 = 16$ possible functions

Figure 2.48 Counting the number of possible Boolean functions of two variables.

Figure 2.49 lists all 16 of those functions. We indicate the 6 familiar functions in the figure. Some of the other functions are 0, a, b, a', b', and 1. The remaining functions are not necessarily common functions, but each could be useful for some particular application. Thus, we don't necessarily need to build logic gates to represent those functions, but we instead would build those functions as a circuit of the basic logic gates.

a	b	f0	f1	f2	f3	f4	f5	f6	f7	f8	f9	f10	f11	f12	f13	f14	f15
0	0	0	0	0	0	0	0	0	0	1	1	1	1	1	1	1	1
0	1	0	0	0	0	1	1	1	1	0	0	0	0	1	1	1	1
1	0	0	0	1	1	0	0	1	1	0	0	1	1	0	0	1	1
1	1	0	1	0	1	0	1	0	1	0	1	0	1	0	1	0	1
		0	a AND b	a		b		a XOR b	a OR b	a NOR b	a XNOR b	b'		a'		a NAND b	1

Figure 2.49 The 16 possible Boolean functions of two variables.

A more general question of interest is how many Boolean functions exist for a Boolean function of N variables. We can determine this number by first noting that an N-variable function will have 2^N rows in its truth table. Then, we note that each row can output one of two possible values. Thus, the number of possible functions will be $2 * 2 * 2 * —2^N$ times. Therefore, the total number of functions is:

$$2^{2^N}$$

So there are: $2^{2^3} = 2^8 = 256$ possible Boolean functions of 3 variables, and $2^{2^4} = 2^{16} = 65,536$ possible functions of 4 variables.

▶ 2.9 DECODERS AND MUXES

Two additional components, a decoder and a multiplexer, are also commonly used as digital circuit building blocks, though they themselves can be built from logic gates.

Decoders

A decoder is a higher-level building block commonly used in digital circuits. A *decoder* decodes an input *n*-bit binary number by setting exactly one of the decoder's 2^n outputs to 1. For example, a 2-input decoder, illustrated in Figure 2.50, would have $2^2=4$ outputs, d3, d2, d1, d0. If the two inputs i1i0 are 00, d0 would be 1 and the remaining outputs would be 0. If i1i0=01, d1 would be 1. If i1i0=10, d2 would be 1. If i1i0=11, d3 would be 1.

The internal design of a decoder is straightforward. Consider a 2x4 decoder. Each output d0, d1, d2, and d3 is a distinct function. d0 should be 1 only when i1=0 and i0=0, so d0 = i1'i0'. Likewise, d1=i1'i0, d2=i1i0', and d3=i1i0. Thus, we build the decoder with one AND gate for each output, connecting the true or complemented values of i1 and i0 to each gate, as shown in Figure 2.50.

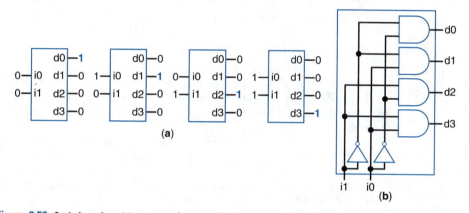

(a)

(b)

Figure 2.50 2x4 decoder: (a) outputs for possible input combinations, (b) internal design.

The internal design of a 3x8 decoder is similar: d0=i2'i1'i0', d1=i2'i1'i0, etc.

A decoder often comes with an extra input called *enable*. When enable is 1, the decoder acts normally. But when enable is 0, the decoder outputs all 0s—no output is a 1. The enable is useful when sometimes you don't want to activate any of the outputs. Without an enable, one output of the decoder *must* be a 1, because the decoder has an output for every possible value of the decoder's *n*-bit input. We created and used a decoder with enable in Figure 2.44. A block diagram of a decoder with enable appears in Figure 2.51.

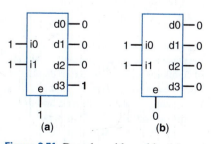

Figure 2.51 Decoder with enable: (a) e=1: normal decoding, (b) e=0: all outputs 0.

When designing a particular system, we check if part (or all) of the system's functionality could be carried out by a decoder. Using a decoder reduces the amount of combinational logic design that we need to perform, as you'll see in Example 2.30.

▶ **EXAMPLE 2.29** Basic questions about decoders

1. What would be a 2x4 decoder's output values when the inputs are 00? *Answer*: $d0=1$, $d1=0$, $d2=0$, $d3=0$.

2. What would be a 2x4 decoder's output values when the inputs are 11? *Answer*: $d0=0$, $d1=0$, $d2=0$, $d3=1$.

3. What input values of a 2x4 decoder cause more than one of the decoder's outputs to be 1 at the same time? *Answer*: No such input values exist. Only one of a decoder's outputs can be 1 at a given time.

4. What would the input values of a decoder be if the output values are $d0=0$, $d1=1$, $d2=0$, $d3=0$? *Answer*: The input values must be $i1=0$, $i0=1$.

5. What would the input values of a decoder be if the output values are $d0=1$, $d1=1$, $d2=0$, $d3=0$? *Answer*: This question is not valid. A decoder only has one output equal to 1 at any time.

6. How many outputs would a 5-input decoder have? *Answer*: 2^5, or 32. ◀

▶ **EXAMPLE 2.30** New Year's Eve countdown display

A New Year's Eve countdown display could make use of a decoder. The display may have 60 light bulbs going up a tall pole. We want one light per second to turn on (with the previous one turning off), starting from bulb 59 at the bottom of the pole, and ending with bulb 0 at the top. We could use a microprocessor to count down from 59 to 0, but the microprocessor probably doesn't have 60 output pins that we could use to control each light. Our microprocessor program could instead output the numbers 59, 58, ..., 2, 1, 0 in binary on a 6-bit output port (thus outputting 111011, 111010, ..., 000010, 000001, 000000). We could connect those six bits to a 6-input, 64 (2^6)-output decoder, with decoder output $d59$ lighting bulb 59, $d58$ lighting bulb 58, etc.

We'd probably want an enable on our decoder in this example, since we'd want all the lights off until we started the countdown. The microprocessor would initially set enable to 0 so that no lights would be illuminated. When the 60 second countdown begins, the microprocessor would set enable to 1, and then output 59, then 58 (1 second later), then 57, etc. The final system would look like that in Figure 2.52.

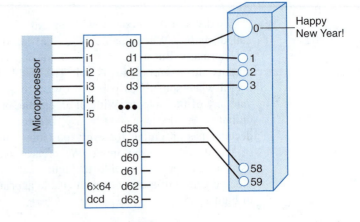

Figure 2.52 Using a 6x64 decoder to interface a microprocessor and a column of lights for a New Year's Eve display. The microprocessor sets $e = 1$ when the last minute countdown begins, and then counts down from 59 to 0 in binary on the pins $i5..i0$. Note that the microprocessor should never output 60, 61, 62, or 63 on $i5..i0$, and thus those outputs of the decoder go unused.

Notice that we implemented this system without having to design any gate-level combinational logic—we merely used a decoder and connected it to the appropriate inputs and outputs. ◀

Whenever you have outputs such that exactly one of those outputs should be set to 1 based on the value of inputs representing a binary number, think about using a decoder.

Multiplexer (Mux)

A multiplexer ("mux" for short) is another higher-level building block in digital circuits. An *Mx1 multiplexer* has *M* data inputs and 1 output, and allows only one input to pass through to that output. A set of additional inputs, known as select inputs, determines which input to pass through. Multiplexers are sometimes called *selectors* because they select one input to pass through to the output.

A mux is like a railyard switch that connects multiple input tracks to a single output track, as shown in Figure 2.53. The switch's control lever causes the connection of the appropriate input track to the output track. Whether a train appears at the output depends on whether a train exists on the presently selected input track. For a mux, the switch's control is not a lever, but rather select inputs, which represent the desired connection in binary. Rather than a train appearing or not appearing at the output, a mux outputs a 1 or a 0 depending on whether the connected input has a 1 or a 0.

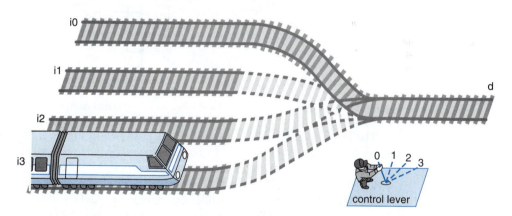

Figure 2.53 A multiplexer is like a railyard switch, determining which input track connects to the single output track, according to the switch's control lever.

A 2-input multiplexer, known as a 2x1 multiplexer, has two data inputs i1 and i0, one select input s0, and one data output d, as shown in Figure 2.54. If s0=0, i0's value passes through. If s0=1, i1's value passes through.

The internal design of a 2x1 multiplexer is shown in Figure 2.54. When s0=0, the top AND gate outputs 1*i0=i0, and the bottom AND gate outputs 0*i1=0. Thus, the OR gate outputs i0+0=i0. So i0 passes through as desired. Likewise, when s0=1, the bottom gate passes i1 while the top gate outputs 0, resulting in the OR gate passing i1.

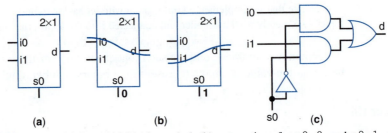

Figure 2.54 2 x 1 multiplexer: (a) block symbol, (b) connections for s0=0, and s0=1, and (c) internal design.

A 4-input multiplexer, known as a 4x1 multiplexer, has four data inputs i3, i2, i1, and i0, two select inputs s1 and s0, and one data output d (a mux *always* has just one data output, no matter how many inputs). A 4x1 mux block diagram is shown in Figure 2.55.

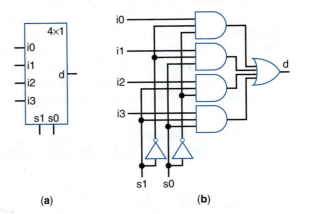

Figure 2.55 4 x 1 multiplexer: (a) block symbol and (b) internal design.

The internal design of a 4x1 multiplexer is shown in Figure 2.55. When s1s0=00, the top AND gate outputs i0*1*1=i0, the next AND gate outputs i1*0*1=0, the next gate outputs i2*1*0=0, and the bottom gate outputs i3*0*0=0. The OR gate outputs i0+0+0+0=i0. Thus, i0 passes through, as desired. Likewise, when s1s0=01, the second AND gate passes i1, while the remaining AND gates all output 0. When s1s0=10, the third AND gate passes i2, and the other AND gates output 0. When s1s0=11, the bottom AND gate passes i3, and the other AND gates output 0. For any value on s1s0, only 1 AND gate will have two 1s for its select inputs and will thus pass its data input; the other AND gates will have at least one 0 for its select inputs and will thus output 0.

An 8x1 multiplexer would have 8 data inputs i7...i0, 3 select inputs s2, s1 and s0, and one data output. More generally, an Mx1 multiplexer has M data inputs, $\log_2(M)$ select inputs, and one data output. Remember, a multiplexer always has just one output.

▶ **EXAMPLE 2.31** Basic questions about multiplexers

Assume a 4x1 multiplexer's four inputs presently have the following values: i0=1, i1=1, i2=0, and i3=0. What would be the value on multiplexer's output d for the following select input values?

1. s1s0 = 01. *Answer:* Because s1s0=01 passes input i1 through to d, then d would have the value of i1, which presently is 1.

2. s1s0 = 11. *Answer:* That configuration of select line input values passes i3 through, so d would have the value of i3, which presently is 0.

3. How many select inputs must be present on a 16x1 multiplexer? *Answer:* Four select inputs would be needed to uniquely identify which of the 16 inputs to pass through to the output since $\log_2(16)=4$.

4. How many select lines are there on a 4x2 multiplexer? *Answer:* This question is not valid—there is no such thing as a 4x2 multiplexer. A multiplexer has exactly one output.

5. How many inputs are there on a multiplexer having five select inputs? *Answer:* Five select inputs can uniquely identify one of $2^5=32$ inputs to pass through to the output. ◀

▶ **EXAMPLE 2.32** Mayor's vote display using a multiplexer

Consider a small town with a very unpopular mayor. During every town meeting, the city manager presents four proposals to the mayor, who then indicates his vote on the proposal (approve or deny). Very consistently, right after the mayor indicates his vote, the town's citizens boo and shout profanities at the mayor—no matter which way he votes. Having had enough of this abuse, the mayor sets up a simple digital system (the mayor happens to have taken a course in digital design), shown in Figure 2.56. He provides himself with four switches that can be positioned up or down, outputting 1 or 0, respectively. When the time comes during the meeting for him to vote on the first proposal, he places the first switch either in the up (accept) or down (deny) position—but nobody else can see the position of the switch. When the time comes to vote on the second

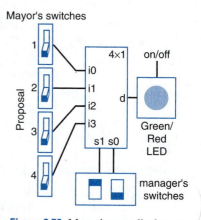

Figure 2.56 Mayor's vote display system implemented using a 4x1 mux.

proposal, he votes on the second proposal by placing the second switch up or down. And so on. When he has finished casting all his votes, he leaves the meeting and heads out for coffee. With the mayor gone, the city manager powers up a large green/red light. When the input to the light is 0, the light lights up red. When the input is 1, the light lights up green. The city manager controls two switches that can route any of the mayor's switch outputs to the light, and so the manager steps through each configuration of the switches, starting with configuration 00 (and calling out "The mayor's vote on this proposal is ..."), then 01, then 10, and finally 11, causing the light to light either green or red for each configuration depending on the positions of the mayor's switches. The system can easily be implemented using a 4x1 multiplexer, as shown in Figure 2.56. ◀

N-bit Mx1 multiplexer

Muxes are often used to selectively pass through not just single bits, but *N*-bit data items. For example, one set of inputs A may consist of four bits a3, a2, a1, a0, and another set of inputs B may also consist of four bits b3, b2, b1, b0. We want to multiplex those inputs to a four-bit output C, consisting of c3, c2, c1, c0. Figure 2.57(a) shows how to accomplish such multiplexing using four 2x1 muxes.

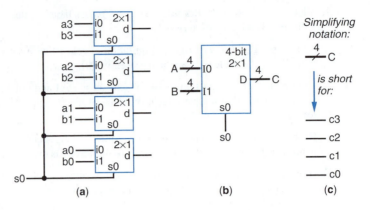

Figure 2.57 4-bit 2x1 mux: (a) internal design using four 2x1 muxes for selecting among 4-bit data items A or B, and (b) block diagram of a 4-bit 2x1 mux component. (c) The block diagram uses a common simplifying notation, using one thick wire with a slanted line and the number 4 to represent 4 single wires.

Because muxing data is so common, another common building block is that of an N-bit-wide Mx1 multiplexer. So in our example, we would use a 4-bit 2x1 mux. Don't get confused, though—an N-bit Mx1 multiplexer is really just the same as N separate Mx1 multiplexers, with all those muxes sharing the same select inputs. Figure 2.57(b) provides the symbol for a 4-bit 2x1 mux.

▶ **EXAMPLE 2.33**   Multiplexed automobile above-mirror display

Some cars come with a display above the rear-view mirror, as shown in Figure 2.58. The car's driver can press a button named mode to select among displaying the outside temperature, the average miles-per-gallon of the car, the instantaneous miles-per-gallon, and the approximate miles remaining until the car runs out of gasoline. Assume the car's central computer sends the data to the display as four 8-bit binary numbers, T (the temperature), A (average mpg), I (instantaneous mpg), and M (miles remaining). T consists of 8 bits: t7, t6, t5, t4, t3, t2, t1, t0. Likewise for A, I, and M. Assume the display system has two additional inputs x and y, which always change according to the fol-

Figure 2.58 Above-mirror display.

lowing sequence—00, 01, 10, 11—whenever the mode button is pressed (we'll see in a later chapter how to create such a sequence). When xy=00, we want to display T. When xy=01, we want to display A. When xy=10, we want to display I, and when xy=11, we want to display M. Assume the outputs D go to a display that knows how to convert the 8-bit binary number on D to a human-readable displayed number like that in Figure 2.58.

We can design the display system using eight 4x1 multiplexers. A simpler representation of that same design uses an 8-bit 4x1 multiplexer, as shown in Figure 2.59.

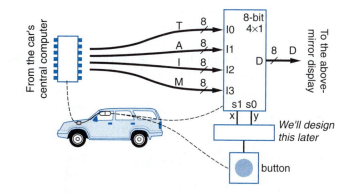

Figure 2.59 Above-mirror display using an 8-bit 4x1 mux.

Notice how many wires must be run from the car's central computer, which may be under the hood, to the above-mirror display—8 * 4 = 32 wires. That's a lot of wires. We'll see in a later chapter how to reduce the number of wires. ◀

Notice in the previous example how simple a design can be when we can utilize higher-level building blocks. If we had to use regular 4x1 muxes, we would have 8 of them, and lots of wires drawn. If we had to use gates, we would have 40 of them. Of course, underlying our simple design in Figure 2.59 are in fact eight 4x1 muxes, and underlying those are 40 gates. And underlying those gates are lots more transistors. We see that the higher-level building blocks make our design task much more managable.

▶ 2.10 ADDITIONAL CONSIDERATIONS

Schematic Capture and Simulation

When we design a circuit, how do we know that we designed the circuit correctly? Perhaps we created the truth table wrong, putting a 0 in an output column where we should have put a 1. Or perhaps we wrote down the wrong minterm, writing xyz when we should have wrote xyz'. For example, consider the number-of-one's counter in Example 2.25. We created a truth table, then equations, and finally a circuit. Is the circuit correct?

One method of checking our work is to reverse engineer the function from the circuit—starting with the circuit, we could convert the circuit to equations, and then the equations to a truth table. If we get the same original truth table, then the circuit should be correct. However, sometimes we start with an equation rather than a truth table, as in Example 2.24. We can reverse engineer the circuit to an equation, but that equation may be different than our original equation, especially if we algebraically manipulated the original equation when designing the circuit. And checking that two equations are equivalent may require converting to canonical form (sum-of-minterms), which may result in huge equations if our function has a large number of inputs.

In fact, even if we didn't make any mistakes in converting our mental understanding of the desired function into a truth table or equation, how do we know that our mental understanding was correct?

A commonly used method for checking that a circuit works as we expect is called simulation. *Simulation* of a circuit is the process of providing sample inputs to the circuit and running a computer program that computes the circuit's output for the given inputs. We can then check that the output matches what we expect. The computer program that performs simulation is called a *simulator*.

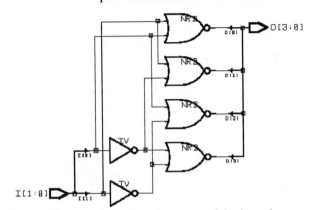

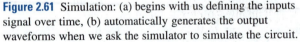

Figure 2.60 Display snapshot of a commercial schematic capture tool.

To use simulation to check a circuit, we must describe the circuit using a method that enables computer programs to read the circuit. One method of describing a circuit is to draw the circuit using a schematic capture tool. A *schematic capture tool* allows a user to place logic gates on a computer screen and to draw wires connecting those gates. The tool allows users to save their circuit drawings as computer files. All the circuit drawings in this chapter have represented examples of schematics—for example, the circuit drawing in Figure 2.50(b), representing a 2x4 decoder, was an example of a schematic. Figure 2.60 shows a schematic for the same design, drawn using a popular commercial schematic capture tool. Schematic capture is used not only to capture circuits for simulator tools, but also for tools that map our circuits to physical implementations, which will be discussed in Chapter 7.

Once we've created a circuit using schematic capture, we must provide the simulator with a set of inputs for which we want to check for proper output. One way of providing the inputs is by drawing waveforms for the circuit's input's. An input's *waveform* is a line that goes from left to right, representing the value of the input as time proceeds to the right. At different times, we draw the line as high to represent 1, and low

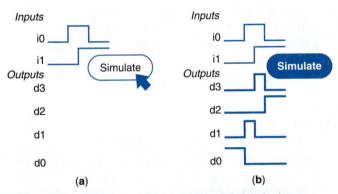

Figure 2.61 Simulation: (a) begins with us defining the inputs signal over time, (b) automatically generates the output waveforms when we ask the simulator to simulate the circuit.

to represent 0, as shown in Figure 2.61(a). After we are satisfied with our input waveforms, we instruct the simulator to simulate our circuit for the given inputs waveforms. The simulator determines what the circuit outputs would be for each unique combination of inputs, and generates waveforms for the outputs, as illustrated in Figure 2.61(b). We can then check that the output waveforms matches the output values that we would expect for each input. Such checking can be done visually, or by providing certain checking statements (often called assertions) to the simulator.

Simulation still does not guarantee that our circuit is correct, but rather increases our *confidence* that our circuit is correct.

Nonideal Gate Behavior—Delay

Ideally, logic gate outputs would change immediately in response to changes in the gate's inputs. The timing diagrams earlier in this chapter all assumed such ideal zero-delay gates, as shown again in Figure 2.62(a) for an OR gate. Unfortunately, real gate outputs don't change immediately, but rather after some short time delay. After all, even the fastest automobiles can't go from 0 to 60 miles-per-hour in 0 seconds. The delay in gates is due in part to the fact that transistors don't switch from nonconducting to conducting (or vice versa) immediately—it takes some time for electrons to accumulate in the channel of an nMOS

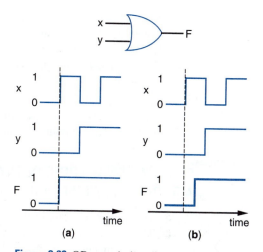

Figure 2.62 OR gate timing diagram: (a) without gate delay, (b) with gate delay.

transistor, for example. Furthermore, electric current travels at the speed of light, which, while extremely fast, is still not infinitely fast. Additionally, wires aren't perfect and can slow down electric current because of "parasitic" characteristics like capacitance and inductance. The timing diagram in Figure 2.62(b) illustrates how a real gate's output changes slightly after changes in the inputs. Gates delays for modern CMOS gates may take less than 1 nanosecond to respond to changes—extremely fast, but still not zero.

Demultiplexers and Encoders

Two additional components, demultiplexers and encoders, can also be considered as combinational building blocks. However, those components are far less commonly used than their counterparts of multiplexers and decoders. Nevertheless, for completeness, we'll briefly introduce those additional components here. You may notice throughout this book that demultiplexers and encoders don't appear in many examples, if in any examples at all.

Demultiplexer

A demultiplexer has roughly the opposite functionality of a multiplexer. Specifically, a 1x*M demultiplexer* has one data input, and based on the values of $\log_2(M)$ select lines, passes that input through to one of M outputs. The other outputs stay 0.

Encoder

An encoder has the opposite functionality of a decoder. Specifically, an n x $\log_2(n)$ encoder has n inputs and $\log_2(n)$ outputs. Of the n inputs, exactly one is assumed to be 1 at any given time (such would be the case if the input consisted of a sliding or rotating switch with n possible positions, for example). The encoder outputs a binary value over the $\log_2(n)$ outputs indicating which of the n inputs was a 1. For example, a 4x2 encoder would have four inputs d3, d2, d1, d0, and two outputs e1, e0. For an input 0001, the output is 00. 0010 yields 01, 0100 yields 10, and 1000 yields 11. In other words, d0=1 results in an output of 0 in binary, d1=1 results in an output of 1 in binary, d2=1 results in an output of 2 in binary, and d3=1 results in an output of 3 in binary.

A *priority encoder* has similar behavior, but handles situations where more than one input is 1 at the same time. A priority encoder gives priority to the highest input that is a 1, and outputs the binary value of that input. For example, if a 4x2 priority encoder has inputs d3 and d1 both equal to 1 (so the inputs are 1010), the priority encoder gives priority to d3, and hence outputs 11 .

▶ 2.11 COMBINATIONAL LOGIC OPTIMIZATIONS AND TRADEOFFS (SEE SECTION 6.2)

The earlier sections in this chapter described how to create basic combinational circuits. This section, Section 2.11, physically appears in this book as Section 6.2, and describes how to make those circuits better (smaller, faster, etc.)—namely, how to make optimizations and tradeoffs. One use of this book covers combinational logic optimizations and tradeoffs immediately after introducing basic combinational logic design, meaning covering that section now (as Section 2.11). An alternative use of the book covers that section later (as Section 6.2), after also introducing basic sequential design, datapath components, and register-transfer level design—namely, after Chapters 3, 4, and 5.

▶ 2.12 COMBINATIONAL LOGIC DESCRIPTION USING HARDWARE DESCRIPTION LANGUAGES (SEE SECTION 9.2)

Hardware description languages (HDLs) allow designers to describe their circuits using a textual language rather than as circuit drawings. This section, Section 2.12, introduces the use of HDLs to describe combinational logic. The section physically appears in the book as Section 9.2. One use of this book introduces HDLs now (as Section 2.12), immediately after introducing basic combinational logic. An alternative use of the book introduces HDLs later (as Section 9.2), after mastery of basic combinational, sequential, and register-transfer level design.

▶ 2.13 CHAPTER SUMMARY

Section 2.1 introduced the idea of using a custom digital circuit to implement a system's desired functionality and defined combinational logic as a digital circuit whose outputs are a function of the circuit's present inputs. Section 2.2 provided a brief history of digital switches, starting from relays in the 1930s to today's CMOS transistors, with the main trend being the amazing pace at which switch size and delay have continued to shrink for the past several decades, leading to ICs capable of containing a billion transistors or more. Section 2.3 described the basic behavior of a CMOS transistor, just enough information to remove the mystery of how transistors work. Section 2.4 introduced three fundamental building blocks for building digital circuits—AND gates, OR gates, and NOT gates (inverters), which are far easier to work with than transistors. Section 2.5 showed how Boolean algebra could be used to represent circuits built from AND, OR, and NOT gates, enabling us to build and manipulate circuits by using math—an extremely powerful concept. Section 2.6 introduced several different representations of Boolean functions, namely equations, circuits, and truth tables. Section 2.7 described a straightforward three-step process for designing combinational circuits, and gave several examples of building real circuits using the three-step process. Section 2.8 described why NAND and NOR gates are actually more commonly used than AND and OR gates in CMOS technology, and showed that any circuit built from AND, OR, and NOT gates could be built with NAND gates alone or NOR gates alone. That section also introduced two other commonly used gates, XOR and XNOR. Section 2.9 introduced two additional commonly used combinational building blocks, decoders and multiplexers. Section 2.10 introduced schematic capture tools, which allow us to draw our circuits such that computer programs can read those circuits, and also introduced simulation, which generates the output waveforms for user-provided input waveforms to help us verify that we created a circuit correctly. That section also discussed how real gates actually have a small delay between the time that inputs change and the time that the gate's output changes. The section also introduced some less commonly used combinational building blocks, demultiplexers and encoders.

▶ 2.14 EXERCISES

Any problem noted with an asterisk (*) represents an especially challenging problem.

SECTION 2.2: SWITCHES

2.1 A microprocessor in 1980 used about 10,000 transistors. How many of those microprocessors would fit in a modern chip having 1 billion transistors?

2.2 The first Pentium microprocessor had about 3 million transistors. How many of those microprocessors would fit in a modern chip having 1 billion transistors?

2.3 Define Moore's Law.

2.4 Assume for a particular year that a particular size chip using state-of-the-art technology can contain 1 billion transistors. Assuming Moore's Law holds, how many transistors will the same size chip be able to contain in ten years?

2.5 Assume a cell phone contains 50 million transistors. How big would such a cell phone be if the phone used vacuum tubes instead of transistors, assuming a vacuum tube has a volume of 1 cubic inch?

2.6 A modern desktop processor, such as the Pentium 4, has about 300 million transistors. How big would a modern desktop processor be if we used vacuum tubes of the 1940s, assuming a vacuum tube has an area of 1 square inch?

SECTION 2.3: THE CMOS TRANSISTOR

2.7 Describe the behavior of the CMOS transistor circuit shown in Figure 2.63, clearly indicating when the transistor circuit conducts.

2.8 If we apply a voltage to the gate of a CMOS transistor, why doesn't the current flow from the gate to the transistor's source or drain?

Figure 2.63 Circuit combining two CMOS transistors.

SECTION 2.4: BOOLEAN LOGIC GATES—BUILDING BLOCKS FOR DIGITAL CIRCUITS

2.9 Which Boolean operation, AND, OR, or NOT, is appropriate for each of the following:

(a) Detecting motion in any motion sensor surrounding a house (each motion sensor outputs 1 when motion is detected).

(b) Detecting that three buttons are being pressed simultaneously (each button outputs 1 when a button is being pressed).

(c) Detecting the absence of light from a light sensor (the light sensor outputs 1 when light is sensed).

2.10 Convert the following English problem statements to Boolean equations:

(a) A flood detector should turn on a pump if water is detected and the system is set to enabled.

(b) A house energy monitor should sound an alarm if it is night and light is detected inside a room but motion is not detected.

(c) An irrigation system should open the sprinkler's water valve if the system is enabled and neither rain nor freezing temperatures are detected.

2.11 Evaluate the Boolean equation F = (a AND b) OR c OR d for the given values of variables a, b, c, and d:

(a) a=1, b=1, c=1, d=0

(b) a=0, b=1, c=1, d=0

(c) a=1, b=1, c=0, d=0

(d) a=1, b=0, c=1, d=1

2.12 Evaluate the Boolean equation F = a AND (b OR c) AND d for the given values of variables a, b, c, and d:

(a) a=1, b=1, c=0, d=1

(b) a=0, b=0, c=0, d=1

(c) a=1, b=0, c=0, d=0

(d) a=1, b=0, c=1, d=1

2.13 Evaluate the Boolean equation F = a AND (b OR (c AND d)) for the given values of variables a, b, c, and d:

(a) a=1, b=1, c=0, d=1

(b) a=0, b=0, c=0, d=1

(c) a=1, b=0, c=0, d=0

(d) a=1, b=0, c=1, d=1

2.14 Show the conduction paths and output value of the OR gate transistor circuit in Figure 2.11 when: (a) x = 1 and y = 0, (b) x = 1 and y = 1.

2.15 Show the conduction paths and output value of the AND gate transistor circuit in Figure 2.13 when: (a) x = 1 and y = 0, (b) x = 1 and y = 1.

2.16 Convert each of the following equations directly to gate-level circuits:

(a) F = ab' + bc + c'

(b) F = ab + b'c'd'

(c) F = ((a + b') * (c' + d)) + (c + d + e')

2.17 Convert each of the following equations directly to gate-level circuits:

(a) F = a'b' + b'c

(b) F = ab + bc + cd + de

(c) F = ((ab)' + (c)) + (d + ef)'

2.18 Convert each of the following equations directly to gate-level circuits:

(a) F = abc + a'bc

(b) F = a + bcd' + ae + f'
(c) F = (a + b) + (c' * (d + e + fg))

2.19 We want to design a system that sounds a buzzer inside our home whenever motion outside is detected at night. Assuming we have a motion sensor with output M that indicates whether motion is detected (M=1 means motion detected) and a light sensor with output L that indicates if light is detected (L=1 means light is detected). The buzzer inside the home has a single input B that when 1 creates a loud warning sound. Using AND, OR, and NOT gates, create a simple digital circuit to implement the motion detector at night system.

2.20 A DJ ("disc jockey," meaning someone who plays the music at a party) would like a system to automatically control a strobe light and disco ball in a dance hall depending on whether music is playing and anyone is dancing. Assume we have a sound sensor with output S that indicates whether music is playing (S=1 means music is playing) and a motion sensor M that indicates whether people are dancing (M=1 means people are dancing). The strobe light has an input L that turns the light on when L is 1, and the disco ball has an input B that turns the ball on when B is 1. The DJ wants the disco ball to turn on only when music is playing and nobody is dancing, and the DJ wants the strobe light to turn on only when music is playing and people are dancing. Using AND, OR, and NOT gates, create a simple digital circuit to activate: (a) the disco ball, and (b) the strobe light.

2.21 We want to concisely describe the following situation using a Boolean equation. We want to fire a football coach (by setting F=1) if he is mean (represented by M=1). If he is not mean, but has a losing season (represented by the Boolean variable L=1), we want to fire him anyway. Write an equation that translates the situation directly to a Boolean equation for F, without any simplification.

SECTION 2.5: BOOLEAN ALGEBRA

2.22 For the function F = a + a'b + acd + c':
   (a) List all the variables.
   (b) List all the literals.
   (c) List all the product terms.

2.23 For the function F = a'd' + a'c + b'cd' + cd:
   (a) List all the variables.
   (b) List all the literals.
   (c) List all the product terms.

2.24 Let variables T represent being tall, H being heavy, and F being fast. Let's consider anyone who is not tall as short, not heavy as light, and not fast as slow. Write a Boolean equation to represent the following:
   (a) You may ride a particular amusement park ride only if you are either tall and light, or short and heavy.
   (b) You may NOT ride an amusement park ride if you are either tall and light, or short and heavy. Use algebra to simplify the equation to sum-of-products.
   (c) You are eligible to play on a particular basketball team if you are tall and fast, or tall and slow. Simplify this equation.
   (d) You are NOT eligible to play on a particular football team if you are short and slow, or if you are light. Simplify to sum-of-products form.
   (e) You are eligible to play on both the basketball and football teams above, based on the above criteria. Hint: combine the two equations into one equation by ANDing them.

2.25 Let variables S represent a package being small, H being heavy, and E being expensive. Let's consider a package that is not small as big, not heavy as light, and not expensive as inexpensive. Write a Boolean equation to represent the following:

(a) You can deliver packages only if the packages are either small and expensive, or big and inexpensive.

(b) You can NOT deliver a package that is listed above. Use algebra to simplify the equation to sum-of-products.

(c) You can load the packages into your truck only if the packages are small and light, small and heavy, or big and light. Simplify the equation.

(d) You can NOT load the packages described above. Simplify to sum-of-products.

2.26 Use algebraic manipulation to convert the following equation to sum-of-products form: F = $a(b + c)(d') + ac'(b + d)$

2.27 Use algebraic manipulation to convert the following equation to sum-of-products form: F = $a'b(c + d') + a(b' + c) + a(b + d)c$

2.28 Use DeMorgan's Law to find the inverse of the following equation: F = $abc + a'b$. Reduce to sum-of-products form. Hint: Start with F' = $(abc + a'b)'$

2.29 Use DeMorgan's Law to find the inverse of the following equation: F = $ac' + abd'$ + acd. Reduce to sum-of-products form.

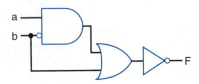

Figure 2.64 Combinational circuit F.

SECTION 2.6: REPRESENTATIONS OF BOOLEAN FUNCTIONS

2.30 Convert the following Boolean equations to a digital circuit:
(a) $F(a,b,c)$ = $a'bc + ab$
(b) $F(a,b,c)$ = $a'b$
(c) $F(a,b,c)$ = $abc + ab + a + b + c$
(d) $F(a,b,c)$ = c'

2.31 Create a Boolean equation representation of the digital circuit in Figure 2.64.

2.32 Create a Boolean equation representation for the digital circuit in Figure 2.65.

2.33 Convert each of the Boolean equations in Exercise 2.30 to a truth table.

2.34 Convert each of the following Boolean equations to a truth table:
(a) $F(a,b,c)$ = $a' + bc'$
(b) $F(a,b,c)$ = $(ab)' + ac' + bc$
(c) $F(a,b,c)$ = $ab + ac + ab'c' + c'$
(d) $F(a,b,c,d)$ = $a'bc + d'$

Figure 2.65 Combinational circuit G.

2.35 Fill in Table 2.8's columns for the equation: $F= ab + b'$.

TABLE 2.8   Truth table.

Inputs					Outputs
a	b	ab	b'	ab+b'	F
0	0				
0	1				
1	0				
1	1				

TABLE 2.9 **Truth table.**

a	b	c	F
0	0	0	0
0	0	1	1
0	1	0	1
0	1	1	1
1	0	0	0
1	0	1	1
1	1	0	1
1	1	1	1

TABLE 2.10 **Truth table.**

a	b	c	F
0	0	0	1
0	0	1	0
0	1	0	1
0	1	1	0
1	0	0	1
1	0	1	1
1	1	0	1
1	1	1	0

TABLE 2.11 **Truth table.**

a	b	c	F
0	0	0	0
0	0	1	1
0	1	0	0
0	1	1	0
1	0	0	0
1	0	1	0
1	1	0	1
1	1	1	1

2.36 Convert the function F shown in the truth table in Table 2.9 to an equation. Don't minimize the equation.

2.37 Use algebraic manipulation to minimize the equation obtained in Exercise 2.36.

2.38 Convert the function F shown in the truth table in Table 2.10 to an equation. Don't minimize the equation.

2.39 Use algebraic manipulation to minimize the equation obtained in Exercise 2.38.

2.40 Convert the function F shown in the truth table in Table 2.11 to an equation. Don't minimize the equation.

2.41 Use algebraic manipulation to minimize the equation obtained in Exercise 2.40.

2.42 Create a truth table for the circuit of Figure 2.64.

2.43 Create a truth table for the circuit of Figure 2.65.

2.44 Convert the function F shown in the truth table in Table 2.9 to a digital circuit.

2.45 Convert the function F shown in the truth table in Table 2.10 to a digital circuit.

2.46 Convert the function F shown in the truth table in Table 2.11 to a digital circuit.

2.47 Convert the following Boolean equations to canonical sum-of-minterms form:
(a) F(a,b,c) = a'bc + ab
(b) F(a,b,c) = a'b
(c) F(a,b,c) = abc + ab + a + b + c
(d) F(a,b,c) = c'

2.48 Determine whether the Boolean functions F = (a + b)'*a and G = a + b' are equivalent, using: (a) algebraic manipulation, and (b) truth tables.

2.49 Determine whether the Boolean functions F = ab' and G = (a' + ab)' are equivalent, using: (a) algebraic manipulation, and (b) truth tables.

2.50 Determine whether the Boolean function G = a'b'c + ab'c + abc' + abc is equivalent to the function represented by the circuit in Figure 2.66.

2.51 Determine whether the two circuits in Figure 2.67 are equivalent circuits using: (a) algebraic manipulation, and (b) truth tables.

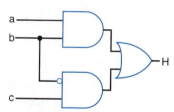

Figure 2.66 Combinational circuit H.

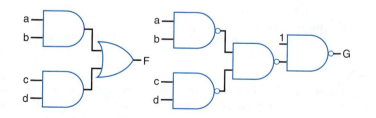
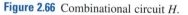

Figure 2.67 Combinational circuits F and G.

2.52 *Figure 2.68 shows two circuits in which the inputs of the circuits are unlabeled.
(a) Determine whether the two circuits are equivalent. Hint: Try all possible labelings of the inputs for both circuits.

(b) How many circuit comparisons will you need to perform to determine if two circuits with 10 unlabeled inputs are equivalent?

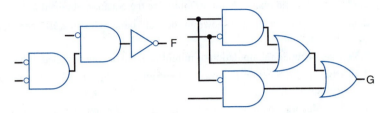

Figure 2.68 Combinational circuits *F* and *G*.

SECTION 2.7: COMBINATIONAL LOGIC DESIGN PROCESS

2.53 A museum has three rooms, each with a motion sensor (m0, m1, and m2) that outputs 1 when motion is detected. At night, the only person in the museum is one security guard who walks from room to room. Create a circuit that sounds an alarm (by setting an output A to 1) if motion is ever detected in more than one room at a time (i.e., in two or three rooms), meaning there must be an intruder or intruders in the museum. Start with a truth table.

2.54 Create a circuit for the musem of Exercise 2.53 that detects whether the guard is properly patrolling the museum, detected by *exactly* one motion sensor being 1. (If no motion sensor is 1, the guard must be sitting or sleeping.)

2.55 Consider the museum security alarm function of Exercise 2.53, but for a museum with 10 rooms. A truth table is not a good starting point (too many rows), nor is an equation describing when the alarm should sound (too many terms). However, the inverse of the alarm function can be straightforwardly captured as an equation. Design the circuit for the 10-room security system by designing the inverse of the function, and then just adding an inverter before the circuit's output.

2.56 A network router connects multiple computers together and allows them to send messages to each other. If two or more computers send messages simultaneously, they collide and the messages must be resent. Using the combinational design process of Table 2.5, create a collision detection circuit for a router that connects 4 computers. The circuit has 4 inputs labeled M0 through M3 that are 1 when the corresponding computer is sending a message and 0 otherwise. The circuit has one output labeled C that is 1 when a collision is detected and 0 otherwise.

2.57 Using the combinational design process of Table 2.5, create a 4-bit prime number detector. The circuit has four inputs, N3, N2, N1, and N0 that correspond to a 4-bit number (N3 is the most significant bit) and one output named P that outputs a 1 when the input is a prime number or 0 otherwise.

2.58 A car has a fuel-level detector that outputs the current fuel-level as a 3-bit binary number, with 000 meaning empty and 111 meaning full. Create a circuit that illuminates a "low fuel" indicator light (by setting an output L to 1) when the fuel level drops below level 3.

2.59 A car has a low-tire-pressure sensor that outputs the current tire pressure as a 5-bit binary number. Create a circuit that illuminates a "low tire pressure" indicator light (by setting an output T to 1) when the tire pressure drops below 16. Hint: you might find it easier to create a circuit that detects the inverse function. You can then just append an inverter to the output of that circuit.

SECTION 2.8: MORE GATES

2.60 Show the conduction paths and output value of the NAND gate transistor circuit in Figure 2.45 when: (a) x = 1 and y = 0, (b) x = 1 and y = 1.

2.61 Show the conduction paths and output value of the NOR gate transistor circuit in Figure 2.45 when: (a) x = 1 and y = 0, (b) x = 0 and y = 0.

2.62 Show the conduction paths and output value of the AND gate transistor circuit in Figure 2.46 when: (a) x = 1 and y = 1, (b) x = 0 and y = 1.

2.63 Two people, denoted using variables A and B, want to ride with you on your motorcycle. Write a Boolean equation that indicates that exactly one of the two people can come (A=1 means A can come, A=0 means A can't come). Then use XOR to simplify your equation.

2.64 Simplify the following equation by using XOR wherever possible: F = a'b + ab' + cd' + c'd + ac.

2.65 Use XOR to create a circuit that outputs a 1 when the number of 1s on inputs a, b, c, d is odd.

2.66 Use XOR or XNOR to create a circuit that detects if all inputs a, b, c, d are 0s.

2.67 Use XOR or XNOR to create a circuit that detects if an even number of the inputs a, b, c, d are 1s.

2.68 Show that a 4-bit XOR gate is an odd function (meaning the output is 1 only if the number of input 1s is odd).

SECTION 2.9: DECODERS AND MUXES

2.69 Design a 3x8 decoder using AND, OR, and NOT gates.

2.70 Design a 4x16 decoder using AND, OR, and NOT gates.

2.71 Design a 3x8 decoder with enable using AND, OR, and NOT gates.

2.72 Design an 8x1 multiplexer using AND, OR, and NOT gates.

2.73 Design a 16x1 multiplexer using AND, OR, and NOT gates.

2.74 Design a 4-bit 4x1 multiplexer using 4x1 multiplexers.

2.75 Create a circuit that rings a bell whenever motion is detected from one of two motion sensors. A switch S determines which sensor to pay attention to: S=0 means ring the bell when there's motion at motion sensor 1, S=1 means motion sensor 2.

2.76 A home entertainment center has four different audio sources that can be played over the same set of speakers. Each audio source, named A, B, C, and D, is connected using 8 wires on which the digitized audio signal is transmitted. The user selects which audio source is to be played using a rotary switch with four outputs, s0, s1, s2, s3, of which exactly one will be '1' at any given time. If s0 = '1', the audio source A should be played, if s1 = '1', the audio source B should be played, and so on. Create a digital circuit with a single 8-bit output O that will output the user's selected audio source.

SECTION 2.10: ADDITIONAL CONSIDERATIONS

2.77 Design a 1x4 demultiplexer using AND, OR, and NOT gates.

2.78 Design a 1x8 demultiplexer using AND, OR, and NOT gates.

2.79 Design a 4x2 encoder using AND, OR, and NOT gates.

2.80 Design an 8x3 encoder using AND, OR, and NOT gates. Assume that only one input will be 1 at any given time.

2.81 Design a 4x2 priority encoder using AND, OR, and NOT gates. Assume that every input being 0 is encoded as 00.

Samson enjoyed physics and math in college, and focused his advanced studies on integrated circuit (IC) design, believing the industry to have a great future. Years later now, he realizes he was right: "Looking back 20 years in high tech, we have experienced four major revolutions: the PC revolution, digital revolution, communication revolution, and Internet revolution—all four enabled by the IC industry. The impact of these revolutions to our daily life is profound."

He has found his job to be "very challenging, interesting, and exciting. I continually learn new skills to keep up, and to do my job more efficiently."

One of Samson's key design projects was for digital television, namely, high-definition TV (HDTV), involving companies like Zenith, Philips, and Intel. In particular, he led the 12-person design team that built Intel's first Liquid Crystal on Silicon (LCoS) chip for rear-projection HDTV. "Traditional LCoS chips are analog. They apply different analog voltages on each pixel of the display chip so it can produce an image. But analog LCoS is very sensitive to noise and temperature variation. We used digital signals to do pulse width modulation on each pixel." Samson is quite proud of his team's accomplishments: "Our HDTV picture quality was much better."

Samson also worked on the 200-member design team for Intel's Pentium II processor. That was a very different experience. "For the smaller team project, each person had more responsibility, and overall efficiency was high. For the large team project, each person worked on a specific part of the project—the chip was divided into clusters, each cluster into units, and each unit had a leader. We relied heavily on design flows and methodologies."

Samson has seen the industry's peaks and valleys during the past two decades: "Like any industry, the IC job market has its ups and downs." He believes the industry survives the low points in large part due to "innovation." "Brand names sell products, but without innovation, markets go elsewhere. So we have to be very innovative, creating new products so that we are always ahead in the global competition."

But, "innovation doesn't grow on trees," Samson points out. "There are two kinds of innovations. The first is invention, which requires a good understanding of the physics behind technology. For example, to make an analog TV into a digital TV, we must know how human eyes perceive video images, which parts can be digitized, how digital images can be produced on a silicon chip, etc. The second kind of innovation reuses existing technology for a new application. For example, we can reuse advanced space technologies in a new non-space product serving a bigger market. e-Bay is another example—it reused Internet technology for on-line auctions. Innovations lead to new products, and thus new jobs for many years.

Thus, Samson points out that "The industry is counting on new engineers from college to be innovative, so they can continue to drive the high tech industry forward. When you graduate from college, it's up to *you* to make things better."

CHAPTER 3

Sequential Logic Design— Controllers

▶ 3.1 INTRODUCTION

The output of a combinational circuit is a function only of the circuit's present inputs. A combinational circuit has no memory—we cannot store bits into a combinational circuit and later read the bits out that we saved. Combinational circuits by themselves are rather limited in their usefulness. Designers instead typically use combinational circuits as part of larger circuits called sequential circuits—circuits that do have memory. A *sequential circuit* is a circuit whose outputs depend not only on the circuit's present inputs, but also on the circuit's present *state*, which is all the bits stored in the circuit. The circuit's state in turn depends on the past *sequence* of values that have appeared at the circuit's inputs.

An everyday example of a combinational circuit is a doorbell—push the button (the input) now, and the bell (the output) rings. Push the button again, and the bell rings again. Push the button tomorrow, or next week, and the bell rings the same each time. A doorbell has no state, no memory—its output value (whether the bell rings or not) depends solely on its present input value (whether the button is pressed or not). In contrast, an example of a sequential circuit is an automatic garage door system—push the button (the input) now, and the door opens. Push the button again, and this time the door closes. Push the button tomorrow, and the door opens again. The system's output (whether the door opens or closes) depends on the state of the system (whether the door is presently open or closed), which in turn depends on the sequence of *past* input values since we turned on the system.

Most digital systems with which you are familiar involve sequential circuits that store bits. A handheld calculator must contain a sequential circuit, because the calculator must store the numbers you enter, in order to operate on those numbers. A digital camera stores pictures. A traffic light controller stores information indicating which light is presently green. A circuit that counts down from 59 to 0 stores the present count value, to know what the next value should be.

In this chapter, we describe basic sequential circuit building blocks, and the design of a certain class of sequential circuits known as controllers.

▶ 3.2 STORING ONE BIT—FLIP-FLOPS

To build a sequential circuit, we need a building block that enables us to store a bit. By store a bit, we mean that we can save a bit in the block (say a 1) and later come back to see what we saved. As an example, suppose we want to build the flight attendant call-button system in Figure 3.1. An airline passenger can push the *Call* button to turn on a small blue light above the passenger's seat, indicating to a flight attendant that the passenger

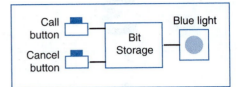

Figure 3.1 Flight attendant call-button system. Pressing Call turns on the light, which stays on after Call is released. Pressing Cancel turns off the light.

needs service. The light stays on even after the call button is released. The light can be turned off by pressing the *Cancel* button. Since the light has to stay on even after the call button is released, we need a way to "remember" that the call button was pressed. We can remember by using a bit storage block, and storing a 1 in the block when the call button is pressed, and storing a 0 when the cancel button is pressed. We connect the output of this bit storage block to the blue light. The light illuminates when the block's output is 1.

To introduce the internal design of such a bit storage block, we'll introduce several increasingly complex circuits able to store a bit—a basic SR latch, a level-sensitive SR latch, a level-sensitive D latch, and an edge-triggered D flip-flop. The D flip-flop will then be used to create a block capable of storing multiple bits, known as a register, which will serve as our primary bit storage block in the rest of the book. Each successive circuit eliminates some problem of the previous one, leading to the robust D flip-flop and then register.

Be aware that designers rarely use bit storage blocks other than D flip-flops. We introduce the other blocks primarily to provide the reader with the underlying intuition of the D flip-flop's design.

Feedback—The Basic Storage Method

The basic method used to store a bit in a digital circuit is *feedback*. You've surely experienced feedback in the form of audio feedback, when someone talking into a microphone stood in front of the speaker, causing a loud continuous humming sound to come out of the speakers (in turn causing everyone to cover their ears and snicker). The talker generated a sound that was picked up by the microphone, came out the speakers (amplified), was picked up *again* by the microphone, came out the speakers again (amplified even more), etc. That's feedback.

Feedback in audio systems is annoying, but in digital systems is extremely useful. Intuitively, we know that we need to somehow feed the output of a logic gate back into the gate itself, so that the stored bit ends up looping around and around, like a dog chasing its own tail. We might try the circuit in Figure 3.2.

Suppose initially Q is 0 and S is 0. At some point, suppose we set S to 1. That causes Q to become 1, and that 1 feeds back into the OR gate, causing Q to be 1, etc. So even when S returns to 0, Q stays 1. Unfortunately, Q stays 1 from then on, and we

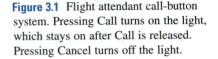

Figure 3.2 First (failed) attempt at using feedback to store a bit.

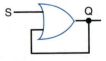

have no way of resetting Q to 0. But hopefully you understand the basic idea of feedback now—we did successfully store a 1 using feedback.

We draw in Figure 3.3 the timing diagram for our attempted feedback circuit from Figure 3.2. Note that we assume the OR gate has a small input to output delay, as was discussed in Section 2.10. Initially, we assume both OR gate inputs are 0 (Figure 3.3(a)). Then we set S to 1 (Figure 3.3(b)), which causes Q to become 1 slightly later (Figure 3.3(c)), which in turn causes t to become 1 slightly later (Figure 3.3(d)). Finally, when we change S back to 0 (Figure 3.3(e)), Q will stay 1 because t is 1. The first curved line with an arrow indicates that the event of S changing from 0 to 1 causes the event of Q changing from 0 to 1. The second curved line with an arrow indicates that the event of Q changing from 0 to 1 in turn causes the event of t changing from 0 to 1. And that 1 then continues to loop around, forever, with no way of S resetting Q to 0.

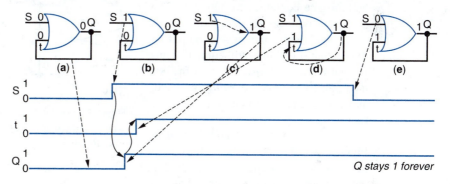

Figure 3.3 Tracing the behavior of our first attempt at bit storage.

SR Latch

Basic SR Latch

It turns out that the simple circuit in Figure 3.4, called a ***basic SR latch***, implements the bit storage building block we desire. The circuit consists of just a pair of cross-coupled NOR gates. Making the circuit's S input equal to 1 causes Q to become 1, while making R equal to 1 causes Q to become 0. Making both S and R equal to 0 causes whatever value Q is to keep looping around. In other words, S "sets" the latch to 1, and R "resets" the latch to 0—hence the letters S (for *set*) and R (for *reset*).

Let's see why the basic SR latch works as it does. Recall that a NOR gate outputs 1 when all the gate's inputs equal 0; if at least one input equals 1, the NOR gate outputs 0.

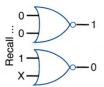

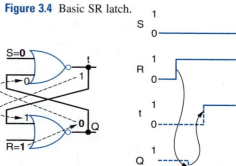

Figure 3.4 Basic SR latch.

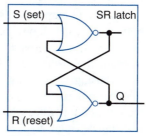

Figure 3.5 SR latch when S = 0 and R = 1.

Suppose that we make S=0 and R=1, as in the SR latch circuit of Figure 3.5, and that we don't initially know the values of Q and t. Since the bottom gate of the circuit has at least one input equal to 1 (R), the gate outputs 0—in the timing diagram, R becoming 1 causes Q to become 0. In the circuit, Q's 0 feeds back to the top NOR gate, which will have both its inputs equal to 0 and its output equal to 1. In the timing diagram, Q becoming 0 causes t to become 1. In the circuit, that 1 feeds back to the bottom NOR gate, which has at least one input equal to 1 (actually, both inputs equal 1), and so the bottom gate will continue to output 0. Thus the output Q equals 0, and all values are stable.

Now suppose we make S=0 and R=0, as in Figure 3.6. The bottom gate still has at least one input equal to 1 (the input coming from the top gate), so the bottom gate continues to output 0. The top gate continues to have both inputs equal to 0 and continues to output 1. The output Q will thus still equal 0. Thus the earlier R=1 *stored* a 0 into the SR latch, also known as *resetting* the latch, and that 0 remains stored even when we return R to 0.

Now let's make S=1 and R=0, as in Figure 3.7. The top gate in the circuit now has one input equal to 1, so the top gate outputs a 0—the timing diagram shows the change of S from 0 to 1 causing t to change from 1 to 0. The top gate's 0 output feeds back to the bottom gate, which now has both inputs equal to 0 and outputs 1—the timing diagram shows the change of t from 1 to 0 causing Q to change from 0 to 1. The bottom gate's (Q) 1 output feeds back to the top gate, which has at least one input equal to 1 (actually, both inputs equal 1 now), so the top gate continues to output 0. The output Q therefore equals 1, and all values are stable.

Now let's make S=0 and R=0 again, as in Figure 3.8. The top gate still has at least one input equal to 1 (the input coming from the bottom gate), so the top gate continues to output 0. The bottom gate continues to have both inputs equal to 0 and continues to output 1. The output Q is still equal to 1. Thus, the

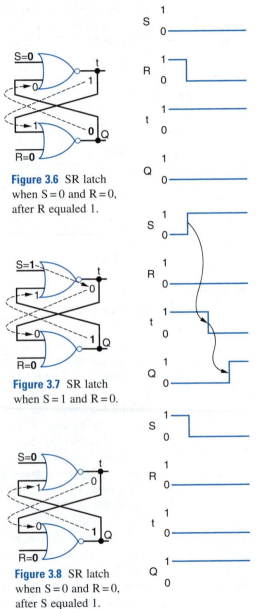

Figure 3.6 SR latch when S = 0 and R = 0, after R equaled 1.

Figure 3.7 SR latch when S = 1 and R = 0.

Figure 3.8 SR latch when S = 0 and R = 0, after S equaled 1.

earlier S=1 *stored* a 1 into the SR latch, also known as *setting* the latch, and that 1 remains stored even when we return S to 0.

The basic SR latch can be used to implement the flight attendant call-button system (Figure 3.9). We connect the call button to S, the cancel button to R, and the light to Q. Pressing the call button sets Q to 1, thus turning on the light. Q stays 1 even when the call button is released. Pressing the cancel button resets Q to 0, thus turning off the light. Q stays 0 even when the cancel button is released.

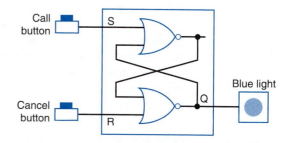

Figure 3.9 Flight attendant call-button system using a basic SR latch.

Level-Sensitive SR Latch

A problem with the basic SR latch is S and R both equaling 1 at the same time causes undefined behavior—we might have stored a 1, we might have stored a 0, or we might even cause the latch output to oscillate from 1 to 0 to 1 to 0, and so on. Let's see why.

If S = 1 and R = 1, both gates have at least one input equal to 1, and thus both gates output 0, as shown in Figure 3.10(a). A problem occurs when we return S and R to 0. Suppose S and R return to 0 at exactly the same time. Then both gates will have all 0s at their inputs, so their outputs will change from 0s to 1s, as shown in Figure 3.10(b). Those 1s feed back to the gate inputs, causing the gates to output 0s, as shown in Figure 3.10(c). Those 0s feed back to the gate inputs again, causing the gates to output 1s. And so on. Going from 1 to 0 to 1 to 0 and so on is called *oscillation*. Oscillation is not a desirable feature of a bit storage block.

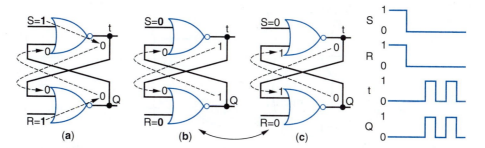

Figure 3.10 The situation of S = 1 and R = 1 causes problems—Q oscillates when SR return to 00.

In a real circuit, the delays of the upper and lower gates and wires would be slightly different from one another. So after a time of oscillation, one of the gates may get ahead of the other (outputting a 1 before the other does, then a 0 before the other one does, etc.), until it gets far enough ahead to cause the circuit to enter a stable situation of either Q=0 or Q=1—which case will happen, we don't know. Such a situation, in which the final value of a memory circuit depends on the delays of gates and wires, is known as a ***race condition***. Figure 3.11 shows a race condition involving oscillation but ending with a stable situation of Q=1. But we didn't know which value Q would eventually settle into (it could have settled into Q=0), so the fact that Q=1 is not useful to us in our use of the bit storage block.

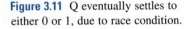

Figure 3.11 Q eventually settles to either 0 or 1, due to race condition.

In our flight attendant call-button system, if the passenger pushes both buttons at the same time, the result could be that the blue light starts oscillating, and then the light either ends up on or off.

S and R should never both equal 1 in an SR latch

In summary, S and R should never both equal 1 in an SR latch.

In practice, we would never actually connect buttons directly to an SR latch's inputs (we did that just for the purpose of an intuitive example). So we can safely assume the S and R inputs come from a digital circuit. Thus, we can design that digital circuit such that S and R should never both equal 1. But even if we try to design that circuit such that S and R should never both be 1, we could still find that S and R inadvertently both become 1 at the same time. For example, consider the simple circuit in Figure 3.12. In theory, S and R can't both be 1—if X=1, then S=1 but R=0. If X=0, R may equal 1 but S=0. So S and R can't both be 1—in theory.

In reality, both S and R could both be 1 for a short time in this circuit, because of the delay of real gates, as introduced in Figure 2.62. Suppose X has been 0 and Y has been 1 for a long time, so S=0 and R=1. Then suppose we change X to 1. S will change to 1 almost immediately, but R will stay 1 for a short while as the new value of X propagates through the inverter and the AND gate, after which R changes to 0. If each component has a delay of 1 ns (nanosecond), then S and R would actually both be 1 for 2 ns (Figure 3.13). Temporary values on signals caused by gate delays are referred to as ***glitches***.

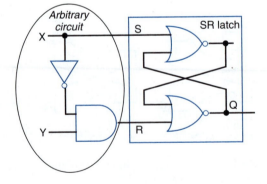
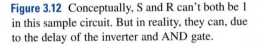

Figure 3.12 Conceptually, S and R can't both be 1 in this sample circuit. But in reality, they can, due to the delay of the inverter and AND gate.

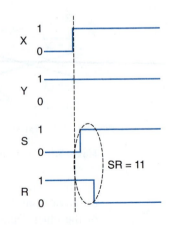

Figure 3.13 Gate delays can cause SR = 11.

A partial solution to this problem is to add an enable input C to the SR latch, as shown in Figure 3.14. When C=1, the S and R signals propagate through the two AND gates to the S1 and R1 inputs of the basic SR latch circuit, because S*1=S and R*1=R. However, when C=0, the two AND gates cause S1 and R1 to be 0, regardless of the values of S and R. Thus, when C=0, the basic latch's value cannot change. (You might note that a difference in the top and bottom AND gate delays could result in S1 and R1 both being 1 for a very short time equal to that difference, but that time is too short to cause a problem.)

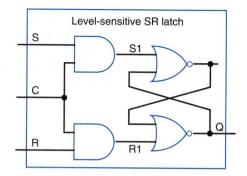

Figure 3.14 Level-sensitive SR latch— an SR latch with enable input C.

The introduction of the enable input leads to the idea of setting the enable to 1 only when we are *sure* that S and R have stable values. Figure 3.15 shows the inverter/AND circuit from Figure 3.12, this time using an SR latch with an enable input. If we change X, we should wait for at least 2 ns before setting the enable input C to 1 in order to ensure that the SR inputs to the latch are stable and are not equal to 11.

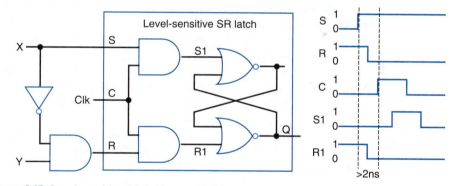

Figure 3.15 Level-sensitive SR latch—an SR latch with enable input C.

An SR latch with an enable is known as a ***level-sensitive SR latch***, because the latch is only sensitive to its S and R inputs when the level of the enable input is 1. Such a latch is also called a ***transparent*** latch, because setting the enable input to 1 makes the internal SR latch transparent to the S and R inputs.

You may have noticed that the top NOR gate of an SR latch outputs the opposite value as the bottom gate, which is connected to the output Q. Thus, we can include an output Q' on an SR latch almost for free, just by connecting the top gate to that output. Most latches do in fact come with both Q and Q' outputs. The symbol for a level-sensitive SR latch with such dual outputs is shown in Figure 3.16.

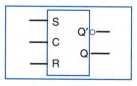

Figure 3.16 Symbol for dual-output level-sensitive SR latch.

Clocks and Synchronous Circuits

The level-sensitive SR latch uses an enable signal C that we must set to 1 after we are sure S and R are stable. But how do we decide when to set the enable C to 1? Most sequential circuits simply use an enable signal that pulses at a constant rate. For example, we could make the enable signal go high for 10 ns, then low for 10 ns, then high for 10 ns, then low for 10 ns, etc., as in Figure 3.17.

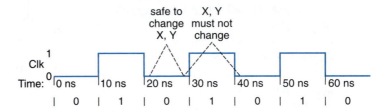

Figure 3.17 An example of a clock signal named *Clk*. Circuit inputs should only change while $Clk = 0$, such that latch inputs will be stable when $Clk = 1$.

The time high and time low need not be the same—for example, we could create a signal that is low for 10 ns, high for 1 ns, low for 10 ns, high for 1 ns, etc.

Such a pulsing enable signal is called a ***clock*** signal, because the signal ticks (high, low, high, low) like a clock. A circuit whose storage elements (in this case latches) can only change when a clock signal is active is known as a synchronous sequential circuit, or just ***synchronous circuit*** (the sequential aspect is implied—there's no such thing as a synchronous combinational circuit). A sequential circuit that does not use a clock is called an ***asynchronous circuit.*** We leave the important but challenging topic of asynchronous circuit design for a more advanced digital design textbook. The majority of sequential circuits designed and used today are synchronous.

Designers typically use an oscillator to generate a clock signal. An ***oscillator*** is a circuit that outputs a signal that alternates between 1 and 0 at a constant frequency, like that in Figure 3.17. An oscillator component typically has no inputs (other than power), and has an output representing the clock signal.

▶ HOW DOES IT WORK?—QUARTZ OSCILLATORS.

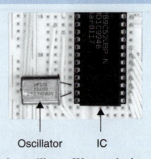

Conceptually, an oscillator can be thought of as an inverter feeding back to itself, as shown on the left. If C is initially 1, the value will feed back through the inverter and so C will become 0, which feeds back through the inverter causing C to become 1 again, and so on. The oscillation frequency would depend on the delay of the inverter. Real oscillators must regulate the oscillation frequency more precisely. A common type of oscillator uses ***quartz,*** a mineral consisting of silicon dioxide in crystal form. Quartz happens to be such that it vibrates if we apply an electric current, and that vibration is at a precise frequency determined by the quartz size and shape. Furthermore, when quartz vibrates, it generates a voltage. So, by making quartz a specific size and shape and then applying a current, we get a precise electronic oscillator. We attach the oscillator to an IC's clock signal input, as shown above. Some ICs come with a built-in oscillator.

Oscillator   IC

A clock signal's ***period*** is the time after which the signal repeats itself—or more simply, the time between successive 1s. The signal in Figure 3.17 has a period of 20 ns. A ***clock cycle*** refers to one such segment of time, meaning one segment where the clock is 1 and then 0. Figure 3.17 shows three and a half clock cycles. A clock signal's ***frequency*** is the number of cycles per second, and is computed as 1/(the clock period). The signal in Figure 3.17 has a frequency of 1/20 ns = 50 MHz. The units of frequency are Hertz, or Hz, where 1 Hz = 1 cycle per second. MHz is short for Megahertz, meaning one million Hz.

Freq.	Period
100 GHz	0.01 ns
10 GHz	0.1 ns
1 GHz	**1 ns**
100 MHz	10 ns
10 MHz	100 ns

A convenient way to mentally convert common computer clock periods to frequencies, and vice versa, is to remember that a 1 ns period equals a 1 GHz (Gigahertz, meaning 1 billion Hz) frequency. Then, if one is slower (or faster) by a factor of 10, the other is slower (or faster) by a factor of 10 also—so a 10 ns period equals 100 MHz, while a 0.1 ns period equals 10 GHz.

D Flip-Flop

While the SR latch is useful for introducing the notion of storing a bit in a digital circuit, most circuits actually use slightly more advanced devices, namely, D latches and D flip-flops, to store bits.

Level-Sensitive D Latch—A Basic Bit Store

The SR latch has the annoying problem of entering an undefined state if the S and R inputs are both 1 when the clock is high. Ensuring that we design circuits that don't set S and R to both 1 imposes a burden on the designer. One way to relieve designers of this burden is to instead use a new type of latch, called a ***D latch***, shown in Figure 3.18.

A D latch stores whatever value is present at the latch's D input when C = 1, and holds that value when C = 0. Internally, the latch's D input connects to S directly, and to R through an inverter. Figure 3.19 provides a timing diagram of the D latch for sample input values on D and C. When D is 1 and C is 1, the latch is set to 1, because S is 1 and R is 0. When D is 0 and C is 1, the latch is reset to 0, because R is 1 and S is 0. By making R the opposite of S, we are assured that S and R won't both be 1 at the same time, as long as we only change S and R when C is 0.

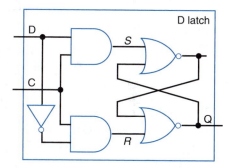

Figure 3.18 D latch internals.

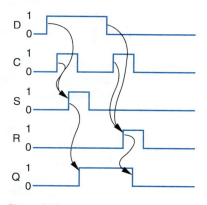

Figure 3.19 D latch timing diagram.

The symbol for a D latch with dual-outputs
(Q and Q') is shown in Figure 3.20.

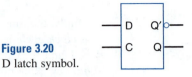

Figure 3.20
D latch symbol.

Edge-Triggered D Flip-Flop—A Robust Bit Store

The D latch still has a potentially nasty problem that can cause unpredictable circuit behavior—namely, signals can propagate from a latch output to another latch's input while the clock signal is 1. For example, consider the circuit in Figure 3.21. When Clk = 1, the value on Y will be loaded into the first latch and appear at that latch's output. If Clk still equals 1, then that value will also get loaded into the second latch. The value will keep propagating through the latches until Clk returns to 0. Through how many latches will the value propagate? It's hard to say—we would have to know the precise timing delay information of each latch.

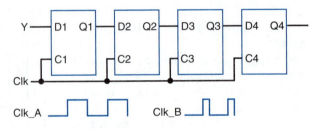

Figure 3.21 A problem with latches—through how many latches will Y propagate for each pulse of Clk_A? For Clk_B?

Figure 3.22 illustrates this propagation problem in more detail. Suppose D1 is initially 0 for a long time, changes to 1 long enough to be stable, and then Clk becomes 1. Q1 will thus change from 0 to 1 after about three gate delays, and thus D2 will also change from 0 to 1, as shown in the left timing diagram. If Clk is still 1, then that new value for D2 will propagate through the AND gates of the second latch, causing S2 to change from 0 to 1 and R2 from 1 to 0, thus changing Q2 from 0 to 1, as shown in the left timing diagram. Also note in the left timing diagram that changing D2 while C2 = 1 causes S2 and R2 to both equal 1 for a short time, due to the extra delay on the path to R2 caused by the inverter, though the time that both are 1 is probably too short to cause a problem.

You might suggest making the clock signal such that the clock is 1 only for a short amount of time, so there's not enough time for the new output of a latch to propagate to the next latch's inputs. But how short is short enough? 50 ns? 10 ns? 1 ns? 0.1 ns? And if we make the clock's time at 1 too short, that time may not be long enough for the bit at a latch's D input to stabilize in the latch's feedback circuit, and we might therefore not successfully store the bit, as illustrated in Figure 3.22 (c).

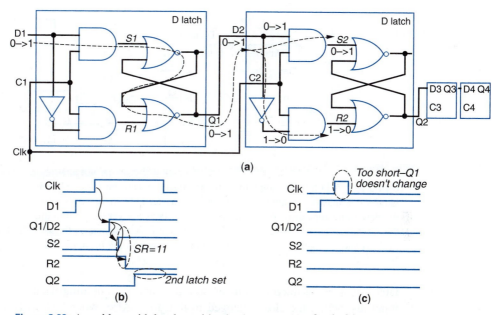

(a)

(b)

(c)

Figure 3.22 A problem with level-sensitive latches: (a) while $C = 1$, $Q1$'s new value may propagate to $D2$, (b) such propagation can cause $S2$ and $R2$ to both be 1 for a short time while the latch's enable is 1 (but $SR = 11$ is never supposed to occur), or can cause an unknown number of latches along a chain to get updated, (c) trying to shorten the clock's high time to avoid propagation to the next latch, but long enough to allow a latch to reach a stable feedback situation, is hard, because making the clock's high time too short prevents proper loading of the latch.

A good solution is to design a more robust block for storing a bit—a block that stores the bit at the D input at the *instant* that the clock rises from 0 to 1. Note that we didn't say that the block stores the bit instantly. Rather, the bit that will eventually get stored into the block is the bit that was stable at D at the instant that the clock rises from 0 to 1. Such a block is called an ***edge-triggered D flip-flop***. The word "edge" refers to the vertical part of the line representing the clock signal, when the signal transitions from 0 to 1. Figure 3.23 shows three cycles of a clock signal, and indicates the three rising clock edges of those cycles.

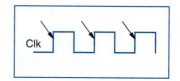

Figure 3.23 Rising clock edges.

Edge-Triggered D Flip-Flop Using a Master-Servant Design. One way to design an edge-triggered D flip-flop is to use *two* D latches, as shown in Figure 3.24.

The first D latch, known as the ***master***, is enabled (can store new values on Dm) when Clk is 0 (due to the inverter), while the second D latch, known as the ***servant***, is enabled when Clk is 1. Thus, while Clk is 0, the bit on D is stored into the master latch, and hence Qm and Ds are updated—but the servant latch does not store this new bit because the servant latch is not enabled since Clk is not 1. When Clk becomes 1, the master

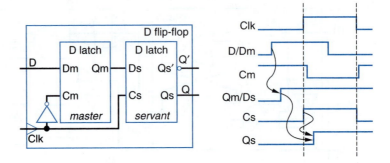

Figure 3.24 A D flip-flop implementing an edge-triggered bit storage block, internally using two latches in a master-servant arrangement. The master D latch stores its Dm input while Clk = 0, but the new value appearing at Qm and hence at Ds does not get stored into the servant latch, because the servant latch is disabled when Clk = 0. When Clk becomes 1, the servant D latch becomes enabled and thus gets loaded with whatever value was in the master latch just before Clk changed from 0 to 1.

latch becomes disabled (retains its stored value), thus holding whatever bit was at the D input just before the clock changed from 0 to 1. Also, when Clk is 1, the servant latch becomes enabled, thus storing the bit that the master is storing, which is the bit that was at the D input just before Clk changed from 0 to 1—hence implementing an edge-triggered storage block.

The edge-triggered block using two internal latches thus prevents the stored bit from propagating through more than one latch when the clock is 1. Consider the chain of flip-flops in Figure 3.25, which is similar to the chain in Figure 3.21 but with D flip-flops in place of D latches.

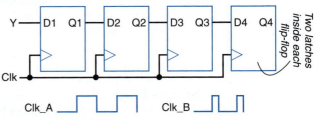

Figure 3.25 Using D flip-flops, we now know through how many flip-flops Y will propagate for Clk_A and for Clk_B— one flip-flop exactly per pulse, for either clock signal.

We know that Y will propagate through exactly one flip-flop on each clock cycle.

The drawback of a master-servant approach is that we now need two D latches to store one bit. So Figure 3.25 shows four flip-flops, but there are two latches inside each flip-flop, for a total of eight latches.

There are many alternative methods other than the master-servant method for designing an edge-triggered flip-flop. In fact, there are hundreds of different designs for latches and flip-flops beyond the designs we showed above, with those designs differing in terms of their size, speed, power, etc. When we use an edge-triggered flip-flop, we usually don't worry about whether the flip-flop achieves edge-triggering using the master-servant method or using some other method. We need only know that the flip-flop is edge-triggered, meaning the data value present when the clock edge is rising is the value that gets loaded into the flip-flop, and that appears at the flip-flop's output some time later.

The common name is actually "master-slave." Some choose instead to use the term "servant" due to some people finding the term "slave" offensive. Others use the terms "primary-secondary."

We've actually been describing what's known as *positive* or *rising* edge-triggered flip-flops, which are triggered by the clock signal going from 0 to 1. There are also flip-flops known as *negative* or *falling* edge-triggered flip-flops, which are triggered by the signal going from 1 to 0. We can build a negative edge-triggered D flip-flop using a master-servant design where the second flip-flop's clock input is inverted, rather than the first flip-flop's.

Positive edge-triggered flip-flops are drawn using a small triangle at the clock input, and negative edge-triggered flip-flops are drawn using a small triangle along with an inversion bubble, as shown in Figure 3.26.

Bear in mind that although our master-servant design doesn't change the output until the falling clock edge, the flip-flop is still positive edge-triggered, because the flip-flop stores the value that was at the D input at the instant that the clock edge is *rising*.

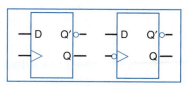

Figure 3.26 Positive (shown on the left) and negative (right) edge-triggered D flip-flops. The sideways triangle input represents an edge-triggered clock input.

Latches versus Flip-Flops: Various textbooks define the terms latch and flip-flop differently. We'll use what seems to be the most common convention among designers, namely:

- A *latch* is level-sensitive, and
- A *flip-flop* is edge-triggered.

So saying "edge-triggered flip-flop" is redundant, since flip-flops are by definition edge-triggered. Likewise, saying "level-sensitive latch" is redundant, since latches are by definition level-sensitive.

Figure 3.27 uses an example timing diagram to illustrate the difference between level-sensitive and edge-triggered bit storage blocks. The figure provides an example of a clock signal and a value on a signal D. The next signal trace is for the Q output of a D latch, which as we know is level-sensitive. The latch ignores the first pulse on D (labeled as *3* in the figure) because Clk is low. However, when Clk becomes high (*1*), the latch output follows the D input, so when D changes from 0 to 1 (*4*), so does the latch output (*7*). The latch ignores the next changes on D when Clk is low (*5*), but then follows D again when Clk is high (*6, 8*).

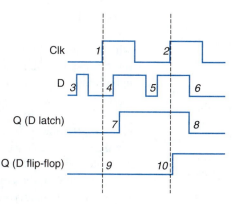

Figure 3.27 Latch versus flip-flop timing.

Compare this with the next signal trace, showing the behavior of a rising-edge-triggered D flip-flop. The flip-flop samples D at the first rising clock edge (*1*), finding D to be 0. The flip-flop thus stores and outputs a 0 (*9*). The flip-flop samples D at the next rising clock edge (*2*), finding D to be 1, and thus stores and outputs a 1 (*10*). Notice that the flip-flop ignores all changes to D that occur between the rising clock edges (*3, 4, 5, 6*)—even ignoring changes on D when the clock is high (*4, 6*).

▶ **EXAMPLE 3.1**   Flight attendant call-button using a D flip-flop

Let's design our flight attendant call-button system using a D flip-flop. If `Call` is pressed, we want to store a 1. If `Cancel` is pressed, we want store a 0. If neither is pressed, we want to store whatever is presently stored, meaning Q. We thus need a simple combinational circuit in front of the D input, described by the truth table in Table 3.1. If `Call`=0 and `Cancel`=0 (the first two rows), D equals Q's value. If `Call`=0 and `Cancel`=1 (the next two rows), D=0. If `Call`=1 and `Cancel`=0 (the next two rows), D=1. And if both `Call`=1 and `Cancel`=1 (the last two rows), we'll give priority to the `Call` button, so D=1.

After some algebraic simplification, we obtain the following equation for D:

$$D = Cancel'Q + Call$$

The final system is shown in Figure 3.28.   ◀

TABLE 3.1 D truth table for call-button system.

Call	Cancel	Q	D
0	0	0	0
0	0	1	1
0	1	0	0
0	1	1	0
1	0	0	1
1	0	1	1
1	1	0	1
1	1	1	1

The D flip-flop-based design uses more gates than the SR latch-based in Figure 3.9 (which could have just as easily used an SR flip-flop). One reason for the extra gates is that a D flip-flop always stores its D input on every clock cycle, so we must explicitly feed Q back into D to maintain the same value. In contrast, we could just set S=R=0 to maintain the same value with an SR flip-flop. Furthermore, we must convert the button presses to the appropriate D input value, requiring extra logic, rather than just setting either S or R to 1. In the late 1970s and early 1980s, those extra gates were a big deal, because ICs came with just a few gates on them, so extra gates often meant extra ICs, meaning extra size, cost, power, etc. But today, in the era of million-gate ICs, the savings of an SR flip-flop are trivial. In modern design, nearly all designs use D flip-flops, not SR flip-flops.

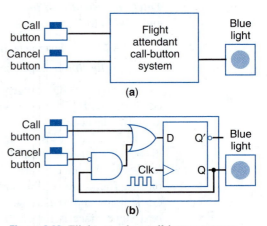

Figure 3.28 Flight attendant call-button system: (a) block diagram, and (b) implemented using a D flip-flop.

As a point of information, designers commonly refer to flip-flops simply as *flops*.

We went through several intermediate designs before arriving at our robust D flip-flop design for our desired bit storage block. Figure 3.29 summarizes those designs, including their features and their problems, leading to the robust edge-triggered D flip-flop. In looking over the summary, notice that the D flip-flop relies on an internal SR latch to maintain a stored bit *between* clock cycles, and relies on the designer to introduce feedback outside the D flip-flop to maintain a stored bit from *across* clock cycles.

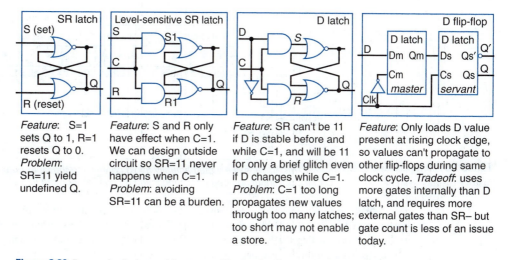

Feature: S=1 sets Q to 1, R=1 resets Q to 0. *Problem*: SR=11 yield undefined Q.

Feature: S and R only have effect when C=1. We can design outside circuit so SR=11 never happens when C=1. *Problem*: avoiding SR=11 can be a burden.

Feature: SR can't be 11 if D is stable before and while C=1, and will be 11 for only a brief glitch even if D changes while C=1. *Problem*: C=1 too long propagates new values through too many latches; too short may not enable a store.

Feature: Only loads D value present at rising clock edge, so values can't propagate to other flip-flops during same clock cycle. *Tradeoff*: uses more gates internally than D latch, and requires more external gates than SR– but gate count is less of an issue today.

Figure 3.29 Increasingly better bit storage blocks, leading to the D flip-flop.

Basic Register—Storing Multiple Bits

A *register* is a sequential component that can store multiple bits. We can build a basic register simply by using multiple flip-flops, as shown in Figure 3.30. That register can hold 4 bits. When the clock rises, all 4 flip-flops get loaded with inputs I0, I1, I2, and I3 simultaneously.

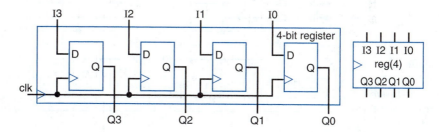

Figure 3.30 A basic 4-bit register internal design (left) and block symbol (right).

This register, made simply from multiple flip-flops, is the most basic form of a register—so basic that some companies refer to such a register simply as a "4-bit D flip-flop." We'll describe more advanced registers, namely, registers with more features and operations, in Chapter 4.

▶ **EXAMPLE 3.2** Temperature history display using registers

We want to design a system that records the outside temperature every hour and displays the last three recorded temperatures, so that an observer can see the temperature trend. An architecture of the system is shown in Figure 3.31.

A timer generates a pulse on signal C every hour. A temperature sensor outputs the present temperature as a 5-bit binary number ranging from 0 to 31, corresponding to those temperatures in Celsius. Three displays convert their 5-bit binary inputs into a numerical display.

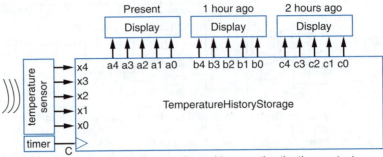

Figure 3.31 Temperature history display system.

(*In practice, we would actually avoid connecting the timer output C to a clock input, instead only connecting an oscillator output to a clock input.*)

We can implement the *TemperatureHistoryStorage* component using three 5-bit registers, as shown in Figure 3.32. Each pulse on signal C loads Ra with the present temperature on inputs x4..x0 (by loading the 5 flip-flops inside Ra with the 5 input bits). At the same time that register Ra gets loaded with that present temperature, register Rb gets loaded with the value that was in Ra. Likewise, Rc gets loaded with Rb's value. All three loads happen at the same time, namely, on the rising edge of C. The effect is that the values that were in Ra and Rb just before the clock edge get shifted into Rb and Rc, respectively.

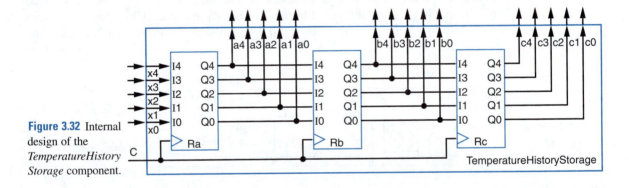

Figure 3.32 Internal design of the *TemperatureHistory Storage* component.

Figure 3.33 shows sample values in the registers for several clock cycles, assuming all the registers initially held 0s, and assuming that as time proceeds the inputs x4..x0 have the values shown at the top of the timing diagram.

Figure 3.33 Example of values in the *TemperatureHistory Storage* registers. One particular data item, 18, is shown moving through the registers on each clock cycle.

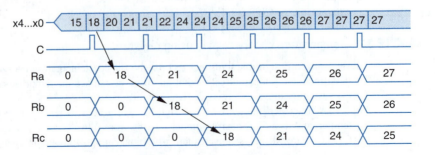

This example demonstrates one of the great things about synchronous circuits built from edge-triggered flip-flops—many things happen at once, yet we need not be concerned about signals propagating too fast through a register to another register. The reason we need not be concerned is because registers *only get loaded on the rising clock edge*, which effectively is an infinitely small period of time, so by the time signals propagate through a register to a second register, it's too late—that second register is no longer paying attention to its data inputs. ◀

We should mention that, in practice, designers typically try to avoid connecting any signal other than an oscillator output to the clock input of a flip-flop or register. So in practice, we might try to avoid connecting the signal C to the registers' clock inputs, since C comes from a timer output, not an oscillator. We'll show in Chapter 4, Example 4.3, how to design a similar system using an oscillator for the clock.

▶ 3.3 FINITE-STATE MACHINES (FSMS) AND CONTROLLERS

Registers store bits in a digital circuit. Stored bits means the circuit has memory, also known as *state*, resulting in what are known as sequential circuits. While a register storing bits happens to result in a circuit with state, we can actually use state to design circuits that have a specific behavior over time. For example, we can specifically design a circuit that outputs a 1 for exactly three cycles whenever a button is pressed. Or we could design a circuit that blinks lights in a specific pattern. Or we could design a circuit that detects if three buttons get pushed in a particular sequence and that then unlocks a door. In all these cases, we would be making use of state to create specific time-ordered behavior for our circuit. A sequential circuit that controls Boolean outputs based on Boolean inputs and a specific time-ordered behavior is often referred to as a *controller*.

▶ EXAMPLE 3.3 Three-cycles-high laser timer—a poorly done first design

Consider the design of a part of a laser surgery system, such as a system for scar removal or corrective vision. Such systems work by turning on a laser for a precise amount of time (see "How does it work?—laser surgery" on page 112). A general architecture of such a system is shown in Figure 3.34.

A surgeon activates the laser by pressing the button. Assume the laser should then stay on for exactly 30 ns.

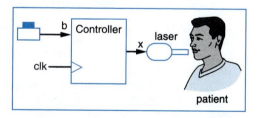

Figure 3.34 Laser timer system.

Assuming our clock's period is 10 ns, 30 ns means 3 clock cycles. (Assume that b is synchronized with the clock and stays high for only 1 clock cycle.) We need to design a controller component that, once detecting that $b = 1$, holds x high for exactly 3 clock cycles, thus turning on the laser for exactly 30 ns.

This is one example for which a software solution may not work. Using just regular programming statements reading input ports and writing output ports, we may not have a way to hold an output port high for exactly 30 ns—for example, when the microprocessor clock frequency is not fast enough, or when each statement takes 2 cycles to execute.

Let's try to create a sequential circuit implementation for the system. After thinking about the problem for a while, we might come up with the (not so good) implementation in Figure 3.35.

Knowing we need to hold the output high for three clock cycles, we used three flip-flops, with the idea being that we'll shift a 1 through those three flip-flops, taking three clock cycles for the bit to move through all three flip-flops. We ORed the flip-flop outputs to generate signal x, so that if any flip-flop contains a 1, the laser will be on. We made b the input to the first flip-flop, so when b=1, the first flip-flop stores a 1 on the next clock cycle. One clock cycle later, the second flip-flop will get loaded with 1, and assuming b has now returned to 0, the first flip-flop will get loaded with 0. One clock cycle later, the third flip-flop will get loaded with 1, and the second flip-flop with 0. One clock cycle later, the third flip-flop will get loaded with 0. Thus, the circuit held the output x at 1 for three clock cycles after the button was pressed. ◀

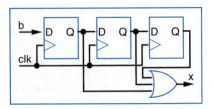

Figure 3.35 First (bad) attempt to implement the laser surgery system.

We did not do a very good job implementing this system. First of all, what happens if the surgeon presses the button a second time before the three cycles are completed? Such a situation could cause the laser to stay on too long. Is there a simple way to fix our circuit to account for that behavior? Second, we didn't use any orderly method for designing the circuit—we came up with the ORing of flip-flop outputs, but how did we come up with that? Will that method work for all time-ordered behavior that we might want to design?

The previous example illustrated the need for a way of describing the desired behavior of a sequential circuit.

We need two things to do a better job at designing circuits having time-ordered behavior. First, we need a way to explicitly represent the desired time-ordered behavior—we'll introduce the finite-state machine representation for this purpose. Second, we need an orderly method for implementing such behavior as a sequential circuit—we'll introduce such a standard method.

Finite-State Machines (FSMs)

In the previous chapter, you saw that we could design a combinational circuit by first describing the desired circuit behavior using a mathematical formalism known as a Boolean equation, and then converting the equation to a circuit. For a sequential circuit, a Boolean equation alone is not sufficient to describe behavior—we need a more powerful mathematical formalism that incorporates time.

Finite-state machines (FSMs) are just such a method. The name is a bit awkward, but the concept is straightforward. An FSM consists of several things, the most important of which is a set of states representing every possible state, or mode, of a system.

Trying to escape

I like to use my daughter's hamster as an intuitive example. After having a hamster as a family pet, I've learned that hamsters basically have four states: *Sleeping, Eating, RunningOnTheWheel*, and *TryingToEscape*. They spend most of their day sleeping (being nocturnal), a bit of time eating or running on the wheel, and the rest of their time desperately trying to escape from their cage.

As a more electronics-oriented example, let's design a system that repeatedly sets an output x to 0 for one clock cycle and to 1 for one clock cycle. The system clearly has only two states, which we'll call *Off* and *On*. In state *Off*, x = 0; in state *On*, x = 1. We can show those states, and the transitions between them, using the state diagram in Figure 3.36.

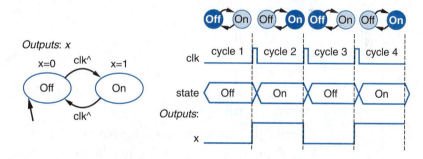

Figure 3.36 A simple state diagram (left) and the timing diagram describing the state diagram's behavior (right). Above the timing diagram, we see the FSM going from one state to the other in each clock cycle. "clk^" represents the rising edge of the clock signal.

Assume we start in state *Off*. The diagram shows that x is set to 0 while the system is in state *Off*. The diagram also shows that on the next rising edge of the clock signal, *clk^*, the system transitions to state *On*, and the diagram shows that x is set to 1 in that state. On the next rising edge of the clock, the diagram shows that the system transitions to state *Off* again. A timing diagram showing the system's behavior is shown in Figure 3.36.

Recall in Example 3.3 that we wanted a system that held its output high for three cycles. Toward that end, let's extend the simple state diagram of Figure 3.36 to have one off state and three on states, as shown in Figure 3.37. The output x will be 0 for one cycle and then 1 for three cycles, as shown in the timing diagram of the figure.

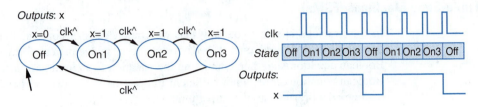

Figure 3.37 Three-cycles-high system: state diagram (left), timing diagram (right).

We can introduce input conditions on the transitions to further extend the behavior. We extend the state diagram in Figure 3.38 by changing the condition on the transition from state *Off* to state *On1*, such that the new condition requires not just a rising clock, but also that b=1. We also add a transition from *Off* back to *Off*, with the condition of a rising clock and b=0. The timing diagram in the figure shows the state and output behavior for the given input values on b.

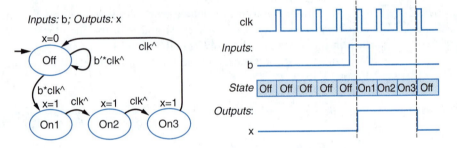

Figure 3.38 Three-cycles-high system: state diagram (left), timing diagram (right).

From the above examples, we can see that a *finite-state machine*, or **FSM**, is a mathematical formalism consisting of several things:

- A set of states. Our example had four states: {*On1, On2, On3, Off*}.
- A set of inputs, and a set of outputs. Our example had one input: {b}, and one output: {x}.
- An initial state, namely, a state to start in when we power up the system. An FSM's initial state can be indicated graphically by a single directed edge, with no source state, that points to the initial state. An FSM can only have one initial state. Our example's initial state was *Off*.
- A description of the next state to go to based on the current state and the values of the inputs. Our example used directed edges with associated input **conditions** to tell us the next state. Those edges with conditions are known as **transitions**.
- A description of what output values to generate in each state. Our example assigns a value to x in every state. Assigning an output in an FSM is known as an **action**.

We used a graphical representation of an FSM, known as a *state diagram*, to show the FSM for our example. We could have represented the FSM textually instead, but state diagrams are very popular for visualizing an FSM's behavior.

▶ **EXAMPLE 3.4** FSM for the three-cycles-high laser timer

We can create an FSM to describe the earlier introduced laser timer system. The system might have four states: *Off, On1, On2,* and *On3*. In the *Off* state, the laser should be off (x=0). The *On1* state would be the first clock cycle the laser is on (x=1), *On2* the second cycle, and *On3* the third cycle. The state diagram of the FSM is in fact identical to that shown in Figure 3.38.

Here's how the FSM should be interpreted. We start in our initial state *Off*. We stay in state *Off* until one of its two outgoing transitions has a true condition. One of those transitions has the condition of b' AND rising clock (b'*clk^)—in that case, we transition right back to state *Off*. The other of those transitions has the condition of a b AND a rising clock (b*clk^)—in that case, we transition to state *On1*. We stay in state *On1* until its one outgoing transition's condition, a rising clock, becomes true—in which case we transition to state *On2*. Likewise, we stay in *On2* until the next rising clock, transitioning to *On3*. We stay in *On3* until the next rising clock, causing a transition back to state *Off*. In state *Off*, we have associated the action of setting x=0, while in states *On1, On2,* and *On3*, we have associated the action of setting x=1.

Thus, we have precisely described the desired time-ordered behavior of the laser timer system using an FSM.

It's interesting to examine the behavior of this FSM if the button is pressed a second time while the laser is on. Notice that the transitions among the *On* states are independent of the value of b. So this system will always turn the laser on for exactly three cycles and then return to the *Off* state to await another press of the button. ◀

Simplifying FSM Notation: Making the Rising Clock Implicit

Thus far, we have included the rising clock edge (clk^) as part of the condition of every FSM transition. We included that edge because we are only considering the design of sequential circuits that are synchronous and that use rising edge-triggered flip-flops to store bits. Synchronous sequential circuits with edge-triggered flip-flops make up the vast majority of sequential circuits in modern design practice. As such, most textbooks and designers, to make their state diagrams more readable, follow the convention that every transition in an FSM is *implicitly ANDed* with a rising clock edge. For example, a transition labeled "a'" actually means "a'*clk^."

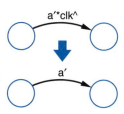

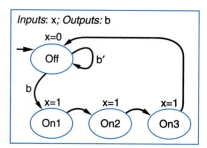

Figure 3.39 Laser timer state diagram assuming every transition is ANDed with a rising clock.

Henceforth, we will not include the rising clock edge when drawing FSM transitions, and we will follow the convention that *every* transition is

implicitly ANDed with a rising clock edge. Figure 3.39 illustrates the laser timer state diagram from Figure 3.40, redrawn using an implicit clock.

A transition with no associated condition simply transitions on the next clock cycle, because of the implicit rising clock edge.

Let's consider a few more examples showing how to describe time-ordered behavior using FSMs.

▶ **EXAMPLE 3.5**   Secure car key

Have you noticed that the keys for many new automobiles have a thicker plastic head than in the past (see Figure 3.40)? The reason is that, believe it or not, there is a computer chip inside the head of the key, implementing a secure car key. In a basic version of such a secure car key, when the driver turns the key in the ignition, the car's computer (which is under the hood and communicates using what's called the *basestation*) sends out a radio signal asking the car key's chip to respond by sending an identifier via a radio signal. The chip in the key then responds by sending the identifier (ID), using what's known as a *transponder* (a transponder "transmits" in "response" to a request). If the basestation does not receive a response or the key's response has an ID different than the ID programmed into the car's computer, the computer shuts down and the car won't start.

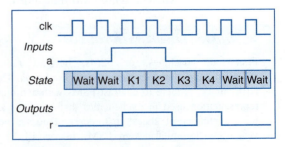

Figure 3.40 Why are the heads of keys getting thicker? Note that the key on the right is thicker than the key on the left. The key on the right has a computer chip inside that sends an identifier to the car's computer, thus helping to reduce car thefts.

Let's design the controller for such a key having an ID of 1011 (real IDs are typically 32 bits long or more, not just 4 bits). Assume the controller has an input a that is 1 when the car's computer requests the key's ID. Thus the controller initially waits for the input a to become 1. The key should then send its ID (1011) serially, starting with the rightmost bit, on an output r; the key sends 1 on the first clock cycle, 1 on the second cycle, 0 on the third cycle, and finally 1 on the fourth cycle. The FSM for the controller is shown in Figure 3.41. Note that the FSM sends the bits starting from the bit on the right, which is known as the *least significant bit* (LSB).

Figure 3.42 provides a timing diagram for the FSM for a particular situation. When we set $a = 1$, the FSM enters state *K1* and outputs $r = 1$. The FSM

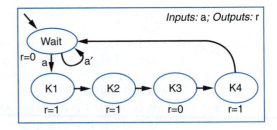

Figure 3.41 Secure car key FSM.

Figure 3.42 Secure car key timing diagram.

then proceeds through *K2*, *K3*, and *K4*, outputting r = 1, 0, and 1, respectively, even though we returned input a to 0.

Timing diagrams represent a particular situation defined by how we set the inputs. What would have happened if we had held a = 1 for many more clock cycles? The timing diagram in Figure 3.43 illustrates that situation. Notice how the FSM, after returning to state *Wait*, proceeds to state *K1* again on the next cycle.

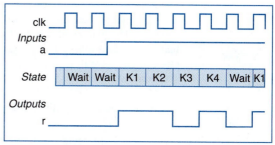

Figure 3.43 Secure car key timing diagram for a different sequence of values on input a.

The computer chip in the car key has circuitry that converts radio signals to bits and vice versa.

"So my car key may someday need its batteries replaced?" you might ask. Actually, no—those chips in keys draw their power as well as their clock from the magnetic component of the radio-frequency field generated from the computer basestation. The extremely low power requirement makes custom digital circuitry, rather than software on a microprocessor, the preferred implementation method.

Computer chip keys make stealing cars a lot harder—no more "hot-wiring" to start a car, since the car's computer won't work unless it also receives the correct identifier. And the method above is actually an overly simplistic method—many cars have more sophisticated communication between the computer and the key, involving several communications in both directions, even using encrypted communication—making fooling the car's computer even harder. A drawback of secure car keys is that you can't just run down to the local hardware store and copy those keys for $5 any longer—copying keys requires special tools that today can run $50-$100. A common problem while computer chip keys were becoming popular was that low-cost locksmiths didn't realize the keys had chips in them, so copies were made and the car owners went home and later couldn't figure out why their car wouldn't start, even though the key fit in the ignition slot and turned. ◀

▶ **EXAMPLE 3.6**   Code detector

You've probably seen doors in airports or hospitals that require a person to press a particular sequence of buttons (i.e., a code) to unlock the door. For example, there might be three buttons, colored red, green, and blue, and a fourth button for starting the code. Pressing the start button, then the following button sequence—red, blue, green, red—unlocks the door, while any other sequence does not unlock the door. Such a system may have the general architecture shown in Figure 3.44. An extra output from the buttons component, a, is 1 whenever *any* button is pressed.

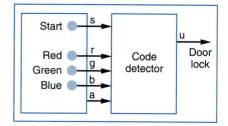

Figure 3.44 Code detector architecture.

We can describe the behavior of the *CodeDetector* block using an FSM captured as the state diagram shown in Figure 3.45.

For simplicity, assume that the buttons each have a special circuit that synchronizes the button with the clock signal, and creates a pulse exactly one clock cycle wide for each unique press of the button. This is necessary to ensure that the current state doesn't inadvertently change to another state if a button press lasts longer than a single clock cycle. (We'll design such a synchronization circuit in Example 3.9.)

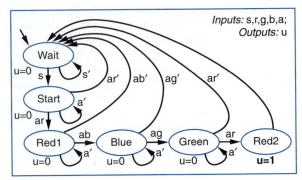

Figure 3.45 Code detector FSM.

- The behavior of the FSM is as follows:

- The FSM begins in the *Wait* state. As long as the start button is not pressed (s'), the FSM stays in *Wait*; when the start button is pressed (s), the FSM goes to the *Start* state.

- Being in the *Start* state means the FSM is now ready to detect the sequence red, blue, green, red. If no button is pressed (a'), the FSM stays in *Start*. If a button is pressed AND that button is the red button (ar), the FSM goes to state *Red1*. If a button is pressed AND that button is not the red button (ar'), the FSM returns to the *Wait* state—note that when in the *Wait* state, further presses of the colored buttons would be ignored, until the start button is pressed again.

- The FSM stays in state *Red1* as long as no button is pressed (a'). If a button is pressed and that button is blue (ab), the FSM goes to state *Blue*; if that button is not blue (ab'), the FSM returns to state *Wait*.

- Likewise, the FSM stays in state *Blue* as long as no button is pressed (a'), and goes to state *Green* on condition ag, and state *Wait* on condition ag'.

- Finally, the FSM stays in *Green* if no button is pressed, and goes to state *Red2* on condition ar, and to state *Wait* on condition ar'.

- If the FSM makes it to state *Red2*, that means that the user pressed the buttons in the correct sequence—thus, *Red2* sets *u=1*, thus unlocking the door. Note that all other states set *u=0*. The FSM then returns to state *Wait*.

Recall that every transition's condition is implicitly ANDed with a rising clock edge.   ◀

Checking FSM Behavior

Correctly defining the behavior of a system is hard. The earlier we find problems, the easier they are to fix. So after we create the FSM, we might take time to ask questions about how the system behaves under certain input situations and then verify that the FSM responds as we expect. Consider the code detector FSM in Figure 3.45. What happens if the user presses the start button and then presses all three colored

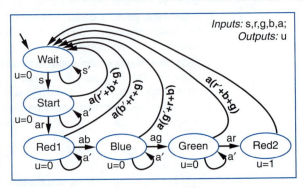

Figure 3.46 Improved code detector FSM.

buttons simultaneously, four times in a row? Well, the way we defined the FSM, the door would unlock! A solution to this undesired situation is to modify the conditions on the arcs that go back to the *Wait* state. Rather than the condition a r ', we could use the condition a (r ' + b + g). Thus, when the FSM expects the red button, then not pressing the red button, or pressing the blue or green button, causes a transition back to the *Wait* state—and so does not unlock the door. Likewise when we are expecting other specific buttons. An improved FSM is shown in Figure 3.46. Fixing the FSM was easy; trying to fix a circuit derived from the FSM would have been much harder.

It turns out that the FSM in Figure 3.46 still has a problem—a fairly serious one. We'll describe that problem in Example 3.13.

Standard Controller Architecture for Implementing an FSM as a Sequential Circuit

Now that we've seen how to describe sequential behavior using an FSM, we need a structured method to convert the FSM to a sequential circuit. The method is actually very straightforward when we use a standard implementation architecture for the circuit, consisting of a state register and combinational logic, together known as a controller. There are many other ways to implement an FSM, but sticking to the standard architecture results in a straightforward design method. The standard architecture may not yield the minimum number of transistors, but as we've mentioned many times, that's not a drawback these days.

A standard controller architecture for an FSM consists of a state register and combinational logic. The standard architecture for the laser timer FSM of Figure 3.39 is shown in Figure 3.47. The architecture consists of a state register and combinational logic.

The state register is a 2-bit register that holds a binary number representing the present state (in this case, the register is 2 bits wide to represent each of the 4 possible states).

The combinational logic's inputs are the inputs of the FSM (in this case, b), as well as the state register's outputs (s1 and s0). The combinational logic's outputs are the outputs of the FSM (x), as well as the next state bits to be loaded into the state register (n1 and n0). The details of the combinational logic determine the behavior of the circuit. The process for creating those details will be covered in the next section.

A more general view of the standard controller architecture appears in Figure 3.48. That figure assumes a state register that is *m* bits wide.

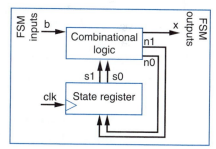

Figure 3.47 Standard controller architecture for the laser timer.

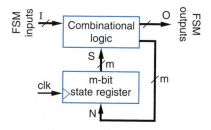

Figure 3.48 Standard controller architecture—general view.

▶ 3.4 CONTROLLER DESIGN

Five-Step Controller Design Process

We can design a controller using a five-step process, summarized in Table 3.2. We'll illustrate this process with some examples.

TABLE 3.2 Controller design process.

	Step	Description
Step 1	*Capture the FSM*	Create an FSM that describes the desired behavior of the controller.
Step 2	*Create the architecture*	Create the standard architecture by using a state register of appropriate width, and combinational logic with inputs being the state register bits and the FSM inputs and outputs being the next state bits and the FSM outputs.
Step 3	*Encode the states*	Assign a unique binary number to each state. Each binary number representing a state is known as an **encoding**. Any encoding will do as long as each state has a unique encoding.
Step 4	*Create the state table*	Create a truth table for the combinational logic such that the logic will generate the correct FSM outputs and next state signals. Ordering the inputs with state bits first makes this truth table describe the state behavior, so the table is a state table.
Step 5	*Implement the combinational logic*	Implement the combinational logic using any method.

▶ **EXAMPLE 3.7**   Three-cycles-high laser timer controller (continued)

We can implement the laser timer (see Example 3.4) as a sequential circuit using the five-step process.

Step 1:   **Capture the FSM.** The FSM was created earlier (see Figure 3.39).

Step 2:   **Create the architecture.**   The standard controller architecture for the laser timer FSM was shown in Figure 3.47. The state register has two bits to represent each of the four states. The combinational logic has external input b and inputs s1 and s0 coming from the state register, and has external output x and outputs n1 and n0 going to the state register.

Step 3:   **Encode the states.**   We can encode the states as follows—*Off*: 00, *On1*: 01, *On2*: 10, *On3*: 11. Remember, any nonredundant encoding is fine. The state diagram with encoded states is shown in Figure 3.49.

Step 4:   **Create the state table.**   Given the implementation architecture and the binary encoding of each state, we can create the state table for the combinational logic, as shown in Table 3.3. Listing the inputs from the state register first in the input columns allows

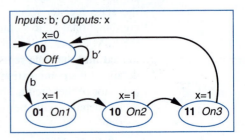

Figure 3.49 Laser timer state diagram with encoded states.

us to easily see which rows correspond to which states. We fill all combinations of inputs on the left, as usual for a truth table. For each row, we look at the state diagram in Figure 3.49 to determine the appropriate outputs. For the two rows starting with $s1s0 = 00$ (state *Off*), x should be 0. If $b = 0$, the controller should stay in state *Off*, so $n1n0$ should be 00. If $b = 1$, the controller should go to state *On1*, so $n1n0$ should be 01.

Likewise, for the two rows starting with $s1s0 = 01$ (state *On1*), x should be 1 and the next state should be *On2* (regardless of the value of b), so $n1n0$ should be 10. We complete the last four rows similarly.

Be careful to note the difference between the FSM inputs and outputs of Figure 3.49, and the combinational logic inputs and outputs of Figure 3.50—the latter includes the bits from and to the state register.

Step 5: **Implement the combinational logic.** We can finish the design by using the combinational logic design process from Chapter 2. From the truth table, we obtain the following equations for the three combinational logic outputs:

TABLE 3.3 State table for laser timer controller.

	Inputs			Outputs		
	s1	s0	b	x	n1	n0
Off	0	0	0	0	0	0
	0	0	1	0	0	1
On1	0	1	0	1	1	0
	0	1	1	1	1	0
On2	1	0	0	1	1	1
	1	0	1	1	1	1
On3	1	1	0	1	0	0
	1	1	1	1	0	0

x = $s1$ + $s0$ (note from the table that $x = 1$ if $s1 = 1$ or $s0 = 1$)

$n1$ = $s1's0b'$ + $s1's0b$ + $s1s0'b'$ + $s1s0'b$
$n1$ = $s1's0$ + $s1s0'$

$n0$ = $s1's0'b$ + $s1s0'b'$ + $s1s0'b$
$n0$ = $s1's0'b$ + $s1s0'$

We then obtain the sequential circuit in Figure 3.50, implementing the FSM.   ◀

Many textbooks will organize the state table in different ways than that in Table 3.3. However, we intentionally organize the table so that it serves both as a state table and a truth table that can be used to design the combinational logic of the controller.

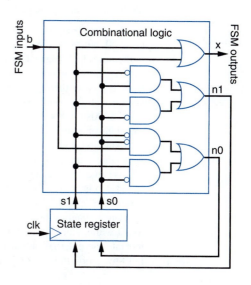

Figure 3.50 Final implementation of the three-cycles-high laser timer controller.

▶ **EXAMPLE 3.8**   Understanding the laser timer controller's behavior

To better understand how a controller implements an FSM, let's trace through the behavior of the three-cycles-high laser timer controller. Assume we are initially in state 00 ($s1s0=00$), b is 0, and the clock is currently low. As shown in Figure 3.51 (left side), based on the combinational logic, x will be 0 (the desired output in state 00), n1 will be 0, and n0 will be 0, meaning the value 00 will be waiting at the state register's inputs. Thus, on the *next* clock edge, 00 will be loaded into the state register, meaning we stay in state 00—which is correct.

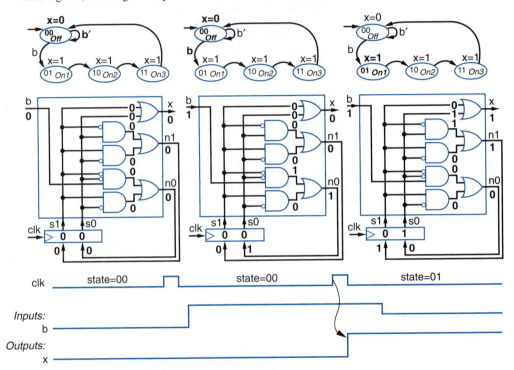

Figure 3.51 Tracing the behavior of the three-cycles-high laser timer controller.

Now suppose b becomes 1. As shown in Figure 3.51 (middle), x will still be 0, as desired. n1 will be 0, but n0 will be 1, meaning the value 01 will be waiting at the state register's inputs. Thus, on the *next* clock edge, 01 will be loaded into the state register, as desired.

As shown in Figure 3.51 (right side), soon after 01 is loaded into the state register, x will become 1 (after the register is loaded, there's a slight delay as the new values for $s1$ and $s0$ propagate through the combinational logic gates). That output is correct—we should output x=1 when in state 01. Also, n1 will become 1 and n0 will equal 0, meaning the value 10 will be waiting at the state register inputs. Thus, on the next clock edge, 10 will be loaded into the state register, as desired.

After 10 is loaded into the state register, x will stay 1, and n1n0 will become 11. When another clock edge comes, 11 will be loaded into the register, x will stay 1, and n1n0 will become 00.

When another clock edge comes, 00 will be loaded into the register. Soon after, x will become 0, and if b is 0, n1n0 will stay 00; if b is 1, n1n0 will become 01. Notice we're back where we started.

Understanding how a state register and combinational logic implement a state machine can take a while, since in a particular state (indicated by the value presently in the state register), we generate the external output for that state, and we generate the signals for the *next* state—but we don't transition to that next state (i.e., we don't load the state register) until the next clock edge. ◀

▷ **EXAMPLE 3.9** Button press synchronizer

We want to build a circuit that synchronizes a button press to a clock signal, such that when a user presses the button, the result is a signal that is high for exactly one clock cycle. Such a synchronized signal is useful to prevent a single button press that lasts multiple cycles from being interpreted as multiple button presses. Figure 3.52 uses a timing diagram to illustrate the desired circuit behavior.

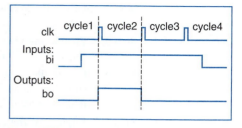

Figure 3.52 Desired timing diagram of the button press synchronizer.

The circuit's input will be a signal bi, and the output a signal bo. When bi becomes 1, representing the button being pressed, we want to set bo to 1 for exactly one cycle. We then wait for bi to return to 0 again, and then wait for bi to become 1 again, which would represent the next pressing of the button.

Step 1: **Capture the FSM.** Figure 3.53(a) shows an FSM describing the circuit's behavior. The FSM waits in state A, outputting bo=0, until bi is 1. The FSM then transitions to state B, outputting bo=1. The FSM will then transition to either state A or C, which both set bo=0 again, so that bo was 1 for just one cycle, as desired. The FSM goes from B to A if bi returned to 0. If bi is still 1, the FSM goes to state C, where the FSM waits for bi to return 0, causing a transition back to state A.

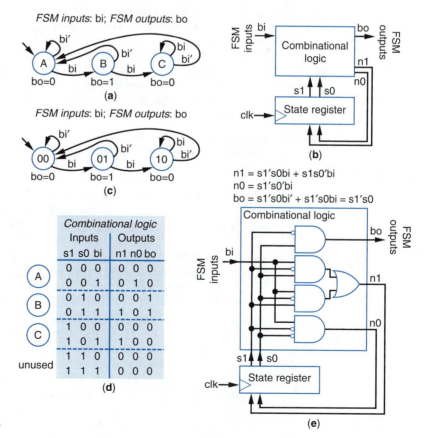

Figure 3.53: Button press synchronizer design steps: (a) initial FSM, (b) architecture, (c) FSM with encoded states, (d) state table, (e) final circuit with implemented combinational logic.

Step 2: **Create the architecture.** Since the FSM has three states, the architecture has a two-bit state register, as shown in Figure 3.53(b).

Step 3: **Encode the states.** We can straightforwardly encode the three states as 00, 01, and 10, as shown in Figure 3.53(c).

Step 4: **Create the state table.** We convert the FSM with encoded states to a state table as shown in Figure 3.53(d). For the unused state 11, we have chosen to output bo=0 and return to state 00.

Step 5: **Implement the combinational logic.** We derive the equations for each combinational logic output, as shown in Figure 3.53(e), and then create the final circuit as shown. ◀

▶ **EXAMPLE 3.10** Sequence generator

We want to design a circuit with four outputs: w, x, y, and z. The circuit should generate the following sequence of output patterns: 0001, 0011, 1100, and 1000. After 1000, the circuit should repeat the sequence, starting at 0001 again. We want the circuit to generate the next pattern only on a rising clock edge.

Sequence generators are common in a wide range of systems. For example, we might want to blink a set of four lights in a particular pattern, such as in a festive lights display. We might instead want to rotate an electric motor a fixed number of degrees on each clock cycle by powering magnets around the motor in a specific sequence to attract the magnetized motor to the next position in the rotation—such a motor is known as a *stepper motor*, since the motor rotates in steps.

We can design the sequence generator controller using our five-step process.

Step 1: **Capture the FSM.** We capture the system's behavior as the FSM shown in Figure 3.54. The FSM has four states, which we've labeled A, B, C, and D (though any other four unique names would do just fine).

Step 2: **Create the architecture.** The standard controller architecture for the sequence generator will have a 2-bit state register to represent the four possible states, no inputs to the logic, and outputs w, x, y, z from the logic, along with outputs n1 and n0, as shown in Figure 3.55.

Step 3: **Encode the states.** We can encode the states as follows—A: 00, B: 01, C: 10, D: 11. Any other encoding with a unique code for each state would also do fine.

Step 4: **Create the state table.** The state table for the FSM with encoded states is shown in Table 3.4.

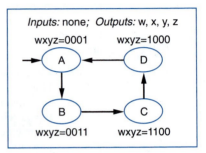

Figure 3.54 Sequence generator FSM.

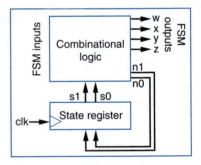

Figure 3.55 Sequence generator controller architecture.

TABLE 3.4 State table for sequence generator controller.

	Inputs		Outputs					
	s1	s0	w	x	y	z	n1	n0
A	0	0	0	0	0	1	0	1
B	0	1	0	0	1	1	1	0
C	1	0	1	1	0	0	1	1
D	1	1	1	0	0	0	0	0

Step 5: **Implement the combinational logic.** We derive the equations for each output of the combinational logic from the table. After some algebraic simplification, the equations are as follows:

$$w = s1$$
$$x = s1s0'$$
$$y = s1's0$$
$$z = s1'$$
$$n1 = s1 \text{ xor } s0$$
$$n0 = s0'$$

The final circuit is shown in Figure 3.56. ◄

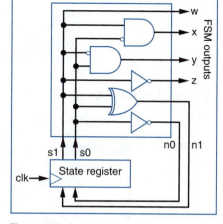

Figure 3.56 Sequence generator controller architecture.

► **EXAMPLE 3.11** Secure car key controller (continued)

Let's complete the design for the secure car key controller from Example 3.5. We already carried out the **Capture the FSM** step of the five-step process, with the FSM shown in Figure 3.41. The remaining steps are as follows.

Step 2: **Create the architecture.** Since the FSM has five states, we'll need a 3-bit state register. A 3-bit state register can represent eight states, so three states will be unused. The input to the logic is signal a, while the outputs are signal r and next state outputs n2, n1, and n0. The architecture is shown in Figure 3.57.

Step 3: **Encode the states.** Let's encode the states using a straightforward binary encoding of 000 through 100. The FSM with state encodings is shown in Figure 3.58.

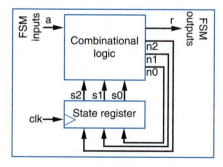

Figure 3.57 Secure car key controller architecture.

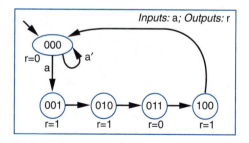

Figure 3.58 Secure car key FSM with encoded states.

Step 4: **Create the state table.** The FSM converted to a state table is shown in Table 3.5. For the unused states, we have chosen to set r = 0 and the next state to 000.

Step 5: **Implement the combinational logic.** We can design four circuits, one for each output, to implement the combinational logic. We leave this step as an exercise for the reader. ◀

More on Controller Design

Converting a circuit to an FSM

We showed in Section 2.6 that a circuit, truth table, and equation were all ways of representing the same combinational function. Similarly, a circuit, state table, and FSM are all ways of representing the same sequential function.

We have been converting an FSM to a circuit using a five-step process. We can also convert a circuit to an FSM by applying the five-step process of Table 3.2 in reverse. In general, converting a circuit to an equation or FSM is known as **reverse engineering** the behavior of the circuit.

TABLE 3.5 State table for secure car key controller.

	s2	s1	s0	a	r	n2	n1	n0
	Inputs				Outputs			
Wait	0	0	0	0	0	0	0	0
	0	0	0	1	0	0	0	1
K1	0	0	1	0	1	0	1	0
	0	0	1	1	1	0	1	0
K2	0	1	0	0	1	0	1	1
	0	1	0	1	1	0	1	1
K3	0	1	1	0	0	1	0	0
	0	1	1	1	0	1	0	0
K4	1	0	0	0	1	0	0	0
	1	0	0	1	1	0	0	0
Unused	1	0	1	0	0	0	0	0
	1	0	1	1	0	0	0	0
	1	1	0	0	0	0	0	0
	1	1	0	1	0	0	0	0
	1	1	1	0	0	0	0	0
	1	1	1	1	0	0	0	0

▶ **EXAMPLE 3.12** Converting a sequential circuit to an FSM

Given the sequential circuit in Figure 3.59, find an equivalent FSM.

We start from step 5 of the 5-step process described in Table 3.2. The combinational circuit has already been implemented, and we can proceed to step 4, where we create a state table.

The combinational logic in the controller architecture has 3 inputs: 2 inputs, s0 and s1, represent the contents of the state register, and 1 input, x, is an external input. Thus our state table will have 8 rows since there are $2^3 = 8$ possible combinations of inputs.

After we set up the state table and enumerate all possible combinations of inputs (e.g., s1s0x = 000, ..., s1s0x = 111), we use the techniques described in Section 2.6 to fill in the values of the outputs. For example, consider the output y. From the combinational circuit, we see that y = s1'. Knowing this,

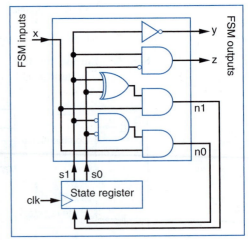

Figure 3.59 A sequential circuit with unknown behavior.

we add a 1 in the y column of the state table in every row where s1 = 0, and we add a 0 in the remaining spaces in the y column. Now consider n0, which we see has the Boolean equation n0 = s1's0'x. Accordingly, we set n0 to 1 when s1 = 0 and s0 = 0 and x = 1. We fill in the columns for z and n1 using a similar analysis and move on to the next step.

In step 3, we must encode the states. Naturally, the states have already been encoded, but we can still name each state. We arbitrarily choose the labels A, B, C, and D, seen in Table 3.6.

Step 2 calls for the creation of the standard controller architecture. This step requires no work since the controller architecture was already defined.

Finally, in step 1, we capture the FSM. Initially, we can set up an FSM diagram with the four states we've labeled in step 3, shown in Figure 3.60(a). Next, we list the values of the FSM outputs y and z next to each state. For example, in state A ($s1s0 = 00$), the outputs y and z are 1 and 0, respectively, so we list "$yz = 10$" with state A in the FSM.

TABLE 3.6 State table for sequential circuit.

	Inputs			Outputs			
	s1	s0	x	n1	n0	y	z
A	0	0	0	0	0	1	0
	0	0	1	0	1	1	0
B	0	1	0	0	0	1	0
	0	1	1	1	0	1	0
C	1	0	0	0	0	0	1
	1	0	1	1	0	0	1
D	1	1	0	0	0	0	0
	1	1	1	0	0	0	0

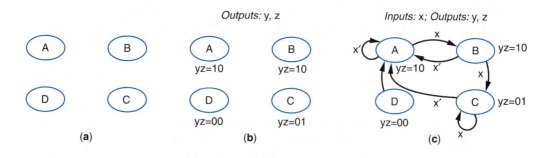

Figure 3.60 Converting a state table to an FSM diagram: (a) initial FSM, (b) FSM with outputs specified, and (c) FSM with outputs and transitions specified.

After listing the outputs for states B, C, and D, shown in Figure 3.60(b), we turn to the state transitions specified in the state table by n1 and n0. Consider the first row of the state table, which says that $n1n0 = 00$ when $s1s0x = 000$. In other words, when in state A ($s1s0 = 00$), the next state is state A ($n1n0 = 00$) if x is 0. We can represent this in the FSM diagram by drawing an arrow from state A back to state A and labeling the new transition "x '." Now consider the second row of the state table, which indicates that from state A, we transition to state B when $x = 1$. We add a transition arrow from state A to B and label it "x." After labeling all the transitions, we are left with the FSM in Figure 3.60(c).

You may notice that state D cannot be reached from any other state and transitions to state A on any input. We can reasonably infer that the original FSM had only three states and state D is an extra, unused state. For completeness, it is preferable to leave state D in the final diagram, however.   ◄

Given any synchronous circuit consisting of logic gates and flip-flops, we can always redraw the circuit as consisting of a state register and logic—our standard controller architecture—just by grouping all the flip-flops together. Thus, the approach described above works for any synchronous circuit, not just a circuit already drawn in the form of our standard controller architecture.

Common Pitfalls

Mistakes are commonly made when capturing an FSM, relating to properties regarding the transitions leaving a state. In short, one and *only* one transition condition should ever evaluate to true during any rising clock edge. The properties are:

ab=11 –
next state?

1. ***Only one*** condition should be true—For a given state, for any rising clock edge, no more than one transition condition should be true. For example, consider an FSM with inputs a and b, and a state *State1* with two outgoing transitions, one labeled "a", and the other labeled "b." What happens when a = 1 and b = 1—which transition should the FSM take? The FSM designer must ensure that the conditions are exclusive—only one could possibly ever be true at one time. In the example, the designer might label the transitions "a" and "a'b" to solve the problem. Actually, a particular type of FSM, known as a ***nondeterministic FSM***, does allow more than one condition to be true and chooses among them in some arbitrary way—but when designing circuits, we usually want deterministic behavior, so we don't consider nondeterministic FSMs further.

what if
ab=00?

2. ***One*** condition should be true—For a given state, for any rising clock edge, *one* of the transitions from that state must be taken. In other words, every input combination should be accounted for in every state. Designers sometimes forget to ensure this. For example, consider an FSM with inputs a and b, and a state *State1* with two outgoing transitions, one labeled "a", and the other labeled "a'b." What happens if the FSM is in *State1*, and a = 0 and b = 0? Neither of the two transitions from *State1* has a true condition. The FSM is not fully specified—we need to add a third transition, indicating what state to go to if a'b' is true. With that third condition, we have covered all possible values of a and b. A commonly forgotten transition is a transition pointing from a state back to itself.

We can verify the above two properties using Boolean algebra. For the first property of only one condition being true, we can check that the *AND of every pair of conditions on transitions of a state always results in 0*. For example, if a state has two transitions, one with condition a and the other with condition a'b, using transformations of Boolean algebra we obtain:

$$a \ * \ a'b$$
$$= \ (a \ * \ a') \ * \ b$$
$$= \ 0 \ * \ b$$
$$= \ 0$$

For the second situation of one condition being true, we can check that the *OR of all the conditions on transitions of a state always results in 1*. Considering the same example of a state that has two transitions, one with condition a and the other with condition a'b, using transformations of Boolean algebra we obtain:

$$a \ + \ a'b$$
$$= \ a*(1+b) \ + \ a'b$$
$$= \ a \ + \ ab \ + \ a'b$$
$$= \ a \ + \ (a+a')b$$
$$= \ a \ + \ b$$

Clearly, the OR of those two conditions is not 1, but rather a+b. Thus, if a and b were both 0, neither condition would be true, and therefore the next state would not be specified in the FSM. Above, we fixed this problem by adding another transition, a'b'. Checking yields:

$$
\begin{aligned}
&a + a'b + a'b' \\
&= a + a'(b+b') \\
&= a + a'*1 \\
&= a + a' \\
&= 1
\end{aligned}
$$

Analyzing the equations made from conditions of every state and proving they equal either 1 or 0 is a lot of work. Therefore, a good FSM capture tool will detect the above two situations and inform the designer of the situation.

► **EXAMPLE 3.13**   Verifying transition properties for the code detector FSM

Figure 3.46 shows an FSM for a code detector. We want to verify the "only one condition should be true" property for the transitions leaving state *Start*. There are three conditions: ar, a', and a(r'+b+g). We thus have three pairs of conditions, which we AND and prove each equal 0 as follows:

```
ar * a'              a' * a(r'+b+g)           ar * a(r'+b+g)
= (a*a')r            = (a'*a)*(r'+b+g)        = (a*a)*r*(r'+b+g)
= 0*r                = 0*(r'+b+g)             = a*r*(r'+b+g)
= 0                  = 0                      = arr'+arb+arg
                                              = 0 + arb+arg
                                              = arb + arg
                                              = ar(b+g)
```

It appears our FSM is not fully specified, as the AND of the third pair of conditions does not result in 0, which in turn means both conditions could be true at the same time—resulting in a non-deterministic FSM (if both conditions are true, what is the next state?). Recall from the code detector problem description that we want to transition from the *Start* state to the *Red1* state when a button is pressed (a=1) and that button is the red button, and no other colored button is pressed. The FSM in Figure 3.46 has the condition ar. Our mistake was underspecifying this condition; it should instead be arb'g'—in other words, a button has been pressed (a) and it is the red button (r) and the blue button has not been pressed (b') and the green button has not been pressed (g'). The transition from *Start1* back to the *Wait* state could then be written as a(rb'g')' (which is the same as in Figure 3.46 after applying DeMorgan's Law). After this change, we can again try to verify the "only one condition is true" property for all pairs of the three conditions arb'g', a', and a(rb'g')':

```
arb'g' * a'          a'*a(rb'g')'             arb'g' * a(rb'g')'
= aa'*rb'g'          = 0*(rb'g')'             = a*a*(rb'g')*(rb'g')'
= 0*rb'g'            = 0                       write rb'g' as Y for clarity...
= 0                                           = a*a*Y*Y'
                                              = a*a*0
                                              = 0
```

We would need to change the transition conditions of the other states similarly, and then check the pairs of conditions for those states' transitions too.

To verify the "one condition is true" property for state *Start*, we OR the three conditions and prove they equal 1:

```
arb'g' + a' + a(rb'g')'
= a' + arb'g' + a(rb'g')'  (write rb'g' as Y for clarity)
= a' + aY + aY'
= a' + a(Y+Y') = a' + a(1)
= a' + a
= 1
```

We would need to check the property for all other states too.   ◀

Simplifying FSM Notations: Unassigned Outputs

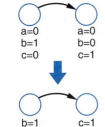

We already introduced the simplifying FSM notation of every transition being implicitly ANDed with a rising clock edge. Another commonly used simplification involves assigning outputs. If an FSM has many outputs, listing the assignment of every output in every state can become cumbersome, and make the relevant behavior of the FSM hard to discern. A common simplifying notation is as follows—if an output is not explicitly assigned in a state, the output is *implicitly* assigned a 0.

Simplifying Circuit Drawings: Implicit Clock Connections

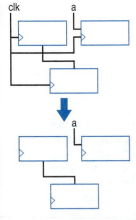

Many if not most sequential circuits have a single clock signal connected to all sequential components. We know a component is sequential because of the small triangle input drawn on the component's block symbol. Many circuit drawings therefore use a simplification wherein the clock signal is assumed to be connected to all sequential components. This simplification leads to less cluttered wiring in the drawing.

Mathematical Formalisms in Combinational and Sequential Circuit Design

We have described two mathematical formalisms, Boolean functions and FSMs, for designing combinational and sequential circuits, respectively. Note that we did not *have* to use those formalisms to design circuits. Recall that our first attempt at building a three-cycles-high laser timer in Figure 3.35 just had us connecting components together in the hopes of creating a correctly working circuit. However, using those formalisms provides for a structured and sound method of designing circuits. Those formalisms also provide the basis for powerful automated tools to assist us with design, such as a tool that would automatically check for the common pitfalls described earlier in this section, tools that automatically convert Boolean equations or FSMs into circuits, tools that verify that two circuits are equivalent, tools that simulate our systems, etc. And, we have scarcely touched on all the benefits of those mathematical formalisms relating to automating the various aspects of designing circuits, and verifying the circuits behave properly. The importance of using sound mathematical formalisms to guide design cannot be overstated.

▷ 3.5 MORE ON FLIP-FLOPS AND CONTROLLERS

Other Flip-Flop Types

Today, designers generally use registers to implement their bit storage needs, and those registers typically are built from D flip-flops. However, in the past, transistors were much more scarce than today. Thus, designers often utilized other types of flip-flops, having more functionality than D flip-flops, to reduce the logic gates required outside of the flip-flops, and hence to reduce the number of ICs necessary to implement a circuit. Those flip-flop types included SR, JK, and T flip-flops.

SR Flip-Flop

The SR flip-flop is similar to the SR latch described earlier, with additional logic to make the circuit triggered by the edge of a clock, rather than just the level of the clock.

JK Flip-Flop

The JK flip-flop is similar to an SR flip-flop, with J corresponding to S, and with K corresponding to R (I remember this by thinking of "K" standing for "Klear" or clear). The JK flip-flop's behavior differs from the SR flip-flop when both inputs are 1. Recall that an SR flip-flop's behavior is undefined when both inputs are 1. A JK flip-flop, in contrast, toggles when both inputs are set to 1 (at the next clock edge, of course). To toggle means to change to the opposite state, meaning if the present stored bit is 1, the next stored bit would be 0. Likewise, if the present stored bit is 0, the next stored bit would be 1.

T Flip-Flop

A T flip-flop acts like a JK flip-flop with the JK inputs tied together to form the T input. In other words, whenever T is 0, the flip-flop maintains its current state, but whenever T is 1, the flip-flop toggles (think of "T" for "Toggle").

Nonideal Flip-Flop Behavior

Generally, when we first learn about digital design, we assume ideal behavior for logic gates and flip-flops, just like when we first learn physics of motion, we assume there's no friction or wind resistance. There is, however, a nonideal behavior of flip-flops—metastability—that is such a common problem in real digital design practice, we feel obliged to discuss the issue briefly here. Digital designers in practice should study metastability and possible solutions quite thoroughly before doing serious designs.

Metastability comes from failing to meet flip-flop setup or hold times, which we now introduce.

Setup Times and Hold Times

Flip-flops are built from wires and logic gates, and wires and logic gates have delays. Thus, a real flip-flop imposes some restrictions on when the flip-flop's inputs can change relative to the clock edge, in order to ensure correct operation despite those delays. Two important restrictions are:

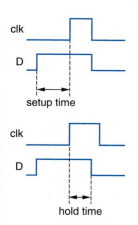

- *Setup time*: The inputs of a flip-flop (e.g., the D input) must be stable for a minimum amount of time, known as the setup time, *before* a clock edge arrives. This intuitively makes sense—the input values must have time to propagate through any internal logic and be waiting at the internal gates' inputs before the clock pulse arrives.

- *Hold time*: The inputs of a flip-flop must remain stable for a minimum amount of time, known as the hold time, *after* a clock edge arrives. This also makes intuitive sense—the clock signal must have time to propagate through the internal gates to create a stable feedback state.

A related restriction is on the minimum clock pulse width—the pulse must be wide enough to ensure that the correct values propagate through the internal logic and create a stable feedback state.

A flip-flop typically comes with a datasheet describing setup times, hold times, and minimum clock pulse widths.

Figure 3.61 illustrates an example of a setup time violation. D changed to 0 too close to the rising clock. The result is that R was not 1 long enough to create a stable feedback in the cross-coupled NOR gates with Q being 0. Instead, Q glitches to 0 briefly. That glitch feeds back to the top NOR gate, causing Q' to glitch to 1 briefly. That glitch feeds back to the bottom NOR gate, and so on. The oscillation would likely continue until a race condition caused the circuit to settle into a stable situation of Q = 0 or Q = 1—or, the circuit could enter a metastable state, which we now describe.

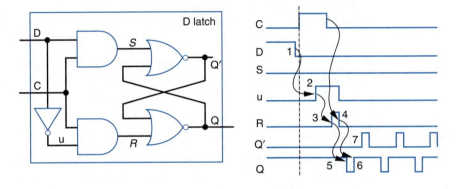

Figure 3.61 Setup time violation: D changed to 0 (1) too close to the rising clock. u changed to 1 after the inverter delay (2), and then R changed to 1 after the AND gate delay (3). But then the clock pulse was over, causing R to change back to 0 (4) before a stable feedback situation with Q=0 occurred in the cross-coupled NOR gates. R's change to 1 did cause Q to change to 0 after the NOR gate delay (5), but R's change back to 0 caused Q to change right back to 1 (6). The glitch of a 0 on Q fed back into the top NOR gate, causing Q' to glitch to 1 (7). That glitch of a 1 fed back to the bottom NOR gate, causing another glitch of a 0 on Q. That glitch runs around the cross-coupled NOR gate circuit (oscillation)—a race condition would eventually cause Q to settle to 1 or 0, or possibly enter a metastable state (to be discussed).

Metastability

If a designer fails to ensure that a circuit obeys the setup and hold times of a flip-flop, the result could be that the flip-flop enters a metastable state. A flip-flop in a *metastable state* is in a state other than a stable 0 or a stable 1. Metastable in general means that a system is only marginally stable—the system has other states that are far more stable. A flip-flop in a metastable state may have an output with a value that is not a 0 or a 1, instead outputting a voltage somewhere between that of a 0 and that of a 1. That voltage may also oscillate somewhat. That's a problem. Since a flip-flop's output is connected to other components like logic gates and other flip-flops, that strange voltage value may cause other components to output strange values, and soon the values throughout our entire circuit can be in bad shape.

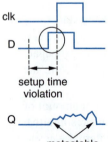

Why would we ever violate setup and hold times? After all, within a circuit we design, we can measure the longest possible path from any flip-flop output to any flip-flop input. As long as we make the clock period sufficiently longer than that longest path, we can ensure our circuit obeys setup times. Likewise, we can ensure that hold times are satisfied too.

The problem is that our circuit likely has to interface to external inputs, and we can't control when those inputs change, meaning those inputs may violate setup and hold times when connected to flip-flop inputs. For example, an input may be connected from a button being pressed by a user—the user can't be told to press the button so many nano-seconds before a clock edge and to be sure to hold the button so many nanoseconds after the clock edge so that setup and hold times are satisfied. So metastability is a problem primarily when a flip-flop has inputs that are not synchronized with the circuit's clock—such inputs are said to be *asynchronous*.

Designers usually try to synchronize a circuit's asynchronous input to the circuit's clock before propagating that input to components in the circuit. A common way to synchronize an asynchronous input is to first *feed the asynchronous input into a single D flip-flop*, and then use the output of that flip-flop wherever the input is needed, as shown for the asynchronous input a i in Figure 3.62. Using a single flip-flop as shown also eliminates a second problem of different values of the same signal appearing at the various internal flip-flops at a clock edge, due to different path delays.

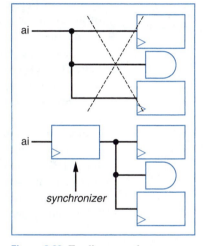

Figure 3.62 Feeding asynchronous external inputs into a single flip-flop can reduce metastability problems.

"Hold on now!" you might say. Doesn't that synchronizing flip-flop experience the setup and hold time problem, and hence the same metasta-bility issue? Yes, that's true. But at least the asynchronous input directly affects only *one* flip-flop, rather than perhaps several or dozens of flip-flops and other components. And that synchronizer flip-flop is specifically introduced for synchronization purposes and has no other purpose, whereas other flip-flops are being used to store bits for other purposes. We can therefore choose a flip-flop for the synchronizer that minimizes the metastability problem—we can choose an extremely fast flip-flop, and/or one with very small setup and hold times, and/or one with special circuitry to minimize metastability. That flip-flop may be bigger than normal or consume more power than normal, but there's only one such flip-flop per asyn-chronous input, so those issues aren't a problem. Bear in mind that no matter what we do, though, the synchronizer flip-flop could still become metastable, but at least we can mini-mize the odds of a metastable state happening by choosing a good flip-flop.

Another thing to consider is that a flip-flop will typically not stay metastable for very long. Eventually, the flip-flop will "topple" over to a stable 0 or a stable 1, like how a coin tossed onto the ground may spin for a while (a metastable state) but will eventually topple over to a stable head or tail. What many designers therefore do is introduce two or more flip-flops in series for synchronization purposes, as shown in Figure 3.63. So even if the first flip-flop becomes metastable, that flip-flop will likely reach a stable state before the next clock cycle, and thus the second flip-flop is even less likely to go metastable. Thus the odds of a metastable signal actually making it to our circuit's normal flip-flops are very low. This approach has the obvious drawback of delaying changes on the input signal by several cycles—in Figure 3.63, the rest of the circuit won't see a change on the input ai for three cycles.

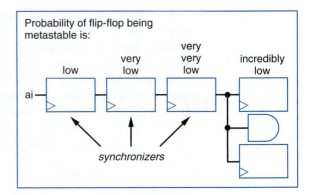

Figure 3.63 Synchronizer flip-flops reduce probability of metastability in our regular flip-flops.

As clock periods become shorter and shorter, the odds of the first flip-flop stabilizing before the next clock cycle decreases, so metastability is becoming a more challenging issue as clock periods shrink. Many advanced methods have been proposed to deal with the issue.

Nevertheless, no matter how hard we try, metastability will always be a possibility, meaning our circuit *may fail*. We can minimize the likelihood of failure, but we can't completely eliminate failures due to metastability. Designers often rate their designs using a measure called *mean time between failures*, or *MTBF*. Designers typically aim for MTBFs of many years. Many students find this concept—that we can't design failproof circuits—somewhat disconcerting. Yet, that concept is the real situation in design.

Designers of serious high-speed digital circuits should study the problem of metastability, and modern solutions to the problem, thoroughly.

Flip-Flop Reset and Set Inputs

Some D flip-flops (as well as other flip-flop types) come with extra inputs that can force the flip-flop to 0 or 1, independently of the D input. One such input is a *clear*, or *reset*, input, which forces the flip-flop to 0. Another such input is a *set* input, which forces the flip-flop to 1. Reset and set inputs are very useful for initializing flip-flops to an initial value (e.g., initializing all flip-flops to 0s) when powering up or reset-

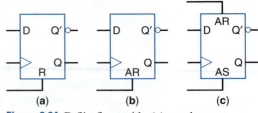

Figure 3.64 D flip-flops with: (a) synchronous reset R, (b) asynchronous reset AR, and (c) asynchronous reset and set.

ting a system. These reset and set inputs should not be confused with the R and S inputs of an RS latch or flip-flop—the reset and set inputs are special control inputs to any type of flip-flop (D, RS, T, JK) that take priority over the normal data inputs of a flip-flop.

The reset and set inputs of a flip-flop may be either synchronous or asynchronous. A *synchronous reset* input forces the flip-flop to 0, regardless of the value on the D input, during a rising clock edge. For the flip-flop in Figure 3.64(a), setting R to 1 forces the flip-flop to 0 on the next clock edge. Likewise, a **synchronous set** input forces the flip-flop to 1 on a rising clock edge. The reset and set inputs thus have priority over the D input. If a flip-flop has both a synchronous reset and a synchronous set input, the flip-flop datasheet must inform the flip-flop user which has priority if both inputs are set to 1.

An **asynchronous reset** forces the flip-flop to 0 independently of the clock signal—the clock does not need to be rising, or even be 1, for the asynchronous reset to occur—hence the term "asynchronous." Likewise, an **asynchronous set**, also known as **preset**, can be used to asynchronously force the flip-flop to 1.

We omit discussion of how synchronous/asynchronous reset/set inputs would be internally designed in a flip-flop.

Sample behavior of a flip-flop's asynchronous reset input is shown in Figure 3.65. We assume the flip-flop initially stores 1. Setting AR to 1 forces the flip-flop to 0, independent of any clock edge. When the next clock edge appears, AR is still 1, so the flip-flop stays 0 even though the input D is 1. When AR returns to 0, the flip-flop follows the D input on successive clock edges, as shown.

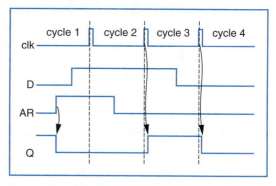

Figure 3.65 Asynchronous reset forces the flip-flop to 0, independent of c̄lk or D.

Initial State of a Controller

Particularly observant readers may have come up with a question when we implemented FSMs as controllers in this section—what happened to the indication of the initial state of an FSM when we designed the controller implementing the FSM? The initial state of an FSM is the state that the FSM starts in when the FSM is first activated—or in controller terms, when the controller is first powered on. For example, the laser timer controller FSM in Figure 3.39 has an initial state of *Off*. When we converted our graphical FSMs to state tables in this section, we ignored the initial state information. Thus, all of our controller circuits start in some random state based on whatever values happen to appear in the state register when we power up the circuit. Not knowing the initial state of a circuit could pose a problem—for example, we don't want our laser timer controller to start in a state that immediately turns on the laser.

One solution is to add an additional input, reset, to every controller. Setting reset to 1 should cause a load of the initial state into the state register. This initial state should be forced into the state register. The reset and set inputs of a flip-flop come in very handy in this situation. We can simply connect the controller's reset input to the reset and set inputs of the state register's flip-flops in a way that sets the flip-flops to the initial state when reset is 1. For example, if the initial state of a 2-bit state register should be 01, then we could connect the controller's reset input to reset and set inputs of the two flip-flops, as shown in Figure 3.66.

Of course, for this reset functionality to work as desired, the designer must ensure that the controller's reset input is 1 when the system is first powered up. Ensuring the reset input is 1 during power up can be handled using an appropriate electronic circuit connected to the on/off switch, the description of which is beyond our scope.

Note that, if the synchronous reset or set inputs of a flip-flop are used, then the earlier-discussed setup and hold times, and associated metastability issues, apply to those reset and set inputs.

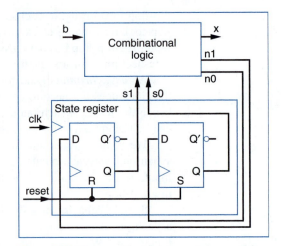

Figure 3.66 Three-cycles-high laser timer controller with a reset input that loads the state register with the initial state 01.

Nonideal Controller Behavior: Output Glitches

Glitching is the presence of temporary values on a wire, typically caused by different delays of different logic paths leading to that wire. We saw an example of glitching in Figure 3.13. Glitching will also often occur when a controller changes states, due to different path lengths from each of the controller's state register flip-flops to the controller's outputs. Consider the three-cycles-high laser timer design in Figure 3.50. The laser should be off (output x=0) in state s1s0=00 and on (x=1) in states s1s0=01, s1s0=10, and s1s0=11. However, the delay from s1 to x's OR gate in the figure could be longer than the delay from s0 to that OR gate. The result could be that when the state register changes state from s1s0=01 to s1s0=10, the OR gate's inputs could momentarily see a 00. The OR gate would thus output 0 momentarily (a glitch). In the laser timer example, that glitch could momentarily shut off the laser—an undesired situation. Even worse would be glitches that momentarily turn *on* a laser.

Real designers must determine whether such glitching would really pose a problem in their particular system, and if so, those designers should take action to avoid such glitching. One solution in the laser timer example might be to insert a D flip-flop after x's OR gate in Figure 3.50. This would shift the x output later by 1 clock cycle (still resulting in three cycles high, however), but should eliminate glitches seen at the x output, as only the stable value appearing at the output would be loaded into the flip-flop on a rising clock edge.

Active-Low Inputs (Negative Logic)

Until now, we have assumed active-high inputs on flip-flops and other components. An *active-high input* is a control input whose associated operation is activated by setting the input to 1. For example, if an input can reset a flip-flop, we assumed that input reset when the input's value was 1. However, a

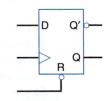

Figure 3.67 D flip-flop with active low synchronous reset input.

component can instead have an active-low input. An ***active-low input*** (also known as a ***negative logic*** input) is a control input whose operation is activated by setting the input to 0. Figure 3.67 depicts a D flip-flop with an active-low synchronous reset input—the circle at the R input indicates that the R input is active-low. Thus, to reset the flip-flop to 0, we would set R to 0, whereas for normal D flip-flop operation, we would set R to 1.

Active-low inputs can occur on any component with a control input, not just on flip-flops. For example, the enable control input on a decoder could be active-low—setting that enable to 0 (meaning the decoder is enabled) would cause normal decoder operation, while setting the input to 1 (meaning the decoder is disabled) would result in all outputs being 0.

When discussing the behavior of a component, designers will often use the term ***assert*** to mean setting a control input to the value that activates the associated operation. Thus, we might say that one must "assert" the R input of the D flip-flop in Figure 3.67 in order to reset the flip-flop to 0. Using the term *assert* avoids possible confusion that could occur when some control inputs are active-high and others are active-low.

Active-low inputs typically exist when the internal design of the component requires fewer gates when implemented with an active-low input than with an active-high input.

▶ 3.6 SEQUENTIAL LOGIC OPTIMIZATIONS AND TRADEOFFS (SEE SECTION 6.3)

The earlier sections described how to design basic sequential logic. This section, which physically appears in this book as Section 6.3, describes how to create *better* sequential logic (smaller, faster, etc.) using optimizations and tradeoffs. One use of this book describes sequential logic design optimizations and tradeoffs immediately after introducing basic sequential logic design, meaning now. An alternative use describes sequential logic design optimizations and tradeoffs later, after completing the introduction of basic datapath components and RTL design (Chapters 4 and 5).

▶ 3.7 SEQUENTIAL LOGIC DESCRIPTION USING HARDWARE DESCRIPTION LANGUAGES (SEE SECTION 9.3)

This section, which physically appears in this book as Section 9.3, introduces the use of HDLs for describing sequential logic. One use of this book introduces such use of HDLs immediately after introducing basic sequential logic design, meaning now. An alternative use introduces such HDL use later.

▶ 3.8 PRODUCT PROFILE—PACEMAKER

A pacemaker is an electronic device that provides electrical stimulation to a heart to help regulate a heart's beating, steadying a heart whose body's natural "intrinsic" pacemaker is not working properly, perhaps due to disease. Implantable pacemakers, which are surgically placed under the skin as shown in Figure 3.68, are worn by over 1/2 million Americans. They are powered by a battery that lasts ten years or more. Pacemakers have improved the quality of life as well as lengthened the lives of many millions of people.

A heart has two atria (left and right) and two ventricles (left and right). The ventricles push the blood out to the arteries, while the atria receive the blood from the veins. A very simple pacemaker has one sensor to detect a natural contraction in the heart's right ventricle, and one output wire to deliver electrical stimulation to that right ventricle if the natural contraction doesn't occur within a specified time period—typically just under one second. Such electrical stimulation causes a contraction, not only in the right ventricle, but also the left ventricle.

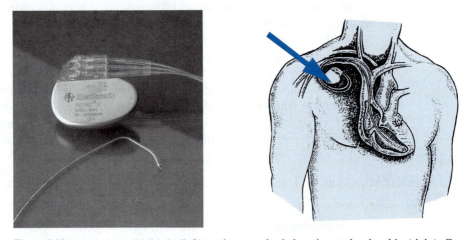

Figure 3.68 Pacemaker with leads (left), and pacemaker's location under the skin (right). Courtesy of Medtronic, Inc.

We can describe the behavior of a simple pacemaker's controller using the FSM in Figure 3.69. The left side of the figure shows the pacemaker consisting of a controller and a timer. The timer has an input t, which resets the timer when $t=1$. Upon being reset, the timer begins counting down from 0.8 seconds. If the timer counts down to 0, the timer sets its output z to 1. The timer could be reset before reaching 0, in which case the timer does not set z to 1, and instead the timer starts counting down from 0.8 seconds again. The controller has an input s, which is 1 when a contraction is sensed in the right ventricle. The controller has an output p, which the controller sets to 1 when the controller wants to cause a paced contraction.

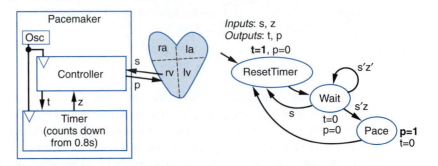

Figure 3.69 A basic pacemaker's controller FSM.

The right side of the figure shows the controller's behavior as an FSM. Initially, the controller resets the timer in state *ResetTimer* by setting $t = 1$. Normally, the controller waits in state *Wait*, and stays in that state as long as a contraction is not detected (s') and the timer does not reach 0 (z'). If the controller detects a natural contraction (s), then the controller again resets the timer and returns to waiting again. On the other hand, if the controller sees that the timer has reached 0 ($z = 1$), then the controller goes to state *Pace*, which paces the heart by setting $p=1$, after which the controller returns to waiting again. Thus, as long as the heart contracts naturally, the pacemaker applies no stimulation to the heart. But if the heart doesn't contract naturally within 0.8 seconds of the last contraction (natural or paced), the pacemaker forces a contraction.

The atria receive blood from the veins, and contract to push the blood into the ventricles. The atrial contractions occur just before the ventricular contractions. Therefore, many pacemakers, known as "atrioventricular" pacemakers, sense and pace not just the ventricular contractions, but also the atrial contractions. Such pacemakers thus have two sensors, and two output wires for electrical stimulation, and may provide better cardiac output, with the desirable result being higher blood pressure (Figure 3.70).

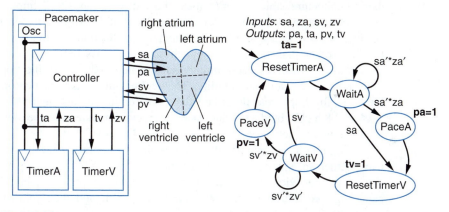

Figure 3.70 An atrioventricular pacemaker's controller FSM (using the convention that FSM outputs not explicitly set in a state are implicitly set to 0).

The pacemaker has two timers, one for the right atrium (*TimerA*) and one for the right ventricle (*TimerV*). The controller initially resets *TimerA* in state *ResetTimerA*, and then waits for a natural atrial contraction, or for the timer to reach 0. If the controller detects a natural atrial contraction (sa), then the controller skips pacing of the atrium. On the other hand, if *TimerA* reaches 0 first, then the controller goes to state *PaceA*, which causes a contraction in the atrium by setting $pa=1$. After an atrial contraction (either natural or paced), the controller resets *TimerV* in state *ResetTimerV*, and then waits for a natural ventricular contraction, or for the timer to reach 0. If a natural ventricular contraction occurs, the controller skips pacing of the ventricle. On the other hand, if *TimerV* reaches 0 first, then the controller goes to state *PaceV*, which causes a contraction in the ventricle by setting $pv=1$. The controller then returns to the atrial states.

Most modern pacemakers can have the timer parameters programmed wirelessly through radio signals so that doctors can try different treatments without having to surgically remove, program, and reimplant the pacemaker.

This example demonstrates the usefulness of FSMs in describing a controller's behavior. Real pacemakers have controllers with tens or even hundreds of states to deal with various details that we left out of the example for simplicity.

With the advent of very low-power microprocessors, a trend in pacemaker design is that of implementing the FSM on a microprocessor rather than with a custom sequential circuit. Microprocessor implementation yields the advantage of easy reprogramming of the FSM, expanding the range of treatments that a doctor can experiment with.

▶ 3.9 CHAPTER SUMMARY

Section 3.1 introduced the concept of sequential circuits, namely circuits that store bits, meaning the circuits have memory, known as state. Section 3.2 developed a series of increasingly robust bit storage blocks, including the SR latch, D latch, D flip-flop, and finally a register, which can store multiple bits. The section also introduced the concept of a clock, which synchronizes the loads of registers. Section 3.3 introduced finite-state machines (FSMs) for capturing the desired behavior of a sequential circuit, and a standard architecture able to implement FSMs, with an FSM implemented using the architecture known as a controller. Section 3.4 then described a five-step process for converting an FSM to a controller implementation. Section 3.5 highlighted some types of flip-flops other than the D flip-flop, those other types being popular in the past. That section also described several timing issues related to the use of flip-flops, including setup time, hold time, and metastability. The section introduced asynchronous clear and set inputs to flip-flops, and described their use for initializing an FSM to its initial state. Section 3.8 highlighted a cardiac pacemaker and illustrated the use of an FSM to describe the pacemaker's behavior.

Designing a combinational circuit begins by capturing the desired circuit behavior using either an equation or a truth table, and then following a several step process to convert the behavior to a combinational circuit. Designing a sequential circuit begins by capturing the desired circuit behavior as an FSM, and then following a several step process to convert the behavior to a circuit consisting of a register and a combinational circuit, known as a controller. Conceptually, then, with the knowledge in Chapters 2 and 3, we can build any digital circuit. However, many digital circuits deal with input data many bits wide, such as five 32-bit inputs. Imagine how complex our equations, truth tables, or FSMs would be if they involved 5*32 = 160 inputs. Fortunately, components have been developed specifically to deal with data inputs and thus simplify the design process—components that will be described in the next chapter.

▶ 3.10 EXERCISES

Any problem noted with an asterisk (*) represents an especially challenging problem.

SECTION 3.2: STORING ONE BIT—FLIP-FLOPS

3.1 Compute the clock period for the following clock frequencies.
   (a) 50 kHz (early computers)
   (b) 300 MHz (Sony Playstation 2 processor)
   (c) 3.4 GHz (Intel Pentium 4 processor)

    (d) 10 GHz (PCs of the early 2000s)

    (e) 1 THz (1 terahertz)

3.2 Compute the clock period for the following clock frequencies.

    (a) 32.768 kHz

    (b) 100 MHz

    (c) 1.5 GHz

    (d) 2.4 GHz

3.3 Compute the clock frequency for the following clock periods.

    (a) 1 s

    (b) 1 ms

    (c) 20 ns

    (d) 1 ns

    (e) 1.5 ps

3.4 Compute the clock frequency for the following clock periods.

    (a) 500 ms

    (b) 400 ns

    (c) 4 ns

    (d) 20 ps

3.5 *Assume scientists have developed a chip having perfect transistors and wires with no resistance, meaning signals within this chip can travel at the speed of light, or 3×10^8 meters/second. Assuming our digital circuit has a width of 25 mm and a height of 25 mm, compute the clock period and clock frequency, where the longest distance any signal must travel during a single clock period is:

    (a) one-eighth of the width of the circuit

    (b) one-half the height of the circuit

    (c) the width of the circuit

    (d) diagonally across the circuit

    (e) the perimeter of the circuit

3.6 Trace the behavior of an SR latch for the following situation: Q, S, and R are 0 and have been for a long time, then S changes to 1 and stays there for a long time, then S changes back to 0. Using a timing diagram, show the values that appear on every wire for every change on a wire. Assume logic gates have a tiny but nonzero delay.

 3.7 Repeat Exercise 3.6, but assume that S was changed to 1 just long enough for the signal to propagate through one logic gate, after which S was changed back to 0—in other words, S did not satisfy the hold time of the latch.

 3.8 Trace the behavior of a level-sensitive SR latch (see Figure 3.14) for the input pattern in Figure 3.71. Assume S1, R1, and Q are initially 0. Complete the timing diagram, assuming logic gates have a tiny but nonzero delay.

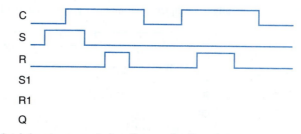

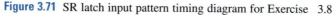

Figure 3.71 SR latch input pattern timing diagram for Exercise 3.8

3.9 Trace the behavior of a level-sensitive SR latch (see Figure 3.14) for the input pattern in Figure 3.72. Assume S1, R1, and Q are initially 0. Complete the timing diagram, assuming logic gates have a tiny but nonzero delay.

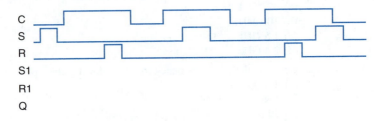

Figure 3.72 SR latch input pattern timing diagram for Exercise 3.9

3.10 Trace the behavior of a level-sensitive SR latch (see Figure 3.14) for the input pattern in Figure 3.73. Assume S1, R1, and Q are initially 0. Complete the timing diagram, assuming logic gates have a tiny but nonzero delay.

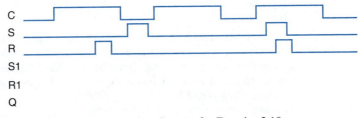

Figure 3.73 SR latch input pattern timing diagram for Exercise 3.10

3.11 Trace the behavior of a D latch (see Figure 3.18) for the input pattern in Figure 3.74. Assume Q is initially 0. Complete the timing diagram, assuming logic gates have a tiny but nonzero delay.

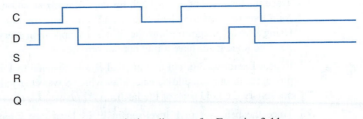

Figure 3.74 D latch input pattern timing diagram for Exercise 3.11

 **3.12** Trace the behavior of a D latch (see Figure 3.18) for the input pattern in Figure 3.75. Assume Q is initially 0. Complete the timing diagram, assuming logic gates have a tiny but nonzero delay.

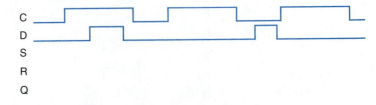

Figure 3.75 D latch input pattern timing diagram for Exercise 3.12

3.13 Trace the behavior of an edge-triggered D flip-flop using a master-servant design (see Figure 3.24) for the input pattern in Figure 3.76. Assume each internal latch initially stores a 0. Complete the timing diagram, assuming logic gates have a tiny but nonzero delay.

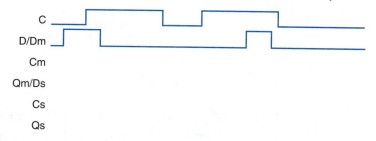

Figure 3.76 Edge-triggered D flip-flop input pattern timing diagram for Exercise 3.13

3.14 Trace the behavior of an edge-triggered D flip-flop using the master-servant design (see Figure 3.24) for the input pattern in Figure 3.77. Assume each internal latch initially stores a 0. Complete the timing diagram, assuming logic gates have a tiny but nonzero delay.

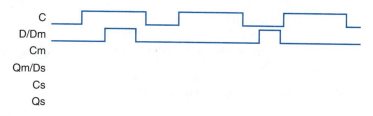

Figure 3.77 Edge-triggered D flip-flop input pattern timing diagram for Exercise 3.14

3.15 Compare the behavior of D latch and D flip-flop devices by completing the timing diagram in Figure 3.78. Assume each device initially stores a 0. Provide a brief explanation of the behavior of each device.

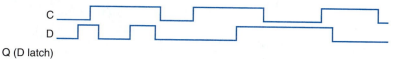

Figure 3.78 D latch and D flip-flop input pattern timing diagram for Exercise 3.15

3.16 Compare the behavior of D latch and D flip-flop devices by completing the timing diagram in Figure 3.79. Assume each device initially stores a 0. Provide a brief explanation of the behavior of each device.

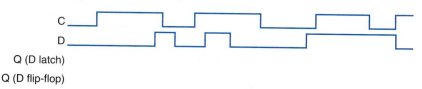
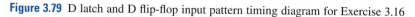

Figure 3.79 D latch and D flip-flop input pattern timing diagram for Exercise 3.16

3.17 Create a circuit of three level-sensitive D latches connected in series (the output of one is connected to the input of the next). Show how a clock with a long high-time can cause the value at the input of the first D latch to trickle through more than one latch during the same clock cycle.

3.18 Repeat Exercise 17 using edge-triggered D flip-flops, and show how the input of the first D latch does not trickle through to the next flip-flop no matter how long the clock signal is high.

3.19 Using D flip-flops, create a circuit with an input X and an output Y, such that Y always equals X delayed by two clock cycles.

3.20 Using four registers, design a circuit that stores the previous four values seen at an 8-bit input D. The circuit should have a single 8-bit output that can be configured using two inputs s1 and s0 to output any one of the four registers. (Hint: use an 8-bit 4x1 mux.)

3.21 Consider three 4-bit registers connected together as shown in Figure 3.80. Assume the initial values in the registers are unknown. Trace the behavior of the registers by completing the timing diagram of Figure 3.81.

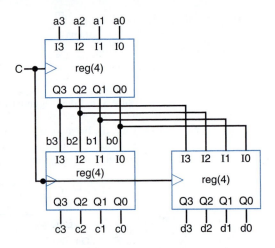

Figure 3.80 Register configuration.

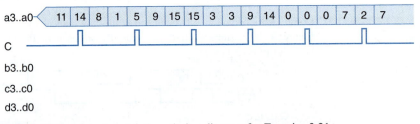

Figure 3.81 4-bit register input pattern timing diagram for Exercise 3.21

3.22 Consider three 4-bit registers connected together as shown in Figure 3.83. Assume the initial values in the registers are unknown. Trace the behavior of the registers by completing the timing diagram of Figure 3.82.

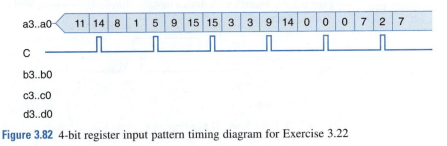

Figure 3.82 4-bit register input pattern timing diagram for Exercise 3.22

SECTION 3.3: FINITE-STATE MACHINES (FSM) AND CONTROLLERS

3.23 Draw a state diagram for an FSM that has an input X and an output Y. Whenever X changes from 0 to 1, Y should become 1 for two clock cycles and then return to 0—even if X is still 1. (Assume for this problem and all other FSM problems that an implicit rising clock is ANDed with every FSM transition condition.)

3.24 Draw a state diagram for an FSM with no inputs and three outputs, x, y, and z. xyz should always follow the following sequence: 000, 001, 010, 100, repeat. The output should change only on a rising clock edge. Make 000 the initial state.

3.25 Do Exercise 24, but add an input I that can stop the sequence when set to 0. When input I returns to 1, the sequence resumes from where it left off.

3.26 Do Exercise 25, except the sequence starts from 000 whenever I returns to 1.

3.27 A wristwatch display can show one of four items: the time, the alarm, the stopwatch, or the date, controlled by two signals s1 and s0 (00 displays the time, 01 the alarm, 10 the stopwatch, and 11 the date—assume s1s0 control an N-bit-wide mux that passes through the appropriate register). Pressing a

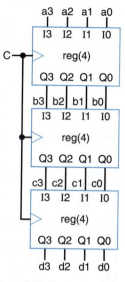

Figure 3.83 Register configuration.

button B (which sets B = 1) sequences the display to the next item (if the presently displayed item is the date, the next item is the current time). Create a state diagram for an FSM describing this sequencing behavior, having an input bit B, and two output bits s1 and s0. Be sure to only sequence forward by one item each time the button is pressed, regardless of how long the button is pressed—in other words, be sure to wait for the button to be released after sequencing forward one item. Use short but descriptive names for each state. Make displaying the time be the initial state.

3.28 Extend the state diagram you created in Exercise 27 by adding an input R. R=1 forces the FSM to return to the state that displays the time.

3.29 Draw a state diagram for an FSM with an input *gcnt* and three outputs, *x*, *y*, and *z*. The *xyz* outputs generate a sequence called a Gray code in which exactly one of the three outputs changes from 0 to 1 or from 1 to 0. The Gray code sequence that the FSM should output is 000, 010, 011, 001, 101, 111, 110, 100, repeat. The output should change only on a rising clock edge when the input *gcnt* = 1. Make the initial state 000.

3.30 Trace through the execution of the FSM you created in Exercise 29 by completing the timing diagram in Figure 3.84, where C is the clock input and S is the n-bit state register. Assume S is initially 000.

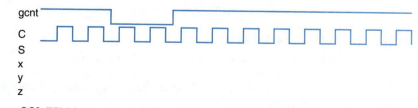

Figure 3.84 FSM input pattern timing diagram for Exercise 3.30

3.31 Draw a timing diagram for the FSM in Figure 3.85, such that the FSM starts in state *Wait*, reaches state *EN,* and returns to *Wait*. Describe the behavior of the circuit in English.

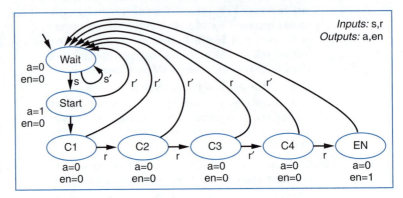

Figure 3.85 FSM for Exercise 3.31

3.32 For FSMs with the following numbers of states, indicate the smallest possible number of bits for a state register representing those states:
(a) 4
(b) 8
(c) 9
(d) 23
(e) 900

3.33 How many possible states can be represented by a 16-bit register?

3.34 If an FSM has N states, what is the maximum number of possible transitions that could exist in the FSM (assuming there are a large number of inputs, meaning the number of transitions is not limited by the number of inputs)?

3.35 *Assuming one input and one output, how many possible four-state FSMs exist?

3.36 *Suppose you are given two FSMs that execute concurrently. Describe an approach for merging those two FSMs into a single FSM with identical functionality as the two separate FSMs, and provide an example. If the first FSM has N states and the second has M states, how many states will the merged FSM have?

3.37 *Sometimes dividing a large FSM into two smaller FSMs results in simpler circuitry. Divide the FSM shown in Figure 3.88 into two FSMs, one containing G0–G3, the other containing G4–G7. You may add additional states, transitions, and inputs or outputs between the two FSMs, as required. Hint: you will need to introduce signals between the FSMs for one FSM to tell the other FSM to go to some state.

SECTION 3.4: CONTROLLER DESIGN

3.38 Using the five-step processor for designing a controller, convert the FSM of Figure 3.86 to a controller, implementing the controller using a state register and logic gates.

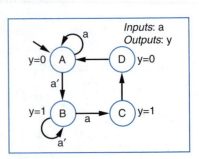

Figure 3.86 FSM for Exercise 3.38

3.39 Using the five-step processor for designing a controller, convert the FSM of Figure 3.87 to a controller, implementing the controller using a state register and logic gates.

3.40 Using the five-step process for designing a controller, convert the FSM you created for Exercise 24 to a controller, implementing the controller using a state register and logic gates.

3.41 Using the five-step process for designing a controller, convert the FSM you created for Exercise 27 to a controller, implementing the controller using a state register and logic gates.

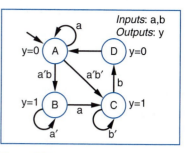

Figure 3.87 FSM for Exercise 3.39

3.42 Using the five-step process for designing a controller, convert the FSM you created for Exercise 29 to a controller, implementing the controller using a state register and logic gates.

3.43 Using the five-step process for designing a controller, convert the FSM in Figure 3.88 to a controller, stopping once you have created the state table. Note: your state table will be quite large, having 32 rows—you might therefore want to use a computer tool, like a word processor or spreadsheet, to draw the table.

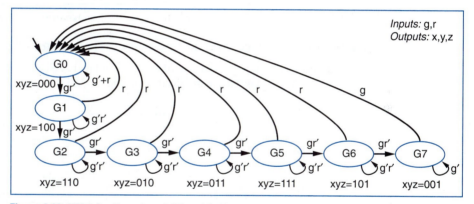

Figure 3.88 FSM for Exercises 3.37 and 3.43.

3.44 Create an FSM that has an input X and an output Y. Whenever X changes from 0 to 1, Y should become 1 for five clock cycles and then return to 0—even if X is still 1. Using the five-step process for designing a controller, convert the FSM to a controller, stopping once you have created the state table.

3.45 The FSM in Figure 3.89 has two problems: one state has two transitions whose conditions could simultaneously evaluate to true, and another states has transitions that aren't guaranteed to have at least one of the transition conditions true. By ORing and ANDing the conditions for each state's transitions, prove that these problems exist. Then, fix these problems by refining the FSM, taking your best guess as to what was the FSM creator's intent.

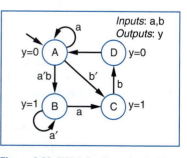

Figure 3.89 FSM for Exercise 3.45

3.46 Reverse engineer the behavior of the sequential circuit shown in Figure 3.90.

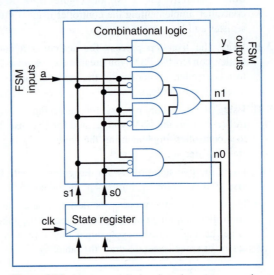

Figure 3.90 A sequential circuit to be reverse engineered.

SECTION 3.5: MORE ON FLIP-FLOPS AND CONTROLLERS

3.47 Consider three T flip-flops connected as shown in Figure 3.92. Trace the behavior of the flip-flops by completing the timing diagram in Figure 3.91. Assume all the flip-flops initially contain 0's.

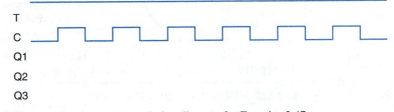

Figure 3.91 T flip-flop input pattern timing diagram for Exercise 3.47

3.48 Show how to connect four T flip-flops together to create a circuit that counts from 0 to 15 in binary and back to 0 again—in other words, that counts 0000, 0001, 0010, ..., 1111, and back to 0000 again. Hint: consider using the Q output of a flip-flop as the clock input of another flip-flop. Assume all the flip-flops initially contain 0's.

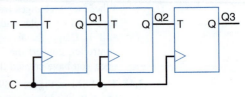

Figure 3.92 Three T flip-flops.

3.49 Define metastability.

3.50 Design a controller with a 4-bit state register that gets synchronously initialized to state 1010 when an input *reset* is set to 1.

3.51 *Design a D flip-flop with asynchronous reset, *AR*, and asynchronous set, *AS*, inputs using basic logic gates.

▶ *DESIGNER PROFILE*

Brian got his bachelors degree in Electrical Engineering and then worked for several years. Realizing the future demand for digital design targeting an increasingly popular type of digital chip known as FPGAs (see Chapter 7), he returned to school to obtain a masters degree in Electrical Engineering with a thesis topic targeting digital design for FPGAs. He has been employed at two different companies, and is now working as an independent digital design consultant.

He has worked on a number of projects, including a system that prevents house fires by tripping a circuit breaker when current running in the circuit indicates arcing is occurring, a microprocessor architecture for speeding up the processing of digitized video, and a mammography machine for precise location detection of tumors in humans.

One of the projects he has found most interesting was a baggage scanner for detecting explosives. "In that system, there is a lot of data being acquired as well as motors running, x-rays being beamed, and other things happening, all at the same time. To be successful, you have to pay attention to detail, and you have to communicate with the other design teams so every one is on the same page." He found that project particularly interesting because "I was working on a small part of a very large, complex machine. We had to stay focused on our part of the design, while at the same time being mindful of how all the parts were going to fit together in the end." Thus, being able to work alone as well as in large groups was important, requiring good communication and team skills. And being able to understand not only a part of the system, but also important aspects of the other parts was also important, requiring knowledge of diverse topics.

Brian is now an independent digital design consultant, something that many electrical engineers, computer engineers, and computer scientists choose to do after getting experience in their field. "I like the flexibility that being a consultant offers. On the plus side, I get to work on a wide variety of projects. The drawback is that sometimes I only get to work on a small part of a project, rather than seeing a product through from start to finish. And of course being an independent consultant means there's less stability than a regular position at a company, but I don't mind that."

Brian has taken advantage of the flexibility provided by consulting by taking a part-time job teaching an undergraduate digital design course and an embedded systems course at a university. "I really enjoy teaching and I have learned a lot through teaching. And I enjoy introducing students to the field of embedded systems."

Asked what he likes most about the field of digital design, he says, "I like building products that make people's lives easier, or safer, or more fun. That's satisfying."

Asked to give advice to students, he says that one important thing is "to ask questions. Don't be afraid of looking dumb when you ask questions at a new job. People don't expect you to know everything, but they do expect you to ask questions when you are unsure. Besides, asking questions is an important part of learning."

CHAPTER 4

Datapath Components

▶ 4.1 INTRODUCTION

Chapters 2 and 3 introduced increasingly complex building blocks that can be used to build digital circuits. Those blocks included logic gates, multiplexors, decoders, basic registers, and finally controllers. Controllers are good for implementing systems having some number of control input signals and generating some number of control output signals. For example, if we see a particular control input become 1 (corresponding perhaps to a button being pressed), then we may want to generate a 1 on a control output (corresponding perhaps to a light turning on). In this chapter, we instead focus on creating building blocks that are good for systems having *data* inputs and outputs. In general, digital systems have two types of inputs (and outputs as well):

- *Control:* A control input is typically one bit, representing a particular event occurring outside the system, like a button being pressed, or representing a particular state of something outside the system, like a door being closed or a car being at an intersection. Control inputs could sometimes be grouped into multiple bits—like 4 bits representing which of 16 buttons is pressed, or 2 bits representing each of 4 possible states of a door (closed, open 1/3rd, open 2/3rd, or fully open). Control inputs are typically used directly to influence a controller's present state.

- *Data:* A data input is typically multiple bits, collectively representing a single entity. For example, a 32-bit input may represent a temperature in binary. A 7-bit input may represent the present floor location of an elevator in a 100-floor building. A data input may be a single bit, differing from a single-bit control input in that we don't directly rely on that bit's value to influence the controller's present state.

Not all inputs can be strictly classified as either control or data—there are some inputs that fall somewhere on the border in between the two types. But most inputs can be classified as one or the other. (And, of course, a digital system also has power inputs, ground inputs, and clock inputs too, in addition to control and data inputs.)

Controllers are a good building block for building systems consisting mainly of control inputs and control outputs. But we also need building blocks for systems consisting of data inputs and outputs. In particular, we need registers to hold the data, and functional units to operate on (e.g. add or divide) the data. Such components are known as *register-transfer level* (*RTL*) components, also known as *datapath components*, and a circuit composed of such components is known as a *datapath*.

Datapaths can become quite complex, and therefore it is crucial to build datapaths from a set of datapath components that each encapsulate an appropriately high level of functionality. For example, if you were asked what components make up an automobile, you would probably list components like an engine, tires, a chassis, a body, and so on. Each of those components encapsulates a high-level function of the automobile. You thought of a tire, not of the rubber, steel wires, valve stem, valve, sidewalls, and other parts that make up the tire. Those detailed parts make up the design of a tire, not an automobile. A tire is an appropriately high level of component when thinking of a car; a valve stem is not. Likewise, when we design datapaths, we must have a set of datapath components at the appropriately high level—logic gates are too low-level.

This chapter defines such a set of datapath components, and also introduces simple datapaths. In Chapter 5, we'll see how to create more advanced datapaths, and how to combine datapaths and controllers to build an even higher-level component known as a processor.

▷ 4.2 REGISTERS

An *N-bit register* is a sequential component able to store N bits. Typical register widths (the number of bits N) are 8, 16, and 32 bits, though any width is possible. The bits in a register often represent data, such as 8 bits representing a temperature as a binary number.

The common name used for storing data into a register is *loading*, although the words *writing* and *storing* are also used. The opposite action of loading a register is known as *reading* a register's contents. Reading consists merely of connecting to the register's outputs—note that reading therefore is not synchronized with the clock, and furthermore, note that reading does not remove the bits from the register or change them in any way.

Registers come in a variety of styles. We'll introduce some of the most common styles in this section. Registers are perhaps the most fundamental datapath component, so we will provide numerous examples of their design and their use.

Parallel Load Register

The most basic type of register, shown in Figure 3.30 in Chapter 3, consists merely of a set of flip-flops that get loaded on every clock cycle. That basic register is useful as the state register in a controller, since the state register is loaded on every clock cycle. However, for most other uses of registers, we want some way to control whether or not a register gets loaded on a particular clock cycle—on some cycles we want to load, whereas on other cycles we just want to keep the previous value.

▶ WHY THE NAME "REGISTER"?

Historically, the term "register" referred to a sign or chalkboard onto which people could temporarily write out cash transactions, and later perform bookkeeping using those transactions. The term generally refers to a device for storing data. In this context, since a collection of flip-flops stores data, the name register seems quite appropriate.

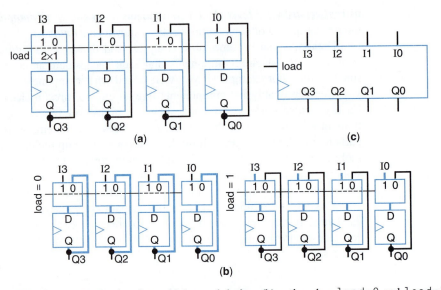

Figure 4.1 4-bit parallel load register: (a) internal design, (b) paths when load=0 and load=1, and (c) register block symbol.

We can achieve control over loading of a register by adding a 2x1 multiplexor in front of each flip-flop, as shown for the 4-bit register in Figure 4.1(a). When the load signal is 0 and the clock signal rises, each flip-flop gets loaded with its own Q value, as shown in Figure 4.1(b). Because Q is the flip-flop's present contents, the register's contents do not change when load is 0. When the load signal is 1 and the clock signal rises, each flip-flop gets loaded with one of the data inputs I0, I1, I2, or I3—thus, the register gets loaded with the data inputs when load is 1.

A register with a load line that controls whether the register is loaded with external inputs, with all those inputs being loaded in parallel, is known as a ***parallel load register***. Figure 4.1(c) provides a block symbol for a 4-bit parallel load register. A ***block symbol*** of a component shows a component's inputs and outputs, without showing the component's internal details.

Because registers are such a fundamental component in datapaths, we present a number of examples involving registers, to ensure the reader gains sufficient comfort with registers.

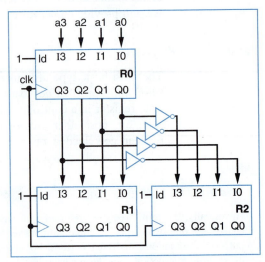

Figure 4.2 Basic register example.

▷ **EXAMPLE 4.1** Basic example using registers

Figure 4.2 shows a simple connection of three registers *R0*, *R1*, and *R2*. Suppose we are told that the input values on a3..a0 have the values shown in the timing diagram in Figure 4.3(a). We can then determine the values in registers $R0$, $R1$, and $R2$, as shown in Figure 4.3(b). Before the first clock edge, we do not know the values in the registers, so we show the registers' contents as "????." The contents are actually some combination of four 0 and 1 values, but we don't know what those particular values are.

Before the first clock edge, we are given that a3..a0 become 1111. Thus, on the first clock edge, $R0$ will be loaded with 1111. At the same moment, $R1$ and $R2$ will be loaded with the value in $R0$, which is "????," so $R1$ and $R2$ will still have contents of "????."

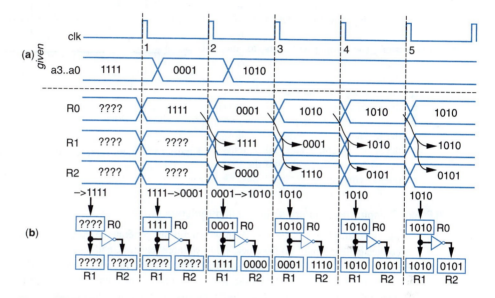

Figure 4.3 Basic register example: (a) timing diagram, and (b) the contents of each register.

Before clock edge 2, we are given that a3..a0 change to 0001. Thus, on the second clock edge, $R0$ will be loaded with 0001. Simultaneously, $R1$ will be loaded with the value of $R0$, which was 1111, and $R2$ will be loaded with the value of $R0$ inverted, meaning 0000.

Before the third clock edge, we are given that a3..a0 change to 1010. On the third clock edge, $R0$ will be loaded with 1010, while simultaneously $R1$ gets 0001, and $R2$ gets 1110.

We are given that a3..a0 stay at 1010 before the fourth clock edge. On the fourth edge, $R0$ again will be loaded with 1010, while simultaneously $R1$ gets 1010 and $R2$ gets 0101.

As a3..a0 stay at 1010 before the fifth clock edge, then on the fourth edge, $R0$ again will be loaded with 1010, while $R1$ again gets 1010 and $R2$ again gets 0101.

The important feature to notice in this example is that the $R0$, $R1$, and $R2$ registers *all get loaded simultaneously*. Thus, even though $R0$ gets loaded with a new value on a clock edge, $R1$ and $R2$ get the *previous* value, not the new value, on that same clock edge. ◄

► **EXAMPLE 4.2** Weight sampler

Consider a scale at a grocery store used to weigh fruit. The scale may have a display that shows the present weight. We want to add a second display, and a button that the user can press to remember the present weight (sometimes called "sampling"), so that when the fruit is removed, the remembered weight continues to be displayed on the second display. A diagram of the system is shown in Figure 4.4.

Assume the scale outputs the present weight as a 4-bit binary number, and the "Present weight" and "Saved weight" displays automatically convert their input binary number to the proper displayed value. We can design the *Weight-Sampler* block using a 4-bit parallel load register. We connect the button signal b to the load input of the register. The output connects to the "Saved weight" display. Whenever b is 1, the weight value gets loaded into the register, and thus appears on the second display. When b returns to 0, the register keeps its value, so the second display continues to show the same weight, even if other items are placed on the scale and the first display changes. ◀

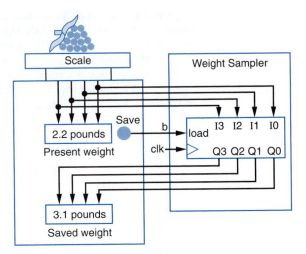

Figure 4.4 Weight sampler implemented using a 4-bit parallel load register.

▶ **EXAMPLE 4.3**   Temperature history display using registers (again)

Recall Example 3.2 of Chapter 3, in which a timer generated a pulse on an input C every hour. We connected that input C to the clock inputs of three registers, and those registers were connected such that the first register would be loaded with the present temperature, the second register would get the previous temperature, and the third register would get the temperature before that one, on the rising edge of C. However, in practice, we typically do not connect any input other than a clock signal (from an oscillator) to a register's clock input. We can therefore redesign the system to use a clock signal as the register clock input, by using a parallel load register. We could then connect the input C to the load inputs of the registers, as shown in Figure 4.5.

The oscillator frequency can be faster than 1 pulse per hour. In fact, due to the nature of how oscillators are made (see "How Does It Work?—Quartz Oscillators" on page 102 in Chapter 3), oscillator frequencies are usually at least in the kilohertz range.

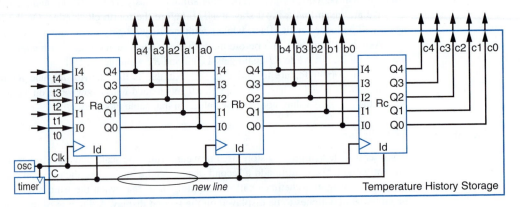

Figure 4.5 Internal design of the *TemperatureHistoryStorage* component, using parallel load registers.

We must ensure that when the timer generates its hourly pulse on C, the pulse is 1 for only one clock cycle. Otherwise, the registers would get loaded more than once during a single pulse (because during that pulse, multiple rising clock edges would occur, and registers get loaded on each rising clock edge), and so the present temperature would get loaded into two or even all three registers. We can accomplish a single-cycle high output by using the same clock as input to the timer, and then designing the timer's internal state machine to only set C=1 for one state—similar to how we set an output to 1 for exactly three states in Example 3.7 in Chapter 3.   ◀

▶ **EXAMPLE 4.4**   Automobile above-mirror display using parallel-load registers

In Chapter 2, we described an example of a system above a rearview mirror that could display one of four 8-bit inputs, T, A, I, and M. In that example, we assumed the car's central computer was connected to the above-mirror system using 32 lines (4*8). Thirty-two wires is a lot of wires to have to connect from the computer to above the rearview mirror. Instead, assume that the computer connects to the above-mirror system using 8 data lines (C), 2 control lines a1a0 that specify which data item presently appears on C (being T when a1a0=00, A when a1a0=01, I when a1a0=10, and M when a1a0=11), and a load control line load, for a total of 11 lines, rather than 32 lines. The computer can send the data items in any order, at any time. The above-mirror system should simply store data items in the appropriate register (according to a1a0) when the data items arrive, and thus the system needs four parallel-load registers in which to store each data item. The control lines a1a0 will therefore serve as the "address" that tells us which register to load. As in the earlier example, inputs xy determine which value to pass through to the 8-bit display output D (with xy sequenced by the user pressing the mode button).

We can design the system as shown in Figure 4.6. The figure uses a popular "shorthand" notation that replaces a group of wires by a single thicker wire having a slanted line and number indicating the number of wires in the group.

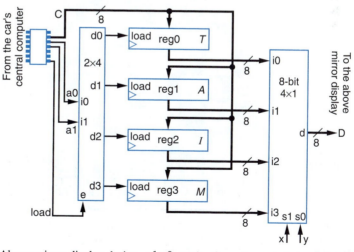

Figure 4.6 Above-mirror display design. a1a0, set by the car's central computer, determines which register to load with C, while load=1 enables such loading. xy, which are independent of a1a0 and are set by the user pressing the mode button, determine which register to output to the display D.

The decoder decodes a1a0 to enable exactly one of the four registers. The load line enables the decoder—if load is 0, no decoder output is 1 and so no register gets loaded. The multiplexer part of the system is the same as in the earlier example.

Let's see how this system works for a sample sequence of inputs. Suppose initially that all registers store 0s and xy=00. Thus, the display will show 0. If the user presses the mode button four times, the inputs xy will sequence through 01, 10, 11, and back to 00, for each press still displaying 0 (since all registers are 0s). Now suppose that during some clock cycle, the car's computer sets a1a0=01, load=1, and C=00001010. Then register 1 will be loaded with 00001010. Since xy=00, the display will still show the contents of register 0, and thus the display will show 0. Now, if the user presses the mode button, xy will become 01, and the display will show the decimal value of register 1's 00001010 value, which is ten in decimal. Pressing mode again will change xy to 10, so the display will show the contents of register 2, which is 0. At any time in the future, the car's computer can load the other registers, or reload register 1, with new values, in any order. Note that the loading of the registers is independent from the display of those registers. ◀

▷ **EXAMPLE 4.5** Computerized checkerboard

Checkers (known in some countries as "draughts") is one of the world's most popular board games. A checkerboard consists of 64 squares, formed from 8 columns and 8 rows. Each player starts with 12 checkers (pieces) on the board. A computerized checkerboard may replace the checkers by using an LED (light-emitting diode) in each square. An on LED represents a checker in a square; an off LED represents no checker. For simplicity of the example, ignore the issue of each player having his own color of checkers. An example board is shown in Figure 4.7(a).

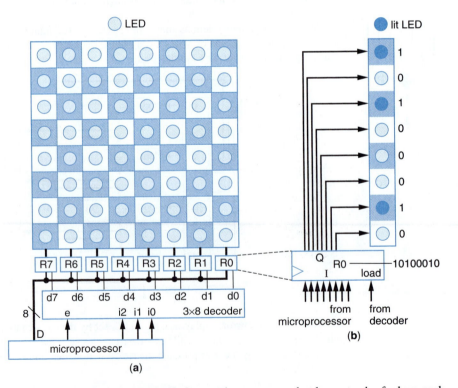

Figure 4.7 An electronic checkerboard: (a) eight 8-bit registers (*R7* through *R0*) can be used to drive the 64 LEDs, using one register per column, and (b) detail of how one register connects to a column's LEDs and how the value 10100010 stored in that register would light three LEDs.

A computerized checkerboard typically has a microprocessor that keeps track of where each piece is located, moves pieces according to user commands or according to a checker-playing program (when playing against the computer), keeps score, etc.

Notice that the microprocessor must set values for 64 bits, one bit for each square. However, the inexpensive type of microprocessor used in such a device probably does not have 64 pins. The microprocessor needs external registers to store those bits that drive the LEDs, and will write to those registers one at a time. The microprocessor writes to the registers so fast, though, that an observer would probably see all the LEDs change at the same time, not noticing that some LEDs are changing microseconds earlier than others.

Let's use one register per column, meaning we'll need eight 8-bit registers total, as shown below the checkerboard in Figure 4.7(a), with those registers named *R7* through *R0*. Each register's 8 bits of data corresponds to a particular row in the register's column, indicating whether the respective LED is on or off, as shown in Figure 4.7(b). The eight registers are connected to the microprocessor. The microprocessor uses eight pins (D) for data, three pins ($i2$, $i1$, $i0$) for addressing the appropriate register (which is decoded into a load line for each of the 8 registers), and one pin (e) for the register load line (implemented using the decoder's enable), for a total of 12 pins—a number much more feasible than 64 pins. To configure the checkerboard for the beginning of a game, the microprocessor would create the following sequence of register writes shown in Figure 4.8. ◀

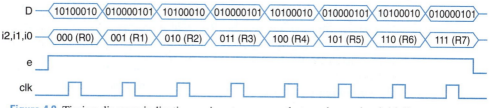

Figure 4.8 Timing diagram indicating an input sequence that can be used to initialize.

▶ *HOW DOES IT WORK? COMPUTERIZED BOARD GAMES.*

Many of you have played a computerized board game, like checkers, backgammon, or chess, either using boards with small displays to represent pieces, or perhaps using a graphics program on a personal computer or website. The main method the computer uses for choosing among possible next moves is called lookahead. For the current configuration of pieces on the board, the computer considers all possible single moves that it might make. For each such move, it might also consider all possible single moves by the opponent. For each new configuration resulting from possible moves, the computer evaluates the configuration's goodness, or quality, and picks a move that may lead to the best configuration. Each move that the computer looks ahead (one computer move, one opponent move, another computer move, another opponent move) is called the *lookahead* amount. Good programs might lookahead three, four, five moves, or more. Looking ahead is costly in terms of compute time and memory—if each player has 10 possible moves per turn, then looking ahead two moves results in 10*10 = 100 configurations to evaluate; three moves in 10*10*10=1000 configurations, four moves in 10,000 configurations, and so on. Good game-playing programs will "prune" configurations that appear to be very bad and thus unlikely to be chosen by an opponent, just as humans do, to reduce the configurations to be considered. Computers can examine millions of configurations, whereas humans can only mentally examine perhaps a few dozen. Chess, being perhaps the most complex of popular board games, has attracted extensive attention since the early days of computing. Alan Turing, considered one of the fathers of Computer Science, wrote much about using computers for chess, and is credited as having written the first computer chess program in 1950. However, humans proved better than computer chess programs until 1997, when IBM's Deep Blue computer defeated the reigning world champion in a classic chess match. Deep Blue had 30 IBM RS-6000 SP processors connected to 480 special purpose chess chips, and could evaluate 200 million moves per second, and hence many billions of moves in a few minutes. Today, chess tournaments not only match humans against computer programs, but also programs against programs, many hosted by the International Computer Games Association.

(Source: *Computer Chess History*, by Bill Wall).

On the first rising clock edge, *R0* gets loaded with 10100010. On the second rising clock edge, *R1* gets loaded with 01000101. And so on. After eight clock cycles, the registers would contain the desired values, and the board's LEDs would be lit, as shown in Figure 4.9. ◀

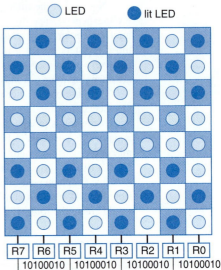

| R7 | R6 | R5 | R4 | R3 | R2 | R1 | R0 |

10100010 10100010 10100010 10100010
01000101 01000101 01000101 01000101

Figure 4.9 Checkerboard after loading registers for initial checker positions.

Shift Register

One thing we might want to do with a register is shift the register's contents to the left or to the right. Shifting to the right means to move each stored bit one flip-flop to the right. If a 4-bit register originally stores 1101, shifting right would result in 0110, as shown in Figure 4.10(a). We dropped the rightmost bit (in this case a 1), and we shifted a 0 into the leftmost bit. To build a register capable of shifting to the right, we conceptually need to connect the register's flip-flops in the manner similar to that shown in Figure 4.10(b).

Figure 4.10 Right shift example: (a) sample contents before and after a right shift, and (b) bit-by-bit view of the shift.

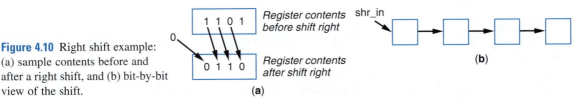

We can create a register able to shift to the right as shown in Figure 4.11. The register includes two control inputs, shr and shr_in. shr=1 causes a right shift on a rising clock edge, while shr=0 causes the register to maintain its present value. shr_in is the bit that we want to shift into the leftmost register bit during a shift operation.

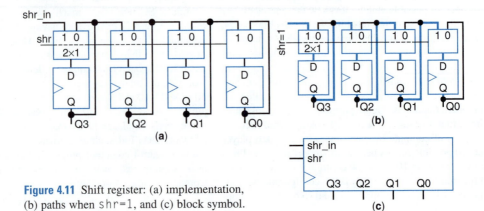

Figure 4.11 Shift register: (a) implementation, (b) paths when shr=1, and (c) block symbol.

Rotate Register

A rotate register is a slight variation of a shift register in which the outgoing bit gets shifted back in as the incoming bit. So on a right rotate, the rightmost bit gets shifted into the leftmost bit, as seen in Figure 4.12.

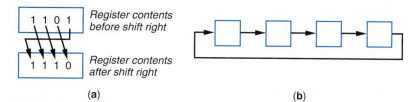

Figure 4.12 Right rotate example: (a) register contents before and after the rotate, and (b) bit-by-bit view of the rotate operation.

Implementing a rotate register is achieved by modifying the design of Figure 4.11, feeding the rightmost flip-flop output, rather than the `shr_in` input, into the leftmost mux's `i1` input. A rotate register needs some way to get values into the register—either via a shift, or via parallel load.

► **EXAMPLE 4.6** *Above-mirror display using shift registers*

In Example 4.4, we redesigned the connection between a car's central computer and an above-mirror display system to reduce the number of wires from 32 down to 8+2+1=11. However, even 11 wires is a lot of wires to have to run from the computer to above the mirror. Let's reduce the wires even further by using shift registers in the above-mirror system. The inputs to the above-mirror system from the car's computer will be one data bit `c`, two address lines `a1a0`, and a shift line `shift`, for a total of only 4 wires.

This bundle should be thin—just a few wires, not eleven wires.

When the computer wants to write to one of the above-mirror system's registers, the computer will set `a1a0` appropriately and will then set `shift` to 1 for exactly eight clock cycles.

For each of those eight clock cycles, the computer will set `c` to one bit of the 8-bit data to be loaded, starting with the least-significant bit on the first clock cycle, and ending with the most-significant bit on the eighth clock cycle. We can thus design the above-mirror system as shown in Figure 4.13.

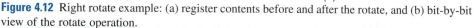

Figure 4.13 Above-mirror display design using shift registers to reduce the number of lines coming from the car's computer. The computer sets `a1a0` to the desired register to load, and then holds `shift=1` for eight clock cycles, with `c` equaling the register contents bit-by-bit, one bit per clock cycle, resulting in the desired register being loaded with the sent 8-bit value.

When shift=1, the appropriate register gets a new value shifted in during the next eight clock cycles. This method achieves the same as a parallel load from eight separate inputs, but utilizes fewer wires.

This example demonstrates a form of communication between digital circuits known as *serial communication*, in which the circuits communicate data by sending the data one bit at a time. ◀

Multifunction Registers

Many registers can perform a variety of operations (also called *functions*), like load, shift right, shift left, rotate right, rotate left, etc. The register user selects the presently desired operation by setting the register's control inputs. We'll now introduce some multifunction registers.

Register with Parallel Load and Shift Right

A popular combination of operations on a register is that of both parallel load and shift. We can design a 4-bit register capable of parallel load and shift right, the details of which are shown in Figure 4.14(a). Figure 4.14(b) shows a block symbol of the register.

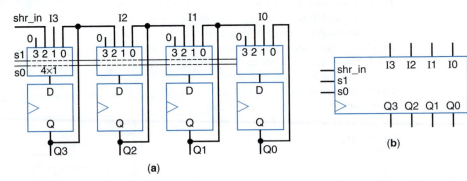

(a)

(b)

Figure 4.14 4-bit register with parallel load and shift right operations: (a) internal design, and (b) block symbol.

Notice that we used a 4x1 mux, rather than a 2x1 mux, in front of each flip-flop, because each flip-flop can now receive its next bit from one of three locations (the fourth mux input is unused). The register has two control inputs, with the control behavior shown in Figure 4.15.

s1	s0	Operation
0	0	Maintain present value
0	1	Parallel load
1	0	Shift right
1	1	(unused – let's load 0s)

Figure 4.15 Operation table of a 4-bit register with parallel load and shift right operations.

Let's examine the mux and flip-flop of the rightmost bit. When s1s0=00, the mux passes the present flip-flop value back to the flip-flop, causing the flip-flop to get reloaded with its present value on the next rising clock, thus maintaining the present value. When s1s0=01, the mux passes the external I0 input to the flip-flop, causing the flip-flop to get loaded. When s1s0=10, the mux passes the present value of the flip-flop output from the left, Q1, thus causing a right shift. s1s0=11 is not a legal input to the register and thus should never occur; the mux passes 0s in this case.

Register with Parallel Load, Shift Left, and Shift Right

Adding a shift left operation to the above 4-bit register is straightforward, and is shown in Figure 4.16. Instead of connecting 0s to the I3 input of each 4x1 mux, we instead connect the output from the flip-flop to the right. The rightmost mux's I3 input would be connected to an additional input shl_in.

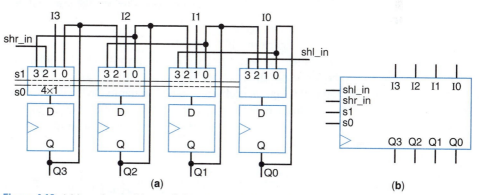

Figure 4.16 4-bit register with parallel load, shift left, and shift right operations: (a) internal design, (b) block symbol.

The register has the operations shown in Figure 4.17.

Load/Shift Register with Separate Control Inputs for Each Operation

Registers typically don't come with control inputs that encode the operation into the minimum number of bits like the control inputs on the registers we designed above. Instead, each operation usually has its own control input.

So a register with the operations of load, shift left, and shift right, might have the inputs and operation table shown in Figure 4.18. The four possible operations (maintain, shift left, shift right and load) really only require two control inputs, but the figure shows that the register has three control inputs—ld, shr, and shl.

Notice that if the user sets more than one control input to 1, we must decide what operation to perform. If the user sets both shr and shl, we'll give priority to shr. If the user asserts ld and either or both of shr and shl, we'll give priority to ld.

The internal design of such a register is similar to the load/shift register designed above, except that the three control inputs of ld, shl, and shr need to be mapped to the two control inputs s1 and s0 of the earlier register, using a simple combinational circuit, as shown in Figure 4.19.

s1	s0	Operation
0	0	Maintain present value
0	1	Parallel load
1	0	Shift right
1	1	Shift left

Figure 4.17 Operation table of a 4-bit register with parallel load, shift left, and shift right operations.

ld	shr	shl	Operation
0	0	0	Maintain present value
0	0	1	Shift left
0	1	0	Shift right
0	1	1	Shift right – shr has priority over shl
1	0	0	Parallel load
1	0	1	Parallel load – ld has priority
1	1	0	Parallel load – ld has priority
1	1	1	Parallel load – ld has priority

Figure 4.18 Operation table of a 4-bit register with separate control inputs for parallel load, shift left, and shift right.

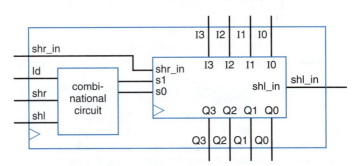

Figure 4.19 A small combinational circuit maps the control inputs ld, shr, and shl to the mux select inputs s1 and s0.

Figure 4.20 Truth tables describing operations of a register with left/right shift and parallel load along with the mapping of the register control inputs to the internal 4x1 mux select lines: (a) complete operation table defining the mapping of `ld`, `shr`, and `shl` to `s1` and `s0`, and (b) a compact version of the operation table.

Inputs			Outputs		Note
ld	shr	shl	s1	s0	Operation
0	0	0	0	0	Maintain value
0	0	1	1	1	Shift left
0	1	0	1	0	Shift right
0	1	1	1	0	Shift right
1	0	0	0	1	Parallel load
1	0	1	0	1	Parallel load
1	1	0	0	1	Parallel load
1	1	1	0	1	Parallel load

(a)

ld	shr	shl	Operation
0	0	0	Maintain value
0	0	1	Shift left
0	1	X	Shift right
1	X	X	Parallel load

(b)

We can design that combinational circuit starting from a simple truth table shown in Figure 4.20(a).

We thus obtain the following equations for the register's combinational circuit:

```
s1 = ld'*shr'*shl + ld'*shr*shl' + ld'*shr*shl
s0 = ld'*shr'*shl + ld
```

Replacing the combinational circuit box in Figure 4.19 by the gates described by the above equations would complete the register's design.

Register datasheets typically show the register operation table in a compact form, taking advantage of the priorities among the control inputs, as shown in Figure 4.20(b). A single X in a row means that row is actually two rows in the complete table, with one row having 0 in the position of the X, the other row having 1. Two Xs in a row means that row is actually four rows in the complete table, one row having 00 in the positions of those Xs, another row having 01, another 10, and another 11. And so on for three Xs, representing 8 rows. Note that putting higher priority control inputs to the left in the table keeps the table's operations nicely organized.

Register Design Process

Table 4.1 describes a general process for designing a register with any number of functions.

TABLE 4.1   Four-step process for designing a multifunction register.

	Step	Description
1.	*Determine mux size*	Count the number of operations (don't forget the maintain present value operation!) and add in front of each flip-flop a mux with at least that number of inputs.
2.	*Create mux operation table*	Create an operation table defining the desired operation for each possible value of the mux select lines.
3.	*Connect mux inputs*	For each operation, connect the corresponding mux data input to the appropriate external input or flip-flop output (possibly passing through some logic) to achieve the desired operation.
4.	*Map control lines*	Create a truth table that maps external control lines to the internal mux select lines, with appropriate priorities, and then design the logic to achieve that mapping

We'll illustrate the register design process with another example.

▶ **EXAMPLE 4.7** Register with load, shift, and synchronous clear and set

We want to design a register with the following operations: load, shift left, synchronous clear, and synchronous set, with unique control inputs for each operation (ld, shl, clr, set). The **synchronous clear** operation on a register means to load all 0s into the register on the next rising clock edge. The **synchronous set** operation means to load all 1s into the register on the next rising clock edge. The term synchronous is included because some registers come with *asynchronous* clear or asynchronous set operations. Following the register design method of Table 4.1, we perform the following steps:

Step 1: **Determine mux size.** There are 5 operations—load, shift left, synchronous clear, synchronous set, and *maintain present value*. Don't forget the maintain present value operation, as that operation is implicit.

Step 2: **Create mux operation table.** We'll use the first 5 inputs of an 8x1 mux for the desired 5 operations. For the remaining 3 mux inputs, we'll choose to maintain the present value, though those mux inputs should never be utilized. The table is shown in Figure 4.21.

Figure 4.21 Operation table for a register with load, shift, and synchronous clear and set.

s2	s1	s0	Operation
0	0	0	Maintain present value
0	0	1	Parallel load
0	1	0	Shift left
0	1	1	Synchronous clear
1	0	0	Synchronous set
1	0	1	Maintain present value
1	1	0	Maintain present value
1	1	1	Maintain present value

Step 3: **Connect mux inputs.** We connect the mux inputs as shown in Figure 4.22, which for simplicity shows only the *n*th flip-flop and mux of the register.

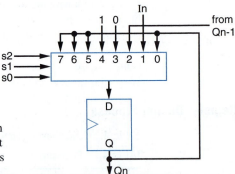

Figure 4.22 *N*th bit-slice of a register with the following operations: maintain present value, parallel load, shift left, synchronous clear, and synchronous set.

Step 4: **Map control lines.** We'll give clr highest priority, followed by set, ld, and shl, so the register control inputs would be mapped to the 8x1 mux select lines as shown in Figure 4.23.

Figure 4.23 Truth table for the control lines of a register with the *N*th bit-slice shown in Figure 4.22.

Inputs				Outputs			
clr	set	ld	shl	s2	s1	s0	Operation
0	0	0	0	0	0	0	Maintain present value
0	0	0	1	0	1	0	Shift left
0	0	1	X	0	0	1	Parallel load
0	1	X	X	1	0	0	Set to all 1s
1	X	X	X	0	1	1	Clear to all 0s

Looking at each output in Figure 4.23, we derive the equations describing the circuit that maps the external control inputs to the mux select lines as follows:

```
s2 = clr'*set
s1 = clr'*set'*ld'*shl + clr
s0 = clr'*set'*ld + clr
```

We could then create a combinational circuit implementing those equations, to map the external register control inputs to the mux select lines, and hence, completing the register's design. ◀

Some registers come with asynchronous clear and/or asynchronous set control inputs. Those inputs could be implemented by connecting them to asynchronous clear or asynchronous set inputs that exist on the flip-flops themselves.

▶ 4.3 ADDERS

Adding two binary numbers is perhaps the most common operation performed on data in a digital system. An **N-bit adder** is a datapath component that adds two N-bit binary numbers A and B, and generates an N-bit sum S and a 1-bit carry C. For instance, a 4-bit adder adds two 4-bit numbers, like 0111 and 0001, resulting in a 4-bit sum, like 1000, with a carry of 0. 1111 + 0001 would result in a carry of 1 and a sum of 0000 (or 10000 if you treat the carry bit and sum bits as one 5-bit result). N is often referred to as the *width* of the adder. Designing fast yet size-efficient adders is a subject that has received considerable attention for many decades.

Although it appears that we could design an N-bit adder by following the combinational logic design process of Table 2.5, it turns out that building an N-bit adder following that process is not very practical when N is much larger than 4. A 4-bit adder has two 4-bit inputs, meaning eight inputs total, and has four sum outputs and a carry output. So we could design the adder using the standard combinational logic design process of Table 2.5. For example, a 2-bit adder, which adds two 2-bit numbers, could be designed by starting with the truth table depicted in Figure 4.24. We could then implement the logic using a two-level logic gate based implementation for each output.

Inputs				Outputs			Inputs				Outputs		
a1	a0	b1	b0	c	s1	s0	a1	a0	b1	b0	c	s1	s0
0	0	0	0	0	0	0	1	0	0	0	0	1	0
0	0	0	1	0	0	1	1	0	0	1	0	1	1
0	0	1	0	0	1	0	1	0	1	0	1	0	0
0	0	1	1	0	1	1	1	0	1	1	1	0	1
0	1	0	0	0	0	1	1	1	0	0	0	1	1
0	1	0	1	0	1	0	1	1	0	1	1	0	0
0	1	1	0	0	1	1	1	1	1	0	1	0	1
0	1	1	1	1	0	0	1	1	1	1	1	1	0

Figure 4.24 Truth table for a 2-bit adder.

The problem with such an approach is that, for wider adders, the approach results in too large of truth tables and too many gates. A 16-bit adder has 16 + 16 = 32 inputs, meaning the truth table would have over *four billion rows*. A two-level logic gate based implementation of that table would likely require millions of gates. To illustrate this point, we performed an experiment in which we used the standard combinational logic design process to create adders of increasing width, starting with 1-bit adders on up. We used the most advanced commercial logic design tool available, and asked the tool to create a design using two levels of logic (one level of AND gates feeding into an OR gate for each output) and using the minimum number of gates (actually, transistors).

The plot in Figure 4.25 summarizes our results. Notice how fast the number of transistors grows as the adder width is increased. This fast growth is an effect of exponential growth—for an adder width of N, the number of truth table rows is proportional to 2^N (more precisely, to 2^{N+N}). Clearly, this exponential growth prohibits us from using the standard design process for adders wider than perhaps 8 to 10 bits. We could not complete our experiments for adders larger than 8 bits—the tool simply could not complete the design in a reasonable

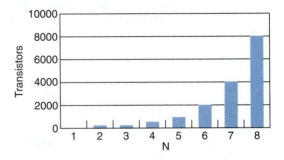

Figure 4.25 Why large adders aren't built using standard two-level combinational logic—notice the exponential growth. How many transistors would a 32-bit adder require?

amount of time. The tool needed 3 seconds to build the 6-bit adder, 40 seconds to build the 7-bit adder, and 30 minutes for the 8-bit adder. The 9-bit adder didn't finish after one full day. Looking at this data, can you predict the number of transistors required by a 16-bit adder or a 32-bit adder using two-levels of gates? From the figure, it looks like the number of transistors is doubling for each increase in N, with about 1000 transistors for $N=5$, 2000 transistors for $N=6$, 4000 transistors for $N=7$, and 8000 transistors for N=8. Assuming that trend continues for larger adders, then a 16-bit adder would have 8 more doublings beyond the 8-bit adder, meaning multiplying the size of the 8-bit adder by $2^8=256$. So a 16-bit adder would require 8000 * 256 = about two million transistors. A 32-bit adder would require an additional $2^{16}=64K$ doublings, meaning 2 million * 64K = over *100 billion transistors*. That's an outrageous number of transistors. We clearly need another approach for designing larger adders.

Adder—Carry-Ripple Style

An alternative approach to the standard combinational logic design process for adding two binary numbers is to instead create a circuit that mimics how we add binary numbers by hand, which is one column at a time. Consider the addition of a binary number A=1111 (15 in base 10) and B=0110 (6 in base 10), column by column, shown in Figure 4.26.

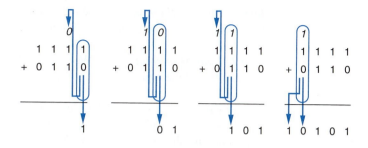

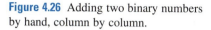

Figure 4.26 Adding two binary numbers by hand, column by column.

For each column, we add three bits together, and we generate a sum bit for the present column and a carry bit for the next column. The first column is an exception in that we only add two bits together, but still generate a sum and a carry bit. The carry of the last column becomes the fifth bit of the sum. The sum is 10101 (21 in base 10).

We can create a combinational component to perform the required addition for a single column. The inputs and outputs of such components are shown in Figure 4.27. Thus, all we need to do is design those components that perform the addition in each column, and connect them together as shown in Figure 4.27 to create a 4-bit adder. Bear in mind, though, that this method of creating an adder is intended to enable efficient design of wider adders, like those with 8 bits and above. We are illustrating the method using only a 4-bit adder because that size adder keeps our figures small and readable, but if all we really needed was a 4-bit adder, the standard combinational logic design process for two-level logic would probably work just fine.

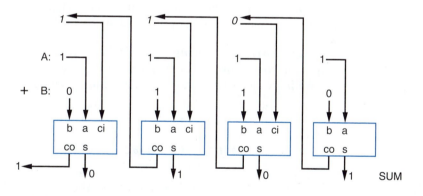

Figure 4.27 Using combinational components to add two binary numbers column by column.

We'll now design the components in each column of Figure 4.27.

Half-Adder

A *half-adder* is a combinational component that adds two bits (a and b), and generates a sum (s) and carry out (co) bit. (Note that we did *not* say that a half-adder adds *two 2-bit numbers*—a half-adder merely adds *two bits*.) The component on the right in Figure 4.27 that adds the rightmost column's two bits (a and b) and generates the sum (s) and carry-out (co) bit is a half adder. We can design a half-adder using the straightforward combinational logic design process from Chapter 2, as follows:

Inputs		Outputs	
a	b	co	s
0	0	0	0
0	1	0	1
1	0	0	1
1	1	1	0

Figure 4.28 Truth table for a half-adder.

Step 1: Capture the function. We'll use a truth table to capture the function. The appropriate truth table is shown in Figure 4.28.

Step 2: Convert to equations. We can clearly see that co = ab and that s = a'b + ab'. Note that the equation s = a'b + ab' is the same as s = a xor b.

Step 3: Create the circuit. The circuit for a half-adder, implementing the above equations, is shown in Figure 4.29(a). Figure 4.29(b) shows a block symbol of a half-adder.

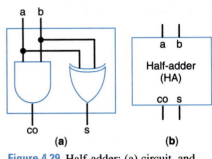

Full-Adder

A ***full-adder*** is a combinational component that adds three bits (a, b, and ci) and generates a sum (s) and a carry-out (co) bit. (Note that we did *not* say that a full-adder adds *two 3-bit numbers*—it merely adds *three bits*.)

Figure 4.29 Half-adder: (a) circuit, and (b) block symbol.

The three components in Figure 4.27 that add the two bits of a column (a and b) along with the carry from the column on the right (ci) and generates the sum (s) and carry out (co) bits are full-adders. We can design a full-adder using the straightforward combinational logic design process, as follows:

Step 1: Capture the function. We'll use a truth table to capture the function, shown in Figure 4.30.

Step 2: Convert to equations. We obtain the following equations for co and s. For simplicity, let's write ci as c. We'll use algebraic methods to simplify the equations.

Inputs			Outputs	
a	b	ci	co	s
0	0	0	0	0
0	0	1	0	1
0	1	0	0	1
0	1	1	1	0
1	0	0	0	1
1	0	1	1	0
1	1	0	1	0
1	1	1	1	1

```
co = a'bc + ab'c + abc' + abc
co = a'bc + abc + ab'c + abc + abc' +
     abc
co = (a'+a)bc + (b'+b)ac + (c'+c)ab
co = bc + ac + ab

s = a'b'c + a'bc' + ab'c' + abc
s = a'(b'c + bc') + a(b'c' + bc)
s = a'(b xor c)' + a(b xor c)
s = a xor b xor c
```

Figure 4.30 Truth table for a full-adder.

During algebraic simplification, for co, we noted that each of the first three terms could be combined with the last term abc, as each of the first three terms differed from the last term in just one literal. We thus created three instances of the last term abc (which doesn't change the function) and combined them with each of the first three terms. Don't worry if you aren't able to come up with that simplification on your own right now—Section 6.2 introduces methods to make such simplification more straightforward. If you have read that section, you might try using a K-map (introduced in that section) to simplify the equations.

Step 3: Create the circuit.

The circuit for a full-adder is shown in Figure 4.31(a), and the full-adder's block symbol is shown in Figure 4.31(b).

4-Bit Carry-Ripple Adder

Using three full-adders and one half-adder, we can design a 4-bit carry-ripple adder, which adds two 4-bit numbers and generates a 4-bit sum, shown in Figure 4.32. The 4-bit carry-ripple adder also generates a carry-out bit.

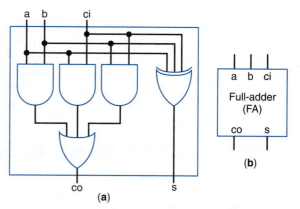

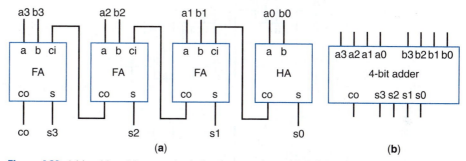

Figure 4.31 Full-adder: (a) circuit, and (b) block symbol.

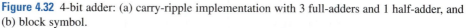

Figure 4.32 4-bit adder: (a) carry-ripple implementation with 3 full-adders and 1 half-adder, and (b) block symbol.

We can include a carry-in bit with the 4-bit adder, which enables us to connect 4-bit adders together to build larger adders. We include the carry-in bit by replacing the half-adder (which was in the rightmost bit position) by a full-adder, as shown in Figure 4.33.

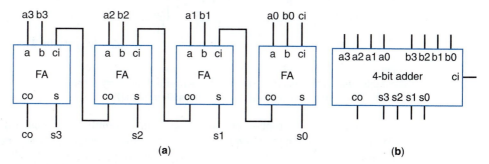

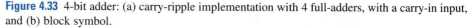

Figure 4.33 4-bit adder: (a) carry-ripple implementation with 4 full-adders, with a carry-in input, and (b) block symbol.

Let's analyze the behavior of this adder. Suppose that all inputs have been 0s for a long time, meaning that S will be 0000, co will be 0, and all ci values of the full adders will also be 0. Now suppose that A becomes 0111 and B becomes 0001 at the same time (whose sum we know should be 1000). Those new values of A and B will propagate through the full-adders. Suppose the delay of a full-adder is 2 ns. So 2 ns after A and B change, the sum outputs of the full-adders will change, as shown in Figure 4.34(a). So s3 will become 0+0+0=0 (with co3=0), s2 will become 1+0+0=1 (with co2=0), s1 will become 1+0+0=1 (with co1=0), and s0 will become 1+1=0 (with co0=1). But, 1111 + 0110 should not be 00110—instead, the sum should be 01000. What went wrong?

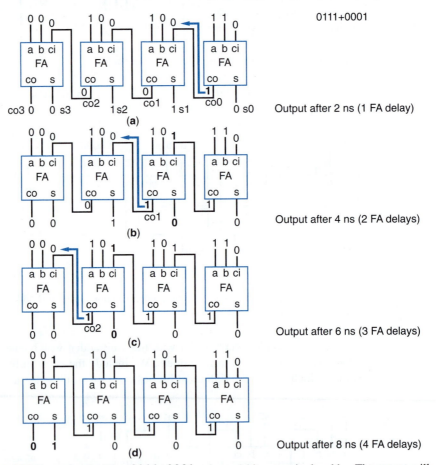

Figure 4.34 Example of adding 0111+0001 using a 4-bit carry-ripple adder. The output will exhibit temporarily incorrect (spurious) results until the carry bit from the rightmost bit has had a chance to propagate (ripple) all the way through to the leftmost bit.

Nothing went wrong—the carry-ripple adder simply isn't done yet after just 2 ns. After 2 ns, co0 changed from 0 to 1. Now, we must allow time for that *new* value of co0 to proceed through the next full-adder. Thus, after another 2 ns, s1 will equal 1+0+1=0, and co2 will become 1. So after 4 ns (two full-adder delays), the output will be 00100, as shown in Figure 4.34(b).

Keep waiting. After a third full-adder delay, the new value of co2 will have propagated through the next full-adder, resulting in s2 becoming 1+0+1=0, with co2 becoming 1. So after three full-adder delays, the output will be 00000, as shown in Figure 4.34(c).

Just a little more patience. After a fourth full-adder delay, co2 has had time to propogate through the last full-adder, resulting in s3 becoming 0+0+1=1, with co3 staying 0. Thus, after four full-adder delays, the output will be 01000, as shown in Figure 4.34(d), and 01000 is the correct result.

To recap, until the carry bits have had time to ripple through all the adders, from right to left, the output was not correct. The intermediate output values are known as ***spurious values***. The delay of the 4-bit adder, meaning the time we must wait until the output is the stable correct value, is equal to the delay of four full-adders, or 8 ns in this case, which is the time for the carry bits to ripple through all the adders—hence, the term ***carry-ripple adder***.

The term "ripple-carry" adder is actually more common. I prefer the term "carry-ripple" for consistent naming with other adder types, like carry-select and carry-lookahead, which we describe in Chapter 6.

Students often intially confuse full-adders and *N*-bit adders. A full-adder adds 3 bits. In contrast, a 3-bit adder adds two 3-bit numbers. A full-adder produces one sum bit and one carry bit. In contrast, a 3-bit adder produces three sum bits and one carry bit. A full-adder is usually used to add only *one column* of two binary numbers, whereas an *N*-bit adder is used to add two *N*-bit numbers.

An *N*-bit adder often comes with a carry-in bit, so that the adder can be cascaded with other *N*-bit adders to form larger adders. Figure 4.35(a) shows an 8-bit adder built from two 4-bit adders. We would set the carry-in bit (ci) on the right to 0 when adding two 8-bit numbers. Figure 4.35(b) shows a block symbol of that 8-bit adder.

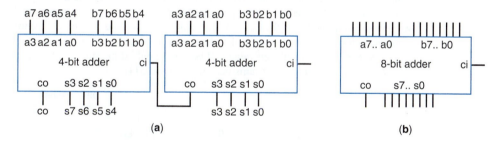

Figure 4.35 8-bit adder: (a) carry-ripple implementation built from two 4-bit carry-ripple adders, and (b) block symbol.

▶ **EXAMPLE 4.8** DIP-switch-based adding calculator

Let's design a very simple calculator that can add two 8-bit binary numbers and produce an 8-bit result. The input binary numbers will come from two 8-switch DIP switches, and the output will be displayed using 8 LEDs, as illustrated in Figure 4.36. An 8-bit ***DIP (Dual Inline Package)*** switch is a simple digital component having switches that a user can by hand move up or down, with up outputting a 1 on the corresponding pin, and down outputting a 0. An ***LED*** (light-emitting diode) is just a small light that illuminates when the LED's input is 1, and is dark when the input is 0.

We can implement this calculator by utilizing an 8-bit carry-ripple adder for the *CALC* block, as shown in Figure 4.36. When a user moves the switches on a DIP switch, the new binary values propagate through the carry-ripple adder's gates, generating intermittent outputs and hence causing

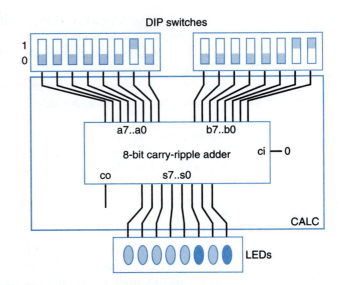

Figure 4.36 8-bit DIP-switch-based adding calculator. The addition 2+3=5 is shown.

rapid blinking of some of the LEDs, until the values have finally propagated through the entire circuit, at which point the output stabilizes and the LEDs display the correct new sum.

If we want to avoid the blinking of the LEDs with the intermittent values, we can introduce a button e (for "equals") to the system, which indicates when the new value should be displayed. We press e only after having configured both DIP switches to represent the new inputs to be summed. We can utilize the e input with a register, as in Figure 4.37. We connect the e input to the load input of a parallel load register. When a user moves switches on the DIP switches, new intermittent values appear at the adder outputs, but are blocked at the register's inputs, as the register holds its previous value and hence the LEDs display that previous value. When the e button is pressed, then on the next clock edge the register will be loaded, and the LEDs will then display the new value.

Notice that the displayed value will be correct only if the sum is 255 or less. We could connect co to a ninth LED to display sums between 256 and 511. ◀

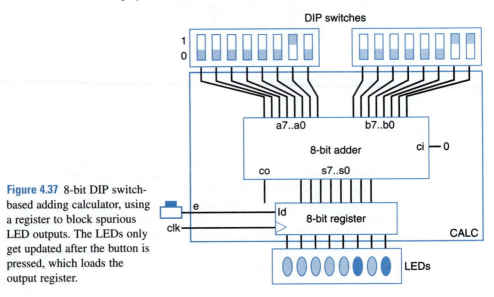

Figure 4.37 8-bit DIP switch-based adding calculator, using a register to block spurious LED outputs. The LEDs only get updated after the button is pressed, which loads the output register.

Delay and Size of an 8-Bit Carry-Ripple Adder

Assuming full-adders are implemented using two levels of gates (ANDs followed by an OR), and that every gate has a delay of 1 ns, let's compute the total delay of a 32-bit carry-ripple adder. Let's also compute the size of such an adder.

To determine the delay, note first that the carry must ripple from the first full-adder to the 32nd full-adder. The delay of the first full-adder is 2 gates * 1 ns/gate = 2 ns. The new carry must now ripple through the second full-adder, resulting in another 2 ns. And so on. Thus, the total delay of the 32-bit carry-ripple adder is 2 ns/full-adder * 32 full-adders = 64 ns.

To determine the size, note that a full-adder requires approximately five gates (we say approximately because the 3-input OR gate in a full-adder requires more transistors than each 2-input AND gates, and the 3-input XOR gate requires even more transistors). Since the 32-bit adder has 32 full-adders, the total size of the 32-bit carry-ripple adder is 5 gates/full-adder * 32 full-adders = 160 gates.

The 32-bit carry-ripple adder has a long delay, but a reasonable number of gates. In Section 6.4, we'll see how to build faster adders, at the expense of using more gates, but still using a reasonable number of gates.

▶ **EXAMPLE 4.9** Compensating weight scale using an adder

A scale, such as a bathroom scale, uses a sensor to determine the weight of an object (e.g., a person) on the scale. The sensor's readings for the same object may change over time, due to wear and tear on the sensing system (such as a spring losing elasticity), resulting perhaps in reporting a weight that is a few pounds too low. Thus, the scale may have a knob that the user can turn to compensate for the low reported weight. The knob indicates the amount to add to a given weight before displaying the weight. Suppose that a knob can be set to change an input compensation amount by a value of 0, 1, 2, ..., 7, as shown in Figure 4.38.

We can implement the system using an 8-bit carry-ripple adder, as shown in the figure. On every rising clock edge, the display register will be loaded with the sum of the currently sensed weight plus the compensation amount. ◀

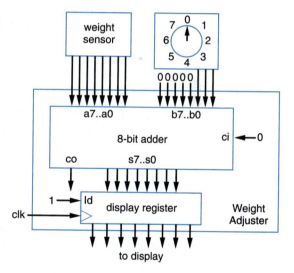

Figure 4.38 Compensating scale: the dial outputs a number from 0 to 7 (000 to 111), which gets added to the sensed weight and then displayed.

▶ **4.4 SHIFTERS**

Shifting is a common operation applied to data. Shifting can be used to manipulate bits, like when we want to reverse the bits of a number. Shifting is useful for communicating data serially, as was done in Example 4.6.

Shifting is also useful for multiplying or dividing by a factor of 2. In base 10, you are familiar with the idea that multiplying by 10 can be done by simply appending a 0 to a number. For example, 5 times 10 is 50. Appending a 0 is the same as shifting left one position. Likewise, in base 2, multiplying by 2 can be done by appending a 0, meaning by shifting left one position. So 0101 times 2 is 1010. Furthermore, in base 10, multiplying by 100 can be done by appending two 0s, or shifting left twice. So in base 2, multiplying by 4 can be done by shifting left twice. Shifting left three times in base 2 is like multiplying by 8. And so on. And since shifting left is the same as multiplying by 2, shifting right is the same as dividing by 2. So 1010 divided by 2 is 0101.

Although shifting can be done using a shift register, sometimes we find the need to use a separate combinational component that performs the shift, and that can shift by different numbers of positions and in different directions.

Simple Shifters

An **N-bit shifter** is a combinational component that can shift an N-bit input by some amount to generate an N-bit output.

The simplest shifter shifts one position in one direction. Say we want a shifter that shifts left by 1 position. That simple shifter's design is straightforward, consisting of just wires, as shown for the 4-bit left shifter Figure 4.39(a). Note that the shifter has an additional input that is the value to shift into the rightmost bit.

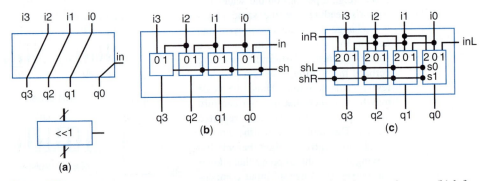

Figure 4.39 Combinational shifters: (a) left shifter with block symbol shown at bottom, (b) left shift or pass component, (c) left/right shift or pass component.

A more advanced shifter can either shift one position when an additional input sh is 1, or can pass the inputs through to the outputs unshifted when sh is 0. We can design that shifter using 2x1 muxes, shown in Figure 4.39(b).

An even more advanced shifter can shift left or right one position, shown in Figure 4.39(c). When both shift control inputs are 0, the inputs pass through unchanged. When shL=1, the shifter shifts left, and when shR=1, the shifter shifts right. When both those control inputs are 1, the shifter could be designed to output 0s by connecting 0s to the I3 inputs of the muxes (not shown). Further extensions of the simple shifter are possible, such as allowing shifts of one position or two positions. Such multifunction shifters' internal designs require larger muxes, and mapping of the control signals to the mux select lines, just as was necessary in designing multifunction registers.

► **EXAMPLE 4.10** Approximate Celsius to Fahrenheit converter using a shifter

We are given a digital thermometer that digitizes a temperature in Celsius into an 8-bit binary number C. So 30 degrees Celsius would be digitized as 00011110. We want to convert that temperature to Fahrenheit, again using 8 bits. The equation for converting is:

```
F = C*9/5 + 32
```

Let's assume that we are not concerned about accuracy, so we'll replace the equation by a simpler one:

```
F = C*2 + 32
```

We can design the converter straightforwardly using a left shifter (with a shift in value of 0) to compute C*2, and then an adder to add 32 (00100000), as in Figure 4.40. ◄

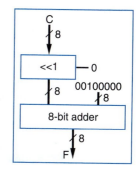

Figure 4.40 Celsius to Fahrenheit converter.

► ***FAHRENHEIT VERSUS CELSIUS.***

The U.S. represents temperature using Fahrenheit, whereas most of the world uses the metric system's Celsius. Presidents and other U.S. leaders have desired to switch to the metric system for almost as long as the U.S. has existed, and several acts have been passed over the centuries, the most recent being the Metric Conversion Act of 1975 (amended several times since). The Act designates the metric system as the preferred system of weights and measures for U.S. trade and commerce. Yet switching to metric has been slow, and few Americans today are comfortable with metric. The problem with such a slow transition was poignantly demonstrated in 1999 when the Mars Climate Orbiter, costing several hundred million dollars, was destroyed when entering the Mars atmosphere too quickly. The reason: "a navigation error resulted from some spacecraft commands being sent in English units instead of being converted to metric units." (Source: www.nasa.gov). Perhaps if all readers of this book in the U.S. use Celsius when they talk, we'll help speed up the transition? So instead of saying "It's a warm ninety degrees outside today," say "It's a warm thirty-two degrees outside today." Actually, we might say "It's a warm three ten and two degrees outside today" (remember correct counting in Chapter 1?).

► **EXAMPLE 4.11** Temperature averager

Recall Example 4.3, in which registers were used to save a history of temperature values over the last three clock periods. We want to extend this system to save the last four values instead of three. We also want the system to compute the average of the last four values and output that average on an output Tavg. The average of four values Ra, Rb, Rc, and Rd is (Ra+Rb+Rc+Rd)/4. Note that dividing by 4 is the same as shifting right by two. Thus, we can design the system using a right shifter that shifts by two places (with a shift in value of 0), as shown in Figure 4.41. ◄

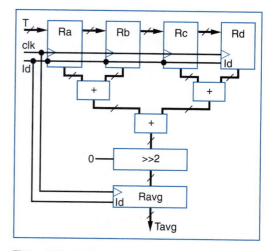

Figure 4.41 Temperature averager using a right-shift-by-2 to divide by 4.

Barrel Shifter

An *N-bit barrel shifter* is a general purpose *N*-bit shifter that can shift or rotate any number of positions. For simplicity, let's consider only left shifts for the moment. An 8-bit barrel shifter can shift left by 1 position, 2 positions, 3 positions, 4 positions, 5 positions, 6 positions, or 7 positions (and of course 0 positions, meaning no shift is done). An 8-bit barrel shifter therefore requires 3 control inputs, say x, y, and z, to specify the distance of the shift. xyz=000 may mean no shift, xyz=001 shift by 1 position, xyz=010 shift by 2 positions, etc.

We could design such a barrel shifter by placing an 8x1 mux in front of each of the 8 shifter outputs, connecting xyz to each of the eight mux's select input, and then connecting the mux inputs with the appropriate shifter inputs for each configuration of x, y, and z. So I0 (corresponding to xyz=000, meaning no shift) of each mux would just get the present bit's shifter input. I1 (corresponding to xyz=001, meaning left shift by one position) would get the shifter input one position to the right. I2 (xyz=010, meaning left shift by two positions) would get the shifter input two positions to the right. And so on.

Such a design, while conceptually straightforward, has too many wires being routed about. And the design does not scale well to larger bit-widths, such as a 32-bit barrel shifter—a 32x1 multiplexor cannot be built with two levels of gates (AND/OR), because gates with 32 inputs are too big to be implemented efficiently, and must instead be implemented using multiple levels of smaller gates.

A more elegant design for an 8-bit barrel shifter consists of 3 cascaded simple shifters, as shown in Figure 4.42. The first simple shifter can shift left four positions (or none), the second can shift left by two positions (or none), and the third by one position (or none). Notice that the shifts "add" to one another—shifting left by two, then by one, results in a total shift of three positions. Thus, by configuring each shifter appropriately, we can obtain a total shift of any amount between zero and seven. Connecting the control inputs xyz to the shifters is easy—just think of xyz as a binary number representing the amount of the shift, x represents shifting by four, y shifting by two, and z shifting by one. So we just connect x to the left-by-four shifter, y to the left-by-two shifter, and z to the left-by-one shifter.

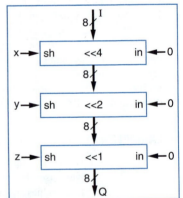

Figure 4.42 8-bit barrel shifter (left shift only).

The above design considered a barrel shifter that could only shift left. We can easily extend the barrel shifter to support both left and right shifts. We would replace the internal left shifters by shifters that could shift left or right, thus each having a control input indicating the direction. The barrel shifter would then have a direction control input also, connected to each internal shifter's direction control input.

Finally, we can easily extend the barrel shifter to support shifts and rotates. We would replace the internal shifters by rotators that could either shift or rotate, thus each having a control input indicating whether to shift or rotate. The barrel shifter would then have a shift-or-rotate control input also, connected to each internal shifter's shift-or-rotate control input.

▶ 4.5 COMPARATORS

We often want to compare two binary numbers to see if they are equal, or if one is greater than the other. For example, we might want to sound an alarm if a thermometer measuring human body temperature reports a temperature greater than 103 degrees Fahrenheit (39.4 degrees Celsius). Comparator components perform such comparison of binary numbers.

Equality (Identity) Comparator

An *N-bit equality comparator* (sometimes called an *identity comparator*) is a datapath component that compares two *N*-bit inputs A and B, setting an output control signal to 1 if the two inputs are equal. Two *N*-bit inputs, say two 4-bit inputs A=a3a2a1a0 and B=b3b2b1b0, are equal if each of their corresponding bit pairs are equal. So A=B if a3=b3, a2=b2, a1=b1, and a0=b0.

Following the combinational logic design process of Table 2.5, we can start by capturing the function of a 4-bit equality comparator as an equation:

```
eq = (a3b3+a3'b3') * (a2b2+a2'b2') * (a1b1+a1'b1') *
     (a0b0+a0'b0')
```

Each term detects if the corresponding bits are equal, namely, if both bits are 1 or both bits are 0. The expressions inside each of the parentheses represent the behavior of an XNOR gate (recall from Chapter 2 that an XNOR gate outputs 1 if the gate's two input bits are equal), so we can replace the above equation by the equivalent equation:

```
eq = (a3 xnor b3) * (a2 xnor b2) * (a1 xnor b1) * (a0
     xnor b0)
```

We convert the equation to the circuit in Figure 4.43.

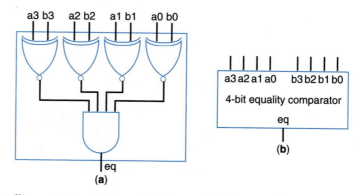

Figure 4.43 Equality comparator: (a) internal design, and (b) block symbol.

Of course, we could have built the comparator starting with a truth table, but that would be cumbersome for a large comparator, with too many rows in the truth table to easily work with by hand. A truth table approach enumerates all the possible situations for which all the bits are equal, since only those situations would have a 1 in the column for the output eq. For two 4-bit numbers, one such situation will be 0000=0000.

Another will be 0001=0001. Clearly, there will be as many situations as there are 4-bit binary numbers—meaning there will be $2^4 = 16$ situations where both numbers are equal. For two 8-bit numbers, there will be 256 equal situations. For two 32-bit numbers, there will be four billion equal situations. A comparator built with such an approach will be large if we don't minimize the equation, and that minimization will be hard with such large numbers of terms. Our XNOR-based design looks to be much simpler and scales to wide inputs wonderfully—widening the inputs by one more bit involves merely adding one more XNOR gate.

Magnitude Comparator—Carry-Ripple Style

An *N-bit magnitude comparator* is a datapath component that compares two *N*-bit binary numbers A and B, and indicates whether A>B, A=B, or A<B.

We have already seen several times that designing certain datapath components by starting with a truth table involves too large of a truth table. Let's instead design a magnitude comparator by considering how we compare numbers by hand. Consider comparing two 4-bit numbers A=a3a2a1a0=1011, B=b3b2b1b0=1001. We start by looking at the high-order bits of A and B, namely, a3 and b3. Since they are equal (both are 1), we look at the next pair of bits, a2 and b2. Again, since they are equal (both are 0), we look at the next pair of bits, a1 and b1. Since a1>b1 (1>0), we conclude that A>B.

Thus, comparing two binary numbers takes place by comparing from the high bit-pairs down to the low bit-pairs. As long as bit-pairs are equal, we need to compare the next lower bit-pair. As soon as a bit-pair is different, we conclude that A>B if ai=1 and bi=0, or that A<B if bi=1 and ai=0. We can thus design a magnitude comparator using the structure shown in Figure 4.44.

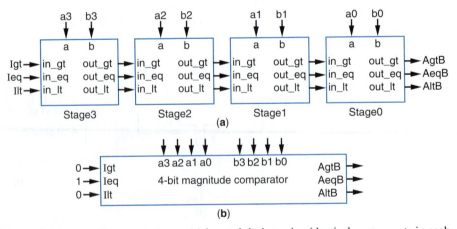

Figure 4.44 4-bit magnitude comparator: (a) internal design using identical components in each stage, and (b) block symbol.

Each stage works as follows. If in_gt=1 (meaning a higher stage determined A>B), this stage need not compare bits, and just sets out_gt=1. Likewise, if in_lt=1 (meaning a higher stage determined A<B), this stage just sets out_lt=1. If in_eq=1 (meaning higher stages were all equal), this stage must compare bits, setting out_gt=1

if a=1 and b=0, setting out_lt=1 if a=0 and b=1, and setting out_eq=1 if a and b both equal 1 or both equal 0.

We could capture the function of a stage's block using a truth table with 5 inputs. For brevity, though, we'll simply use the following equations derived from the earlier explanation of how each stage works; the circuit for each stage would follow directly from these equations:

```
out_gt = in_gt + (in_eq * a * b')
out_lt = in_lt + (in_eq * a' * b)
out_eq = in_eq * (a XNOR b)
```

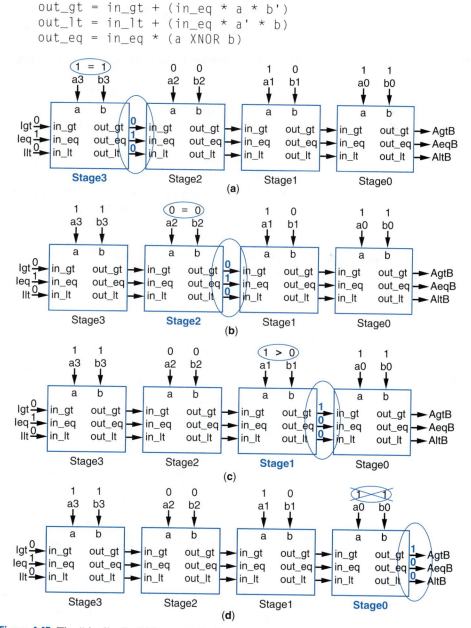

Figure 4.45 The "rippling" within a magnitude comparator.

Figure 4.45 shows how this comparator works for an input of A=1011 and B=1001. We can view the comparator's behavior as consisting of four stages:

- In *Stage3* shown in Figure 4.45(a), we start by setting the external input Ieq=1, to force the comparator to actually do the comparison. *Stage3* has in_eq=1, and since a3=1 and b3=1, then out_eq will become 1, while out_gt and out_lt will become 0.

- In *Stage2* shown in Figure 4.45(b), we see that since out_eq of *Stage3* connects to in_eq of *Stage2*, then *Stage2*'s in_eq will be 1. Since a2=0 and b2=0, then out_eq will become 1, while out_gt and out_lt will be 0.

- In *Stage1* shown in Figure 4.45(c), we see that since *Stage2*'s out_eq is connected to *Stage1*'s in_eq, *Stage1*'s in_eq will be 1. Since a1=1 and b1=0, out_gt will become 1, while out_eq and out_lt will be 0.

- In *Stage0* shown in Figure 4.45(d), we see that the outputs of *Stage1* cause *Stage0*'s in_gt to become 1, which directly causes *Stage0*'s out_gt to become 1, and causes out_eq and out_lt to be 0. Notice that the values of a0 and b0 are irrelevant. Since *Stage0*'s outputs connect to the comparator's external outputs, AgtB will be 1, while AeqB and AltB will be 0.

Because of the way the result ripples through the stages in a manner similar to a carry-ripple adder, a magnitude comparator built this way is often referred to as having a *carry-ripple* style implementation, even though what's rippling is not really a "carry" bit.

The 4-bit magnitude comparator can be connected straightforwardly with another 4-bit magnitude comparator to build an 8-bit magnitude comparator, and likewise to build any size comparator, simply by connecting the comparison outputs of one comparator (AgtB, AeqB, AltB) with the comparison inputs of the next comparator (Igt, Ieq, Ilt).

If each stage is built from two levels of logic, and a gate has a 1 ns delay, then each stage will have a 2 ns delay. So the delay of a carry-ripple style 4-bit magnitude comparator is 4 stages * 2 ns/stage = 8 ns. A 32-bit comparator built with this style will have a delay of 32 stages * 2 ns/stage = 64 ns.

▶ **EXAMPLE 4.12** Computing the minimum of two numbers using a comparator

We want to design a combinational component that takes two 8-bit inputs A and B, and outputs an 8-bit output C that is the minimum of A and B. We can use a magnitude comparator and an 8-bit 2x1 multiplexor to implement this component, as shown in Figure 4.46.

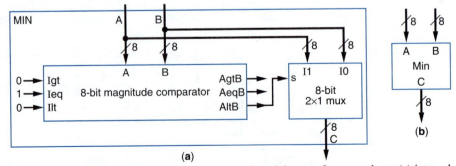

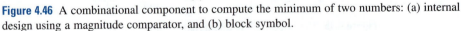

Figure 4.46 A combinational component to compute the minimum of two numbers: (a) internal design using a magnitude comparator, and (b) block symbol.

If A<B, the comparator's A1tB output will be 1. In this case, we want to pass A through the mux, so we connect A1tB to the 8-bit 2x1 mux select input, and A to the mux's I1 input. If A1tB is 0, then either AgtB=1 or AeqB=1. If AgtB=1, we want to pass B. If AeqB=1, we can pass either A or B (since they are identical), and so let's pass B. We thus simply connect B to the I0 input of the 8-bit 2x1 mux. In other words, if A<B, we'll pass A, and if A is not less than B, we'll pass B.

Notice that we set the comparator's Ieq control input to 1, and the Igt and Ilt inputs to 0. These values force the comparator to compare its data inputs. ◄

► 4.6 COUNTERS

An *N-bit counter* is an extended *N*-bit register component that can increment or decrement its own value on each clock cycle, when a count enable control input is 1. *Increment* means to add 1, while *decrement* means to subtract 1. A counter that can increment is known as an *up-counter*, a counter that can decrement is known as a *down-counter*, and a counter that can increment and decrement is known as an *up/down-counter*. A 4-bit up-counter would thus count the following sequence: 0000, 0001, 0010, 0011, 0100, 0101, 0110, 0111, 1000, 1001, 1010, 1011, 1100, 1101, 1110, 1111, 0000, 0001, etc. Notice that a counter *wraps around* (also known as *rolling over*) from the highest value (1111) to 0. Likewise, a down-counter would wrap around from 0 to the highest value. A control output on the counter, often called *terminal count*, or tc, becomes 1 during the clock cycle that the counter has reached its last (terminal) count value, after which the counter will roll over.

Figure 4.47 shows the block symbol of a 4-bit up-counter. When cnt=1, the counter increments its own value on every clock cycle. When cnt=0, the counter maintains its present value. On the cycle that the counter rolls over from 1111 to 0000, the counter sets tc=1 for that cycle, returning tc to 0 on the next cycle.

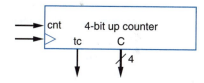

Figure 4.47 4-bit up-counter block symbol.

Up-Counter

We can design an *N*-bit up-counter using the register design process described in Table 4.1—the incremented value of the register would be fed into a mux input, and the counter's control lines would be mapped to the mux select lines. A simpler view of an up-counter design is shown in Figure 4.48, assuming an incrementer component exists to add 1 to the present value. When cnt=0, the register should maintain its present value. When cnt=1, the register should be loaded with its present value plus 1. Note that the 4-input AND gate causes terminal count tc to become 1 when the counter reaches 1111.

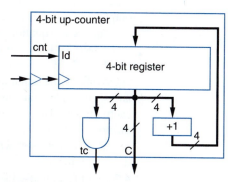

Figure 4.48 4-bit up-counter internal design.

Incrementer

We need to design a combinational circuit for the incrementer. We could simply use an N-bit adder, by setting the B input to 0001 and the carry-in to 0. But using an N-bit adder is overkill—we don't need all the logic involved in an N-bit adder, because B is always just 0001. Instead, observe in Figure 4.49 that adding 1 to a binary number involves only two bits per column, not three bits per column like when adding two general binary numbers.

Recall that a half-adder adds two bits (see Section 4.3). Thus, a simple incrementer could be built using half-adders, as shown in Figure 4.50.

Figure 4.49 Adding 1 to a binary number requires only 2 bits per column.

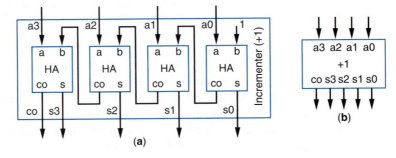

Figure 4.50 4-bit incrementer: (a) internal design, and (b) block symbol.

We could instead design an incrementer using the combinational logic design process from Chapter 2. We would start with a truth table, shown in Figure 4.51. We obtain each output row simply by adding 1 to the corresponding input row binary number. We would then derive an equation for each output. For example, we can easily see that the equation for c0 is c0=a3a2a1a0. We can also easily see that s0=a0'. We would derive equations for the remaining outputs, and then implement the circuit for each output. The resulting incrementer would have a total delay of only two gate levels, which is less delay than the incrementer in Figure 4.50 built from half-adders.

Inputs				Outputs				
a3	a2	a1	a0	c0	s3	s2	s1	s0
0	0	0	0	0	0	0	0	1
0	0	0	1	0	0	0	1	0
0	0	1	0	0	0	0	1	1
0	0	1	1	0	0	1	0	0
0	1	0	0	0	0	1	0	1
0	1	0	1	0	0	1	1	0
0	1	1	0	0	0	1	1	1
0	1	1	1	0	1	0	0	0
1	0	0	0	0	1	0	0	1
1	0	0	1	0	1	0	1	0
1	0	1	0	0	1	0	1	1
1	0	1	1	0	1	1	0	0
1	1	0	0	0	1	1	0	1
1	1	0	1	0	1	1	1	0
1	1	1	0	0	1	1	1	1
1	1	1	1	1	0	0	0	0

Figure 4.51 Truth table for four-bit incrementer.

We could use the same combinational logic design process to build larger incrementers. Recall that we said in Section 4.3 that building adders using the combinational logic design process was not very practical. Yet here we built an incrementer using the combinational logic design process. A key difference to note is that a 4-bit adder has 8 inputs, whereas a 4-bit incrementer has only 4 inputs. Thus, we can build wider incrementers as two-level logic implementations using the combinational logic design process. Of course, at some point, even the number of inputs for an incrementer gets too large, in which case we might chain smaller incrementers together to make a wider incrementer.

► **EXAMPLE 4.13** Up-counter used in the above-mirror display

In Example 4.4 and Example 4.6, we assumed pressing a mode button would cause inputs xy to sequence from 00, 01, 10, 11, and back to 00 again. A simple design to achieve such sequencing, assuming the mode input is 1 for exactly one clock cycle per button press (see Example 3.9), utilizes an up-counter, as shown in Figure 4.52. ◄

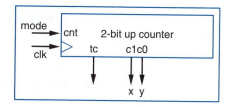

Figure 4.52 Sequencer for xy inputs of above-mirror display.

► **EXAMPLE 4.14** 1 Hz pulse generator using a 256 Hz oscillator

Suppose we have a 256 Hz oscillator, but we want a 1 Hz pulse signal. We can convert the 256 Hz signal to a 1 Hz signal p using an 8-bit counter. The 8-bit counter wraps around every 256 cycles, so we can simply connect the oscillator signal to the counter's clock input, set the counter's load input to 1, and then use the counter's tc output as the pulse signal, as shown in Figure 4.53. A 1 Hz signal may be useful for driving a clock or a watch, for example, since 1 Hz means 1 pulse per second. ◄

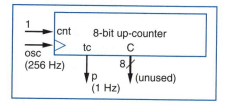

Figure 4.53 Clock divider.

Down-Counter

A down-counter can be designed similarly to an up-counter, replacing the incrementer by a decrementer, as shown for the 4-bit down-counter in Figure 4.54. A decrementer could be designed in a similar manner as an incrementer, starting from a truth table like that in Figure 4.51. Note that the terminal count tc becomes 1 when the down-counter reaches 0000, implemented using a NOR gate—recall that NOR outputs 1 when all its inputs are 0. The reason the down-counter detects 0000 for tc, rather than 1111 like the up-counter, is because a down-counter wraps around after 0000, as in the following count sequence: 0100, 0011, 0010, 0001, **0000**, 1111, 1110, ...

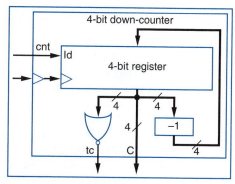

Figure 4.54 4-bit down-counter design.

Up/Down-Counter

An up/down-counter can count either up or down. It requires an input signal dir to indicate the count direction, in addition to the count enable signal cnt. We'll let dir=0 mean to count up and dir=1 mean to count down. Figure 4.55 shows the design of such a 4-bit up/down-counter with synchronous clear. A 2x1 mux passes either the decremented or incremented value, with dir selecting among the two—dir=0 (count up) passes the incremented value and dir=1 (count down) passes the decremented value. The

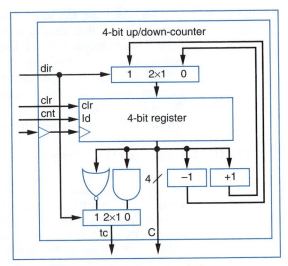

Figure 4.55 4-bit up/down-counter design.

passed value gets loaded into the 4-bit register if cnt=1. dir also selects whether to pass the NOR or AND output to the terminal count tc external output—dir=0 (count up) selects the AND, while dir=1 (count down) selects the NOR.

Alternatively, we could design an up/down-counter using the register design process of Section 4.2, by directly connecting the incrementer and decrementer outputs to muxes in front of each flip-flop, and mapping the clr, cnt, and dir control signals to the mux select lines.

Notice that we also added a control input clr, which we could have added to the up-counter and down-counter too, that when 1 **synchronously clears** the register, meaning resetting the register to all 0s on a rising clock edge. We used a 4-bit register with clear to support the clear operation.

▷ **EXAMPLE 4.15** Light sequencer

We want to design a strip of 8 light bulbs, such that the bulbs illuminate one at a time, right to left, and then repeat illuminating in that sequence. The sequence should proceed at the rate of one bulb per second. Such a lighting display might be attractive outside a restaurant or movie theater, for example.

For simplicity, assume we have an oscillator that generates a 1 Hz clock signal (meaning one rising clock edge per second). We'll connect this clock to a 3-bit up-counter, and connect the counter's three outputs to a 3x8 decoder, as shown in Figure 4.56.

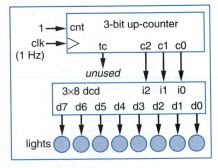

Figure 4.56 Light sequencer.

When the power is on, the system counts up (we don't know what the initial value of the counter was, but it doesn't really matter), wrapping around from 111 to 000. We don't need the tc output in this example.

Notice that we used a *3-bit counter with a decoder*, and *not an 8-bit counter*, even though there were 8 outputs. An 8-bit counter would generate the sequence 00000000, 00000001, 00000010, ..., 11111110, 11111111. That sequence is *not* the desired sequence. ◁

Counter with Parallel Load

Counters often come with the ability to initialize the count value, achieved by loading the counter's register with parallel data. Figure 4.57 shows the design of a 4-bit up-counter with parallel load. When control input ld is 1, the 2x1 mux passes load data input L to the register; when ld is 0, the mux passes the incremented value. Furthermore, we OR the counter's ld and cnt signals to generate the load signal for the register. When cnt is 1, the incremented value will be loaded. When ld is 1, the parallel load data will be loaded. Even if cnt is 0, ld=1 causes the register to be loaded. A down-counter or up/down-counter could similarly be extended to have a parallel load.

Parallel load is useful when we want to generate a pulse signal that is not directly obtainable from letting a counter wrap around and pulse its tc output naturally. An N-bit counter naturally wraps around every 2^N cycles. What if we want a pulse every X cycles, where X is not a

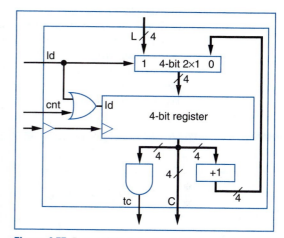

Figure 4.57 Internal design of a 4-bit up-counter with load.

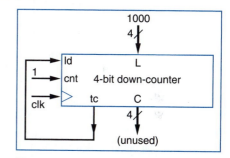

Figure 4.58 A counter setup that pulses tc every 9 cycles.

power of 2? For example, say we have a 4-bit down-counter, which normally pulses the tc output and wraps around every 16 cycles, and suppose we want to pulse every 9 cycles. We can achieve a pulse every 9 cycles by setting the load data input L to 9-1, or 8 (1000), and by connecting the tc output to the load control input ld, as shown in Figure 4.58. When the counter reaches its lowest value (0000), tc will become 1, causing the ld input to become 1. Thus, on the next clock cycle, the counter will load 1000, rather than wrapping around to 1111. (Note: the load occurs on the *next* cycle, not the present cycle, because tc changes to 1 *after* the rising clock edge, so the new value for ld doesn't get seen until the next clock edge.) The counter would thus count in the sequence 8, 7, 6, 5, 4, 3, 2, 1, 0, pulsing tc and then returning to 8. The reason we load 9-1, rather than 9, even though we want a pulse every 9 cycles, is because we must remember that 0 is included in the count sequence—just as the count from 15 down to 0 takes 16 cycles.

We could instead use an up-counter for the same purpose, but we must make the load value equal to the total cycles minus the desired cycles. So for the above example, we would use a load value of 16 - 9 = 7 (0111). The counter would count the sequence 7, 8, 9, 10, 11, 12, 13, 14, 15, pulsing tc and then returning to 7.

▶ **EXAMPLE 4.16**   New Year's Eve countdown display

In Example 2.30, we utilized a microprocessor to output the numbers 59 down to 0, and a decoder to illuminate one of 60 lights based on that output. In this example, we'll replace the microprocessor by a down-counter with parallel load to output 59 down to 0. Suppose we have an 8-bit down-counter available, which can count from 255 down to 0. We need to load 59 and then count down. Assume the user can press a button called reset to load 59 into the counter, and then the user can move a switch countdown from the 0 position (don't count) to the 1 position (count) to begin the countdown. The system implementation is shown in Figure 4.59.

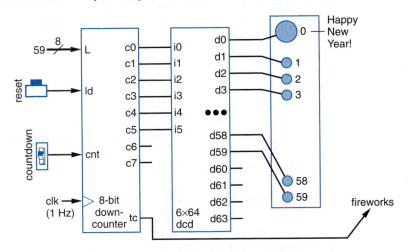

Figure 4.59 Happy New Year countdown system using a down-counter.

Notice that the tc signal is our "Happy New Year" indication. We've connected that signal to an output called fireworks, which we'll assume activates a device that ignites fireworks. Happy New Year! ◀

▶ **EXAMPLE 4.17**   1 Hz pulse generator using a 60 Hz oscillator

In the U.S., electricity to the home operates as an alternating current with a frequency of 60 Hz. Many appliances convert this signal to a 60 Hz digital signal, and then convert the 60 Hz digital signal to a 1 Hz signal, to drive a clock or other device needing to keep track of time at the granularity of seconds. Unlike Example 4.2, we can't simply use a counter of a particular bitwidth, since no basic up-counter wraps around after 60 cycles—a 5-bit counter wraps around every 32 cycles, while a 6-bit counter wraps every 64 cycles. Let's start with a 6-bit counter, which counts from 0 to 63 and then wraps around to 0. We'll add some some extra logic, as shown in Figure 4.60. The extra logic should detect when the counter has counted up to 59, and should clear the counter back to 0 on the next rising clock edge rather than letting the counter continue counting to 60 and beyond. Fifty-nine as a 6-bit binary number is 111011. Thus the AND gate in Figure 4.60 detects 111011, in which case the AND

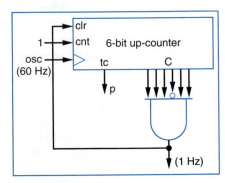

Figure 4.60 Clock divider.

gate output sets the counter clear input to 1. We assume the counter's clear input *clr* takes precedence over the counter's count input *cnt*. Since the AND gate's output will pulse every 60 cycles and the input clock frequency is 60 Hz, this circuit converts a 60 Hz input clock into a 1 Hz output clock. A circuit that converts an input clock into a new clock with a lower frequency is known as a *clock divider*.

◀

Timer

We load 999, rather than 1000, because we must remember that 0 is part of the count. Try counting from 9 down to 0, raising a finger each time you say a number. Notice that when you reach 0, ten fingers are up.

A common use of a counter is as the central component within another device called a timer. A ***timer*** is a special type of counter that measures time. Measuring time is a very common task in a digital system.

One type of timer is based on a down-counter. We store a value into the counter, and wait for the terminal count (0) to be reached. If we know the counter's oscillator frequency, then we can load a value corresponding to a desired time interval. For example, suppose we want to know when one second has passed, using a counter having a clock frequency of 1 kHz. We would thus load 999 (in binary, meaning 1111100111) into the counter and enable counting. After 1 second, the counter would reach 0 and assert its terminal count output, notifying us that 1 second has passed. A timer may repeat this process automatically, using the terminal count to automatically reload the desired time value (999 in our example) into the counter. Such a timer might be used in any type of watch or clock. Our earlier three-cycles-high laser timer (from chapter 3) could have been built using a timer component, especially if instead of wanting the laser high for three cycles, we wanted the laser high for a period of time like 1.5 seconds.

Another type of timer is based on an up-counter. We reset that counter to 0, and then enable counting when some event occurs that we want to time. When the event ends, we disable the counter, after which the counter contains the number of cycles that occurred during the event. Knowing the time of one clock cycle, we multiply the number of cycles by the time of one clock cycle to obtain the total time for the event. For example, if we time an event as lasting 500 clock cycles, and the timer's oscillator frequency is 1 kHz, then the time for the event was 500 cycles * 0.001 s/cycle = 0.5 s. We illustrate this type of timer using an example.

▶ **EXAMPLE 4.18** Highway speed measuring system

Many highways and freeways have systems that measure the speed of cars at various parts of the highway and upload that speed information to a central computer. Such information is used by law enforcement, traffic planners, and radio and Internet traffic reports.

One technique for measuring the speed of a car uses two sensors embedded under the road, as illustrated in Figure 4.61. When a car is over a sensor, the sensor outputs a 1; otherwise, the sensor outputs a 0. A sensor's output travels on underground wires to a speed-measuring computer box, some of which are above the ground and others of which are underground. The speed measurer determines speed by dividing the distance between the sensors (which is fixed and known) by the time required for a vehicle to travel from the first sensor to the second sensor. If the distance between the sensors is 0.01 miles, and a vehicle takes 0.5 seconds to travel from the first to the second sensor, then the vehicle's speed is 0.01 miles / (0.5 seconds * (1 hour / 3600 seconds)) = 72 miles per hour.

To measure the time between the sensors, we can construct a simple FSM that controls a 16-bit timer, as shown in Figure 4.61. State *S0* clears the timer to 0. The FSM transitions to state *S1* when a car passes over the first sensor. *S1* starts the timer counting up. The FSM stays in *S1* until the car

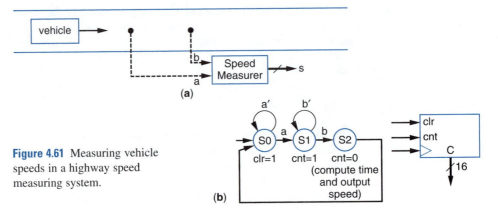

Figure 4.61 Measuring vehicle speeds in a highway speed measuring system.

passes over the second sensor, causing a transition to state *S2*. *S2* stops the counting and computes the time using the timer's output C. Assuming a 1 kHz clock input to the timer, meaning each cycle is 0.001 seconds, then the time would be C * 0.001 s. That result would then be multiplied by 0.01/3600 to obtain the speed. We omit the implementation details of the speed computation, which would most likely be implemented as software on a microprocessor. ◀

▶ HOW DOES IT WORK? CAR SENSORS IN ROADS.

How does a highway speed sensor or a traffic light car sensor know that a car is present in a particular lane? The main method today uses what's called an *inductive loop*. A loop of wire is placed just under the pavement—you can usually see the cuts, as in Figure 4.62(a). That loop of wire has a particular "inductance," which is an electronics term describing the wire's opposition to a change in electric current—higher inductance means the wire has higher opposition to changes in current. It turns out that placing a big hunk of metal (like a car) near the loop of wire changes the wire's inductance. (Why? Because the metal disrupts the magnetic field created by a changing current in the wire—but that's getting beyond our scope.) The traffic light control circuit keeps checking the wire's inductance (perhaps by trying to change the current and seeing how much the current really changes in a certain time period), and if inductance is more than normal, the circuit assumes a car is above the loop of wire.

Many people think that the loops seen in the pavement are scales that measure weight—I've seen bicyclists jumping up and down on the loops trying to get a light to change. That doesn't work, but it sure is entertaining to watch.

Many others believe that small cylinders attached to a traffic light's support arms, like that in Figure 4.62(b), detect vehicles. Those instead are typically devices that detect a special encoded radio or infrared-light signal from emergency vehicles, causing the traffic light to turn green for the emergency vehicle (e.g., 3M's "Opticom" system). Such systems are another example of digital systems, reducing the time needed by emergency vehicles to reach the scene of an emergency as well as reducing accidents involving the emergency vehicle itself proceeding through a traffic light, thus often saving lives.

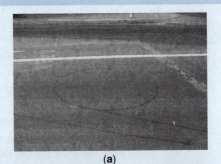

(a)

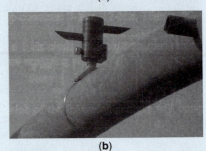

(b)

Figure 4.62 (a) Inductive loop for detecting a vehicle on a road, (b) emergency vehicle signal sensor for changing an intersection's traffic light to green for the approaching emergency vehicle.

An *NxN multiplier* is a datapath component that multiplies two *N*-bit input binary numbers A (the multiplicand) and B (the multiplier), and outputs an (*N*+*N*)-bit result. For example, an 8x8 multiplier multiplies two 8-bit binary numbers and outputs a 16-bit result. Designing an *NxN* multiplier in two levels of logic using the standard combinational design process will result in too complex of a design, as we've already seen for previous operations like addition and comparison. For multipliers with *N* greater than 4 or so, we need a more efficient method.

We can create a reasonably sized multiplier by mimicking how we perform multiplication by hand. Consider multiplying two 4-bit binary numbers 0110 and 0011 by hand:

```
    0110     (the top number is called the multiplicand)
    0011     (the bottom number is called the multiplier)
    ----     (each row below is called a partial product)
    0110     (because the rightmost bit of the multiplier is 1, and 0110*1=0110)
   0110      (because the second bit of the multiplier is 1, and 0110*1=0110)
  0000       (because the third bit of the multiplier is 0, and 0110*0=0000)
 +0000       (because the leftmost bit of the multiplier is 0, and 0110*0=0000)
 --------
 00010010    (the product is the sum of all the partial products: 18, which is 6*3)
```

Each partial product is easily obtained by ANDing the present multiplier bit with the multiplicand. Thus, multiplication of two 4-bit numbers A (a3a2a1a0) and B (b3b2b1b0) can be represented as follows:

```
              a3    a2    a1    a0
         x    b3    b2    b1    b0
    ---------------------------------------
              b0a3  b0a2  b0a1  b0a0          (pp1)
        b1a3  b1a2  b1a1  b1a0    0           (pp2)
  b2a3  b2a2  b2a1  b2a0    0     0           (pp3)
+ b3a3  b3a2  b3a1  b3a0    0     0     0     (pp4)
    ---------------------------------------
p7 p6   p5    p4    p3    p2    p1    p0
```

After generating the partial products (*pp1*, *pp2*, *pp3*, and *pp4*) by ANDing the present multiplier bit with each multiplicand bit, we merely need to sum those partial products together. We can use three adders of varying widths for computing that sum. The resulting design is shown in Figure 4.63.

This design has a reasonable size, about three times bigger than a carry-ripple adder. The design has reasonable speed. The delay consists of 1 gate-delay for generating the partial products, plus the delay of the adders. If each adder is a carry-ripple adder, then the 5-bit adder delay will be 5*2 = 10 gate-delays, the 6-bit adder delay will be 6*2 = 12 gate-delays, and the 7-bit adder delay will be 7*2 = 14 gate-delays. If we assume that the total delay of the adders is simply the sum of the adder delays, then the total delay would thus be 1 + 10 + 12 + 14 = 37 gate-delays. However, the total delay of carry-ripple adders when chained together is actually less than their sum—see Exercise 4.15.

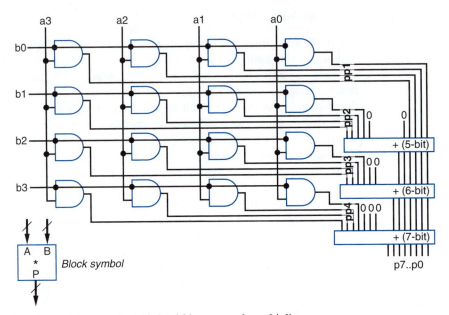

Figure 4.63 Internal design of a 4-bit by 4-bit array-style multiplier.

Delays for larger multipliers, which will have an even longer chain of adders, will be even slower. Faster mutiplier designs are possible, at the expense of more gates.

▶ 4.8 SUBTRACTORS

An *N*-bit ***subtractor*** is a datapath component that takes two *N*-bit binary inputs A and B, and outputs an *N*-bit result S equaling A-B.

Subtractor for Positive Numbers Only

Subtraction gets slightly more complex when we consider negative results, like 5 − 7 = −2, because thus far we haven't discussed representation of negative numbers. For now, let's assume we are only dealing with positive numbers, so the subtractor's inputs are positive, and the result is always positive. This could be the case, for example, when we are designing a system that only subtracts smaller numbers from larger numbers, such as when compensating a sampled temperature that will always be greater than 80 using a small compensation value that will always be less than 10.

Designing an *N*-bit subtractor using the standard combinational logic design process suffers from the same exponential size growth problem as an *N*-bit adder. (See Section 4.3.) Instead, we can again try to mimic subtraction by hand in hardware.

Figure 4.64 shows subtraction of 4-bit binary numbers "by hand." Starting with the first column, we see that a is less than b (0 < 1), necessitating a borrow from the previous column. The first column result is then 10 − 1 = 1 (in base ten, two minus one equals one). The second column has a 0 for a because of the borrow by the first column, making a < b (0 < 1), generating a borrow from the third column—which must itself borrow from the fourth column. The result of the second column is then $10 - 1 = 1$. The third column, because of the borrow generated by the second column, has an a of 1, which is not less than b, so the result of the third column is $1-1=0$. The fourth column has $a=0$ due to the borrow from the third column, and since b is also 0, the result is $0-0=0$.

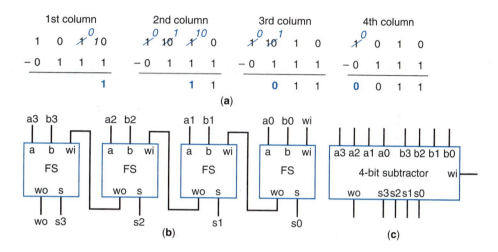

Figure 4.64 Design of a 4-bit subtractor: (a) subtraction "by hand", (b) borrow-ripple implementation with four full-subtractors with a borrow-in input wi, and (c) block symbol.

Based on the above-described behavior, we could create the internal design of a full-subtractor combinational component to implement the behavior of each column, with a full-subtractor having an input wi representing a borrow by the previous column, and an output wo representing a borrow from the next column, in addition to the inputs a and b and the output s. (We use w's for the borrows rather than b's because b is already used for the input; the w comes from the end of the word borrow.) We leave the design of a full-subtractor as an exercise for the reader.

► **EXAMPLE 4.19**   DIP-switch-based adding/subtracting calculator

In Example 4.8, we designed a simple calculator that could add two 8-bit binary numbers and produce an 8-bit result, using DIP switches for inputs, and a register plus LEDs for output. Let's extend that calculator to allow the user to choose among addition and subtraction operations. We'll introduce a single-switch DIP switch that sets a signal f (for "function") as another system input. When $f=0$, the calculator should add; when $f=1$, the calculator should subtract.

One implementation of this calculator would use an adder, a subtractor, and a multiplexor, as in Figure 4.65. The f input chooses which component, the adder or subtractor, to pass through the mux to the register inputs. When the user presses e, either the addition or subtraction result gets loaded into the register and displayed at the LEDs.

This example assumes the result of a subtraction is always a positive number, never negative. It also assumes that the result is always between 0 and 255.

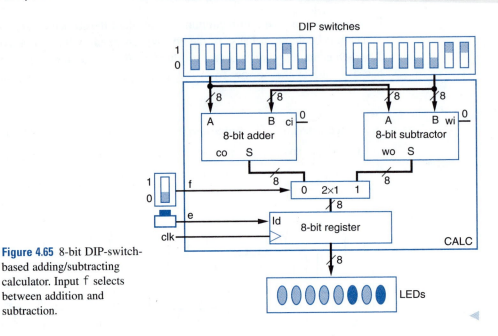

Figure 4.65 8-bit DIP-switch-based adding/subtracting calculator. Input f selects between addition and subtraction.

▶ **EXAMPLE 4.20**   Color space converter—RGB to CMYK

Computer monitors, digital cameras, scanners, printers, and other electronic devices deal with color images. Those devices treat an image as millions of tiny **pixels** (short for "picture elements"), which are indivisible dots representing a tiny part of the image. Each pixel has a color, so an image is just a collection of colored pixels. A good computer monitor may support over 10 million unique colors for each pixel. How does a monitor create each unique color for a pixel? In a common method used in what are known as RGB monitors, the monitor has three light sources inside—red, green, and blue. Any color of light can be created by adding specific intensities of each of the three colors. Thus, for each pixel, the monitor shines a specific intensity of red, of green, and of blue at that pixel's location on the monitor's screen, so that the three colors add together to create the desired pixel color. Each subcolor (red, green, or blue) is typically represented as an 8-bit binary number (thus each ranging from 0 to 255), meaning a color is represented by 8+8+8=24 bits. An (R, G, B) value of (0, 0, 0) represents black. (10, 10, 10) represents a very dark gray, while (200, 200, 200) represents a light gray. (255, 0, 0) represents red, while (100, 0, 0) represents a darker (nonintense) red. (255, 255, 255) represents white. (109, 35, 201) represents some mixture of the three base colors. Representing color using intensity values for red, green, and blue is known as an **RGB color space**.

RGB color space is great for computer monitors and certain other devices, but not the best for some other devices, like printers. Mixing red, green, and blue ink on paper will not result in white, but rather in black. Why? Because ink is not light; rather, ink reflects light. So red ink *reflects* red light, absorbing green and blue light. Likewise, green ink absorbs red and blue light. Blue ink absorbs red and green light. Mix all three inks together on paper, and the mixture absorbs *all* light, reflecting none, thus yielding black. Printers therefore use a different color space based on the complementary colors of red/green/blue, namely, cyan/magenta/yellow, known as a **CMY color space**. Cyan ink *absorbs* red, reflecting green and blue (the mixture of which is cyan). Magenta ink *absorbs* green light, reflecting red and blue (which is magenta). Yellow ink *absorbs* blue, reflecting red and green (which is yellow).

Notice that a color printer may have three color ink cartridges, one cyan, one magenta, and one yellow. Figure 4.66 shows the ink cartridges for a particular color printer. Some printers have a single cartridge for color instead of three, with that single cartridge internally containing separated fluid compartments for the three colors.

A printer must convert a received RGB image into CMY. Let's design a fast circuit to perform that conversion. Given three 8-bit values for R, G, and B for a particular pixel, the equations for C, M, and Y are simply:

```
C = 255 - R
M = 255 - G
Y = 255 - B
```

(255 is the maximum value of an 8-bit number). A circuit to perform such conversion can be built using subtractors, as shown in Figure 4.67.

Actually, the conversion needs to be slightly more complex. Ink isn't perfect, meaning that mixing cyan, magenta, and

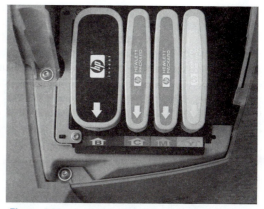

Figure 4.66 A color printer mixes cyan, magenta, and yellow inks to create any color. The picture shows inside a color printer having those three colors' cartridges on the right, labeled C, M, and Y. Such printers may use black ink directly (the big cartridge on the left), rather than mixing the three colors, to make grays and blacks, in order to create a better-looking black and to conserve the more expensive color inks.

yellow yields a black that doesn't look as black as you might expect. Furthermore, colored inks are expensive compared to black ink. Therefore, color printers use black ink whenever possible. One way to maximize use of black ink is to factor out the black from the C, M, and Y values. In other words, a (C, M, Y) value of (250, 200, 200) can be thought of as (200, 200, 200) plus (50, 0, 0).

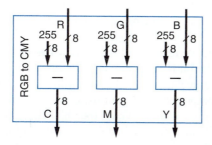

Figure 4.67 RGB to CMY converter.

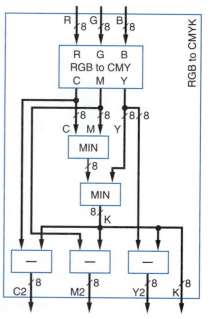

Figure 4.68 RGB to CMYK converter.

The (200, 200, 200), which is a light gray, can be generated using black ink. The remaining (50, 0, 0) can be generated using a small amount of cyan, and using no magenta or yellow ink at all, thus saving precious color ink. A CMY color space extended with black is known as a **CMYK color space** (the "K" comes from the last letter in the word "black." "K" is used instead of "B" to avoid confusion with the "B" from "blue").

An RGB to CMYK converter can thus be described as:

```
K = Minimum (C, M, Y)
C2 = C - K
M2 = M - K
Y2 = Y - K
```

where C, M, and Y are defined as earlier. We thus create the circuit in Figure 4.68 for converting an RGB color space to a CMYK color space. We've used the *RGBtoCMY* component from Figure 4.67. We've also used two instances of the *MIN* component that we created in Example 4.12 to compute the minimum of two numbers; using two such components computes the minimum of three numbers. Finally, we use three more subtractors to remove the K value from the C, M, and Y values. In a real printer, the imperfections of ink and paper require even more adjustments. A more realistic color space converter multiplies the R, G, and B values by a series of constants, which can be described using matrices:

$$
|C|\quad |m00\ m01\ m02|\quad |R|
$$
$$
|M| = |m10\ m11\ m12| * |G|
$$
$$
|Y|\quad |m20\ m21\ m22|\quad |B|
$$

Further discussion of such a matrix-based converter is beyond the scope of this example. ◀

Representing Negative Numbers: Two's Complement

The subtractor design in the previous section assumed we only dealt with positive input numbers and positive results. But in many systems, we may obtain results that are negative, and in fact, our input values may even be negative numbers. We thus need a way to represent negative numbers using bits.

One obvious but not very effective representation is known as **signed-magnitude**. In this representation, the highest-order bit is used only to represent the number's sign, with 0 meaning positive and 1 meaning negative. The remaining low-order bits represent the magnitude of the number. In this representation, and using 4-bit numbers, 0111 would represent +7, while 1111 would represent –7. Thus, four bits could represent –7 to 7. (Notice, by the way, that both 0000 and 1000 would represent 0, the former representing 0, the latter ⁻0.) Signed-magnitude is easy for humans to understand, but doesn't lend itself easily to the design of simple arithmetic components like adders and subtractors. For example, if an adder's inputs use signed-magnitude representation, the adder would have to look at the highest-order bit, and then internally perform either an addition or a subtraction, using different circuits for each.

Instead, the most common method of representing negative numbers and performing subtraction in a digital system actually uses a trick that allows us to *use an adder to perform subtraction*. Using an adder to perform subtraction would enable us to keep our simple adder, and to use the same component for both addition and subtraction.

The key to performing subtraction using addition lies in what are known as *complements*. We'll first introduce complements in the base ten number system just so you can

We are introducing ten's complement just for intuition purposes—we'll actually be using two's complement.

familiarize yourself with the concept, but bear in mind that the intention is to use complements in base two, not base ten.

Consider subtraction involving two single-digit base ten numbers, say 7 – 4. The result should be 3. Let's define the **complement** of a single-digit base ten number A as *the number that when added to A results in a sum of ten*. So the complement of 1 is 9, of 2 is 8, and so on. Figure 4.69 provides the complements for the numbers 1 through 9.

The wonderful thing about a complement is that you can use it to perform subtraction using addition, by replacing the number being subtracted with its complement, then by adding, and then by finally throwing away the carry. For example:

$$7 - 4 \longrightarrow 7 + 6 = 13 \longrightarrow \cancel{1}3 = 3$$

1	→	9
2	→	8
3	→	7
4	→	6
5	→	5
6	→	4
7	→	3
8	→	2
9	→	1

Figure 4.69 Complements in base ten.

We replaced 4 by its complement, 6, and then added 6 to 7 to obtain 13. Finally, we then threw away the carry, leaving 3, which is the correct result. Thus, *we performed subtraction using addition*.

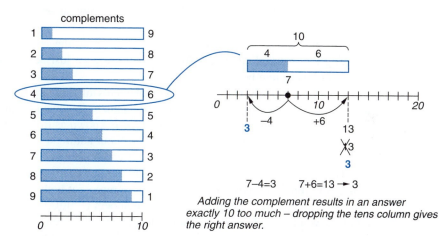

Adding the complement results in an answer exactly 10 too much – dropping the tens column gives the right answer.

Figure 4.70 Subtracting by adding—subtracting a number (4) is the same as adding the number's complement (6) and then dropping the carry, since by definition of the complement, the result will be exactly 10 too much. After all, that's how the complement was defined—the number plus its complement equals 10.

A number line helps us visualize why complements work, as shown in Figure 4.70.

Complements work for any number of digits. Say we want to perform subtraction using two two-digit base ten numbers, perhaps 55 – 30. The complement of 30 would be the number that when added to 30 results in 100, so the complement of 30 is 70. 55 + 70 is 125. Throwing away the carry yields 25, which is the correct result for 55 – 30.

So using complements achieves subtraction using addition.

"Not so fast!" you might say. In order to determine the complement, don't we have to perform subtraction? We know that 6 is the complement of 4 by computing 10 – 4 = 6. We know that 70 is the complement of 30 by computing 100 – 30 = 70. So haven't we just moved the subtraction to another step—the step of computing the complement?

Yes. Except, it turns out that *in base two, we can compute the complement in a much simpler way—just by inverting all the bits and adding 1.* For example, consider computing the complement of the 3-bit base-two number 001. The complement would be the number that when added to 001 yields 1000—you can probably see that the complement should be 111. Using the same method for computing the complement as we did in base ten, we compute the two's complement of 001 as: 1000 - 001 = 111—so 111 is the complement of 001. However, it just so happens that if we invert all the bits of 001 and add 1, we get the same result! Inverting the bits of 001 yields 110; adding 1 yields 110+1 = 111—the correct complement.

Thus, to perform a subtraction, say 011 – 001, we would perform the following:

```
011 – 001
—> 011 + ((001)'+1)
= 011 + (110+1)
= 011 + 111
= 1010  (throw away the carry)
—> 010
```

That's the correct answer, and didn't involve any subtractions—only an invert and additions.

We omit discussion as to why one can compute the complement in base two by inverting the bits and adding 1—for our purposes, we just need to know that that trick works for binary numbers.

There are actually two types of complements of a binary number. The type we've been using above is known as the **two's complement,** obtained by inverting all the bits of the binary number and adding 1. Another type is known as the **one's complement,** which is obtained simply by inverting all the bits, without adding a 1. The two's complement is much more commonly used in digital circuits and results in simpler logic.

Two's complement leads to a simple way to represent negative numbers. Say we have four bits to represent numbers, and we want to represent both positive and negative numbers. We can choose to represent positive numbers as 0000 to 0111 (0 to 7). Negative numbers would be obtained by taking the two's complement of the positive numbers, because a – b is the same as a + (–b). So –1 would be represented by taking the two's complement of 0001, or (0001)'+1 = 1110+1 = 1111. Likewise, -2 would be (0010)'+1 = 1101+1 = 1110. -3 would be (0011)'+1 = 1100+1 = 1101. And so on. –7 would be (0111)'+1 = 1000+1 = 1001. Notice that the two's complement of 0000 is 1111+1 = 0000. Two's complement representation has only one representation of 0, namely, 0000 (unlike signed-magnitude representation, which had two representations of 0). Also notice that we can represent –8 as 1000. So two's complement is slightly asymmetric, representing one more negative number than positive numbers. A 4-bit two's-complement number can represent any number from –8 to +7.

Say you have 4-bit numbers and you want to store –5. –5 would be (0101)'+1 = 1010+1 = 1011. Now you want to add –5 to 4 (or 0100). So we simply add: 1011 + 0100 = 1111, which is –1—the correct answer.

Note that negative numbers all have a 1 in the highest-order bit; thus, the highest-order bit in two's complement is often referred to as the **sign bit**, 0 indicating a positive number, 1 a negative number.

If you want to know the magnitude of a two's complement negative number, you can obtain the magnitude by taking the two's complement again. So to determine what number 1111 represents, we can take the two's complement of 1111: (1111)'+1 = 0000+1 = 0001. We put a negative sign in front to yield –0001, or –1.

A quick way for humans to mentally figure out the magnitude of a negative number in 4-bit two's complement (having a 1 in the high order bit) is to subtract the magnitude of the three lower bits from 8. So for 1111, the low three bits are 111 or 7, so the magnitude is 8 – 7 = 1, which in turn means that 1111 represents –1. For an 8-bit two's complement number, we would subtract the magnitude of the lower 7 bits from 128. So 10000111 would be –(128–7) = –121.

To summarize, we can represent negative numbers using two's complement representation. Addition of two's complement numbers proceeds unmodified—we just add the numbers. Even if one or both numbers are negative, we simply add the numbers. We perform subtraction of A – B by taking the two's complement of B and then adding that two's complement to A, resulting in A + (–B). We compute the two's complement of B by simply inverting the bits of B and then adding 1.

Building a Subtractor Using an Adder and Two's Complement

With knowledge of the two's complement representation, we can now see how to subtract using an adder. To compute A – B, we compute A + (–B), which is the same as A + B' + 1 because –B can be computed as B'+1 in two's complement. Thus, to perform subtraction, we invert B, and input a 1 to the carry-in of an adder, as shown in Figure 4.71.

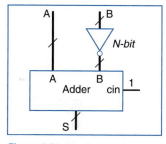

Figure 4.71 Two's complement subtractor built with an adder.

Adder/Subtractor

We can straightforwardly design an adder/subtractor component, having an input sub, such that when sub=1, the component subtracts, but when sub=0, the component adds, as shown in Figure 4.72(a). The *N*-bit 2x1 multiplexor passes B when sub=0, and passes B' when sub=1. sub is connected to cin also, so that cin is 1 when subtracting. Actually, XORs can be used instead of the inverters and mux, as shown in Figure 4.72(b). When sub=0, the output of XOR equals the other input's value. When sub=1, the output of the XOR is the inverse of the other input's value.

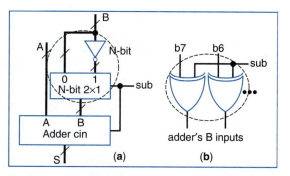

Figure 4.72 (a) Two's complement adder/subtractor using a mux, and (b) alternative circuit for B using XOR gates.

▷ **EXAMPLE 4.21**   DIP-switch-based adding/subtracting calculator (continued)

Let's revisit our DIP-switch-based adding/subtracting calculator of Example 4.19. Observe that at any given time, the output displays the results of either the adder or subtractor, but never both simultaneously. Thus, we really don't need both an adder and a subtractor operating in parallel; instead, we can use a single adder/subtractor component. Assuming DIP switches have been set, setting f=0 (add) versus f=1 (subtract) should result in the following computations:

```
00001111 + 00000001 (f=0) = 00010000
00001111 - 00000001 (f=1) = 00001111 + 11111110 + 1 =
   00001110
```

We achieve this simply by connecting f to the sub input of the adder/subtractor, as shown in Figure 4.73.

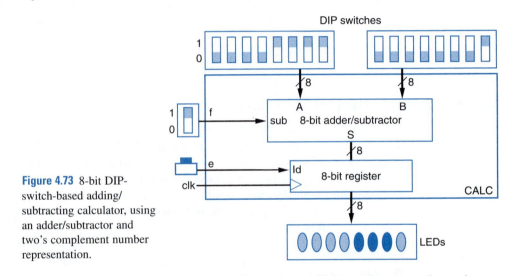

Figure 4.73 8-bit DIP-switch-based adding/subtracting calculator, using an adder/subtractor and two's complement number representation.

Let's consider signed numbers using two's complement. If the user is unaware that two's complement representation is being used and the user will only be inputting positive numbers using the DIP switches, then the user should only use the low-order 7 switches of the 8-switch DIP inputs, leaving the eighth switch in the 0 position, meaning the user can only input numbers ranging from 0 (00000000) to 127 (01111111). The reason the user can't use the eighth bit is that in two's complement representation, making the highest-order bit a 1 causes the number to represent a negative number.

If the user is aware of two's complement, then the user could use the DIP switches to represent negative numbers too, from –1 (11111111) down to –128 (10000000). Of course, the user will need to check the leftmost LED to determine whether the output represents a positive number or a negative number in two's complement form. ◀

Detecting Overflow

When we perform arithmetic using binary numbers of a fixed bitwidth, sometimes the result is wider than the fixed bitwidth, a situation known as **overflow**. For example, consider adding two 4-bit binary numbers (just regular binary numbers for now, not two's complement numbers) and storing the result as another 4-bit number. Adding 1111 + 0001 yields a result of 10000—a 5-bit number, which is bigger than the 4 bits we have to store the result. In other words, 15 + 1 = 16, and 16 requires 5 bits to represent in binary. We can easily detect overflow when adding two binary numbers simply by looking at the carry-out bit of the adder—if the carry-out bit is 1, overflow has occurred. So a 4-bit adder adding 1111 + 0001 would output 1 + 0000, where the 1 is the carry out—indicating overflow.

When using two's complement numbers, detecting overflow is somewhat more complicated. Suppose again we have 4-bit numbers but now those numbers are in two's complement form. Consider the addition of two positive numbers, such as 0111 and 0001 in Figure 4.74(a). A 4-bit adder would output 1000, but that is incorrect—the result of 7 + 1 should be 8, but 1000 represents –8 in two's complement. The problem is that the largest positive number we can represent in 4-bit two's comple-

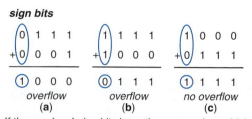

sign bits

If the numbers' sign bits have the same value, which differs from the result's sign bit, overflow has occurred.

Figure 4.74 Two's complement overflow detection comparing sign bits: (a) when adding two positive numbers, (b) when adding two negative numbers, (c) no overflow.

ment form is 7. Thus, when adding two positive numbers, we can detect overflow by checking whether the most significant bit is a 1 in the result.

Likewise, consider the addition of two negative numbers, such as 1111 and 1000 in Figure 4.74(b). An adder would output a sum of 0111 (and a carry out of 1). 0111 is incorrect: −1 + −8 should be −9, but 0111 is +7. The problem is that the most negative number we can represent with 4-bit two's complement is −8. Thus, when adding two negative numbers, we can detect overflow by checking whether the most significant bit is a 0 in the result.

Notice that adding a positive with a negative, or a negative with a positive, can never result in overflow. The result will always be less negative than the most negative number, or less positive than the most positive number. For example, the extreme is the addition of −8 + 7, which is −1. Increasing −8 or decreasing 7 in that addition still results in a number between −8 and 7.

So detecting overflow in two's complement involves detecting that both input numbers were positive but yielded a negative result, or that both input numbers were negative but yielded a positive result. Restated, detecting overflow in two's complement involves detecting that the sign bits of both inputs are the same as one another but differ from the result's sign bit. If we call the sign bit of one input a and the sign bit of the other input b, and the sign bit of the result r, then the following equation outputs 1 when there is overflow:

```
overflow = abr' + a'b'r
```

Although the circuit implementing the above overflow detection equation is quite simple and intuitive, we can create an even simpler circuit if our adder generates a carry-out. The simpler method merely compares the carry into the sign bit column with the carry out of the sign bit column—if the carry in and carry out differ, overflow has occurred.

Figure 4.75 illustrates this method for several cases. In Figure 4.75(a), the carry into the sign bit is 0, whereas the carry out is 0. Because the carry in and carry out differ, overflow has occurred. A circuit detecting whether two bits differ is just an XOR gate, which is slightly simpler than the circuit of the previous method. We omit discussion as to why this method works, but looking at the cases in Figure 4.75 should help provide the intuition.

```
  1 1 1          0 0 0          0 0 0
  0 1 1 1        1 1 1 1        1 0 0 0
+ 0 0 0 1      + 1 0 0 0      + 0 1 1 1
───────────    ───────────    ───────────
0 1 0 0 0      1 0 1 1 1      0 1 1 1 1
  overflow       overflow      no overflow
    (a)            (b)            (c)
```

If the carry into the sign bit column differs from the carry out of that column, overflow has occurred.

Figure 4.75 Two's complement overflow detection comparing carry into and out of the sign bit column: (a) when adding two positive numbers, (b) when adding two negative numbers, (c) no overflow.

▶ *WHY SUCH CHEAP CALCULATORS?*

Several earlier examples dealt with designing simple calculators. Cheap calculators, costing less than a dollar, are easy to find. Calculators are even given away for free by many companies selling something else. But a calculator internally contains a chip implementing a digital circuit, and chips normally aren't cheap. Why are some calculators such a bargain?

The reason is known as *economy of scale*, which means that products are often cheaper when produced in large volumes. Why? Because the design and setup costs can be amortized over larger numbers. Suppose it costs $1,000,000 to design a custom calculator chip and to setup the chip's manufacturing (not so unreasonable a number)—design and setup costs are often called *nonrecurring engineering*, or *NRE*, costs. If you plan to produce and sell one such chip,

then you need to add $1,000,000 to the selling price of that chip if you want to break even (meaning to recover your design and setup costs) when you sell the chip. If you plan to produce and sell 10 such chips, then you need to add $1,000,000/10 = $100,000 to the selling price of each chip. If you plan to produce and sell 1,000,000 such chips, then you need to add only $1,000,000/1,000,000 = $1 to the selling price of each chip. And if you plan to produce and sell 10,000,000, you need to add a mere $1,000,000/10,000,000 = $0.10 = 10 cents to the selling price of each chip. If the actual raw materials only cost 20 cents per chip, and you add another 10 cents per chip for profit, then I can buy the chip from you for a mere 40 cents. And I can then give away such a calculator for free, as many companies do, as an incentive for people to buy something else.

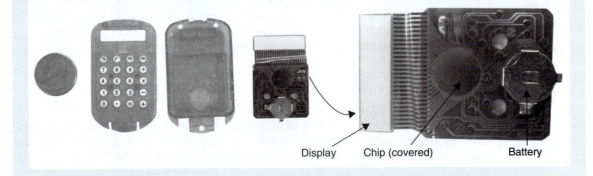

Display   Chip (covered)   Battery

► 4.9 ARITHMETIC-LOGIC UNITS—ALUS

An *N-bit arithmetic-logic unit (ALU)* is a datapath component able to perform a variety of arithmetic and logic operations on two *N*-bit wide data inputs, generating an *N*-bit data output. Example arithmetic operations include addition and subtraction. Example logic operations include AND, OR, XOR, etc. Control inputs to the ALU indicate which particular operation to perform.

To understand the need for an ALU component, consider Example 4.22.

► EXAMPLE 4.22 Multi-function calculator without using an ALU

Let's extend our earlier DIP-switch-based calculator to support eight operations, determined by a three-switch DIP switch that provides three inputs x, y, and z to our system, as shown in Figure 4.76. For each combination of the three switches, we want to perform the operations shown in Table 4.2, on the 8-bit data inputs A and B, generating the 8-bit output on S.

TABLE 4.2 Desired calculator operations

Inputs			Operation	Sample output if A=00001111, B=00000101
x	y	z		
0	0	0	S = A + B	S=00010100
0	0	1	S = A - B	S=00001010
0	1	0	S = A + 1	S=00010000
0	1	1	S = A	S=00001111
1	0	0	S = A AND B (bitwise AND)	S=00000101
1	0	1	S = A OR B (bitwise OR)	S=00001111
1	1	0	S = A XOR B (bitwise XOR)	S=00001010
1	1	1	S = NOT A (bitwise complement)	S=11110000

The table includes several bitwise operations (AND, OR, XOR, and complement). A *bitwise* operation applies to each corresponding pair of bits of A and B separately.

We can design a circuit for our calculator as shown in Figure 4.76, using a separate datapath component to compute each operation: we use an adder to compute the addition, a subtractor to compute the subtraction, an incrementer to compute the increment, and so on. However, that circuit is very inefficient with respect to the number of wires, power consumption, or delay. There are too many wires that must be routed to all those components, and especially to the mux, which will have 8*8 = 64 inputs. Furthermore, every operation is computed all the time, which wastes power. Imagine instead that we were dealing not with 8-bit numbers, but instead with 32-bit numbers, and we wanted to support not just 8 operations but 32 operations. Then we would have even more wires (32*32 = 1024 wires at the mux inputs), and even more power consumption. Furthermore, a 32x1 mux will require several levels of gates, because due to practical reasons, a 32-input logic gate (inside the mux) will likely need to be implemented using several levels of smaller logic gates.

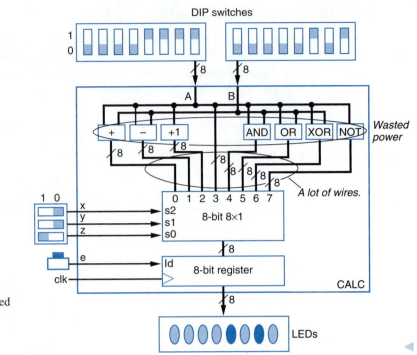

Figure 4.76 8-bit DIP-switch-based multifunction calculator, using separate components for each function.

We saw in the above example that using separate components for each operation is not efficient. To solve the problem, we observe that the calculator can only be configured to do one operation at a time, so there is no need to compute all the operations in parallel as was done in the example. Instead, we can create a single component (an ALU) that can compute any of the eight operations. Such a component would be more area and power efficient, and would have less delay because a large mux would not be needed.

Let's start with an adder as our base internal ALU design. To avoid confusion, we'll call the inputs to the internal adder IA and IB, short for "internal A" and "internal B," to distinguish those inputs from the external ALU inputs A and B. We start with the design shown in Figure 4.77(a). The ALU consists of an adder, and some logic in front of the adder's inputs. We'll call that logic an arithmetic/logic extender, or *AL-extender*. The purpose of the *AL-extender* is to set the adder's inputs based on the values of the ALU's

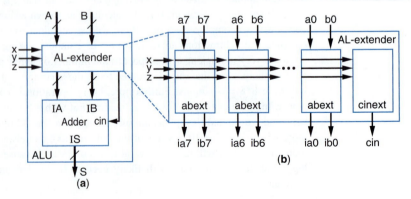

Figure 4.77 Arithmetic-logic unit: (a) ALU design based on a single adder, with an arithmetic/logic extender, and (b) arithmetic/logic extender detail.

control inputs x, y, and z, such that the desired arithmetic or logic result appears at the adder's output. The *AL-extender* actually consists of eight identical components labeled *abext*, one for each pair of bits a i and b i, as shown in Figure 4.77(b). It also has a component *cinext* to compute the c i n bit.

Thus, we need to design the *abext* and *cinext* components to complete the ALU design. Consider the first four calculator operations from Table 4.2, which are all arithmetic operations:

- When xyz=000, S=A+B. So in that case, we want IA=A, IB=B, and cin=0.
- When xyz=001, S=A-B. So we want IA=A, IB=B', and cin=1.
- When xyz=010, S=A+1. So we want IA=A, IB=0, and cin=1.
- When xyz=011, S=A. So we want IA=A, IB=0, and cin=0. Notice that A will pass through the adder, because A+0+0=A.

The last four ALU operations are all logical operations. We can compute the desired operation in the *abext* component, and input the result to IA. We then set IB to 0 and cin to 0, so that the value on IA passes through the adder unchanged.

One possible design of *abext* places an 8x1 mux in front of each output of the *abext* and *cinext* components, with x, y, and z as the select inputs, in which case we would set each mux data input as described above. A more efficient and faster design would create a custom circuit for each component output. We leave the completion of the internal design of the *abext* and *cinext* components as an exercise for the reader.

Example 4.23 redesigns the multifunction calculator of Example 4.22, this time utilizing an ALU.

▶ EXAMPLE 4.23 Multi-function calculator using an ALU

Example 4.22 built an eight-function calculator without an ALU. The result was wasted area and power, complex wiring, and long delay. Using the above-designed ALU, the calculator could instead be built as shown in Figure 4.78. Notice the simple and efficient design.　　　◀

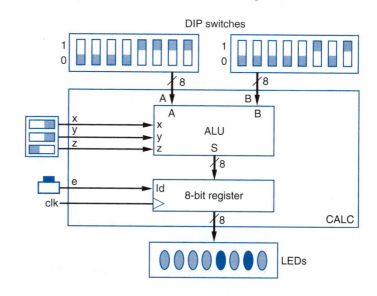

Figure 4.78 8-bit DIP-switch-based multi-function calculator, using an ALU.

▶ 4.10 REGISTER FILES

An *MxN register file* is a datapath memory component that provides efficient access to a collection of *M* registers, where each register is *N* bits wide. To understand the need for a register file component in building good datapaths, rather than just using *M* separate registers, consider Example 4.24.

▶ **EXAMPLE 4.24**   Above-mirror display system using 16 32-bit registers

Recall the above-mirror display system from Example 4.4. Four 8-bit registers were multiplexed to an 8-bit output. Suppose instead that the system required sixteen 32-bit registers, to display more values, each of more precision. We would therefore need a 32-bit-wide 16x1 multiplexor, as shown in Figure 4.79. From a purely digital logic perspective, the design is just fine. But in practice, that multiplexor is very inefficient. Count the number of wires that would be fed into that multiplexor—16x32 = 512 wires. That's a lot of wires to try to route from the registers to the muxes—try plugging 512 wires into the back of one stereo system for a hands-on demonstration. Having too many wires in a small area is known as *congestion*.

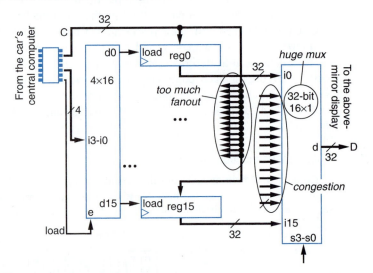

Figure 4.79 Above-mirror display design, assuming sixteen 32-bit registers. The mux has too many input wires, resulting in congestion. Also, the data lines C are fanned out to too many registers, resulting in weak current.

Likewise, consider routing the data input to all sixteen registers. Each data input wire is being branched into sixteen subwires. Imagine electric current being like a river of water—branching a main river into sixteen smaller rivers will yield much less water flow in each smaller river than in the main river. Likewise, branching a wire, known as *fanout*, can only be done so many times before the branched wires' currents are too small to sufficiently control transistors. Furthermore, low-current wires may be very slow also, so fanout can create long delays over wires too.   ◀

The fanout and congestion problems illustrated in the previous example can be solved by observing that we never need to load more than one register at a time, and that we never need to read more than one register at a time either. An *MxN* register file solves the fanout and congestion problems by grouping the *M* registers into a single component, with that component having a single *N*-bit wide data input, and a single *N*-bit wide data output. The wiring inside the component is done carefully to handle fanout and congestion. Figure 4.80 shows a block symbol of a 16x32 register file (16 registers, each 32-bits wide).

Consider writing a value to a register in a register file. We would place the data to be written on the input W_data. We then need a way to indicate which register we actually want to write. Since there are 16 registers, we need four bits to specify a particular register. Those four bits are called the register's ***address***. We would thus write the desired register's address on the input W_addr. For example, if we wanted to write to register 7, we would set W_addr=0111. To indicate that we actually want to write on a particular clock cycle

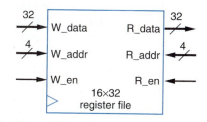

Figure 4.80 16x32 register file block symbol.

(we won't want to write on every cycle), we would set the input W_en to 1. The collection of inputs W_data, W_addr, and W_en is known as a register file's ***write port***.

Reading is similar. We would specify the register to read on input R_addr, and set R_en=1. Those values would cause the register file to output the addressed register's contents onto output R_data. R_data, R_addr, and R_en are known as a register file's ***read port***. The read port and write port are independent of one another. Thus, during the same clock cycle, we can write to one register, and read from another (or the same) register.

Let's consider how to internally design a register file. For simplicity, consider a 4×32 register file, rather than the 16×32 register file described above. One internal design of a 4x32 register file is shown in Figure 4.81. Let's consider the circuitry for writing to this register file, found in the left half of the figure. If W_en=0, the register file won't write to any register, because the write decoder's outputs will be all 0s. If W_en=1, then the write decoder decodes W_addr and sets to 1 the load input of exactly one register. That register will be written on the next clock cycle with the value on W_data.

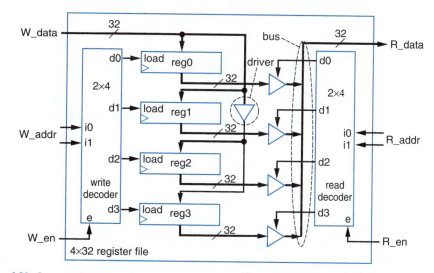

Figure 4.81 One possible internal design of a 4x32 register file.

Notice the circled triangular one-input one-output component placed on the W_data line (there would actually be 32 such components since W_data is 32 bits wide). That component is known as a ***driver***, sometimes called a ***buffer***, illustrated in Figure 4.82(a). A driver's output equals its input, but the output is a stronger (higher current) signal. Remember the fanout problem we described in Example 4.24? A driver reduces the fanout problem. In Figure 4.81, the W_data lines only fanout to two registers before they go through the driver. The driver's output then fans out to only two more registers. Thus, instead of a fanout of four, the W_data lines have a fanout of only two (actually three if you count the driver itself). The insertion of drivers is beyond the scope of this book, and is instead a subject for a VLSI design book or an advanced digital design book. But seeing at least one example of the use of a driver hopefully gives you an idea of one reason why a register file is a useful component—the component hides the complexity of fanout from a designer.

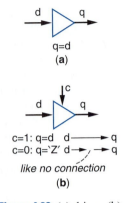

Figure 4.82 (a) driver, (b) three-state driver.

To understand the read circuitry, you must first understand the behavior of another new component that we've introduced—the triangular component having two inputs and one output. That component is known as a ***three-state driver*** or ***three-state buffer***, illustrated in Figure 4.82(b). When the control input c is 1, the component acts like a regular driver—the component's output equals its input. However, when the control input c is 0, the driver's output is neither 0 or 1, but instead what is known as high-impedance, written as 'Z'. High-impedance can be thought of as no connection at all between the driver's input and output. "Three-state" means the driver has three possible output states—0, 1, and Z.

Let's now consider the circuitry for reading from the register file, found in the right half of Figure 4.81. If R_en=0, the register file won't read from any register, since the read decoder's outputs will be all 0s, meaning all the three-state drivers will output Z's, and thus the output R_data will be high-impedance. If R_en=1, then the read decoder decodes R_addr and sets to 1 the control input of exactly one three-state driver, which will pass its register value through to the R_data output.

Be aware that each shown three-state driver actually represents a set of 32 three-state drivers, one for each of the 32 wires coming from the 32-bit registers and going to the 32-bit R_data output. All 32 drivers in a set are controlled by the same control input.

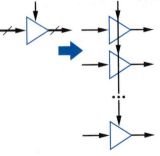

The wires fed by the various three-state drivers are known as a ***bus***, as indicated in Figure 4.81. A bus is a popular alternative to a multiplexor when each mux data input is many bits wide and/or when there are many mux data inputs, because a bus results in less congestion.

Notice that the register file design scales well to larger numbers of registers. The write data lines can be driven by more drivers if necessary. The read data lines are fed from three-state drivers and thus there is no congestion at a single multiplexor. The reader may wish to compare the register file design in Figure 4.81 with the design in Figure 4.6, which was essentially a poor design of a register file.

Figure 4.83 provides example timing diagrams describing writing and reading of a register file. During *cycle1*, we do not know the contents of the register file, so the register file's contents are shown as "?." During *cycle1*, we set W_data=9 (in binary, of course), W_addr=3, and W_en=1. Those values cause a write of 9 to register file location 3 on the first clock edge. Notice that we had set R_en=0, so the register file outputs nothing ("Z"), and the value we put on R_addr does not matter (the value is a "don't care", written as "X").

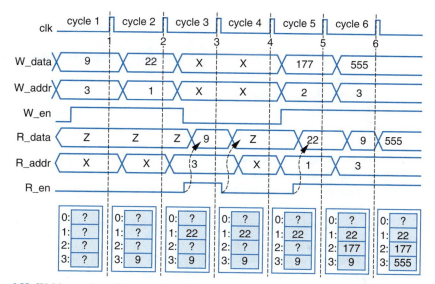

Figure 4.83 Writing and reading a register file.

During *cycle2*, we set W_data=22, W_addr=1, and W_en=1. These values cause a write of 22 to register file location 1 on clock edge 2.

During *cycle3*, we set W_en=0, so then it doesn't matter to what values we set W_data and W_addr. We also set R_addr=3 and R_en=1. Those values cause the register file to read out the contents of register file location 3 onto R_data, causing R_data to output 9. Notice that the reading is not synchronized to clock edge 3—R_data changes soon after R_en becomes 1. Examining the design of Figure 4.81 should make clear why reading is not synchronous—setting R_en to 1 simply enables the output decoder to turn on one set of the three-state buffers.

During *cycle4*, we return R_en to 0. Note that this causes R_data to become "Z" again.

During *cycle5*, we want to simultaneously write and read the register file. We read location 1 (which causes R_data to become 22) while simultaneously writing location 2 with the value 177.

Finally, during *cycle6*, we want to simultaneously read and write the same register file location. We set R_addr=3 and R_en=1, causing location 3's contents of 9 to appear on R_data shortly after setting those values. We also set W_addr=3, W_data=555, and W_en=1. On clock edge 6, 555 thus gets stored into location 3. Notice that soon after that clock edge, R_data also changes to 555.

The ability to simultaneously read and write locations of a register file, even the same location, is a widely used feature of register files. The next example makes use of that feature.

▶ **EXAMPLE 4.25** *Above-mirror display system using a 16x32 register file*

Example 4.4 used four 8-bit registers for an above-mirror display system. Example 4.24 extended the system to use sixteen 32-bit registers, resulting in fanout and congestion problems. We can redo that example using a register file. The design is shown in Figure 4.84. Since the system always outputs one of the register values to the display, we tied the R_en input to 1. Notice that the writing and reading of particular registers are independent of one another.

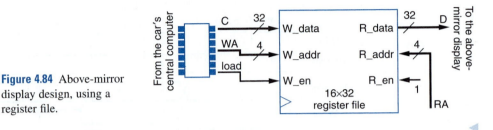

Figure 4.84 Above-mirror display design, using a register file.

◀

A register file having one read port and one write port is sometimes referred to as a **dual-ported register file**. To make clear that the two ports consist of one read port and one write port, such a register file may be referred to as follows: *dual-ported (1 read, 1 write) register file*.

A register file may actually have just one port, which would be used for both reading and writing. Such a register file has only one set of data lines that can serve as inputs or outputs, one set of address inputs, an enable input, and one more input indicating whether we wish to write or read the register file. Such a register file is known as a **single-ported register file**.

Multiported (2 Read, 1 Write) Register File. Many register files have three ports: one write port, and two read ports. Thus, in the same clock cycle, two registers can be read simultaneously, and another register written. Such a register file is especially useful in a microprocessor, since a typical microprocessor instruction operates on two registers and stores the result in a third register, like in the instruction "R0 <— R1 + R2."

We can create a second read port in a register file by adding another set of lines, Rb_data, Rb_addr, and Rb_en. We would introduce a second read decoder with inputs Rb_addr and enable input Rb_en, a second set of three-state drivers, and a second bus connected to the Rb_data output.

Other Register File Variations. Register files come in all sorts of configurations. Typical numbers of registers in a register file range from 4 to 1024, and typical register widths range from 8 bits to 64 bits per register, but sizes may vary beyond those ranges. Registers files may have one port, two ports, three ports, or even more, but increasing to many more than three ports can slow down the register file's performance and increase its size significantly, due to the difficulty of routing all those wires around inside the register file. Nevertheless, you'll occasionally run across register files with perhaps 3 write ports and 3 read ports, when concurrent access is critical.

The most ports I've seen on a register file in a product was 10 read ports and 5 write ports.

► 4.11 DATAPATH COMPONENT TRADEOFFS (SEE SECTION 6.4)

For each datapath component that we introduced in previous sections, we created the most basic and easy-to-understand implementation. In this section, which physically appears in the book as Section 6.4, we describe alternative implementations of several datapath components. Each alternative trades off one design criteria for another—most of those alternatives trade off larger size in exchange for less delay. One use of this book covers those alternative implementations immediately after introducing the basic implementations (meaning now). Another use of the book covers those alternative implementations later, after showing how to use datapath components during register-transfer level design.

► 4.12 DATAPATH COMPONENT DESCRIPTION USING HARDWARE DESCRIPTION LANGUAGES (SEE SECTION 9.4)

This section, which physically appears in the book as Section 9.4, shows how to use HDLs to describe several datapath components. One use of the book describes such HDL use now, while another use describes such HDL use later.

► 4.13 PRODUCT PROFILE: AN ULTRASOUND MACHINE

If you or someone you know has ever had a baby, then you may have seen ultrasound images of that baby before he/she was born, like the images of a fetus' head in Figure 4.85(a).

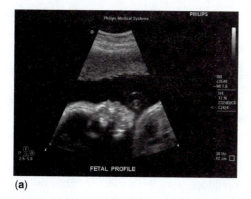

(a)

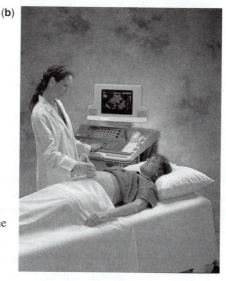

(b)

Figure 4.85 (a) Ultrasound image of a fetus, created using an ultrasound device that is simply placed on the mom's abdomen (b) and that forms the image by generating sound waves and listening to the echoes. Photos courtesy of Philips Medical Systems.

That image wasn't taken by a camera somehow inserted into the uterus, but rather by an ultrasound machine pressed against the mom's skin and pointed toward the fetus. Ultrasound imaging is now common practice in obstetrics—mainly helping doctors to track the fetus' progress and correct potential problems early, but also giving parents a huge thrill when they get their first glimpse of their baby's head, hands, and little feet!

Functional Overview

This section briefly describes the key functional ideas of how ultrasound imaging works. Digital designers don't typically work in a vacuum—instead, they apply their skills to particular applications, and thus designers typically learn the key functional ideas underlying those applications. We therefore introduce you to the basic ideas of ultrasound applications. Ultrasound imaging works by sending sound waves into the body and listening to the echoes that return. Objects like bones yield different echoes than objects like skin or fluids, so an ultrasound machine processes the different echoes to generate images like those in Figure 4.85(a)—strong echoes might be displayed as white, weak ones as black. Today's ultrasound machines rely heavily on fast digital circuits to generate the sounds waves, listen to the echoes, and process the echo data to generate good quality images in real time.

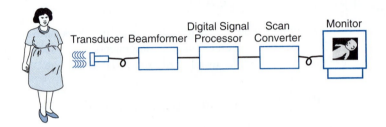

Figure 4.86 Basic components of an ultrasound machine.

Figure 4.86 illustrates the basic parts of an ultrasound machine. Let's discuss each part individually.

Transducer

A *transducer* converts energy from one form to another. You're certainly familiar with one type of transducer, a stereo speaker, which converts electrical energy into sound by changing the current in a wire, which causes a nearby magnet to move back and forth, which pushes the air and hence creates sound. Another familiar transducer is a dynamic microphone, which converts sound into electrical energy by letting sound waves move a magnet, which induces current changes in a nearby wire. In an ultrasound machine, the transducer converts electrical pulses into sound pulses, and sound pulses (the echoes) into electrical pulses, but the tranducer uses piezoelectric crystals instead of magnets. Applying electric current to such a crystal causes the crystal to change shape rapidly, or vibrate, thus generating sound waves—typically in the 1 to 30 Megahertz frequency range. Humans can't hear much above 30 kilohertz—the term "ultrasound" refers to the fact that the frequency is beyond human hearing. Inversely, sound waves (echoes) hitting the crystal create electric current. An ultrasound machine's transducer component may contain hundreds of such crystals, which we can think of as hundreds of transducers. Each such transducer is considered to form a *channel*.

Beamformer

A *beamformer* electronically "focuses" and "steers" the sound beam of an array of transducers to or from particular focal points, without actually moving any hardware like a dish to obtain such focusing and steering.

Real designers must often learn about the domain for which they will design. Many designers consider such learning about domains, like ultrasound, as one of the fascinating features of the job.

To understand the idea of beamforming, we must first understand the idea of additive sound. Consider two loud fireworks exploding at the same time, one 1 mile away from you, and the other 2 miles away. You'll hear the closer firework after about 5 seconds—assuming sound travels 0.2 miles/second (or 1 mile every 5 seconds)—a reasonable approximation. You'll hear the farther firework after about 10 seconds. So you'll hear "boom ... (five seconds pass) ... boom." However, suppose instead that the closer firework exploded 5 seconds later than the farther one. Then you'll hear both at the same time—one big "BOOM!" That's because the two sounds add together. Now suppose there are 100 fireworks spread throughout a city, and you want all the sound from those fireworks to reach one particular house (perhaps somebody you don't like very much) at the same time. You can do this by exploding the closer fireworks later than the farther fireworks. If you time everything just right, that particular house will hear a tremendously loud single "BOOOOOM!!!!," probably rattling the house's walls pretty good, as if one huge firework had exploded. Other houses throughout the city will instead hear a series of quieter booms, since the timing of the explosions don't result in all the sounds adding at those other houses.

Now you understand a basic principle of beamforming: If you have multiple sound sources (fireworks in our example, transducers in an ultrasound machine) in different locations, you can cause the sound to add together at any desired point in space, by carefully timing the generation of sound from each source such that all the sound waves arrive at the desired point at the same time. In other words, you can *electronically* focus and steer the sound beam by introducing appropriate delays. Focusing and steering the sound to a particular point is useful because then *that point will produce a much louder echo than all other points*, so we can easily hear the echo from that point over all the echoes from other points.

Figure 4.87 illustrates the concept of electronic focusing and steering, using two sound sources to focus and steer a beam to a desired point X.

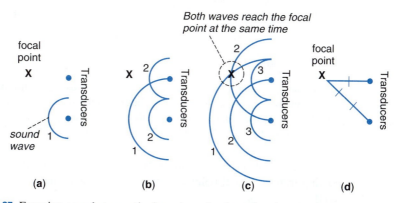

Figure 4.87 Focusing sound at a particular point using beamforming: (a) first time step—only the bottom transducer generates sound, (b) second time step—the top transducer now generates sound too, (c) third time step—the two sound waves add at the focal point, (d) an illustration showing that the top transducer is two time steps away from the focal point, while the bottom transducer is three time steps away, meaning the top transducer should generate sound one time step later than the bottom transducer.

At the first time step (Figure 4.87(a)), the bottom source has begun transmitting its sound wave. After two time steps (Figure 4.87(b)), the top source has begun transmitting its sound wave. After three time steps (Figure 4.87(c)), the waves from both sensors reach the focal point, adding together. They'll continue adding as long as the waves from both sources are in phase with one another. We can simplify the drawing by showing only the lines from the sources to the focal point, as shown in Figure 4.87(d).

An ultrasound machine uses this ability to electronically focus and steer sound, in order to scan, point by point, the entire region in front of the transducers. The machine does such scanning perhaps tens or hundreds of times per second.

For each focal point, the machine needs to listen to the echo that comes back from whatever object is located at the focal point, to determine if that object is bone, skin, blood, etc., utilizing the fact that each such object generates a different echo. Remember, the echo from the focal point will be louder than echoes from other points, because the sound adds at that point. We can use beamforming to also focus in on a particular point in space that we want to *listen* to. In the same way that we generated sound pulses with particular delays to focus the sound on a particular point, likewise, to "listen" to the sounds from a particular point, we also want to introduce delays to the signals received by the transducers. That's because the sounds will arrive at the closer transducers sooner than at the farther transducers, so by using appropriate delays, we can "line up" the signals from each transducer so that the sounds coming from the focal point all add together. This concept is shown in Figure 4.88.

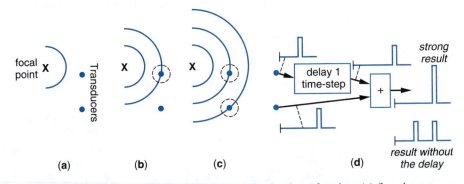

(a)   **(b)**   **(c)**   **(d)**

Figure 4.88 Listening to sound from a particular point using beamforming: (a) first time step, (b) second time step—the top transducer has heard the sound first, (c) third time step—the bottom transducer hears the sound at this time, (d) delaying the top transducer by one time step results in the waves from the focal point adding, amplifying the sound.

Note that there will certainly be echoes from other points in the region, but those coming from the focal point will be much stronger—hence, the weaker echoes can be filtered out.

Notice that beamforming can be used to listen to a particular point even if the sounds coming from that point are not echoes coming back from our own sound pulses—the sound could be coming from the object at the point itself, such as a car engine or a person talking. Beamforming is the electronic equivalent to pointing a big parabolic dish in a particular direction, but beamforming requires no moving parts.

Beamforming is tremendously common in a wide variety of sonar applications, such as observing a fetus, observing a human heart, searching for oil underground, monitoring the surroundings of a submarine, spying, etc. Beamforming is used in some hearing aids having multiple microphones, to focus in on the source of detected speech—in that case, the beamforming must be adaptive. Beamforming can be used in multimicrophone cell phones to focus in on the user's voice, and can even be used in cellular telephone base stations (using radio signals though, not sound waves) to focus a signal going to or coming from a cell phone.

Signal Processor, Scan Converter, and Monitor

The signal processor analyzes the echo data of every point in the scanned region, by filtering out noise (see Section 5.11 for a discussion on filtering), interpolating between points, assigning a level of gray to each point depending on the echoes heard (echoes corresponding to bones might be shaded as white, liquid as black, and skin as gray, for example), and other tasks. The result is a gray-scale image of the region. The scan converter steps through this image to generate the necessary signals for a black-and-white monitor, and the monitor displays the image.

Digital Circuits in an Ultrasound Machine's Beamformer

Much of the control and signal processing tasks in an ultrasound machine are carried out using software running on one or more microprocessors, typically special microprocessors specifically designed for digital signal processing, known as digital signal processors, or DSPs. But certain tasks are much more amenable to custom digital circuitry, such as those in the beamformer.

Sound Generation and Echo Delay Circuits

Beamforming during the sound generation step consists of providing appropriate delays to hundreds of transducers. Those delays vary depending on the focal point, so they can't be built into the transducers themselves. Instead, we can place a delay circuit in front of each transducer, as shown in Figure 4.89. For a given focal point, the DSP writes the appropriate delay value into each delay circuit, by writing the delay value on the bus labeled delay_out, writing the "address" on the lines labeled addr, and enabling the decoder. The decoder will thus set the load line of one of the *OutDelay* components.

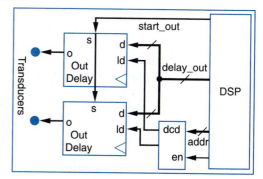

Figure 4.89 Transducer output delay circuits for two channels.

After writing to every such component, the DSP starts all of them simultaneously by setting start_out to 1. Each *OutDelay* component will, after the specified delay, pulse its o output, which we'll assume causes the transducer to generate sound. The DSP would then set start_out to 0, and then listen for the echo.

We can implement the *OutDelay* component using a down-counter with parallel load, as shown in Figure 4.90. The parallel load inputs L and ld load the down-counter with its count value. The cnt input commences the down-counting—when the counter reaches zero, the counter pulses tc. The data output of the counter is unused in this implementation.

After the ultrasound machine sends out sound waves focused on a particular focal point, the machine must listen to the echo coming back from that focal point. This listening requires appropriate delays for each transducer to account for the differing distances of each transducer from the focal point. Thus, each transducer needs another delay circuit for delaying the received echo signal, as shown in Figure 4.91. The *EchoDelay* component receives on input t the signal from the transducer, which we'll assume has been digitized into a stream of *N*-bit values. The component should output that signal on output t_delayed, delayed by the appropriate amount. The delay amount can be written by the DSP using the component's d and ld inputs.

We can implement the *EchoDelay* component using a series of registers, as shown in Figure 4.92. That implementation can delay the output signal by 0, 1, 2, or 3 clock cycles, simply using the appropriate select line values for the 4x1 mux. A longer register chain, along with a larger mux, would support longer delays. The DSP configures the delay amount by writing to the top register, which sets the 4x1 mux select lines. A more flexible implementation of the *EchoDelay* component would instead use a timer component.

Summation Circuits—Adder Tree

The output of each transducer, appropriately

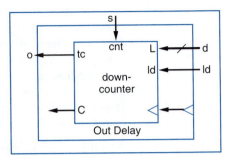

Figure 4.90 OutDelay circuit.

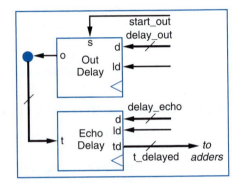

Figure 4.91 Transducer output and echo delay circuits for one channel.

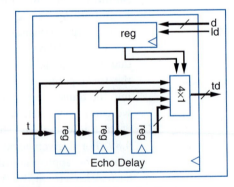

Figure 4.92 EchoDelay circuit.

delayed, should be summed to create a single echo signal from the focal point, as was illustrated in Figure 4.88. That illustration had only two transducers, and thus only one adder. What if we have 256 transducers, as would be more likely in a real ultrasound machine? How do we add 256 values? We could add the values in a linear way, as illustrated on the left side of Figure 4.93(a) for eight values. The delay of that circuit is roughly equal to the delay of seven adders. For 256 values, the delay would roughly be that of 255 adders. That's a very long delay.

We can do better by reorganizing how we compute the sum, using a configuration of adders known as an ***adder tree***. In other words, rather than computing $((((((A+B)+C)+D)+E)+F)+G)+H$, depicted in Figure 4.93(a), we could instead compute $((A+B)+(C+D)) + ((E+F)+(G+H))$, as shown in Figure 4.93(b). The answer comes out the same, and uses the same number of adders, but the latter method computes four additions in parallel, then two additions in parallel, and then performs a last addition. The delay is thus only that of three adders. For 256 values, the tree's first level would compute 128 additions in parallel, the second level would compute

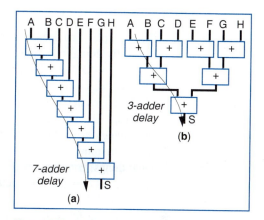

Figure 4.93 Adding many numbers: (a) linearly, (b) using an adder tree. Note that both methods use seven adders.

64 additions, then 32, then 16, then 8, then 4, then 2, and finally 1 last addition. Thus, that adder tree would have eight levels, meaning a total delay equal to eight adder delays. That's a lot faster than 256 adder delays—*32 times faster*, in fact.

The output of the adder tree can be fed into a memory to keep track of the results for the DSP, which may access the results sometime after they are generated.

Multipliers

We presented a greatly simplified version of beamforming above. In reality, many other factors must be considered during beamforming. Several of those considerations can be accounted for by multiplying each channel with specific constant values, which the DSP again sets individually for each channel. For example, focusing on a point close to the handheld device may require us to more heavily weigh the incoming signals of transducers near the center of the device. A channel may therefore actually include a multiplier, as shown in Figure 4.94. The DSP could write to the register shown,

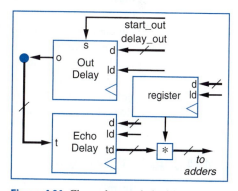

Figure 4.94 Channel extended with a multiplier.

which would represent a constant by which the transducer signal would be multiplied.

Our introduction of the ultrasound machine is greatly simplified from a real machine, yet even in this simplified introduction, you can see many of this chapter's datapath components in use. We used a down-counter to implement the *OutDelay* component, and several registers along with muxes for the *EchoDelay* component. We used many adders to sum the incoming transducer signals. And we used a multiplier to weigh those incoming signals.

Future Challenges in Ultrasound

Over the past two decades, ultrasound machines have moved from mostly analog machines to mostly digital machines. The digital systems consist of both custom digital circuits and software on DSPs and microprocessors, working together to create real-time images.

One of the main trends in ultrasound machines involves creating three-dimensional (3-D) images in real time. Most ultrasound machines of the 1990s and 2000s generated two-dimensional images, with the quality of those images (e.g., more focal points per image) improving during those decades. In contrast to two-dimensional ultrasound, generating 3-D images requires viewing the region of interest from different perspectives, just like people view things from their two eyes. Such generation also requires extensive computations to create a 3-D image from the two (or more) perspectives. The result is a picture like that in Figure 4.95.

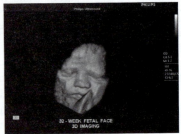

Figure 4.95 3-D ultrasound image of a fetus's face. Photo courtesy of Philips Medical Systems.

That's a fetus' face. Impressive, isn't it? Keep in mind that image is made solely from sound waves bouncing into a woman's womb. Color can also be added to distinguish among different fluids and tissues. Those computations take time, but faster processors, coupled with clever custom digital circuits, are bringing real-time 3-D ultrasound closer to reality.

Another trend is toward making ultrasound machines smaller and lighter, so that they can be used in a wider variety of health care situations. Early machines were big and heavy, with more recent ones coming on rollable carts. Some recent versions are handheld. A related trend is making ultrasound machines cheaper, so that perhaps every doctor could have a machine in every examination room, every ambulance could carry a machine to help emergency personnel ascertain the extent of certain wounds, and so on.

Ultrasound is used for numerous other medical applications, such as imaging of the heart to detect artery or valve problems. Ultrasound is also used in various other applications, like submarine region monitoring.

▶ 4.14 CHAPTER SUMMARY

In this chapter, we began (Section 4.1) by introducing the idea of new building blocks intended for common operations on multibit data, with those blocks being known as datapath components, or register-transfer-level components. We then introduced a number of datapath components, including registers, shifters, adders, comparators, counters, multipliers, subtractors, arithmetic-logic units, and register files. For each component, we examined two aspects: the internal design of the component, and the use of the component in applications.

We ended (Section 4.13) by describing some basic principles underlying the operation of an ultrasound machine, and showing how several of the datapath components might be used to implement parts of such a machine. One thing you might notice is how designing a real ultrasound machine would require some knowledge of the domain of ultrasound. The requirement that a software programmer or digital designer have some understanding of an application domain is quite common.

In the coming chapter, you will apply your knowledge of combinational logic design, sequential logic design (controller design), and datapath components, to build digital circuits that can implement very general and powerful computations.

▶ 4.15 EXERCISES

Exercises marked with an asterisk (*) represent especially challenging problems.

For exercises relating to datapath components, each problem indicates whether the problem emphasizes the component's internal design or the component's use.

SECTION 4.2: REGISTERS

4.1 Trace the behavior of an 8-bit parallel load register with input I, output Q, and load control input *ld* by completing the following timing diagram.

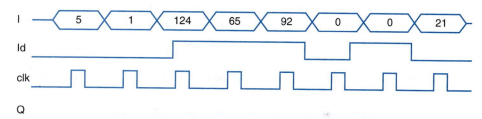

4.2 Trace the behavior of an 8-bit parallel load register with input I, output Q, load control input *ld,* and synchronous clear input *clr* by completing the following timing diagram.

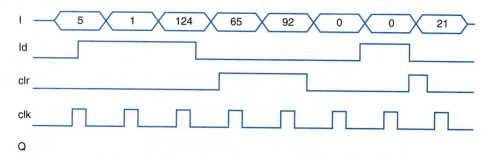

4.3 Design a 4-bit register with 2 control inputs s1 and s0, 4 data inputs I3, I2, I1, and I0, and 4 data outputs Q3, Q2, Q1, and Q0. When s1s0=00, the register maintains its value. When s1s0=01, the register loads I3..I0. When s1s0=10, the register clears itself to 0000. When s1s0=11, the register complements itself, so, for example, 0000 would become 1111, and 1010 would become 0101. *(Component design problem.)*

4.4 Repeat the previous problem, but when s1s0=11, the register reverses its bits, so 1110 would become 0111, and 1010 would become 0101. *(Component design problem.)*

4.5 Design an 8-bit register with 2 control inputs s1 and s0, 8 data inputs I7..I0, and 8 data outputs Q7..Q0. s1s0=00 means maintain the present value, s1s0=01 means load, and s1s0=10 means clear. s1s0=11 means to swap the high nibble with the low nibble (a nibble is 4 bits), so 11110000 would become 00001111, and 11000101 would become 01011100. *(Component design problem.)*

4.6. The radar gun used by a police officer is always outputting a radar signal and measuring the speed of the cars as they pass. However, when the officer wants to ticket an individual for speeding, he must save the measured speed of the car on the radar unit. Build a system to implement a speed save feature for the radar gun. The system has an 8-bit speed input S, an input B from the save button on the radar gun, and an 8-bit output D that will be sent to the radar's gun speed display. (*Component use problem.*)

SECTION 4.3: ADDERS

4.7. Trace the values appearing at the outputs of a 3-bit carry-ripple adder for every one full-adder-delay time period, when adding 111 with 011. Assume all inputs were previously zero for a long time.

4.8. Assuming all gates have a delay of 1 time unit, compute the longest time required to add two numbers using an 8-bit carry-ripple adder.

4.9. Assuming AND gates have a delay of 2 time units, OR gates have a delay of 1 time unit, and XOR gates have a delay of 3 time units, compute the longest time required to add two numbers using an 8-bit carry-ripple adder.

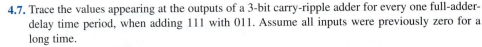

4.10 Design a 10-bit carry-ripple adder using 4-bit carry-ripple adders. (*Component use problem.*)

4.11 Design an adder that computes the sum of three 8-bit numbers, using 8-bit carry-ripple adders. (*Component use problem.*)

4.12 Design an adder that computes the sum of four 8-bit numbers, using 8-bit carry-ripple adders. (*Component use problem.*)

4.13 Design a digital thermometer that can compensate for errors in the temperature sensing device's output T, which is an 8-bit input to our system. The compensation amount can be positive only, and comes to our system via inputs a, b, and c, from a 3-pin DIP switch. Our system should output the compensated temperature on an 8-bit output U. (*Component use problem.*)

4.14 Repeat the previous problem, except that the compensation amount can be positive or negative, coming to our system via four inputs a, b, c, and d from a 4-pin DIP switch. The compensation amount is in two's complement form (so the person setting the DIP switch better know that!). Design the circuit. What is the range by which the input temperature can be compensated? (*Component use problem*).

4.15 We can add three 8-bit numbers by chaining one 8-bit carry-ripple adder to the output of another 8-bit carry-ripple adder. Assuming every gate has a delay of 1 time-unit, compute the longest delay of this three 8-bit number adder. Hint: you may have to look carefully inside the carry-ripple adders, even inside the full-adders, to correctly compute the longest delay from any input to any output. (*Component use problem.*)

SECTION 4.4: SHIFTERS

4.16 Design an 8-bit shifter that shifts its inputs two bits to the right (shifting in 0s) when the shifter's shift control input is 1. (*Component design problem.*)

4.17 Design a circuit that outputs the average of four 8-bit inputs representing binary numbers (not in two's complement form). (*Component use problem.*)

4.18 Design a circuit that takes an 8-bit input D representing binary numbers (not in two's complement form), and outputs two times that value. (*Component use problem.*)

4.19 Design a circuit that outputs nine times its 8-bit input D representing binary numbers (not in two's complement form). Hint: Use a shifter and an adder. (*Component use problem.*)

4.20 Design a special multiplier circuit that can multiply its 16-bit input by 1, 2, 4, 8, 16, or 32, specified by three inputs a, b, c (abc=000 means no multiply, abc=001 means multiply by 1, abc=010 means by 4, abc=011 means by 8, abc=100 means by 16, abc=101 means by 32). Hint: Use a predefined component described in this chapter. *(Component use problem.)*

4.21 Trace through the execution of the barrel shifter shown in Figure 4.42, when I=01100101, x = 1, y = 0, z = 1. Be sure to show how the input I is shifted after each internal shifter stage.

4.22 Trace through the execution of the barrel shifter shown in Figure 4.42, when I=10011011, x = 0, y = 1, z = 0. Be sure to show how the input I is shifted after each internal shifter stage.

4.23 Using the barrel shifter shown in Figure 4.42, what settings of the inputs x, y, and z are required to shift the input I left by six positions?

SECTION 4.5: COMPARATORS

4.24 Trace through the execution of the 4-bit magnitude comparator shown in Figure 4.45 when a=15 and b=12. Be sure to show how the comparisons propagate thought the individual comparators.

4.25 Design a comparator that determines if three 4-bit numbers are equal, by connecting 4-bit magnitude comparators together and using additional components if necessary. *(Component use problem.)*

4.26 Design a 4-bit carry-ripple style magnitude comparator that has two outputs, a greater-than or equal-to output *gte*, and a less-than or equal-to output *lte*. Be sure to clearly show the equations used in developing the individual 1-bit comparators and how they are connected to form the 4-bit circuit. *(Component design problem.)*

4.27 Design a 5-bit magnitude comparator. *(Component design problem.)*

4.28 Design a circuit that outputs 1 if the circuit's 8-bit input equals 99:
(a) using an equality comparator,
(b) using gates only.
Hint: In the case of (b), you need only 1 AND gate and some inverters. *(Component use problem.)*

4.29 Use magnitude comparators and logic to design a circuit that computes the minimum of three 8-bit numbers. *(Component use problem.)*

4.30 Use magnitude comparators and logic to design a circuit that computes the maximum of two 16-bit numbers. *(Component use problem.)*

4.31 Use magnitude comparators and logic to design a circuit that outputs 1 when an 8-bit input is between 75 and 100, inclusive. *(Component use problem.)*

4.32 You are to design a human body temperature alarm system for a hospital. Your system takes an 8-bit input representing the temperature, which can range from 0 to 255. If the measured temperature is 95 or less, you should set output A to 1. If the temperature is 96 to 104, you should set output B to 1. If the temperature is 105 or above, you should set output C to 1. *(Component use problem.)*

4.33 You are working as a weight guesser in an amusement park. Your job is to try to guess the weight of an individual before they step on the scale. If your guess is not within ten pounds of the individual's actual weight (higher or lower), the individual wins a prize. Build a weight guess analyzer system that outputs whether the guess was within ten pounds. The weight guess analyzer has an 8-bit guess input G, an 8-bit input from the scale W with the correct weight, and a single output C that is 1 if the guessed weight was within the defined limits of the game. *(Component use problem.)*

SECTION 4.6: COUNTERS

4.34 Design a 4-bit up-counter that has two control inputs: *cnt* enables counting up, while *clear* synchronously resets the counter to all 0s:
(a) using a parallel load register as a building block,
(b) using flip-flops and muxes directly by following the register design process of Section 4.2. *(Component design problem.)*

4.35 Design a 4-bit down-counter that has three control inputs: *cnt* enables counting up, *clear* synchronously resets the counter to all 0s, and *set* synchronously sets the counter to all 1s:
(a) using a parallel load register as a building block,
(b) using flip-flops and muxes directly by following the register design process of Section 4.2. *(Component design problem.)*

4.36 Design a 4-bit up-counter with an additional output *upper. upper* outputs a 1 whenever the counter is within the upper half of the counter's range, 8 to 15. Use a basic 4-bit up-counter as a building block. *(Component design problem.)*

4.37 Design a 4-bit up/down-counter that has four control inputs: *cnt_up* enables counting up, *cnt_down* enables counting down, *clear* synchronously resets the counter to all 0s, and *set* synchronously sets the counter to all 1s. If both count control inputs *cnt_up* and *cnt_down* are 1, the counter will retain its current count value. Use a parallel load register as a building block. *(Component design problem.)*

4.38 Design a circuit for a 4-bit decrementer. *(Component design problem.)*

4.39 Design an electronic turnstile system using a 64-bit counter. The input is a bit A, which is 1 for exactly one clock cycle whenever a person walks through the turnstile. The output is a 64-bit binary number. A second input B is 1 whenever a reset button is pressed, and should reset the output to 0s. Knowing that California's Disneyland attracts about 15,000 visitors per day, and assuming they all pass through your one turnstile, how many days would pass before your counter would roll over? *(Component use problem.)*

4.40 (a) Using an up-counter with a synchronous clear control input, and extra logic, design a circuit that outputs a 1 every 99 clock cycles.
(b) Design the counter from part (a), but use a down-counter with parallel load.
(c) What are the tradeoffs between the two designs from parts (a) and (b)?
(Component use problem.)

4.41 (a) Give the count range for the following sized up-counters: 8-bits, 12-bits, 16-bits, 20-bits, 32-bits, 40-bits, 64-bits, and 128-bits.
(b) For each size of counter in part (a), assuming a 1 Hz clock, indicate how many minutes, hours, days, etc., the counter would count before wrapping around.

SECTION 4.7: MULTIPLIER—ARRAY STYLE

4.42 Assuming all gates have a delay of 1 time-unit, which of the following designs will compute the 8-bit multiplication A*9 faster:
(a) a circuit as designed in Exercise 4.19. or
(b) an 8-bit array style multiplier with one of its inputs connected to a constant value of nine.

4.43 Design an 8-bit array-style multiplier. *(Component design problem.)*

4.44 Design a more accurate version of the Celsius to Fahrenheit converter from Example 4.10. The new conversion circuit receives a digitized temperature in Celsius as a 16-bit binary number C and outputs the temperature in Fahrenheit as a 16-bit output F. Our more accurate equation for calculating an approximate conversion from Celsius to Fahrenheit is: F = C*30/16 + 32. *(Component use problem.)*

SECTION 4.8: SUBTRACTORS

4.45 Create the internal design of a full-subtractor. *(Component design problem.)*

4.46 Convert the following two's complement binary numbers to decimal numbers:
(a) 00001111
(b) 10000000
(c) 10000001
(d) 11111111
(e) 10010101

4.47 Convert the following two's complement binary numbers to decimal numbers:
(a) 01001101
(b) 00011010
(c) 11101001
(d) 10101010
(e) 11111100

4.48 Convert the following two's complement binary numbers to decimal numbers:
(a) 11100000
(b) 01111111
(c) 11110000
(d) 11000000
(e) 11100000

4.49 Convert the following 9-bit two's complement binary numbers to decimal numbers:
(a) 011111111
(b) 111111111
(c) 100000000
(d) 110000000
(e) 111111110

4.50 Convert the following decimal numbers to 8-bit two's complement binary form:
(a) 2
(b) −1
(c) −23
(d) −128
(e) 126
(f) 127
(g) 0

4.51 Convert the following decimal numbers to 8-bit two's complement binary form:
(a) 29
(b) 100
(c) 125
(d) −29
(e) −100
(f) −125
(g) −2

4.52 Convert the following decimal numbers to 8-bit two's complement binary form:
   (a) 6
   (b) 26
   (c) –8
   (d) –30
   (e) –60
   (f) –90
   (g) –120

4.53 Convert the following decimal numbers to 9-bit two's complement binary form:
   (a) 1
   (b) –1
   (c) –256
   (d) –255
   (e) 255
   (f) –8
   (g) –128

4.54 Using 4-bit subtractors, build a subtractor that has three 8-bit inputs, A, B, and C, and a single 8-bit output F, where F=(A–B) – C. *(Component use problem.)*

4.55 You are given a digital thermometer that digitizes a temperature into a 16-bit binary number K in Kelvin. Build a system to convert that temperature to a 16-bit Fahrenheit value. Use the following equation to provide an approximate conversion: F= (K-273)*2+32. *(Component use problem.)*

SECTION 4.9:   ARITHMETIC-LOGIC UNITS—ALUS

4.56 Design an ALU with two 8-bit inputs A and B, and control signals x, y, and z. The ALU should support the operations described in Table 4.3. Use an 8-bit adder and an arithmetic/logic extender. *(Component design problem.)*

TABLE 4.3   Desired ALU operations.

Inputs			Operation
X	y	z	
0	0	0	S = A – B
0	0	1	S = A + B
0	1	0	S = A * 8
0	1	1	S = A / 8
1	0	0	S = A NAND B (bitwise NAND)
1	0	1	S = A XOR B (bitwise XOR)
1	1	0	S = Reverse A (bit reversal)
1	1	1	S = NOT A (bitwise complement)

4.57 Design an ALU with two 8-bit inputs A and B, and control signals x, y, and z. The ALU should support the operations described in Table 4.4. Use an 8-bit adder and an arithmetic/logic extender. *(Component design problem.)*

TABLE 4.4   Desired ALU operations.

Inputs			Operation
x	y	z	
0	0	0	S = A + B
0	0	1	S = A AND B (bitwise AND)
0	1	0	S = A NAND B (bitwise NAND)
0	1	1	S = A OR B (bitwise OR)
1	0	0	S = A NOR B (bitwise NOR)
1	0	1	S = A XOR B (bitwise XOR)
1	1	0	S = A XNOR B (bitwise XNOR)
1	1	1	S = NOT A (bitwise complement)

4.58 An instructor teaching Boolean algebra wants to help her students learn and understand basic Boolean operators by providing the students with a calculator capable of performing bitwise AND, NAND, OR, NOR, XOR, XNOR, and NOT operations. Using the ALU specified in Exercise 4.57, build a simple logic calculator using DIP switches for input and LEDs for output. The logic calculator should have three DIP switch inputs to select which logic operation to perform. *(Component use problem.)*

SECTION 4.10: REGISTER FILES

4.59 Design an 8x32 two port (1 read, 1 write) register file. *(Component design problem.)*

4.60 Design a 4x4 three port (2 read, 1 write) register file. *(Component design problem.)*

4.61 Design a 10x14 register file (one read port, one write port). *(Component design problem.)*

4.62 *Create a speed-dial system for a telephone. Eight special buttons b0–b7 access each stored number. The most recently dialed number exists as nine digits stored in nine 8-bit registers R0–R8. When the phone user presses another button S simultaneously with any button b0–b7, the most recently dialed number gets stored in the button's corresponding storage. When the user presses a button b0–b7 by itself, the number in that button's storage gets read out and placed on nine 8-bit outputs P0–P8. Hint: use nine register files and some extra logic. *(Component use problem.)*

Roman began studying Computer Science in college due to his interest in software development. During his undergraduate studies, his interests expanded to include digital design and embedded systems and eventually led him to become involved in research developing new methods to help designers quickly build large integrated circuits (IC). Roman continued his education through graduate studies and received his M.S. in Computer Science, after which Roman worked for both a large company designing integrated circuits (IC) for consumer electronics as well as a start-up company focusing on high-performance processing.

Roman enjoys working as both a software developer and hardware engineer and believes that "fundamentally software and hardware design are very similar, both relying on efficiently solving difficult problems. While good problem solving skills are important, good learning skills are also important." Contrary to what many students may believe, he points out that "learning is a fundamental activity and skill that does not end when you receive your degree. In order to solve problems, you often are required to learn new skills, adopt new programming languages and tools, and determine if existing solutions will help you solve the problems you face as an engineer." Roman points out that digital design has changed at a rapid pace over the last few decades, requiring engineers to learn new design techniques, learn new programming languages, such as VHDL or SystemC, and be able to adopt new technologies to stay successful. "As the industry continues to advance at such a rapid pace, companies do not only hire engineers for what they already know, but more so on how well those engineers can continue to expand their knowledge and learn new skills." He points out that "college provides students with an excellent opportunity to not only learn the essential information and skills from their course work but also to learn additional information on their own, possibly by learning different programming languages, getting involved in research, or working on larger design projects."

Roman is motivated by his enjoyment of the work he does as well being able to work with other engineers who share his interests. "Motivation is one of the keys to success in an engineering career. While motivation can come from many different sources, finding a career that you are truly interested in and enjoy really helps. Co-workers are also a great source of motivation as well as knowledge and technical advice. Working as a member of a team that communicates well is very rewarding. You are able to motivate each other and use your strengths along with the strengths of your co-workers to achieve goals far beyond that which you could achieve on your own."

5

Register-Transfer Level (RTL) Design

▶ 5.1 INTRODUCTION

In the previous chapters, we've defined the combinational and sequential components needed to build digital systems. In this chapter, we'll learn to build interesting and useful digital systems from those components. In particular, we'll put together datapath components to build datapaths, and we'll use controllers to control those datapaths. The combination of a controller and datapath is known as a ***processor***. Some processors, like those in personal computers, are programmable—those processors are the focus of Chapter 8. Other processors are custom-designed for a particular task, and are not programmable—design of such custom processors is the focus of this chapter.

Digital designers today focus largely on designing custom processors, as opposed to designing lower-level digital components. We can define a custom processor as a digital circuit that implements a computer algorithm—a sequence of instructions that carry out a particular task. For example, we can define an algorithm to filter out noise from a digitized stream of audio, and we can then create a processor to implement that algorithm. Another algorithm might encrypt data for secure electronic commerce purposes. An algorithm might compare a fingerprint to a set of 10,000 fingerprints to quickly enable a police officer to determine if someone is a wanted criminal. An image processing algorithm might detect a tank in a large video image. Beamforming, part of the ultrasound machine example in the previous chapter, can be thought of as another algorithm, implemented using the processor design described in that chapter. In fact, several of our examples in the previous chapter, like the above-mirror display, DIP-switch-based calculator, and color space converter, can actually be thought of as very simple processors implementing simple algorithms.

Processors can be designed using different design methods. The most common method in practice today is known as register-transfer level design. ***Register-transfer level design***, or ***RTL design***, actually consists of a wide variety of approaches, but in general, a designer specifies the registers of a design, describes the possible transfers and operations performed on input, output, or register data, and defines the control that specifies when to transfer and operate on data.

Recall the design processes we defined for combinational logic design in Chapter 2, and for sequential logic (controller) design in Chapter 3:

- In the combinational logic design process outlined in Table 2.5,
    1. The first step was to *capture* the desired behavior of the combinational logic, with either a truth table or an equation.
    2. The remaining steps were to *convert* the behavior to a circuit.
- In the sequential logic (controller) design process in Table 3.2,
    1. The first step was to *capture* the desired behavior of the sequential logic, using a finite-state machine.
    2. The remaining steps were to *convert* the behavior to a circuit.

It should therefore come as no surprise that:

1. The first step of an RTL design method will be to *capture* the desired behavior of the processor. We'll introduce the concept of a high-level state machine for capturing RTL behavior.

2. The remaining steps will be to *convert* the behavior to a circuit.

Figure 5.1 illustrates the idea that the design process can be viewed as first capturing behavior and then converting the behavior to structure. That process applies regardless of whether we are performing combinational logic design, sequential logic design, or RTL design.

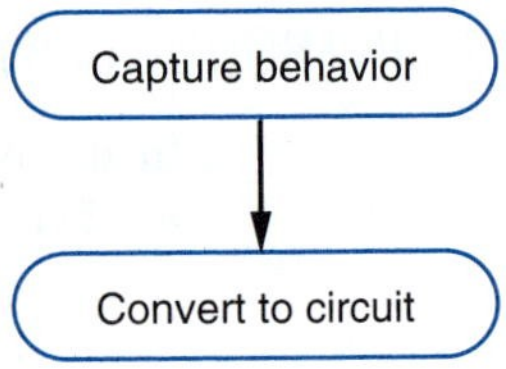

In this chapter, we will introduce the RTL design process, also known as the RTL design method. As the process is largely creative, we will utilize numerous examples to illustrate the process. We will also introduce several high-level components that are useful during RTL design, including memory components and queue components.

Figure 5.1 The design process.

▶ 5.2 RTL DESIGN METHOD

RTL design is carried out using a wide variety of methods in practice, but it may be useful to define a general method as in Table 5.1

TABLE 5.1 RTL design method.

	Step	Description
Step 1	*Capture a high-level state machine*	Describe the system's desired behavior as a high-level state machine. The state machine consists of states and transitions. The state machine is "high-level" because the transition conditions and the state actions are more than just Boolean operations on bit inputs and outputs.
Step 2	*Create a datapath*	Create a datapath to carry out the data operations of the high-level state machine.
Step 3	*Connect the datapath to a controller*	Connect the datapath to a controller block. Connect external Boolean inputs and outputs to the controller block.
Step 4	*Derive the controller's FSM*	Convert the high-level state machine to a finite-state machine (FSM) for the controller, by replacing data operations with setting and reading of control signals to and from the datapath.

A fifth step may be necessary, in which one selects a clock frequency. Designers seeking high performance may choose a clock frequency that is the fastest possible based on the longest register-to-register delay in the final circuit.

Implementing the controller's FSM as a sequential circuit, as we learned in Chapter 3, would then complete the design.

Notice that the first step *captures* the desired behavior, while the remaining steps *convert* that behavior to a circuit.

We'll first provide a small and simple example as a "preview" of the RTL design method's steps, before we define each step in more detail.

► **EXAMPLE 5.1** Soda machine dispenser

We are to design a processor for a soda dispenser. A coin detector provides our processor with a 1-bit input c that becomes 1 for one clock cycle when a coin is detected, and an 8-bit input a indicating the coin's value in cents. Another 8-bit input s indicates the cost of a soda (this cost can be set by the machine owner). Once the processor has seen coins whose value equals or exceeds the cost of a soda, the processor should set an output bit d to 1 for one clock cycle, causing a soda to be dispensed (this machine has only one type of soda). The system does not give change—any excess money is kept. Figure 5.2 provides a block symbol of the system.

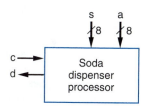

Figure 5.2 Soda dispenser block symbol.

Step 1 of our RTL design method is to capture the desired behavior of the system. Figure 5.3 shows a high-level state machine describing the desired behavior. The first state, *Init*, sets the output d to 0 and initializes a local register tot to 0. tot will keep track of how many cents the system has seen so far. The state machine then enters state *Wait*. (Recall from Chapter 3 that a transition with no condition has an implicit "true" condition, and thus transitions on the next rising clock edge.) The FSM stays there as long as no coin is detected and the total cents seen so far is less than the cost of a soda. When a coin is detected, the state machine goes to state *Add*, which adds the coin's value to tot, and then returns to state *Wait*. Once tot is greater than or equal to (in other words, not less than) the cost of a soda, the state machine goes to state *Disp*, which dispenses a soda by setting d to 1. The state machine then returns to state *Init*.

Step 2 is to create a datapath. We'll need a local *register* for tot, an *adder* connected to tot and a to compute tot + a, and a *comparator* connected to tot and s to compute tot<s. The resulting datapath appears in Figure 5.4.

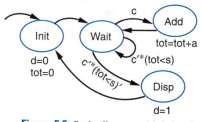

Figure 5.3 Soda dispenser high-level state machine.

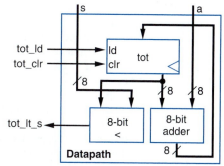

Figure 5.4 Soda dispenser datapath.

Step 3 is to connect the datapath to a controller. Figure 5.5 shows the connections. Notice that the controller's inputs and outputs are all just one-bit signals.

Step 4 is to derive the controller's FSM. The FSM has the same states and transitions as the high-level state machine, but utilizes the datapath to perform any data operations. Figure 5.6 shows the FSM for the controller. In the high-level state machine, state *Init* had a data operation of tot = 0 (tot is 8 bits wide, so that assignment of 0 is not a single-bit operation). We replace that assignment by setting tot_clr=1, which clears the tot register to 0. State *Wait*'s transitions had data operations comparing tot < s. Now we have a comparator computing that comparison for the controller, so the controller need only look at the result of that comparison in the signal tot_lt_s. State *Add* had a data operation of tot = tot + a. The datapath computes that addition for the controller using the adder, so the controller merely needs to set tot_ld = 1 to cause the addition result to be loaded into the tot register.

To complete the design, we would implement the controller's FSM as a state register and combinational logic. Figure 5.7 shows a partial state table for the controller, with the states encoded as *Init*: 00, *Wait*: 01, *Add*: 10, and *Disp*: 11. To complete the controller design, we would complete the state table, create a 2-bit state register, and create a circuit for each of the five outputs from the table, as discussed in Chapter 3. Appendix C provides details of completing the controller's design. That appendix also traces through the functioning of the controller and datapath with one another. ◀

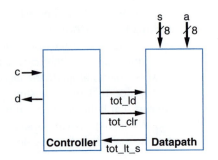

Figure 5.5 Soda dispenser controller and datapath connections.

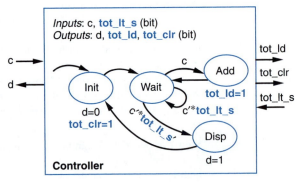

Figure 5.6 Soda dispenser contoller FSM.

	s1	s0	c	tot_lt_s	n1	n0	d	tot_ld	tot_clr
Init	0	0	0	0	0	1	0	0	1
	0	0	0	1	0	1	0	0	1
	0	0	1	0	0	1	0	0	1
	0	0	1	1	0	1	0	0	1
Wait	0	1	0	0	1	1	0	0	0
	0	1	0	1	0	1	0	0	0
	0	1	1	0	1	0	0	0	0
	0	1	1	1	1	0	0	0	0
Add	1	0	0	0	0	1	0	1	0
			•••				•••		
Disp	1	1	0	0	0	0	1	0	0
			•••				•••		

Figure 5.7 Soda dispenser controller's state table (partial).

The previous example gave a preview of the RTL design method. Notice that we started with a high-level state machine, which wasn't just an FSM because there were local registers declared, and because there were data operations (rather than just Boolean operations) in the states and on the transitions. We then created a datapath to implement those local registers and to carry out the data operations. We further needed a controller to control that datapath. We defined the behavior of that controller to be the same as the behavior of the high-level state machine, except the controller's FSM used datapath control signals to carry out and evaluate the datapath operations. Finally, we could design the controller using Chapter 3's controller design process.

We now discuss each RTL design method step in more detail, while illustrating each step with another example.

Step 1—Creating a High-Level State Machine

A high-level state machine is a computation model similar to a finite-state machine, but with additional features that enable the description of computations involving more than just Boolean data.

Recall that a finite-state machine (FSM) consists of inputs, outputs, states, state actions (a mapping of states to output values), and state transitions (a mapping of states and inputs to next states). However, the inputs and outputs of an FSM are limited to Boolean types, actions are limited to Boolean equations, and transition conditions are limited to Boolean expressions. These limitations make specifying of computations involving data cumbersome, other than for just single-bit data.

Figure 5.3 showed a high-level state machine describing the behavior of a soda dispenser processor. Notice that the state machine is *not* an FSM because of the several reasons highlighted in Figure 5.8. One reason is because the state machine has inputs that are 8-bit types, whereas FSMs only allow inputs and outputs of Boolean types (a single bit each). Another reason is because the state machine declares a local register tot to store intermediate data, whereas FSMs don't allow local data storage—the only "stored" item in an FSM is the state itself. A third reason is because the state actions and transition conditions involve data operations, like

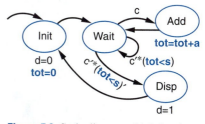

Inputs: c (bit), **a (8 bits), s (8 bits)**
Outputs: d (bit)
Local registers: **tot (8 bits)**

Figure 5.8 Soda dispenser high-level state machine with non-FSM constructs highlighted.

tot = 0 (remember that tot is 8-bits wide), tot < s (there's no "<" Boolean operator), and tot = tot + a (where the "+" is addition, not OR, and there's no addition Boolean operator), whereas an FSM allows only Boolean equations and expressions.

Therefore, a useful form of high-level state machine is an extension of an FSM in which:

- inputs and outputs may involve *data types beyond just single bits*,
- *local registers* may be declared (of various data types), and
- actions and conditions may involve general *arithmetic equations* and expressions, rather than just Boolean equations and expressions.

Such a high-level state machine is not the only possible extension to an FSM. Dozens of varieties of extended FSMs exist. However, we will be utilizing the above-described extended FSM variety throughout this chapter. That particular variety of high-level state machine is sometimes called an *FSM with data*, or *FSMD*.

We will continue to use the following conventions for high-level state machines, which we also used for FSMs:

• Each transition is implicitly ANDed with a rising clock edge.

• Any *bit* output not explicitly assigned a value in a state is implicitly assigned a 0. Note: this convention does not apply for multibit outputs.

We now provide another example of describing a system using a high-level state machine.

▶ **EXAMPLE 5.2** Laser-based distance measurer—High-level state machine

There are countless applications that require one to accurately measure the distance of an object from a known point. For example, road builders need to accurately determine the length of a stretch of road. Map makers need to accurately determine the locations and heights of hills and mountains and the sizes of lakes. A giant crane for constructing skyrise buildings needs to accurately determine the distance of the sliding crane arm from the base. In all of these applications, stringing out a tape measure to measure the distance is not very practical. A better method involves laser-based distance measurement.

In laser-based distance measurement, a laser is pointed at the object of interest. The laser is briefly turned on, and a timer is started. The laser light, traveling at the speed of light, travels to the object and reflects back. A sensor detects the reflection of the laser light, causing the timer to stop. Knowing the time T taken by the light to travel to the object and back, and knowing that the speed of light is $3x10^8$ meters/second, we can compute the distance D easily by the equation: $2D = T$ seconds $* 3x10^8$ meters/second. Laser-based distance measurement is illustrated in Figure 5.9.

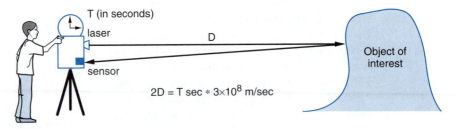

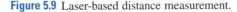

Figure 5.9 Laser-based distance measurement.

Let's design a processor to control the laser and the timer and to compute distances up to 2000 meters. A block diagram of the system is shown in Figure 5.10. The system has a bit input B, which equals 1 when the user presses a button to start the measurement. Another bit input S comes from the sensor, and is 1 when the reflected laser is detected. A bit output L controls the laser, turning the laser on when L is 1. Finally, an N-bit output D indicates the distance in binary, in units of meters—we'll assume a display converts that binary number into a decimal number and displays the results on an LCD for the user to read. D will have to be at least 11 bits, since 11 bits can represent the numbers 0 to 2047, and we want to measure distances up to 2000 meters. Let's make D 16 bits.

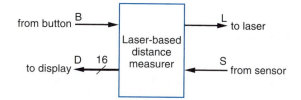

Figure 5.10 Block diagram of the laser-based distance measurement system.

Step 1—Create a high-level state machine.

We can describe the overall control of the system using a high-level state machine. To facilitate the creation of the state machine, we enumerate the sequence of events underlying the measurement system:

* The system powers on. Initially, the system's laser is off and the system outputs a distance of 0 meters.

* The system should then wait for the user to initiate measurement by pressing a button, B.

* After the button is pressed, the system should turn the laser on. We'll choose to leave the laser on for one clock cycle.

* After the laser is pulsed, the system should wait for the sensor to detect the laser's reflection. Meanwhile, the system should count how much time passes from the time the laser was pulsed until the reflection is sensed.

* After the reflection is detected, the system should use the amount of time passed since the laser was pulsed to compute the distance to the object of interest. The system should then return to waiting for the user to press the button so that a new measurement can be taken.

The above sequence guides our construction of a high-level state machine. We begin with an initial state, which we call *S0*. *S0's* task is to ensure that when our system powers on, it does not output an incorrect distance, and it does not turn the laser on (possibly injuring the unsuspecting user). Specifying this behavior as a high-level state machine is straightforward and seen in Figure 5.11. Notice that the high-level state machine differs from an FSM in that the state's actions use a data type that is larger than one bit (namely, D is 16 bits). However, the

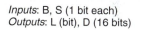

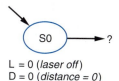

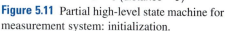

Figure 5.11 Partial high-level state machine for measurement system: initialization.

high-level state machine itself follows the convention that every transition is implicitly ANDed with a rising clock edge, so the state machine only transitions during clock edges (just like for an FSM). Note that even though the assignments L = 0 and D = 0 look the same, the assignment L = 0 assigns a 0 bit to the one-bit output L, whereas the assignment D = 0 assigns the 16-bit binary number 0 (which is actually 0000000000000000) to the 16-bit output D. Some other notations distinguish bit assignments from data assignments using different notations, such as enclosing a bit in single quotes. For example, the bit assignment L = 0 could be written instead as L = '0'.

After initialization, the measurement system waits for the user to press the button B, which initiates the measurement process. When the user presses the button, B will equal 1, and the measurement system should proceed to activate the laser. To perform the waiting, we add a state after *S0*, which we call *S1*, shown in Figure 5.12. The shown transitions cause the state machine to remain in state *S1* while B = 0 (meaning B' is true).

When B=1, the laser should stay on for one cycle. In other words, when B=1, the state machine should transition to a state that turns the laser on, followed by a state that turns the laser off. We'll call the laser-on state *S2* and the laser-off state *S3*. Figure 5.13 shows how *S2* and *S3* are connected in the high-level state machine.

In state *S3*, the state machine should wait until the sensor detects the laser's reflection (S=1). The state machine remains in *S3* while S=0. As mentioned in the earlier sequence of events, the state machine should meanwhile count the duration between the laser being pulsed and the laser's reflection being sensed. From the discussion of timers in Chapter 4, we know that with a given clock period, we can measure time by counting the number of clock cycles and multiplying that number by the clock period (time = cycles * (1/clock frequency)). Thus, we use a *local register*, which we'll call Dctr, to count clock cycles. The state machine increments Dctr as long as the state machine is waiting for the laser's reflection. (For simplicity, we ignore the possibility that no reflection is ever detected.) We must also initialize Dctr to 0, which we choose to do in state *S1*. With these modifications, our high-level state machine is seen in Figure 5.14.

Inputs: B, S (1 bit each)
Outputs: L (bit), D (16 bits)

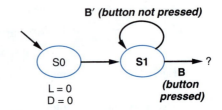

Figure 5.12 Partial high-level state machine for measurement system: waiting for a button press.

Inputs: B, S (1 bit each)
Outputs: L (bit), D (16 bits)

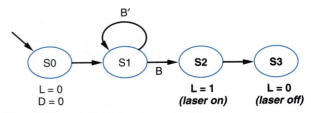

Figure 5.13 Partial high-level state machine for measurement system: pulsing the laser for one cycle.

Inputs: B, S (1 bit each)   *Outputs*: L (bit), D (16 bits)
Local Registers: Dctr (16 bits)

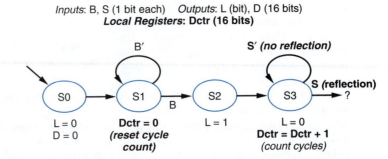

Figure 5.14 Partial high-level state machine for measurement system: waiting for the laser reflection and counting clock cycles.

Once the reflection is detected (S=1), our high-level state machine should compute the distance D that is being measured. From Figure 5.9, we know that $2*D = Tsec * 3 \times 10^8$ m/sec. We also know that the time T in seconds is Dctr * (1 / clock frequency). To simplify the system's design, let's assume the clock frequency is 3×10^8 Hz, or 300 MHz. Since light travels 3×10^8 meters per second, each clock cycle would thus correspond to one meter. Thus with a 300 MHz clock, Dctr counts the number of meters that the laser beam traveled from the measurer to the object and back to the measurer. To count just the distance from the measurer to the object, we divide Dctr by 2 (algebraic simplification of the equations in this paragraph verify that D = Dctr/2). We'll perform this calculation in a state we will call *S4*. Our final high-level state machine is shown in Figure 5.15.

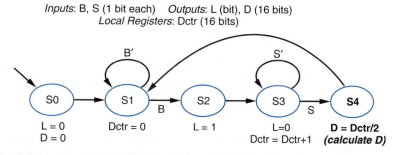

Inputs: B, S (1 bit each)   *Outputs*: L (bit), D (16 bits)
Local Registers: Dctr (16 bits)

Figure 5.15 High-level state machine for measurement system: calculating the value of D.

We can summarize the behavior of the high-level state machine in Figure 5.15 as follows:

- S0 is the initial state. In state S0, the state machine initializes the laser to off by setting L=0 and sets the output D=0 too. The machine then transitions to S1.

- S1 clears Dctr to 0 and then waits until the button is pressed. When the button is pressed, the machine transitions to state S2.

- S2 turns on the laser. The machine then transitions to S3.

- S3 turns off the laser and increments Dctr every clock cycle (with a 300 MHz clock, every cycle corresponds to one meter). The machine stays in S3, incrementing Dctr during each clock cycle, until the reflection is sensed, at which time the machine transitions to state S4.

- S4 sets the output D to the counted number of cycles divided by two, which corresponds to the measured distance in meters. The machine then returns to state S1, which waits for the button to be pressed again.

A real laser-based distance measurer might use a faster clock frequency in order to measure distance with a greater precision than just 1 meter.   ◀

The high-level state machine described above is just one type of FSM variation. A different state machine variation that was previously quite popular was called ***Algorithmic State Machines***, or ***ASMs***. ASMs are similar to flowcharts, except that ASMs include a notion of a clock that enables transitions from one state to another (a traditional flowchart does not have an explicit clock concept). ASMs, like flowcharts, contain more "structure" than a state machine. A state machine can transition from any state to any other state, whereas an ASM restricts transitions in a way that causes the computation to look more like an algorithm—an ordered sequence of instructions. An ASM uses several types of boxes, including state boxes, condition boxes, and output boxes. ASMs typically also allowed local data storage and data operations.

The advent of hardware description languages (see Chapter 9) seems to have largely replaced the use of ASMs, as hardware description languages contain the constructs supporting algorithmic structure, and much more. Thus, we do not describe ASMs further.

Step 2—Creating a Datapath

Given a high-level state machine, we want to create a datapath that can implement all the data storage and computations on non-Boolean data types present in the high-level state machine. Doing so will enable us to then replace the high-level state machine by an FSM that merely controls the datapath. We can decompose the "create a datapath" step into several substeps:

Step 2: Create a datapath

(a) Make all *data* inputs and outputs to be datapath inputs and outputs.

(b) Implement the data storage by adding a register component into the datapath for every declared register in the high-level state machine. Furthermore, we typically want to add a register component for every data output.

(c) Methodically examine each state and each transition, adding and connecting new datapath components to implement new data computations. We add multiplexors in front of component inputs as they become necessary in order to share a component among multiple signals that use the same component in different states. Sometimes we find that a component already exists (e.g., a register) but that we need to add a new control input to that component (e.g., a clear input on a register to set the register to 0).

A common term used to describe the adding of a component into a design is ***instantiation***. Thus, we say that we "instantiate a new register" rather than we "add a new register." Using the term "instantiate" rather than "add" helps avoid possible confusion with the use of the term "add" to mean arithmetic addition (e.g., saying "we add two registers" could otherwise be confusing). When we instantiate a new component, we should give that component a name that is unique from any other datapath component name. So if we instantiate a register, we might call it "*Register1*." If we instantiate another register, we might call it "*Register2*." Actually, we should give meaningful names whenever possible. So we might call one register "*TemperatureReg*," and another register "*HumidityReg*."

When we instantiate a new component, we may create additional datapath inputs corresponding to the control inputs of the component. For example, instantiating a register will create a new datapath input corresponding to the register's load and clear control inputs. We should give unique names to each new datapath control input, ideally describing which component the input controls and the control operation performed. For example, if we instantiate a register named *Register1*, we might then create two new datapath inputs named *Register1_load* and *Register1_clear*. Likewise, we may need to utilize control outputs of a component, like the output of a comparator, in which case we should give those outputs unique names too.

▶ **EXAMPLE 5.3**   Laser-based distance measurer—Creating a datapath

We now continue Example 5.2 by proceeding to the second step of the RTL design method.

Step 2—Create a datapath

We can follow the substeps of this step to create the datapath shown in Figure 5.17:

(a) Output D is a data output (16 bits), so we make D an output of the datapath, as shown in Figure 5.16(i).

(b) We need a register to implement the 16-bit local register Dctr. Noting that the operations on Dctr are *clear* (in state *S1*) and *increment* (in state *S3*), we can implement that register by instantiating a 16-bit up-counter, as shown in Figure 5.16(ii). Furthermore, as we want to control when the output D changes (notice that we only change D in state *S4*), we instantiate a 16-bit register Dreg at the output D, as shown in Figure 5.16(iii). We extend the Dctr counter and Dreg register control signals to be inputs to the datapath, with each signal having a unique name, as in Figure 5.16(iv).

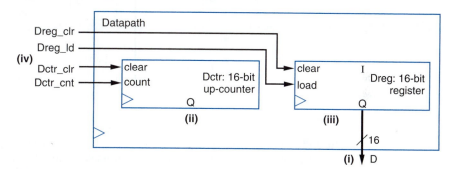

Figure 5.16 Partial datapath for the laser-based distance measurer.

(c) Noting that *S3* writes D with Dctr divided by 2, we insert a right shifter between Dctr and Dreg to implement the divide by 2, as shown in Figure 5.17.

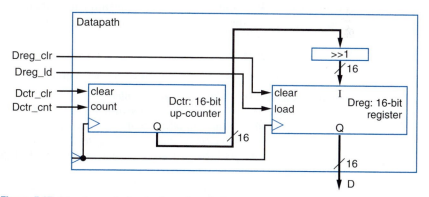

Figure 5.17 The datapath for the laser-based distance measurement system.

The resulting datapath in Figure 5.17 is a very simple datapath, but a datapath nonetheless. ◀

The previous example did not require any multiplexors, so we'll illustrate separately why sometimes multiplexors must be instantiated. Consider the sample high-level state machine portion shown in Figure 5.18(a). Figure 5.18(b) shows the datapath after implementing the actions of state *T0*. Those actions require an adder, with the *E* and *F* registers connected to the *A* and *B* inputs of that adder. Figure 5.18(c) shows that datapath after implementing the actions of state *T1*. That state also requires an adder, but because one already exists in the datapath, we need not instantiate another adder. However, the *R* and *G* registers must connect to the *A* and *B* inputs of that adder, but those inputs of the adder already have connections from *E* and *F*. We therefore need to instantiate multiplexors, as shown in Figure 5.18(d). Notice that we create unique names for each mux's control input.

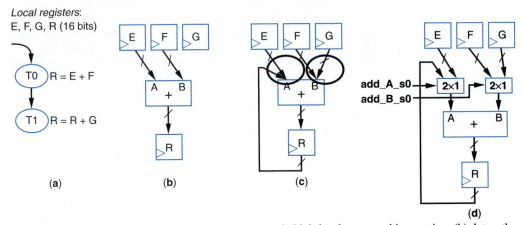

Figure 5.18 Instantiating datapath muxes: (a) sample high-level state machine portion, (b) datapath after implementing T0's actions, (c) datapath after implementing T1's actions, resulting in two sources for each adder input, (d) datapath after instantiating muxes to handle the multiple sources.

Step 3—Connecting the Datapath to a Controller

Step 3 of the RTL design method is actually quite straightforward. We simply create a controller block having the system's Boolean inputs and outputs, and we connect the controller block with the datapath control inputs and outputs.

▶ **EXAMPLE 5.4** Laser-based distance measurer—Connecting the datapath to a controller

Continuing the previous example, we proceed to step 3 of the RTL design method:

Step 3—Connect the datapath to a controller.
We connect the datapath to a controller as shown in Figure 5.19. We connect the control inputs and outputs (*B*, *L*, and *S*) to the controller, and the data output (D) to the datapath. We also connect the controller to the datapath control inputs (*Dreg_clr*, *Dreg_ld*, *Dctr_clr*, *Dctr_cnt*). Normally we don't draw the clock generator block, but we've explicitly shown the clock generator in the figure to make clear that the generator must be exactly 300 MHz.

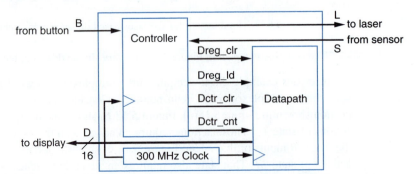

Figure 5.19 Controller/datapath (processor) design for the laser-based distance measurer.

Step 4—Deriving the Controller's FSM

If we created our datapath correctly, deriving an FSM for the controller is straightforward. The FSM will have the same states and transitions as the high-level state machine. We merely define the FSM's inputs and outputs (all will now be single bits), and replace any data computations in the actions and conditions by the appropriate datapath control signal values. Remember, we created the datapath specifically to carry out those computations, and therefore we should only need to appropriately configure the datapath control signals to implement each particular computation at the right time.

▶ **EXAMPLE 5.5** Laser-based distance measurer—Deriving the controller's FSM

We continue the previous example by going to step 4 of the RTL design method.

Step 4—Derive the controller's FSM.

The last step is to design the controller's internals. We can describe the controller's behavior by refining our high-level state machine from Figure 5.15 into an FSM, replacing the "high-level" actions and conditions, like `Dctr=0`, by actual controller input and output signal assignments and conditions, like `Dctr_clr=1`, as shown in Figure 5.20. Notice that the FSM does not directly indicate the computations that are happening in the datapath. For example, *S4* loads `Dreg` with `Dctr/2`, but the FSM itself only shows `Dreg`'s load signal being activated. Thus, the overall system behavior can be determined from the FSM by looking also at the datapath.

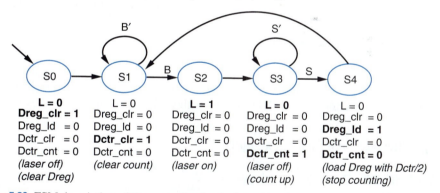

Inputs: B, S   Outputs: L, Dreg_clr, Dreg_ld, Dctr_clr, Dctr_cnt

S0	S1	S2	S3	S4
L = 0	L = 0	**L = 1**	L = 0	L = 0
Dreg_clr = 1	Dreg_clr = 0	Dreg_clr = 0	Dreg_clr = 0	Dreg_clr = 0
Dreg_ld = 0	Dreg_ld = 0	Dreg_ld = 0	Dreg_ld = 0	**Dreg_ld = 1**
Dctr_clr = 0	**Dctr_clr = 1**	Dctr_clr = 0	Dctr_clr = 0	Dctr_clr = 0
Dctr_cnt = 0	Dctr_cnt = 0	Dctr_cnt = 0	**Dctr_cnt = 1**	Dctr_cnt = 0
(laser off)	*(clear count)*	*(laser on)*	*(laser off)*	*(load Dreg with Dctr/2)*
(clear Dreg)			*(count up)*	*(stop counting)*

Figure 5.20 FSM description of the controller for the laser-based distance measurer. The desired action in each state is shown in italics in the bottom row; the corresponding bit signal assignment that achieves that action is shown in bold.

▶ *HOW DOES IT WORK?—AUTOMOTIVE ADAPTIVE CRUISE CONTROL*

The early 2000s saw the advent of automobile cruise control systems that not only maintained a particular speed, but also maintained a particular *distance* from the car in front—thus slowing the automobile down when necessary. Such "adaptive" cruise control thus adapts to changing highway traffic. Adaptive cruise controllers must measure the distance to the car in front. One way to measure that distance uses a laser-based distance measurer, with the laser and sensor placed in the front grill of the car, connected to a circuit and/or microprocessor that computes the distance. The distance is then input to the cruise control system, which determines when to increase or decrease the automobile's speed.

Recall from Chapter 3 that we typically follow the convention that FSM output signals not explicitly assigned in a state are implicitly assigned 0. Following that convention, the FSM would look as in Figure 5.21. We may still choose to explictly show the assignment of 0 (e.g., $L = 0$ in state $S3$) when that assignment is a key action of a state. The key actions of each state were bolded in Figure 5.20.

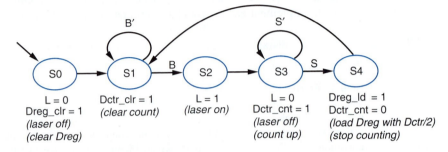

Inputs: B, S   *Outputs*: L, Dreg_clr, Dreg_d, Dctr_clr, Dctr_cnt

Figure 5.21 FSM description of the controller for the laser-based distance measurer, using the convention that FSM outputs not explicitly assigned a value in a state are implicitly assigned 0.

We would complete the design by implementing this FSM, using a 3-bit state register and combinational logic to describe the next state and output logic, as was described in Chapter 3. ◀

▶ 5.3 RTL DESIGN EXAMPLES AND ISSUES

RTL design involves a certain amount of creativity and insight. Thus, a good way to begin to learn RTL design is perhaps through seeing several examples. We now provide additional examples of the RTL design method, through which we also explain some detailed issues.

Simple Bus Interface Design Example

▶ **EXAMPLE 5.6**   Simple bus interface

Processors typically need to transfer data to and from other processors. They typically communicate such data over a bus, to reduce wire congestion problems that might otherwise occur (see Section 4.10). Suppose 16 different processors each has a 32-bit output connected to a single 32-bit bus named D. Suppose another processor, a master processor, may want to read the output of any of those 16 processors. (Let's call those 16 processors *peripherals*, which is a common term for a processor that is auxiliary to a master processor). The master processor outputs a 4-bit address, A, that all the 16 peripherals can read, with each peripheral having its own unique address (0000, or 0001, or 0010, etc.). Because the master processor must always set the address lines to a value, but might not always want to read, the master processor has another output, rd, that the master processor sets to 1 when reading, and 0 when not reading. So if the master processor wants to read the value in peripheral number five, the master processor would set the address lines A to 0101, then set rd to 1. The master processor would then read the data lines D (perhaps storing the read data into a local register), and then return rd to 0. Additionally, the value on D should not change while the master processor is reading.

A block diagram of the system is shown in Figure 5.22. Such an arrangement is very similar to the arrangement in a desktop computer, where a master processor can read peripheral processor registers—peripherals might include a disk drive, a CD-ROM drive, a keyboard, a modem, etc.

We have just described what is known as a bus protocol. A **bus protocol** defines a sequence of actions over a set of data, address, and control lines, to carry out a data transfer over those lines from one processor to another.

A **bus interface** implements a bus protocol for a processor. Let's implement the bus interface for one of the peripheral processors. Figure 5.23 provides a block diagram for a peripheral divided into a main part and a bus interface part. The main part's output Q is an input to the bus interface. Let's assume the peripheral's own address is another input, called Faddr, to the bus interface. Faddr might come from a DIP switch, or perhaps another register. The bus interface also has inputs and outputs that connect to the bus signals rd, D, and A.

Step 1 of our RTL design method is to create a high-level state machine. Based on the bus protocol we defined, a peripheral's bus interface part sends data only if the address on input A

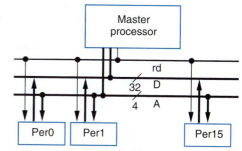

Figure 5.22 Bus interface example.

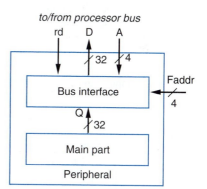

Figure 5.23 Bus interface block diagram.

matches the address on input Faddr AND the processor requests a read by setting rd to 1. While the bus interface waits for an instruction from the master processor to send data, the bus interface should not interfere with what another processor may be writing to the shared data lines, D. Thus, while waiting for a matching address and rd=1, the bus interface should drive D with no value (known as **high impedance**, represented as "**Z**").

When the bus interface detects a matching address and rd=1, the bus interface should output data from the input Q (from the main part) to the output D. However, we must also ensure that D does not change while the master processor is reading from the bus interface. We can keep the value on D stable by storing Q into a local register Q1. As long as the bus interface is not sending data, the bus

interface updates Q1 with the current value of Q. When the bus interface is sending data, the bus interface does not update Q1 and outputs Q1 on D, causing D to not change during a send.

We can see that the bus interface's implementation of the bus protocol can be described by a high-level state machine using two states, shown in Figure 5.24: a state in which the bus interface waits to be able to send data (*WaitMyAddress*) and a state in which the bus interface sends data (*SendData*).

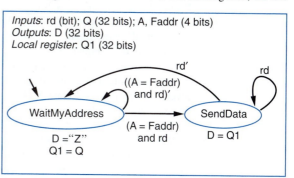

Figure 5.24 High-level state machine of the sending half of a simple bus interface.

Figure 5.25 provides a sample timing diagram of the state machine's behavior. (*W* stands for state *WaitMy-Address*, *SD* for *SendData*). As long as the system is in the *W* state, the system outputs Z on D. When rd=1 and A=Faddr, the system outputs the contents of Q1 beginning at the next clock cycle's rising edge. The system continues to output Q1 as long as rd=1. When read returns to 0, the system returns to the *WaitMyAddress* state at the next rising clock edge and hence outputs Z again.

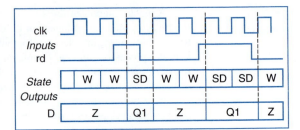

Figure 5.25 Bus interface timing diagram.

Step 2 is to create a datapath, as shown on the right in Figure 5.26. The datapath contains a 4-bit equality comparator to compare A and Faddr, a 32-bit register Q1, and a 32-bit wide three-state driver to enable driving of D by nothing or by Q1. A, Faddr, and Q are the datapath's data inputs, and D is the only data output.

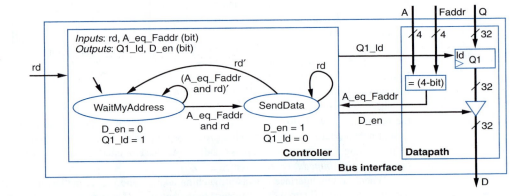

Figure 5.26 Datapath (right) and controller FSM description (left) for the simple bus interface.

Step 3 is to connect the datapath to a controller, as shown in Figure 5.26. The controller has one external control input, rd, and also gets a control input from the datapath, A_eq_Faddr, indicating whether A equals Faddr. The controller has two control outputs to the datapath, with Q1_ld causing Q1 to be loaded with Q, and D_en controlling the three-state driver.

Step 4 is to derive the controller's FSM. We simply replace the data operations in the high-level state machine of Figure 5.24 by the appropriate control signals, as shown on the left side of Figure 5.26. We replace A=Faddr by the signal A_eq_Faddr, the actions of D="Z" and of D=Q by D_en=0 and D_en=1, and the action of Q1=Q by Q1_ld=1. We would then implement the FSM using a state register (in this case only 1 bit) and combinational logic.

You may have heard of several popular buses, like the PCI (Peripheral Component Interface) bus in a personal computer. Those are the buses that a PC "card" plugs into in a PC, like the card shown in Figure 5.27. You can see on the card the metal pads of the buses—each pad corresponds to one wire of the bus. The bus protocol for PCI is far more complex than the protocol in the above example. Hundreds of other "standard" bus protocols exist. Designers not needing to interface to other chips often define their own bus protocol for communication. ◀

Figure 5.27 PCI card plugged into a PC's PCI slot.

▶ *ALL ='s ARE NOT EQUAL.*

Figure 5.24 showed two distinct uses of the "=" symbol. In a state's actions, "=" meant "assign the value of the right side to the left side," e.g., D = Q1. On a transition, "=" meant "the left and right sides are the same," e.g., A = Faddr. Be careful not to confuse those two meanings of the "=" symbol. Some languages use different symbols to distinguish the two meanings. For example, the C language uses "=" for "assign" and "==" for "the same." VHDL uses ":=" (or "<=") for "assign", and "=" for "the same."

Video Compression—Sum-of-Absolute Differences (SAD) Design Example

▶ **EXAMPLE 5.7**   Video compression—sum-of-absolute differences

After a 2004 natural disaster in Indonesia, a TV news reporter reported from the scene by "camera phone." The video was smooth as long as the scene wasn't changing significantly. When the scene changed (like panning across the landscape), the video became very jerky, because the camera phone had to transmit complete pictures rather than just differences, resulting in fewer frames transmitted over the limited bandwidth of the camera phone.

Digitized video is becoming increasingly commonplace, like in the case of the increasingly popular DVD (see Section 6.7 for further information on DVDs). A straightforward digitized video consists of a sequence of digitized pictures, where each picture is known as a *frame*. However, such digitized video results in huge data files. Each pixel of a frame is stored as several bytes, and let's say a frame contains about a million pixels. Let's assume then that we require about 1 Mbyte per frame, and we play approximately 30 frames per second (a normal rate for a TV), so that's 1 Mbyte/frame * 30 frames/sec = 30 Mbytes/sec. One minute of video would require 60 sec * 30 Mbytes/sec = 1.8 Gbytes, and 60 minutes would require 108 Gbytes. A 2-hour movie would require over 200 Gbytes. That's a lot of data, more than can be downloaded quickly over the Internet, or stored on a DVD, which can only hold between 5 Gbytes and 15 Gbytes. In order to make practical use of digitized video with web pages, digital camcorders, cellular telephones, or even with DVDs, we need to compress those files into much smaller files. A key technique in compressing video is to recognize that successive frames often have much similarity, so instead of sending a sequence of digitized pictures, we can send one digitized picture frame (a "base" frame), followed by data describing just the difference between the base frame and the next frame. We can send just the difference data for numerous frames, before sending another base frame. Such a method results in some loss of quality, but as long as we send base frames frequently enough, the quality may be acceptable.

Of course, if there's a major change from one frame to the next (like for a change of scene, or lots of activity), we can't use the difference method. Video compression devices therefore need to quickly estimate the similarity between two successive digitized frames to determine whether frames can be sent using the difference method. A common way to determine the similarity of two frames is to compute what is known as the *sum-of-absolute-differences (SAD)*. For each pixel in frame 1, we compute the difference between that pixel with the corresponding pixel in frame 2. Each pixel is represented by a number, so difference means the difference in numbers. Suppose we represent a pixel with a byte (real pixels are usually represented by at least three bytes), and we are comparing the pixel at the upper left of frames 1 and 2 in Figure 5.28(a). Say frame 1's upper-left pixel has a value of 255. Frame 2's pixel is clearly the same, so would have a value of 255 also.

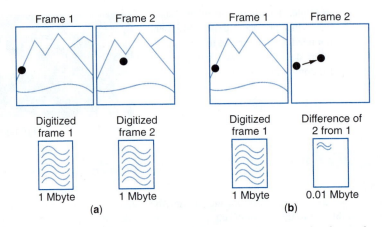

Figure 5.28 A key principle of video compression recognizes that successive frames have much similarity: (a) sending every frame as a distinct digitized picture, (b) instead, sending a base frame and then difference data, from which the original frames can later be reconstructed. If we could do this for 10 frames, (a) would require 1 Mbyte * 10 = 10 Mbytes, while (b) (compressed) would require only 1 Mbyte + 9 * 0.01 Mbyte = 1.09 Mbytes, an almost 10x size reduction.

Thus, the difference of these two pixels is 255 − 255 = 0. We might compare the next pixels of both frames in that row, finding the difference to be 0 again. And so on for all the pixels in that row for both frames, as well as the next several rows. However, when we compute the difference of the left-most pixel of the middle row, where that black circle is located, we see that frame 1's pixel will be black, say with a value of 0. On the other hand, frame 2's corresponding pixel will be white, say with a value of 255. So the difference is 255 − 0 = 255. Likewise, somewhere in the middle of that row, we'll find another difference, this time with frame 1's pixel white (255) and frame 2's pixel black (0)—the difference is again 255 − 0 = 255. Note that we only care about the difference, not which is bigger or smaller, so we are actually looking at the absolute value of the difference between frame 1 and frame 2 pixels. By summing the absolute value of the differences for every pair of pixels, we get a number representing the similarity of the two frames—0 means identical, and bigger numbers means less similar. If the resulting sum is below some threshold (e.g., below 1,000), we might then apply the method of sending the difference data, as in Figure 5.28(b)—we don't explain how to compute the difference data here, as that is beyond the scope of this example. If the sum is above the threshold, then the difference between the blocks is too great, so we might instead send the full digitized frame for frame 2. Thus, video with similarity among frames will achieve a higher compression than video with plenty of differences.

Actually, most video compression methods compute similarity not between two entire frames, but rather between corresponding 16x16 pixel blocks—yet the idea is the same.

Computing the sum of absolute differences is slow in software, so that task may be done using a custom digital circuit, while other tasks may remain in software. For example, you might find an SAD circuit inside a digital camcorder, or inside a cellular telephone that supports video. Let's design such a circuit. A block diagram is shown in Figure 5.29. The circuit's inputs will be a 256-byte memory A, holding the contents of a 16x16 block of pixels of frame 1, and another 256-byte memory B, holding the corresponding block of frame 2. Memories will be discussed in Section 5.6; for now, consider the memory as a register file, and ignore details of the interface to the memories. Another circuit input go tells the circuit when to begin computing. An output sad will present the result after some number of clock cycles.

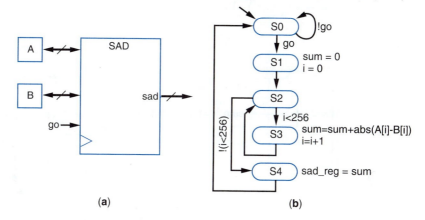

Figure 5.29 Sum-of-absolute-differences (SAD) component: (a) block diagram, and (b) high-level state machine.

Step 1 of our RTL design method is to create a high-level state machine. We can describe the behavior of the SAD component using the high-level state machine shown in Figure 5.29(a). We declare the inputs, outputs, and local registers sum, i, and sad_reg. The sum register will hold the running sum of differences; we make this register 32 bits wide. The i register will be used to index into the current pixel in the block memories; i will range from 0 to 256, and therefore we'll make it 9 bits wide. sad_reg will be connected to the output sad (it's good practice to register your data outputs), so will be 32 bits wide, like the sad output. The state machine initially waits for the input go to become 1. The state machine then initializes registers sum and i to 0. The state machine then enters a loop: if i is less than 256, the state machine computes the absolute value of the difference of the two blocks' pixels indexed by i (the notation A[i] refers to the data in word i of memory A), updates the running sum, increments i, and repeats. Otherwise, the state machine loads sad_reg with the sum, which now represents the final sum, and returns to the first state to wait for the go signal to become 1 again.

One point to re-emphasize is that the order of actions in a state does not impact the results, because all those actions occur simultaneously. Thus, for the state inside the loop, arranging the actions as "sum = sum + abs(A[i]-B[i]); i = i + 1" or as "i = i + 1; sum = sum + abs(A[i]-B[i])" does not impact the results. Either arrangement uses the old value of i.

Step 2 of our RTL design method is to create a datapath. We see from the high-level state machine that we'll need a subtractor, an absolute-value component (which we have not designed earlier, but is straightforward to design), an adder, and a comparison of i to 256. We build the datapath shown in Figure 5.30. The adder will be 32-bits wide, so the 8-bit input coming from the *abs* component will need to have 0s appended for its high 24 bits.

Step 3 is to connect the datapath to a controller block, as shown in Figure 5.30. Note that we've defined the interface to the A and B memories, consisting of a read line, address lines, and data lines. Also note that we haven't explicitly listed the inputs and outputs of the controller's FSM, as they can be seen at the periphery of the controller's block.

Step 4 is to convert the high-level state machine to an FSM. We show the FSM on the left side of Figure 5.30. For convenience, we've shown the original high-level actions (crossed out), and we've shown their replacement by the FSM actions.

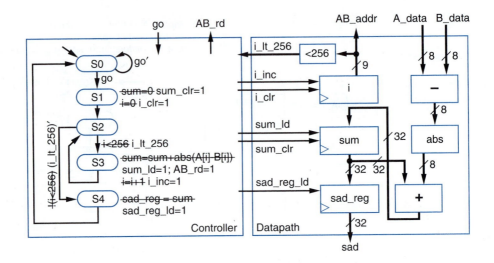

Figure 5.30 SAD datapath and controller FSM.

To complete the design, we would convert the FSM to a controller implementation (a state register and combinational logic), as described in Chapter 3. ◀

Comparing Software and Custom Circuit Implementations

In Example 5.7, we said that the output appears after some number of clock cycles. Let's determine exactly how many cycles. After go becomes 1, our state machine will spend one cycle initializing registers in *S1*, then will spend two cycles in each of the 256 loop iterations (states *S2* and *S3*), and finally one more cycle to update the output register in state *S4*, for a total of 1 + 2*256 + 1 = 514 cycles.

If we executed SAD in software, we would likely need more than two clock cycles per loop iteration. We would need perhaps two cycles to load internal registers, then a cycle for subtract, perhaps two cycles for absolute value, and a cycle for sum, for a total of six cycles per iteration. The custom circuit we built, at two cycles per iteration, is thus about three times faster for computing SAD, assuming equal clock frequencies.

We'll see in Section 6.5 that we could actually build a SAD circuit that is *much* faster.

▶ *DIGITAL VIDEO—IMAGINING THE FUTURE.*

People seem to have an insatiable appetite for good quality video, and thus much attention is placed on developing fast and/or power-efficient encoders and decoders for digital video devices, like DVD players and recorders, digital video cameras, cell phones supporting digital video, video conferencing units, TVs, TV set-top boxes, etc. It's interesting to think toward the future—assuming video encoding/decoding becomes even more powerful and digital communication speeds increase, we might imagine video displays (with audio) on our walls at home or work that continually display what's happening at another home (perhaps our mom's house) or at a partner office on the other side of the country—like a virtual window to another place. Or we might imagine portable devices that enable us to continually see what someone else wearing a tiny camera—perhaps our child or spouse—sees. Those developments could significantly change our living patterns.

RTL Design Pitfalls and Good Practice

Pitfall: Assuming a Register Is Updated in the State in Which the Register Is Written

Perhaps the most common mistake in creating a high-level state machine is assuming that a register is updated in the state in which the register is written. Such an assumption is incorrect, and can lead to unexpected behavior when the state machine reads the register in the same state, and likewise when the state machine reads the register in a transition condition leaving that state. For example, Figure 5.31(a) shows a simple high-level state machine. Examine the state machine, and then answer the following two questions:

- What will be the value of Q after state *A*?
- What will be the final state: *C* or *D*?

The answers may surprise you. The value of Q will not be 99; Q's value will actually be unknown. The reason is illustrated by the timing diagram in Figure 5.31(b). State *A* configures the datapath to load a 99 into R on the next clock edge, and configures the datapath to load the value of register R into register Q on the next clock edge. When the next clock edge occurs, both those loads occur *simultaneously*. Q therefore gets whatever value was in *R* just before the next clock edge, which is unknown.

Furthermore, the final state will not be *D*, but will rather be *C*. The reason is illustrated by the timing diagram in Figure 5.31(b). State *B* configures the datapath to load 100 into R on the next clock cycle, and configures the controller to load the

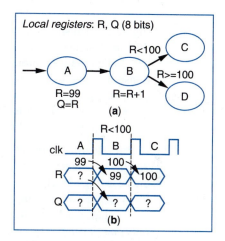

Figure 5.31 High-level state machine that behaves different than some people may expect, due to reads of a register in the same state as writes to that register: (a) state machine, (b) timing diagram.

next state based on the transition condition. R is 99, and therefore the transition condition R<100 is true, meaning the controller will be configured to load state *C* into the state register, not state *D*. On the next clock edge, R becomes 100, and the next state become *C*.

The key is to always remember that *a state's actions* **configure** *the datapath and controller such that the next clock edge will load the desired values—but those values* ***don't actually get loaded*** *until that next clock edge.* Thus, any expressions in a state's actions or outgoing transition conditions will be using the previous values of registers, not the values being assigned in that state itself. By the same reasoning, all the actions of a state occur simultaneously on the next clock edge, and thus could be written in any order.

Assuming that the designer actually wants Q to equal 99 and the final state to be *D*, then a solution is to add an extra state before reading the value of a register that we assign. Figure 5.32(a) shows a new state machine in which the assignment of Q=R has been moved to state *B*, after R=99 has taken effect. Furthermore, the state machine has a new state, *B2*, that simply allows R to be updated with the new value before we read that value in the transition conditions. The timing diagram in Figure 5.32(b) shows the behavior that the designer expected.

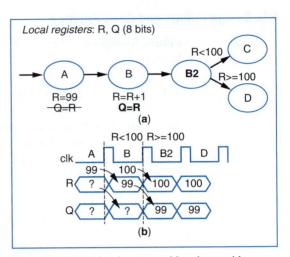

Figure 5.32 High-level state machine that avoids reading just-assigned registers: (a) state machine, (b) timing diagram.

An alternative solution for the transition issue in this case would be to utilize comparison values that take into account that the old value is being used. So instead of comparing R to 100, the comparisons might instead compare to 99.

Avoiding this pitfall is the reason that we included state *S2* in Example 5.7.

Pitfall: Reading Outputs

Another common mistake is to create a high-level state machine in which an external output is read in the state machine. Outputs can only be written and cannot be read. For example, Figure 5.33(a) shows an invalid high-level state machine—the read of P in state *T* is not allowed. If you wish to read an output, then create and use a local register. Figure 5.33(b) shows use of a local register R to avoid reading output P.

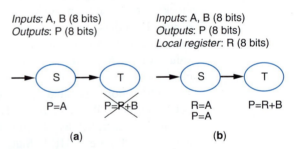

Figure 5.33 (a) Reading an output is not allowed, (b) using a local register.

Good Design Practice: Registered Data Outputs

It's a good idea to always ensure your design has a register at every data output. Doing so prevents those outputs from displaying spurious values. For example, the state machine of Figure 5.33(b) could be implemented as a datapath in which output P is directly connected to the output of an adder, as shown in Figure 5.34. P will therefore output spurious values for some time after R is loaded with A, while the addition is being computed. Furthermore, if B or A changes in some other states, P will also change, but such change is likely not the intended behavior of the state machine—P should only change when we explicitly assign P in a state. Another problem is that any processor using the P output must take into account the adder when computing longest register-to-register delays to determine a circuit's critical path (see Section 5.4).

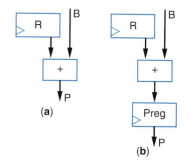

Therefore, we will follow the design practice of always putting a register directly before the data output, as shown in Figure 5.34(b). Even if we don't explicitly declare the register as a local register, we always assume it is there in interpreting the high-level state machine, and we always add that register when creating the datapath. Alternatively, we can explicitly declare that register, and then assume that the output is

Figure 5.34 (a) P will exhibit spurious values, (b) registering P solves the problem.

directly connected to that register—this is the approach we took in Example 5.7, in which we declared the register `sad_reg`. It's good practice to *not* read this register; the register's only purpose is to connect to the output port.

Registering data outputs does have the potential disadvantage of delaying writes to the output port by one cycle, depending on the example.

Data-Dominated RTL Design

We can consider RTL designs as falling into one of two categories: control-dominated designs and data-dominated designs.

A ***control-dominated design*** is a design whose controller contains most of the complexity of the design. When creating such a design, a designer focuses mostly on the design of the controller, meaning design effort goes mostly into defining the state behavior of the system. Once the designer has defined that state behavior, he/she can derive the datapath straightforwardly from that state behavior. A control-dominated design typically responds to external inputs in a precise amount of time, and typically has a simple datapath.

A ***data-dominated design*** is a design whose datapath contains most of the complexity of the design. When creating such a design, a designer focuses mostly on the design of the datapath, meaning design effort goes mostly into instantiating and interconnecting datapath components. Once the designer has defined the datapath, he/she can define the controller's state behavior straightforwardly. A data-dominated design typically has a lot of parallelism in its datapath, and the datapath may be large. For a data-dominated design, designers often skip the first step of our RTL design method of Table 5.1.

The laser-based distance measurer example in the previous section was an example of control-dominated design, since the complexity of the design was really in the controller, not the datapath.

The terms "control-dominated" and "data-dominated" are merely descriptive, and can't be used to strictly categorize designs. Some designs will exhibit properties of both types of designs. It's like the terms "introvert" and "extrovert" for describing people—while the terms are useful, people can't be strictly categorized as either introverts or extroverts, since many people are somewhere in between, or exhibit features of both categories. The example of the simple bus interface was an example of a design that has a similar amount of control and data design. The video compression SAD circuit, at least the way we designed it, was also a mix of control and data.

RTL design is very much a creative process. Two designers may come up with very different designs for the same system, following perhaps different design methods, with those designs differing in terms of performance, size, and other metrics.

FIR Filter Design Example

As our previous examples were either control-dominated or a mix of control and data, we now provide an example of a data-dominated design.

▶ **EXAMPLE 5.8** FIR filter

A digital filter takes a stream of digital inputs and generates a stream of digital outputs with some feature of the input stream removed or modified. Figure 5.35 shows a block diagram of a popular digital filter known as an FIR filter. X and Y are *N*-bits wide each, such as 12 bits each. As a filtering

Figure 5.35 General block diagram of an FIR filter.

example, consider the following stream of digital temperature values on X coming from a car engine temperature sensor sampled every second: 180, 180, 181, *240*, 180, 181. That 240 is probably not an accurate measurement, as a car engine's temperature cannot jump 60 degrees in one second. A digital filter would remove such "noise" from the input stream, generating perhaps an output stream on Y like: 180, 180, 181, *181*, 180, 181.

An FIR filter (usually pronounced by saying the letters "F" "I" "R"), short for "Finite Impulse Response" filter, is a popular general digital filter design that can be used for a wide variety of filtering goals. Figure 5.35 shows a block diagram of an FIR filter. The basic idea of an FIR filter is simple: the present output is obtained by multiplying the present input value by a constant, and adding that result to the previous input value times a constant, and adding that result to the next earlier input value times a constant, and so on. In a sense, adding to previous values in this manner results in a weighted average. We describe digital filtering and FIR filters in more detail in Section 5.11. For the purpose of this example, we merely need to know that an FIR filter can be described by the following equation:

$$y(t) = c0 \times x(t) + c1 \times x(t-1) + c2 \times x(t-2)$$

An FIR filter with three terms, as in the above equation, is known as a *3-tap* FIR filter. Real FIR filters typically have many tens of taps—we use only three taps for the purpose of illustration. A filter designer using an FIR filter achieves a particular filtering goal *simply by choosing the FIR filter's constants*.

We wish to design a circuit to implement an FIR filter. Because the FIR filter equation is just data transformation and no control, let's skip **Step 1** of the RTL design method and go straight to **Step 2**—designing the datapath. We'll need a register for each tap to hold *x(t)*, *x(t-1)*, and *x(t-2)*. On each clock cycle, we'll want to move *x(t-1)* to *x(t-2)*, to move *x(t)* to *x(t-1)*, and to load *x(t)* with the present input. We thus start the datapath with three registers, connected as shown in Figure 5.36.

Notice how the data moves to the right on each clock cycle, so that register *xt0* holds the current input sample, $\texttt{xt1}$ holds the previous input sample, and $\texttt{xt2}$ holds the sample before the previous one. For the example, we'll assume data is 12 bits wide.

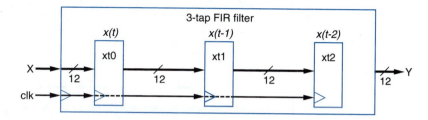

Figure 5.36 Beginning to build the datapath for the FIR filter—inserting and connecting the *x(t)*, *x(t-1)*, and *x(t-2)* registers.

Now we need another register for each tap to hold the constant value $\texttt{c0}$, $\texttt{c1}$, or $\texttt{c2}$—we'll worry later about how those registers will be loaded. We'll also need a multiplier for each tap, to multiply the tap's $\texttt{x}$ value by the constant $\texttt{c}$ value. The datapath with the constant registers and multipliers is shown in Figure 5.37.

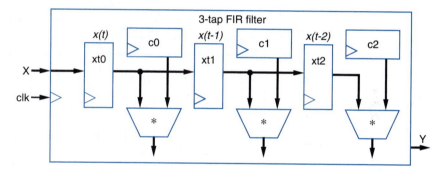

Figure 5.37 Extending the datapath for the FIR filter—inserting and connecting the $\texttt{c0}$, $\texttt{c1}$, and $\texttt{c2}$ registers, along with the multipliers, for each tap. For simplicity, clock connections are not shown, and all data lines are assumed to be 12 bits wide.

The output $\texttt{Y}$ is the sum of each tap's product. We can thus insert adders to compute the sum, and we can connect that sum to the output $\texttt{Y}$, as shown in Figure 5.38.

We have completed the heart of the FIR filter datapath design. We now need to provide a method for a user to load values into the constant registers $\texttt{c0}$, $\texttt{c1}$, and $\texttt{c2}$. Let's create another input $\texttt{C}$ to the filter, a load line $\texttt{CL}$, and a 2-bit address $\texttt{Ca1}$ and $\texttt{Ca0}$, that the filter user can use to load a particular constant register. $\texttt{Ca1Ca0=00}$ indicates that register $\texttt{c0}$ should be loaded, $\texttt{01}$ indicates that $\texttt{c1}$ should be loaded, and $\texttt{10}$ indicates that *c2* should be loaded. Loading of the value on input $\texttt{C}$ into the appropriate register occurs on a clock edge only when $\texttt{CL=1}$. We can straightforwardly design the circuit for such loading using a decoder, as shown in Figure 5.39. The address lines $\texttt{Ca1}$ and $\texttt{Ca0}$ feed into a 2x4 decoder, thus enabling the appropriate register (note that address $\texttt{11}$ is unused). The load input $\texttt{CL}$ is connected to the decoder's enable input. Note that we've also added a register at the $\texttt{Y}$ output, which is generally good design practice, since such a register ensures the output doesn't fluctuate as intermediate products and sums are computed, and reduces the likelihood of the user accidentally extending the critical path by connecting $\texttt{Y}$ through a lot of combinational logic before loading $\texttt{Y}$ into a register.

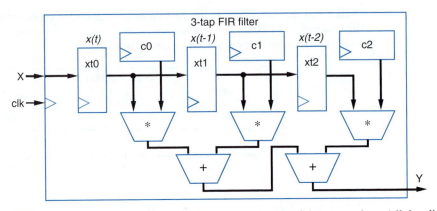

Figure 5.38 Computing the output Y in the FIR filter as the sum of the tap products (all data lines are assumed to be 12 bits wide).

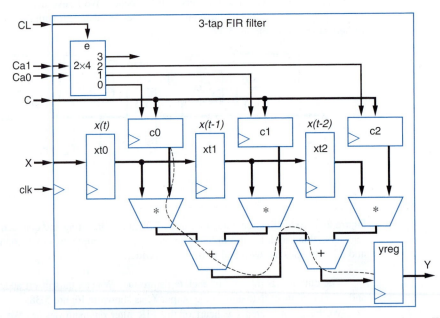

Figure 5.39 Finalizing the FIR filter datapath with circuitry for loading the constant registers. We've also added a register on the Y output, which is good design practice. The critical path—the longest register-to-register delay—is shown as a dotted line.

Our RTL design method involves two steps after designing the datapath to complete the controller. However, this particular design does not require a controller, not even a simple one! *This example is indeed an extreme example of a data-dominated design.* ◀

Comparing Software and Custom Circuit Implementations
It is interesting to compare the performance of the hardware implementation of a 3-tap FIR filter with a software implementation. The critical path goes from the xt and c registers, through one multiplier, and through two adders, before reaching the Y register yreg.

For hardware implementation, let's assume that the adder has a 2 ns delay. Let's also assume that chaining the adders together results in the delays adding, so that two adders chained together have a delay of 4 ns (detailed analysis of the internal gates of the adders could show the delay to actually be slightly less). Let's assume the multiplier has a 20 ns delay. Then the critical path, or longest register-to-register delay (to be discussed further in Section 5.4), would be from *c0* to *yreq*, going through the multiplier and two adders as shown in Figure 5.39. That path's length would be 20+4 = 24 ns. Note that the path from *c1* to *yreg* would be equally long, but not longer. A critical path of 24 ns means the datapath could be clocked at a frequency of 1 / 24 ns = 42 MHz. In other words, a new sample could appear at X every 24 ns, and new outputs would appear at Y every 24 ns.

Now let's consider the hardware performance of a larger sized filter: a 100-tap FIR filter rather than a 3-tap filter. The main performance difference is that we'll need to add 100 values rather than just three. Recall from Section 4.13 that an adder tree is a fast way to add many values. One hundred values will require a tree with seven levels—50 additions, then 25, then 13 (roughly), then 7, then 4, then 2, then 1. So the total delay would be 20 ns (for the multiplier) plus seven adder-delays (7*2ns = 14ns), for a total delay of 34 ns.

For a software implementation, we'll assume 10 ns per instruction. Assume each multiplication or addition would require two instructions. A 100-tap filter would need approximately 100 multiplications and 100 additions, so the total time would be (100 multiplications * 2 instr/mult + 100 additions * 2 instr/add) * 10 ns per instruction = 4000 ns.

In other words, the hardware implementation would be over 100 times faster (4000 ns / 34 ns) than the software implementation. A hardware implementation could therefore process 100 times more data than a software implementation, resulting in much better filtering.

▶ 5.4 DETERMINING CLOCK FREQUENCY

RTL design produces a processor, consisting of a datapath and a controller. Inside the datapath and controller are registers, and registers require a clock signal. A clock signal must have a particular frequency. The frequency will determine how fast the system will execute its specified task. Obviously, a lower frequency will result in slower execution, while a higher frequency will result in a faster execution. Conversely stated, a larger period is slower, while a smaller period is faster.

Designers of digital circuits often (but not always) want their systems to execute as fast as possible. However, a designer cannot choose an arbitrarily high clock frequency (meaning an arbitrarily small period). Consider, for example, the simple circuit in Figure 5.40, in which registers *a* and *b* feed through an adder into register *c*. The adder has a delay of 2 ns, meaning that when the adder's inputs change, the adder's outputs will not be stable until after 2 ns—before 2 ns, the adder's outputs will have spurious values (see Section 4.3 for a description of spurious values appearing at an adder's outputs). If the designer chooses a clock period of 10 ns, the circuit should work fine. Shortening the period to 5 ns will speed the execution. But shortening the period to 1 ns will result in incorrect circuit behavior. One clock cycle might load new values into registers *a* and *b*. The next clock cycle will load register *c* 1 ns later (as well as *a* and *b*), but the output of the adder won't be stable until 2 ns have passed. The value loaded into register *c* will thus be some spurious value that has no useful meaning, and will not be the sum of *a* and *b*.

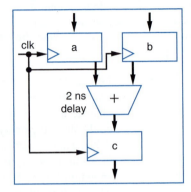

Figure 5.40 Longest path is 2 ns.

Thus, a designer must be careful not to set the clock frequency too high. To determine the highest possible frequency, a designer must analyze the entire circuit, and find the longest path delay from any register to any other register, or from any circuit input to any register. The longest register-to-register or input-to-register delay in a circuit is known as the circuit's **critical path**. Designers then choose a clock whose period is *longer* than the circuit's critical path.

Figure 5.41 illustrates a circuit with at least four possible paths from any register to any other register:

- One path starts at register *a*, goes through the adder, and ends at register *c*. This path's delay is 2 ns.

- Another path starts at register *a*, goes through the adder, through the multiplier, and ends at register *d*. This path's delay is 2 ns + 5 ns = 7 ns.

- Another path starts at register *b*, goes through the adder, through the multiplier, and ends at register *d*. This path's delay is also 2 ns + 5 ns = 7 ns.

- The last path starts at register *b*, goes through the multiplier, and ends at register *d*. This path's delay is 5 ns.

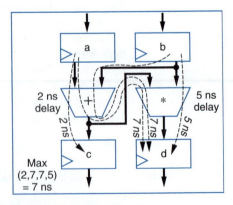

Figure 5.41 Determining the critical path.

The longest path is thus 7 ns (there are actually two such paths). Thus, the clock period must be at least 7 ns.

The above analysis assumes that the only delay between registers is caused by logic delays. In reality, *wires* also have a delay. In the 1980s and 1990s, the delay of logic dominated over the delay of wires— wire delays were often negligible. But in modern chip technologies, the delay of wires may equal or even exceed the delay of logic, and thus wire delays cannot be ignored. Wire delays add to a path's length just as logic delays do. Figure 5.42 illustrates a path length calculation with wire delays included.

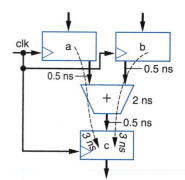

Figure 5.42 Longest path is 3 ns considering wire delays.

Furthermore, the above analysis does not consider setup times for the registers. Recall from Section 3.5 that flip-flop inputs (and hence register inputs) must be stable for a specified amount of time *before* a clock edge. The setup time adds to the path length.

Even considering wire delays and setup times, designers typically choose a clock period that is still *longer* than the critical path by an amount depending on how conservative the designer wants to be with respect to ensuring the circuit works under a variety of operating conditions. Certain conditions can change the delay of circuit components, conditions like very high temperature, very low temperature, vibration, age, etc. Generally, the longer the period beyond the critical path, the more conservative the design. For example, we might determine that the critical path is 7 ns, but we might choose a clock period of 10 ns, or even 15 ns, the latter being quite conservative.

If low power is a design goal, then a designer might choose an even longer period, such as 100 ns, to reduce circuit power. Why reducing the clock frequency reduces power will be discussed in Section 6.6.

When analyzing a processor (controller and datapath) to find the critical path, a designer must be aware that register-to-register paths exist not just within the datapath (Figure 5.43(a)), but also within the controller (Figure 5.43(b)), between the controller and datapath (Figure 5.43(c)), and even between the processor and external components.

The number of possible paths in a circuit can be quite large. Consider a circuit with N registers that has paths from every register to every other register. Then there are $N*N$, or N^2 possible register-to-register paths. For example, if N is 3 and the three registers are named A,

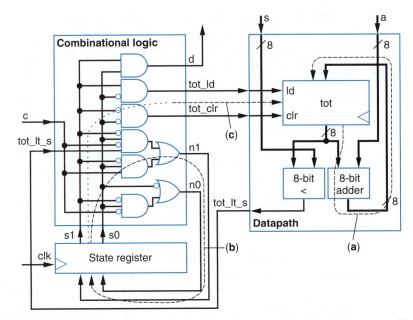

Figure 5.43 Critical paths throughout a circuit: (a) within a datapath, (b) within a controller, (c) between a controller and datapath.

B, and C, then the possible paths are: A—>A, A—>B, A—>C, B—>A, B—>B, B—>C, C—>A, C—>B, C—>C, for 3*3 = 9 possible paths. For N=50, there may be up to 2500 possible paths. Because of the large number of possible paths, automated tools can be of great assistance. **Timing analysis** tools automatically analyze all paths to determine the longest path, and may also ensure that setup and hold times are satisfied throughout the circuit.

▷ 5.5 BEHAVIORAL-LEVEL DESIGN: C TO GATES (OPTIONAL)

As transistors per chip continue to increase and hence designers build more complex digital systems that use those additional transistors, digital system behavior becomes increasingly difficult to understand. Frequently, a designer building a new digital system finds it useful to first describe the desired system behavior using a programming language, like C, C++, or Java, in order to first get that desired behavior correct. (Alternatively, the designer may use the high-level programming constructs in a hardware description language, like VHDL or Verilog, to first get the desired behavior correct.) Then, the designer converts that programming language description to an RTL design, by following the RTL design method that usually starts with a high-level state machine RTL description. Converting a system's programming language description to an RTL description is known as **behavioral-level design**. We'll introduce behavioral-level design using an example.

▷ EXAMPLE 5.9   Sum-of-absolute-differences in C for video compression

Recall Example 5.7, in which we created a sum-of-absolute-differences component. In that example, we started with a high-level state machine—but that state machine wasn't very easy to understand. We can more easily describe the computation of the sum of absolute differences using C code, as shown in Figure 5.44.

```
int SAD (byte A [256], byte B [256]) / / not quite C syntax
{
    uint sum; short uint i;
    sum = 0;
    i = 0;
    while (i < 256) {
        sum = sum + abs (A[i] – B[i]);
        i = i + 1;
    }
    return (sum);
}
```

Figure 5.44 C program description of a sum-of-absolute differences computation—the C program may be easier to develop and easier to understand than a state machine.

That code is much easier to understand for most people than the high-level state machine in Figure 5.29. Thus, for some designs, C code (or something similar) is the most natural starting point.

To begin the RTL design method, we could convert this code to a high-level state machine, like that in Figure 5.29, and then proceed to complete the RTL design method and hence design the circuit. ◀

It is instructive to define a structured method for converting C code to a high-level state machine. Defining such a method makes clear to us that C code can be *automatically compiled* to either software on a programmable processor, or *to a custom digital circuit*. We point out that most designers that start with C code and then continue with RTL design do *not* necessarily follow a particular method in performing such conversion. However, automated tools *do* follow a method having some similarities to the one we now describe. We also point out that the conversion method will sometimes result in "extra" states that you might notice could be combined with other states—these extra states would be combined by a later optimization step, though we'll combine some of them as we follow the method.

We consider three types of statements in C code—assignment statements, while loops, and condition statements (if-then-else)—and provide high-level state machine templates for each such statement.

An assignment statement in C translates simply into a state in a state machine, with the state's actions carrying out the assignment, as shown in Figure 5.45.

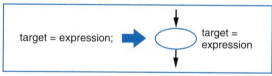

Figure 5.45 State machine template for assignment statement.

An *if-then* statement in C translates into a state that checks the condition of the *if* statement, and branches to the states for the *then* part if the condition is true, otherwise branching past those states to an end state, as shown in Figure 5.46.

We can translate an *if-then-else* statement in C into a similar state machine with a state that checks the condition of the *if* statement, but

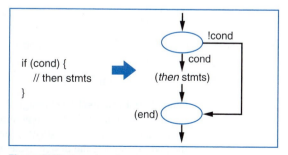

Figure 5.46 Template for if-then statement.

this time branching to states for the *else* part if the *if* condition is false, as shown in Figure 5.47.

The *else* part commonly contains another *if* statement as C programmers may have multiple *else if* parts in a region of code.

Finally, a *while* loop statement in C translates into states similar to an if-then statement, except that after executing the while's statements, if the *while* condition is true, the state machine branches back to the condition check, rather than to the end state, as shown in Figure 5.48. Only when the condition is false can we reach the end state.

Given these simple templates, we can convert a wide variety of C programs to high-level state machines, from which we already know how to create circuit designs following our RTL design method.

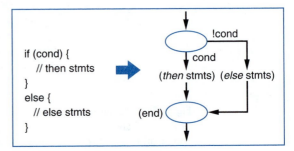

Figure 5.47 Template for if-then-else statement.

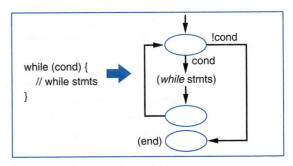

Figure 5.48 Template for while loop statement.

▶ **EXAMPLE 5.10**   Converting an if-then-else statement to a state machine

We are given the C-like code shown in Figure 5.49(a), which computes the maximum of two data inputs X and Y. We can translate that code to a state machine by first translating the if-then-else statement to states using the method of Figure 5.47, as shown in Figure 5.49(b). We then translate the *then* statements to states, and then the *else* statements, yielding the final state machine in Figure 5.49(c).

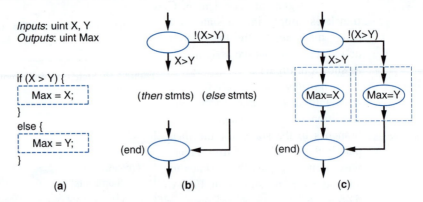

Figure 5.49 Behavioral-level design starting from C code: (a) C code for computing the max of two numbers, (b) translating the if-then-else statement to a high-level state machine, (c) translating the *then* and *else* statements to states. From the state machine in (c), we could use our RTL design method to complete the design. Note: max can be implemented more efficiently; we use max here to provide an easy-to-understand example.   ◀

▷ **EXAMPLE 5.11** SAD C code to high-level state machine conversion

We wish to convert the C program description of the sum-of-absolute differences example of Example 5.9 to a high-level state machine. The code is shown in Figure 5.50(a), written as an infinite loop rather than a procedure call, and using an input "go" to indicate when the system should compute the SAD. The "while (1)" statement, after some optimization, translates just to a transition from the last state back to the first state, so we'll hold off on adding that transition until we have formed the rest of the state machine. We begin with the statement "while (!go)," which based on the template approach translates to the states shown in Figure 5.50(b). Since the loop has no statements

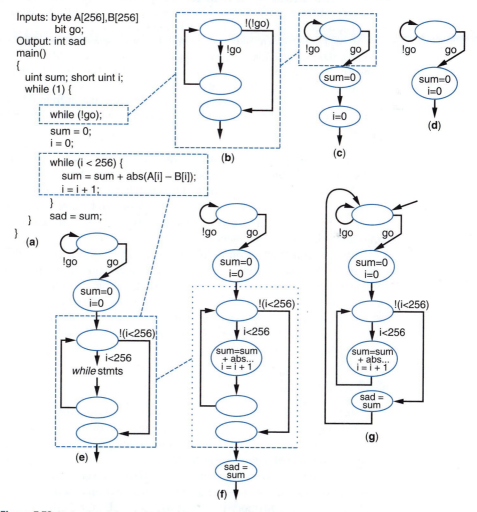

Figure 5.50 Behavioral-level design of the sum-of-absolute difference code: (a) original C code, written as an infinite loop, (b) translating the statement "while (!go);" to a state machine, (c) simplified states for "while (!go);" and states for the assignment statements that follow, (d) merging the two assignment states into one, (e) inserting the template for the next while loop, (f) inserting the states for that while loop, merging two assignment statements into one, (g) the final high-level state machine, with the "while (1)" included by transitioning from the last state back to the first state, and with obviously unnecessary states removed.

in the loop body, we can simplify the loop's states as shown in Figure 5.50(c). Figure 5.50(c) also shows the states for the next two statements, which are assignment statements. Since those two assignments could be done simultaneously, we merge the two states into one, as shown in Figure 5.50(d). We then translate the next *while* loop, using the *while* loop template, to the states shown in Figure 5.50(e). We fill in the states for the *while* loop's statements in Figure 5.50(f), merging the two assignment statement states into one state since the assignments can be done simultaneously. Figure 5.50(f) also shows the state for the last statement of the C code, which assigns *sad=sum*. Finally, we eliminate obviously unnecessary empty states, and add a transition from the last state to the first state to account for the entire code being enclosed in a "while (1)" loop.

Notice the similarity between our final high-level state machine in Figure 5.50(g) and the high-level state machine we designed from scratch in Figure 5.29.

We will need to map the C data types to bits at some point. For example, the C code declares i to be a short unsigned integer, which means 16 bits. So we could declare i to be 16 bits in the high-level state machine. Or, knowing the range of i to be 0 to 256, we could instead define i to be 9 bits (C doesn't have a 9-bit wide data type).

We could then proceed to design a controller and datapath from this state machine, as was done in Figure 5.30. Thus, we can translate C code to gates, using a straightforward automatable method. ◀

Through the previous examples, you have seen how C code can be converted to a custom digital circuit using methods that are fully automatable.

General C code can contain additional types of statements, some of which can be easily translated to states. For example, a *for* loop can be translated to states by first transforming the *for* loop into a *while* loop. A *switch* statement can be translated by first translating the *switch* statement to *if-then-else* statements.

Some C constructs pose problems for converting to a circuit, though. For example, pointers and recursion are not easy to translate. Thus, tools that automate behavioral design from C code typically impose restrictions on the allowable C code that can be handled by the tool. Such restrictions are known as **subsetting** the language.

While we have emphasized C code in this section, obviously any similar language, such as C++, Java, VHDL, Verilog, etc., can be converted to custom digital circuits—with appropriate language subsetting.

▶ 5.6 MEMORY COMPONENTS

Register-transfer level design involves instantiating and connecting datapath components to form datapaths, controlled by controllers. RTL design often utilizes some additional components outside the datapath and controller.

One such component is a memory. An **MxN memory** is a memory component able to store *M* data items of *N* bits each. Each data item in a memory is known as a **word**. Figure 5.51 depicts the storage available in an *MxN* memory.

We can generally categorize memories into two groups: RAM memory, which can be written to and read from, and ROM memory, which can only be read from. However, as we shall see, the distinction between the two categories is blurring due to new technologies.

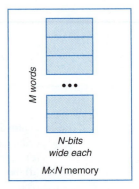

Figure 5.51 Logical view of a memory.

Random Access Memory (RAM)

A RAM is logically the same as a register file (see Section 4.10)—both components are memories whose words (each of which can be thought of as a register) can be individually read and written using address inputs. The differences between a RAM and a register file are:

* The size of *M*—We typically refer to smaller memories (from 4 to 512 or perhaps even 1024 words or so) as register files, and larger memories as RAMs.

* The bit storage implementation—For large numbers of words, a compact implementation becomes increasingly important. Thus, a RAM typically uses a very compact implementation for bit storage, rather than using a flip-flop.

* The memory's physical shape—For large numbers of words, the physical shape of the memory's implementation becomes important. A tall rectangular shape will have some short wires and some long wires, whereas a square shape will have all medium length wires. A RAM therefore typically has a square shape, to reduce the memory's critical path. Reads are performed by first reading out an entire row of words, and then selecting the appropriate word (column) out of that row.

There's no clear-cut border between what defines a register file and what defines a RAM. Smaller memories (typically) tend to be called register files, and larger memories tend to be called RAMs. But you'll often see the terms used quite interchangeably.

A typical RAM is single-ported. Some RAMs are dual-ported. Adding more ports to RAMs is much less common than to register files, because a RAM's larger size makes the delay and size overhead of extra ports much more costly. Nevertheless, conceptually, a RAM can have an arbitrary number of read ports and write ports, just like a register file.

Figure 5.52 shows a block diagram for a 1024x32 single-port RAM ($M = 1024$, $N = 32$). data is a 32-bit wide set of data lines that can serve either as input lines during writes or as output lines during reads. addr is a 10-bit input serving as the address lines during reads or writes. rw is a 1-bit control input that indicates whether the present operation should be a read or a write (e.g., rw = 0 means read, rw = 1 means write). en is a 1-bit control input that enables the RAM for reading or writing—if we don't want to read nor write during a particular clock cycle, we set en to 0 to prevent a read or write (regardless of the value of rw).

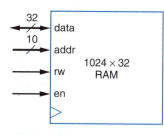

Figure 5.52 1024x32 RAM block symbol.

▶ *WHY IS IT CALLED "RANDOM ACCESS" MEMORY?*

In the early days of digital design, RAMs did not exist. If you had information you wanted your digital circuit to store, you stored it on a magnetic drum, or a magnetic tape. Tape drives (and drum drives too) had to spin the tape to get the head, which could read or write onto the tape, above the desired memory location. If the head was currently above location 900, and you wanted to write to location 999, the tape would have to spin past 901, 902, ...998, until location 999 was under the head. In other words, the tape was accessed *sequentially*. When RAM was first released, its most appealing feature was that any "random" address could be accessed in the same amount of time as any other address—regardless of the previously read address. That's because there is no "head" used to access a RAM, and no spinning of tapes or drums. Thus, the term "random access" memory was used, and has stuck to this day.

Figure 5.53 shows the logical internal structure of an *MxN* RAM. By "logical" structure, we mean that we can think of the structure being implemented in that way, although a real physical implementation may possess a different actual structure. (As an analogy, a logical structure of a telephone includes a microphone and a speaker connected to a phone line, although real physical telephones vary tremendously in their implementations, including handheld devices, headsets, wireless connections, built-in answering machines, etc.) The main part of the RAM structure is the grid of bit storage blocks, also known as *cells*. A collection of N cells forms a word, and there are M words. The address inputs feed into a decoder, each output of which enables all the cells in one word corresponding to the present address values. The enable input en can disable the decoder and prevent any word from being enabled. The read/write control input rw also connects to every cell to control whether the cell will be written with wdata, or read out to rdata. The data lines are connected through one word's cell to the next word's cell, so each cell must be designed to only output its contents when enabled and thus output nothing when disabled, to avoid interfering with another cell's output.

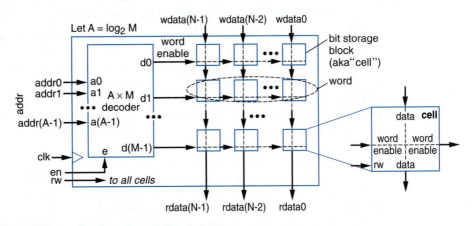

Figure 5.53 Logical internal structure of a RAM.

Notice that the RAM in Figure 5.53 has the same inputs and outputs as the RAM block diagram in Figure 5.52, except that the RAM in Figure 5.53 has separate write and read data lines whereas Figure 5.52 has a single set of data lines (a single port). Figure 5.54 shows how the separate lines might be combined inside a RAM having just a single set of data lines.

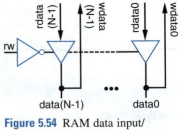

Figure 5.54 RAM data input/output for a single port.

Bit Storage in a RAM

Compared to a register file, the key feature of RAM is its compactness. Recall from Chapter 3 that we implemented a bit storage block using a D flip-flop. Because RAMs store large numbers of bits, RAMs utilize a bit storage block that is more compact than a flip-flop. We thus discuss briefly the internal design of the bit storage blocks inside two popular types of RAM—static RAM and dynamic RAM. However, be forewarned that the internal design of those blocks involves electronics issues beyond the scope of this book, and instead is within the scope of textbooks on VLSI or advanced digital design. Fortunately, a RAM component hides the complexity of its internal electronics by using a memory controller, and thus a digital designer's interaction with a RAM remains as discussed in the previous section.

Static RAM

Static RAM uses a bit storage block involving two inverters connected in a loop, as shown in Figure 5.55. A bit d will go through the bottom inverter to become d', then back through the top inverter to become d again—thus, the bit is stored in the inverter loop. Notice that this bit storage block has an extra line, data', passing through it, compared with the "logical" RAM structure in Figure 5.53.

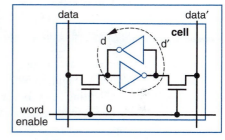

Figure 5.55 SRAM cell.

To write a bit into this inverter loop, we set the data line to the value of the desired bit, and data' to the complement. So to store a 1, the memory controller sets data=1 and data'=0, as shown in Figure 5.56. (To store a 0, the controller would have set data=0 and data'=1.) The controller then sets enable=1, which turns on both shown transistors. The data and data' values thus appear in the inverter loop as shown (overwriting whatever value was there before). Fully understanding why this circuit works involves electrical details beyond the scope of this discussion.

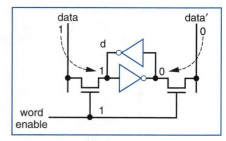

Figure 5.56 Writing a 1 to an SRAM cell.

Reading the stored bit can be done by first setting the data and data' lines *both* to 1 (an act known as ***precharging***), and then by setting enable to 1. One of the enabled transistors will have a 0 at one end, causing the precharged 1 on the data or data' to drop to a voltage slightly less than a regular logic 1. Both the data and data' lines connect to a special circuit called a ***sense amplifier*** that detects whether the voltage on data is slightly higher than data', meaning logic 1 is stored, or whether the voltage on data' is slightly higher than on data, meaning logic 0 is stored. Again, details of the electronics are beyond the scope of this discussion.

Notice that the bit storage block of Figure 5.57 utilizes six transistors—two inside each of the two inverters, and two transistors outside the inverters. Six transistors are fewer than needed inside a D flip-flop. A tradeoff is that special circuitry must be used to read a bit stored in this bit storage block, whereas a D flip-flop outputs regular logic values directly. Such special circuitry slows the access time of the stored bits.

RAM based on a six-transistor bit storage block, or similar such block, is known as a *static RAM*, or *SRAM*. A static RAM maintains the stored bit as long as power is supplied to the transistors. Except, of course, when the block is being written, the stored bit does *not change*—it is static (not changing).

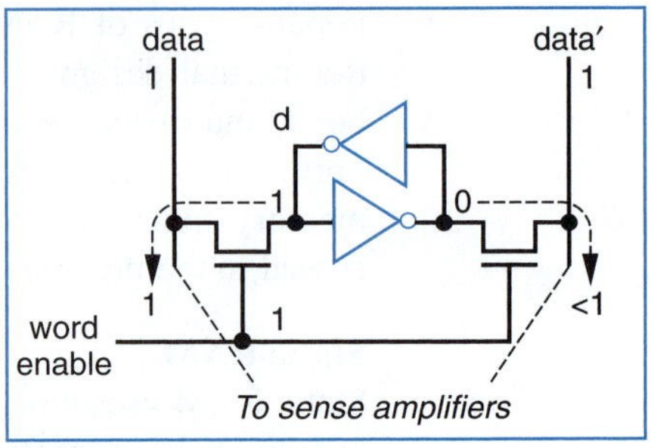

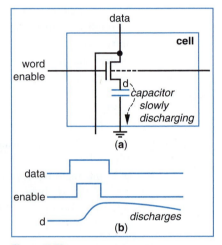

Figure 5.57 Reading an SRAM.

Dynamic RAM

An alternative popular bit storage block used in RAM has only a single transistor per block. Such a block utilizes a (relatively large) capacitor at the output of the transistor, as shown in Figure 5.58(a).

Writing can occur when enable is 1: data=1 will charge the top plate of the capacitor to a 1, while data=0 will make it 0. When enable is returned to 0, a 1 on the top plate will begin to discharge across to the bottom plate of the capacitor on to ground (Why? Because that's what a capacitor does.) However, the capacitor is intentionally designed to be relatively large, so that the discharge takes a long time, during which time the bit d is effectively stored in the capacitor. Figure 5.58(b) provides a timing diagram illustrating the charge and discharge of the capacitor.

Figure 5.58 DRAM bit storage (a) bit storage block, (b) discharge.

Reading can be done by first setting data to a voltage midway between 0 and 1, and then setting enable to 1. The value stored in the capacitor will alter the voltage on the data line, and that altered voltage can be sensed by special circuits connected to the data line that amplify the sensed value to either a logic 1 or a logic 0.

It turns out that reading the charge stored in the capacitor discharges the capacitor. Thus, the RAM must immediately write the read bit back to the bit storage block after reading the block. The RAM must contain a memory controller that automatically performs such a write back.

Because a bit stored in the capacitor gradually discharges to ground, the RAM must *refresh* every bit storage block before the bits completely discharge and hence the stored bit is lost. To refresh a bit storage block, the RAM must read the block and then write the read bit back to the block. Such refreshing may be done every few microseconds. The RAM must include a built-in memory controller that automatically performs these refreshes.

DRAM chips first appeared in the early 1970s, and could hold only a few thousand bits. Modern DRAMs can hold many billions of bits.

Note that the RAM may be busy refreshing itself at a time that we wish to read the RAM. Furthermore, every read must be followed by an automatic write. Thus, RAM based on one-transistor plus capacitor technology may be slower to access.

Because the stored bit *changes* (discharges) even when power is supplied and we are not writing the bit storage block, RAM based on the one transistor plus capacitor bit storage block is known as *dynamic RAM*, or *DRAM*.

Compared to SRAM, DRAM is even more compact, requiring only one transistor per bit storage block rather than six transistors. The tradeoff is that DRAM requires refreshing, which ultimately slows the access time. Another tradeoff, not alluded to above, is that creating the relatively large capacitor in a DRAM requires a special chip fabrication process, and thus incorporating DRAM with regular logic can be costly. In the 1990s, incorporating DRAM with regular logic on the same chip was nearly unheard of. Technology advancements, however, have led to DRAM and logic appearing on the same chip in more and more cases.

Figure 5.59 graphically depicts the compactness advantages of SRAM over register files, and DRAM over SRAM, for storing the *same* number of bits.

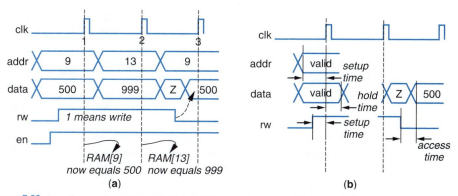

Figure 5.59 Depiction of compactness benefits of SRAM and DRAM (not to scale).

Using a RAM

Figure 5.60 shows timing diagrams describing how to write and read the RAM of Figure 5.52. The timing diagram in Figure 5.60 shows how to write a 9 and a 13 into locations 500 and 999 during clock edges 1 and 2, respectively. The next cycle shows how to read location 9 of the RAM, by setting `addr=9`, `data=Z`, and `rw=0` (meaning read). Shortly after `rw` becomes 0, `data` becomes 500 (the value we had previously stored in location 9). Notice that we had to disable our writing of `data` first (by setting it to `Z`), so as not to interfere with the data being read from the RAM. Also notice that this RAM's read functionality is asynchronous.

Figure 5.60 Reading and writing a RAM: (a) timing diagrams, (b) setup, hold, and access times.

The delay between our setting the `rw` line to read and the read data stabilizing at the `data` output is known as the RAM's *access time* or *read time*.

We now provide an example of using a RAM in an RTL design.

► **EXAMPLE 5.12** Digital sound recorder using a RAM

Let's design a system that can record sound, and can play back that recorded sound. Such a recorder is found in various toys, in telephone answering machines, in cell phone outgoing announcements, and numerous other devices. We'll need an analog-to-digital converter to digitize the sound, a RAM to store the digitized sound, a digital-to-analog converter to output the digitized sound, and a processor to control both converters and the RAM. Figure 5.61 shows a block diagram of the system.

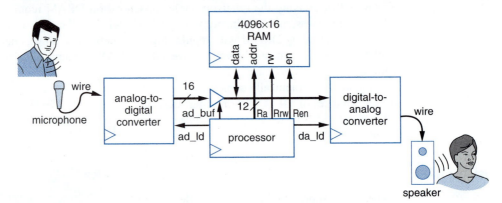

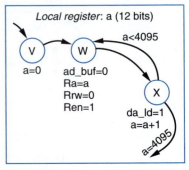

Figure 5.61 Utilizing a RAM in a digital sound recorder system.

To store digitized sound, the processor block can implement the high-level state machine segment shown in Figure 5.62. The machine first intializes its internal address counter a to 0 in state *S*. Next, in state *T*, the machine loads a value into the analog-to-digital converter to cause a new analog sample to be digitized, and sets the three-state buffer to pass that digitized value to the RAM's data lines. That state also sets the RAM address to the counter a's value, and sets the control lines to enable writing. The machine then transitions to state *U*, whose transitions check the value of a against 4095. That state also increments a. (Remember that the transitions from *U* will use the old value, not the incremented value, of a. Thus, the transitions compare with 4095, not 4096.) The machine returns to state *T* and hence continues writing samples in sequential memory addresses as long as the memory is not yet filled (a < 4095). Notice that the comparison is with 4095, not 4096. This is because the action in state X of a = a + 1 does not occur until the next clock edge, so the comparison of a < 4095 on state *X*'s outgoing transition uses the old value of a, not the incremented value (See Section 5.3 discussion of common pitfalls.)

To playback the stored digitized sound, the processor block can implement the high-level state machine segment shown in Figure 5.63. After initializing the counter a in state *V*, the machine enters state *W*. State *W*

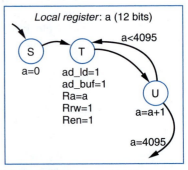

Figure 5.62 State machine for storing digitized sound in RAM.

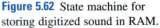

Figure 5.63 State machine for playing sound from the RAM.

disables the three-state buffer, to avoid interfering with the RAM's output data that will appear during RAM reads. That state also sets the RAM address lines, and sets the RAM control lines to enable reading. Read data will thus appear on data lines. The next state *X* loads a value into the digital-to-analog converter, to convert the data just read from RAM to the analog signal. That state also increments the counter a. The machine returns to state *W* to continue reading, until the entire memory has been read.   ◀

Read-Only Memory (ROM)

A Read-Only Memory (ROM) is a memory that can be read from, but not written to. Because of being read only, the bit-storage mechanism in a ROM can be made to have several advantages over a RAM, including:

- *Compactness*—a ROM's bit storage may be even smaller than a RAM's.

- *Nonvolatility*—A ROM's bit storage maintains its contents even after the power supply to the ROM is shut off—when turned back on, the ROM's contents can be read again. In contrast, a RAM loses its contents when power is shut off. A memory that loses its contents when power is shut off is known as **volatile**, while a memory that maintains its contents without power is known as **nonvolatile**.

- *Speed*—A ROM may be faster to read than a RAM, especially than a DRAM.

- *Low-power*—A ROM does not consume power to maintain its contents, in contrast to a RAM. Thus, a ROM consumes less power than a RAM.

Therefore, when the data stored in a memory will not change, we might choose to store that data in a ROM to gain the above advantages.

Figure 5.64 shows a block symbol of a 1024x32 ROM. The logical internal structure of an *M*x*N* ROM is shown in Figure 5.65. Notice that the internal structure is very similar to the internal structure of a RAM shown in Figure 5.53. Bit storage blocks forming a word are enabled by a decoder output, with the decoder input being the address. However, because a ROM can only be read and cannot be written, there is no need for a rw input control to specify read versus write, nor for wdata inputs to provide data being written. Also, because no synchro-

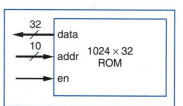

Figure 5.64 1024x32 ROM block symbol.

nous writes occur in a ROM, the ROM does not have a clock input. In fact, not only is a ROM an asynchronous component, but in fact a ROM can be thought of as a *combinational* component (when we only read from the ROM; we'll see variations later).

Some readers might at this point be wondering how we write the initial contents of a ROM that we then can only read. After all, if we can't write the contents of a ROM at all, then the ROM is really of no use to us. Obviously, there must be a way to write the contents of a ROM, but in ROM terminology, the writing of the initial contents of a ROM is known as **ROM programming**. ROM types differ in their bit storage block implementations, which in turn causes differences in the methods used for ROM programming. We now describe several popular bit storage block implementations for ROM.

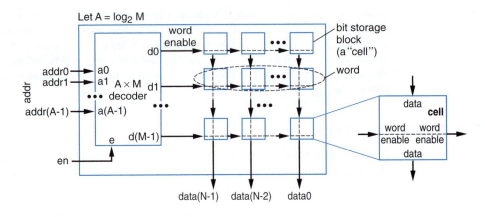

Figure 5.65 Logical internal structure of a ROM.

ROM Types

Mask-programmed ROM

Figure 5.66 illustrates the bit storage cell for a mask-programmed ROM. A *mask-programmed ROM* has its contents programmed when the chip is manufactured, by directly *wiring* 1s to cells that should store a 1, and 0s to cells that should store a 0. Recall that a "1" is actually a higher-than-zero voltage coming from one of several power input pins to a chip—thus, wiring a 1 means wiring the power input pin directly to the cell. Likewise, wiring a 0 to a cell means wiring the ground pin directly to the cell. Be aware that Figure 5.66 presents a *logical* view of a mask-pro-

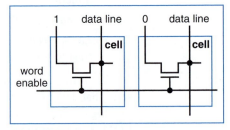

Figure 5.66 Mask-programmed ROM cells: left cell programmed with 1, right cell with 0.

grammed ROM cell—the actual physical design of such cells may be somewhat different—for example, a common design strings several vertical cells together to form a large NOR-like logic gate. We leave details for more advanced textbooks on CMOS circuit design.

Wires are placed onto chips during manufacturing by using a combination of light-sensitive chemicals and light passed through lenses and "masks" that block the light from reaching regions of the chemicals. (See Chapter 7 for further details.) Hence the term "mask" in mask-programmed ROM.

Mask-programmed ROM has the best compactness of any ROM type, but the contents of the ROM must be known during chip manufacturing. This ROM type is best suited for high-volume well-established products in which compactness or very low cost is critical, and in which programming of the ROM will never be done after the ROM's chip is manufactured.

Fuse-Based Programmable ROM—One-Time Programmable (OTP) ROM

Figure 5.67 illustrates the bit storage cell for a fuse-based ROM. A *fuse-based ROM* uses a fuse in each cell. A fuse is an electrical component that initially conducts from one end to the other just like a wire, but whose connection from one end to the other can be destroyed ("blown") by passing a higher-than-normal current through the fuse. A blown fuse does not conduct and is instead an open circuit (no connection). In the figure, the cell on the left has its fuse intact, so when the cell is enabled, a 1 appears on the data line. The

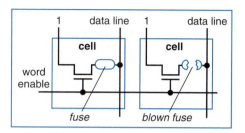

Figure 5.67 Fuse-based ROM cells: left cell programmed with 1, right cell with 0.

cell on the right has its fuse blown, so when the cell is enabled, nothing appears on the data line (special electronics will be necessary to convert that nothing to a logic 0).

A fuse-based ROM is manufactured with all fuses intact, so the initially stored contents are all 1s. A user of this ROM can program the contents by connecting the ROM to a special device, known as a *programmer*, that provides higher than normal currents to only those fuses in cells that should store 0s. Because a user can program the contents of this ROM, the ROM is known as a programmable ROM, or *PROM*.

A blown fuse cannot be changed back to its initial conducting form. Thus, a fuse-based ROM can only be programmed once. Fuse-based ROM are therefore also known as *one-time programmable (OTP) ROM*.

Erasable PROM—EPROM

Figure 5.68 depicts a logical view of an erasable PROM cell. An *erasable PROM*, or *EPROM*, cell uses a special type of transistor, having what is known as a floating gate, in each cell. The details of a floating gate transistor are beyond the scope of this section, but briefly—a floating gate transistor has a special gate in which electrons can be "trapped." A transistor with electrons trapped in its gate stays in the nonconducting situation, and thus is programmed to store a 0. Otherwise, the cell is considered to store a 1.

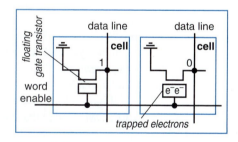

Figure 5.68 EPROM cells: left cell programmed with 1, right cell with 0.

Special electronic circuitry converts sensed currents on the data lines as logic 1 or 0.

An EPROM cell initially has no electrons trapped in any floating gate transistors, so the initially stored contents are all 1s. A programmer device applies higher-than-normal voltages to those transistors in cells that should store 0s. That high voltage causes electrons to *tunnel* through a small insulator into the floating gate region. When the voltage is removed, the electrons do not have enough energy to tunnel back, and thus are trapped as shown in the right cell of Figure 5.68.

The electrons can be freed by exposing the electrons to ultraviolet (UV) light of a particular wavelength. The UV light energizes the electrons such that they tunnel back through the small insulator, thus escaping the floating gate region. Exposing an EPROM chip to UV light therefore "erases" all the stored 0s, restoring the chip to having all 1s as contents, after which the EPROM can be programmed again. Hence the term "erasable" PROM. Such a chip can typically be erased and reprogrammed about ten thousand times or more, and can retain its contents without power for ten years or more. Because a chip usually appears inside a black package that doesn't pass light, a chip with an EPROM requires a window in that package through which UV light can pass, as shown in Figure 5.69.

Figure 5.69 The "window" in the package of a microprocessor that uses an EPROM to store programs.

EEPROM and Flash Memory

An *electrically erasable PROM*, or *EEPROM*, utilizes the EPROM programming method of using high voltage to trap electrons in a floating gate transistor. However, unlike an EPROM that requires UV light to free the electrons and hence erase the PROM, an EEPROM uses another high voltage to free the electrons. EEPROMs thus avoid the need for placing the chip under UV light.

Because EEPROMs use voltages for erasing, those voltages can be applied to specific cells only. Thus, while EPROMs must be erased in their entirety, EEPROMs can be erased one word at a time. Thus, we can erase and reprogram certain words in an EEPROM without changing the contents of other words.

Some EEPROMs require a special programmer device for programming. However, most modern EEPROMs do not require special voltages to be applied to the pins, and also include internal memory controllers that manage the programming process. Thus, we can reprogram an EEPROM's contents (or part of its contents) without ever removing the chip from the system that the EEPROM serves—such an EEPROM is known as being *in-system programmable*. Most such devices can therefore be read and written in a manner very similar to a RAM.

Figure 5.70 shows a block diagram of an EEPROM. Notice that the data lines are bidirectional, just as was the case for RAM. The EEPROM has a control input write—write=0 indicates a read operation (when en=1), while write=1 indicates that the data on the data lines should be programmed into the word at the address specified by the address lines. Programming a word into an EEPROM takes time, though, perhaps several, dozens, hundreds, or even thousands of clock cycles. Therefore, EEPROMs may have a control output busy to indicate that programming is not yet complete. While the device is busy, the EEPROM user should not try writing to a different word. Fortunately, most EEPROMs will load

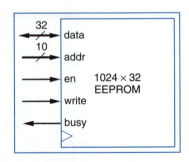

Figure 5.70 1024x32 EEPROM block symbol.

the data to be programmed and the address into internal registers, freeing the circuit that is writing the EEPROM from having to hold these values constant during programming.

Modern EEPROMs can be programmed tens of thousands to millions of times or more, and can retain their contents for tens to one hundred years or more without power.

While erasing one word at a time is fine for some applications that utilize EEPROM, other applications need to erase large blocks of memory quickly—for example, a digital camera application would need to erase a block of memory corresponding to an entire picture. *Flash memory* is a type of EEPROM in which all the words with a large block of memory can be erased very quickly, perhaps simultaneously, rather than one word at a time. A flash memory may be completely erased by setting an `erase` control input to `1`. Many flash memories also allow only a specific region, known as a block or sector, to be erased while other regions are left untouched.

Using a ROM

We now provide examples of using a ROM in RTL designs.

► **EXAMPLE 5.13** Talking doll using a ROM

We wish to design a doll that speaks the message "Nice to meet you" whenever the doll's right arm is moved. A block diagram of the system is shown in Figure 5.71. A vibration sensor in the doll's right arm has an output `v` that is `1` when vibration is sensed. A processor detects the vibration and should then output a digitized version of the "Nice to meet you" message to a digital-to-analog converter attached to a speaker. The "Nice to meet you" message will be the prerecorded voice of a professional actress. Because that message will not change for the lifetime of the doll product, we can store that message in a ROM.

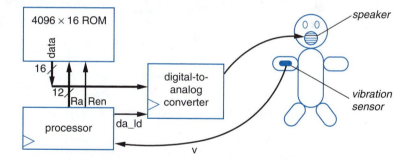

Figure 5.71 Utilizing a ROM in a talking doll system.

Figure 5.72 shows a high-level state machine segment that plays the message after detecting vibration. The machine starts in state *S*, initializing the ROM address counter a to 0, and waiting for vibration to be sensed. When vibration is sensed, the machine proceeds to state *T*, which reads the current ROM location. The machine moves on to state *U*, which loads the digital-to-analog converter with the read value from ROM, increments a, and proceeds back to *T* as long as a hasn't reached 4095 (remember that the transition from *U* uses the value of a before the increment, so compares to 4095, not to 4096).

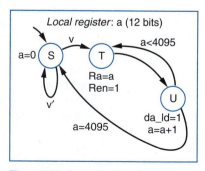

Figure 5.72 State machine for reading the ROM.

Because this doll's message will never change, we might choose to use a mask-programmed ROM or an OTP ROM. We might utilize OTP ROM during prototyping or during initial sales of the doll, and then produce mask-programmed ROM versions during high-volume production of the doll. ◀

▶ **EXAMPLE 5.14** Digital telephone answering machine using a flash memory

We are to design the outgoing announcement part of a telephone answering machine (e.g., "We're not home right now, leave a message."). That announcement should be stored digitally, should be recordable by the machine owner any number of times, and should be saved even if power is removed from the answering machine. Recording begins immediately after the owner presses a record button, which sets a signal rec to 1. Because we must be able to record the announcement, we cannot use a mask-programmed ROM or OTP ROM. Because removing power should not cause the announcement to be lost, we cannot use a RAM. Thus, we might choose an EEPROM or a flash memory. We'll use a flash memory, as shown in Figure 5.73. Notice that the flash memory has the same interface as a RAM, except that the flash memory has an extra input named erase. erase on this particular flash memory clears the contents of the entire flash. While the flash memory is erasing itself, the flash sets an output busy to 1, during which time we cannot write to the flash memory.

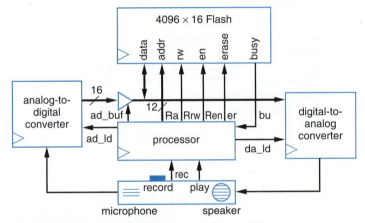

Figure 5.73 Utilizing a flash memory in a digital answering machine.

Figure 5.74 shows a high-level state machine segment for recording the announcement. The state machine segment begins when the record button is pressed. State *S* activates the erase of the flash memory (er=1), and then state *T* waits for the erasing to complete (bu'). Such erasing should occur in just a few milliseconds, so we shouldn't miss any of the spoken announcement. The state machine then transitions to state *U*, which copies a digitized sample from the analog-digital converter to the flash memory, writing to the current address a. State *U* also increments a. The next state (*V*) checks to see if the memory is filled with samples by checking if a<4096, returning to state *U* until the memory is filled.

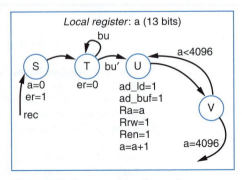

Figure 5.74 State machine for storing digitized sound in a flash memory.

Notice that, unlike Examples 5.12 and 5.13, this state machine increments a before the state that checks for the last address (state *V*), so *V*'s transitions use 4096, not 4095. We show this version just for variety. The version in Example 5.12 may be slightly better because that version requires that a, and the comparator, only be 12 bits wide (to represent 0 to 4095) rather than 13 bits wide (to represent 0 to 4096).

This state machine assumes that writes to the flash occur in one clock cycle. Some flash memories require more time for writes, asserting their busy output until the write has completed. For such a flash, we would need to add a state between states *U* and *V*, similar to the state *T* between *S* and *U*.

To prevent missing sound samples while waiting, we might want to first save the entire sound sample in a 4096x16 RAM, and then copy the entire RAM contents to the flash. ◀

The Blurring of the Distinction between RAM and ROM

Notice that EEPROM and flash ROM blur the distinction between RAM and ROM. Many modern EEPROM devices are writable just like a RAM, having nearly the same interface, with the only difference being longer write times to an EEPROM than to a RAM. However, the difference between those times is shrinking each year.

Further blurring the distinction are ***nonvolatile RAM*** (***NVRAM***) devices, which are RAM devices that retain their contents even without power. Unlike ROM, NVRAM write times are just as fast as regular RAM—typically one clock cycle. One type of NVRAM simply includes an SRAM with a built-in battery, with the battery able to supply power to the SRAM for perhaps ten years or more. Another type of NVRAM includes both an SRAM and an EEPROM—the NVRAM controller automatically backs up the SRAM's contents into the EEPROM, typically just at the time when power is being removed. Furthermore, extensive research and development into new bit storage technologies are leading to NVRAMs that are even closer to RAM in terms of performance and density while being nonvolatile. One such technology is known as MAGRAM, short for magnetic RAM, which uses magnetism to store charge, having access times similar to DRAM, but without the need for refreshing, and with nonvolatility.

Thus, digital designers have a tremendous variety of memory types available to them, with those types differing in their cost, performance, size, nonvolatility, ease-of-use, write time, duration of data retention, and other factors.

▶ 5.7 QUEUES (FIFOs)

Sometimes our data storage needs specifically require that we read items in the same order that we wrote them, and that reading removes the item from the list. For example, a busy restaurant may maintain a waiting list of customers—the host writes customer names to the *rear* of the list, but when a table becomes available, the host reads the next customer's name from the *front* of the list and removes that name from the list. Thus, the first customer written to the list is the first customer read from the list. A ***queue*** is

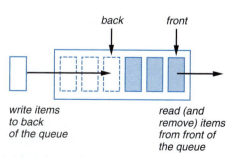

write items
to back
of the queue

read (and
remove) items
from front of
the queue

Figure 5.75 Conceptual view of a queue.

PLEASE
QUEUE
FROM
THIS
END

a list that is written at the rear of the list but read from the beginning of the list, with a read also removing the read item from the list, as illustrated in Figure 5.75. The common term for a queue in American English is a "line"—for example, you stand in a line at the grocery store, with people entering the rear of the line, and being served from the front of the line. In British English, the word queue is used directly in everyday language (which sometimes confuses Americans who visit other English-speaking countries). Because the first item written into the list will be the first item read out of the list, a queue is known as being *first-in first-out* (FIFO). As such, sometimes queues are called *FIFO queues*, although that term is redundant because a queue is by definition first-in first-out. The term *FIFO* itself is often used to refer to a queue. The term *buffer* is also sometimes used. A write to a queue is sometimes called a *push* or *enqueue*, and a read is sometimes called *pop* or *dequeue*.

We can implement a queue using a memory—either a register file or a RAM, depending on the queue size needed. When using a memory, the front and rear will move to different memory locations as the queue is written and read, as illustrated in Figure 5.76. The figure shows an initially empty eight-word queue with front and rear both set to memory address 0. The first action on the queue is a write of item *A*, which goes to the rear (address 0), and the rear increments to address 1. The next action is a write of item *B*, which goes to the rear (address 1), and the rear increments to 2. The next action is a read, which comes from the front (address 0) and thus reads out item *A*, and the front increments to 1.

Subsequent reads and writes continue likewise, except that when the rear or front reaches 7, its next value should be 0, not 8. In other words, the memory can be thought of as a circle, as shown in Figure 5.77.

Two conditions of a queue are of interest:

- *Empty*: there are no items in the queue. This condition can be detected as *front = rear*, as seen in the topmost queue of Figure 5.76.

- *Full*: there is no more room to add items to the queue, meaning there are *N* items in a queue of size *N*. This comes about when the rear wraps around and catches back up to the front, meaning *front = rear*.

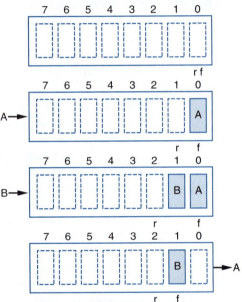

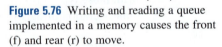

Figure 5.76 Writing and reading a queue implemented in a memory causes the front (f) and rear (r) to move.

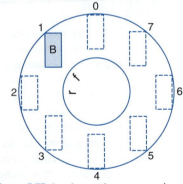

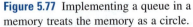

Figure 5.77 Implementing a queue in a memory treats the memory as a circle.

Unfortunately, notice that the conditions detecting the queue being empty and the queue being full are the same—the front address equals the rear address. One way to tell the two conditions apart is to keep track of whether a write or a read preceded the front and rear addresses becoming equal.

In many uses of a queue, the circuit writing the queue operates independently from the circuit reading the queue. Thus, a queue implemented with a memory may use a two-port memory having separate read and write ports.

We can implement an 8-word queue using an 8-word two-port register file and additional components, as depicted in Figure 5.78. A 3-bit up-counter maintains the front address, while another 3-bit up-counter maintains the rear address. Notice that these counters will naturally wrap around from 7 to 0, or from 0 to 7, as desired when treating the memory as a circle. An equality comparator detects whether the front counter equals the rear counter. A controller writes the write data to the register file and increments the rear counter during a write, reads the read data from the register file and increments the front counter during a read, and determines whether the queue is full or empty based on the equality comparison as well as whether the previous operation was a write or a read. We omit further description of the queue's controller, but it can be built by starting with an FSM.

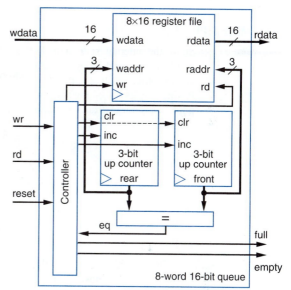

Figure 5.78 Architecture of an 8-word 16-bit queue.

A user of the queue should never read an empty queue or write a full queue—depending on the controller design, such an action might just be ignored or might put the queue into a misleading internal state (e.g., the front and rear addresses may cross over).

Most queues come with one or more additional control outputs that indicate whether the queue is half full, or perhaps 80% full.

Queues are commonplace in digital systems. Some examples include:

- A computer keyboard writes the pressed keys into a queue and meanwhile requests that the computer read the queued keys. You might at some time have typed faster than your computer was reading the keys, in which case your additional keystrokes were ignored—and you may have even heard beeps each time you pressed additional keys, indicating the queue was full.

- A digital video camera may write recently captured video frames into a queue, and concurrently may read those frames from the queue, compress them, and store them on tape or another medium.

- A computer printer may store print jobs in a queue while those jobs are waiting to be printed.

- A modem stores incoming data in a queue and requests a computer to read that data. Likewise, the modem writes outgoing data received from the computer into a queue and then sends that data out over the modem's outgoing medium.

- A computer network router receives data packets from an input port and writes those packets into a queue. Meanwhile, the router reads the packets from the queue, analyzes the address information in the packet, and then sends the packet along one of several output ports.

▶ **EXAMPLE 5.15**   Using a queue

Show the internal state of a 8-word queue, and popped data values, after each of the following sequences of pushes and pops, assuming an initially empty queue:

1. Push 9, 5, 8, 5, 7, 2, and 3.

2. Pop

3. Push 6

4. Push 3

5. Push 4

6. Pop

   Figure 5.79 shows the queue's internal states. After the first sequence of seven pushes (step 1), we see that the rear address points to address 7. The pop (step 2) reads from the front address of 0, returning data of 9. The front address increments to 1. Note that although the queue might still contain the value of 9 in address 0, that 9 is no longer accessible during proper queue operation, and thus is essentially gone. The push of 6 (step 3) increments the rear address, which wraps around from 7 to 0.

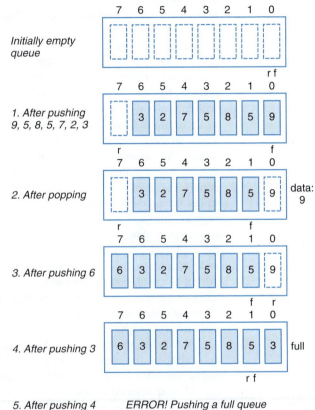

Figure 5.79 Example pushes and pops of a queue.

The push of 3 (step 4) increments the rear address to 1, which now equals the front address, meaning the queue is now full. If a pop were to occur now, it would read the value 5. But instead, a push of 4 occurs (step 5)—this push should not have been performed, because the queue is full. Thus, this push puts the queue into an erroneous state, and we cannot predict the behavior of any subsequent pushes or pops.   ◀

A queue could of course come with some error-tolerance behavior built in, perhaps ignoring pushes when full, or perhaps returning some particular value (like 0) if popped when empty.

▶ 5.8 HIERARCHY—A KEY DESIGN CONCEPT

Managing Complexity

Throughout this book, we have been utilizing a powerful design concept known as hierarchy. ***Hierarchy*** in general is defined as an organization with a few "things" at the top, and each thing possibly consisting of several other things. Perhaps the most widely known type hierarchy involves a country. At the top is a country, which consists of many states or provinces, each of which in turn consists of many cities. A hierarchy involving a country, provinces, and cities is shown in Figure 5.80. That figure shows all three levels of the hierarchy—country, provinces, and cities.

Figure 5.81 shows the same country, but this time showing only the top two levels of hierarchy—countries and provinces. Indeed, most maps of a country only show these top two levels (possibly showing key cities in each province/state, but certainly not all the cities)—showing all the cities also makes the map far too detailed and cluttered. A map of a province/state, however, might then show all the cities within that state. Thus, we see that hierarchy plays an important role in understanding countries (or at least their maps).

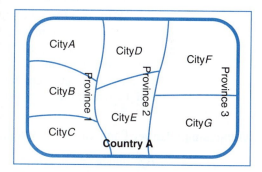

Figure 5.80 Three-level hierarchy example: a country, made up of provinces, each made up of cities.

Likewise, hierarchy plays an important role in digital design. In Chapter 2, we introduced the most fundamental component in digital systems—the transistor. In Chapters 2 and 3, we introduced several basic components composed from transistors, like AND gates, OR gates, and NOT gates, and then some slightly more complex components composed from gates: multiplexers, decoders, flip-flops, etc. In Chapter 4, we composed the basic components into a higher level of components, datapath components, like registers, adders, ALUs, multipliers, etc. In Chapter 5, we introduced components composed of datapath components, including controllers, datapaths, processors (made up of controllers and datapaths), memories, and queues.

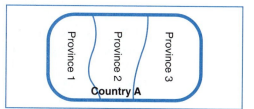

Figure 5.81 Hierarchy showing just the top two levels.

Use of hierarchy enables us to manage complex designs. Imagine trying to comprehend the design of Figure 5.30 at the level of logic gates—that design likely consists of several thousand logic gates. Humans can't comprehend several thousand things at once. But they can comprehend a few dozen things. As the number of things grows beyond a few dozen, we therefore group those things into a new thing, to manage the complexity. However, hierarchy alone is not sufficient—we must also associate an understandable meaning to the higher-level things we create, a task known as abstraction.

Abstraction

Hierarchy may not only involve grouping things into a larger thing, but may also involve associating a higher-level behavior to that larger thing. So when we grouped transistors to form an AND gate, we didn't just say that an AND gate was a group of transistors—rather, we associated a specific behavior with the AND gate, with that behavior describing the behavior of the group of transistors in an easily understandable way. Likewise, when we grouped logic gates into a 32-bit adder, we didn't just say that an adder was a group of logic gates—rather, we associated a specific understandable behavior with the adder: A 32-bit adder adds two 32-bit numbers.

Associating higher-level behavior with a component to hide the complex inner details of that component is a process known as ***abstraction***.

Abstraction frees a designer from having to remember, or even understand, the low-level details of a component. Knowing that an adder adds two numbers, a designer can use an adder in a design. The designer need not worry about whether the adder internally is implemented using a carry-ripple design, or using some complicated design that is perhaps faster but larger. Instead, the designer just needs to know the delay of the adder and the size of the adder, which are further abstractions.

Composing a Larger Component from Smaller Versions of the Same Component

A common design task is to create a larger version of a component from smaller versions of the same component. For example, suppose you have 3-input AND gates available to you, but you need a 9-input AND gate. You could compose several 3-input AND gates to form a 9-input AND gate, as shown in Figure 5.82. You could compose OR gates into a larger OR gate, and XOR gates into larger XOR gates, similarly. Some compositions might require more than two levels—composing an 8-bit AND from 2-input ANDs requires four 2-input ANDs in the first level, two 2-input ANDs in the second level, and a 2-input AND in the third level. Some compositions might end up with extra

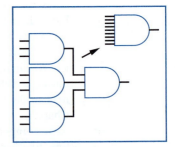

Figure 5.82 Composing a 9-input AND gate from 3-input AND gates.

inputs that must be hardwired to 0 or 1—an 8-input AND built from 3-input ANDs would look similar to Figure 5.82, but with the bottom input of the bottom AND gate hardwired to 1. After trying a few examples of composing AND gates into larger ones, you can come up with a general rule to compose any size AND gates into a larger gate: fill the first level with (the largest available) AND gates until the sum of their inputs equal the desired number of inputs, then fill the second level similarly (feeding first level outputs to the second level gates), until a level has just one gate (that's the last level). Connect any unused AND gate inputs to 1. Composing NAND, NOR, or XNOR gates into larger gates of the same kind would require a few more gates to maintain the same behavior.

Multiplexers can also be composed together to form a larger multiplexer. For example, suppose you had 4x1 and 2x1 muxes available, but you needed an 8x1 mux. You could compose the smaller muxes into an 8x1 mux as shown in Figure 5.83. Notice that s2 selects among group i0-i3 and i4-i7, while s1 and s0 select one input from the group. You can check that select line values pass the appropriate input through, for example, s2s1s0 = 000 passes i0, s2s1s0 = 100 passes i4, and s2s1s0 = 111 passes i7.

One particularly commonly occurring composition problem is that of creating a larger memory from smaller ones. The larger memory may have wider words, may have more words, or both.

For example, suppose you have available a large number of 1024x8 ROMs, but you want a 1024x32 ROM. Composing the smaller ROMs into the larger one is straightforward, and shown in Figure 5.84. We'll need four 1024x8 ROMs to obtain 32 bits per word. We connect the 10 address inputs to all four ROMs. Likewise, we connect the enable input to all four ROMs. We group the four 8-bit outputs into our desired 32-bit output. Thus, each ROM stores one byte of the 32-bit word. Reading a location, say location 99, results in four simultaneous reads, of the byte at location 99 of each ROM.

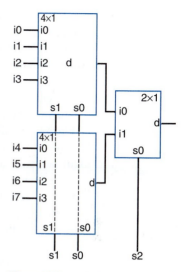

Figure 5.83 An 8x1 mux composed from 4x1 and 2x1 muxes.

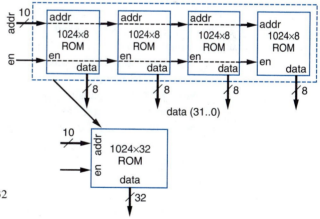

Figure 5.84 Composing a 1024x32 ROM from 1024x8 ROMs.

As another example using ROM, suppose you again have 1024x8 ROMs available, but this time you need a 2048x8 ROM. So you have an extra address line because you have twice as many words to address. Figure 5.85 shows how to use two 1024x8 ROMs to create a 2048x8 ROM. The top ROM represents the top half of the memory (1024 words), and the bottom ROM the bottom half (1024 words). We use the 11th address line (a10) to enable either the top ROM or the bottom ROM—the other 10 bits represent the offset into the ROM. That 11th bit feeds into a 1x2 decoder, whose outputs feed into the ROM enables. Figure 5.86 uses a table of addresses to show how the 11th bit selects among the two smaller ROMs.

Actually, we could use any bit to select between the top ROM and bottom ROM. Designers commonly use the lowest-order bit (a0) to select. The top ROM would thus represent all evenly addressed words, the bottom ROM all oddly addressed words.

Finally, since only one ROM will be active at any time, we can tie together the output data lines to form our 8-bit output, as shown in Figure 5.85.

As a final example using ROM, suppose you needed a 4096x32 ROM, but had only 1024x8 ROMs available. In this situation, we need both to create more words, and wider words. The approach is straightforward: first, create a 4096x8 ROM by using 4 ROMs one on top of the other and by feeding the top two address lines to a 2x4 decoder to select the appropriate ROM, and then second, widen the ROM by adding 3 more ROMs to each row.

Most of the datapath components we introduced in Chapter 4 can be composed into larger versions of the same type of component.

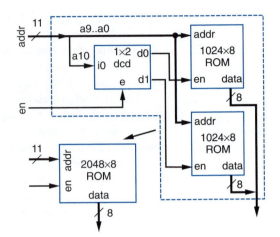

Figure 5.85 Composing a 2048x8 ROM from 1024x8 ROMs.

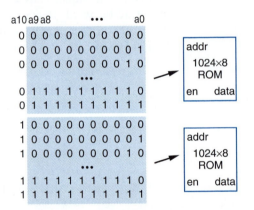

Figure 5.86 When composing a 2048x8 ROM from two 1024x8 ROMs, we can use the highest address bit to choose among the two ROMs; the remaining address bits offset into the chosen ROM.

▶ 5.9 RTL DESIGN OPTIMIZATIONS AND TRADEOFFS (SEE SECTION 6.5)

Previous sections in this chapter described how to perform register-transfer level design to create processors consisting of a controller and a datapath. This section, which physically appears in the book as Section 6.5, describes how to create processors that are better optimized, or that trade off one feature for another (e.g., size for performance). One use of this book covers such RTL optimizations and tradeoffs immediately after introducing RTL design, meaning now. Another use introduces them later.

▶ 5.10 RTL DESIGN USING HARDWARE DESCRIPTION LANGUAGES (SEE SECTION 9.5)

This section, which physically appears in the book as Section 9.5, describes use of HDLs during RTL design. One use of this book describes such HDL use immediately after introducing RTL design (meaning now). Another use describes use of HDLs later.

▶ 5.11 PRODUCT PROFILE: CELL PHONE

A cell phone, short for cellular telephone and also known as a mobile phone, is a portable wireless telephone that can be used to make phone calls while moving about a city. Cell phones have made it possible to communicate with distant people nearly anytime and anywhere. Before cell phones, most telephones were tied to physical places like a home or an office. Some cities supported a radio-based mobile telephone system using a powerful central antenna somewhere in the city, perhaps atop a tall building. Because radio frequencies are scarce and thus carefully doled out by governments, such a radio telephone system could only use perhaps tens or a hundred different radio frequencies, and thus could not support large numbers of users. Those few users therefore paid a very high fee for the service, limiting such mobile telephone use to a few wealthy individuals and to key government officials. Those users had to be within a certain radius of the main antenna, measured in tens of miles, to receive service, and that service typically didn't work in another city.

Cells and Basestations

Cell phone popularity exploded in the 1990s, growing from a few million users to hundreds of millions of users in that decade (even though the first cell phone call was made way back in 1973, by Martin Cooper of Motorola, the inventor of the cell phone), and today it is hard for many people to remember life before cell phones. The basic technical idea behind cell phones divides a city into numerous smaller regions, known as *cells* (hence the term "cell phone"). Figure 5.87 shows a city divided into three cells. A typical city might actually be divided into dozens, hundreds, or even thousands of cells. Each cell has its own radio antenna and equipment in the

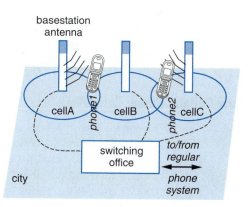

Figure 5.87 Phone1 in cell A can use the same radio frequency as phone 2 in cell C, increasing the number of possible mobile phone users in a city.

center, known as a *basestation*. Each basestation can use dozens or hundreds of different radio frequencies. Each basestation antenna only needs to transmit radio signals powerful enough to reach the basestation's cell area. Thus, nonadjacent cells can actually *reuse* the same frequencies, so the limited number of radio frequencies allowed for mobile phones can be thus shared by more than one phone at one time. Hence, far more users can be supported, leading to reduced costs per user. Figure 5.87 illustrates that *phone1* in cell *A* can use the same radio frequency as *phone2* in cell *C*, because the radio signals from cell *A* don't reach cell *C*. Supporting more users means greatly reduced cost per user, and more basestations means service in more areas than just major cities.

Figure 5.88(a) shows a typical basestation antenna. The basestation's equipment may be in a small building or commonly in a small box near the base of the antenna. The antenna shown actually supports antennas from two different cellular service providers—one set on the top, one set just under, on the same pole. Land for the poles is expensive, which is why providers share, or sometimes find existing tall structures on which to mount the antennas, like buildings, park light posts, and other interesting places (e.g., Figure 5.88(b)). Some providers try to disguise their antennas to make them more soothing to the eye, as in Figure 5.88(c)—the entire tree in the picture is artificial.

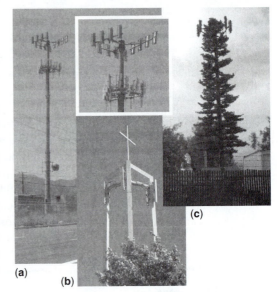

(a) (b) (c)

Figure 5.88 Basestations found in various locations.

All the basestations of a service provider connect to a central switching office of a city. The switching office not only links the cellular phone system to the regular "landline" phone system, but also assigns phone calls to specific radio frequencies, and handles switching among cells of a phone moving between cells.

How Cellular Phone Calls Work

Suppose you are holding *phone1* in *cell A* of Figure 5.87. When you turn on the cell phone, the phone listens for a signal from a basestation on a control frequency, which is a special radio frequency used for communicating commands (rather than voice data) between the basestation and cell phone. If the phone finds no such signal, the phone reports a "No Service" error. If the phone finds the signal from basestation *A*, the phone then transmits its own identification (ID) number to basestation *A*. Every cell phone has its own unique ID number. (Actually, there is a nonvolatile memory card inside each phone that has that ID number—a phone user can potentially switch cards among phones, or have multiple cards for the same phone, switching cards to change phone numbers.) Basestation *A* communicates this ID number to the central switching office's computer, and thus the service provider computer database now records that your phone is in *cell A*. Your phone intermittently sends a control signal to remind the switching office of the phone's presence.

If somebody then calls your cell phone's number, the call may come in over the regular phone system, which goes to the switching office. The switching office computer database indicates that your phone is in *cell A*. In one type of cell phone technology, the switching office computer assigns a specific radio frequency supported by basestation *A* to the call. Actually, the computer assigns two frequencies, one for talking, one for listening, so that talking and listening can occur simultaneously on a cell phone—let's call that frequency pair a channel. The computer then tells your phone to carry out the call over the assigned channel, and your phone rings. Of course, it could happen that there are so many phones already involved with calls in *cell A* that basestation *A* has no available frequencies—in that case, the caller may hear a message indicating that user is unavailable.

Placing a call proceeds similarly, but your cell phone initiates the call, ultimately resulting in assigned radio frequencies again (or a "system busy" message if no frequencies are presently available).

Suppose that your phone is presently carrying out a call with basestation *A*, and that you are moving through *cell A* toward *cell B* in Figure 5.87. Basestation *A* will see your signal weakening, while basestation *B* will see your signal strengthening, and the two basestations transmit this information to the switching office. At some point, the switching office computer will decide to switch your call from basestation *A* to basestation *B*. The computer assigns a new channel for the call in *cell B* (remember, adjacent cells use different sets of frequencies to avoid interference), and sends your phone a command (through basestation *A*, of course) to switch to a new channel. Your phone switches to the new channel and thus begins communicating with basestation *B*. Such switching may occur dozens of times while a car drives through a city during a phone call, and is transparent to the phone user. Sometimes the switching fails, perhaps if the new cell has no available frequencies, resulting in a "dropped" call.

Inside a Cell Phone

Basic Components

A cell phone requires sophisticated digital circuitry to carry out calls. Figure 5.89 shows the insides of a typical basic cell phone. The printed-circuit boards include several chips implementing digital circuits. One of those circuits performs analog-to-digital conversion

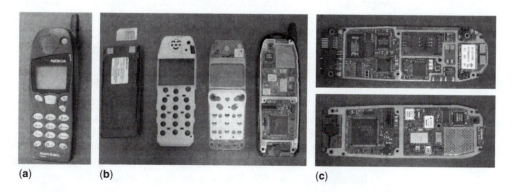

(a)   **(b)**   **(c)**

Figure 5.89 Inside a cell phone: (a) handset, (b) battery and ID card on left, keypad and display in center, digital circuitry on a printed-circuit board on right, (c) the two sides of the printed-circuit board, showing several digital chip packages mounted on the board.

of a voice (or other sound) to a signal stream of 0s and 1s, and another performs digital-to-analog conversion of a received digital stream back to an analog signal. Some of the circuits, typically software on a microprocessor, execute tasks that manage the various features of the phone, such as the menu system, address book, games, etc. Note that any data that you save on your cell phone (e.g., an address book, customized ring tones, game high score information, etc.) will likely be stored on a flash memory, whose nonvolatility ensures the data stays saved in memory even if the battery dies or is removed. Another important task involves responding to commands from the switching office. Another task carried out by the digital circuits is filtering. One type of filtering removes the carrier radio signal from the incoming radio frequency. Another type of filtering removes noise from the digitized audio stream coming from the microphone, before transmitting that stream on the outgoing radio frequency. Let's examine filtering in more detail.

Filtering, and FIR Filters

Filtering is perhaps the most common task performed in digital signal processing. Digital signal processing operates on a stream of digital data that comes from digitizing an input signal, such as an audio, video, or radio signal. Such streams of data are found in countless electronic devices, such as CD players, cell phones, heart monitors, ultrasound machines, radios, engine controllers, etc. *Filtering* a data stream is the task of removing particular aspects of the input signal, and outputting a new signal without those aspects.

A common filtering goal is to remove noise from a signal. You've certainly heard noise in audio signals—it's that hissing sound that's so annoying on your stereo, cell phone, or cordless phone. You've also likely adjusted a filter to reduce that noise, when you adjusted the "treble" control of your stereo (though that filter may have been implemented using analog methods rather than digital). Noise can appear in any type of signal, not just audio. Noise might come from an imperfect transmitting device, an imperfect listening device (e.g., a cheap microphone), background noise (e.g., freeway sounds coming into your cell phone), electrical interference from other electric appliances, etc. Noise typically appears in a signal as random jumps from a smooth signal.

Another common filtering goal is to remove a carrier frequency from a signal. A carrier frequency is a signal added to a main signal for the purpose of transmitting that main signal. For example, a radio station might broadcast a radio signal at 102.7 MHz. 102.7 MHz is the carrier frequency. The carrier signal may be a sine wave of a particular frequency (e.g., 102.7 MHz) that is added to the main signal, where the main signal is the music signal itself. A receiving device locks on to the carrier frequency, and then filters out the carrier signal, leaving the main signal.

An FIR filter (usually pronounced by saying the letters "F" "I" "R"), short for "Finite Impulse Response," is a very general filter design that can be used for a huge variety of filtering goals. The basic idea of an FIR filter is very simple: multiply the present input value by a constant, and add that result to the previous input value times a constant, and add that result to the next earlier input value times a constant, and so on. A designer using an FIR filter achieves a particular filtering goal *simply by choosing the FIR filter's constants*.

Mathematically, an FIR filter can be described as follows:

$$y(t) = c0 \times x(t) + c1 \times x(t-1) + c2 \times x(t-2) + c3 \times x(t-3) + c4 \times x(t-4) + \ldots$$

t is the present time step. x is the input signal, and y is the output signal. Each term (e.g., $c0*x(t)$) is called a *tap*. So the above equation represents a 5-tap FIR filter.

Let's see some examples of the versatility of an FIR filter. Assume we have a 5-tap FIR filter. For starters, to simply pass a signal through the filter unchanged, we set $c0$ to 1, and we set $c1=c2=c3=c4=0$. To amplify an input signal, we can set $c0$ to a number larger than 1, perhaps setting $c0$ to 2. To create a smoothing filter that outputs the average of the present value and the past four input values, we can simply set all the constants to equivalent values that add to 1, namely, $c1=c2=c3=c4=c5=0.2$. The results of such a filter applied to a noisy input signal are shown in Figure 5.90. To smooth and amplify, we can set all constants to equivalent values that add to something greater than 1, for example, $c1=c2=c3=c4=c5=1$, resulting in 5x amplification. To create a smoothing filter that only includes the previous two rather than four input values, we simply set $c3$ and $c4$ to 0. We see that we can build all the above different filters just by changing the constant values of an FIR filter. The FIR filter is indeed quite versatile.

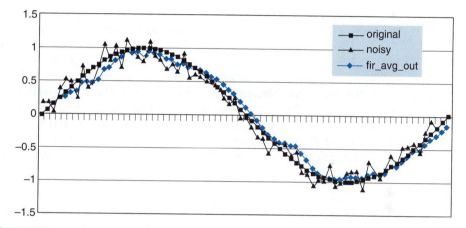

Figure 5.90 Results of a 5-tap FIR filter with $c0=c1=c2=c3=c4=0.2$ applied to a noisy signal. The original signal is a sine wave. The noisy signal has random jumps . The FIR output (fir_avg_out) is much smoother than the noisy signal, approaching the original signal. Notice that the FIR output is slightly shifted to the right, meaning the output is slightly delayed in time (probably a tiny fraction of a second delayed). Such slight shifting is usually not important to a particular application.

That versatility extends even further. We can actually filter out a carrier frequency using an FIR filter, by setting the coefficients to different values, carefully chosen to filter out a particular frequency. Figure 5.91 shows a main signal, *in1*, that we want to transmit. We can add that to a carrier signal, *in2*, to obtain the composite signal, *in_total*. The signal *in_total* is the signal that would be the signal that is transmitted by a radio station, for example, with *in1* being the signal of the music, and *in2* the carrier frequency.

Now say a stereo receiver receives that composite signal, and needs to filter out the carrier signal, so the music signal can be sent to the stereo speakers. To determine how to filter out the carrier signal, look carefully at the samples (the small filled squares in Figure 5.91) of that carrier signal. Notice that the sampling rate is such that if we take any sample, and add it to a sample from three time steps back, we get 0. That's because for a positive point, three samples earlier was a negative point of the same magnitude. For a negative point, three samples earlier was a positive point of the same magnitude. And for a zero point, three samples earlier was also a zero point. Likewise, adding a carrier signal

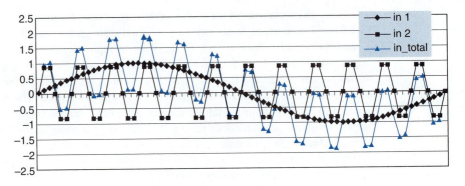

Figure 5.91 Adding a main signal, *in1*, to a carrier signal, *in2*, resulting in a composite signal *in_total*.

sample to a sample three steps later also adds to zero. So to filter out the carrier signal, we can add each sample to a sample three time steps back. Or we can add each sample to 1/2 times a sample three steps back, plus 1/2 times a sample three steps ahead. We can achieve this using a 7-tap FIR filter with the following seven coefficients: 0.5, 0, 0, 1, 0, 0, 0.5. Since that sums to 2, we can scale the coefficients to add to 1, as follows: 0.25, 0, 0, 0.5, 0, 0, 0.25. Applying such a 7-tap FIR filter to the composite signal results in the FIR output shown in Figure 5.92. The main signal is restored. We should point out that we chose the main signal such that this example would come out very nicely—other signals might not be restored so perfectly. But the example demonstrates the basic idea.

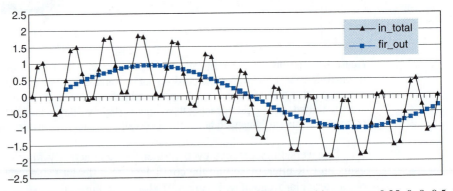

Figure 5.92 Filtering out the carrier signal using a 7-tap FIR filter with constants 0.25, 0, 0, 0.5, 0, 0, 0.25. The slight delay in the output signal typically poses no problem.

While 5-tap and 7-tap FIR filters can certainly be found in practice, many FIR filters may contain tens or hundreds of taps. FIR filters can certainly be implemented using software (and often are), but many applications require that the hundreds of multiplications and additions for every sample be executed faster than is possible in software, leading to custom digital circuit implementations. Example 5.8 illustrated the design of a circuit for an FIR filter.

Many types of filters exist other than FIR filters. Digital signal filtering is part of a larger field known as digital signal processing, or DSP. DSP has a rich mathematical foundation and is a field of study in itself. Advanced filtering methods are what make cell phone conversations as clear as they are today.

▶ 5.12 CHAPTER SUMMARY

In this chapter, we described (Section 5.1) that much digital design today involves designing processor-level components, and that design is done at what is called the register-transfer level (RTL). We introduced (Section 5.2) a four-step RTL design method for converting RTL behavior to a processor implementation, with that implementation consisting of a datapath controlled by a controller. The RTL design method made use of the datapath components defined in Chapter 4, and the controller design process defined in Chapter 3, which built on the combinational design process of Chapter 2. We provided several examples of RTL design (Section 5.3), while pointing out several pitfalls and good design practices, and discussing the characteristics of control- versus data-dominated designs. We discussed (Section 5.4) how to set a circuit's clock frequency based on the circuit's critical path. We demonstrated (Section 5.5) how a sequential program, like a C program, could conceptually be converted to gates using some straightforward transformations that transform the C into RTL behavior, which as we know can then be converted to gates using the four-step RTL design method. That demonstration should make it clear that a digital system's functionality can be implemented as either software on a microprocessor or as a custom digital circuit (or even as both). The differences among software and custom circuit implementations are not related to what each can implement—they can both implement any functionality. The differences are instead related to design metrics like system performance, power consumption, size, cost, design time, and so on. Modern digital designers must therefore be comfortable migrating functionality between software on a microprocessor and custom digital circuits, in order to obtain the best overall implementation with respect to constraints on design metrics. We introduced (Section 5.6) several memory components commonly used in RTL design, including RAM and ROM components. We also introduced (Section 5.7) a queue component that can be useful during RTL design. We took a moment to discuss (Section 5.8) a general technique that we've been using throughout the book, hierarchy, which helps a designer to manage complexity.

In Chapters 1 through 5, we have emphasized straightforward design methods for increasingly complex systems, but we have not emphasized how to design those systems *well*. Improving on our designs will be the focus of the next chapter.

▶ 5.13 EXERCISES

Any problems noted with an asterisk (*) represent especially challenging problems.

SECTION 5.2: RTL DESIGN METHOD

5.1 (a) Create a high-level state machine that describes the following system behavior. The system has an 8-bit input A, a single-bit input d, and a 32-bit output S. On every clock cycle, if d=1, the system should add A to a running sum and output that sum on S. If d=0, the system should instead subtract. Ignore issues of overflow and underflow. Don't forget to include an initialization state. *Hint:* Declare and use an internal register to keep the sum.

(b) Add a 1-bit input rst to the system. When rst=1, the system should clear its sum back to 0.

5.2 Create a high-level state machine for a simple data encryption/decryption device. If a bit-input b is 1, the device stores the data from a 32-bit input I as what is known as an offset value. If b is 0 and another bit-input e is 1, then the device "encrypts" its input I by adding the stored offset value to I, and outputs this encrypted value over a 32-bit output J. If instead another bit-input d is 1, the device should "decrypt" the data on I by subtracting the offset value before outputting the decrypted value over J. Be sure to explicitly handle all possible combinations of the three input bits.

5.3 Create a high-level state machine for a digital bath-water controller. The system has a 3-bit input ratio indicating the desired ratio of cold water to hot water, and a bit input on indicating that the water should flow. The system has two 4-bit outputs hflow and cflow, controlling the hot water flow rate and the cold water flow rate. The sum of these two rates should always equal 16. Your high-level state machine should determine the output values for hflow and cflow such that the ratio of hot water to cold water is as close as possible to the desired ratio, while the total flow is always 16. *Hint:* As there are only 8 possible ratios, a reasonable solution may use one state for each ratio.

5.4 Create a high-level state machine that initializes a 16x32 register file's contents to all 0s, beginning the initialization when an input rst is 1.

5.5 (a) Create a high-level state machine that adds each register of one 128x8 register file to the corresponding registers of another 128x8 register file, storing the results in a third 128x8 register file. The system should only begin the addition when a bit-input add is 1, and should not perform the addition again until it has finished adding (only adding again if add is 1).

(b) Extend this system to either add or subtract, using an additional bit-input op, where op = 1 means add, and op = 0 means subtract.

5.6 Design a high-level state machine for a 4-bit up-counter with count control input cnt, count clear input clr, and a terminal count output tc. Use the RTL design method of Table 5.1 to convert the high-level state machine to a controller and a datapath. Use a register and incrementer in the datapath, not a counter itself. Design the controller down to a state register and logic gates.

5.7 Compare the up-counter designed in Exercise 5.6 with the up-counter design shown in Figure 4.48.

5.8 Create a datapath for the high-level state machine in Figure 5.93.

5.9 *Starting with the soda machine dispenser design described in Example 5.1, create a block diagram and high-level state machine for a soda machine dispenser that has a choice of two soda types, and that also provides change to the consumer. A coin detector provides the circuit with a 1-bit input c that becomes 1 for one clock cycle when a coin is detected, and an 8-bit input a indicating the coin's value in cents. Two 8-bit inputs s1 and s2 indicate the cost of the two soda choices. The user's soda selection is controlled by two buttons b1 and b2 that when pushed will output 1 for one clock cycle. If the user has inserted enough change for their selection, the circuit should set either output bit d1 or d2 to 1 for one clock cycle, causing the selected soda to be dispensed. The soda dispenser circuit should also set an output bit cr to 1 for one clock cycle if change is required, and should output the amount of change required using an 8-bit output ca. Use the RTL design method shown in Table 5.1 to convert the high-level state machine to a controller and a datapath. Design the datapath to structure, but design the controller to the point of an FSM only, as was done in Figure 5.26.

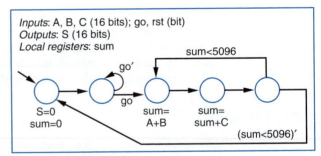

Figure 5.93 Sample high-level state machine.

5.10 (a) Use the RTL design method of Table 5.1 to convert the high-level state machine in Figure 5.94 to a controller and a datapath. Design the datapath to structure, but design the controller to an FSM only, as was done in Figure 5.26.

(b) *Design the controller's FSM down to structure.

5.11 Create an FSM that interfaces with the datapath in Figure 5.95. The FSM should use the datapath to compute the average value of the 16 32-bit elements of any

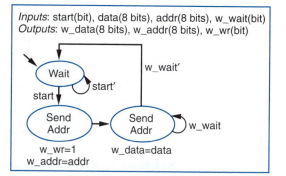

Figure 5.94 High-level state machine of bus interface with bus wait signal.

Array A. Array A is stored in a memory, with the first element at address 25, the second at address 26, and so on. Assume that putting a new value onto the address lines M_addr causes the memory to almost immediately output the read data on the M_data lines. Ignore the possibility of overflow.

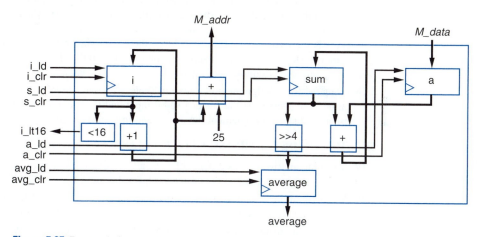

Figure 5.95 Datapath for computing the average of 16 elements of an array.

5.12 Using the RTL design method shown in Table 5.1, create an RTL design of a reaction timer circuit that measures the time elapsed between the illumination of a light and the pressing of a button by a user. The reaction timer has three inputs, a clock input *clk*, a reset input *rst,* and a button input *B*, and three outputs, a light enable output *len*, a 10-bit reaction time output *rtime,* and a *slow* output indicating the user was not fast enough. The reaction timer works as follows. On reset, the reaction timer waits for 10 seconds before illuminating the light by setting *len* to 1. The reaction timer then measures the length of time in milliseconds before the user presses the button *B*, outputting the time as a 12-bit binary number on *rtime*. If the user did not press the button within 2 seconds (2000 milliseconds), the reaction timer will set the output *slow* to 1 and output 2000 on *rtime*. Assume your clock input has a frequency of 1 kHz. *Hint:* This is a control-dominated RTL design problem. Design the datapath to structure, but design the controller to an FSM only, as was done in Figure 5.26.

5.13 Use the RTL design method shown in Table 5.1 to convert the high-level state machine in Figure 5.74 to a controller and a datapath. Design the datapath to structure, but design the controller to the point of an FSM only, as was done in Figure 5.26.

SECTION 5.3: RTL DESIGN EXAMPLES AND ISSUES

For the following problems, design the datapath to structure, but design the controller to an FSM only, as done in Figure 5.26.

5.14 Using the RTL design method shown in Table 5.1, create an RTL design that computes the sum of all positive numbers within a 512-word register file *A* consisting of 32-bit numbers stored in two's complement form.

5.15 Using the RTL design method shown in Table 5.1, create an RTL design that computes the sum of all positive numbers from a set of 16 separate 32-bit registers storing numbers in two's complement form. Make the design as fast as possible by performing as many computations concurrently as possible. *Hint:* This is a data-dominated design.

5.16 Using the RTL design method shown in Table 5.1, create an RTL design that outputs the maximum value found within a register file *A* consisting of 64 32-bit numbers.

5.17 Using the RTL design method shown in Table 5.1, create an RTL design that outputs a warning signal whenever the average temperature over the past four samples exceeds a user-defined value. The circuit has a 32-bit input *CT* indicating the current temperature reading, a 32-bit input *WT* indicating the user-specified temperature at which the warning should be enabled, and a button input *clr* that will disable the warning. When the average temperature exceeds the user-specified warning level, the circuit should assert the output *W* to enable the warning. The warning output should remain high until the *clr* button is pressed. *Hint:* You can use a right shift to implement the divide within your datapath.

5.18 Using the RTL design method shown in Table 5.1, create an RTL design for a digital filter that outputs the average of the current 32-bit input and the previous 32-bit sample. *Hint:* You can use a right shift to implement the divide within your datapath.

SECTION 5.4: DETERMINING CLOCK FREQUENCY

5.19 Assuming an inverter has a delay of 1 ns, all other gates have a delay of 2 ns, and wires have a delay of 1 ns, determine the critical path for the full-adder circuit shown in Figure 4.31.

5.20 Assuming an inverter has a delay of 1 ns, all other gates have a delay of 2 ns, and wires have a delay of 1 ns, determine the critical path for the 3x8 decoder of Figure 2.50.

5.21 Assuming an inverter has a delay of 1 ns, all other gates have a delay of 2 ns, and wires have a delay of 1 ns, determine the critical path for a 4x1 multiplexer.

5.22 Assuming an inverter has a delay of 1 ns, and all other gates have a delay of 2 ns, determine the critical path for an 8-bit carry-ripple adder:
(a) assuming wires have no delay,
(b) assuming wires have a delay of 1 ns.

5.23 (a) Convert the laser-based distance measurer's FSM, shown in Figure 5.21, to a state register and logic.
(b) Assuming all gates have a delay of 2 ns and the 16-bit up-counter has a delay of 5 ns, and wires have no delay, determine the critical path for the laser-based distance measurer.
(c) Calculate the corresponding maximum clock frequency for the circuit.

SECTION 5.5: BEHAVIORAL-LEVEL DESIGN: C TO GATES (OPTIONAL)

5.24 Convert the following C-like code, which calculates the greatest common divisor (GCD) of the two 8-bit numbers *a* and *b*, into a high-level state machine.

```
Inputs: byte a, byte b, bit go
Outputs: byte gcd, bit done
GCD:
while(1) {
  while(!go);
  done = 0;
  while ( a != b ) {
    if( a > b ) {
      a = a - b;
    }
    else {
      b = b - a;
    }
  }
  gcd = a;
  done = 1;
}
```

5.25 Use the RTL design method shown in Table 5.1 to convert the high-level state machine you created in Exercise 5.24 to a controller and a datapath. Design the datapath to structure, but design the controller to the point of an FSM only.

5.26 Convert the following C-like code, which calculates the maximum difference between any two numbers within an array *A* consisting of 256 8-bit values, into a high-level state machine.

```
Inputs: byte a[256], bit go
Outputs: byte max_diff, bit done
MAX_DIFF:
while(1) {
  while(!go);
  done = 0;
  i = 0;
  max = 0;
  min = 255; // largest 8-bit value
  while( i < 256 ) {
    if( a[i] < min ) {
      min = a[i];
    }
    if( a[i] > max ) {
      max = a[i];
    }
    i = i + 1;
  }
  max_diff = max - min;
  done = 1;
}
```

5.27 Use the RTL design method shown in Table 5.1 to convert the high-level state machine you created in Exercise 5.26 to a controller and a datapath. Design the datapath to structure, but design the controller to the point of an FSM only.

5.28 Convert the following C-like code, which calculates the number of times the value b is found within an array A consisting of 256 8-bit values, into a high-level state machine.

```
Inputs: byte a[256], byte b, bit go
Outputs: byte freq, bit done
FREQUENCY:
while(1) {
   while(!go);
   done = 0;
   i = 0;
   freq = 0;
   while( i < 256 ) {
      if( a[i] == b ) {
         freq = freq + 1;
      }


   }
   done = 1;
}
```

5.29 Use the RTL design method shown in Table 5.1 to convert the high-level state machine you created in Exercise 5.28 to a controller and a datapath. Design the datapath to structure, but design the controller to the point of an FSM only.

5.30 Develop a template for converting a do{ }while loop of the following form to a high-level state machine.

```
do {
   // do while statements
} while (cond);
```

5.31 *Convert the while(a != b) loop within the C code description of Exercise 24 into a do{ }while loop as described in Exercise 5.30. Using the do{ }while loop template you created in Exercise 5.30, convert the revised C code into a high-level state machine. Use the RTL design method shown in Table 5.1 to convert the high-level state machine you created in the previous problem to a controller and a datapath. Design the datapath to structure, but design the controller to the point of an FSM only.

5.32 Develop a template for converting a for() loop of the following form to a high-level state machine.

```
for(i=start; i<cond; i++)
{
   // for statements
}
```

5.33 *Convert the while(a != b) loop within the C code description of Exercise 5.24 to a for() loop as described in Exercise 5.32. Using the for() loop template you created in

Exercise 5.32, convert the revised C code into a high-level state machine. Use the RTL design method shown in Table 5.1 to convert the high-level state machine you created in the previous problem to a controller and a datapath. Design the datapath to structure, but design the controller to the point of an FSM only.

5.34 *Convert the `while( i < 256 )` loop within the C code description of Exercise 5.26 to a `for()` loop as described in Exercise 5.32. Using the `for()` loop template you created in Exercise 5.32, convert the revised C-like code into a high-level state machine. Use the RTL design method shown in Table 5.1 to convert the high-level state machine you created in the previous problem to a controller and a datapath. Design the datapath to structure, but design the controller to the point of an FSM only.

5.35 Compare the time required to execute the following computation using a custom circuit versus using software. Assume a gate has a delay of 1 ns. Assume a microprocessor executes one instruction every 5 ns. Assume that n=10 and m=5. Estimates are acceptable; you need not design the circuit, or determine exactly how many software instructions will execute.

```
for (i = 0; i<n, i++) {
    s = 0;
    for (j = 0; j < m, j++) {
        s = s + c[i]*x[i + j];
    }
    y[i] = s;
}
```

SECTION 5.6: MEMORY COMPONENTS

5.36 Calculate the approximate number of DRAM bit storage cells that will fit on an IC with a capacity of 10 million transistors.

5.37 Calculate the approximate number of SRAM bit storage cells that will fit on an IC with a capacity of 10 million transistors.

5.38 Summarize the main differences between DRAM and SRAM memories.

5.39 Draw a complete logic internal structure for a 4x2 DRAM (four words, 2 bits each), clearly labeling all internal components and connections.

5.40 Draw a complete logic internal structure for a 4x2 SRAM (four words, 2 bits each), clearly labeling all internal components and connections.

5.41 *Design an SRAM memory cell with a reset input that when enabled will set the memory cell's contents to 0.

SECTION : READ-ONLY MEMORY (ROM)

5.42 Summarize the main differences between EPROM and EEPROM memories.

5.43 Summarize the main differences between EEPROM and flash memories.

SECTION 5.7: QUEUES (FIFOS)

5.44 For an 8-word queue, show the queue's internal state and provide the value of popped data for the following sequences of pushes and pops: (1) push A, B, C, D, E, (2) pop, (3) pop, (4) push U, V, W, X, Y, (5) pop, (6) push Z, (7) pop, (8) pop, (9) pop.

5.45 Create an FSM describing the queue controller of Figure 5.78. Pay careful attention to correctly setting the `full` and `empty` outputs.

5.46 Create an FSM describing the queue controller of Figure 5.78, but with error-preventing behavior that ignores any pushes when the queue is full, and ignores pops of an empty queue (outputting 0).

SECTION 5.8: HIERARCHY—A KEY DESIGN CONCEPT

5.47 Compose a 20-input AND gate from 2-input AND gates.

5.48 Compose a 16x1 mux from 2x1 muxes.

5.49 Compose a 4x16 decoder with enable from 2x4 decoders with enable.

5.50 Compose a 1024x8 RAM using only 512x8 RAMs.

5.51 Compose a 512x8 RAM using only 512x4 RAMs.

5.52 Compose a 1024x8 ROM using only 512x4 ROMs.

5.53 Compose a 2048x8 ROM using only 256x8 ROMs.

5.54 Compose a 1024x16 RAM using only 512x8 RAMs.

5.55 Compose a 1024x12 RAM using 512x8 and 512x4 RAMs.

5.56 Compose a 640x12 RAM using only 128x4 RAMs.

5.57 *Write a program that takes a parameter N, and automatically builds an N-input AND gate from 2-input AND gates. Your program merely need indicate how many 2-input AND gates exist in each level, from which we could easily determine the connections.

Chi-Kai started college as an engineering major, and became a Computer Science major due to his developing interests in algorithms and in networks. After graduating, he worked for a Silicon Valley startup company that made chips for computer networking. His first task was to help simulate those chips before the chips were built. For over 10 years now, he has worked on multiple generations of networking devices that buffer, schedule, and switch ATM network cells and Internet Protocol packets. "The chips required to implement networking devices are complex components that must all work together almost perfectly to provide the building blocks of telecommunication and data networks. Each generation of devices becomes successively more complex."

When asked what skills are necessary for his job, Chi-Kai says "More and more, breadth of one's skill set matters more than depth. Being an effective chip engineer requires the ability to understand chip architecture (the big picture), to design logic, to verify logic, and to bring up the silicon in the lab. All these parts of the design cycle interplay more and more. To be truly effective at one particular area requires hands-on knowledge of the others as well. Also, each requires very different skills. For example, verification requires good software programming ability, while bring up requires knowing how to use a logic analyzer—good hardware skills."

High-end chips, like those involved in networking, are quite costly, and require careful design. "The software design process and the chip design process are fundamentally different. Software can afford to have bugs because patches can be applied. Silicon is a different story. The one time expenses to spin a chip are on the order of $500,000. If there is a show-stopping bug, you may need to spend another $500,000. This constraint means the verification approach taken is quite different—effectively: there can be no bugs." At the same time, these chips must be designed quickly to beat competitors to the market, making the job "extremely challenging and exciting."

One of the biggest surprises Chi-Kai encountered in his job is the "incredible importance of good communication skills." Chi-Kai has worked in teams ranging from 10 people to 30 people, and some chips require teams of over 100 people. "Technically outstanding engineers are useless unless they know how to collaborate with others and disseminate their knowledge. Chips are only getting more complex—individual blocks of code in a given chip have the same complexity as an entire chip only a few years ago. To architect, design, and implement logic in hardware requires the ability to convey complexity." Furthermore, Chi-Kai points out that "just like any social entity, there are politics involved. For example, people are worried about aspirations for promotion, financial gain, and job security. In this greater context, the team still must work together to deliver a chip." So, contrary to the conceptions many people have of engineers, engineers must have excellent people skills, in addition to strong technical skills. Engineering is a social discipline.

6

Optimizations and Tradeoffs

▶ 6.1 INTRODUCTION

The previous chapters described how to design digital circuits using straightforward techniques. This chapter will describe how to design *better* circuits. For our purposes, *better* means circuits that are smaller, faster, or consume less power. Real world design may involve additional criteria.

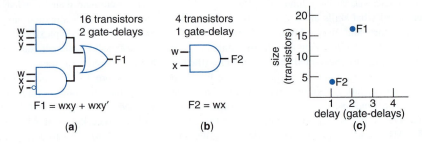

Figure 6.1 A circuit transformation that improves both size and delay, that is, an *optimization*: (a) original circuit, (b) optimized circuit, (c) plot of size and delay of each circuit.

Consider the circuit for the equation involving F1 shown in Figure 6.1(a). The circuit's size, *assuming two transistors per gate input* (and ignoring inverters for simplicity), is 8 * 2 = 16 transistors. The circuit's delay, which is the longest path from any input to the output, is two gate-delays. We could algebraically transform the equation into that for F2, shown in Figure 6.1(b). F2 represents the same function as F1, but requires only four transistors (instead of 16) and has a delay of only one gate-delay (instead of two). The transformation improved both size and delay, as shown in Figure 6.1(c). When we perform transformations that improve all criteria of interest to us, we have performed an **optimization**.

Now consider the circuit for a different function, implementing the equation for G1 in Figure 6.2(a). The circuit's size (assuming 2 transistors per gate input) is 14 transistors and the circuit's delay is two gate-delays. We could algebraically transform the equation into that shown for G2 in Figure 6.2(b), which results in a circuit having only 12 transistors. However, the reduction in transistors comes at the expense of a longer delay of three

*A **tradeoff** improves some criteria at the expense of other criteria of interest to us. An **optimization** improves all criteria of interest to us, or improves some of those criteria without worsening the others.*

gate-delays, as shown in Figure 6.2(c). Which circuit is better, that for G1 or for G2? The answer depends on whether the size or delay criteria is more important to us. When we improve one criteria at the expense of another criteria of interest to us, we have performed a **tradeoff**.

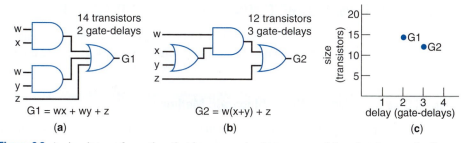

| 14 transistors | 12 transistors |
| 2 gate-delays | 3 gate-delays |

G1 = wx + wy + z

G2 = w(x+y) + z

(a)   **(b)**   **(c)**

Figure 6.2 A circuit transformation that improves size but worsens delay, that is, a *tradeoff:* (a) original circuit, (b) transformed circuit, (c) plot of size and delay of each circuit.

You likely perform optimizations and tradeoffs every day. Perhaps you regularly commute by car from one city to another via a particular route. You might be interested in two criteria: commute time and safety. Other criteria, such as scenery along the route, may not be of interest to you. If you choose a new route that improves both commute time and safety, you have optimized your commute. If you instead choose a route that improves safety at the expense of increased commute time, you have made a tradeoff (and perhaps a wise one at that).

Figure 6.3 illustrates optimizations versus tradeoffs for three different starting designs, with the criteria of delay and size, smaller being better for each criteria. Obviously, we prefer optimizations over tradeoffs, since optimizations improve both criteria (or at least improve one criteria without worsening another criteria, as shown by the horizontal and vertical arrows on the left side of the figure). But we can't always improve one criteria without

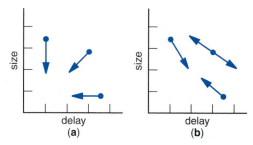

Figure 6.3 (a) Optimizations, versus (b) tradeoffs.

worsening another criteria. For example, if a car designer wants to improve a car's fuel efficiency, the designer may have to make the car smaller—a tradeoff among the criteria of fuel efficiency and comfort.

Some general criteria commonly of interest to digital system designers include:

- **Performance**: a measure of execution time for a computation on the system.
- **Size**: a measure of the number of transistors, or silicon area, of a digital system.
- **Power**: a measure of the energy consumed per second of a system, directly relating to both the heat generated by the system and to the battery energy consumed by computations.

Dozens of other criteria exist.

Optimizations and tradeoffs can be made throughout nearly all stages of digital design. This chapter describes some common optimizations and tradeoffs for some common criteria, at various stages of digital design.

▶ 6.2 COMBINATIONAL LOGIC OPTIMIZATIONS AND TRADEOFFS

In Chapter 2, we described how to design combinational logic, namely, how to convert desired combinational behavior into a circuit of gates. There are optimization and tradeoff methods we can apply to make those circuits better.

Two-Level Size Optimization Using Algebraic Methods

Implementing a Boolean function using only two levels of gates—a level of AND gates followed by one OR gate—usually results in a circuit having minimum delay. Recall from Chapter 2 that any Boolean equation can be written in sum-of-products form, simply by "multiplying out" the equation—for example, $xy(w+z) = xyw + xyz$. Thus, any Boolean function can be implemented using two levels of gates, simply by converting its equation to sum-of-products form and then using AND gates for the products followed by an OR gate for the sum.

In the 1970s/ 1980s, when transistors were costly (e.g., cents each), minimization <u>meant</u> size minimization, which dominated digital design. Today's cheaper transistors (e.g., 0.0001 cents each) make optimizations of other criteria equally or more critical.

A popular optimization is to *minimize the number of transistors* of a two-level logic circuit implementation of a Boolean function. Such optimization is traditionally called **two-level logic optimization**, or sometimes **two-level logic minimization**. We'll refer to it as **two-level logic size optimization**, to distinguish such optimization from the increasingly popular optimizations of *performance* and *power*, as well as other possible optimizations.

To optimize size, we need a method to determine the number of transistors for a given circuit. We'll use a simple method for determining the number of transistors:

- We'll assume every logic gate input requires two transistors. So a 3-input logic gate (whether an AND, OR, NAND, or NOR) would require 3 * 2 = 6 transistors. The circuits inside logic gates shown in Section 2.4 should clarify why we assume two transistors per gate input.
- We'll ignore inverters when determining the number of transistors, for simplicity.

We can view the problem of two-level logic size optimization *algebraically* as the problem of *minimizing the number of literals and terms of a Boolean equation that is in sum-of-products form*. The reason we can view the problem algebraically is because, recall from Section 2.4, we can translate a sum-of-products Boolean equation directly to a circuit using a level of AND gates followed by an OR gate. For example, the equation $F = wxy + wxy'$ from Figure 6.1(a) has six literals, w, x, y, w, x, and y', and two terms, wxy and wxy', for a total of 6 + 2 = 8 literals and terms. Each literal and each term translates approximately to a gate input in a circuit, as shown in Figure 6.1(a)—the literals translate to AND gate inputs, and the terms to OR gate inputs. The circuit thus has 3 + 3 + 2 = 8 gate inputs. With two transistors per gate input, the circuit has 8 * 2 = 16 transistors. We can minimize the number of literals and terms *algebraically*: $F = wxy + wxy' = wx(y+y') = wx$, which has only two literals, w and x, resulting in 2 gate inputs, or 2 * 2 = 4 transistors, as shown in Figure 6.1(b). (Note that a one-term equation doesn't require an OR gate.)

▶ **EXAMPLE 6.1**   Two-level logic size optimization using algebraic methods

Minimize the number of literals and terms in a two-level implementation of the equation:

$$F = xyz + xyz' + x'y'z' + x'y'z$$

Let's minimize using algebraic transformations:

$$F = xy(z + z') + x'y'(z + z')$$
$$F = xy*1 + x'y'*1$$
$$F = xy + x'y'$$

There doesn't seem to be any further minimization we can perform. Thus, we've reduced the circuit from 12 literals and 4 terms (meaning 12 + 4 = 16 gate inputs, or 32 transistors), down to only 4 literals and 2 terms (meaning 4 + 2 = 6 gate inputs, or 12 transistors). ◀

The previous example showed the most common algebraic transformation used to simplify a Boolean equation in sum-of-products form, a transformation that generally can be written as:

$$ab + ab' = a(b+b') = a*1 = a$$

Let's call this transformation ***combining terms to eliminate a variable***. More formally, this transformation is known as the ***uniting theorem***. In the previous example, we applied this transformation twice, once with xy being a and z being b, and a second time with $x'y'$ being a and z being b.

Sometimes we need to duplicate a term in order to increase opportunities for combining terms to eliminate a variable, as illustrated in the next example.

▶ **EXAMPLE 6.2**   Reusing a term during two-level logic size optimization

Minimize the number of literals and terms in a two-level implementation of the equation:

$$F = x'y'z' + x'y'z + x'yz$$

You might notice two opportunities to combine terms to eliminate a variable:

$$1: x'y'z' + x'y'z = x'y'$$
$$2: x'y'z + x'yz = x'z$$

Notice that the term $x'y'z$ appears in both opportunities, but that term only appears once in the original equation. We'll therefore first replicate the term in the original equation (such replication doesn't change the function, because $a = a + a$) so that we can use the term twice when combining terms to eliminate a variable, as follows:

$$F = x'y'z' + x'y'z + x'yz$$
$$F = x'y'z' + x'y'z + x'y'z + x'yz$$
$$F = x'y'(z+z') + x'z(y'+y)$$
$$F = x'y' + x'z$$ ◀

After we have combined terms to eliminate a variable, the resulting term might also be combinable with other terms to eliminate a variable, as shown in the following example.

▶ **EXAMPLE 6.3** Repeatedly combining terms to eliminate a variable

Minimize the number of literals and terms in a two-level implementation of the equation:

$$G = xy'z' + xy'z + xyz + xyz'$$

We can combine the first two terms to eliminate a variable, and the last two terms also:

$$G = xy'(z'+z) + xy(z+z')$$
$$G = xy' + xy$$

We can combine the two remaining terms to eliminate a variable:

$$G = xy' + xy$$
$$G = x(y'+y)$$
$$G = x$$ ◀

In the previous examples, how did we "see" the opportunities to combine terms to eliminate a variable? The examples' original equations happened to be written in a way that made seeing the opportunities easy—terms that could be combined were side-by-side. Suppose instead the equation in Example 6.1 had been written as:

$$F = x'y'z + xyz + xyz' + x'y'z'$$

That's the same function, but the terms appear in a different order. We might see that the middle two terms can be combined:

$$F = x'y'z + xyz + xyz' + x'y'z'$$
$$F = x'y'z + xy(z+z') + x'y'z'$$
$$F = x'y'z + xy + x'y'z'$$

But then we might not see that the left and right terms can be combined. We therefore might stop minimizing, thinking that we had obtained a fully minimized equation.

There is a visual method to help us *see* opportunities to combine terms to eliminate a variable, a method we now describe.

A Visual Method for Two-Level Size Optimization—K-Maps

Karnaugh Maps, or *K-maps* for short, are a visual method intended to assist humans to algebraically minimize Boolean equations having a few (two to four) variables. They actually are not commonly used any longer in design practice, but nevertheless, they are a very effective means for *understanding* the basic optimization methods underlying today's automated tools. A K-map is essentially a graphical representation of a truth table, meaning a K-map is yet another way to represent a function (the other ways including an equation, truth table, and circuit). The idea underlying a K-map is to graphically place minterms adjacent to one another if those minterms differ in one variable only, so that we can actually "see" the opportunity for combining terms to eliminate a variable.

Three-Variable K-Maps

Figure 6.4 shows a K-map for the equation:

$$F = x'y'z + xyz + xyz' + x'y'z'$$

which is the equation from Example 6.1 but with terms appearing in a different order. The map has eight cells, one for each possible combination of variable values. Let's examine the cells in the top row. The upper-left cell corresponds to xyz=000, meaning x'y'z'. The next cell to the right corresponds to xyz=001, meaning x'y'z. The next cell to the right corresponds to xyz=011, meaning x'yz. And the rightmost top cell corresponds to xyz=010, meaning x'yz'. Notice that the ordering of those top cells is *not* in increasing binary order. Instead, the order is 000, 001, *011*, 010, rather than 000, 001, *010*, 011. The ordering

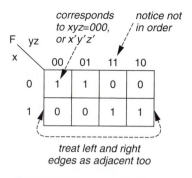

Figure 6.4 Three-variable K-map.

In a K-map, adjacent cells differ in exactly one variable.

is such that *adjacent cells differ in exactly one variable*. For example, the cells for x'y'z (001) and x'yz (011) are adjacent, and differ in exactly one variable, namely, y. Likewise, the cells for x'y'z' and xy'z' are adjacent, and differ only in variable x. The map is also assumed to have its *left and right edges adjacent*, so the rightmost top cell (010) is adjacent to the leftmost top cell (000)—note those cells too differ in exactly one variable. Adjacent means abutted either horizontally or vertically, but *not diagonally*, because diagonal cells differ in more than one variable. Adjacent bottom row cells also differ in exactly one variable. And cells in a column also differ in exactly one variable.

We can represent a Boolean function as a K-map by placing 1s in the cells corresponding to the function's minterms. So for the equation F above, we place a 1 in cells corresponding to minterms x'y'z, xyz, xyz', and x'y'z', as shown in Figure 6.4. We place 0s in the remaining cells. Notice that a K-map is just another representation of a truth table. Rather than showing the output for every possible combination of inputs using a table, a K-map uses a graphical map. Therefore, a K-map is yet another representation of a Boolean function, and in fact is another standard representation.

*K-maps enable us to **see** opportunities to combine terms to eliminate a variable.*

The usefulness of a K-map for size minimization is that, because the map is designed such that adjacent cells differ in exactly one variable, then we know that *two adjacent 1s in a K-map indicate that we can combine the two minterms to eliminate a variable*. In other words, a K-map lets us easily see when we can combine two terms to eliminate a variable. We indicate such combining by drawing a circle around two adjacent 1s, and then we show the resulting term after the differing variable is removed. We illustrate in the following example.

▶ **EXAMPLE 6.4** Two-level logic size optimization using a K-map

Minimize the number of literals and terms in a two-level implementation of the equation:

F = xyz + xyz' + x'y'z' + x'y'z

Note that this is the same equation as in Example 6.1. We create a K-map representing the function, shown in Figure 6.5. We see adjacent 1s at the upper left of the map, so we circle those 1s to yield the term x'y'—in other words, *the circle is a shorthand notation for* x'y'z' + x'y'z

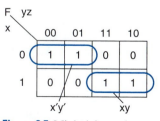

Figure 6.5 Minimizing a three-variable function using a K-map.

= x'y'. Likewise, we see adjacent 1s at the bottom right circle of the map, so we draw a circle representing xyz + xyz' = xy. Thus, F = x'y' + xy. ◀

Recall from Example 6.3 that sometimes terms can be repeatedly combined to eliminate a variable, resulting in even fewer terms and literals. We can redo that example using a different order of simplifications as follows:

$$G = xy'z' + xy'z + xyz + xyz'$$
$$G = x(y'z' + y'z + yz + yz')$$
$$G = x(y'(z'+z) + y(z+z'))$$
$$G = x(y'+y)$$
$$G = x$$

Notice that the second line above ANDs x with the OR of all possible combinations of variables y and z. Obviously, one of those combinations of y and z will be true for any values of y and z, and thus the subexpression in parentheses will always evaluate to 1, as we algebraically affirmed in the latter lines above.

K-maps also help us graphically see this situation. In addition to helping us see when we can combine two minterms to eliminate a variable, K-maps give us a graphical way to see when we can combine four minterms to eliminate two variables. We merely need to look for four adjacent cells, where the cells form either a rectangle or a square (but not a shape like an "L"). Those four cells will have one variable the same, and all possible combi-

Figure 6.6 Four adjacent 1s.

nations of the other two variables. Figure 6.6 shows the earlier function G as a three-variable K-map. The map has four adjacent 1s in the bottom row. The four minterms corresponding to those 1s are xy'z', xy'z, xyz, and xyz'— note that x is the same in all four minterms, while all four combinations of y and z appear in those minterms. We draw a circle around the bottom four 1s to represent the simplification of G shown in the equations above. The result is G = x. In other words, the circle is a shorthand notation for the algebraic simplification of G shown in the five equations above.

Always draw the largest circles possible to cover the 1s in a K-map.

Note that we could have drawn circles around the left two 1s and the right two 1s of the K-map, as shown in Figure 6.7, resulting in G = xy' + xy. Clearly, G can be further simplified to x(y'+y)=x. Thus, we should always draw the biggest circle possible, in order to best minimize the equation.

As another example of four adjacent 1s, consider the equation:

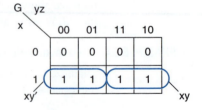

Figure 6.7 Nonoptimal circles.

$$H = x'y'z + x'yz + xy'z + xyz$$

Figure 6.8 shows the K-map for that equation's function. Circling the four adjacent 1s yields the minimized equation, H = z.

Sometimes, we need to draw circles that include the same 1 twice. That's okay. For example, consider the equation:

$$I = x'y'z + xy'z' + xy'z + xyz + xyz'$$

Figure 6.9 shows the K-map for that equation's function. We can draw a circle around the bottom four 1s to reduce those four minterms to just x. But that leaves the single 1 in the top row, corresponding to minterm x'y'z. We have to include that minterm in the minimized equation, since if we left that minterm out, we would be changing the function. We could include the minterm itself, yielding I = x + x'y'z. But that's not minimized, because the original equation included minterm xy'z, and xy'z + x'y'z = (x+x')y'z = y'z. On the K-map, we draw a circle around that top 1 that also includes the 1 in the cell below. The minimized function is thus I = x + y'z.

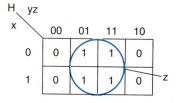

Figure 6.8 Four adjacent 1s.

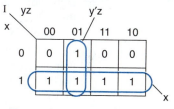

Figure 6.9 Circling a 1 twice.

It's OK to cover a 1 more than once to minimize multiple terms.

It's OK to include a 1 twice—that doesn't change the function. Think about it: the function doesn't change if we duplicate a minterm (don't forget, a = a + a), and duplicating a minterm can allow for more optimization. In other words:

$$I = x'y'z + xy'z' + xy'z + xyz + xyz'$$
$$I = x'y'z + xy'z + xy'z' + xy'z + xyz + xyz'$$
$$I = (x'y'z + xy'z) + (xy'z' + xy'z + xyz + xyz')$$
$$I = (y'z) + (x)$$

We duplicated a minterm, which resulted in better optimization.

On the other hand, there's no reason to circle 1s more than once if the 1s are already included in a minimized term. For example, the K-map for the equation:

$$J = x'y'z' + x'y'z + xy'z + xyz$$

appears in Figure 6.10. There's no reason to draw the circle resulting in the term y'z. The other two circles cover all the 1s, meaning those two circles' terms cause the equation to output 1 for all the required input combinations. The third circle just results in an extra term without changing the function. Thus, we not only want to draw the largest circles possible to cover all the 1s, but we also want to draw the *fewest* circles.

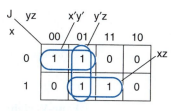

Figure 6.10 An unnecessary term.

Draw the fewest circles possible, to minimize the number of terms.

We mentioned earlier that the left and right sides of a K-map are adjacent. Thus, we can draw circles that wrap around the sides of a K-map. For example, the K-map for the equation:

$$K = xy'z' + xyz' + x'y'z$$

appears in Figure 6.11. The two cells in the corners with 1s are adjacent since the left and right sides of the map are adjacent, and therefore we can draw one circle that covers both, resulting in the term xz'.

Sometimes a 1 does not have any adjacent 1s. In that case, we simply circle the single 1, resulting in a term that is a minterm. The term $x'y'z$ in Figure 6.11 is an example of such a term.

A circle in a three-variable K-map must involve one cell, two adjacent cells, four adjacent cells, or eight adjacent cells. A circle can *not* involve only three, five, six, or seven cells. The reason is because the circle must represent algebraic transformations that eliminate variables appearing in all possible combinations, since those variables can be factored out and then combined to a 1. Three adjacent cells don't have all combinations of two variables—one combination is missing. Thus, the circle in Figure 6.12 would not be valid, since it corresponds to $xy'z' + xy'z + xyz$, which doesn't simplify down to one term. To cover that function, we would need two circles, one around the left pair of 1s, the other around the right pair.

If all the cells in a K-map have 1s, like for the function E in Figure 6.13, then we would have eight adjacent 1s. We can draw a circle around those eight cells. Since that circle represents the ORing of all possible combinations of the function's three variables, and since obviously one of those combinations will be true for any combination of input values, the equation would minimize to just $E = 1$.

Whenever in doubt as to whether a circle is valid, just remember that the circle represents a shorthand for algebraic transformations that combine terms to eliminate a variable. A circle must represent a set of terms for which all possible combinations of some variables appear while other variables are identical in all terms. The changing variables can be eliminated, resulting in a single term without those variables.

Four-Variable K-Maps

K-maps are also useful for minimizing four-variable Boolean functions. Figure 6.14 shows a four-variable K-map for the following equation:

$$F = w'xy'z' + w'xy'z + w'x'yz + w'xyz$$
$$+ wxyz + wx'yz$$

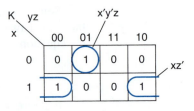

Figure 6.11 Sides are adjacent.

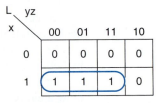

Figure 6.12 Invalid circle.

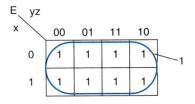
Figure 6.13 Four adjacent 1s.

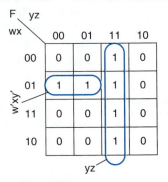
Figure 6.14 Four-variable K-map.

Again, notice that every adjacent pair of cells differs by exactly one variable. The left and right sides of the map are considered adjacent, and the top and bottom edges of the map are also adjacent—note that the left and right cells differ by only one variable, as do the top and bottom cells.

We cover the 1s in the map with the two circles shown in Figure 6.14, resulting in the terms $w'xy'$ and yz, so the minimized equation is $F = w'xy' + yz$.

A circle covering eight adjacent cells would represent all combinations of three variables, so algebraic manipulation would eliminate all three variables and yield one term. For example, the function in Figure 6.15 simplifies to a single term, z, as shown.

Legal-sized circles in a four-variable K-map are one, two, four, eight, or sixteen adjacent cells. Circling all sixteen cells yields a function that equals 1.

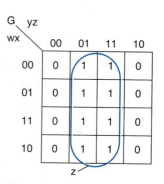

Figure 6.15 Eight adjacent cells.

Larger K-Maps

K-maps for five and six variables have been proposed, but are rather cumbersome to use effectively. Thus, we do not discuss them further.

K-maps for two variables also exist, as shown in Figure 6.16. However, they aren't particularly useful, because two-variable functions are very easy to minimize algebraically.

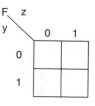

Using a K-Map

Given any Boolean function of three or four variables, the following method summarizes how to use a K-map to minimize the function:

Figure 6.16 Two-variable K-map.

1. *Convert* the function's equation into sum-of-minterms form.
2. *Place* a 1 in the appropriate K-map cell for each minterm.
3. *Cover* all the 1s by drawing the *minimum* number of *largest* circles such that every 1 is included at least once, and write the corresponding term.
4. *OR* all the resulting terms to create the minimized function.

The first step, converting to sum-of-minterms form, can be done algebraically, as was done in Chapter 2. Alternatively, many people find it easier to combine steps 1 and 2, by converting the function's equation to sum-of-products form (where each term is not necessarily a minterm), and then filling in the 1s on the K-map corresponding to each term. For example, consider the four-variable function:

$$F = w'xz + yz + w'xy'z'$$

The term $w'xz$ corresponds to the two lightly shaded cells in Figure 6.17, so we put 1s in those cells. The term yz corresponds to the entire dark-shaded column in the figure. The term $w'xy'z'$ corresponds to the single unshaded cell shown on the left with a 1.

Minimization would proceed by covering the 1s with circles and ORing all the terms. The function in Figure 6.17 is identical to the function in Figure 6.14, for which we obtained the minimized equation:

$$F = w'xy' + yz.$$

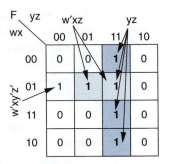

Figure 6.17 w'xz and yz terms.

▶ **EXAMPLE 6.5** Two-level logic size optimization using a three-variable K-map

Minimize the following equation:

$$G = a + a'b'c' + b*(c' + bc')$$

Let's begin by converting the equation to sum-of-products:

$$G = a + a'b'c' + bc' + bc'$$

We place 1s in a three-variable K-map corresponding to each term, as in Figure 6.18. The bottom row corresponds to the term a, the top left cell to term a'b'c', and the right column to the term bc' (which appears twice in the equation).

We then cover the 1s using the two circles shown in Figure 6.19. ORing the resulting terms yields the minimized equation $G = a + c'$. ◀

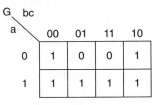

Figure 6.18 Terms on the K-map.

▶ **EXAMPLE 6.6** Two-level logic size optimization using a four-variable K-map

Minimize the following equation:

$$H = a'b'(cd' + c'd') + ab'c'd' + ab'cd' + a'bd + a'bcd'$$

Converting to sum-of-products form yields:

$$H = a'b'cd' + a'b'c'd' + ab'c'd' + ab'cd' + a'bd + a'bcd'$$

We fill in the 1s corresponding to each term, resulting in the K-map shown in Figure 6.20. The term a'bd corresponds to the two cells whose 1s are in italics. All the other terms are minterms and thus correspond to one cell.

We cover the 1s using circles as shown. One "circle" covers the four corners, resulting in the term b'd'. That circle may look strange, but remember that the top and bottom cells are adjacent, and the left and right cells are adjacent. Another circle results in the term a'bd, and a third circle in the term a'bc. The minimized two-level equation is therefore:

$$H = b'd' + a'bc + a'bd$$ ◀

Note the bolded 1 in Figure 6.20. We covered that 1 by drawing a circle that included the 1 to the

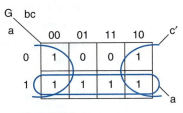

Figure 6.19 A cover.

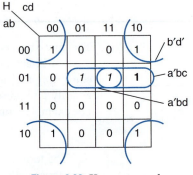

Figure 6.20 K-map example.

left, yielding the term $a'bc$. Alternatively, we could have drawn a circle that included the 1 above, yielding the term $a'cd'$, resulting in the minimized equation:

$$H = b'd' + a'cd' + a'bd$$

Not only does that equation represent the same function as the previous equation, that equation would also require the same number of transistors as the previous equation. Thus, we see that there may be multiple minimized equations that are equally good.

Don't Care Input Combinations

Sometimes, we are guaranteed that certain input combinations of a Boolean function can never appear. For those combinations, we don't care whether the function outputs a 1 or a 0, because the function will never actually see those input values—the output for those inputs just doesn't matter. As an intuitive example, if you became ruler of the world, would you live in a palace or a castle? Your answer (the output) doesn't matter, because the input (you becoming ruler of the world) simply won't happen.

Thus, when given a don't care input combination, we can choose whether to output a 1 or a 0 for each input combination, such that we obtain the best minimization possible. We can choose whatever output yields the best minimization, because the output for those don't care input combinations doesn't matter, as those combinations simply won't happen.

Algebraically, we can use don't care terms by introducing them into an equation during algebraic minimization to create the opportunity to combine terms to eliminate a variable. As a simple example, consider a function $F = xy'z'$, for which we are for some reason guaranteed that the terms $x'y'z'$ and $xy'z$ can each never evaluate to 1. We notice that adding the first don't care term to the equation would result in $xy'z' + x'y'z' = (x+x')y'z' = y'z'$. Thus, introducing that don't care term $x'y'z'$ into the equation yields a minimization benefit. However, introducing the second don't care term does not yield such a benefit, so we choose not to introduce that term.

In a K-map, don't care input combinations can be easily handled by placing an X in a K-map for each don't care minterm. We don't *have* to cover the Xs with circles, but we *can* cover some Xs if that helps us draw bigger circles while covering the 1s, meaning fewer literals will appear in the term corresponding to the circle. For the above example, we would draw the K-map shown in Figure 6.21, having one 1 corresponding to $xy'z'$, when the function *must* output 1, and having two Xs corresponding to $x'y'z'$ and $xy'z$, when the function *may* output 1 if that helps us minimize the function. Drawing a single circle results in the minimized equation $F = y'z'$. (Be careful in this discussion not to confuse the uppercase X, corresponding to a don't care, with the lowercase x, corresponding to a variable.)

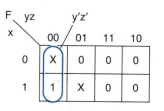

Figure 6.21 Map with don't cares.

Remember, don't cares don't *have* to be covered. The cover in Figure 6.22 gives an example of a

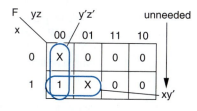

Figure 6.22 Wasteful use of Xs.

wasteful use of don't cares. The circle covering the bottom X, yielding term xy', is not needed. That term is not wrong, because we don't care whether the output is 1 or 0 when xy' evaluates to 1. But, that term would result in a larger circuit, because the resulting equation is $F = y'z' + xy'$. Since we don't care, why not make the output 0 when $xy'z$ is 1, and thus obtain a smaller circuit?

▶ **EXAMPLE 6.7** Two-level logic size minimization with don't cares on a K-map

Minimize the following equation:

$$F = a'bc' + abc' + a'b'c$$

given that terms $a'bc$ and abc are don't cares. Intuitively, those don't cares mean that bc can never be 11.

We begin by creating the 3-variable K-map in Figure 6.23. We place 1s in the three cells for the function's minterms. We then place Xs in the two cells for the don't cares. We can cover the upper-left 1 using a circle that includes an X. Likewise, including the two Xs in a circle covers the two 1s on the right with a bigger circle. The resulting minimized equation is $F = a'c + b$.

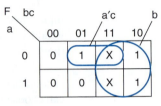

Figure 6.23 Using don't cares.

Without don't cares, the equation would have minimized to $F = a'b'c + bc'$. Assuming two transistors per gate input and ignoring inverters, the equation minimized without don't cares would require $(3+2+2) * 2 = 14$ transistors (3 gate inputs for the first AND gate, 2 for the second AND gate, and 2 for the OR gate, times 2 transistors per gate input). In contrast, the equation minimized with don't cares requires only $(2 + 0 + 2)*2 = 8$ transistors. ◀

▶ **EXAMPLE 6.8** Don't care input combinations in a sliding switch example

Consider a sliding switch, shown in Figure 6.24, that can be in one of five positions, with three outputs x, y, and z indicating the position in binary. So xyz can take on the values of 001, 010, 011, 100, and 101. The other values for xyz are not possible, namely, the values 000, 110, and 111 (or $x'y'z'$, xyz', and xyz). We wish to design combinational logic, with x, y, and z inputs, that outputs 1 if the switch is in position 2, 3, or 4, corresponding to xyz values of 010, 011, or 100.

A Boolean equation describing the desired logic is: $G = x'yz' + x'yz + xy'z'$. We can minimize the equation using a K-map, as shown in Figure 6.25. The minimized equation that results is: $G = xy'z' + x'y$.

However, if we consider don't cares, we can obtain a simpler minimized equation. In particular, we know that none of the three

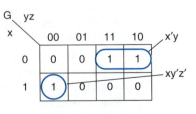

Figure 6.24 Sliding switch example.

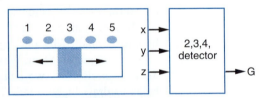

Figure 6.25 Without don't cares.

minterms $x'y'z'$, xyz', and xyz can ever be true, because the switch can only be in one of the above-stated five positions. So it doesn't matter whether we output a 1 or a 0 for those three other minterms. We can include these don't care input combinations as Xs on the K-map, as shown in Figure 6.26. When covering the 1s in the top right, we can now draw a larger circle, resulting in the term y. When covering the 1 at the bottom left, we can draw a larger circle also, resulting in the term z'. Although we ended up covering all the Xs in this example, recall that we do not have to cover the Xs—we only use them if they help us cover the 1s with larger circles. The minimized equation that results is: $G = y + z'$.

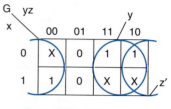

Figure 6.26 With don't cares.

That minimized equation using don't cares looks a lot different than the minimized equation without don't cares. But keep in mind the circuit still works the same. For example, if the switch is in position 1, then xyz will be 001, so $G = y + z'$ evaluates to 0, as desired. ◁

Don't cares must be used with caution. We must balance the criteria of size with other criteria, like reliable, error-tolerant, and safe circuits, when deciding whether to use don't cares. We must ask ourselves—is it *ever* possible that the don't care input combination *might* occur, even if in an error situation? And if it *is* possible, then do we *really* not care at all what our circuit outputs in that situation? Often, we really *do* care, and will want to ensure our circuit outputs a particular value. For example, in the sliding switch example above, perhaps temporary values could appear at the xyz outputs as the switch is being moved. We might therefore want to ensure we output 0 for the don't care values.

Several common situations lead to don't cares. Sometimes don't cares come from physical limits on the inputs—a switch can't be in two positions at once, for example. If you've read Chapter 3, then you may realize that another common situation in which don't cares may appear is in controller design, when a controller uses a state register that can represent more states than the controller requires. For example, a controller with 17 states may use a 5-bit state register, meaning that 15 of the 32 possible states of the state register would be unutilized. Those 15 states could be treated as don't cares (although to be safe, we might actually want to transition back to an initial state if we ever enter one of those 15 unused states due to noise or some other error). If you've read Chapter 5, then you may realize that another common situation where don't cares arise is in a controller controlling a datapath. If we aren't reading or writing to a particular memory or register file in a given state, then we don't care what address appears at the memory or register file during that state. Likewise, if a mux feeds into a register and we aren't loading the register in a given state, then we really don't care which mux data input passes through the mux during that state. If we aren't going to load the output of an ALU into a register in a given state, then we really don't care what function the ALU computes during that state.

Automating Two-Level Logic Size Optimization

Visual Use of K-Maps Is Rather Limited

Although the visual K-map method is helpful in two-level optimization of three- and four-variable functions, the visual method is unmanageable for functions with many more variables. One problem is that we can't effectively visualize maps beyond 5 or 6 variables. Another problem is that humans make mistakes, and might accidentally not draw the biggest circle possible on a K-map. Furthermore, the order in which a designer begins covering 1s may result in a function that has more terms than would have been obtained using a different order. For example, consider the function shown in the K-map of Figure 6.27(a). Starting from the left, a designer might first draw the circle yielding the term y'z', then the circle yielding x'y', then the circle yielding yz, and finally the circle yielding xy, for a total of four terms. The K-map in Figure 6.27(b) shows an alternative cover. After drawing the circle yielding the term y'z', the designer draws the circle yielding x'z, and then the circle yielding xy. The alternative cover uses only three terms instead of four.

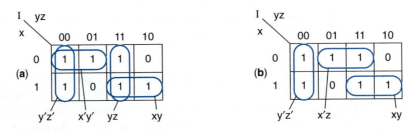

Figure 6.27 A cover is not necessarily optimal: (a) a four-term cover, and (b) a three-term cover of the same function.

Concepts Underlying Automated Two-Level Size Optimization

Because of the above-mentioned problems, two-level logic size optimization is done primarily using automated computer-based tools executing heuristics or exact algorithms. A *heuristic* is a problem solving method that *usually* yields a good solution, which is ideally close to the optimal, but *not necessarily* optimal. An *exact algorithm*, or just algorithm, is a problem solving method that yields the optimal solution. An *optimal solution* is as good or better than any other possible solution, with respect to the criteria of interest to us.

We first define some concepts underlying heuristics and exact algorithms for two-level logic size optimization. We will illustrate those concepts graphically on K-maps, but such illustration is only intended to provide the reader with an intuition of the concepts—automated tools do *not* use K-maps.

Recall that a function can be written as a sum-of-minterms equation. A *minterm* is a product term that includes all the function's variables exactly once, in either true or complemented form. The *on-set* of a function is the set of minterms that define when the function should evaluate to 1 (i.e., when the function is "on"). For the function in Figure 6.28, the on-set is: {x'y'z, xyz, xyz'}. The *off-set* of a function is all the remaining minterms. For the function in Figure 6.28, the off-set is: {x'y'z', x'yz', x'yz, xy'z', xy'z}. Using compact minterms representation (see Section 2.6), the on-set is {1,6,7}, and the off-set is {0,2,3,4,5}.

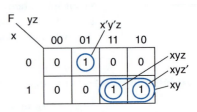

Figure 6.28 Implicants.

An ***implicant*** is a product term that may include fewer than all the function's variables, but is a term that only evaluates to 1 if the function should evaluate to 1—in other words, an implicant of a function is a term that should evaluate to 1 for a particular set of variable values only if at least one of the function's on-set minterms evaluates to 1 for those variable values. For example, the function F = x'y'z + xyz' + xyz has four implicants: x'y'z, xyz', xyz, and xy. Graphically, an implicant is any legal (but not necessarily the biggest possible) circle on a K-map, as shown in Figure 6.28. All minterms are obviously implicants, but not all implicants are minterms.

We say that the implicant xy ***covers*** minterms xyz' and xyz of function F. Graphically, an implicant's circle encircles the 1s of the covered minterms. Intuitively, we know that we can replace the covered minterms by the covering implicant and still obtain the same function. In other words, we can replace xyz'+ xyz by xy. A set of implicants that covers the on-set of a function (and covers no other minterms) is known as a ***cover*** of the function. For the above function, one function cover is x'y'z + xyz + xyz'; another cover is x'y'z + xy; yet another cover is x'y'z + xyz + xyz'+ xy.

Removing a variable from a term is known as ***expanding*** the term, which is the same as expanding the size of a circle on a K-map. For example, for the function in Figure 6.28, expanding the term xyz to the term xy (by eliminating z) results in an implicant of the function. Expanding the term xyz' to xy also results in an implicant (the same one). But, expanding xyz to xz (by eliminating y) does not result in an implicant—xz covers minterm xy'z, which is not in the function's on-set.

A ***prime implicant*** of a function is an implicant with the property that if any variable were eliminated from the implicant, the result would be a term covering a minterm not in the function's on-set. Graphically, a prime implicant corresponds to circles that are the largest possible—enlarging the circle further would result in covering 0s, which changes the function. In Figure 6.28, x'y'z and xy are prime implicants. Removing any variable from implicant x'y'z, say z, would result in a term (x'y') that covers a minterm that is not in the on-set—x'y' covers x'y'z', for example, which is not in the function's on-set. Likewise, removing x' or y' from that term would cover a minterm not in the function's on-set. Removing any variable from implicant xy, say y, would result in a term (x) that covers minterms not in the on-set. On the other hand, xyz is not a prime implicant, because z can be removed from that implicant without changing the function, since xy covers minterms xyz and xyz', both of which are in the on-set. Likewise, xyz' is not a prime implicant, because z' can be removed. There is no reason to cover a function with anything other than prime implicants, since a prime implicant achieves the same function with fewer literals than nonprime implicants (which is why we always draw the biggest circles possible in K-maps).

An ***essential prime implicant*** is a prime implicant that is the *only* prime implicant that covers a particular minterm in the function's on-set. Graphically, an essential prime implicant is the only circle (the largest possible, of course, since the circle must represent a prime implicant) that covers a particular 1. In Figure 6.28, x'y'z is an essential prime implicant, as is xy, because each is the only prime implicant covering a particular 1. A nonessential prime implicant is a prime implicant whose covered minterms are also covered by one or more other prime implicants. Figure 6.29 shows a different function that has four prime implicants, but only two of which are essential. x'y' is an essential prime implicant because it is the only prime implicant that covers minterm x'y'z'. xy is an essential prime implicant because it is the only prime implicant that covers minterm xyz'. y'z is a nonessential prime implicant because both of its covered minterms are covered by other implicants (those other prime implicants may or may not be essential prime implicants). Likewise, xz is not essential. The importance of essential prime implicants is as follows: we know that we *must* include all essential prime implicants in a function's cover, otherwise there would be some minterms that could not be covered. We may or may not need to include nonessential prime implicants to completely cover the function, but we must include all essential prime implicants.

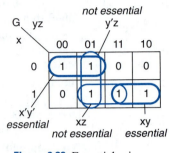

Figure 6.29 Essential prime implicants.

Given the notions of prime implicants and essential prime implicants, a simple approach for two-level logic optimization is given in Table 6.1.

TABLE 6.1 Approach for automated two-level logic size optimization.

Step	Description
1 *Determine prime implicants*	For every minterm in the function's on-set, maximally expand the term (meaning eliminate literals from the term) such that the term still only covers minterms in the function's on-set (like drawing the biggest circle possible around each 1 in a K-map). Repeat for each minterm. If don't cares exist, use them to maximally expand minterms into prime implicants (like using X's to create the biggest circles possible for a given 1 in a K-map).
2 *Add essential prime implicants to the function's cover*	Find any minterms covered by only one prime implicant (i.e., by an essential prime implicant). Add those prime implicants to the cover, and mark the minterms covered by those implicants as already covered.
3 *Cover remaining minterms with nonessential prime implicants*	Cover the remaining minterms using the minimal number of remaining prime implicants.

The first two steps are exact. The last step is a bit tricky. How do we choose which prime implicants to use to cover the remaining minterms? Recall the example of Figure 6.27, in which the cover in Figure 6.27(a) used two prime implicants to cover the two 1s that would be left after adding essential prime implicants, while the cover in Figure 6.27(b) used only one prime implicant to cover those remaining two 1s. When there are only two possibilities, we can try each possibility and pick the one with fewest prime implicants in the final cover. But what if there were millions, or billions, of possibilities? We may not have enough compute time to try all those possibilities. For large functions with hundreds of minterms and thousands of prime implicants, there may indeed be millions of possible covers to consider in the last step.

If an approach tries all such possibilities, the approach is an exact algorithm. If an approach just tries a few such possibilities, the overall two-level size optimization approach may be a heuristic (unless the approach can guarantee that the ignored possibilities couldn't possibly be part of an optimal solution).

We'll demonstrate the approach for automated two-level logic size optimization with the following example.

▶ **EXAMPLE 6.9**   Two-level logic size optimization with the approach of Table 6.1, illustrated on a K-map

Figure 6.30 shows a K-map for the function from Figure 6.27, for which we saw that different covers yielded different numbers of terms. The first step is to determine all prime implicants, shown in the top part of the figure. For each 1, we draw every possible circle involving adjacent 1s, ensuring that each circle is the largest possible.

The second step is to add essential prime implicants to the function's cover. Notice that the 1 corresponding to minterm x'yz (the top right 1) is covered only by one prime implicant, namely, x'z. Thus, we know we'll need to use that prime implicant, so we'll include prime implicant x'z in the cover. Also notice that the 1 corresponding to minterm xyz' (the bottom right 1) is only covered by one prime implicant, namely, xz', so we'll include that prime implicant in the cover too. We mark all the 1s covered by these essential prime implicants, noted by italicized 1s in the figure.

The last step is to cover the remaining 1s with the fewest number of prime implicants. There is only one 1 uncovered, and that 1 is covered by two prime implicants. We can choose either prime implicant for the cover—let's choose y'z'. Thus, the final cover is:

$$I = x'z + xz' + y'z'$$

This example uses a K-map merely to illustrate to the reader the steps occurring within an automated tool—such a tool does *not* use K-maps internally, but rather other means of representing the terms of a function.   ◀

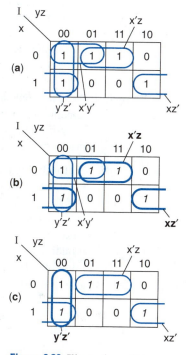

Figure 6.30 Illustration of two-level optimization: (a) all prime implicants, (b) including essential prime implicants in the cover, (c) covering remaining 1s.

Automated Two-Level Logic Size Optimization Using the Quine-McCluskey Method

The most well-known, and in fact the original, approach for automated two-level logic size optimization is the **Quine-McCluskey** method, sometimes called the **tabular method**.

The first step of this method finds all prime implicants. The step starts with the function's minterms—if we are minimizing a three-variable function, then we might call these three-variable terms. To find all the prime implicants, the method first compares each three-variable term with every other three-variable term, and if two terms are found that differ by only one variable, the method adds a new term (without the differing variable) to a new set of two-variable terms. For example, xyz' and xyz differ by one variable z, resulting in a new term xy being added to the two-variable set. Once done comparing all three-variable terms, the method compares every pair of two-variable terms for terms that differ by only one variable, resulting in a set of one-variable terms. One-variable terms can then be compared for terms that differ by one variable, but if such terms are found, then the function evaluates simply to 1. Actually, not all terms in a set need to be compared—only those terms whose *number* of uncomplemented literals differs by one need to be compared. For example, x'yz' and xyz need not be compared, because the number of uncomplemented literals differs by two, not one, and thus can't be simplified to a new term by eliminating a variable. If at any time in this step a term cannot be combined with any other term, we mark that term as a prime implicant. Thus, after this step, all *marked* terms represent all prime implicants. The method thus provides an approach for finding prime implicants, more efficient than just maximally expanding every term.

The second step is to add all the essential prime implicants to the cover, and to mark as "covered" all minterms covered by those prime implicants.

The final step is to cover all remaining uncovered minterms by selecting the fewest remaining prime implicants to cover those minterms. Trying all the possibilities results in a version of the Quine-McCluskey method that is an exact algorithm. Trying just a subset may result in a heuristic.

Methods That Enumerate All Minterms or Compute All Prime Implicants May Be Inefficient

The Quine-McCluskey method works reasonably for functions with perhaps tens of variables. However, for larger functions, just listing all the minterms could result in a huge amount of data. A function of 10 variables could have up to 2^{10} minterms—that's 1024 minterms, which is fairly reasonable. But a function of 32 variables could have up to 2^{32} minterms, or up to about four billion minterms. Representing those minterms in a table requires prohibitive computer memory. And comparing those minterms with other minterms could require on the order of (four billion)^2 computations, or quadrillions of computations (a quadrillion is a thousand times a trillion). Even a computer performing 10 billion computations per second would require 100,000 seconds to perform all those computations, or 27 hours. And for 64 variables, the numbers go up to 2^{64} possible minterms, or quadrillions of minterms, and quadrillions^2 of computations, which could require a month of computation. Functions with 100 inputs, which are not that uncommon, would require an absurd amount of memory, and many years of computations. Even computing all prime implicants, without first listing all minterms, is computationally prohibitive for many modern-sized functions.

Iterative Heuristic for Two-Level Logic Size Optimization

Because enumerating all minterms of a function, or even just all prime implicants, is prohibitive in terms of computer memory and computation time for functions with many variables, most automated tools use methods that instead just iteratively transform the original function's equation, in an attempt to find improvements to the equation. *Iterative improvement* means repeatedly making small changes to an existing solution until we decide to stop, perhaps because we can't find a better solution, or perhaps because the tool has run for enough time. As an example of making small changes to an existing solution, consider the equation:

```
F = abcdefgh + abcdefgh'+ jklmnop
```

Clearly, we can reduce this equation simply by combining the first two terms and removing variable h, resulting in F = abcdefg + jklmnop. However, enumerating the minterms, as required in the earlier-described size optimization methods, would have resulted in roughly 1000 minterms and then millions of computations to find the prime implicants—but such enumeration and computation are obviously not necessary to minimize this equation.

Modern automated logic optimization tools therefore don't try to enumerate all the minterms for functions with many variables. Instead, those tools start with a given sum-of-products equation of the function, like the description for F above. Those tools then try to transform the equation little by little into a better equation, meaning an equation with fewer terms and/or fewer literals. Those tools repeat, or *iterate*, until they find no further improvement or until some maximum time allocated for the tool's execution has expired.

Heuristics for such two-level logic optimization in modern tools can be quite complex. However, a simple heuristic that is reasonably effective uses repeated application of the expand operation. The ***expand*** operation means to remove a literal from a term and then check whether the new term is legal. Removing a literal makes that term cover more minterms, like drawing a bigger circle on a K-map—thus the name "expand." For example, consider the function F = x'z + xy'z + xyz. We might try to expand the term x'z by removing x', or by removing z. Note that expanding a term *reduces* the number of literals—the concept that *expanding* a term *reduces* the number of literals in a term may take a while for you to get used to. Thinking of K-map circles may help, as shown in Figure 6.31—the bigger the circle, the fewer the resulting literals. An expansion is legal if the new term covers only minterms in the function's on-set, or equivalently, does *not* cover a minterm in the function's off-set—in other words, an expansion is legal if the new term is still an implicant of the function. Figure 6.31(a) shows that expanding term x'z to z for the given function is legal, as the expanded term covers only 1s, whereas expanding x'z to x' is not legal, as the expanded term covers at least one 0. If an expansion is legal, we replace the original term by the expanded term, and *we look for and remove any other term covered by the expanded term*. In Figure 6.31(a), the expanded term z covers terms xy'z and xyz, so both those latter terms can be removed.

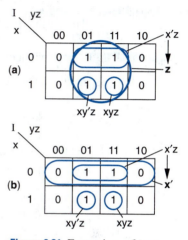

Figure 6.31 Expansions of term x'z in the function F = x'z + xy'z + xyz: (a) legal, (b) not legal (because the expanded term covers 0s).

Note that we illustrated the expand operation on a K-map merely to aid in understanding the intuition of the operation—K-maps are nowhere to be found in heuristic two-level logic size minimization tools.

As another example, for the earlier introduced function:

$$F = abcdefgh + abcdefgh' + jklmnop$$

We might start by trying to expand the first term, abcdefgh. One expansion of that term is bcdefgh (i.e., we removed the literal a). However, that term covers the term a'bcdefgh, which covers minterms that are not in the function's on-set, so that expansion is not legal. We might try other expansions, finding them not legal too, until we come across the expansion to abcdefg (i.e., we removed the literal h). That term strictly covers abcdefgh and abcdefgh', both of which are clearly implicants because they appear in the original function, and thus the new term must also be an implicant. Therefore, we replace the first term by the expanded term:

$$F = abcdefg\cancel{h} + abcdefgh' + jklmnop$$

and we also remove the second term, since that term is covered by the expanded term:

$$F = abcdefg\cancel{h} + \cancel{abcdefgh'} + jklmnop$$
$$F = abcdefg + jklmnop$$

Thus, using just the expand operation, we have improved the equation.

▶ **EXAMPLE 6.10**   Iterative heuristic two-level logic size optimization using *expand*

Minimize the following equation, which was also minimized in Example 6.4, using repeated application of the expand operation:

$$F = xyz + xyz' + x'y'z' + x'y'z$$

In other words, the on-set consists of the minterms: {7, 6, 0, 1}, and so the off-set consists of the minterms: {2, 3, 4, 5}.

Let's expand the terms from left to right, so we'll start with xyz. We can try to expand xyz to xy. Is that a legal expansion? xy covers minterms xyz' (minterm 6) and xyz (minterm 7), both in the on-set. Thus, the expansion is legal, so we replace xyz by xy, yielding the new equation:

$$F = xy\cancel{z} + xyz' + x'y'z' + x'y'z$$

We also look for implicants covered by the new implicant xy. xyz' is covered by xy, so we eliminate xyz', yielding:

$$F = xy + \cancel{xyz'} + x'y'z' + x'y'z$$

Let's continue trying to expand that first term. We can try expanding it from xy to x. The term x covers minterms xy'z' (minterm 4), xy'z (minterm 5), xyz' (minterm 6), and xyz (minterm 7). The term x thus covers minterms 4 and 5, which are not in the on-set, but instead in the off-set. Thus, that expansion is not legal. We can also try expanding xy to y, but we'll find again the expansion is not legal.

We might then consider the next term, x'y'z'. Let's try expand it to x'y'. That term covers minterms x'y'z' (minterm 0) and x'y'z (minterm 1), both in the on-set, so the expansion is legal. We thus replace the term by the expanded one:

$$F = xy + x'y'\cancel{z'} + x'y'z$$

We check for other terms covered by the expanded term, and find that x'y'z is covered by x'y', so we remove x'y'z, leaving:

$$F = xy + x'y' \cancel{+ x'y'z}$$

We can try expanding the term x'y' further, but will find that both possible expansions (x', or y') are not legal. Thus, the above equation represents the minimized equation. Notice that this happens to be the same result as we obtained when we minimized the same initial equation in Example 6.4.   ◀

Even though the heuristic based on expand happened to generate the optimally minimized equation in the previous example, there is no guarantee the results from the heuristic will always be optimal.

More advanced heuristics utilize additional operations beyond just the expand operation. One such operation is the reduce operation, which can be thought of as the opposite of expand. The **reduce** operation takes a term, and tries to add a literal to the term, checking that the equation with the new term still covers the function. Adding a literal to a term is like reducing the size of a circle on a K-map. Adding a literal to a term reduces the number of minterms covered by the term, hence the name *reduce*. Another operation is **irredundant**, which tries to remove a term entirely, checking that the new equation still covers the function. If so, the removed term was "redundant," hence the name *irredundant*. Heuristics may iterate among the expand, reduce, irredundant, and other operations, such as in the following heuristic: Try 10 random expansion operations, then 5 random reduce operations, then 2 irredundant operations, and then repeat (iterate) the whole sequence until no improvement occurs from one iteration to the next. Modern two-level size optimization tools differ largely in their ordering of operations and their number of iterations.

Recall that we said that modern heuristics don't enumerate all of a function's minterms, yet in the previous example we did enumerate all the minterms—actually, we were given the minterms in the initial equation. When we don't initially know the minterms, many advanced methods exist to efficiently represent a function's on-set and off-set without enumerating the minterms in those sets, and also to quickly check if a term covers terms in the off-set. Those methods are beyond the scope of the book, and instead the subject of textbooks on digital design synthesis. But hopefully you now get the basic idea of heuristic two-level minimization.

One of the original tools that performed automated heuristics as well as exact two-level logic optimization was called **Espresso**, developed at the University of California, Berkeley. The algorithms and heuristics in Espresso formed the basis of many modern commercial logic optimization tools.

Multilevel Logic Optimization—Performance and Size Tradeoffs

We have thus far discussed two-level logic size optimization. However, in practice, we may not need the speed of two levels of logic. We may be willing to use three, four, or more levels of logic if those additional levels reduce the amount of required logic. As a simple example, consider the equation:

$$F1 = ab + acd + ace$$

This equation can't be minimized. The resulting two-level circuit is shown in Figure 6.32(a).

We could, however, algebraically manipulate the equation as follows:

$$F2 = ab + ac(d + e) = a(b + c(d + e))$$

That equation can be implemented with the circuit shown in Figure 6.32(b). That multilevel logic implementation results in fewer transistors, at the expense of more gate-delays, as illustrated in Figure 6.32(c). The multilevel implementation thus represents a *tradeoff* compared to the two-level implementation.

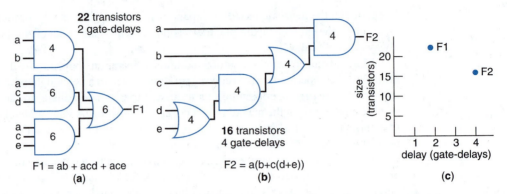

Figure 6.32 Using multilevel logic to tradeoff performance and size: (a) two-level circuit, (b) multilevel circuit with fewer transistors, (c) illustration of the size versus delay tradeoff. Numbers inside gates represent transistor counts.

Automated heuristics for multilevel logic optimization iteratively transform the initial function's equation, much like for two-level logic optimization, optimizing one of the criteria at the expense of another.

▶ **EXAMPLE 6.11** Multilevel logic optimization

Minimize the following function's circuit size, at the expense of perhaps slower performance, using algebraic manipulation. Plot the tradeoff of the initial and size-optimized circuits with respect to size and delay.

$$F1 = abcd + abcef$$

The circuit corresponding to this equation is shown in Figure 6.33(a). The circuit requires 22 transistors and has a delay of 2 gate-delays.

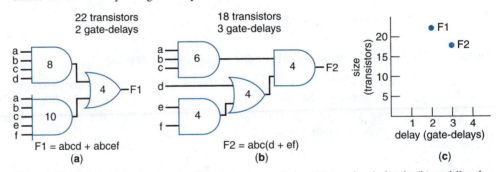

Figure 6.33 Multilevel logic to tradeoff performance and size: (a) two-level circuit, (b) multilevel circuit with fewer transistors, (c) tradeoff of size versus delay. Numbers inside gates represent transistor counts.

We can algebraically manipulate the equation by factoring out the abc term from the two terms, as follows:

$$F2 = abcd + abcef = abc(d + ef)$$

The circuit for that equation is shown in Figure 6.33(b). The circuit requires only 18 transistors, but has a longer delay of 3 gate-delays. The plot in Figure 6.33(c) shows the size and performance for each design. ◀

► **EXAMPLE 6.12**   Reducing noncritical path size with multilevel logic

Use multilevel logic to reduce the size of the circuit in Figure 6.34(a), without extending the circuit's delay. Note that the circuit initially has 26 transistors. Furthermore, the longest delay from any input to the output is three gate-delays. That delay occurs through the path shown by the dashed line in the figure. The longest path through a circuit is the circuit's **critical path**.

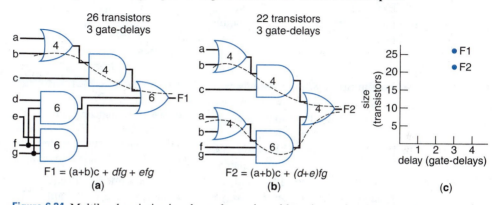

F1 = (a+b)c + *dfg* + *efg*

(a)

F2 = (a+b)c + *(d+e)fg*

(b)

(c)

Figure 6.34 Multilevel optimization that reduces size without increasing delay, by altering a noncritical path: (a) original circuit, (b) new circuit with fewer transistors but same delay, (c) illustration of the size optimization with no tradeoff of delay.

The other paths through the circuit are only two gate-delays. Thus, if we reduce the size of the logic for the noncritical paths and extend those paths to three gate-delays, we would not have extended the overall delay of the circuit. We focus on the noncritical parts of the equation for F1 in Figure 6.34(a); the equation has its noncritical parts italicized. We can algebraically modify the noncritical parts by factoring out the term fg, resulting in the new equation and circuit shown in Figure 6.34(b). One of the modified paths is now also three gate-delays, so we now have two equally long critical paths, both having three gate-delays. The resulting circuit has only 22 transistors compared to 26 in the original circuit, yet still has the same delay of three gate-delays, as illustrated in Figure 6.34(c). So overall, we've performed a size optimization with no penalty in performance.   ◄

Generally, multilevel logic optimization uses factoring (e.g., abc + abd = ab(c+d)) to reduce the number of gates.

Multilevel logic optimization is probably more commonly used today than two-level logic optimization. Multilevel logic optimization is also extensively used by automatic tools that map circuits to FPGAs. FPGAs will be discussed in Chapter 7.

► **6.3 SEQUENTIAL LOGIC OPTIMIZATIONS AND TRADEOFFS**

In Chapter 3, we described the design of sequential logic, namely, of controllers. When creating the FSM, and converting the FSM to a state-register and logic, we can apply some optimizations and tradeoffs.

State Reduction

State reduction, also known as *state minimization*, is an optimization that reduces the number of FSM states without changing the FSM's behavior. By reducing the number of states, we may reduce the size of the required state register that implements the FSM, thus reducing circuit size. Reducing the number of states is possible when the FSM contains states that are equivalent to one another. For example, consider the FSM of Figure 6.35(a), having input x and output y. Examination reveals that states *S2* and *S3* appear to be the same as states *S0* and *S1*. Regardless of whether we start in *S0* or *S2*, the outputs will be identical. For example, if we start in *S0* and the input sequence for four clock edges is 1, 1, 0, 0, the state sequence will be *S0*, *S1*, *S1*, *S2*, *S2*, so the output sequence

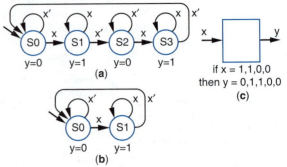

Inputs: x; Outputs: y

(a)

(b)

if x = 1,1,0,0
then y = 0,1,1,0,0

(c)

Figure 6.35 Eliminating redundant states: (a) original FSM, (b) equivalent FSM with fewer states, (c) the FSMs are indistinguishable from the outside, providing identical output behavior for any input sequence.

will be 0, 1, 1, 0, 0. If instead we start in *S2*, the same input sequence will result in a state sequence of *S2*, *S3*, *S3*, *S0*, *S0*, so the output sequence will again be 0, 1, 1, 0, 0. In fact, if we tried all possible input sequences, we would find that the output sequence starting from state *S0* would be identical to the output sequence starting from state *S2*. States *S0* and *S2* are thus equivalent. Likewise, states *S1* and *S3* are equivalent for the same reason. Thus, we can redraw the FSM as in Figure 6.35(b). The FSMs in Figure 6.35(a) and (b) have exactly the same behavior—for any sequence of inputs, the two FSMs provide exactly the same sequence of outputs. If we encapsulate the FSM as a box as in Figure 6.35(c), the outside world cannot distinguish between the two FSMs based on the outputs.

   Two states are equivalent if:

   - they assign the same values to outputs, AND
   - for all possible sequences of inputs, the FSM outputs will be the same starting from either state.

   For large FSMs, visual inspection cannot guarantee that we've removed all redundant states—a more systematic approach is needed, which we now introduce.

Implication Tables

Intuitively, we know that two states cannot be equivalent if they produce different outputs for the same sequence of inputs. Consider the FSM in Figure 6.36, which is almost identical to the FSM in Figure 6.35 with a slight modification — in state *S2*, the FSM now outputs y=1 instead of y=0. States *S0* and *S2* therefore clearly are not equivalent, because they have different output values. States *S1* and *S3* produce the same output, but when we transition from either state to the corresponding next state, the output differs. For example, if the FSM starts in state *S1* and x becomes 0, the next state (*S2*) outputs y=1, but if

Inputs: x; Outputs: y

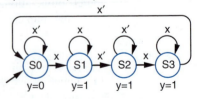

Figure 6.36 A variant of the FSM in Figure 6.35—states *S0* and *S2* cannot be equivalent because they output different values, and states *S1* and *S3* can't be equivalent because they have nonequivalent next states for the same input values.

the FSM had started in *S3*, the next state (*S0*) would output y=0. Thus, *S1* and *S3* cannot be equivalent, because the same input sequence results in a different output sequence.

If two states' outputs are not equivalent, the two states clearly are not equivalent. Furthermore, if two states' *next states* are not equivalent for a given input value, then the two states are also not equivalent. Using these concepts of nonequivalent states, Table 6.2 describes an algorithm for reducing an FSM's number of states.

TABLE 6.2 Algorithm for state reduction.

Step		Description
1	*Mark state pairs having different outputs as nonequivalent*	States having different outputs obviously cannot be equivalent.
2	*For each unmarked state pair, write the next state pairs for the same input values*	
3	*For each unmarked state pair, mark state pairs having nonequivalent next-state pairs as nonequivalent. Repeat this step until no change occurs, or until all states are marked.*	States with nonequivalent next states for the same input values can't be equivalent. Each time through this step is called a **pass**.
4	*Merge remaining state pairs*	Remaining state pairs must be equivalent.

When comparing all possible pairs of states by hand, using a graphical table ensures that we don't miss any pairs. Consider the FSM of Figure 6.35(a). The FSM has 4 states, therefore there are $4^2 = 16$ possible state pairs. Figure 6.37(a) shows those possible pairs graphically in a table, with the states listed along the row and column headings. Each cell corresponds to a state pair. We can simplify the table size by removing redundant cells (e.g., row *S0*, column *S1* is the same as row *S1*, column *S0*) and removing meaningless cells along the diagonal of the table (state *S0* is obviously equivalent to state *S0*). The reduced table is shown in Figure 6.37(b).

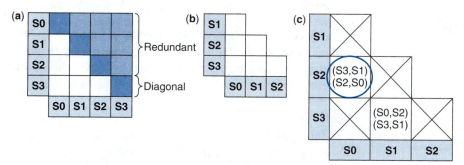

Figure 6.37 Table of state pairs: (a) original table comparing all pairs, (b) simpler table comparing only unique and relevant pairs, (c) after initial filling in with FSM state information.

Figure 6.37(c) steps through the state reduction algorithm of Table 6.2 for the FSM of Figure 6.35(a).

Step 1 involves looking at every table cell and marking that cell with a large "X" if the states for that cell have different outputs. We refer to such cells as being *marked*. The first state pair (*S1,S0*) is not equivalent because *S0* outputs $y = 0$, while *S1* outputs $y = 1$. We then look at state pair (*S2,S0*), (*S2,S1*), and so on, and finally (*S3,S2*), marking state pairs having different outputs, resulting in the Xs shown in Figure 6.37(c).

Step 2 involves writing the next state pairs for each remaining unmarked cell. There are two unmarked cells:

- (*S2,S0*) (circled in Figure 6.37(c)): When x=1, state *S2*'s next state is *S3,* while state *S0*'s next state is *S1* (we see this by looking at the FSM in Figure 6.35(a)). Thus, we write "(*S3,S1*)" in that cell (the order doesn't matter), meaning that for states *S2* and *S0* to be equivalent, *S3* and *S1* must be equivalent. We then consider the case when input x=0, in which case the next states are *S2* and *S0*, so we write "(*S2,S0*)" in that cell also.

- (*S3,S1*): When x=0, the next states are *S0* and *S2*, so we write (*S0,S2*) in the cell. For x=1, we write (*S3,S1*) in the cell.

Step 3 involves marking as nonequivalent any unmarked cells whose next state pairs are already marked as nonequivalent. Looking at cell (*S2,S0*), the next state pair (*S3,S1*) is not marked, nor is next state pair (*S2,S0*) (which happens to be the current cell), so we can't mark this cell. Likewise, for cell (*S3,S1*), the next state pair (*S0,S2)* is not marked, nor is the next state pair (*S3,S1*), so we can't mark this cell.

Because we made a pass through step 3 without any changes, we don't repeat step 3, and instead move on to step 4.

Step 4 involves declaring the unmarked state pairs as equivalent, so *S2* and *S0* are equivalent, and *S3* and *S1* are equivalent. To finalize step 4 of the algorithm, we combine the equivalent states in the FSM. After combining states *S2* and *S0*, and combining states *S3* and *S1*, we obtain the FSM in Figure 6.35(b).

The method we have just employed is known as the ***implication table*** method for state reduction.

Naturally, not every FSM can have its number of states reduced. For example, let's use the implication table method on the FSM in Figure 6.36. With 4 states, the FSM's implication table will be the same size as the previous example, as shown in Figure 6.38(a). **Step 1** marks state pairs with different outputs, shown in Figure 6.38(a). **Step 2** lists, for each unmarked cell, the next state pairs for identical input values, as also shown in Figure 6.38(a).

In **step 3's first pass**, we first examine the cell for state pair (*S2, S1*). Naturally, the next state pair (*S2, S2*) is equivalent. The next state pair (*S3, S1*) is unmarked, so we cannot mark (*S2, S1*). We then examine the cell for state pair (*S3,S1*), and find that the next state pair (*S0,S2*) has its cell marked. This tells us that *S3* and *S1* cannot be equivalent (because they could transition to nonequivalent states for the same input values), so we mark the cell for *(S3,S1)*. Similarly, we mark (*S3,S2*) since its first next state pair, (*S0,S2*), has its cell marked. Completing step 3's first pass results in the table of Figure 6.38(b).

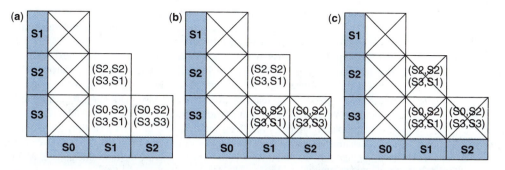

Figure 6.38 Implication table for FSM in Figure 6.36: (a) table after initial setup and steps 1 and 2, (b) after step 3's first pass through the table, (c) after step 3's second and final pass through the table.

Because the table changed during the first pass (we marked two state pairs), we must make a **second pass**, because changes in the table may affect state pairs that we already looked at and left unmarked. In the second pass, we again look at state pair (*S2,S1*). Naturally, the next state pair (*S2,S2*) is equivalent. The next state pair (*S3,S1*), however, is now marked, and therefore we mark (*S2,S1*).

With all pairs in the table marked, as seen in Figure 6.38(c), we can conclude that no states in the FSM are equivalent, and thus we leave the FSM unchanged.

We now provide another example of state reduction.

► **EXAMPLE 6.13** Minimizing states in an FSM using an implication table

Consider the FSM in Figure 6.39(a). Unlike previous examples, this FSM has 5 states, resulting in more possible state pairs than in previous examples. The first task in minimizing the FSM's states is to construct an implication table so we can compare every state with each other as a state pair.

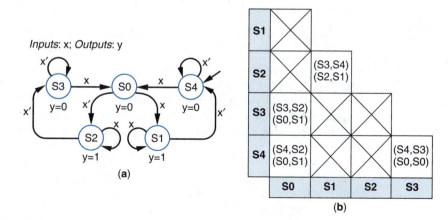

Figure 6.39 An FSM needing state reduction: (a) original FSM, (b) implication table after steps 1 and 2.

In **step 1** of our state reduction algorithm, we mark with an X state pairs that we can easily tell are not equivalent because their outputs differ, as shown in Figure 6.39(b).

In **step 2**, we write in all the next state pairs for unmarked cells of the implication table, as shown in Figure 6.39(b). Since there are only two possible combinations of inputs (either x=0 or x=1), each unmarked cell will have two next state pairs.

In **step 3's first pass**, we mark each state pair if one of their next state pairs is marked. During our first pass through the table, we will examine four state pairs. Starting with (S2,S1), we see that both of its next state pairs are unmarked. Looking at (S3,S0), we see one of its next state pairs, (S3,S2), is marked, so we mark (S3,S0)'s cell. We also mark (S4,S0) because its next state pair (S4,S2) is marked. We leave (S4,S3) unmarked as both of its next state pairs are unmarked, thus completing the first pass. Figure 6.40(a) reflects the results of our first pass through the implication table.

Because we marked new state pairs in the first pass, we conduct a **second pass** through step 3. During that pass, we find no new cells to mark, leaving the table unchanged. We thus move on to step 4.

In **step 4**, we declare the unmarked state pair (S2,S1) as equivalent, and the unmarked state pair (S4,S3) as equivalent. We combine states S2 and S1, and we combine states S4 and S3, resulting in the new FSM shown in Figure 6.40(b). Note that the two transitions with conditions x' and x from S0 could be replaced by one transition with no conditions.

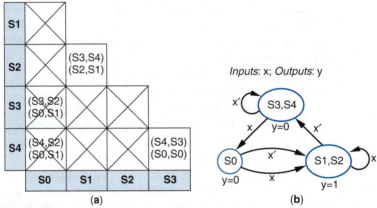

Figure 6.40 Implication table and minimized FSM: (a) implication table after first pass, (b) minimized state machine with states S1 and S2 combined, and S3 and S4 combined.

In this example, by reducing the number of states from 5 down to 3, we have reduced the minimum state register size from 3 bits down to 2 bits, perhaps reducing circuit size. ◀

Sometimes equivalent states may overlap. For example, assume that for some FSM with states {T0, T1, T2, T3, T4}, you find that state pairs (T0,T1), (T1,T2) and (T2,T0) are equivalent. How do you deal with the overlapping equivalencies? The answer is simple: the three states, T0, T1, and T2 can be combined into a single state.

The implication table method is suitable for hand-optimizing small FSMs such as those introduced in the previous examples, but can quickly become unwieldy for FSMs with more states. Consider the 15-state FSM in Figure 6.41. Its reduced implication table would require 14 rows and 14 columns, and 105 state pairs. With two combinations of inputs (namely, a = 0 or a = 1), each state pair would have two next state pairs, and, in the worst case, we would need to check 105*2 = 210 next state pairs during our first pass alone. What if the same FSM had four inputs (say, a, b, c, and d) instead of one? With four inputs, there would be 4^2=16 combinations of inputs (i.e. a'b'c'd', a'b'c'd, a'b'cd', ..., abcd) and up to 16 next state pairs in each cell in the implication table. If instead the FSM had, say, 100 states (a reasonable number), the implication table would have on the order of 100*100 = 10,000 state pairs.

Inputs: x; Outputs: z

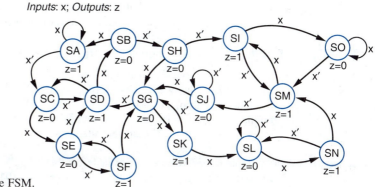

Figure 6.41 A 15-state FSM.

State reduction is therefore typically performed using automated tools. For smaller FSMs, the tools may implement the implication table method. For larger FSMs, the tools may need to resort to heuristics to avoid inordinately large table sizes or numbers of next state pairs.

Even when we reduce the number of states, we are not guaranteed that such state reduction actually reduces the size of the resulting logic. One reason is because reducing the states might not reduce the number of required state register bits—reducing the states from 15 down to 12 does not reduce the minimum state register size, which is four in either case. Another reason is because, even if the state reduction reduces the state register size, the combinational logic size could possibly *increase* with a smaller state register, due to the logic having to decode the state bits. Thus, automated state reduction tools may need to actually implement the combinational logic before and after state reduction, to determine if state reduction ultimately yields improvements for a particular FSM.

State Encoding

State encoding is the task of assigning a unique bit representation for each state in an FSM. Some state encodings may optimize the resulting controller circuit by reducing circuit size, or may trade off size and performance in the circuit. We now discuss several methods for state encoding.

Alternative Minimum-Bitwidth Binary Encodings

Previously, we assigned a unique binary encoding to each state in an FSM using the fewest number of bits possible, representing a *minimum-bitwidth binary encoding*. If there were four states, we used two bits. If there were five, six, seven, or eight states, we used three bits. The encoding represented the state in the controller's state register. There are many ways to map minimum-bitwidth binary encodings to a set of states. Say we are given four states, A, B, C, and D. One encoding is A:00, B:01, C:10, D:11. Another encoding is A:01, B:10, C:11, D:00. In fact, there are 4*3*2*1 = 4! = 24 possible encodings into two bits (4 encoding choices for the first state, 3 for the next state, 2 for the next, and 1 for the last state). For eight states, there are 8!, or over 40,000, possible encodings into three bits. For N states, there are $N!$ (N factorial) possible encodings—a huge number for any N greater than 10 or so. One encoding may result in less combinational logic than another encoding. Automated tools may try several different encodings (but not all *N!* encodings) to reduce combinational logic in the controller.

▶ **EXAMPLE 6.14**   Alternative binary encoding for three-cycles-high laser timer

In Example 3.7, we encoded states using a straightforward binary encoding, starting with 00, then 01, then 10, and then 11. The resulting design had 15 gate inputs (ignoring inverters). We can try instead the alternative binary encoding shown in Figure 6.42.

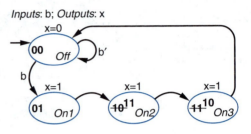

Inputs: b; Outputs: x

Figure 6.42 Laser timer state diagram with alternative binary state encoding.

Table 6.3 provides the state table for the new encoding, showing the differences from the original encoding.

From the state table, we obtain the following equations for the three combinational logic outputs of a controller:

x = s1 + s0 (note from the table that x=1 if s1=1 or s0=1)

n1 = s1's0b' +s1's0b + s1s0b' + s1s0b

n1 = s1's0 + s1s0

n1 = s0

n0 = s1's0'b + s1's0b + s1's0b'

n0 = s1's0'b + s1's0b + s1's0b + s1's0b'

n0 = s1'b(s0' + s0) + s1's0(b + b')

n0 = s1'b + s1's0

The resulting circuit would have only 8 gate inputs: 2 for x, 0 for n1 (n1 is connected to s0 directly with wire), and 4+2 for n0. The 8 gate inputs is significantly less than the 15 gate inputs needed for the binary encoding of Example 3.7. This encoding reduces size without any increase in delay, thus representing an optimization.   ◀

TABLE 6.3 State table for laser timer controller with alternative encoding.

	Inputs			Outputs		
	s1	s0	b	x	n1	n0
Off	0	0	0	0	0	0
	0	0	1	0	0	1
On1	0	1	0	1	1	1
	0	1	1	1	1	1
On2	1	1	0	1	1	0
	1	1	1	1	1	0
On3	1	0	0	1	0	0
	1	0	1	1	0	0

One-Hot Encoding

There is no requirement that we encode a set of states using the fewest number of bits. For example, we could encode four states *A, B, C,* and *D* using three bits instead of just two bits, such as *A:*000, *B:*011, *C:*110, *D:*111. Using more bits requires a larger state register, but possibly less logic. A popular encoding scheme is called *one-hot encoding*, wherein we use the same number of bits for encoding as there are states, and each bit corresponds to exactly one state. For example, a one-hot encoding of four states *A, B, C,* and *D* uses four bits, such as *A:*0001, *B:*0010, *C:*0100, *D:*1000. The main advantage of one-hot encoding is speed—because the state can be detected from just one bit and thus need not be decoded using an AND gate, the controller's next state and output logic may involve fewer gates and/or gates with fewer inputs, resulting in a shorter delay.

▶ **EXAMPLE 6.15** One-hot encoding example

Consider the simple FSM of Figure 6.43, which repeatedly generates the output sequence 0, 1, 1, 1, 0, 1, 1, 1, etc. A straightforward minimal binary encoding is shown, which is then crossed out and replaced with a one-hot encoding.

The binary encoding results in the state table shown in Table 6.4. The resulting equations are:

```
n1 = s1's0 + s1s0'
n0 = s0'
x  = s1 + s0
```

The one-hot encoding results in the state table shown in Table 6.5. The resulting equations are:

```
n3 = s2
n2 = s1
n1 = s0
n0 = s3
x  = s3 + s2 + s1
```

Figure 6.44 shows the resulting circuits for each encoding. The binary encoding yields more gates, but more importantly, requires two levels of logic. The one-hot encoding in this example requires only one level of logic. Notice that the logic to generate the next state is just wires in this example (other examples may require some logic). Figure 6.44(c) illustrates that the one-hot encoding has less delay, meaning we could use a faster clock frequency for that circuit.   ◀

Inputs: none; *Outputs*: x

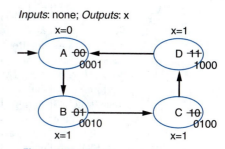

Figure 6.43 FSM for given sequence.

TABLE 6.4 State table using binary encoding.

	Inputs		Outputs		
	s1	s0	n1	n0	x
A	0	0	0	1	0
B	0	1	1	0	1
C	1	0	1	1	1
D	1	1	0	0	1

TABLE 6.5 State table using one-hot encoding.

	Inputs				Outputs				
	s3	s2	s1	s0	n3	n2	n1	n0	x
A	0	0	0	1	0	0	1	0	0
B	0	0	1	0	0	1	0	0	1
C	0	1	0	0	1	0	0	0	1
D	1	0	0	0	0	0	0	1	1

Figure 6.44 One-hot encoding can reduce delay: (a) minimum binary encoding, (b) one-hot encoding, (c) though total sizes may be roughly equal (one-hot encoding uses fewer gates but more flip-flops), one-hot yields a shorter critical path.

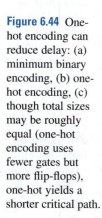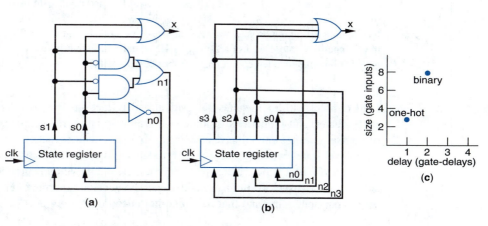

▶ **EXAMPLE 6.16**   Three-cycles-high laser timer using one-hot encoding

In Example 3.7, we encoded states using a straightforward binary encoding, starting with 00, then 01, then 10, and then 11. Here, we'll perform a one-hot encoding of the four states, requiring four bits, as shown in Figure 6.45.

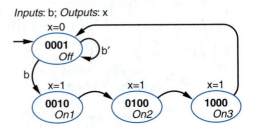

Figure 6.45 One-hot encoding of laser timer.

Table 6.6 shows a state table for the FSM of Figure 6.45, using the one-hot encoding of the states. We don't show all possible rows, since the table would be too large.

The last step is to design the combinational logic. Deriving equations for each output directly from the table (assuming all other input combinations are don't-cares), and minimizing those equations algebraically, results in the following:

$$x = s3 + s2 + s1$$
$$n3 = s2$$
$$n2 = s1$$
$$n1 = s0*b$$
$$n0 = s0*b' + s3$$

This circuit would require $3+0+0+2+(2+2) = 9$ gate inputs. Thus, the circuit has fewer gate inputs than the original binary encoding's 15 gate inputs—but one must also consider that a one-hot encoding uses more flip-flops.

TABLE 6.6 State table for laser timer controller with one-hot encoding.

	Inputs					Outputs				
	s3	s2	s1	s0	b	x	n3	n2	n1	n0
Off	0	0	0	1	0	0	0	0	0	1
	0	0	0	1	1	0	0	0	1	0
On1	0	0	1	0	0	1	0	1	0	0
	0	0	1	0	1	1	0	1	0	0
On2	0	1	0	0	0	1	1	0	0	0
	0	1	0	0	1	1	1	0	0	0
On3	1	0	0	0	0	1	0	0	0	1
	1	0	0	0	1	1	0	0	0	1

More importantly, the circuit with one-hot encoding is slightly faster. The critical path for that circuit is n0 = s0*b' + s3. The critical path for the circuit with regular binary encoding is n0 = s1's0'b + s1s0'. The regular binary encoded circuit requires a 3-input AND gate feeding into a 2-input OR gate, whereas the one-hot encoded circuit has a 2-input AND gate feeding in a 2-input OR gate. Because a 2-input AND actually has slightly less delay than a 3-input AND gate, the one-hot encoded circuit has a shorter critical path.   ◀

For examples with more states, the critical path reductions from one-hot encoding may be even greater, and reductions in logic size may also be more pronounced. At some point, of course, one-hot encoding results in too big of a state register—for example, an FSM with 1000 states would require a 10-bit state register for a binary encoding, but would require a 1000-bit state register for a one-hot encoding, which is probably too big to consider. In such cases, we might consider encodings using a number of bits in between that for a binary encoding and that for a one-hot encoding.

Output Encoding

Some problem descriptions require us to generate a particular sequence of values on a set of outputs. For example, a problem might require us to repeatedly output the following sequence on a pair of outputs x and y: 00, 11, 10, 01. We can capture the behavior using the FSM with four states, *A, B, C,* and *D,* as shown in Figure 6.46. A straightforward binary encoding for those states would be: *A*:00, *B*:01, *C*:10, *D*:11, as shown in Figure 6.46. When we design a controller for this system, we'll have a two-bit state register, logic to determine the next state, and logic to generate the output from the present state. But might it make more sense to use a state encoding that is identical to the output values in each state? If we use such an encoding, then we will still have a two-bit state register, and we will still have logic to generate the next state, but we won't have logic to generate the output from the present state. Instead, each output will simply be connected by a wire to a bit in the state register—thus reducing the required number of logic gates.

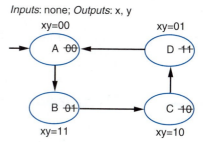

Figure 6.46 FSM for given sequence.

If an FSM has at least as many outputs as needed for a binary encoding, and if each state has a unique output combination, then we may consider using a state's output combination as the state's encoding. Such an encoding may reduce the amount of logic required, by eliminating the need for logic to generate the outputs from the present state encoding—that logic is reduced to just wires.

Output encoding requires that the system have at least as many outputs as it has bits in a minimal binary encoding, otherwise the outputs can't represent enough encodings to uniquely identify each state. Furthermore, we can't use output encoding if the desired output sequence contains the same output values in two different states, since every state's encoding must be unique. For example, if we wish to repeatedly generate the sequence 00, 11, 01, 11, we cannot use output encoding, because if we did, then two states would have the same encoding. Even in such a situation, though, we might try to output encode as many states as possible.

▶ **EXAMPLE 6.17** Sequence generator using output encoding

Example 3.10 involved design of a sequence generator, in which we were to generate the sequence 0001, 0011, 1100, 1000 on a set of four outputs, as shown in Figure 6.47. In that example, we encoded the states using a two-bit binary encoding, with *A* being 00, *B* being 01, *C* being 10, and *D* being 11. In this example, we'll instead use output encoding. The outputs have enough bits, four, whereas we need at least two bits to encode the four states. The sequence also has a different output combination for each state. Thus, we can consider output encoding for this example.

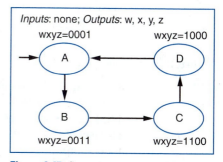

Figure 6.47 Sequence generator FSM.

Table 6.7 shows a partial state table for the sequence generator, using an output encoding. Notice that the outputs themselves w, x, y, and z, don't need to appear in the table, as they will be the same as s3, s2, s1, and s0. We use a partial table to avoid having to show all 16 rows, and we assume that all unspecified rows represent don't cares.

From the table, we derive equations for each output as follows:

$$n3 = s1 + s2$$
$$n2 = s1$$
$$n1 = s1's0$$
$$n0 = s1's0 + s3s2'$$

We obtained those equations by looking at all the 1s for a particular output, and visually determining a minimal input equation that would generate those 1s and 0s for the other shown column entries (all other output values, not shown, are don't cares).

Figure 6.48 shows the final circuit. Notice that there is no output logic—the outputs w, x, y, and z connect directly to the state register.

Compared to the circuit obtained in Example 3.10 using a binary encoding, the output encoded circuit in Figure 6.48 actually appears to use more transistors. In other examples, an output encoded circuit might use fewer transistors. ◀

Whether one-hot encoding, binary encoding, output encoding, or some variation thereof results in fewest transistors or a shorter critical path depends on the example itself. Thus, modern tools may try a variety of different encodings for a given problem to see which works best.

TABLE 6.7 Partial state table for sequence generator controller using output encoding.

	Inputs				Outputs			
	s3	s2	s1	s0	n3	n2	n1	n0
A	0	0	0	1	0	0	1	1
B	0	0	1	1	1	1	0	0
C	1	1	0	0	1	0	0	0
D	1	0	0	0	0	0	0	1

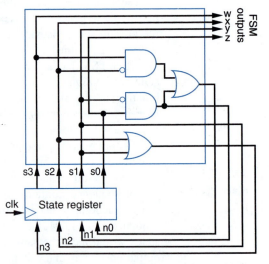

Figure 6.48 Sequence generator controller with output encoding.

Moore versus Mealy FSMs

Basic Mealy Architecture

The FSMs described in this book have thus far all been a type of FSM known as a Moore FSM. A *Moore FSM* is an FSM whose outputs are a function of the FSM's state. An alternative type of FSM is a Mealy FSM. A *Mealy FSM* is an FSM whose outputs are a function of the FSM's states *and inputs*. Sometimes a Mealy FSM results in fewer states than a Moore FSM, representing an optimization. Sometimes those fewer states come at the expense of timing complexities that must be handled, representing a tradeoff.

Recall the standard controller architecture of Figure 3.48, reproduced in Figure 6.49. The architecture shows one block of combinational logic, responsible for converting the present state and external inputs into the next state and external outputs.

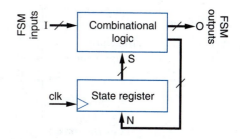

Because a Moore FSM's outputs are solely a function of the present state (and not the external inputs), then we can refine the architecture to have two combinational logic blocks: the **next-state logic** block converts the present state and external

Figure 6.49 Standard controller architecture—general view.

inputs into a next state, and the **output logic** block converts the present state (but *not* the external inputs) into external outputs, as shown in Figure 6.50(a).

In contrast, a Mealy FSM's outputs are a function of both the present state and the external inputs. Thus, the output logic block for a Mealy FSM takes both the present state *and* the external FSM inputs as input, rather than just the present state, as shown in Figure 6.50(b). The next-stage logic is the same as for a Moore, taking as input both the present state and the external FSM inputs.

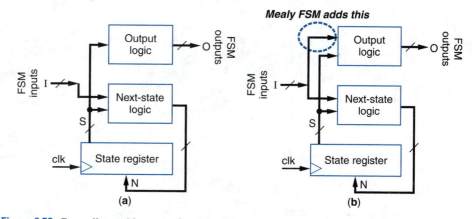

(a)   **(b)**

Figure 6.50 Controller architectures for: (a) a Moore FSM, (b) a Mealy FSM.

Graphically, the FSM output assignments of a Mealy FSM would be listed with each transition, rather than each state, because each transition represents a present state and a particular input value. Figure 6.51 shows a two-state Mealy FSM with an input b and an output x. When in state *S0* and b=0, the FSM outputs x=0 and stays in state *S0*, as indicated by the transition labeled "b'/x=0". When in state *S0* and b = 1, the FSM outputs x = 1 and goes to state *S1*. We use the "/" simply to separate the transition's

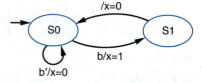

Figure 6.51 A Mealy FSM associates outputs with transitions, not states.

input conditions from the output assignments—the "/" does not mean "divide" here. Because the transition from *S1* to *S0* is taken no matter what the input value, we list the transition simply as "/x=0," meaning there's no input condition, but there is an output assignment.

Mealy FSMs May Have Fewer States

The seemingly minor difference between a Mealy and a Moore FSM, namely, that a Mealy FSM's output is a function of the state *and* the current inputs, can lead to fewer states for some behaviors when implemented as a Mealy machine. For example, consider the simple soda dispenser controller FSM in Figure 6.52(a). Setting d=1 dispenses a soda. The FSM starts in state *Init*, which sets d=0 and sets an output clear=1, which we assume clears a device keeping count of the amount of money deposited into the soda dispenser machine. The FSM transitions to state *Wait*, where the FSM waits to be informed, through the enough input, that enough money has been deposited. Once enough money has been deposited, the FSM transitions to state *Disp*, which dispenses a soda by setting output d=1, and the FSM then returns to state *Init*. (Readers who have read Chapter 5 may notice this example is a simplified version of Example 5.1; familiarity with that example is not required, though, for the present discussion.).

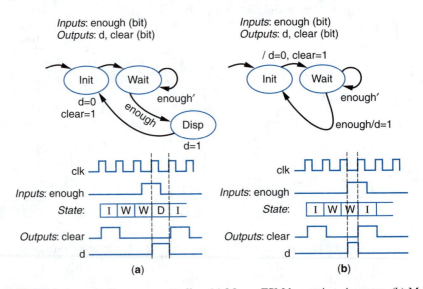

Figure 6.52 FSMs for soda dispenser controller: (a) Moore FSM has actions in states, (b) Mealy FSM has actions on transitions, resulting in this case in fewer states.

Like with Moore FSMs, we follow the convention that unassigned outputs in a Mealy FSM state diagram are implicitly assigned 0.

Figure 6.52(b) shows a Mealy FSM for the same controller. The initial state *Init* has no actions itself, but rather has a conditionless transition to state *Wait* that has the initialization actions d=0 and clear=1. In state *Wait*, a transition with condition enough' returns to state *Wait* without any actions listed. Another transition with condition enough has the action d=1, and takes the FSM back to the *Init* state. Notice that the Mealy FSM does not need the *Disp* state to set d=1; that action occurs on a transition. Thus, we were able to create a Mealy FSM with fewer states than in a Moore FSM.

The Mealy state diagram in Figure 6.52(b) uses a convention similar to the convention we used for Moore FSMs (Section 3.4), namely, that any outputs not explicitly assigned on a transition are implicitly assigned a 0. As with Moore FSMs, we still list an assignment to 0 explicitly if the assignment is key to the FSM's behavior (such as the assignment of d=0 in Figure 6.52(b)).

► **EXAMPLE 6.18**   Beeping wristwatch FSM using a Mealy machine

Create an FSM for a wristwatch that can display one of four registers by setting two outputs s1 and s0, which control a 4x1 multiplexer that passes one of the four registers through. The four registers correspond to the watch's present time (s1s0=00), the alarm setting (01), the date (10), and a stopwatch (11). The FSM should sequence to the next register, in the order listed above, each time a button b is pressed (assume b is synchronized with the clock as to be high for only 1 clock cycle on each unique button press). The FSM should set an output p to 1 each time the button is pressed, causing an audible beep to sound.

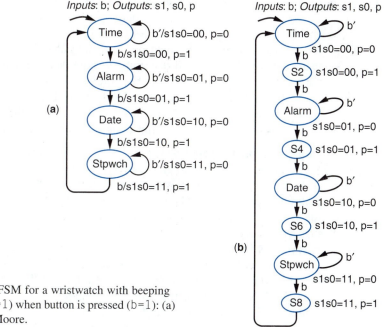

(a)

(b)

Figure 6.53 FSM for a wristwatch with beeping behavior (p=1) when button is pressed (b=1): (a) Mealy, (b) Moore.

Figure 6.53(a) shows a Mealy FSM describing the desired behavior. Notice that the Mealy FSM easily captures the beeping behavior, simply by setting p=1 on the transitions that correspond to button presses. In the Moore FSM of Figure 6.53(b), we had to add an extra state in between each pair of states in Figure 6.53, with each extra state having the action p=1 and having a conditionless transition to the next state.

Notice that the Mealy FSM has fewer states than the Moore machine. A drawback is that we aren't guaranteed that a beep will last at least one clock cycle, due to timing issues that we will describe. ◄

Timing Issues with Mealy FSMs

Mealy FSM outputs are not synchronized with clock edges, but rather can change in between clock edges if an input changes. For example, consider the timing diagram shown in Figure 6.52(a) for a soda dispenser's Moore FSM. Note that the output d becomes 1 *not right after* the input enough became 1, but rather *on the first clock edge after* enough became 1. In contrast, the timing diagram for the Mealy FSM in Figure 6.52(b) shows that the output d becomes 1 *right after* the input enough becomes 1. Moore outputs are synchronized with the clock; in particular, Moore outputs only change on entering a new state, which means Moore outputs only change slightly after a rising clock edge loads a new state into the state register. In contrast, Mealy outputs can change not just on entering a new state, but also any time an input changes, because Mealy outputs are a function of both the state and the inputs. We took advantage of this fact to eliminate the *Disp* state from the soda dispenser's Mealy FSM in Figure 6.52(b). Notice, however, in the timing diagram that the d output of the Mealy FSM *does not stay 1 for a complete clock cycle*. If we are unsure as to whether d's high time is long enough, we could include a *Disp* state in the Mealy FSM. That state would have a single transition, with no condition and with action d=1, pointing back to state *Init*. In that case, d would be 1 for longer than one clock cycle (but less than two cycles).

The Mealy FSM feature of outputs being a function of states and inputs, which enables the reduction in number of states in some cases, also has an undesirable characteristic—the outputs may glitch if the inputs glitch in between clock cycles. A designer using a Mealy FSM should determine whether such glitching could pose a problem in a particular circuit. One solution to the glitching is to insert flip-flops between an asynchronous Mealy FSM's inputs and the FSM logic, or between the FSM logic and the outputs. Such flip-flops make the Mealy FSM synchronous, and the outputs will change at predictable intervals. Of course, such flip-flops introduce a one clock cycle delay.

Implementing a Mealy FSM

We create a controller implementing a Mealy FSM in nearly the identical way that we created a controller for Moore FSMs in Section 3.4, using the method of Table 3.2. The only difference is that when we create a state table, the FSM outputs' values for all the rows of a particular state won't necessarily be identical. For example, Table 6.8 shows a state table for the Mealy FSM of Figure 6.52(b). Notice that the output d should be 0 in state *Wait* (s0=1) if enough=0, but should

TABLE 6.8 Mealy state table for soda dispenser

	Inputs		Outputs		
	s0	enough	n0	d	clear
Init	0	0	1	0	1
	0	1	1	0	1
Wait	1	0	1	0	0
	1	1	0	1	0

be 1 if enough=1. In contrast, in a Moore state table, an output's values were identical within a given state. Given the state table of Table 6.8, we would proceed to implement the combinational logic in the same manner as described in Section 3.4.

Combining Moore and Mealy FSMs

Viewing the two "o's" in the word Moore *as states may help you remember that a Moore FSM's actions occur in the states, while Mealy is on the transitions.*

Designers often utilize FSMs that are a combination of Moore and Mealy types. Such a combination allows the designer to specify some actions in states, and others on transitions. Such a combination provides the reduced number of states advantage of a Mealy FSM, yet avoids having to replicate a state's actions on every outgoing transition of a state. This simplification is really just a convenience to a designer describing the FSM; the underlying implementation will likely be the same as for the Mealy FSM having replicated actions on a state's outgoing transitions.

EXAMPLE 6.19 Beeping wristwatch FSM using a combined Moore/Mealy machine

Figure 6.54 shows a combined Moore/
Mealy FSM state diagram describing the
beeping wristwatch of Example 6.18. The
FSM has the same number of states as
did the Mealy FSM in Figure 6.53(a),
because the FSM still associates the beep
behavior p=1 with transitions, avoiding
the need for extra states to describe the
beep. But the combined FSM state
diagram is easier to comprehend than the
Mealy FSM state diagram, because the
assignments to s1s0 are associated with
each state, and not duplicated on every
outgoing transition. ◄

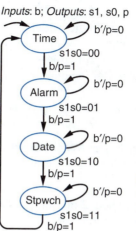

Inputs: b; Outputs: s1, s0, p

Figure 6.54 Combining Moore and Mealy FSMs yields a simpler wristwatch FSM.

6.4 DATAPATH COMPONENT TRADEOFFS

In Chapter 4, we created several components that are useful in datapaths. In that chapter, we
created the most basic, easy to understand versions of those components. In this section, we
describe methods to build faster or smaller versions of some of those components.

Faster Adders

Adding two numbers is an extremely common operation in digital circuits, so it makes
sense for us to try to create an adder that is faster than a carry-ripple adder. Recall that a
carry-ripple adder requires that the carry bits ripple through all the full-adders before all
the outputs are correct. The longest path through the circuit, shown in Figure 6.55, is
known as the circuit's *critical path*. Since each full-adder has a delay of two gate-delays,
then a 4-bit carry-ripple adder has a delay of 4 * 2 = 8 gate-delays. A 32-bit carry-ripple
adder's delay is 32 * 2 = 64 gate-delays. That's rather slow, but the nice thing about a
carry-ripple adder is that it doesn't require very many gates. If a full-adder uses 5 gates,
then a 4-bit carry-ripple adder requires only 4 * 5 = 20 gates, and a 32-bit carry-ripple
adder would only require 32 * 5 = 160 gates.

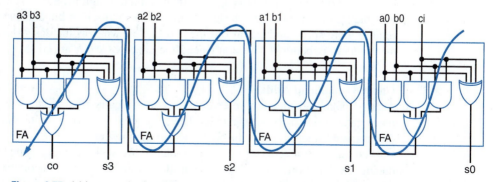

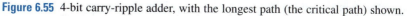

Figure 6.55 4-bit carry-ripple adder, with the longest path (the critical path) shown.

We would like to design an adder that is much closer to the delay of just a few gates, perhaps about 5 or 6 gate-delays, at the possible expense of more gates.

Two-Level Logic Adder

One obvious way to create a faster adder at the expense of more gates is to use our earlier-defined two-level combinational logic design process. An adder designed using two levels of logic has a delay of only two gate-delays. That's certainly fast. But recall from Figure 4.25 that building an N-bit adder using two levels of logic results in excessively large circuits as N increases beyond 8 or so. To be sure you get this point, let's restate the previous sentence slightly:

> Building an N-bit adder using two levels of logic results in *shockingly large circuits* as N increases beyond 8 or so.

For example, we estimated (in Chapter 4) that a two-level 16-bit adder would require about 2 million transistors, and that a two-level 32-bit adder would require about 100 billion transistors.

On the other hand, building a 4-bit adder using two levels of logic results in a big, but reasonably sized adder—about 100 gates, as was shown in Figure 4.25. We could build a larger adder by cascading such fast 4-bit adders together. Say we wanted an 8-bit adder. We could build this

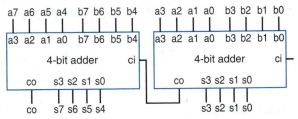

Figure 6.56 8-bit adder built from two fast 4-bit adders.

by cascading two fast 4-bit adders together, as shown in Figure 6.56. If each 4-bit adder is built from two levels of logic, then each 4-bit adder has a delay of 2 gate-delays. The 4-bit adder on the right takes 2 gate-delays to generate the sum and carry out bits, after which the 4-bit adder on the left takes another 2 gate-delays to generate its outputs, resulting in a total delay of 2 + 2 = 4 gate-delays. For a 32-bit adder built from eight 4-bit adders, the delay would be 8 * 2 = 16 gate-delays, and the size would be about 8 * 100 gates = 800 gates. That's much better than the 32 * 2 = 64 gate-delays of a carry-ripple adder, though the improved speed comes at the expense of more gates than the 32 * 5 = 160 gates of the carry-ripple adder. Which design is better? The answer depends on your requirements—the design using two-level logic 4-bit adders is better if you require more speed and can afford the extra gates, whereas the design using carry-ripple 4-bit adders is better if you don't need the speed or can't afford the extra gates. It's a tradeoff.

Carry-Lookahead Adder

A carry-lookahead adder improves on the speed of a carry-ripple adder, but without using as many gates as a two-level logic adder. The basic idea is to "look ahead" into lower stages to determine whether a carry will be created in the present stage. This lookahead concept is very elegant and generalizes to other problems. We will therefore spend some time introducing the intuition underlying lookahead. Consider the addition of two 4-bit numbers shown in Figure 6.57(b), with the carries in each column labeled $c0$, $c1$, $c2$, $c3$, and $c4$.

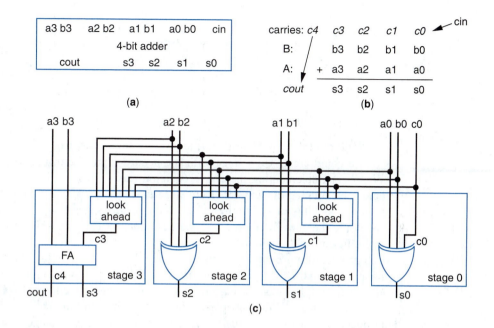

Figure 6.57 Adding two binary numbers by a naive inefficient carry-lookahead scheme—each stage looks at all earlier bits and computes whether the carry-in bit to that stage would be a 1. The longest delay is stage 3, which has 2 logic levels for the lookahead, and 2 for the full-adder, for a total delay of only four gate-delays.

A Naive Inefficient Carry-Lookahead Scheme. One simple but not very efficient way of carry-lookahead is as follows. Recall that the output equations for a full-adder having inputs a, b, and c, and outputs co and s, are:

$$s = a \text{ xor } b \text{ xor } c$$
$$co = bc + ac + ab$$

So we know that the equations for c1, c2, and c3 in a 4-bit adder will be:

$$c1 = co0 = b0c0 + a0c0 + a0b0$$
$$c2 = co1 = b1c1 + a1c1 + a1b1$$
$$c3 = co2 = b2c2 + a2c2 + a2b2$$

In other words, the equation for the carry-in to a particular stage is the same as the equation for the carry-out of the previous stage.

We can substitute the equation for c1 into c2's equation, resulting in:

```
c2 = b1c1 + a1c1 + a1b1
c2 = b1(b0c0 + a0c0 + a0b0) + a1(b0c0 + a0c0 + a0b0) + a1b1
c2 = b1b0c0 + b1a0c0 + b1a0b0 + a1b0c0 + a1a0c0 + a1a0b0 +
     a1b1
```

We can then substitute the equation for c2 into c3's equation, resulting in:

$$c3 = b2c2 + a2c2 + a2b2$$
$$c3 = b2(b1b0c0 + b1a0c0 + b1a0b0 + a1b0c0 + a1a0c0 +$$
$$\quad a1a0b0 + a1b1) + a2(b1b0c0 + b1a0c0 + b1a0b0$$
$$\quad + a1b0c0 + a1a0c0 + a1a0b0 + a1b1) + a2b2$$
$$c3 = b2b1b0c0 + b2b1a0c0 + b2b1a0b0 + b2a1b0c0 +$$
$$\quad b2a1a0c0 + b2a1a0b0 + b2a1b1 + a2b1b0c0$$
$$\quad + a2b1a0c0 + a2b1a0b0 + a2a1b0c0 + a2a1a0c0$$
$$\quad + a2a1a0b0 + a2a1b1 + a2b2$$

We'll omit the equation for $c4$, in order to save a few pages of paper.

We could create each stage with the needed inputs, and include a lookahead logic component implementing the above equations, as shown in Figure 6.57(c). Notice that there is no rippling of carry bits from stage to stage—each stage computes its own carry-in bit by "looking ahead" to the values of the previous stages.

While the above demonstrates the basic idea of carry-lookahead, the scheme is not very efficient. $c1$ requires 4 gates, $c2$ requires 8 gates, and $c3$ requires 16 gates, with each gate requiring more inputs in each stage. If we count gate inputs, $c1$ requires 9 gate inputs, $c2$ requires 27 gate inputs, and $c3$ requires 71 gate inputs. Building a larger adder, say an 8-bit adder, using this lookahead scheme would thus likely result in excessively large size. While the presented scheme is therefore not practical, it serves to introduce the basic idea of carry-lookahead: by having each stage looking ahead at the inputs to the previous stages and computing for itself whether that stage's carry-in bit should be 1, rather than waiting for the carry-in bit to ripple from previous stages, we get a four-bit adder with a delay of only 4 gate-delays.

An Efficient Carry–Lookahead Scheme. A more efficient carry-lookahead scheme is as follows. Consider again the addition of two 4-bit numbers A and B, shown in Figure 6.58(a). Suppose that we add each column's two operand bits (e.g., $a0 + b0$) using a half-adder, ignoring the carry-in bit of that column. The resulting half-adder outputs (carry-out and sum) give us some useful information about the carry for the next stage. In particular:

- If the addition of $a0$ with $b0$ results in a carry-out of 1, then we know for sure that $c1$ will be 1, regardless of whether $c0$ is a 1 or 0. Why? Because considering adding $a0+b0+c0$, then $1+1+0=10$, and $1+1+1=11$ (the "+" represents add here, not OR)—both cases generate a carry-out of 1. Recall that a half-adder computes its carry-out as ab.
- If the addition of $a0$ with $b0$ results in a sum of 1, then $c1$ will be 1 only if $c0$ is 1. In particular, considering $a0+b0+c0$, then $1+0+1=10$ and $0+1+1=10$. Recall that a half-adder computes its sum as a xor b.

In other words, $c1$ will be 1 if $a0b0=1$, OR if $a0$ xor $b0 = 1$ AND $c0=1$. So we get the following equations for the carry bits:

$$c1 = a0b0 + (a0 \text{ xor } b0)c0$$
$$c2 = a1b1 + (a1 \text{ xor } b1)c1$$
$$c3 = a2b2 + (a2 \text{ xor } b2)c2$$
$$c4 = a3b3 + (a3 \text{ xor } b3)c3$$

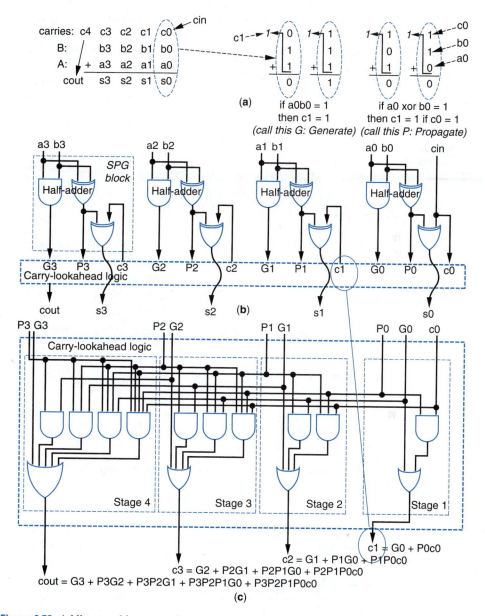

Figure 6.58 Adding two binary numbers using a fast carry-lookahead scheme: (a) idea of using propagate and generate terms, (b) computing the propagate and generate terms and providing them to the carry-lookahead logic, (c) using the propagate and generate terms to quickly compute the carries for each column. The correspondence between $c1$ in figures (c) and (b) is shown by two circles connected by the line; similar correspondences exist for $c2$ and $c3$.

Let's include a half-adder in each stage to add the two operand bits for that column, as shown in Figure 6.58(b). Each half-adder outputs a carry-out bit (which is ab) and a sum bit (which is a xor b). Note in the figure that for a given column, we just need to xor the half-adder's sum output with the column's carry-in bit to compute that column's sum bit, because the sum bit for a column is just `a xor b xor c` (see Section 4.3, page 188).

*Why those names? When a0b0=1, we know we should **generate** a 1 for c1. When a0 xor b0 = 1, we know we should **propagate** the c0 value as the value of c1, meaning c1 should equal c0.*

Let's rename the carry-output of the half-adder **generate**, symbolized as G—so `G0` means `a0b0`, `G1` means `a1b1`, `G2` means `a2b2`, and `G3` means `a3b3`. Let's also rename the sum output of the half-adder as **propagate**—so `P0` means `a0 xor b0`, `P1` means `a1 xor b1`, `P2` means `a2 xor b2`, and `P3` means `a3 xor b3`. In short:

$$Gi = aibi \text{ (generate)}$$
$$Pi = ai \text{ xor } bi \text{ (propagate)}$$

When we perform carry-lookahead, rather than looking directly at the operand bits of previous stages as we did in the naive lookahead scheme (e.g., stage 1 looking at `a0` and `b0`), let's look instead at the half-adder outputs of the previous stage (e.g., stage 1 looks at `G0` and `P0`). Why? Because the lookahead logic will turn out to be simpler than in the naive lookahead scheme.

We can therefore rewrite our equations for each carry bit as follows:

$$c1 = G0 + P0c0$$
$$c2 = G1 + P1c1$$
$$c3 = G2 + P2c2$$
$$c4 = G3 + P3c3$$

Substituting like we did for the naive scheme, we get the following carry-lookahead equations:

$$c1 = G0 + P0c0$$
$$c2 = G1 + P1c1 = G1 + P1(G0 + P0c0)$$
$$c2 = G1 + P1G0 + P1P0c0$$
$$c3 = G2 + P2c2 = G2 + P2(G1 + P1G0 + P1P0c0)$$
$$c3 = G2 + P2G1 + P2P1G0 + P2P1P0c0$$
$$c4 = G3 + P3G2 + P3P2G1 + P3P2P1G0 + P3P2P1P0c0$$

Remember, the P and G symbols represent simple terms: `Gi = ai*bi`, `Pi = ai xor bi`.

Figure 6.58(c) shows the circuits implementing the carry-lookahead equations for computing each stage's carry.

Figure 6.59 shows a high-level view of the carry-lookahead adder's design from Figure 6.58(b) and (c). The four blocks on the top are responsible for generating the sum,

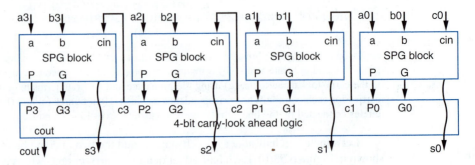

Figure 6.59 High-level view of a 4-bit carry-lookahead adder.

propagate, and generate bits—let's call those "*SPG blocks*," and you'll recall from Figure 6.58(b) that each SPG block consists of just three gates. The 4-bit carry-lookahead logic uses the propagate and generate bits to precompute the carry bits for high-order stages, using only two levels of gates.

The complete 4-bit carry-lookahead adder requires only 26 gates (4*3=12 gates for the nonlookahead logic, and then 2+3+4+5=14 gates for the lookahead logic).

The delay of this 4-bit adder is only 4 gate-delays—1 gate through the half-adder, 2 gates through the carry-lookahead logic, and 1 to finally generate the sum bit (we can see those gates in Figure 6.58(b) and (c)). An 8-bit adder built using the same carry-lookahead scheme would still have a delay of only 4 gate-delays, but would require 64 gates (8*3=24 gates for the nonlookahead logic, and 2+3+4+5+6+7+8+9 = 44 gates for the lookahead logic). A 16-bit carry-lookahead adder would still have a delay of 4 gate-delays, but would require 200 gates (16*3=48 gates for the nonlookahead logic, and 2+3+4+5+6+7+8+9+10+11+12+13+14+15+16+17=152 gates for the lookahead logic). A 32-bit carry-lookahead adder would have a delay of 4 gate-delays, but would require 656 gates (32*3=96 gates for the nonlookahead logic, and 152+18+19+20+21+22+23+24+25+26+27+28+29+30+31+32+33=560 gates).

Unfortunately, there are problems that make the size and delay of large carry-lookahead adders less attractive. First, the above analysis counts gates, but not gate inputs, whereas gate inputs better tell us the number of transistors needed. Notice in Figure 6.58 that the gates keep getting wider in higher stages. For example, stage 3 has a 4-input OR gate and 4-input AND gate, while stage 4 has a 5-input OR gate and 5-input AND gate as highlighted in Figure 6.60. Stage 32 of a 32-bit carry-lookahead adder would have 33-input OR and AND gates, along with other large gates. Since gates with more inputs need more transistors, then in terms of transistors, the carry-lookahead design is actually quite large. Furthermore, those huge gates would not have the same delay as a 2-input AND or OR gate. Such huge gates are typically built using a tree of smaller gates, so we would have more gate-delays.

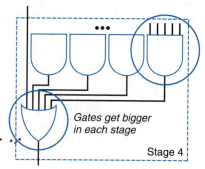

Figure 6.60 Gate size problem.

Gates get bigger in each stage

Stage 4

Hierarchical Carry-Lookahead Adders.

Building a 4-bit or even 8-bit carry-lookahead adder using the previous section's method may be reasonable with respect to gate sizes, but larger carry-lookahead adders begin to involve gates with too many inputs.

We can build a larger adder by connecting smaller adders in a carry-ripple manner. For example, suppose we have 4-bit carry-lookahead adders available. We can build a 16-bit adder by connecting four 4-bit carry-lookahead adders, as shown in Figure 6.61. If each 4-bit carry-lookahead adder had a 4-gate-delay, then the total delay of the 16-bit adder would be 4+4+4+4 = 16 gate-delays. Compare this to the delay of a 16-bit carry-ripple adder—if each full-adder has a two gate-delay, then a 16-bit carry-ripple adder would have a delay of 16*2 = 32 gate-delays. Thus, the 16-bit adder built from four carry-lookahead adders connected in a carry-ripple manner is twice as fast as the 16-bit carry-ripple adder.

(Actually, careful observation of Figure 6.55 reveals that the carry-out of a four-bit carry-lookahead adder would be generated in three gate-delays rather than four, resulting in even faster operation of the 16-bit adder built from four carry-lookahead adders—but for simplicity, let's not look inside the components for such detailed timing analysis.) Sixteen gate-delays is good, but can we do better? Can we avoid having to wait for the carries to ripple from the lower-order 4-bit adders to the higher-order adders?

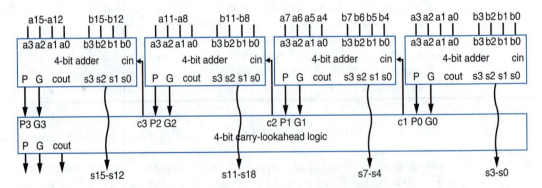

Figure 6.61 16-bit adder implemented using four 4-bit adders connected in a carry-ripple manner.

In fact, avoiding the rippling is exactly what we did in developing the 4-bit carry-lookahead adder itself. Thus, we can *repeat the same carry-lookahead process outside* of the 4-bit adders, to quickly provide the carry-in values to the higher-order 4-bit adders. To accomplish this, we add another 4-bit carry-lookahead logic block outside the four 4-bit adders, as shown in Figure 6.62. The carry-lookahead logic block has exactly the same internal design as was shown in Figure 6.58(c). Notice that the lookahead logic needs propagate (P) and generate (G) signals from each adder block. Previously, each input block output the P and G signals just by ANDing and XORing the block's a i and b i input bits. However, in Figure 6.62, each block is a 4-bit carry-lookahead adder. We therefore must modify the internal design of a 4-bit carry-lookahead adder to output P and G signals, so that those adders can be used with a second level carry-lookahead generator.

Figure 6.62 16-bit adder implemented using four CLA 4-bit adders and a second level of lookahead.

Thus, let's extend the 4-bit carry-lookahead logic of Figure 6.58 to output P and G signals. The equations for the P and G outputs of a 4-bit carry-lookahead adder can be written as follows:

$$P = P3P2P1P0$$
$$G = G3 + P3G2 + P3P2G1 + P3P2P1G0$$

To understand these equations, recall that propagate meant that the output carry for a column should equal the input carry of the column (hence propagating the carry through the column). For that to be the case for the carry in and carry out of a 4-bit adder, the first stage of the 4-bit adder must propagate its input carry to its output carry, the second stage must propagate its input carry to its output carry, and so on for the third and four stages. In other words, each internal propagate signal must be 1, hence the equation P = P3P2P1P0.

Likewise, recall that generate meant that the output carry of a column should be a 1 (hence generating a carry of 1). Generate should thus be 1 if the first stage generates a carry (G0) and all the higher stages propagate the carry through (P3P2P1), yielding the term P3P2P1G0. Generate should also be a 1 if the second stage generates a carry and all higher stages propagate the carry through, yielding the term P3P2G1. Likewise for the third stage, whose term is P3G2. Finally, generate should be 1 if the fourth stage generates a carry, represented as G3. ORing all four of these terms yields the equation G = G3 + P3G2 + P3P2G1 + P3P2P1G0.

We would then revise the 4-bit carry-lookahead logic of Figure 6.58(c) to include two additional gates in stage four, one AND gate to compute P = P3P2P1P0, and one OR gate to compute G = G3 + P3G2 + P3P2G1 + P3P2P1G0 (note that stage four already has AND gates for each term, so we need only add an OR gate to OR the terms). For conciseness, we omit a figure showing these two new gates.

We can introduce additional levels of 4-bit carry-lookahead generators to create even larger adders. Figure 6.63 illustrates a high-level view of a 32-bit adder built using 32 SPG blocks and three levels of 4-bit carry-lookahead logic. Notice that the carry-lookahead logic forms a tree. Total delay for the 32-bit adder is only two gate-delays for the

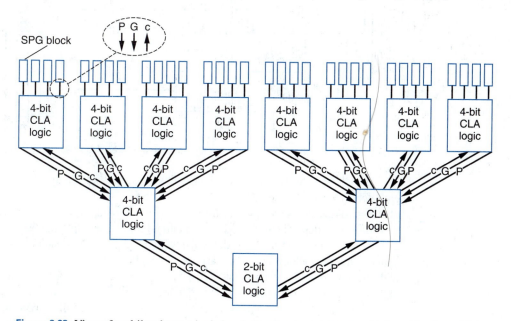

Figure 6.63 View of multilevel carry-lookahead, showing tree structure, which enables fast addition with reasonable numbers and sizes of gates. Each level adds only two gate-delays.

SPG blocks, and two gate-delays for each level of carry-lookahead (CLA) logic, for a total of $2+2+2+2 = 8$ gate-delays. (Actually, closer examination of gate delays within each component would demonstrate that total delay of the 32-bit adder is actually less than 8 gate-delays.) Carry-lookahead adders built from multiple levels of carry-lookahead logic are known as *multilevel* or *hierarchical carry-lookahead adders*.

In summary, the carry-lookahead approach results in faster additions of large binary numbers (more than 8 bits or so) than a carry-ripple approach, at the expense of more gates. However, by clever hierarchical design, the carry-lookahead gate size is kept reasonable.

Carry-Select Adders

Another way to build a larger adder from smaller adders is known as carry-select. Consider building an 8-bit adder from 4-bit adders. A carry-select approach uses two 4-bit adders for the high-order four bits, which we've labeled *HI4_1* and *HI4_0* in Figure 6.64. *HI4_1 assumes* the carry-in will be 1, while *HI4_0 assumes* the carry-in will be 0, so both generate stable output at the same time that *LO4* generates stable output—after 4 gate-delays (assuming the 4-bit adder has a delay of four gate-delays). We use the *LO4* carry-out value to select among *HI4_1* or *HI4_0*, using a 5-bit-wide 2x1 multiplexer—hence the term *carry-select adder*.

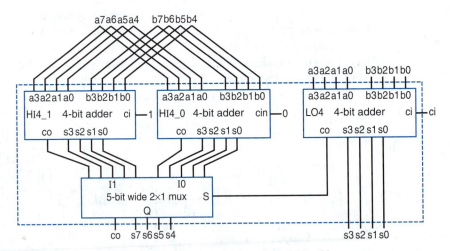

Figure 6.64 8-bit carry-select adder implemented using three 4-bit adders.

The delay of a 2x1 mux is 2 gate-delays, so the total delay of the 8-bit adder is 4 gate-delays for *HI4_1* and *HI4_0* to generate correct sum bits (*LO4* executes in parallel), plus 2 gate-delays for the mux (whose select line is ready after only 3 gate-delays), for a total of 6 gate-delays. Compared with a carry-lookahead implementation using two 4-bit adders, we've reduced the total delay from 7 gate-delays down to 6 gate-delays. The cost is one extra 4-bit adder. If a 4-bit carry-lookahead adder requires 26 gates, then the design with two 4-bit adders requires $2*26 = 52$ gates, while the carry-select adder requires $3*26 = 78$ gates, plus the gates for the 5-bit 2x1 mux.

We could also build a 16-bit carry-select adder using 4-bit carry-lookahead adders, by using multiple levels of multiplexing. Each nibble (four bits) would have two 4-bit adders, one assuming a carry-in of 1, the other assuming 0. Nibble0's carry-out would select, using a multiplexer, the appropriate adder for Nibble1. Nibble1's selected carry-out would then select the appropriate adder for Nibble2. Nibble2's selected carry-out would finally select the appropriate adder for Nibble3. The delay of such an adder would be 6 gate-delays for Nibble1, plus 2 gate-delays for Nibble2's selection, plus 2 gate-delays for Nibble3's selection—for a total of only 10 gate-delays. Cascading four 4-bit adders would have required $4+4+4+4 = 16$ gates-delays. The speedup of the carry-select version over the cascaded version would be $16 / 10 = 1.6$. Total size would be $7*26 = 182$ gates, plus the gates for the three 5-bit 2x1 muxes. That's pretty efficient size for pretty good speed.

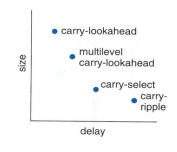

Figure 6.65 illustrates the tradeoffs among adder designs. Carry-ripple is the smallest but has the longest delay. Carry-lookahead is the fastest but has the largest size. Carry-select is a compromise between the two, involving some lookahead and some rippling. The choice of the most appropriate adder for a design depends on the speed and size constraints of the design.

Figure 6.65 Adder tradeoffs.

Smaller Multiplier—Sequential (Shift-and-Add) Style

An array-style multiplier can be fast, but may require a lot of gates for wide-bitwidth multipliers, like 32-bit multipliers. In this section, we create a sequential multiplier instead of a combinational one, in order to reduce the size of the multiplier. The idea of a sequential multiplier is to keep a running sum of the partial products and compute each partial product one at a time, rather than computing all the partial products at once and summing them.

Figure 6.66 provides an example of 4-bit multiplication. Assume we start with a running of sum of 0000. Each step corresponds to a bit in the multiplier (the second number). In step 1, we compute the partial product as 0110, which we add to the running sum of 0000 to obtain 00110. In step 2, we compute the partial product as 0110, which we add to the proper columns of the running sum of 00110 to obtain 010010. In step 3, we compute the partial product as 0000, which we add to the proper columns of the running sum. Likewise for step 4. The final running sum is 00010010, which is the correct product of 0110 and 0011.

Step 1	Step 2	Step 3	Step 4	
0 1 1 0	0 1 1 0	0 1 1 0	0 1 1 0	
× 0 0 1 *1*	× 0 0 *1* 1	× 0 *0* 1 1	× *0* 0 1 1	
0 0 0 0	0 0 1 1 0	0 1 0 0 1 0	0 0 1 0 0 1 0	**(running sum)**
+ 0 1 1 0	+ 0 1 1 0	+ 0 0 0 0	+ 0 0 0 0	(partial product)
0 0 1 1 0	0 1 0 0 1 0	0 0 1 0 0 1 0	0 0 0 1 0 0 1 0	(new running sum)

Figure 6.66 Multiplication done by generating a partial product for each bit in the multiplier (the number on the bottom), accumulating the partial products in a running sum.

Computing each partial product is easy—we just AND the current multiplicand bit with every bit in the multiplier to obtain the partial product. So if the current multiplicand bit is 1, the AND creates a copy of the multiplier as the partial product. If the current multiplicand bit is 0, the AND creates 0 as the partial product.

We need to determine how to add each partial product to the proper columns of the running sum. Notice that the partial product should be moved to the left by one bit relative to the running sum after each step. We can look at this another way—the running sum should be moved to the *right* by one bit after each step. Look at the multiplication illustration in Figure 6.66, until you "see" how the running sum moves one bit to the right relative to each partial product.

Therefore, we can compute the running sum by initializing an 8-bit register to 0. In each step we add the partial product for the current multiplicand bit to the leftmost four bits of the running sum, and we shift the running sum one bit to the right, shifting in a 0 into the leftmost bit. So the running sum register should have a clear function, a parallel load function, and a shift right function. A circuit showing the running sum register and an adder to add each partial product to that register is shown in Figure 6.67.

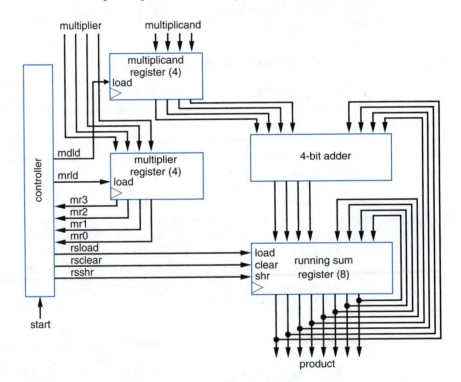

Figure 6.67 Internal design of a 4-bit by 4-bit sequential multiplier.

The last thing we need to figure out is how to control the circuit so that the circuit does the right thing during each step—that's exactly what controllers are for. Figure 6.68 shows an FSM describing the desired controller behavior of our sequential multiplier.

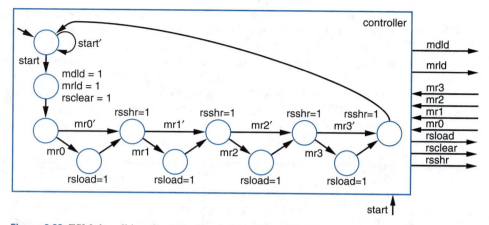

Figure 6.68 FSM describing the controller for the 4-bit multiplier.

In terms of performance, the sequential multiplier requires two cycles per bit, plus 1 cycle for initialization. So a 4-bit multiplier would require 9 cycles, while a 32-bit multiplier would require 65 cycles. The longest register-to-register delay is from a register through the adder to a register. If we built the adder as a carry-lookahead adder having only 4 gate-delays, then the total delay for a 4-bit multiplication would be 9 cycles * 4 gate-delays/cycle = 36 gate-delays. The total delay for a 32-bit multiplication would be 65 cycles * 4 gate-delays/cycle = 260 gate-delays. While slow, notice that this multiplier's size is quite good, requiring only an adder, a few registers, and a state-register and some control logic for the controller. For a 32-bit multiplier, the size would be far smaller than an array-style multiplier requiring 31 adders.

The multiplier's design can be further improved by using a shifter in the datapath, but we omit details of that improved design.

▶ 6.5 RTL DESIGN OPTIMIZATIONS AND TRADEOFFS

In Chapter 5, we described the process of RTL design. While creating the datapath during RTL design, there are several optimizations and tradeoffs that we might make to create smaller or faster designs.

Pipelining

Microprocessors continue to become smaller, faster, and less expensive, and thus designers use microprocessors whenever possible to implement desired digital system behavior. But designers continue to choose to build their own digital circuits to implement desired behavior of many digital systems, with the main reason for that choice being *speed*. One method of obtaining speed from digital circuits is through the use of pipelining. **Pipelining** means to break a large task down into a sequence of stages

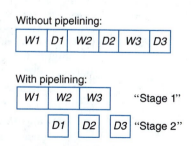

Figure 6.69 Applying pipelining to dishwashing—washing and drying dishes can be done concurrently.

such that data moves through the stages like parts move through a factory assembly line. Each stage produces output used by the next stage, and all stages operate concurrently, resulting in better performance than if data had to be fully processed by the task before new data could begin being processed. An example of pipelining is washing dishes with a friend, with you washing and your friend drying (Figure 6.69). You (the first stage) pick up a dish (dish 1) and wash it, then hand it to your friend (the second stage). You pick up the next dish (dish 2) and wash it *concurrently* to your friend drying dish 1. You then wash dish 3 while your friend drys dish 2. Dishwashing this way is nearly twice as fast as when washing and drying aren't done concurrently.

Consider a system with data inputs W, X, Y, and Z, that should repeatedly output the sum S = W + X + Y + Z. We could implement the system using an adder tree as shown in Figure 6.70(a). The fastest clock for this design must not be faster than the longest path between any pair of registers, known as the critical path. There are four possible paths from any register output to any register input, and each path goes through two adders. If each adder has a delay of 2 ns, then each path is 2+2 = 4 ns long. Thus, the critical path is 4 ns, and so the fastest clock has a period of at least 4 ns, meaning a frequency of no more than 1 / 4 ns = 250 MHz.

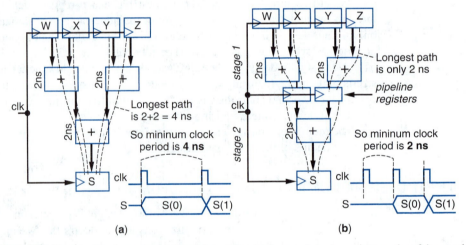

Figure 6.70 Nonpipelined versus pipelined datapaths: (a) four register-to-register paths of 4 ns each, so longest path is 4 ns, meaning minimum clock period is 4 ns, or 1/4 ns = 250 MHz, (b) six register-to-register paths of 2 ns each, so longest path is 2 ns, meaning minimum clock period of 2 ns, or 1/2 ns = 500 MHz.

Figure 6.70(b) shows a pipelined version of this design. We merely add registers between the first and second rows of adders. Since the purpose of these registers is solely related to pipelining, they are known as **pipeline registers**, though their internal design is the same as any other register. The computations between pipeline registers are known as **stages**. By inserting those registers and thus creating a two-stage pipeline, we've reduced the critical path from 4 ns down to only 2 ns, and so the fastest clock has a period of at least 2 ns, meaning a frequency of no more than 1/2 ns = 500 MHz. In other words, just by inserting those pipeline registers, we've *doubled the performance* of our design!

Latency versus Throughput

The term "performance" needs to be refined due to the pipelining concept. Notice in Figure 6.70(b) that the first result S(0) doesn't appear until after two cycles, whereas the design in Figure 6.70(a) outputs the first result after only one cycle. That's because data must now pass through an extra row of registers. The term *latency* refers to delay for new input data to result in new output data. Latency is one kind of performance. Both designs in the figure have a latency of 4 ns. Figure 6.70(b) also shows that a new value for S appears every 2 ns, versus every 4 ns for the design in Figure 6.70(a). The term *throughput* refers to the rate at which new data can be input to the system, and similarly, the rate at which new outputs appear from the system. The throughput of the design in Figure 6.70(a) is 1 sample every 4 ns, while the throughput of the design in Figure 6.70(b) is 1 sample every 2 ns. Thus, we can more precisely describe the performance improvement of our pipelined design as having *doubled the throughput* of the design.

▶ **EXAMPLE 6.20**   Pipelined FIR filter

Recall the 100-tap FIR filter from Example 5.8. We estimated that implementation on a microprocessor would require 4000 ns, while a custom digital circuit implementation would require only 34 ns. That custom digital circuit utilized an adder tree, with seven levels of adders—50 additions, then 25, then 13 (roughly), then 7, then 4, then 2, then 1. The total delay was 20 ns (for the multiplier) plus seven adder-delays (7*2ns = 14ns), for a total delay of 34 ns. We can further improve the throughput of that filter using pipelining. Noticing that the multipliers' delay of 20 ns is roughly equal to the adder tree delay of 14 ns, we might decide to insert pipeline registers (50 of them since there are 50 multipliers feeding into 50 adders at the top of the adder tree) between the multipliers and adder tree, resulting in dividing the computation task into two stages, as shown in Figure 6.71. Those pipeline registers shorten the critical path from 34 ns down to only 20 ns, meaning we can clock the circuit faster and hence improve the throughput. The throughput speedup of the unpipelined design compared to the microprocessor implementation was 4000/34 = 117, while the throughput speedup of the pipelined design is 4000/20 = 200. Quite a nice additional speedup for just inserting some registers!

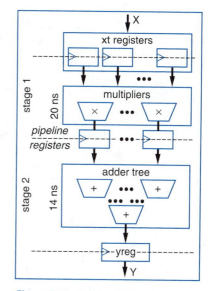

Figure 6.71 Pipelined FIR filter.

Although we could pipeline the adder tree also, that would not gain us higher throughput, since the multiplier stage would still represent the critical path. We can't clock a pipelined system any faster than the longest stage, since otherwise that stage would fail to load correct values into the stage's output pipeline registers.

The latency of the nonpipelined design is one cycle of 34 ns, or 34 ns total. The latency of the pipelined design is two cycles of 20 ns, or 40 ns total. Thus, we see that pipelining improves the throughput at the expense of latency.   ◀

Concurrency

A key reason for designing a custom digital circuit, rather than writing software that executes on a microprocessor, is to achieve improved performance. A common method of achieving performance in a custom digital circuit is through concurrency. **Concurrency** in digital design means to divide a task into several independent subparts, and then to execute those subparts simultaneously. As an analogy, if we have a stack of 200 dishes to wash, we might divide the stack into 10 substacks of 20 dishes each, and then give 10 of our neighbors each a substack. Those neighbors simultaneously go home, wash and dry their respective substacks, and return to us their completed dishes. We would get a ten times speedup in dishwashing (ignoring the time to divide the stack and move substacks from home to home).

We have used concurrency in several examples already. For example, the FIR filter datapath of Figure 5.38 had three multipliers executing concurrently.

Let's use concurrency to create a faster version of an earlier example.

▶ **EXAMPLE 6.21**   Sum-of-absolute-difference component with concurrency

In Example 5.7, we designed a custom circuit for a sum-of-absolute-difference (SAD) component, and we estimated that component to be three times faster than a software-on-microprocessor solution. We can do even better. Notice that comparing one pair of corresponding pixels of two frames is independent of comparing another pair. Thus, such comparisons are an ideal candidate for concurrency.

We first need to be able to read the pixels concurrently. We can do this by redesigning the block memories A and B, which earlier were designed as 256-byte memories. Instead, let's design them as 16 word memories, where each word is 16 bytes (the total is still 256 bytes). Thus, each memory read corresponds to reading an entire pixel row of a 16x16 block. We can then concurrently determine the differences among all 16 pairs of pixels from A and B. Figure 6.72 shows a new datapath and controller FSM for a more concurrent SAD component.

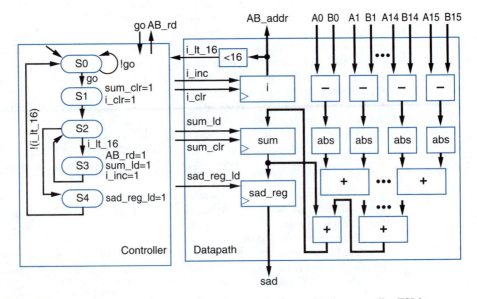

Figure 6.72 SAD datapath using concurrency for speed, along with the controller FSM.

The datapath consists of 16 subtractors operating concurrently on the 16 pixels of a row, followed by 16 absolute value components. The 16 resulting differences feed into an adder tree, whose result gets added with the present sum, for writing back into the sum register. The datapath compares its counter *i* with 16, since there are 16 rows in a block, and so we must compute the difference between rows 16 times. The controlling FSM loops 16 times to accumulate the differences of each row, and then loads the final result into the register *sad_reg*, which connects to the SAD component's output sad.

In Example 5.7, we estimated that a software solution would require about six cycles per pixel pair comparison. Since there are 256 pixels in a 16x16 block, the software would require 256*6 = 1536 cycles to compare a pair of blocks. Our SAD circuit with concurrency instead requires only 1 cycle to compare each row of 16 pixels, which the circuit must do 16 times for a block, resulting in only 16*1 = 16 cycles. Thus, the SAD circuit's speedup over software is 1536 / 16 = 96. In other words, the relatively simple SAD circuit using concurrency runs nearly 100 times faster than a software solution. That sort of speedup eventually translates to better quality digitized video from whatever video appliance we are designing. ◄

Pipelining and concurrency can be combined to achieve even greater performance improvements.

Component Allocation

When the same operation is used in two different states of a high-level state machine, we can choose to either instantiate two functional units, one for each state, or one functional unit, which will be shared among the two states. For example, Figure 6.73 shows a portion of a state machine with two states, *A* and *B*, that each have a multiplication operation. We can choose to use two distinct multipliers as shown in Figure 6.73(a) (we assume the t variables represent registers). The figure also shows the control signals that would be set in each state of the FSM controlling that datapath, with the t1 register being loaded in the first state (t1ld=1), and the t4 register being loaded in the second state (t4ld=1).

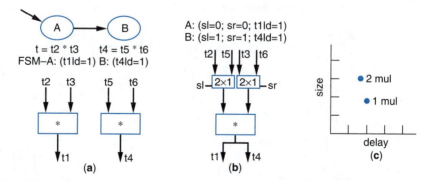

Figure 6.73 Two different component allocations: (a) two multipliers, (b) one multiplier, (c) the one multiplier allocation represents a tradeoff of smaller size for slightly more delay.

However, because a state machine can't be in two states at the same time, then we know that the FSM will perform only one multiplication at a time, so we can share one multiplier among the two states. Because fast multipliers are big, such sharing could save a lot of gates. A datapath with only one multiplier appears in Figure 6.73(b). In each state of the state machine, the controller FSM would configure the multiplexer select lines to pass the appropriate operands through to the multiplier, as well as loading the appropriate destination register as before. So in the first state A, the FSM would set the select line for the left multiplexer to 0 to let t2 pass through (sl=0) and would set the select line for the right multiplexer to 0 to let t3 pass through (sr=0), in addition to setting t1ld=1 to load the result of the mutliplication into the t1 register. Likewise, the FSM in state B sets the muxes to pass t5 and t6, and loads t4.

Figure 6.73(c) illustrates that the one-multiplier design would have smaller size, at the expense perhaps of slightly more delay due to the multiplexers.

The terms "operator" and "operation" refers to behavior, like addition or multiplication. The term "component" (aka "functional unit") refers to hardware, like an adder or a multiplier.

A component library might consist of numerous different functional units that could potentially implement a desired operation—for a multiplication, there may be several multiplier components: MUL1 might be very fast but large, while MUL2 might be very small but slow, and MUL3 may be somewhere in between. There may also be fast but large adders, small but slow adders, and several choices in between. Furthermore, some components might support multiple operations, like an adder/subtractor component, or an ALU. Choosing a particular set of functional units to implement a set of operations is known as **component allocation**. Automated RTL design tools consider dozens or hundreds of possible component allocations to find the best ones that represent a good tradeoff among size and performance.

Operator Binding

Given an allocation of components, we still have to choose which operations to map to which components. For example, Figure 6.74 shows three multiplication operations, one in state A, one in state B, and one in state C. Figure 6.74(a) shows one possible component binding to two multipliers, resulting in two multiplexers. Figure 6.74(b) shows an alternative binding to two multipliers, which results in only one multiplexer, since the same operand (t3) is fed to the same multiplier *MULA* in two different states and thus that multiplier's input doesn't require a mux. Thus, the second binding results in fewer

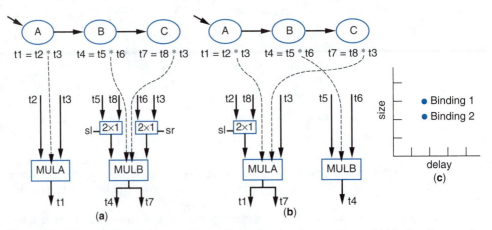

Figure 6.74 Two different operator bindings: (a) binding 1 uses two muxes, (b) binding 2 uses only one mux, (c) binding 2 represents an optimization compared to binding 1.

gates, with no performance loss—an optimization, as shown in Figure 6.74(c). Note that that binding not only maps operators to components, but also chooses which operand to map to which component input; if we had mapped t3 to the left operand of *MULA* in Figure 6.74(b), then *MULA* would have required two muxes rather than just one.

Mapping a given set of operations to a particular component allocation is known as **operator binding**. Automated tools typically explore hundreds of different bindings for a given component allocation.

Of course, the tasks of component allocation and operator binding are interdependent. If we allocate only one component, then all operators must be bound to that component. If we allocate two components, then we have some choices in binding. If we allocate many components, then we have many more binding choices. Thus, some tools will perform allocation and binding simultaneously, or the tools will iterate among the two tasks. Together, component allocation and operator binding are sometimes referred to as **resource sharing**.

Operator Scheduling

Given a high-level state machine, we may introduce additional states to enable us to create a smaller datapath. For example, consider the high-level state machine in Figure 6.75(a). The state machine has three states, with state *B* having two multiplications. Since

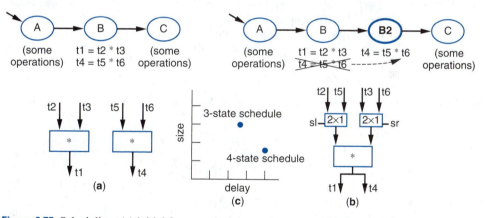

Figure 6.75 Scheduling: (a) initial 3-state schedule requires two multipliers, (b) new 4-state schedule requires only one multiplier, (c) new schedule trades off size for delay (extra state).

those two multiplications occur in the same state, and we know that each state will be a single clock cycle, then we will need two multipliers (at least) in the datapath to support the two simultaneous multiplications in state *B*. But what if we only have enough gates for one multiplier? In that case, we can reschedule the operations so that there is at most only one multiplication needed in any one state, as in Figure 6.75(b). Thus, when we allocate components, we need only allocate one multiplier as shown, and as was also done in Figure 6.73(b). The result is a smaller but slower design, as illustrated in Figure 6.75(c). That scheduling example assumed that the computation of t4 could not be moved to state *A* or state *C*, perhaps because those states already used a multiplier, or perhaps because t5 and t6 were not ready yet in state *A*, and the new result in t4 was needed in state *C*.

Converting a computation from occurring concurrently in one state to occurring across several states is known as *serializing* a computation.

Of course, the inverse rescheduling is also possible. Suppose we started with the high-level state machine of Figure 6.75(b). If we have plenty of gates available and want to improve our design's performance, we might reschedule the operations such that we merge the operations of state B2 and B into the one state B, as in Figure 6.75(a). The result is a faster but larger design, requiring two multipliers instead of one.

Generally, introducing or merging states, and assigning operations to those states, is a task known as *operator scheduling*.

You may have noticed that operator scheduling is interdependent with component allocation, which you may recall was interdependent with operator binding. Thus, the tasks of scheduling, allocation, and binding are all interdependent. Modern tools may combine the tasks somewhat, and/or may iterate among the tasks several times, in search of good designs.

▶ **EXAMPLE 6.22** Smaller FIR filter using operator scheduling

Consider the 3-tap FIR filter of Example 5.8. That design had no controller, meaning the high-level state machine actually had just one state containing all the datapath actions, as shown in Figure 6.76(a). We could reduce the size of the datapath by scheduling the operations across several states, such that at most one multiplication and one addition occurs per state, as shown in Figure 6.76(b). The first state loads the x registers with samples—note that the ordering of those actions next to the state doesn't matter, since all the actions occur simultaneously. That state also clears a new register named sum, which we had to introduce to keep track of the intermediate tap sums to be computed in the later states. The second state computes the first tap of the filter result, the next state computes the second tap, and the next state computes the third tap. The last state outputs the result, and then the state machine returns to the first state again.

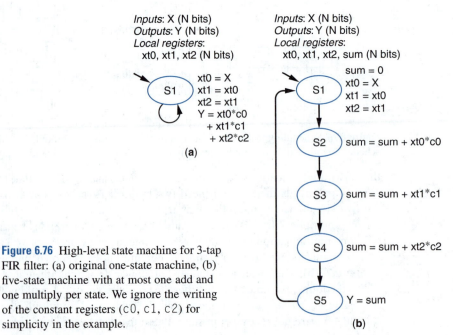

Figure 6.76 High-level state machine for 3-tap FIR filter: (a) original one-state machine, (b) five-state machine with at most one add and one multiply per state. We ignore the writing of the constant registers (c0, c1, c2) for simplicity in the example.

A datapath for this state machine is shown in Figure 6.77. The datapath requires only one multiplier and one adder, because there is at most one multiplication and one addition in any given state in Figure 6.76. The particular configuration of the multiplier, adder, and register in Figure 6.77 is extremely common in single processing circuits, and is generally known as a ***multiply-accumulate*** (***MAC***) unit. The datapath multiplexes the inputs to the MAC unit.

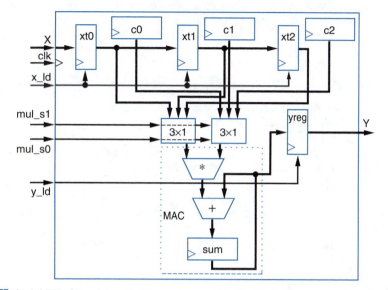

Figure 6.77 Serial FIR filter datapath. The components in the dashed box comprise what is known as a multiply-accumulate (MAC) component.

One further difference between this datapath and the concurrent datapath of Example 5.8 is that this datapath has load lines on the x registers and on yreg. The concurrent design loaded those registers every clock cycle, but the serial design only loads those registers during particular states—other states compute intermediate results.

We estimated the performance of the concurrent design of Example 5.8 assuming 1 ns per gate, 2 ns per adder, and 20 ns per multiplier. The design had a critical path of 20 ns for the multiplier and then 4 ns for two adders in series, for a total of 24 ns. That was also the time between new results being taken in at the inputs and generated at the output: 24 ns. Using the more precise performance measures of latency and throughput defined in Section 6.5, the concurrent design has a latency of 24 ns (delay from input to output), and a throughput of 1 sample every 24 ns. The serial design has a critical path equal to the delay through a mux, multiplier, and adder. Assuming two gate-delays for the mux, we obtain a delay of 2 ns + 20 ns + 2 ns, or 24 ns. The latency from input to output is five states, meaning 5 * 24 ns = 120 ns. The throughput is 1 sample every 120 ns. Thus, the concurrent 3-tap FIR filter has 120/25 = 5 times faster latency, as well as 5 times faster throughput, compared to the serial FIR filter. Recall from Example 6.20 that a pipelined concurrent FIR filter has even faster throughput.

The performance difference between serial and concurrent becomes even more pronounced if we look at an FIR filter with more taps. We estimated the latency of a concurrent 100-tap FIR filter in Section 5.3, after Example 5.8 to be 34 ns (the delay is greater than the concurrent 3-tap filter because the 100-tap filter needs an adder tree). The serial design would still have a 24 ns critical path, but would require 102 states (1 to initialize, 100 to compute the taps, and 1 to output), for a latency of 102 * 24 ns = 2448 ns. Thus, the latency speedup of the concurrent design would be 2448 / 34 = 72.

We should also consider the size difference between the serial and concurrent designs. Let's assume for illustrative purposes that an adder requires approximately 500 gates and a multiplier requires 5000 gates. The serial design's one multiplier and one adder would thus require only 5500 gates. For a 3-tap FIR filter, the concurrent design's 3 multipliers and 2 adders would require 5000*3 + 500*2 = 16,000 gates. For a 100-tap FIR filter, the concurrent design's 100 multipliers alone would require 100*5000 = 500,000 gates—100 times more gates than the serial design.

Intuitively, these numbers make sense. A concurrent design for 100 taps uses about 100 times more gates (due to using 100 multipliers instead of just 1) compared to a serial design, yet achieves about 100 times better performance (due to computing 100 multiplications concurrently rather than computing one multiplication at a time).

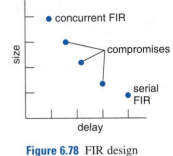

Depending on our performance needs and size constraints, we might consider designs in between the two extremes of serial and concurrent, such as a design with two multipliers, which would be roughly twice as big and twice as fast as the serial design, or ten multipliers, which would be roughly ten times as big and ten times as fast as the serial design. Figure 6.78 illustrates tradeoffs among serial and concurrent designs for an FIR filter. ◀

Figure 6.78 FIR design tradeoffs.

The above sections should have made it quite clear that RTL design presents an enormous range of possible solutions to the designer. A single high-level state machine can be implemented as any of a huge variety of possible implementations that differ tremendously in their sizes and performance.

Moore versus Mealy High-Level State Machines

In the same way that we can create either a Moore or a Mealy FSM (see Section 6.3), we can create Moore or Mealy high-level state machines. In the case of a high-level state machine, a Moore type can only have actions associated with the states, while a Mealy type can have actions associated with the transitions. As was the case with FSMs, a Mealy type may result in fewer states. Mixing Moore and Mealy types is commonly done in high-level state machines.

▶ 6.6 MORE ON OPTIMIZATIONS AND TRADEOFFS

Serial versus Concurrent Computation

Having seen in this chapter numerous examples of tradeoff techniques at various levels of design, we can detect a common theme underlying some of those tradeoffs. The common theme is that of serial versus concurrent computation. *Serial* means to perform tasks one at a time. *Concurrent* means to perform tasks at the same time.

For example, in combinational logic design, we can reduce logic size by factoring out terms. By factoring out terms, we are essentially serializing the computation, by computing the factored out terms first, and then combining the results with other terms. In datapath component design, we can improve an adder's speed by computing carries concurrently, rather than waiting for the carry to ripple serially. In RTL design, we can schedule operations across several states, serializing the operations to reduce size compared to concurrent operations in a single state. Example 6.21 and Example 6.22 both illustrated serial versus concurrent computation tradeoffs, for an SAD circuit and an FIR circuit, respectively.

Trading off between serial and concurrent computation is a fundamental concept spanning all levels of digital design. As a general rule, a concurrent design is faster but larger, while a serial design is smaller but slower.

Typically, numerous design options exist that span the range in between fully serial and fully concurrent designs.

Optimizations and Tradeoffs at Higher versus Lower Levels of Design

As a general rule, the optimizations and tradeoffs made at the higher levels of design may have a much greater impact on design criteria than the optimizations and tradeoffs made at lower levels of design. For example, imagine wanting to drive to a city on the other side of the country in as little time as possible. We could reduce time by reducing the number of stops we make to eat, meaning we carry our own food in the car. We could also reduce time by reducing stops for fuel, meaning we use a car with the longest driving capacity per gas tank. Some people (not you, of course) might even consider driving faster than the legal speed limit. But those are not the first things you typically think of when trying to reduce driving time for a cross-country trip. The most important decision is which route to take. One route might be 4000 miles long, while another route may be only 2000 miles. The high-level decision of which route to take has far more impact than all the lower-level decisions mentioned previously. Those lower-level decisions are only really useful to us if we made the right high-level decision, and then if we still want to reduce the time further.

In digital design, optimization/tradeoff decisions at the higher levels (e.g., RTL decisions) may have a much larger impact than decisions at the lower levels (e.g., datapath component decisions or multilevel logic decisions). For example, the RTL decision to build a serial or concurrent FIR filter (Example 6.22) will have a far greater impact on circuit size and performance than the datapath-component-level decision to use a carry-ripple or carry-lookahead adder, or the combinational-logic-

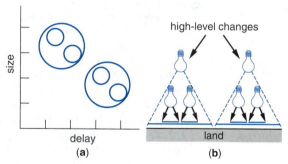

Figure 6.79 Higher- versus lower-level decisions: (a) higher-level decisions (denoted by the larger two circles) focus the design into a region, while lower-level decisions tune within the region, (b) spotlight analogy.

level decision to use two-level or multilevel logic. Those lower-level decisions merely tune the size and performance of the higher-level decision. Figure 6.79(a) illustrates this concept. An analogy might be a spotlight shining down on land, illustrated in Figure 6.79(b)— moving the spotlight left or right at high altitude (higher-level decisions) has a larger impact on which land region (possible solutions) is illuminated than do lower-altitude movements (lower-level decisions).

Algorithm Selection

When attempting to implement a system as a digital circuit, perhaps the highest-level design decision, having therefore the most signficant impact on design criteria like size, performance, power, etc., is the selection of an algorithm. An ***algorithm*** is a set of steps that solve a problem. The same problem can be solved by different algorithms. Algorithms for the same problem, when implemented as a digital circuit, may result in tremendously different performance and/or size. Some algorithms may simply be better than others (optimization without much tradeoff), while other algorithms may represent tradeoffs between performance, size, and other criteria. Selecting an algorithm for a digital design problem is perhaps the highest level of design, and can have the biggest impact on design criteria. For example, earlier examples showed various implementations of an FIR filter. But there are many other algorithms for filtering very different from the algorithm used in FIR. Some algorithms may provide higher-quality filtering at the expense of more required computation, others may provide lower quality but need less computation.

We illustrate algorithm selection using an example.

▶ **EXAMPLE 6.23**   Data compression using different table lookup algorithms

We wish to compress data being sent over a long-distance computer network in order to achieve faster communication by sending fewer bits. One method for such compression is to use short codes for frequently appearing data values. For example, suppose each data item is 32 bits long. We might analyze the data we expect to send and find the 256 most frequently appearing data values. We could then assign a unique 8-bit code to each of those 256 values. When sending data over the network, we first send a bit indicating whether we are about to send an encoded 8-bit data item or a raw 32-bit data item—if the first bit is 1, that might mean encoded, and a 0 might mean raw. If all the data items being sent happen to be among the top 256 most frequent ones, then we'd be sending 9 bits per data item (1 bit indicating whether encoded, plus 8 bits of encoded data) rather than 32 bits per data item—a compression of nearly 4x, which could translate to about 4 times faster communication.

We might design the encoder using a 256-word memory that stores the 256 most frequent values in sorted order, from smallest to largest in binary. The code would then be the address of that word in the memory. Figure 6.80 shows sample contents of such a memory, in hexadecimal. The contents vary depending on the communicating applications we are considering.

One algorithm for searching a list of values in a memory is known as ***linear search***. Starting at address 0, we compare each memory word's contents with the data item we are looking for (known as the key), incrementing the address and repeating until we find a match, at which point we treat the address at which there was a match as the encoded value. If we get to address 255 and don't find a match, we will transmit the raw data. The linear search algorithm is a slow way to search a sorted list in memory. The algorithm requires 256 reads and compares for data items that aren't in the memory, which may translate to 256 cycles. For data items that are in the memory, we would require on average 128 reads.

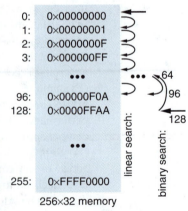

Figure 6.80 Searching a sorted memory for the key 0x00000F0A —linear search requires 97 reads/ compares, binary search only 3.

A faster algorithm for searching a list of items in a memory is known as ***binary search***. We first sort the list and then store the list in the memory (we need only sort once). To look up an item, we start in the middle of the memory, meaning address 128, and compare that word's contents with the key. If the content's value is less than 128, then we know that the key, if it exists in the memory, must be somewhere between 0 and 127. So we go to the middle of that range, meaning address 64, and again compare. If the value there is less than the key, we search 0 to 63; if greater, we search 65–127. So after each comparison, we decrease the remaining possible range of addresses in which the key lies by one half. Halving 256 repeatedly can only be done 8 times: 256, 128, 64, 32, 16, 8, 4, 2, 1. In other words, after at most 8 comparisons, we've either seen the key, or shrunk the range to 1, meaning the key can't be found in the memory. Binary search is 256/8 = 32 times faster than linear search when the key does not exist in the memory, and roughly that much faster when the key exists in the memory too. Yet binary search only requires a slightly smarter controller.

We see that the choice of the right algorithm makes a big difference in performance for this example—much bigger a difference than determined by, say, the speed of the comparator being used. ◀

Power Optimization

Power is becoming an important design criteria, both in high-end computing as well as in embedded computing. The unit of power is ***watts***, which represents the energy per second (i.e., joules per second). In high-end computing, like desktop PCs, servers, or video-game consoles, the chips inside a computer consume a lot of power, causing the chips to become very hot. For example, a typical chip inside a PC may consume 60 watts—think about touching a 60 watt light bulb (but don't actually touch one) to understand how hot that is. Designing low-power chips reduces the need for expensive chip cooling methods beyond simple fans in high-end computing, and also reduces the electricity costs, which can be quite significant for companies operating large numbers of computers.

In embedded computing, even simple cooling methods likes fans are often not available—for example, your cell phone does not have a fan (if it did, people might find their tie or scarf getting stuck in that fan). Portable embedded devices might have chips that run at only 1 watt or less.

Furthermore, portable devices typically get their energy from batteries, and thus low power chips are necessary to extend battery life—especially considering the fact that batteries are not improving fast enough to keep pace with increasing power consumption. By some measures, energy demand per chip is doubling about every three years (going along with Moore's Law). Figure 6.81 plots such energy demands compared to battery energy densities improving at their present rate of only about 8% per year. The increasing gap shown translates to shorter battery lifetimes for a device like a cell phone, or translates to bigger batteries.

The most popular IC technology today uses CMOS transistors, and the biggest contributor to

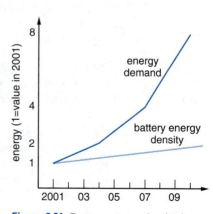

Figure 6.81 Battery energy density is improving slower than the increasing energy demands of digital chips.

power consumption in CMOS is the switching of values from 0 to 1. The reason for this is that wires aren't perfect, having capacitance (we don't put a capacitor there on purpose—it is simply a result of the fact that wires aren't perfect conductors of electricity). Switching the wire from 0 to 1 requires charging that capacitor. Switching from 1 back to 0 causes that charge to be discharged to ground. That switching results in power being consumed. This power is known as ***dynamic power***, since this power comes from the changing of signals (dynamic means changing). Dynamic power consumption of a CMOS wire is proportional to the size of the capacitance (C) of the wire, multiplied by the voltage (V) squared, multiplied by the frequency at which the wire switches (f), namely:

$$P = k * CV^2f \quad \text{(equation for CMOS dynamic power consumption)}$$

where k is some constant. To compute the dynamic power of a circuit, we would add up the power computed by the above equation for every wire.

Looking at the above equation, one can clearly see that lowering the voltage will cause the greatest reduction in dynamic power, because of the voltage having a quadratic (squared) contribution to dynamic power. Low-level circuit designers seek to reduce power by creating transistors that operate at the lowest voltage possible, to reduce the V term, and that have the smallest wire capacitance possible, to reduce the C term. Digital designers can therefore choose to utilize gates that operate with a lower voltage.

Unfortunately, lower voltage gates have a longer delay than higher voltage gates, resulting in a tradeoff between power and performance.

Another way to reduce the dynamic power consumed by a circuit is to reduce the circuit's clock frequency, which obviously reduces the f term for all the clock wires in the circuit, as well as for the many other wires that change on each clock edge (like register wires and the logic connected to those registers' outputs). But again, reducing the clock frequency slows performance, resulting in a tradeoff between power and performance.

The chief technical officer at a major chip design company told me in 2004 that, for their company, "Power is enemy number one." The reason is that they had scaled their voltage down nearly as low as possible, yet are putting more transistors on each IC every year due to the shrinking of transistor sizes, meaning more wires switching. And capacitance isn't decreasing at the same rate as transistor sizes. The result is that an IC consumes more power as we put more transistors on the IC, which can result in problems due to too much heat and due to fast battery energy consumption.

Clock Gating (Advanced Technique)

Assuming the C and V terms have been reduced to the extent possible using transistor-level design techniques, power can be reduced further by reducing f, the frequency at which wires switch. One method for reducing such power is known as clock gating. ***Clock gating*** is the disabling of the clock signal in regions of the chip that we know are not computing anything at a given time. Clock gating saves power because a significant percentage of the wires switching in a chip are the wires that distribute the clock to all the registers and flip-flops— perhaps 20%–30% of the power consumption is due to the clock signal switching throughout the chip. Clock gating reduces f without slowing the clock frequency itself.

In clock gating, the clock signal is disabled by ANDing the clock signal with an enable signal that is set in the state machine. Recall that a register with parallel load internally reloads the same value from the register's flip-flops back into the flip-flops on a rising clock edge. Preventing the clock edge from appearing keeps the same values in the flip-flops, yielding the same net result—the register's contents don't change.

Clock gating is not something that digital designers typically do themselves. Rather, modern synthesis tools may allow us to specify clock enable and disable using special commands in each state. These tools must use extreme caution, because adding a gate on a clock signal delays the clock signal, resulting in clock signals in different parts of the circuit being slightly different from one another, an effect known as ***clock skew***. The tools must perform careful timing analysis to ensure that the clock skew does not change overall circuit behavior. Furthermore, putting gates on a clock signal can reduce the sharpness of the clock edges, and so must be done carefully, sometimes using special gates. Nevertheless, the technique is widely used by low-power tools in practice.

We demonstrate clock gating with an example.

▶ **EXAMPLE 6.24**   Serial FIR filter with clock gating to reduce power

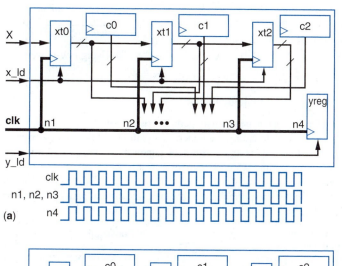

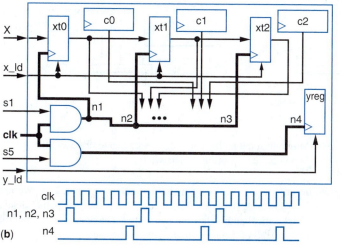

We designed a serial FIR filter in Example 6.22. A five-state state machine controlled the datapath. The state machine loaded the three xt registers only in the first state, state $S1$, and loaded the yreg register only in the last state, state $S5$. Yet, the design routed the clock signal to all four registers utilizing four wires, labeled n1-n4 in Figure 6.82(a). Notice from the timing diagram at the top of the figure that n1-n4 change identically as the clock signal changes, and remember that every such change consumes dynamic power.

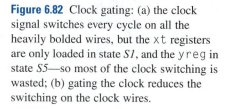

Figure 6.82 Clock gating: (a) the clock signal switches every cycle on all the heavily bolded wires, but the xt registers are only loaded in state $S1$, and the yreg in state $S5$—so most of the clock switching is wasted; (b) gating the clock reduces the switching on the clock wires.

Figure 6.82(b) shows a design using clock gating. The controller gates the clock to the xt registers by setting s1 to 0 in all states but S1. Likewise, the controller gates the clock to the yreg register by setting s5 to 0 in all states but s5. Notice the significant decrease in signal switching on the clock's wires n1-n4, shown at the bottom of Figure 6.82. ◄

Low-power gates on noncritical paths

Not all gates are equally fast. Engineers that build gates from transistors can make a gate faster by increasing the size of the gate's transistors, or by operating the gate at a higher voltage, or by any of several other means. Thus, one two-input AND gate might have a 1 ns delay, while another two-input AND gate might have a 2 ns delay. The latter AND may consume less power, due to its smaller size or lower voltage.

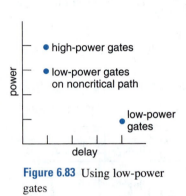

Figure 6.83 Using low-power gates

If we want to reduce the power consumed by a circuit, we can build the entire circuit using low-power gates to achieve low power at the expense of slower performance, as illustrated in Figure 6.83.

Alternatively, we can put low-power gates only on the noncritical paths, such that we lengthen those paths to have delays no longer than the critical path, as shown in the following example.

► **EXAMPLE 6.25** Reducing noncritical path power with multilevel logic

In Example 6.12, we reduced the size of a noncritical path by using multilevel logic. In this example, we instead reduce the power consumed by the noncritical path by using low-power gates. Assume that normal gates have a delay of 1 ns and consume 1 nanowatt of power, and that low-power gates have a delay of 2 ns and consume 0.5 nanowatts of power.

The left side of Figure 6.84 shows the same circuit from Example 6.12, having a critical path of 3 gate-delays. Assume that all the gates are normal gates, meaning the critical path delay is 3 ns, and the total power consumption is 5 nanowatts.

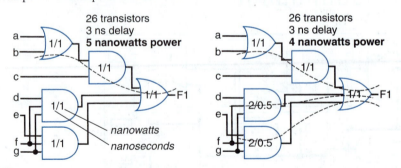

Figure 6.84 Using low-power gates on noncritical paths. Numbers inside a gate represent the gate's delay in nanoseconds, and the gate's power consumption in nanowatts.

The bottom two AND gates lie on two noncritical paths having delays of only 2 ns. We can thus replace those AND gates by low-power AND gates. The result is that the two paths' delays lengthen to 3 ns, so become equal to the critical path delay, but not longer. The result is also that the total power becomes only 4 nanowatts instead of 5 nanowatts (a 20% reduction). ◄

▶ 6.7 PRODUCT PROFILE: DIGITAL VIDEO PLAYER/RECORDER

Digital Video Overview

In the 1990s, the digitization of video became practical due to faster, smaller, and lower-power digital circuits. Previously, video was largely captured, stored, and played using analog methods. Digitized video works by sampling an analog video signal and transforming the samples to digital values. Such digitization is similar to the audio digitization example from Figure 1.1, but with some additional work.

A video is actually a series of quickly displayed still pictures, known as *frames*, as shown in Figure 6.85(a). One second of video might consist of about 30 frames—the human eyes and brain see such a rapid sequence of frames as a smooth, continuous video.

A digital display may be divided into several hundred thousand tiny "picture elements," or *pixels*. A typical size might be about 720 across and 480 down. For each frame, a digitized sample captures several values for each pixel, like the intensity of the red, blue, and green components of the light at that pixel, converting analog measurements of those intensities into digital numbers. The result is the representation of a digitized frame as a (large) series of 0s and 1s, and the representation of a digitized video as a large series of digitized frames. Digitized video can be transmitted, stored, replayed, and copied with much higher quality than analog video. Furthermore, digitized video can be compressed, resulting possibly in higher quality video than analog video transmitted or stored using the same medium.

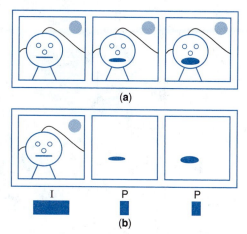

Figure 6.85 Video: (a) is a series of pictures, or frames, with much interframe redundancy, (b) can be constructed from I (intra) frames and P (predicted) frames, shown with relative bit encoding sizes.

DVD—One Form of Digital Video Storage

Digital video discs (also known as digital versatile discs), or *DVDs*, store video in a digital format. First sold in 1997, DVDs replaced the analog video technology known as VHS tape. DVD players appear in home entertainment centers, personal computers, automobiles (especially family-oriented vehicles), and even as stand-alone portable units. In 2001, consumer electronic companies introduced the first DVD *recorder* to market, allowing individuals to record television shows to special recordable DVDs. The popularity of DVDs compared to the previously popular analog-based VHS technology stems from several advantages, including better quality video, no deterioration in video quality over time, and the ability to jump directly to particular parts in a video without having to sequentially forward or rewind.

DVDs store large amounts of data on a thin reflective layer of metal. Although the metal layer within a DVD looks flat from our perspective, there are actually billions of tiny pits on the metal layer that store the data. These pits, or lack of pits (called *lands*), store the binary data on the DVD. Figure 6.86 shows how a DVD player reads the information off a DVD. Using a very precise laser, the laser's light is focused onto the metal layer within the DVD. The metal layer reflects the light onto an optical sensor that can detect if the light is reflected off of a pit or a land. By detecting the different regions, the optical sensor creates a stream of binary values as it reads the DVD.

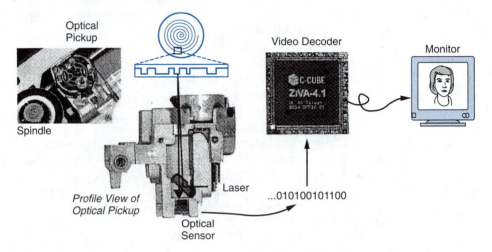

Figure 6.86 How a DVD player reads a DVD. The DVD player's optical pickup element shines a laser on the surface of the DVD. The DVD reflects the laser back to an optical sensor, and the optical sensor uses the intensity of the reflected laser to output the sequence of 0s and 1s stored on the DVD. A video decoder circuit converts the binary data to a sequence of frames that humans interpret as a moving picture.

The DVD's binary data is organized into a series of tracks that spiral outward from the center of the DVD. As the DVD player is reading the data, the laser and optical sensor must slowly move outward from the center of the DVD to the outer edge. If a DVD is dual-layered, the data on the disk's second layer is stored in a spiral that moves from the disk's outer to inner edge. The motivation for the second layer's reverse spiral is to prevent the laser and optical sensor from needing to reposition itself to the center of the disk after focusing on the second layer during a layer change. (You may have noticed a DVD pause momentarily at a certain point in a movie during a layer change.)

A single-layer single-sided DVD can store 4.7 gigabytes of data (meaning 37.6 giga-bits), but that amount is not enough for a movie unless the data is compressed. Consider a video with a resolution of 720 pixels by 480 pixels, using 24 bits of information per pixel, and displayed at 30 frames per second. One frame would require 720*480*24 = 8,294,400 bits, or about 8 Mbits. One second of video, or 30 frames, would require 30*8,294,400 = 248,832,000 bits, or about 250 Mbits. A 100-minute movie would thus require about 250 Mbits/sec * 100 min * 60 sec/min = 1500 Gbits. But a DVD can only hold 37.6 Gbits. To store a movie, a DVD must store the video in a compressed format.

A DVD is only one of many different digital video storage media. Digitized video may be stored on any storage media capable of storing 0s and 1s in some form, such as on tape (used in many digital video cameras), on a flash memory (used in digital cameras and cell phones with video recording capability), on a CD, or on a computer hard drive. All such media are typically still quite limited and thus require compression methods.

MPEG-2 Video Encoding—Sending Frame Differences Using I-, P-, and B-Frames

MPEG-2 video compression was defined and standardized by the Motion Picture Expert Group in 1994 (as an improvement over the 1992 MPEG-1 standard), and is used in DVDs, digital television, and numerous other digital video devices. MPEG-2 compression ratios range from 30:1 to 100:1 or more. The compression ratio is determine by dividing the number of bits of the digitized video before compression, by the number of bits after compression. So if a digitized video requires 400 gigabytes uncompressed but only 4 gigabytes compressed, the compression ratio would be 400/4 = 100:1. Note that packing 1500 Gbits of a movie into 37.6 Gbits would require a compression ratio of 1500 Gbits/37.6 Gbits = 40:1.

The key observation leading to MPEG-2's compression method is that typically very little difference exists between two successive frames in a video—in other words, video typically has much interframe redundancy. For example, a frame may consist of a person standing in front of a mountain, as in Figure 6.85(a). The next frame (which represents perhaps 1/30th of a second later) may be almost identical to the previous frame, except that the person's mouth has opened slightly. The next frame may still be almost identical, with the person's mouth opened slightly more. And so on.

Therefore, MPEG-2 does not merely encode each frame as a distinct picture. Instead, to take advantage of the interframe redundancy, MPEG-2 may choose to encode each frame as one of the following:

- An *I-frame*, or Intracoded frame, is a complete picture.
- A *P-frame*, or Predicted frame, is a frame that merely describes the difference between the current frame and the previous frame. Thus, to derive the picture for this frame, one must combine the P-frame with the previous frame.

For example, Figure 6.85(b) shows P-frames that contain only the differences from the previous frame. A P-frame will obviously require fewer bits than an I-frame. Example frame sizes might be about 8 Mbits for an I-frame, but only 2 Mbits for a P-frame. Thus, instead of representing 30 frames as 30 complete pictures (30 I-frames), a compression method might represent those frames using the following sequence of frames: **I** P P P P P P P P P P P P P P **I** P P P P P P P P P P P P P P P. The compression ratio in this example would thus be 8 Mbits * 30 / (2 * 8 Mbits + 28 * 2 Mbits) = 240 / 72 = 3.3:1. Obviously, a picture created by combined predicted frames with a previous frame won't be a perfect representation of the original picture, especially if there is a lot of motion in the video. MPEG-2 thus trades off some quality for compression.

To achieve even further reductions, MPEG-2 uses a third frame type:

- a *B-frame*, or Bidirectional predicted frame, is a frame that can store differences from previous and *future* frames.

B-frames can thus be even smaller than P-frames. An example B-frame size might be just 1 Mbit.

▶ **EXAMPLE 6.26** Computing compression ratios involving I-, P- and B-frames

Assume a 30-frame MPEG-2 sequence has the following frame sequence: **I** B B P B B P B B P B B P B B **I** B B P B B P B B P B B P B B. Assume average frame sizes of 8 Mbits for I-frames, 2 Mbits for P-frames, and 1 Mbit for B-frames. Compute the compression ratio.

The compression ratio in this example would be 8 Mbits * 30 / (2 * 8 Mbits + 8 * 2 Mbits + 20 * 1 Mbits) = 240 / 52 = 4.6 : 1.

The example sequence of frames is in fact fairly typical for MPEG-2 video, with I-frames occurring about every 12–15 frames.   ◀

MPEG-2 video encoders may seek to create about 30 frames per second. With hundreds of thousands of pixels per frame that must be compared with another frame, MPEG-2 encoding requires a large amount of computation to determine which frames should be I, P, and B, and what should be the values for the P- and B-frames. Furthermore, much of that computation will consist of the *same* computation performed between corresponding regions of two frames. Thus, many MPEG-2 encoders utilize custom digital circuits to parallelize those computations at the expense of more hardware size. For example, Example 6.21 built a sum-of-absolute-differences circuit using more parallelism than in Example 5.9, at the expense of a larger circuit size. Such a circuit would be useful in a video encoder needing to quickly determine whether a frame should be encoded as a P- or B-frame, or instead should be encoded as an I-frame. Additional circuits might compute the actual values of P- and B-frames.

Likewise, an MPEG-2 video decoder might use circuits to quickly recompose I-, P- and B-frames back into full picture frames—although decoding MPEG-2 video is easier than encoding because the actual determination of P- and B-frame contents is only done during encoding; decoding merely needs to combine P- and B-frames with their surrounding frames.

Transforming to the Frequency Domain for Further Compression

DCT—Discrete Cosine Transform

We saw in the previous section that sending a frame (P or B) that is just the difference from a previous or future frame can result in some compression. However, the compression ratios achieved were only about 4:1. Recall earlier that a DVD needs perhaps a 40:1 compression ratio to store a full length movie. Thus, further compression is needed.

MPEG-2 therefore further compresses each I-, P- and B-frame individually. The compression method involves applying what is known as a discrete cosine transform to 8x8 blocks of pixel values within each frame. The discrete cosine transform is also used in the well-known JPEG standard for compressing still images, like those in a digital camera. The *discrete cosine transform*, or *DCT*, transforms information from the spatial domain to the frequency domain. (The DCT is similar to another popular technique known as the Fast Fourier Transform, or FFT, also used for translating to the frequency domain.)

Translating to the frequency domain is a powerful concept, which is widely used in digital signal processing. To understand this concept, consider wanting to digitally store the analog signal shown in Figure 6.87, using the fewest bits possible. The signal is a 1 Hz cosine wave with an amplitude of 10. To store the signal digitally, we could sample the signal at frequent intervals, perhaps every millisecond, and record the measured signal value as a binary number, perhaps 8-bits wide. One second would thus result in 1000 * 8 = 8000 bits. On the other hand, we could just store the fact that the signal is a cosine wave with a frequency of 1 Hz and an amplitude of 10. If we store each of those numbers as an 8-bit value, then we only need to store 8 + 8 = 16 bits. Sixteen bits is far less than 8000 bits.

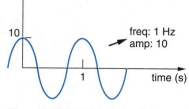
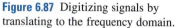

Figure 6.87 Digitizing signals by translating to the frequency domain.

Of course, not all signals that we want to digitize are simple cosine waves. But—and this is the key idea underlying frequency domain representation—*we can approximate any original signal as a sum of cosine waves of different frequencies and amplitudes.* If we break the original signal into small regions, we obtain even better approximation. For example, we might approximate one region as the sum of a 1 Hz cosine wave of amplitude 5 plus a 2 Hz cosine wave of amplitude 3. We might approximate another region as the sum of 50 different cosine waves of different frequencies and amplitudes. The smaller the region we consider, and the more different cosine wave frequencies we consider, the more accurate will be our approximation to the real signal.

Rather than storing the actual frequencies along with the amplitudes of the cosine waves, we could instead decide only to consider using particular frequencies, such as: 1 Hz, 2 Hz, 4 Hz, 8 Hz, 16 Hz, and so on. Then, we can simply send the amplitudes of those particular cosine waves: (5, 3, 0, 0, 0, ...). Let's refer to these amplitudes as coefficients.

The DCT in MPEG-2 converts an input 8x8 block, whose values represent pixel intensities, to an 8x8 block representing the coefficients of predetermined "frequencies." In the video domain, each frequency represents a different block pattern, with low frequency being an almost constant pattern and high frequency being a changing pattern (like a checkerboard). The DCT determines a set of coefficients such that adding the predetermined patterns together with each pattern multiplied by its coefficient yields one resulting pattern very similar to the original input block.

The equation for a two-dimensional DCT applied to an 8x8 block of numbers is:

$$F(u, v) = \frac{1}{4}C(u)C(v) \sum_{x=0}^{8} \sum_{y=0}^{8} D[x, y]\cos\left(\frac{\pi(2x+1)u}{16}\right)\cos\left(\frac{\pi(2y+1)v}{16}\right)$$

$$C(h) = \begin{cases} \frac{1}{\sqrt{2}}, h = 0 \\ 1, otherwise \end{cases}$$

The input is an 8x8 block, $D[x, y]$. The output is another 8x8 block, with $F(u,v)$ computing the coefficient at row u, column v for the output block.

An MPEG-2 encoder may utilize custom digital circuits for fast DCT computation. Notice that computing each coefficient requires evaluating the rightmost term (let's call that term the inner term) 64 times, and that must be done for each of the 64 coefficients, meaning 64*64 = 4096 evaluations of the term. And that inner term itself requires several multiplications. Furthermore, the DCT operates on 8x8 blocks, but in a 720x480 I-frame there will be 5400 such blocks. Thus, the DCT for one I-frame could require 5400*4096 = 22 million computations of the inner term. And that encoding may have to occur at 30 frames per second. You can begin to see why an MPEG-2 encoder may need to use custom digital circuits to compute the DCT quickly, using extensive parallelism and pipelining to obtain the necessary performance.

The DCT computation can be sped up further by precomputing the cosine terms of the inner term. Notice that the DCT computes two cosines based on the input values of u and x and the input values of v and y. However, because the DCT operates on 8x8 blocks, the variables u, v, x, and y only range in value from 0 to 7. Therefore, we can precompute the 64 possible cosine values needed for the DCT computation and store those values in an 8x8 table, which may be programmed into a ROM. We can then rewrite the DCT transform as follows:

$$F(u, v) = \frac{1}{4}C(u)C(v)\sum_{x=0}^{8}\sum_{y=0}^{8} D[x, y]\cos[x, u]\cos[y, v]$$

Using a ROM to store the precomputed cosine values speeds up the computation of the inner term of the DCT.

Quantization

Translating to the frequency domain using the DCT does not directly perform compression—we merely converted an input 8x8 block to an output 8x8 block. That output 8x8 block represents amplitudes of particular cosine wave frequencies. We can achieve compression by rounding those amplitudes, such that we use fewer bits to represent the amplitudes. For example, suppose we use 8 bits to represent the amplitude, meaning we can represent amplitudes ranging from 0 to 255. Suppose we only represent even amplitudes, meaning 2, 4, ..., 254. In that case, we can drop the lowest order bit, in the representation of the amplitude, resulting in only 7 bits. The decoder would merely append a 0 to the 7-bit number to obtain an 8-bit number again. For example, the 8-bit number 0000111**1** would be compressed to the 7-bit number 0000111 with an implicit **0** in the eighth bit. The decoder would expand that 7-bit number back to the 8-bit number 0000111**0**—notice that the decoded number is slightly different than the original, being 14 rather than the original 15 (an example of why MPEG-2 compression loses some image quality). We could take this rounding concept further, only representing amplitudes that are multiples of 4 (thus dropping the two lowest order bits, yielding a 6-bit representation), or are multiples of 8 (dropping the three lowest order bits, yielding a 5-bit representation). 00001**111** might be represented as 00001 with three implicit 0s, thus decoded back to 00001**000**. The decoded number of 8 is different from the original number 15 due to the rounding.

The rounding described above, achieved by dropping low order bits to achieve compression, is known as *quantization*. Notice the tradeoff—more rounding yields more compression, at the expense of accuracy. Fortunately, *humans don't notice such rounding in the high-frequency components of the picture*—our vision just isn't that precise. We also don't notice minor differences in the high-frequency components of sound—our hearing isn't that precise. Think of a very high-pitched sound, so high it could perhaps break glass. You probably couldn't tell the difference between two such high-pitched sounds of slightly different frequencies—they are both just high. Likewise, our eyes can't detect slight rounding of color values in a highly complex scene. So MPEG-2 applies quantization more aggressively on the DCT output block's high-frequency coefficients than on the low-frequency coefficients.

After quantization, the 64 values in the 8x8 block are treated as a list of 64 numbers. Those 64 numbers are then run-length encoded. **_Run-length encoding_** is a compression method that reduces consecutive occurrences of zeros by a number indicating the number of consecutive zeros rather than representing those zeros themselves. For example, consider wanting to represent the following 5 numbers: 0, 0, 0, 0, 24. If each value is 6 bits, the 5 numbers require 5*6 = 30 bits. On the other hand, we could just send a pair of numbers, the first indicating the number of leading zeros, the second indicating the nonzero number. So 0, 0, 0, 0, 24 would be encoded as (4, 24)—4 leading zeros, followed by the number 24. If each value is 6 bits, the run-length encoded version requires only 2*6=12 bits. Any sequence of numbers could similarly be replaced by a sequence of number pairs, each pair replacing a sequence of zeros and a number. The sequence 0, 0, 0, 0, 24, 0, 0, 8, 0, 0, 0, 0, 0, 0, 16 could thus be replaced by three pairs: (4, 24), (2, 8), (6, 16), reducing the number of bits from 15*6=90 down to 6*6=36 bits. Note that the number of zeros at the beginning of the sequence or in between nonzero numbers may be zero, and the last number may be zero. For example, the sequence 2, 0, 0, 63, 2, 0, 0, 0, 0, 0 could be encoded as (0,2), (2,63), (0,2), (4,0).

Run-length encoding achieves good compression only if there are many 0s in the sequence of numbers. Fortunately, the nature of the DCT leads to many 0 numbers (not all cosine frequencies are needed to approximate a signal region, so those frequencies will have 0 coefficients), especially after quantization (many coefficients are just small numbers, which become 0 during quanitization). Thus, applying run-length encoding after quantization leads to further compression.

▶ **EXAMPLE 6.27** Computing compression ratios involving quantization and run-length encoding

Continuing Example 6.26, assume that the 30-frame MPEG-2 sequence has the same frame sequence and average sizes as that example, but that each frame is further compressed by DCT conversion to the frequency domain followed by quantization and run-length encoding. Assume the DCT output block consists of 64 8-bit numbers, that quantization reduces the average number size to 5-bit numbers, and that run-length encoding reduces the resulting number sequence size to 30% of its size.

The compression ratio would be 8 Mbits * 30 / 5/8 * 0.30 *(2 * 8 Mbits + 8 * 2 Mbits + 20 * 1 Mbits) = 240 / 9.7 = 25:1. ◀

Huffman Coding

After run-length encoding, each block consists of a sequence of numbers. Some numbers will occur in that sequence more frequently than others. **_Huffman coding_** is a method of reducing the number of bits required to represent a set of values, by creating shorter encodings for the frequently occurring values, and longer encodings for the less frequent value.

Huffman coding, a form of encoding known as entropy encoding, is another powerful concept in digital data compression. Suppose you wish to represent an original sequence of 16 numbers 0, 3, 3, 31, 0, 3, 5, 8, 9, 7, 15, 14, 3, 0, 3, 0. Assuming 5 bits per number, a straightforward binary encoding would be: 00000 00011 00011 11111 00000 00011 00101, and so on, for a total of 16*5 = **80 bits**. We can reduce this total by first observing that there are only 9 unique symbols: 0, 3, 5, 7, 8, 9, 14, 15, and 31. We really only need 4 bits to uniquely identify each symbol. We could thus assign the nine unique symbols to 4-bit encodings using the following definitions: 0=0000, 3=0001, 5=0010, 7=0011, ..., 31=1001 (note that the encodings are no longer the binary number representations of the original numbers). Thus, the original sequence of numbers (0, 3, 3, 31, 0, 3, 5, ...) would be encoded as 0000 0001 0001 1001 0000 0001 0010 etc., for a total of 16*4 = **64 bits**. The key observation here is that we can encode numbers using any arbitrary unique bit patterns we desire, as long as the encoder and decoder are both aware of the encoding definitions.

We can take this definitions concept a step further, by using encodings of different lengths. Observing that 3 and 0 occur more frequently than the other numbers, we might give 3 and 0 shorter encodings. So we might create the following encoding definitions: 0=00, 3=10, 5=010, 7=0110, 8=0111, 9=1100, 14=1101, 15=1110, 31=1111. How these definitions were created is just beyond the scope of this discussion, though it's really not hard to learn. Notice that the encodings are such that the shorter encodings do not appear at the left of any of the longer encodings. For example, 00 does not appear at the left of any of the longer encodings, like 010, 0110, 0111, etc. This feature allows the decoder to know when it has reached the end of the code word—when the decoder has seen 00, it knows it has found an encoded 0 (because no other encoding starts with 00); when it sees 10, it knows it has found a 3 (because no other encoding starts with 10). But when the decoder sees 01, it must look at the next bit, and if it sees 010, it knows it has found a 5 (because no other encoding starts with 010). Using this variable-length encoding scheme, the original sequence (0, 3, 3, 31, 0, 3, 5, ...) would be encoded as 00 10 10 1111 00 10 010 etc. We have inserted the spaces just for readability; the actual encoding would just be 00101011110010010 etc. The total number of bits would be 4 * 2 (for the four 0s, encoded with the two bits 00) + 5 * 2 (for the five 3s, encoded with the two bits 10) + 1*3 (for the one 5, encoded with the three bits 010) plus 6*4 (for the six remaining numbers 31, 8, 9, 7, 15, and 14, each encoded as 4 bits), totaling **45 bits**—much reduced from the original 80 bits required by the straightforward binary encoding.

Huffman coding achieves good compression when some numbers occur much more frequently than other numbers in the sequence of numbers to be encoded. Fortunately, this is indeed the case after DCT, quantization, and run-length tasks are performed on a block of a frame. For example, there may be plenty of 0s, 1s, 2s, etc., and fewer occurrences of higher numbers.

▶ **EXAMPLE 6.28** Computing compression ratios involving Huffman coding

Continuing Example 6.27, assume that pairs of numbers after quantization and run-length encoding are Huffman coded, and that such encoding reduces the number of bits by 50%.

The compression ratio would thus be 240 / 0.50* 9.7 = 50:1. ◀

Summary

Summarizing MPEG-2 video encoding:

- The use of I-, P-, and B-frames achieves compression by not resending redundant information of successive frames, but rather just sending the differences.

- The DCT transforms 8x8 blocks of frames to the frequency domain, which doesn't achieve compression itself, but rather enables compression in the next steps.

- Quantization achieves further compression by reducing the number of bits needed to represent the DCT coefficients, through rounding.

- Run-length encoding achieves further compression by replacing sequences of zero coefficients by a number indicating the number of such zeros.

- Huffman coding achieves further compression by encoding frequently occurring coefficient numbers with shorter encodings than less frequently occurring coefficient numbers.

The sequence of steps is shown graphically in Figure 6.88.

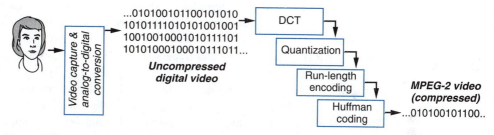

Figure 6.88 MPEG-2 video compression encoding overview.

Our example compression ratio calculations yielded a ratio of about 50:1. In fact, the compression ratio can be varied by varying each of the above steps. We can use fewer I-frames to achieve even higher compression at the cost of degraded video quality, or more I-frames for improved video quality at the cost of more bits. Likewise, we can vary the amount of quantization to trade off quality and compression ratio. Because a typical movie will have some slow-changing scenes and other rapidly changing scenes, and some complex colored frames and other simpler frames, the compression ratio for different parts of a video may actually vary. Notice the permeating presence of *tradeoffs* (primarily between quality and compression ratio) throughout MPEG-2 encoding.

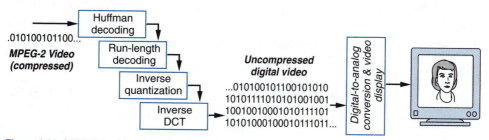

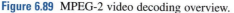

Figure 6.89 MPEG-2 video decoding overview.

An MPEG-2 decoder merely needs to apply the above steps in reverse, as illustrated in Figure 6.89, to convert an MPEG-2 stream of bits back into a series of pictures, or video.

Clearly, MPEG-2 encoding and decoding require a lot of computations performed at speeds fast enough to create smooth-looking, good-quality video. Custom digital circuits can help achieve those required speeds.

▶ 6.8 CHAPTER SUMMARY

In this chapter, we introduced (Section 6.1) the idea that sometimes we can improve a particular design criteria without hurting other criteria (optimization), but usually we can improve one criteria at the expense of another criteria (tradeoff). We described (Section 6.2) the problem of two-level size minimization, introducing K-maps as a visual method, and then describing automated heuristics for two-level as well as multilevel logic size minimization. We discussed (Section 6.3) methods for optimization and tradeoffs in designing sequential logic, including state minimization, state encoding, and Moore versus Mealy type FSMs. We highlighted (Section 6.4) several alternative methods for implementing some datapath components, including a faster adder using carry-lookahead, and a smaller multiplier using sequential multiplication. We described (Section 6.5) methods for RTL optimizations and tradeoffs, including the powerful concepts of pipelining and concurrency as means of achieving parallel execution—a key purpose of custom digital design. We also described the RTL methods of component allocation, operator binding, and operator scheduling. We briefly mentioned (Section 6.6) some higher-level methods, including the general idea of serial versus concurrent computation, and the selection of efficient algorithms. We also introduced some basic concepts of power reduction, including clock gating, and using low-power gates.

As you can see from this chapter, there are many methods for improving our designs. Yet, this chapter just scratched the surface of such methods. An entire multibillion-dollar-per-year industry exists that specializes in making automated tools for converting behavioral descriptions of desired system functionality into highly optimized circuit implementations—that industry is known as Electronic Design Automation (EDA) or as Computer-Aided Design (CAD). This chapter hopefully gave you enough exposure at least to understand the basic idea behind circuit optimization at various levels of design abstraction, ranging from the gate level up to the RTL level and beyond.

▶ 6.9 EXERCISES

SECTION 6.1: INTRODUCTION

6.1 Define the terms "optimization" and "tradeoff," and provide everyday examples of each.

SECTION 6.2: COMBINATIONAL LOGIC OPTIMIZATIONS AND TRADEOFFS

6.2 Perform two-level logic size optimization for the equation $F(a,b,c) = ab'c + abc + a'bc + abc'$ using (a) algebraic methods, (b) a K-map. Express the answers as sum-of-products.

6.3 Perform two-level logic size optimization for the equation F(a,b,c) = a + a'b'c + a'c using a K-map. Express the answer as sum-of-products.

6.4 Perform two-level logic size optimization for the equation `F(a,b,c,d)` = `a'bc'` + `abc'd'` + `abd` using a K-map. Express the answer as sum-of-products.

6.5 Perform two-level logic size optimization for the equation `F(a,b,c,d)` = `ab` + `a'b'd'` using a K-map. Express the answer as sum-of-products.

6.6 Perform two-level logic size optimization for the equation `F(a,b,c)` = `a'b'c` + `abc`, assuming that input combinations `a'bc` and `ab'c` can never occur (those two minterms represent don't cares). Express the answer as sum-of-products.

6.7 Perform two-level logic size optimization for the equation `F(a,b,c,d)` = `a'bc'd` + `ab'cd'`, assuming that a and b can never both be 1 at the same time, and that c and d can never both be 1 at the same time (i.e., there are don't cares).

6.8 Consider the equation `F(a,b,c)` = `a'c` + `ac` + `a'b`. Using a K-map, determine which of the following terms are implicants (but not necessarily prime implicants) of the equation: `a'b'c'`, `a'b'`, `a'bc`, `a'c`, `c`, `bc`, `a'bc'`, `a'b`.

6.9 Repeat the previous problem, but this time determine which of the terms are prime implicants of the function.

6.10 For the equation `F(a,b,c)` = `a'c` + `ac` + `a'b`, determine all prime implicants and all essential prime implicants of the function.

6.11 For the equation `F(a,b,c,d)` = `ab'c'` + `abc'd` + `abcd` + `a'bcd` + `a'bcd'`, determine all prime implicants, and all essential prime implicants.

6.12 For the previous problem, use the heuristic method of Table 6.1 to obtain a two-level size optimized equation expressed in sum-of-products form.

6.13 Use repeated application of the expand operation to heuristically minimize the equation `F(a,b,c)` = `a'b'c` + `a'bc` + `abc`. Try expanding each term for each variable. Give the minimized equation in sum-of-products form.

6.14 Use repeated application of the expand operation to heuristically minimize the equation `F(a,b,c,d,e)` = `abcde` + `abcde'` + `abcd'e'`. Try expanding each term for each variable.

6.15 Using algebraic methods, reduce the number of gate inputs for the following equation by creating a multilevel circuit: `F(a,b,c,d,e,f,g)` = `abcde` + `abcd'e'fg` + `abcd'e'f'g'`. Assume only AND, OR, and NOT gates will be used. Draw the circuit for the original equation and for the multilevel circuit, and clearly list the delay and number of gate inputs for each circuit.

SECTION 6.3: SEQUENTIAL LOGIC OPTIMIZATIONS AND TRADEOFFS

6.16 Reduce the number of states for the FSM in Figure 6.90 by eliminating redundant states by using an implication table.

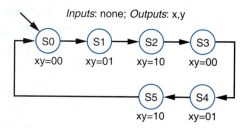

Inputs: none; *Outputs*: x,y

S0 xy=00 → S1 xy=01 → S2 xy=10 → S3 xy=00 → S4 xy=01 → S5 xy=10 →

Figure 6.90 FSM example.

6.17 Reduce the number of states for the FSM in Figure 6.91 by using an implication table.

6.18 Reduce the number of states for the FSM in Figure 6.92 by using an implication table.

6.19 Compare the logic size (as number of gate inputs) and the delay (as number of gate-delays) of a straightforward 2-bit binary encoding of the FSM in Figure 6.93 with a 3-bit output encoding and with a one-hot encoding of the same FSM.

6.20 Compare the logic size (as number of gate inputs) and the delay (as number of gate-delays) of a minimal bit width state encoding and an output encoding for laser-based distance measurer FSM shown in Figure 5.20.

6.21 Compare the logic size (as number of gate inputs) and the delay (as number of gate-delays) of a minimum binary encoding (if not possible, indicate why), output encoding, and one-hot encoding of the FSM in Figure 3.39.

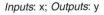

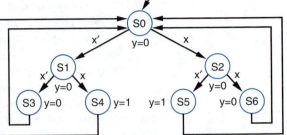

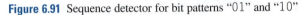

Figure 6.91 Sequence detector for bit patterns "01" and "10"

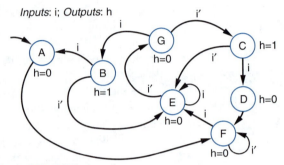

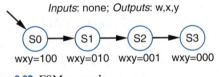

Figure 6.92 FSM example.

Figure 6.93 FSM example.

6.22 Convert the Moore FSM for the code detector circuit shown in Figure 3.46 to the nearest Mealy FSM equivalent.

6.23 Convert the following Moore FSM to the nearest Mealy FSM equivalent.

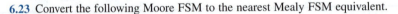

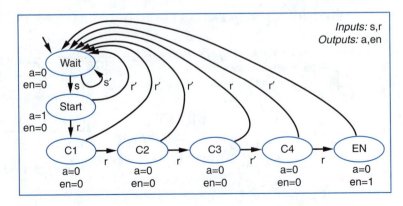

6.24 Convert the following Mealy FSM to the nearest Moore equivalent.

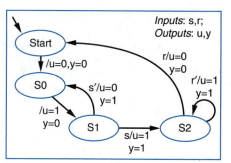

6.25 Convert the following Mealy FSM to the nearest Moore equivalent.

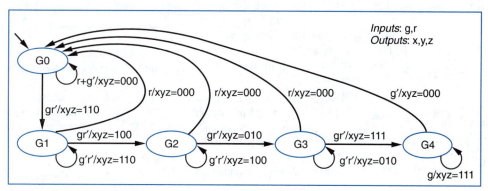

SECTION 6.4: DATAPATH COMPONENT TRADEOFFS

6.26 Trace the execution of the 4-bit carry-lookahead adder shown in Figure 6.59 when $a = 11$ and $b = 7$.

6.27 Trace the execution of the 4-bit carry-lookahead adder shown in Figure 6.59 when $a = 5$ and $b = 4$.

6.28 Trace the execution of the 16-bit carry-lookahead adder shown in Figure 6.59 when $a = 43690$ and $b = 21845$. Do not trace internal behavior of the individual 4-bit carry-lookahead adders.

6.29 Design a 64-bit hierarchical carry-lookahead adder using 4-bit carry-lookahead adders. What is the total delay through the 64-bit adder? How much faster is the carry-lookahead adder compared to a 64-bit carry-ripple adder (compute as slower time/faster time).

6.30 Design a 24-bit hierarchical carry-lookahead adder using 4-bit carry-lookahead adders.

6.31 Design a 16-bit carry-select adder using 4-bit ripple carry adders.

SECTION 6.5: RTL DESIGN OPTIMIZATIONS AND TRADEOFFS

6.32 The adder tree shown in Figure 6.94 is used to compute the sum of eight inputs on every clock cycle, where the sum is $S = R + T + U + V + W + X + Y + Z$.

(a) Design a pipelined version of the adder tree to maximize the speed at which we can operate our clock input clk.

(b) Create a timing diagram.

6.33 Assume the delay of an adder is 3 ns. How fast can we execute the adder tree shown in Figure 6.94 and how fast can we execute the pipelined adder tree designed in Exercise 6.32?

6.34 What are the latency and throughput of the pipelined adder tree you designed in Exercise 6.32?

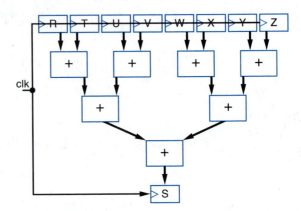

Figure 6.94 Adder tree used to compute the sum of eight inputs every clock cycle.

6.35 (a) Convert the following C-like code to a high-level state machine.

(b) Use the RTL design process shown in Table 5.1 to convert the high-level state machine for the C code to a controller and a datapath. Design the datapath to structure, but design the controller to the point of an FSM only.

(c) Redesign your datapath to allow for concurrency in which four multiplications and two additions can be performed concurrently.

```
Inputs: byte a[256], b[256]
Output: byte sum, byte c[256]
MULT:
int i=0;
int sum = 0;
while( i < 256 ) {
    c[i] = a[i] * b[i];
    sum = sum + c[i];
    i++;
}
```

6.36 Redesign the datapath and controller designed in Exercise 6.35 by allowing up to four concurrent additions and inserting pipeline registers to your datapath and updating the controller if necessary. Assuming an adder has a delay of 3 ns and a multiplier has a delay of 20 ns, how long will the circuit take to finish its computation?

6.37 (a) Convert the following C-like code to high-level state machine.

(b) Use the RTL design process shown in Table 5.1 to convert the high-level state machine for the C code to a controller and a datapath. Design the datapath to structure, but design the controller to the point of an FSM only.

(c) Redesign your datapath to allow for concurrency in which three comparisons, three additions, and three multiplications can be performed concurrently.

```
Inputs: byte a[256], byte b[256], byte cy
Output: byte sumx, byte sumy, byte c[256]
MULT_OR_ADD:
int i=0;
int sumx = 0;
int sumy = 0;
while( i < 256 ) {
  if( a[i] > 128 ) {
    c[i] = a[i] * b[i];
    sumx = sumx + c[i];
  } else {
    c[i] = a[i] * (b[i] + cy);
    sumy = sumy + c[i];
  }
  i++;

}
```

6.38 Redesign the datapath and controller designed in Exercise 6.37 by allowing up to nine concurrent additions and inserting pipeline registers to datapath and updating the controller if necessary. Assuming a comparator has a delay of 4 ns, an adder has a delay of 3 ns, and a multiplier has a delay of 20 ns, how long will the circuit take to finish its computation?

6.39 Given the high-level state machine in Figure 6.95, create two different designs: one design optimized for minimum circuit speed and one design optimized for minimum circuit size. Be

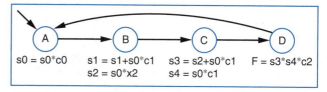

Figure 6.95 High-level state machine for Exercise 6.39.

sure to clearly indicate the component allocation, operator binding, and operator scheduling used to design the two circuits.

SECTION 6.6: MORE ON OPTIMIZATIONS AND TRADEOFFS

6.40 Trace through the execution of the binary search algorithm when searching for the number 86 in the following sorted list of 15 numbers: 1, 10, 25, 62, 74, 75, 80, 84, 85, 86, 87, 100, 106, 111, 121. How many comparisons were required to find the number using the binary search and how many comparisons would have been required using a linear search?

6.41 Trace through the execution of the binary search algorithm when searching for the number 99 in the following list of 15 numbers: 1, 10, 25, 62, 74, 75, 80, 84, 85, 87, 99, 100, 106, 111, 121. How many comparisons were required to look for the number using the binary search and how many comparisons are required using a linear search?

6.42 Trace through the execution of the binary search algorithm when searching for the number 121 in the list of numbers from the previous example. How many comparisons were required to find the number using the binary search and how many comparisons are required using a linear search?

6.43 Using the list of 15 numbers from Exercise 6.41, how many numbers could we find faster using a linear search algorithm compared with the binary search algorithm?

SECTION 6.7: POWER OPTIMIZATION

6.44 Given the logic gates shown in Figure 6.96, optimize the following circuit by reducing power consumption without increasing the circuit's delay.

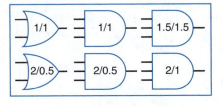

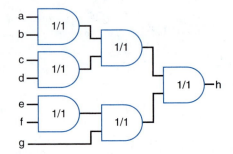

Figure 6.96 Logic gate library. 2/0.5 format means 2 ns delay/0.5 nw power.

6.45 Given the logic gates shown in Figure 6.96, optimize the following circuit by reducing power consumption without increasing the circuit's delay.

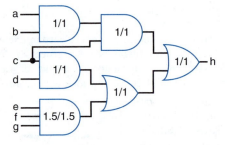

6.46 Given the logic gates shown in Figure 6.96, optimize the following circuit by reducing power consumption without increasing the circuit's delay.

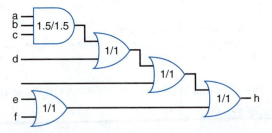

6.47 Given the logic gates shown in Figure 6.96, optimize the following circuit by reducing power consumption without increasing the circuit's delay.

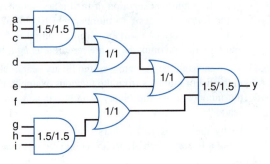

Smita has degrees in Electronics Engineering and in Computer Science, and has worked in the digital design field for nearly a decade. She spent a lot of time thinking about the choice of a college major. "What major should I invest my focus, energy, heart, and soul for what will be some of the most productive years of my life?" She chose engineering, for several reasons. "First, engineering is a career in itself—unlike some other majors, jobs specifically for engineering majors are out there. With engineering, I would learn the most valuable and universal of skills: problem solving. Second, engineers have many options, because engineers are highly valued for their problem solving skills by other professions, such as management consulting, marketing, and investment banking. And electrical and computer engineers can choose from a range of industries in which to work: telecommunications, image processing, medical devices, IC fabrication, and even banking. This was a phenomenal discovery for me!"

Smita continued her education by doing graduate studies in Computer Science, researching methods for automatically designing integrated circuits (IC) or chips— "a fascinating field because it involves a mix of hardware and software skills and knowledge. I continued in this profession after school and worked for a company that develops Computer-Aided Design (CAD) software used by hardware designers who work with a type of chip called an FPGA (Field Programmable Gate Array). FPGAs can be used for an amazing variety of applications all the way from high-speed telecommunication chips to low-speed and low-cost chips that go into electronic toys and games. Our software saves designers many months or even years of time. In fact, without our software, it would be absolutely impossible for people to design most chips even if they had a decade or more to do it."

Smita (shown mountain climbing above) loves her work. "My work is intellectually stimulating and I have an opportunity to innovate, create, and actually build something really useful." She also enjoys the people-aspect of her work. "I work in teams of dynamic people because most projects, hardware or software, are done in teams of 3–8 people these days. The people on my team are also my friends and it's a lot of fun to work with them."

In her decade of work so far, Smita has taken on some management responsibilities. "As manager of one of the four products that my company develops, I play a variety of different roles. I work with my team of 7 software developers to determine what features to build in the product and how best to build those features. I work with the marketing and sales team to understand what the customers need and how best to message and position our product. Finally, I work with other groups that are involved in releasing a product — technical publications, application engineering, and product engineering. The diversity of my job makes it very interesting.

Smita enjoys the respect that engineers receive. "As an engineer, I am highly respected by customers, partner companies, and by our marketing and sales organizations because I have a deep understanding of our products. I really know my stuff since I built it and I get recognized for it." And regarding the pay: "I get compensated very well for my skills." She also likes the lifestyle: "I get in to work around 10 a.m. and leave around 7 p.m. I don't have early morning meetings unlike the folks in marketing and sales, and I can work from home once a week or more often if I wish. This is also a great career for women - I can take time off and return to my job without much penalty when I have children. I can tailor my work hours as I need as my children are growing up. Lastly, I realize that I can move from engineering to other functions such as marketing and sales, but not the other way around! That's a great benefit of being an engineer - more options."

Smita recommends engineering and computer science students focus on certain things while in college.

"First, get a good understanding of both hardware and software. Systems are highly integrated today and there are very few companies that develop one without paying very close attention to the other. For instance, though I write software, I need to completely understand the hardware for which it will be used. My husband, on the other hand, designs telecommunication chips but works very closely with his software team, especially during the initial design stages when they decide what to implement in hardware versus software and how to design the hardware interface so that the software algorithms work efficiently."

"So, what do I mean by a good understanding of hardware and software? In software, I think it is most important to develop good software "habits". Treat your program like a well-landscaped garden—you want it beautiful and weed-free. Understand data structures well and know when one is more appropriate than the other. Organize your code, be disciplined, cross the Ts and dot the Is, document diligently, have your code reviewed by friends, and finally, don't be afraid to throw away code and rewrite it if you discover a better way."

"In hardware, understand the basics of logic design and then make sure you also understand the capacitive, inductive, and resistive properties of circuits since these play a big role in designing the high-speed circuits of today."

"Other than these hardware and software skills, become adept at math and analysis. Learn to frame problems and break them down until you can solve them. Be experimental and try different tools and methods. Have a hypothesis and then go about proving or disproving it. If you haven't already, you will soon discover that engineering is not only fun, but also provides you with many fulfilling career opportunities—so stick with it and make the most of it!"

7

Physical Implementation

▶ 7.1 INTRODUCTION

A digital circuit design that we've created but just drawn out, perhaps with pencil on paper or as a figure in this book, is just a drawing. Somehow, we must eventually implement that digital circuit design on a real physical device, so that the device can then be placed in some electronic product to carry out the desired function. Nowadays, such a device is usually some form of integrated circuit, or IC, also known as a computer chip, or just chip. In other words, looking at Figure 7.1, how do we get from (a), the seat belt warning light circuit we designed in Chapter 2, to (b), a physical implementation using an IC?

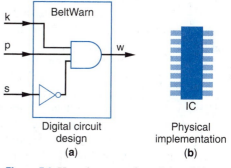

Figure 7.1 How do we get from (a) to (b)?

In this chapter, we will describe several popular physical implementation technologies for digital circuits.

▶ 7.2 MANUFACTURED IC TECHNOLOGIES

If we are willing to wait weeks or months for a physical implementation of our digital circuit design, and if we are willing to spend tens of thousands of dollars to millions of dollars for that physical implementation, then we might consider implementing our circuit using one of several technologies that involve the manufacture of a custom or semicustom IC.

Full-Custom Integrated Circuits

One physical implementation technology is known as a custom IC. A *full-custom IC* is a chip created specifically to implement the gates (actually, the transistors) of the desired digital circuit design (Figure 7.2). We digital designers wouldn't usually build full-custom ICs ourselves, but rather we would send our desired digital circuit design out to a group or company that specializes in transforming digital designs into custom ICs. Engineers, assisted by computer-aided design (CAD) tools, convert our desired digital circuit design into a circuit of transistors, and then decide where to place each transistor on the surface of the chip, how to orient each transistor (e.g., left to right, right to left, top to bottom, etc.), how big to make each transistor, etc. All that information about how the transistors should be layed out on a chip's surface is known as a *layout*. Then, the full-custom IC engineers send that layout information to a special factory that specializes in fabricating ICs, known as a fabrication plant, or *fab* for short. Fabricating an IC is often referred to as a silicon *spin*.

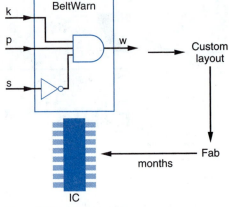

Figure 7.2 Full-custom IC design.

Fabricating an IC is an extremely costly, delicate, error-prone process, utilizing state-of-the-art photographic, laser, and chemical equipment that costs hundreds of millions of dollars. The fabrication process may take many weeks or even months, because transistors and wires are formed as layers on the surface of a chip, and each layer may take hours or even days to form through chemical processes.

Implementing a digital circuit on a full-custom IC is a complex and expensive task. Costs for setting up the fabrication of an IC, known as *nonrecurring engineering (NRE) costs*, can easily exceed many millions of dollars for a full-custom IC. Furthermore, that setup takes time, perhaps months, and that time may be costly to us too—the product for which we are fabricating the chip may be losing market share to a competing product already completed and being sold while we wait for our chip to be fabricated. Once we've set up the details needed for fabrication, the fabrication process itself is less expensive. But because we custom designed everything, the probability is high that we made a mistake somewhere in the transistors or wiring. Therefore, after fabricating a full-custom IC, we may find errors that necessitate refabricating the IC, known as a *respin*. Respinning may happen two or three times, each time requiring weeks or months, thus costing us even more. We ought to either be making millions of chips, or charging large amounts of money per chip, to earn back the large NRE costs.

According to one survey, only about 10% of 2002 digital circuits were implemented as custom ICs.

Needless to say, full-custom IC fabrication is not extremely common. Designers choose to implement a digital circuit on a full-custom IC when they know they will produce the chip in extremely high volumes, such as a mass-produced chip found inside calculators or wristwatches, or a mass-produced microprocessor chip like a Pentium. High volumes in the tens of millions or more are needed to offset the cost and time needed to produce a custom IC. Alternatively, designers may choose to implement a digital circuit on a custom IC if cost is not tightly constrained but maximum performance is a must, as might be the case in military or space applications.

Semicustom (Application-Specific) Integrated Circuits—ASICs

Because physical implementation on full-custom ICs is so costly and time-consuming, semicustom technologies evolved during the 1980s and 1990s that reduce the costs and the time of fabricating a chip, known as *Application-Specific Integrated Circuits*, or *ASICs*. Two popular ASIC technologies are gate array and standard cell.

Gate Arrays

The hardest part of custom IC design is designing and fabricating the transistors that will go onto the surface of the chip. Designing and fabricating the *wires* that connect those transistors is somewhat simpler. **Gate array** ASIC technology utilizes a chip whose transistors are predesigned to form rows (*arrays*) of logic *gates* on the chip, as shown in Figure 7.3. Gate arrays are sometimes referred to as **sea-of-gates**. To implement a desired digital circuit on a gate array chip, we merely need to create the *wires* that connect those gates. Creating the wires represents just the last steps of fabrication, and thus gate array technology eliminates much of the time and cost of fabricating a chip for a particular design. A gate array company predesigns and mass-produces the gate array chip, and then customizes some of those chips for each client's circuit—the chip is somewhat customized, hence the term *semicustom*, and the customization is for a particular circuit application, hence the term *application-specific*. Figure 7.3 illustrates how we might implement our seat belt warning light circuit (Figure 7.3(a)) using a gate array chip (Figure 7.3(b)). Figure 7.3(c) shows how we might map the desired 3-input AND gate to two 2-input gate array AND gates, and the inverter to one of the gate array inverters. The figure also shows how we might implement the desired wiring among the gate array's pins, the gate array AND gate, and the gate array inverter. The remaining gates and pins on the gate array chip would be unutilized. Fabricating these wires would result in the IC being customized to our seat belt application (Figure 7.3(d)).

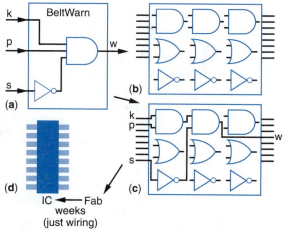

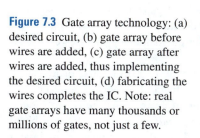

Figure 7.3 Gate array technology: (a) desired circuit, (b) gate array before wires are added, (c) gate array after wires are added, thus implementing the desired circuit, (d) fabricating the wires completes the IC. Note: real gate arrays have many thousands or millions of gates, not just a few.

We point out that the actual mapping of our desired digital circuit to a gate array would typically be carried out by an automated tool. Designers rarely, if ever, carry out that mapping manually, and in fact usually don't even see that mapping in any form—the mapping is all done by tools, resulting in huge data files that can be processed by other tools at a fab to control the fabrication process. We also point out that a typical gate array chip may hold *many thousands or millions of gates*; the gate array shown in Figure 7.3, having less than ten gates, is trivially small and is for illustration purposes only—*gate arrays with only 10 gates do not exist*. Furthermore, we would typically not use gate arrays unless our design contained thousands of gates or more. For designs with only a few gates, we would instead use logic ICs; see Section 7.4.

Gate array technology is far cheaper than full-custom IC technology, costing perhaps tens of thousands to hundreds of thousands of dollars for set up (NRE costs), rather than many millions of dollars. Furthermore, the fabrication time is typically just several weeks or perhaps just a month or two, rather than many months. Respins are also less common. The drawback is that the implementation is less optimized, having slower performance, bigger size, and more power consumption than is possible using full-custom IC technology. For example, notice that the gate array implementation in Figure 7.3 utilizes an extra level of logic than the original circuit, has long wires, and has wasted area due to unused gates and pins. Nevertheless, those drawbacks are often outweighed by the savings in cost and fabrication time compared to custom IC technology.

► **EXAMPLE 7.1**   Implementing a half-adder on a gate array

Let's implement a half-adder component on the gate array chip of Figure 7.3. Recall that the equations for a half-adder are: co = ab, and s = a'b + ab'. Thus, we need one AND gate for co, and two inverters, two AND gates, and one OR gate for s. The gate array chip in Figure 7.3 has three AND gates, three OR gates, and three inverters, so the chip has enough gates to implement our desired circuit. We can implement the half-adder circuit on the gate array chip as shown in Figure 7.4. ◄

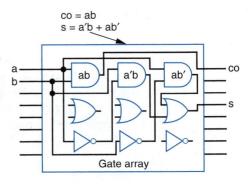

Figure 7.4 Half-adder on a gate array.

Standard Cells

Standard cell technology is another ASIC technology that reduces physical implementation costs and design time compared to full-custom IC technology. *Standard cell* ASIC technology uses libraries of pre-layed-out gates or small pieces of logic, known as *cells*, that a designer must instantiate and connect with wires to implement a digital circuit. In contrast, a gate array's gates are all preinstantiated—the designer merely connects those gates with wires.

A cell might be a 2-input AND gate, or a 2x1 mux, or a common combination of gates like two 2-input AND gates connected to an OR gate connected to an inverter (known as an AND-OR-INVERT, or AOI, cell). All cells are typically the same *standard* height (hence the term *standard cells*), so that cells can be placed in standard-height rows on a chip. A standard cell company predesigns the layout for each cell. We can convert our seat belt warning light digital circuit (Figure 7.5(a)) to a physical implementation by choosing the appropriate cells from a cell library (Figure 7.5(b)), instantiating and wiring those cells (Figure 7.5(c)), and then fabricating an IC (Figure 7.5(d)).

Like with gate arrays, designers themselves don't typically choose standard cells and map their circuits onto those cells. Rather, automated tools convert the desired digital circuits onto standard cells and output results in large data files that can be processed by fabs to control the fabrication process. We also point out that a typical cell library might contain hundreds or thousands of cells; the cell library shown in Figure 7.5(b), having just five cells, is *trivially small and for illustrative purposes only*. Furthermore, we would typically not use standard cells unless our design required thousands of cells or more.

Compared to gate array technology, standard cell technology can be better optimized, since we decide on which cells to include, and where to place them in each row. Comparing Figure 7.5(c) and Figure 7.3(c) illustrates that standard cell technology's flexibility of choosing and placing cells results in a more compact design, with fewer gates and fewer wires, than gate array technology. However, standard cell technology may take somewhat longer to design than gate arrays, because the transistors cannot be prefabricated.

Compared to full-custom IC technology, standard cell is less

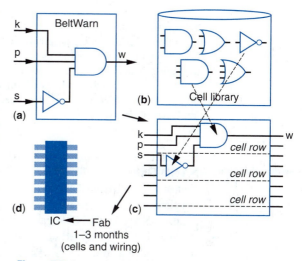

Figure 7.5 Standard cell technology: (a) desired circuit, (b) cell library, (c) standard cell layout, (d) fabricating the transistors and wires creates the IC.

optimized because the cells are restricted in their size and variety, and their placement is restricted to predetermined rows. But standard cell requires less NRE and time, because we need not perform any of the transistor-level design or layout, as those were done beforehand by the standard cell company. Furthermore, respins, though still common, are less frequent. Compared to gate array technology, standard cell is more optimized, but more expensive and takes more time.

Cell Array and Structured ASICs

Another technology that has become popular is a cross between gate array and standard cell technologies, known as cell array. In a *cell array*, standard cells are preplaced on the IC (just like gates were preplaced in a gate array), with only the wiring left to be completed to create a particular circuit. Cell arrays are sometimes referred to as *sea-of-cells*. The difference between a gate array and a cell array is just the complexity of the cell— cell array cells can be more complex than just logic gates. Of course, gate array makers also use more complex items than just gates, and cell arrays include cells that are just gates, so the terms somewhat blur. Generally, the term *structured ASICs* has become popular in describing ASICs whose gates or cells have been preplaced, meaning that only that wiring needs to be completed to implement a circuit on the IC (and the term "gate array" seems to be fading).

▶ **EXAMPLE 7.2**   Implementing a half-adder using standard cells

Using the standard cell library in Figure 7.5, let's implement a half-adder on a standard cell ASIC. Recall that the equations for a half-adder are: $co = ab$, and $s = a'b + ab'$. Thus, we'll use two inverter cells, three two-input AND cells, and a two-input OR cell from the library. We implement the half-adder using cells as shown in Figure 7.6, assuming each cell row can hold at most three cells.

Notice that our standard cell implementation places the cells such that wiring is minimized, whereas the gate array implementation of Figure 7.4 required us to run the wires to the pre-existing gate locations, resulting in longer wires. Thus, the standard cell implementation may be faster than the gate array implementation, since shorter wires typically have shorter delay. ◂

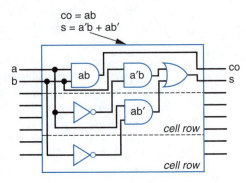

Figure 7.6 Half-adder using standard cells.

Implementing Circuits Using Only NAND Gates

You may recall from Chapter 2 that CMOS transistors lend themselves more readily to creating NAND and NOR gates rather than AND and OR. The stated underlying reason was that pMOS transistors conduct 1s well but not 0s, while nMOS transistors conduct 0s well but not 1s. In any case, gate arrays typically contain plenty of NAND and/or NOR gates, rather than AND and OR gates. And standard cell designs will also be more efficient if implemented using NAND or NOR gates rather than AND and OR. Furthermore, creating a gate array is much easier using just one type of gate, like just NANDs, or just NORs, rather than having to decide how many AND gates, OR gates, and NOT gates to pre-instantiate in the arrays. Given the ready availability of NAND or NOR gates in CMOS ASIC technologies, we therefore want a method for converting AND/OR circuits to NAND circuits or to NOR circuits.

Fortunately, converting any AND/OR circuit to a NAND-only circuit is possible because NAND is a universal gate, as was mentioned in Section 2.8. A ***universal gate*** is a logic gate type that can implement any Boolean function using gates of that one type only. One way to understand NAND's universality is to recognize that we can implement a NOT gate, an AND gate, and an OR gate by substituting each by an equivalent circuit of NAND gates. Therefore any circuit of NOT, AND, and OR gates can be implemented using NAND gates only.

To implement a NOT gate using NAND gates, we can substitute the NOT gate by a two-input NAND gate with its two inputs tied together, as shown in Figure 7.7. The truth table in the figure shows that the NAND gate with its inputs tied together acts the same as an inverter. When the input x is 0, both inputs of the NAND gate are 0, causing the NAND gate to output 1. When the input x is 1, both inputs of the NAND gate are 1, causing the NAND gate to output 0.

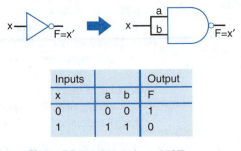

Inputs			Output
x	a	b	F
0	0	0	1
1	1	1	0

Figure 7.7 Implementing a NOT gate using a NAND gate

Alternatively, we could simply connect x to one NAND input, and a 1 to the other NAND input. Then if x is 0, the NAND outputs 1, and if x is 1, the NAND outputs 0, achieving the desired NOT gate behavior.

To implement an AND gate using NAND gates, we can substitute the AND gate by a NAND gate followed by a NOT gate (which we know to be a two-input NAND gate with its inputs tied together), as shown in Figure 7.8. This works because given inputs a, b, the first NAND computes (ab)', and then the NOT gate computes (ab)'' = ab, which is AND.

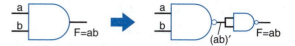

Figure 7.8 Implementing an AND gate using NAND gates.

To implement an OR gate using NAND gates, we can substitute the OR gate by a NAND gate with each input inverted, as shown in Figure 7.9. This works because given inputs a, b, the circuit of NAND gates in Figure 7.9 computes (a'b')', which by DeMorgan's Law is a'' + b'', which simplifies to a + b — which is OR.

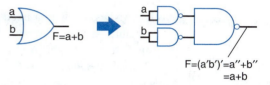

$$F=(a'b')'=a''+b''$$
$$=a+b$$

Figure 7.9 Implementing an OR gate using NAND gates.

When we replace a circuit originally consisting of AND/OR/NOT gates by a circuit with NAND gates only using the above substitutions, we may find that certain signals get double-inverted—the signal feeds into an inverter and then immediately feeds into another inverter. Double-inverting a signal yields the original signal, so double inversions can be replaced by just a wire, as shown in Figure 7.10. Such elimination reduces the transistors needed without changing the circuit's function.

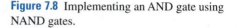

Figure 7.10 Double inversions can be eliminated.

► **EXAMPLE 7.3** Implementing a half-adder's sum circuit using NAND gates

Figure 7.11(a) shows the sum circuit for a half-adder (see Section 4.3), using AND, OR, and NOT gates. We can implement that circuit using NAND gates only by substituting each gate with an equivalent NAND circuit, as shown in Figure 7.11(b). After the substitutions, we note that there are two signals that are double-inverted. Eliminating the double inversions results in the circuit shown in Figure 7.11(c).

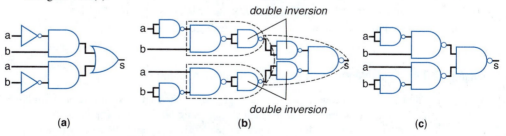

(a)   **(b)**   **(c)**

Figure 7.11 Implementing a half-adder's sum circuit using NAND gates only: (a) original AND/OR/NOT circuit, (b) circuit obtained after substituting equivalent NAND circuits for each gate, (c) circuit after eliminating double inversions.

When converting AND/OR/NOT circuits by hand to NAND circuits, some people find it easier to simply draw inversion bubbles rather than the NAND-based inverters, as shown in Figure 7.12. Then, double inversion bubbles on a signal cancel. Any remaining isolated inversion bubbles become a NAND-based NOT gate. Thus, the circuit in Figure 7.12 would end up identical to the circuit in Figure 7.11(c).

If NAND gates with a fixed number of inputs are available, such as 2-input NAND gates only, we can first modify the AND/OR circuit to use only 2-input AND/OR gates (by composing larger gates from smaller ones—see Section 5.8), before converting to NAND gates.

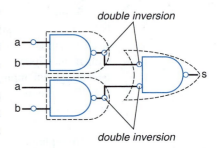

Figure 7.12 Drawing inverters as inversion bubbles during conversion to NAND.

Implementing Circuits Using NOR Gates

Converting AND/OR/NOT circuits to NOR gate circuits is similar to converting to NAND circuits, as a NOR gate is also a universal gate. The process of transforming a circuit into NOR gates replaced each AND, OR, and NOT gate with equivalent NOR-based circuits, as shown in Figure 7.13. We can replace a NOT gate with a two-input NOR gate with the inputs tied together (or alternatively, by a two-input NOR

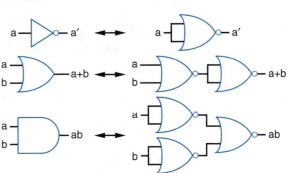

Figure 7.13 NOR gate equivalencies.

gate with one input tied to 0). We can replace an OR gate with a NOR gate followed by an inverter, yielding (a+b)'' = a+b. We can substitute an AND gate with a NOR gate having inverted inputs, yielding (a'+b')' = a''*b'' = ab (notice the use of DeMorgan's Law).

▶ **EXAMPLE 7.4** Implementing a half-adder's sum circuit using NOR gates

Earlier, we demonstrated how to represent the half-adder's sum output with NAND gates; we can just as easily implement the sum output using NOR gates. The half-adder's sum circuit is shown again in Figure 7.14(a). We replace each NOT, AND, and OR gate by its equivalent NOR circuit in Figure 7.14(b), using inversion bubbles instead of NOR-based NOT gates for convenience. We eliminate double inversions, and replace stand-alone inversion bubbles by NOR-based NOT gates, as shown in Figure 7.14(c).

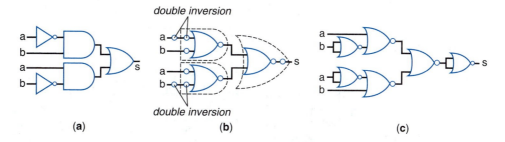

Figure 7.14 Implementing an AND/OR/NOT circuit using NORs only: (a) original circuit, (b) circuit obtained by substituting AND/OR/NOT gates by equivalent NOR circuits, using inversion bubbles for ease of drawing, (c) final circuit after eliminating double inversions and replacing standalone inversion bubbles by NOR-based NOT gates.

The half-adder's sum circuit was implemented with fewer NAND gates than NOR gates. Depending on the original circuit, the reverse could be true. We saw that NAND gates were well-suited for circuits in the sum-of-products form. NOR gates are best used when a circuit is in product-of-sums form (a level of OR gates feeding into a single AND gate).

Gate array and standard cell libraries typically include additional components, beyond just NAND or NOR gates, that have efficient CMOS implementations. For example, a popular such component is known as AND-OR-INVERT, or *AOI* for short. Such a component has two 2-input AND gates (thus four inputs total), feeding into a 2-input NOR gate. That circuit can be efficiently designed using CMOS transistors. Thus, we would want to utilize AOI components, and other similarly compact available components in a library, as much as possible.

The task of converting a general logic circuit to a circuit using only components from a particular technology's library (e.g., a particular gate array library or standard cell library) is known as *technology mapping*. The task of determining where to place those components on a chip is known as *placement*, and the task of connecting those components by wires is known as *routing*. All three tasks, collectively known as *physical design*, are typically done by automated tools today.

▶ **EXAMPLE 7.5**   Implementing the seat belt warning light on a NOR-based gate array

Implement the *BeltWarn* circuit of Figure 7.15(a) using the NOR-based gate array of Figure 7.15(a). Noticing that the gate array has only 2-input NOR gates, we first convert the *BeltWarn* circuit to use AND/OR gates with 2 inputs only, as shown in Figure 7.15(b). We then convert the AND/OR circuit to the NOR-only circuit in Figure 7.15(c), using the equivalencies in Figure 7.13, and using inversion bubbles rather than NOR-based inverters. We then see a double inversion on the wire from input S, so we eliminate those two inversions. Note that we do not eliminate the double inversion between points 3 and 4 in Figure 7.15(c), because the first inversion is part of a NOR gate—eliminating that first inversion would convert the NOR gate to an OR, defeating our goal of having NOR gates only. After converting remaining stand-alone inversions to NOR-based inverters, we map the circuit to the gate array's 2-input NOR gates as in Figure 7.15(d)—we numbered the NOR gates of Figure 7.15(c) and (d) to show the correspondence between the two circuits.

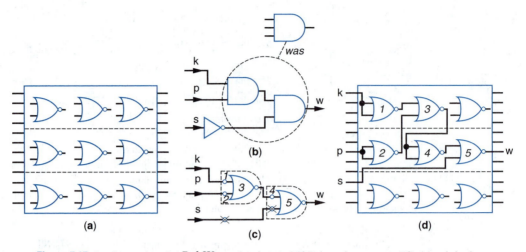

Figure 7.15 Implementing the *BeltWarn* circuit on a NOR-based gate array IC: (a) original gate array, (b) - (c) converting the desired circuit to two-input NOR gates only, (d) final gate array with wires. ◀

▶ 7.3 PROGRAMMABLE IC TECHNOLOGY—FPGA

Manufactured IC technologies require at least a few weeks, and usually more like several months, to convert a desired digital circuit design into a physical IC. What if we are developing a circuit that we want to implement *today*? In that case, we can utilize one of several programmable IC technologies. In a ***programmable IC technology***, we implement a desired circuit simply by writing a particular sequence of bits into a memory (or number of memories) contained in the IC. Using a programmable IC technology has the drawback of worse performance, size, and power compared to custom or semicustom IC technologies. But we get our implementation today, and the benefits of that fact may outweigh the drawbacks.

The most popular form of programmable IC technology is known as a ***Field-Programmable Gate Array***, or ***FPGA***. An FPGA company prefabricates an FPGA chip, meaning that the chip contains all the transistors and all wires that the chip will ever have. We buy those FPGA chips, and then *program* the chips to implement our desired circuit. To *program* in this context means simply to download a series of bits into the chip's memories—not to be confused with writing high-level software programs like C or C++ code. Such programming

Figure 7.16 FPGA chips.

occurs in the *field*, meaning in our lab, or office, or home, as opposed to in a fabrication plant. Hence the words "*field-programmable*" in the FPGA name. Furthermore, programming typically takes only seconds, or perhaps minutes at most. Figure 7.16 shows some FPGA chips. The chip at the top, with its front and back shown, measures about 3/4 inch on each side. The chip on the bottom measures just over 1 inch on each side.

Field-programmable gate arrays (FPGAs) have no "gate arrays" inside them—the name is there due to historical reasons.

The words "*gate array*" are there in the name because, when FPGAs first became popular in the mid-1980s, they were marketed as an alternative to gate array technology, which was very popular at that time. Thus, an FPGA was a semicustom IC (nearly synomous with gate array at that time) that could be programmed in the field instead of at a fabrication plant. However, be forewarned that the internal design of an FPGA chip looks nothing like a gate array—the naming is somewhat unfortunate.

The two basic types of components inside an FPGA are lookup tables and switch matrices. Those components are replicated hundreds of times in regular patterns inside an FPGA. We now describe each type of component.

Lookup Tables

A basic idea underlying FPGAs is that *a memory can implement combinational logic*. More specifically, a 1-bit wide memory with N address lines, and hence 2^N words, configured to read the word corresponding to the present address, can implement any Boolean combinational function of N variables.

Recall that a memory configured to be read will output the contents of the word corresponding to the present address at the memory's address lines. So if a 4x1 memory's address lines a1a0 are 00, the memory will output the contents of word 0. If the address lines are 01, the memory outputs the contents of word 1. Likewise, 10 reads word 2, and 11 reads word 3.

The key idea underlying FPGAs is that a memory with N-address lines can implement any combinational function with N-inputs.

Implementing a Boolean function with a memory can therefore be done simply by connecting the function's inputs to the memory address lines, and storing a 0 or 1 in each memory word to match the desired function output for each combination of input values. For example, consider the function F(x,y) = x'y' + xy. The truth table for the function is shown in Figure 7.17(a). To implement the example function, we can connect x and y to a 4x1 memory's address lines a1 and a0, respectively, and based on the truth table, we store a 1 in word 0, a 0 in word 1, a 0 in word 2, and a 1 in word 3—in other words, we store the truth table outputs in the memory. The memory then implements the desired function, as shown in Figure 7.17(b). For example, when xy=00, we want the output to be 1. Figure 7.17(c) shows that when xy=00, the memory's address lines will be 00, and thus the memory will output the contents of word 0, which is the value 1, as desired.

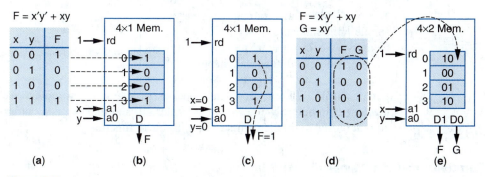
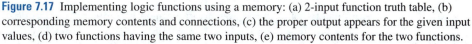

Figure 7.17 Implementing logic functions using a memory: (a) 2-input function truth table, (b) corresponding memory contents and connections, (c) the proper output appears for the given input values, (d) two functions having the same two inputs, (e) memory contents for the two functions.

A memory with M bits per word, rather than just 1 bit per word, can implement M functions, as long as all those M functions have the same inputs. For example, consider the two functions F(x,y) = x'y' + xy and G(x,y) = xy'. The truth table for these two functions is shown in Figure 7.17(d). A 4x2 memory, which has 2 bits per word, can implement those two functions, as shown in Figure 7.17(e).

A memory used to implement a combinational circuit is known (in FPGA terminology) as a ***lookup table***. When used as a lookup table, we typically refer to the memory by the number of *inputs* (address lines) and the number of outputs (bits per word), rather than by the number of *words* and the number of outputs. For example, we would refer to an 8x2 memory being used as a lookup table as a "3-input 2-output lookup table," rather than as an 8x2 lookup table

From this point forward, we'll assume the memory is configured for read, and thus we won't show the read line set to 1.

▶ **EXAMPLE 7.6** Implementing the seat belt warning light with a lookup table

Use a lookup table to implement the seat belt warning light circuit from Figure 7.1, whose circuit appears in Figure 7.18(a) and whose equation is:

w = kps'

We generate the truth table for the function, as shown in Figure 7.18(b). Because the circuit has three inputs, we know we'll need a 3-input 1-output lookup table (memory). We connect the inputs to the memory's address lines, and store the truth table in the memory, as shown in Figure 7.18(c), thus implementing the desired function. If the 3-input 1-output memory is an IC, then we are done implementing our design, and can insert the IC into the electronic system with which the IC should interact. ◀

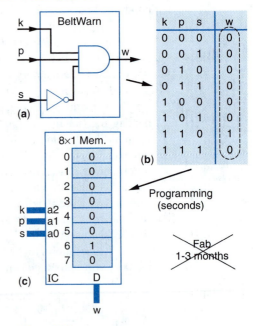

Figure 7.18 Lookup table implementation.

You've just seen an example of a very simple programmable IC technology—a memory. We can use a memory chip with N address lines and hence 2^N words, and with M bits per word, to implement M different Boolean functions of the same N inputs. We can purchase a memory chip before we need it for our design, and then we can "program" the memory chip in our lab to implement a desired Boolean function.

Partitioning a Circuit among Lookup Tables

Unfortunately, using a memory to implement a Boolean function does not work well for functions with numerous inputs. For example, while a 4-input function would need only a

16-word memory, a 16-input function would require a 64 Kword memory; a 32-input function would require a 4-billion-word memory. The needed memory size grows the same as the size of the function's truth table, which we know grows as 2^N, where N is the number of function inputs. In short, a truth table is *not* an efficient Boolean function representation for functions with numerous inputs, and thus a lookup table is not an efficient implementation for functions with numerous inputs.

Partitioning a function's circuit among multiple lookup tables can yield more efficient implementations for larger functions. Consider the extended seat belt warning circuit from Example 2.8. Let's extend the circuit even more by adding a third "diagnostic" input called d that forces the warning light to turn on when d=1—perhaps a mechanic investigating a faulty warning light might want to force the warning light on to isolate whether the light has blown out or to help determine if a seat belt sensor has failed. The extended circuit is shown in Figure 7.19(a). That circuit can't be mapped to a 3-input 1-output lookup table because the circuit has 5 inputs, but the circuit could be mapped onto a 5-input 1-output lookup table. Alternatively, we could implement the circuit by using a 3-input 1-output lookup table connected to another 3-input 1-output lookup table, as shown in Figure 7.19(c). We do so by partitioning the original circuit into two groups, such that the first group has 3 inputs and 1 output, and the second group has 3 inputs and 1 output, as circled in Figure 7.19(b). The first group's output, which we've labeled as x, has the equation x = kps'. The second group's output has the equation w = x + t + d. We would program the lookup tables to implement these functions, as shown in Figure 7.19(c), thus implementing the desired circuit using two lookup tables.

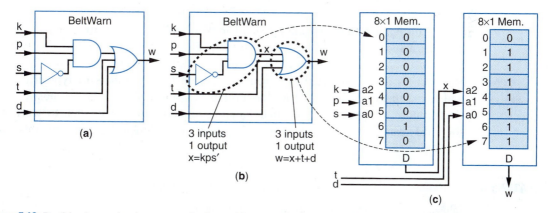

Figure 7.19 Partitioning a circuit onto two lookup tables: (a) desired circuit, (b) circuit partitioned into groups with at most 3 inputs and 1 output, (c) groups mapped to two 3-input 1-output lookup tables.

Notice that the implementation with two lookup tables has a total of 8 + 8 = 16 words, compared to 32 words that would have been present with a 5-input lookup table. Thus, partitioning a circuit among small lookup tables can result in better efficiency than using one larger lookup table.

This efficiency can be seen even more dramatically for examples with more inputs. For example, the function F = abc + def + ghi, shown in Figure 7.20(a), has 9 inputs. Implementing the function on a single lookup table would require a table with $2^9 = 512$ words. However, we can partition the circuit into groups such that each group has 3 inputs and 1 output—the first group would compute `abc`, the second `def`, the third `ghi`, and the fourth would OR the outputs of the first three groups to generate the output `F`. Each group could be implemented using a 3-input 1-output lookup table, meaning 8x1 memories. The resulting implementation would have four such lookup tables, as shown in Figure 7.20(b). The total words for that four-table implementation would be a mere $8 + 8 + 8 + 8 = 32$ words—far less than the 512 words required for a single 9-input lookup table. Figure 7.20(c) compares the relative sizes of a 512-word and four 8-word memories. Notice the tremendous reduction in size.

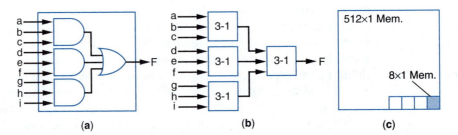

(a)   **(b)**   **(c)**

Figure 7.20 Dividing a many-input circuit among smaller lookup tables reduces total lookup table size: (a) 9-input circuit, (b) circuit mapped to 3-input 1-output lookup tables, (c) size savings compared to 9-input 1-output lookup table.

Partitioning a function among small lookup tables is more efficient than implementing a function on one large lookup table. But what is a "small" lookup table—a table with 2 inputs, 3 inputs, 4 inputs, 7 inputs, or maybe even 10 inputs? Researchers have conducted numerous studies on large numbers of typical circuits, and found that 3-input or 4-input lookup tables seem to work best for most circuits. Furthermore, researchers found that 2-output lookup tables also seem to work well for most examples. Thus, we'll use 3-input 2-output lookup tables from this point forward.

▶ **EXAMPLE 7.7** Partitioning a circuit among 3-input 2-output lookup tables

Implement the circuit shown in Figure 7.21(a) using 3-input 2-output lookup tables. We begin by trying to partition the circuit into groups such that each group has at most 3 inputs and 2 outputs. However, the 4-input AND gate prevents us from successfully performing such partitioning, because whatever gate that group is in will have at least four inputs. To remedy this problem, we decompose that gate into two smaller gates, while maintaining the same functionality, as shown in Figure 7.21(b). We can then partition the circuit into two groups, each with 3 inputs and 1 output, as shown in the figure—we've numbered the inputs to each group to make clear that each group has three inputs. We then map those groups onto two 3-input 2-output lookup tables as shown in Figure 7.21(c). Notice that the first lookup table's `D1` output is unused, and the second table's `D0` output is unused. The first table's `D0` column implements `t=abc`. The second table's `D1` column implements `F = td + e`.

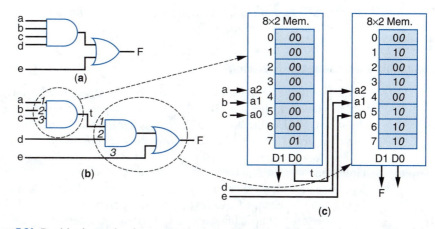

Figure 7.21 Partitioning a circuit onto two lookup tables: (a) original circuit, (b) transformed circuit that breaks the 4-input AND gate into two smaller gates, and then that shows the 3-input 1-output groupings, (c) mapping of each group to a lookup table, with the group's function converted to programmed bits in the lookup table. Italicized bits are unused. ◀

In the previous example, notice that we did not use one of the columns in the first lookup table, and did not use one of the columns in the second lookup table either. Using lookup tables sometimes results in unused memory cells. Using lookup tables also sometimes results in unused lookup table words, as illustrated in the following example.

▶ **EXAMPLE 7.8** Mapping a 2x4 decoder to 3-input 2-output lookup tables

Let's implement a 2x4 decoder, without enable, using 3-input 2-output lookup tables. A 2x4 decoder has two inputs, i1 and i0, and four outputs, d0, d1, d2, and d3. A mapping is shown in Figure 7.22. The equations for each output are d0 = i1'i0', d1=i1'i0, d2=i1i0', and d3=i1i0. The lookup tables implement those equations using the top halves of the tables' words; the bottom halves are unused.

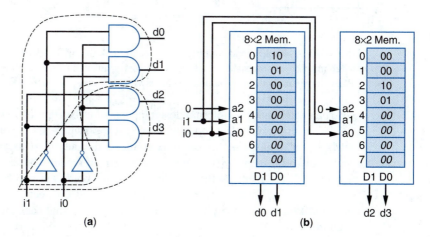

Figure 7.22 Mapping a 2x4 decoder to two 3-input 2-output lookup tables: (a) desired circuit, (b) mapping to two lookup tables. Italicized bits are unused. ◀

An FPGA may come with tens, hundreds, or even thousands of lookup tables, and thus can implement large amounts of combinational logic.

Programmable Interconnects (Switch Matrices)

In the previous examples, we have been creating customized connections between lookup tables. However, the point of FPGAs is that the entire chip is prefabricated—including the wires. FPGAs therefore come with *programmable interconnects*, sometimes called *switch matrices*, which allow us to *program* the connections among lookup tables. Figure 7.23 shows a simple FPGA chip having six inputs (*P0–P5*), two 3-input 2-output lookup tables, one 4-input 2-output switch matrix, and four outputs (*P6–P9*). All three of the left lookup table's inputs come from the external inputs *P1*, *P2*, and *P3*—that lookup table's inputs can't be changed. However, two of the right lookup table's inputs may come from either the left lookup table's outputs, or from the external inputs *P4* and *P5*. The switch matrix determines which of those connections will be made.

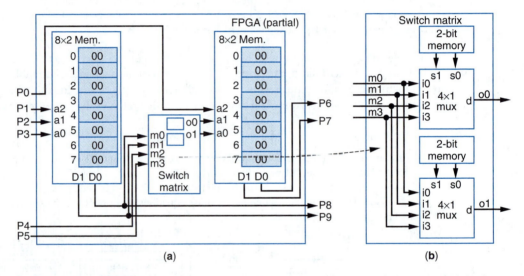

Figure 7.23 A simple FPGA architecture: (a) an FPGA that includes a switch matrix, and (b) the switch matrix's internals showing two 4x1 muxes controlled by two 2-bit registers. Note: real FPGAs have hundreds of lookup tables and switch matrices, not just a few. ◀

The switch matrix's internal design appears on the right of Figure 7.23. It consists of two 4x1 multiplexers. The top mux connects the switch matrix output *o0* to one of the matrix's four inputs. The bottom mux connects the output *o1* to one of the matrix's four inputs. A two-bit memory (which is actually a 2-bit register, but called a memory for consistency with the memory inside a lookup table) holds the two bits that set each mux's two select lines. Thus, we can program the desired connections simply by writing the appropriate bits into those two 2-bit memories. Notice that each switch matrix output can be configured independently of the other. In fact, we could even make the same input appear at both outputs, though that's probably not useful in this FPGA design.

We'll illustrate the use of the switch matrix with an example.

► **EXAMPLE 7.9**   A 2x4 decoder on an FPGA with a switch matrix

We repeat Example 7.8 here using the FPGA shown in Figure 7.23(a). We can easily get the proper inputs to the first lookup table the same as in Example 7.8, by connecting 0, external input $i1$, and external input $i0$ to the appropriate FPGA inputs, as shown in Figure 7.24(a). To get the proper inputs to the second lookup table, we first connect external input $i1$ and external input $i0$ to the FPGA inputs that feed into the switch matrix. We then configure the switch matrix such that switch matrix input $m2$ passes through to switch matrix output $o0$, which means that external input $i1$ passes through to switch matrix output $o0$. We achieve that configuration by programming 10 into the top 2-bit register in the switch matrix, as shown in Figure 7.24(b). Likewise, we configure the switch matrix such that switch matrix input $m3$ passes through to switch matrix output $o1$, meaning external input $i0$ passes through to switch matrix output $o1$. We achieve that configuration by programming 11 into the bottom 2-bit register in the switch matrix. Because the switch matrix outputs connect to the right lookup table's inputs, we've successfully connected external inputs $i1$ and $i0$ to the second lookup table's inputs, as desired. We program the two lookup tables as we did in Example 7.8. Thus, external outputs $d0$–$d3$ can be found at the FPGA external pins, as shown in Figure 7.24(a).

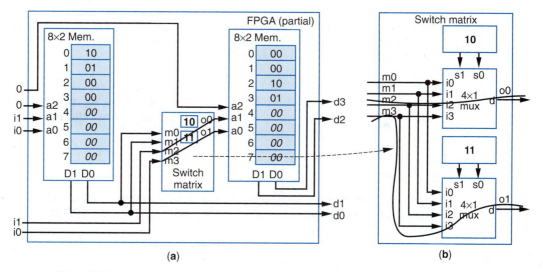

Figure 7.24 Implementing a 2x4 decoder on the FPGA fabric having a switch matrix: (a) external connections and programmed bits in the lookup tables and switch matrix, and (b) a look inside the switch matrix, showing the programmed connections between the outputs and inputs. Italicized bits in the lookup tables are unused.   ◄

► **EXAMPLE 7.10**   Extended seat belt warning light on an FPGA

We are to implement the extended seat belt warning light system of Example 2.8 on the FPGA shown in Figure 7.23. (Figure 7.19 showed how to partition a similar circuit in two groups, with equations x = kps' and w = x + t + d. For this example, w = x + t.) We connect k, p, and s to the FPGA pins going to the left lookup table, and we program that lookup table to implement the function kps', as shown in Figure 7.25. We connect an output of the left lookup table, representing x, to the right lookup table, by programming the switch matrix to connect m0 to o0. We connect t to the right lookup table also, by connecting t to an external pin connected to switch matrix input m2, and then by configuring the switch matrix to connect m2 to o1. We then program the right lookup table to implement the function x + t, as shown in Figure 7.25.

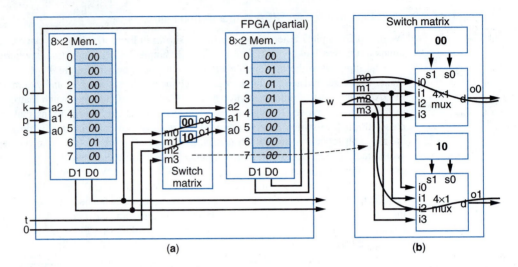

Figure 7.25 Implementing the extended seat belt warning light circuit on the FPGA fabric having a switch matrix: (a) external connections and programmed bits, (b) a look inside the switch matrix, showing the programmed connections. Italicized bits in the lookup tables are unused.   ◀

Notice that, in the previous two examples, we implemented *two different circuits* using the *same FPGA chip*. To implement the two different circuits, we merely had to program different bits into the lookup tables and switch matrices. That's the appeal of FPGAs— they implement our circuit just by programming.

Configurable Logic Block

In the previous section, the illustrated FPGAs were missing a critical element needed to implement general circuits, namely, *flip-flops*. Without flip-flops, FPGAs could not implement sequential circuits.

FPGAs may include a flip-flop with each output of a lookup table—two flip-flops in the case of a 2-output lookup table. The lookup table and its flip-flops together are known as a **configurable logic block**, or **CLB**. A simple CLB is shown in Figure 7.26. Each configurable logic block has a 3-input 2-output lookup table, and has two outputs and two flip-flops. Each flip-flop is loaded every clock cycle with the corresponding lookup table output. Each output of the CLB can be configured to either come from the output's flip-flop, or directly from the corresponding lookup table output. That configuration is done by programming a 1-bit memory (which itself is a flip-flop, but we'll call it a memory to avoid confusion), shown in Figure 7.26, that controls a 2x1 mux for each CLB output.

The output flip-flops enable us to implement sequential circuits, that is, circuits having registers, on the FPGA.

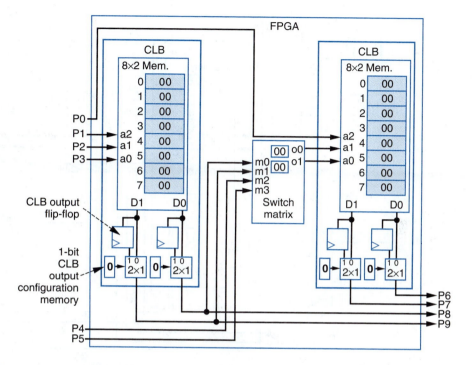

Figure 7.26 An FPGA with configurable logic blocks, which contain flip-flops along with a lookup table. We've put 0s in all the configuration memory bit cells in the figure.

▶ **EXAMPLE 7.11**   Implementing a sequential circuit on an FPGA

We wish to implement the circuit shown in Figure 7.27(a) on the FPGA of Figure 7.26. We first connect a and b to the left lookup table, and c and d to the right lookup table through the switch matrix, as shown in Figure 7.27(c). We program the left lookup table to output the functions a ' and b ', as shown in Figure 7.27(b). Likewise, we program the right lookup table to output c and d. We program all the configurable logic block outputs to connect to their flip-flops, by programming 1s into the CLB output configuration memories, as shown in Figure 7.27(c).   ◀

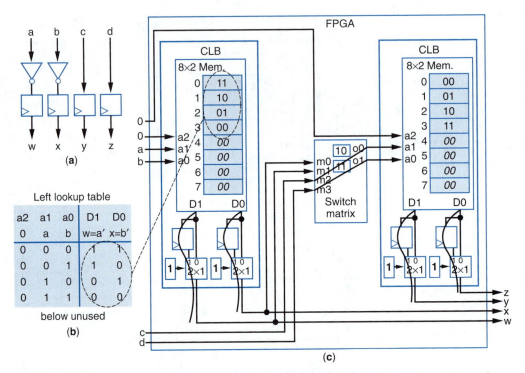

Figure 7.27 Implementing a sequential circuit on an FPGA: (a) desired sequential circuit, (b) left CLB's lookup table program bits, (c) programmed FPGA. Unused bits are italicized

Care should be taken to avoid confusing the output flip-flops themselves and the CLB output configuration "memories"—the configuration memories store bits that program the FPGA to implement the desired circuit, before circuit operation, while the output flip-flops store the bits that the circuit loads during circuit operation.

The storage elements for the lookup table, the CLB output configuration, and the switch matrices, are collectively known as an FPGA's *configuration memory*, although that "memory" is comprised of numerous smaller memories and even registers or flip-flops.

Overall FPGA Architecture

Grid of CLBs and switch matrices

A commercial FPGA contains hundreds or even thousands of CLBs and switch matrices, arranged in a regular pattern on the chip. A sample arrangement is shown in Figure 7.28. CLBs connect with horizontal and vertical routing channels, which connect to switch matrices. A sample connection of a CLB to the routing channels is shown for the top center CLB. The routing channels consist of tens of wires, represented in the figure just as single bolded wires.

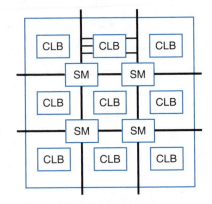

Figure 7.28 FPGA architecture.

CLBs and switch matrices in commercial FPGAs are more complex than described in this chapter. For example, CLBs may contain two lookup tables, or direct connections to adjacent CLBs to support carry chains. Switch matrices may contain more inputs and outputs and more flexible switching options. Furthermore, commercial FPGAs may also include large embedded RAM memories for data storage, and embedded multipliers or multiply-accumulate units for fast multiplications.

Programming an FPGA

We haven't said anything yet about how we actually program the lookup table, switch matrix configuration memories, and CLB-output configuration memories; in particular, how do we get the program bits into the configuration memories? The configuration memories are all the lookup table memories, the switch matrix memories, and the CLB-output configuration memories. Conceptually, programming is enabled by the FPGA having all the configuration memory bit storage cells connected as one big shift register. That shift register's bit storage cells are spread out across the chip, so don't represent a traditional register whose bits are usually in one place, but thinking of them as a shift register helps understand their connectivity. Actually, storage cells connected as a shift register are typically referred to as a *scan chain*. The FPGA will have an extra input pin for programming that serves as the shift input for the shift register. Another extra input pin indicates that programming is taking place. During programming, we shift in the bits necessary to implement our desired circuit. Remember that the configuration memory cells only get written during programming of the FPGA—during normal FPGA operation, those configuration memory cells become read-only. Thus, one can conceive of FPGAs whose configuration memories are made from programmable read-only memory technology (PROM, EPROM, or EEPROM), although today most FPGAs use RAM and flip-flop components for configuration memories. RAM and flip-flops are used probably because those components need to be programmed quickly using the scan chain method, easily achieved using RAM/flip-flop components, but not so easily using EPROM or EEPROM components.

Automated tools that program FPGAs usually start with a file containing the bits to be shifted into the FPGA chain—that file is known as a *bit file*. The tool that creates the bit file obviously must know the number and purpose of every bit cell in the FPGA scan chain, so such tools will generate a different bit file for different FPGA devices.

▶ **EXAMPLE 7.12** Programming an FPGA

This example demonstrates programming an FPGA for the FPGA and desired circuit shown in Example 7.11. Figure 7.27 from Example 7.11 showed the required contents of the configuration memory on the FPGA to implement the desired circuit. We replicate the contents in Figure 7.29(a), this time illustrating the manner in which the FPGA has the configuration memory bits connected as a scan chain. Figure 7.29(b) shows how that scan chain conceptually forms a 40-bit shift register. Figure 7.29(c) shows the contents of a bit file that could be used to program the FPGA to implement the desired circuit. We created that bit file simply by following the dashed line that represents the scan chain, placing 1s and 0s into the bit file as we see them in the figure. ◀

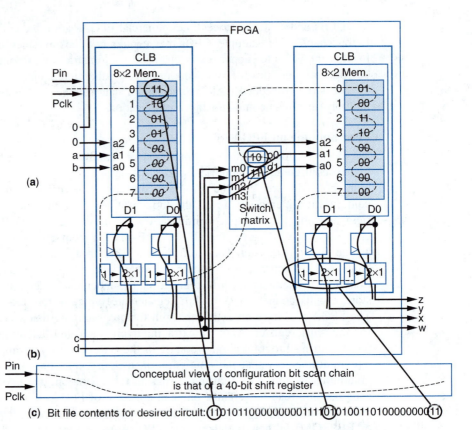

Figure 7.29 Programming an FPGA: (a) all configuration bit cells exist in a scan chain, (b) a scan chain conceptually is a big shift register, (c) a bit file's contents would be shifted in during programming—some relationships between the file's bits and configuration bit cells are shown.

How Many Gates Does an FPGA Implement?

We usually think of a digital circuit's size using the notion of "gates" to represent design size. A design with 3000 gates is likely bigger than a design with 2000 gates. Of course, whether that statement is true depends on the type of gates used in each design (e.g., because XOR gates are bigger than NAND gates, 2000 XOR gates may actually be bigger than 3000 NAND gates), as well as the number of inputs to each gate (a 20-input gate is bigger than a 2-input gate). Thus, a common method of indicating design size for a circuit *approximates the number of 2-input NAND gates* that would be required to implement the circuit. So when we say that a circuit consists of 3000 gates or 2000 gates, we typically mean that if those circuits were implemented using 2-input NAND gates, they would require 3000 2-input NAND gates and 2000 2-input NAND gates, respectively.

FPGAs have lookup tables and switch matrices inside, not gates. FPGA sizes are therefore typically reported by considering how large of a circuit made up of 2-input NAND gates could be implemented using the FPGA architecture. FPGA vendors may report FPGA size by saying a particular FPGA has a "density of 100,000 system gates" or "100,000 typical gates." These numbers are *approximations*, and many people view such reported numbers very skeptically (because sometimes companies like to exaggerate). FPGA vendors might also describe FPGA size as the number of "logic blocks" or "lookup tables," which is useful when comparing sizes of FPGAs having the same types of logic blocks or lookup tables.

FPGA versus ASICs and Microprocessors

FPGAs are less efficient than ASICs in terms of delay, size, and power. For example, the circuit of Figure 7.22(a) could be implemented with a delay of just one gate-delay in a custom or semicustom IC technology. However, when mapped to the FPGA of Figure 7.26, that circuit will have a longer delay—the inputs must pass through the left CLB's lookup table (which may have a delay of two gate-delays), through the left CLB's output muxes (another two gate-delays), through the switch matrix (another two gate-delays), through the right CLB's lookup table (another two gate-delays), and finally through the right CLB's output muxes, resulting in a total of ten gate-delays. In terms of size, an ASIC implementation of the circuit of Figure 7.22(a) would require about 20 transistors, whereas the FPGA implementation using two CLBs and a switch matrix would require several hundred transistors.

An FPGA implementation of a circuit will therefore be slower and bigger than an ASIC implementation of the same circuit. Some studies have shown that FPGAs are approximately 10 times slower, and 10–30 times bigger, than ASIC implementations of the same circuit. Similarly, a circuit implemented on an FPGA may consume about 10 times more power than when implemented on an ASIC. But the advantage of being able to program FPGAs immediately and for almost no cost, rather than having to wait weeks or months while spending tens of thousands of dollars, often outweighs those disadvantages.

Despite the performance, size, and power overhead compared to ASICs, FPGAs are still much faster than software on a microprocessor for many tasks, in part because FPGAs can effectively implement concurrency, pipelining, and bit-level operations. Thus, FPGAs possess the programming flexibility of software on a microprocessor, yet approach the performance of an ASIC, representing an excellent implementation option for many designs.

▶ 7.4 OTHER TECHNOLOGIES

In this section, we describe other technologies for physically implementing digital circuits. Some of those technologies are older technogies that are still useful for particular situations. Others are newer technologies that are beginning to gain popularity.

Off-the-Shelf Logic (SSI) IC

Sometimes we need only implement a circuit having just a few gates. In these cases, using an FPGA may be overkill, as FPGAs typically support thousands or millions of gates. Likewise, using an ASIC would also be overkill. For cases where we only need a few gates, we might instead use one or more off-the-shelf logic ICs. A *logic IC* typically contains a few, perhaps ten or less, gates connected directly to the IC's pins, as shown in Figure 7.30. The IC shown has four AND gates and 14 pins. One pin is for power to the IC (known as *VCC*), the other for ground (*GND*). The remaining pins connect to the four AND gates in the IC, as shown in the figure. Different logic ICs have gate types other than AND, such as OR, NAND, NOR, or NOT. To build a small circuit from these off-the-shelf logic ICs, we would simply place the ICs on a board and connect the appropriate pins. ICs with only a few gates are known as *Small-Scale Integration* chips, or *SSI* chips.

7400 ICs

The most popular off-the-shelf SSI ICs are known generally as *7400-series* ICs. A 7400 IC typically contains four to six logic gates, and about 14 pins. A particular 7400 IC is shown in Figure 7.31. The IC measures about 1/2 inch across. The IC package shown has two rows, or lines, of pins, and is thus known as a *dual-inline package*, or *DIP*.

7400 ICs first became available in the early 1960s. The original 7400 chip had four NAND gates, and cost about $1000 each, in 1962. That's right—$1000. And that's in 1960s dollars, when a U.S. engineer earned only about $10,000/year. The price dropped significantly during that decade, thanks in large part to the use of huge numbers of the devices by the U.S. Minuteman Missile and the Apollo rocket programs, and has continued to drop since then due to cheaper transistors and huge volumes. Today, you can buy 7400-series ICs for just tens of cents each.

Parts with different gates have different part numbers. Table 7.1 shows some commonly used 7400 parts from

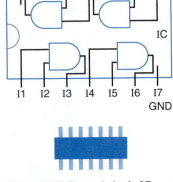

Figure 7.30 Example logic IC.

Figure 7.31 7400-series IC.

TABLE 7.1: Commonly used 7400-series ICs.

Part	Description	Pins
74LS00	Four 2-input NAND	14
74LS02	Four 2-input NOR	14
74LS04	Six inverters	14
74LS08	Four 2-input AND	14
74LS10	Three 3-input NAND	14
74LS11	Three 3-input AND	14
74LS14	Six inverters (Schmitt trigger)	14
74LS20	Two 4-input NAND	14
74LS27	Three 3-input NOR	14
74LS30	One 8-input NAND	14
74LS32	Four 2-input OR	14
74LS74	Two D flip-flop, positive edge triggered, with preset and reset	14
74LS83	4-bit binary full-adder	16
74LS85	4-bit magnitude comparator	16

Source: www.digikey.com

Fairchild's 74LS00 subfamily of the 7400 series. In addition to basic gates, the table shows an IC with D flip-flops, full-adders, or a magnitude comparator. Parts also exist for XOR, XNOR, buffers, decoders, multiplexers, up-counters, up-down-counters, and more.

There are several different subfamilies of 7400-series parts—parts from a subfamily can be used with other parts from the subfamily, but generally not with parts from other subfamilies. The reason is that the voltage and current setting of a subfamily are designed such that the ICs can be connected without worrying about adjusting the voltage and current between ICs. The *74* series (e.g., 7400, 7402, etc.), is the basic subfamily, based on a type of transistor known as TTL—designers using logic ICs today only use 74-series ICs if they must integrate with old designs, and typically don't use the series for new designs. The *74LS* subfamily (e.g., 74LS00, 74LS02) uses a special type of TTL technology known as Schottky that results in lower power and slightly higher speed than the 74 series—the "L" in the name means low-power, the "S" means Schottky. The *74HC* subfamily uses high-speed (denoted by the "H") CMOS (denoted by the "C") transistors. The *74F* subfamily was introduced by Fairchild, consisting of fast (hence the "F") advanced Schottky TTL logic. Numerous other 7400 subfamilies exist, with new subfamilies still being introduced.

Furthermore, additional series of off-the-shelf SSI ICs also exist in addition to the 7400 series. Another popular series is the *4000 series* of ICs, a CMOS series that evolved in the 1970s as a low-power alternative to the TTL-based 7000 series. More series exist too.

▶ **EXAMPLE 7.13** Seat belt warning implementation using off-the-shelf 7400 ICs

Using 74LS-series ICs shown in Table 7.1, physically implement the seat belt warning light circuit of Figure 7.1, shown again in Figure 7.32(a). We could implement the inverter using a 74LS04. The 74LS08 has 2-input AND gates, and we need a 3-input AND gate. A simple solution is to decompose the 3-input AND into two 2-input ANDs, as shown in Figure 7.32(b). The final implementation is shown in Figure 7.32(c).

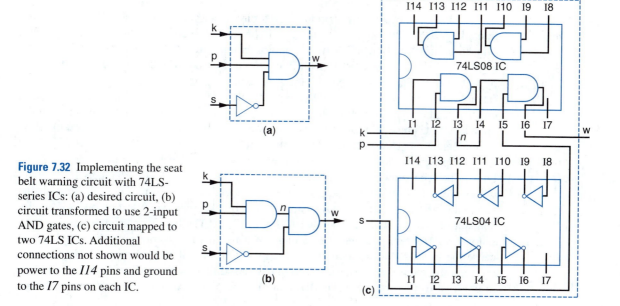

Figure 7.32 Implementing the seat belt warning circuit with 74LS-series ICs: (a) desired circuit, (b) circuit transformed to use 2-input AND gates, (c) circuit mapped to two 74LS ICs. Additional connections not shown would be power to the *I14* pins and ground to the *I7* pins on each IC.

Preferably, we would implement the circuit using just one IC, to reduce board size, cost, and power. Converting the circuit to use only one type of gate, like NAND gates only, or NOR gates only, could result in just one IC. For example, if we could convert to 3-input NOR gates, we could use the 74LS27 chip. We start by converting the circuit to NORs only, as in Figure 7.33(a). We remove the double inversion, and replace the single inversions by 3-input NOR gates. The implementation using a 74LS27 IC is shown in Figure 7.33(c).

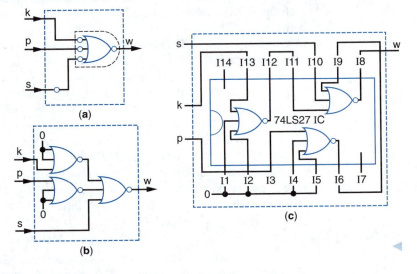

Figure 7.33 Implementing the seat belt warning circuit with one 74LS IC, namely, the 74LS27 consisting of three 3-input NOR gates: (a) desired circuit transformed to NOR gates with inversion bubbles, (b) circuit with double inversions eliminated and single inversions replaced by 1-input NOR gates, (c) circuit mapped to a 74LS27 chip. Additional connections not shown would be power to the *I14* pin, and ground to the *I7* pin.

Simple Programmable Logic Device (SPLD)

A *programmable logic device*, or *PLD*, is an IC that can be configured to implement a variety of logic functions, ranging from tens to thousands of gates. PLDs became popular in the 1970s (thus predating FPGAs), as they could implement far more functionality in a single IC than possible using SSI ICs.

A PLD device contains a prefabricated circuit with a set of external inputs feeding into a large AND-OR circuit structure, with the special feature that the user can configure (via "programming") which external inputs connect to the AND gates. For example, Figure 7.34 shows a basic PLD with three inputs feeding into three AND gates followed by an OR gate. The inputs feed into the AND gates in both true and complemented forms. Each wire feeding into each AND gate passes through a programmable node, which can either pass the node's input to the node's output, or disconnect the node's input from the node's output. Thus, by programming the programmable nodes, we can program the PLD to implement *any* 3-term function of three inputs.

The programmable node design varies among types of PLDs. Figure 7.35 shows two types. The type shown in Figure 7.35(a) is based on a fuse. A fuse conducts like a wire, unless we "blow" the fuse, meaning we pass a higher-than-normal current through the fuse, causing the fuse to literally burn up and break. A blown fuse obviously does not conduct electricity. The type shown in Figure 7.35(b) is based on memory and a transistor—we program a 1 into the memory to cause the transistor to conduct, and a 0 to cause the transistor to not conduct. We omit the details of how to program the fuses or program the memories themselves. Memory-based PLDs can usually be reprogrammed, in contrast to fuse-based PLDs that can only be programmed once and are known as

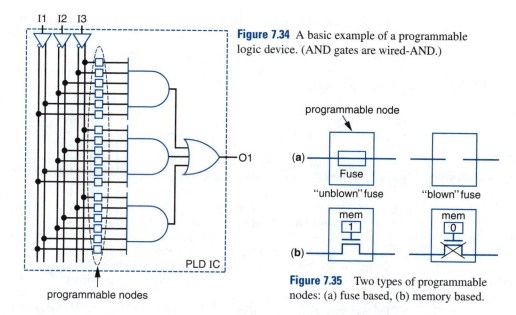

Figure 7.34 A basic example of a programmable logic device. (AND gates are wired-AND.)

Figure 7.35 Two types of programmable nodes: (a) fuse based, (b) memory based.

one-time programmable (*OTP*) devices. Fuse-based PLDs are popular in electrically noisy applications, like space applications, since memories can have their contents changed from radiation in space. They are also popular in applications demanding high security, since malicious enemies can't reprogram the device. Memory-based devices are more common, however, since they can be reprogrammed and thus reduce costs when we make design changes. The memories used are almost always nonvolatile, meaning the memories don't need power to retain their stored bits. (See Section 5.6 for more information on nonvolatile memories.)

You might be wondering how those AND gates work when the programmable node is programmed to disconnect an input—how does the AND gate treat an input with no connection? As a 0, as a 1, or as something else? Actually, PLDs don't use normal AND gates. Instead, they typically use what is known as "wired-AND." Explaining how wired AND works is beyond the scope of this book, and instead the subject of a course on transistor-level circuits. For our purposes, we can think of a wired-AND gate as an AND gate that simply ignores unconnected inputs.

Real PLDs have more than just three inputs, three AND gates, and one output. PLD structure drawings thus need a more concise way of drawing the circuits. A concise method of drawing PLDs is shown in Figure 7.36. Such a drawing doesn't show the programmable nodes, and simply utilizes an "x" to indicate a connection. In the drawing, wires that cross each other are *not* connected unless an "x" exists at the crossing. Furthermore, such a drawing uses a single wire to represent all the AND gate inputs, representing the

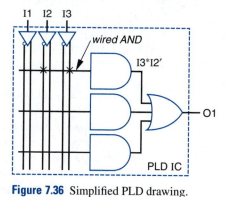

Figure 7.36 Simplified PLD drawing.

wired-AND. The figure shows how we would use such a drawing to indicate the connections needed to generate the term $I3*I2'$. The "x" on the left represents $I2'$ feeding into the top AND gate. The "x" on the right indicates $I3$ feeding into the top AND gate.

▶ **EXAMPLE 7.14**   Seat belt warning light using a simple PLD

We are to implement the seat belt warning light system of Figure 7.1 using the PLD of Figure 7.36. We can do so by programming the PLD as shown in Figure 7.37. We generate the desired term kps' by programming the connections for the top AND gate as shown. We want the bottom two AND gates to output 0s so that the OR gate's output equals the top AND gate's output. We can achieve 0s by ANDing an input with its complement—the result of $a*a'$ is always 0. The figure shows two ways of achieving 0s, with the middle gate using just one of the inputs, and the bottom gate using all three inputs—the result is the same.   ◀

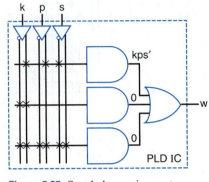

Figure 7.37 Seat belt warning system on a simple PLD.

PLDs typically have more than just one output. Figure 7.38(a) shows a PLD with two outputs instead of just one. Each output is an OR of up to three terms.

Many PLDs have a D flip-flop that stores each output's bit, and the PLD's output pin can be programmed to connect from the OR gate output or the flip-flop output, known as combinational or registered output, respectively. A PLD supporting combinational/registered output is shown in Figure 7.38(b).

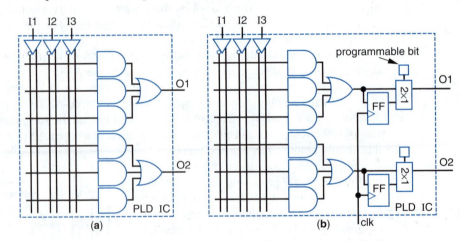

Figure 7.38 (a) PLD with two outputs, (b) PLD with programmable registered outputs.

Another extension is to allow the PLD output to be either the true or complemented value of the OR gate or flip-flop output, using a 2x1 mux controlled by a programmable bit. Yet another extension is for the output to feed back to the input array. One use of feedback is to implement functions with more terms, achieved by feeding back the combinational output value. Another very common use of feedback, achieved by feeding back the registered output, is to implement a state register and control logic (i.e., a controller)—the AND array gets its inputs from the registered outputs and external inputs, and the OR gates then generate the external outputs and the next values for the state register.

Some PLDs not only have a programmable AND array, but also have a programmable OR array, meaning the OR gate can get its inputs from any of the AND gates.

SPLD versus PAL versus GAL versus PLA

Like so many names in the rapidly evolving field of high technology, names for PLDs are a bit blurred and confusing. Originally (1970s), PLDs consisted of programmable AND arrays and programmable OR arrays, and were known as *programmable logic arrays*, or *PLAs*. In the mid-1970s, a company named AMD (Applied Micro Devices, Inc.) developed PLDs that instead had OR gates with fixed rather than programmable inputs, as in Figure 7.38 and the other PLD figures we've shown, and referred to such devices as *Programmable Array Logic*, or *PALs* ("PAL" is a registered trademark of AMD). PALs were originally fuse-based and hence one-time-programmable. A company named Lattice Semiconductor Corporation developed a PLD using a memory-based programming approach rather than fuses, resulting in reprogrammability, and referred to such devices as *Generic Array Logic*, or *GAL* (which are registered trademarks of Lattice Semiconductor Corporation). As PLDs became more complex (as we'll discuss in the next section), PLDs based on PAL or GAL architectures (PLA architectures seem to be pretty rare) became known as *Simple PLDs*, or *SPLDs*, to contrast them with the more complex PLD varieties. Today, numerous companies manufacture SPLDs, and often state that their SPLD architecture is based on "PAL" or "PAL/GAL" architectures, with the distinction between PAL and GAL not seemingly relevant in that context.

SPLDs typically support tens to hundreds of logic gates.

Complex Programmable Logic Device (CPLD)

As IC transistor densities grew in the 1980s, companies began to build PLDs to support thousands of gates. However, the PLD architecture described in the previous section does not scale well to thousands of gates—who needs one big huge circuit of two-level logic? Instead, architectures evolved that consisted of numerous SPLDs on a single device, connected using switch matrices (also known as programmable interconnect)—see Section 7.3 for details on switch matrices. These devices today are known as *Complex PLDs*, or *CPLDs*. CPLDs can typically implement designs with thousands of gates.

SPLDs versus CPLDs versus FPGAs

What's the difference among SPLDs, CPLDs, and FPGAs? In general, the term SPLD is used for devices that support tens to hundreds of gates, CPLD for devices that support thousands of gates, and FPGAs for devices that support tens of thousands of gates to millions of gates.

Furthermore, today, SPLDs and CPLDs are almost always nonvolatile, meaning they can store their program even after power is removed, whereas FPGAs are almost always volatile, meaning they lose their program when power is removed—and thus must include external circuitry that stores the program in nonvolatile memory and that programs the FPGA from that memory on power up of the FPGA. FPGAs today are likely volatile because of the way they are programmed using a scan chain, which is easy using flip-flops and RAM cells, but would be difficult using nonvolatile memory bits. However, conceptually, any of SPLDs, CPLDs and FPGAs could be made to be volatile or nonvolatile, and one might anticipate that future FPGAs will include FPGAs that are nonvolatile.

New FPGA-to-ASIC Flows

An interesting new technology that has evolved in the early 2000s is that of creating an ASIC from an FPGA-based design. Many designers use FPGAs for ASIC prototyping. They use automated tools to implement their circuit on FPGAs, and they then extensively test the circuit in the circuit's environment, for example, in a prototype DVD player. The FPGA-based prototype implementation may be larger, costlier, and more power-hungry than an ASIC-based implementation, but can be very useful for detecting and correcting errors in the circuit, as well as for demonstrating the eventual product. Once satisfied with the circuit, designers might then use automated tools to reimplement the circuit on an ASIC. The ASIC implementation traditionally did not utilize any information from the FPGA implementation.

Implementing large circuits on ASICs is a difficult task, even with automated tools. Nonrecurring engineering costs may exceed hundreds of thousands or even millions of dollars, and fabricating the IC may take many weeks or months. Furthermore, any problem with the fabricated ASIC may require a second fabrication cycle, requiring additional weeks or months. Problems may arise in the ASIC that didn't appear in the FPGA due to the completely new implementation of the circuit as an ASIC—perhaps timing problems might arise, for example, due to the circuit being placed and routed in a completely different fashion than was the case in the FPGA.

To ease the migration of a circuit from FPGA to ASIC, some FPGA vendors offer a structured ASIC approach. In a *structured ASIC* approach, an automated tool converts the *FPGA implementation* to an ASIC implementation, in contrast to converting the *original circuit* to an ASIC implementation. In other words, a structured ASIC will reflect the lookup table and switch matrix structure of the original FPGA. However, the structured ASIC will not be programmable, and thus will have faster lookup tables and faster switch matrices, because their contents will have been "hardwired" into the ASIC. The structured ASIC's cells can be preplaced, with only wires left to be completed to implement a particular circuit. The result is less NRE cost (tens of thousands of dollars rather than hundreds of thousands or millions) and less time-to-silicon (weeks rather than months), as well as less chance of unforeseen problems. The drawback is that the ASIC will be larger, slower, and more power-hungry than a traditional ASIC, but still better than an FPGA.

SOCs

The advent of ICs containing a billion transistors has led to ICs that contain what used to exist on multiple ICs. Thus, a single IC may contain dozens or hundreds of microprocessors, custom digital circuits, memories, buses, etc. An IC with numerous processors, custom circuits, and memories is known as a *System-on-a-Chip*, or *SOC*.

While many SOCs are created by designers for a particular application (e.g., for a particular DVD player), other SOCs are created to be used in a variety of different applications. Such *platform SOCs* might contain processors and custom circuits specifically for an application domain. For example, a platform SOC for video processing might contain custom digital circuits having hardware optimized for high-speed low-power video compression and decompression (known as *codecs*)—such platforms often contain codecs for a wide variety of protocols (e.g., MPEG 2, MPEG 4, H.264, etc.), since the platform could be used in different products supporting different standards. An example is the Nexperia platform from Philips. Furthermore, some platform SOCs contain FPGA in addition to one or more microprocessors and custom digital circuits on the IC. Examples include the Virtex II Pro platform from Xilinx and the Excalibur platform from Altera. Designers might utilize a platform SOC to prototype an ASIC, or to physically implement a system in a final product.

▶ 7.5 IC TECHNOLOGY COMPARISONS

Relative Popularity of IC Technologies

We've described numerous technologies in this chapter. In this section, we'll give you some idea of the relative popularity of some of those technologies. Table 7.2 provides the relative percentage of designs that were physically implemented in various technologies in 2001, based on a particular study. The table considers each new unique design only once, meaning that it doesn't matter how many copies of the same design were manufactured. That table's data does not include off-the-shelf SSI ICs or SPLDs (both represent only a tiny fraction of the IC market from a total dollars perspective, and are thus often excluded from such surveys). A different study describes 2002 IC revenues (as opposed to unique designs) totaling $11 billion as follows: standard cell 54%, full custom 20%, gate array 10%, PLD/FPGA 17%, and other 5% (source: WSTS, IC Insights). Yet another study lists 2002 ASIC revenues at $10.9 billion, PLD/FPGA revenues at $2.5 billion, and SOC revenues at $7.6 billion (source: Business Communications Company, 2003). Numbers from different studies vary; we provide these numbers just to give you a general feel for the popularity of the various technologies.

In 2002 alone, nearly 80 billion ICs (of all types) were produced. (Source: IC Insights McClean Report, 2003.)

TABLE 7.2: Sample % of new implementations in various technologies. Total is more than 100% due to overlap among categories.

Technology	%
Standard cell	55%
Gate array	5%
System-on-a-Chip	30%
Full-custom	10%
CPLD/FPGA	10%
Other	5%

Source: Synopsys, DAC 2002 panel.

Some general trends seem to include the increasing popularity of FPGAs, the increasing use of structured ASIC approaches, and the increasing appearance of system-on-a-chip.

The tools used to map digital designs to physical implementations, collectively known as **Electronic Design Automation** tools, or **EDA**, themselves form a market with revenues of $3 billion in 2002, $3.6 billion in 2003, and predicted revenues of $5 billion in 2006 (source: Gartner Dataquest, 2004).

Tradeoffs among IC Technologies

Figure 7.39 illustrates the general tradeoffs among the key IC technologies described in this chapter. Technologies toward the right can be more customized to a particular desired circuit, and thus may have faster performance, higher density (smaller chip for a given circuit), lower power, and larger chip capacity (more circuits on a single chip). But such customized technologies will be more costly to design and will take time to design. Technologies toward the left are less customized to a particular desired circuit, and thus may be more quickly available and have lower design cost, but at the expense of slower performance, less density, higher power, and less chip capacity (fewer of our circuits on a single chip). More generally, technologies toward the right allow for more optimization. Technologies to the left yield less optimization, but yield easier design.

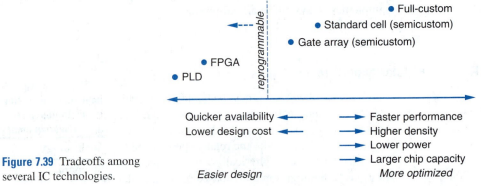

Figure 7.39 Tradeoffs among several IC technologies.

Furthermore, FPGAs and PLDs not only enable easier design, but may be reprogrammable, a feature that enables changes to the circuit late in the design cycle, or even after the circuit's IC has been deployed in a final product.

Choosing an IC technology for a particular design will therefore depend on the constraints imposed on that design. If a design needs to get to market quickly, that constraint favors PLD and FPGA technologies. If a design must be extremely fast, that constraint favors semicustom or full-custom technology. If a design must consume very little power or take up very little space, those constraints favor semicustom or full-custom technology. If changes to the circuit are likely, that constraint favors PLD and FPGA technologies. Choosing the best technology is a hard problem, requiring careful consideration of numerous competing constraints.

IC Technologies versus Processor Varieties

IC technologies and processor varieties are orthogonal implementation features. Two implementation features are ***orthogonal*** if we can select each independently (in mathematics, orthogonal means forming a right angle). We know that there are several processor varieties that can each implement a desired system function, including a custom processor, or a programmable processor. Figure 7.40 illustrates that the choice of processor variety is independent of the choice of IC technology. Point *1* illustrates the choice of implementing desired system functionality using a custom processor circuit with a full-custom IC technology. That choice results in a highly optimized design. Point *2* illustrates the choice of implementing a custom processor circuit on an FPGA. While the circuit may be optimized, the FPGA IC technology results in a less-optimized implementation (compared to full-custom) but an easier design. Point *3* illustrates the choice of implementing desired system functionality as software executing on a programmable processor, where the programmable processor is implemented in standard cells. Point *4* illustrates the choice of implementing software on a programmable processor, where the programmable processor is actually implemented on an FPGA. While that concept may seem strange, a programmable processor is just another circuit, so that circuit can be mapped to an FPGA just like any other circuit. Programmable processors mapped to FPGAs are in fact becoming increasingly popular, because a designer can choose how many processors to put on a single IC (perhaps the

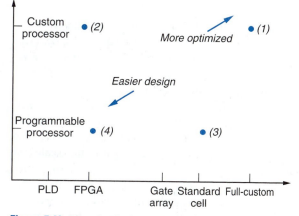

Figure 7.40 IC technologies and processor varieties are orthogonal implementation features. Four of the ten possible choices are shown.

designer wants 9 programmable processors on one IC), and because a designer can put single-purpose processors alongside programmable processors—all without having to fabricate a new IC.

Of course, programmable processors can often be purchased as off-the-shelf ICs, so a designer using a programmable processor may not have to worry about the processor's IC technology.

But increasingly, designers must place a programmable processor within their own IC, coexisting with other processors. When a programmable processor coexists on an IC along with other processors (programmable or custom), that programmable processor is often referred to as a ***core***.

Our discussion of IC technologies and processor varieties has thus far assumed just one type of each item (e.g., one type of FPGA). In reality, each type itself has many varieties. For example, dozens of different types of FPGAs are available, varying in their size, speed, power, cost, etc. Likewise, dozens of different types of programmable processors are available, also varying in those features. And we know that we can create different types of custom processors, varying also in their size, speed, power, etc. Thus, each point in Figure 7.39 and Figure 7.40 is actually a large collection of points that spread out in different directions on the plots, and may even overlap with other types. Furthermore, other IC technologies as well as processor varieties exist and continue to evolve.

We also point out that a single IC may actually incorporate several different IC technologies. So a single IC may have some circuits created using full-custom technology, and other circuits created using ASIC or even FPGA technology. Likewise, a single processor may have different parts implemented in different IC technologies. For example, a common situation is for a programmable processor to have its datapath implemented in full-custom technology, but its controller implemented in ASIC technology—the reason being that the datapath is very regular, while the controller is mostly unstructured combinational logic.

In summary, designers have a *huge* number of choices in choosing processor varieties and IC technologies to implement their systems.

IC Technology Trend—Moore's Law

Understanding the trends of IC technologies requires knowledge of Moore's Law. *Moore's Law* roughly states that IC capacity doubles every 18 months. Figure 7.41 plots such doubling, beginning with about 10 million transistors per IC in 1997. The plot uses a logarithmic scale for the *Y*-axis—each tick mark represents 10 times more than the previous tick mark. The growth rate is astounding—ICs increase from 10 million transistors in

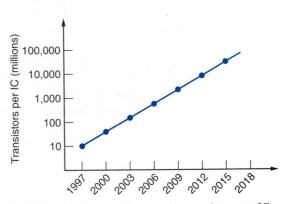

Figure 7.41 The trend of increasing transistors per IC.

1997 to over 10 *billion* transistors in 2015. That means that the 2015 IC can hold 1000 times more transistors than the 1997 IC. In other words, the 2015 IC is as powerful as about 1000 1997 ICs. This increasing capacity trend has also resulted in the cost per transistor dropping at nearly the same astounding rate.

In a 2004 speech, an Intel vice-president suggested that we might now consider transistors as essentially free.

The IC capacity trend has many implications. One implication is that digital designers can create massively parallel designs that use huge numbers of functional units and registers, to create high-performance systems not previously practical. The number of required transistors for such designs might have been considered absurd just a decade earlier. Another implication is that the size overhead of FPGAs compared to ASICs (about 10x) becomes less relevant, making FPGAs an increasingly popular choice in more systems. Yet another implication is that designers increasingly need automated tools to help build these multimillion transistor circuits, and may increasingly wish to use RTL and even higher levels of design (e.g., C-based design) as the method for describing circuits, leaving the remaining design to tools.

At some point, Moore's Law must come to an end, because transistors cannot shrink to an infinitely small size. When that end will occur has been a subject of debate for many years. Some people have predicted Moore's Law will continue a couple decades into the 2000s.

▶ 7.6 PRODUCT PROFILE: GIANT VIDEO DISPLAY

In the late 1990s and 2000s, giant color video displays became popular at sport stadiums, car dealerships, casinos, freeway billboards, and various other locations. Most such video displays utilize a huge grid of light-emitting diodes (LEDs) driven by digital circuits.

A *light-emitting diode* (*LED*) is a semiconductor device that emits light when current passes through the device. In contrast, a traditional "incandescent" light bulb emits light when current passes through the bulb's internal filament, which is a high-resistance wire that heats up and glows when current flows through the wire—the wire, however, doesn't burn because it is enclosed in a vaccum or inert gas within the bulb. Because LED light comes from a semiconductor material and not from a hot glowing filament in a bulb, LEDs use less power, last longer, and can handle vibrations that would break a regular light bulb.

LEDs have long been used to display simple device status (e.g., on or off), text messages, or even simple graphics. However, until recently, LEDs were only available in white, yellow, red, and green colors, and were not very bright. Thus, earlier LED video displays were typically small, used only a single color, and were designed for indoor use. However, with the development of the blue LED in 1993, and the development of brighter LEDs, full-color LED displays evolved that can display video in much the same way as a computer monitor or television, even in sunny outdoor environments. In fact, LEDs, being a semiconductor technology, have been improving at a rate similar to transistors (which also use semiconductor technology). The improvement has followed what is known as ***Haitz's Law*** (the LED equivalent of Moore's Law), stating that the LED "flux per package" doubles every 18–24 months, which has been the case for several decades. Due to this improvement, many people predict that LEDs will replace incandescent light bulbs for home and office lighting. LEDs have already begun to replace incandescent bulbs in traffic lights, as illustrated in Figure 7.42.

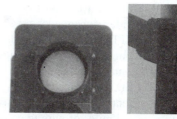

Traffic light using incandescent light and red plastic cover

Traffic light made from several hundred red LEDs

Figure 7.42 LEDs are replacing incandescent bulbs in traffic lights, as well as other areas.

Figure 7.43(a) shows a large LED video display capable of displaying full-color video on a 15 x 8 yard screen. Because each LED is relatively large (1/8th of an inch wide, for example) in comparison to the pixels of a computer monitor, one has to stand several feet away from the LED display to view the image without noticing the individual LEDs. If we look closer at the LED display, as seen in Figure 7.43(b), we can see the individual lines of the displays. If we look even closer at the display, we can finally see the individual LEDs within the display, as shown in Figure 7.43(c). That figure shows that the LEDs are clustered into groups of red, green, and blue LEDs—each cluster represents one pixel. For the LED video display shown in Figure 7.43, each cluster of LEDs consists of five LEDs: two red, two green, and one blue LED. Giant video displays are indeed intended to be viewed from a distance, so most viewers don't see the individual LEDs.

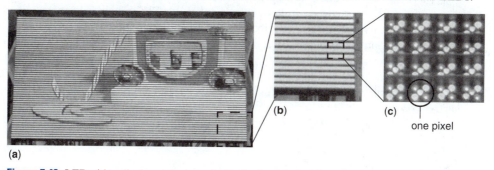

(b)

(c)

one pixel

(a)

Figure 7.43 LED video display: (a) a large LED display (about 10 yards wide and 5 yards tall), (b) a closer view showing about 1 square yard, (c) a very close view showing about 1 square inch—16 "pixels" can be seen, each pixel having 2 red (upper-left and lower-right of pixel), 2 green (upper-right and lower-left of pixel), and 1 blue LED (center of pixel).

Assume we want to create an LED video display capable of displaying a 720x480 pixel video, where each pixel simply consists of one red, one green, and one blue LED. If each LED cluster has a width of just over 3/8 inch (10 millimeters) and a height of 3/8 inch, our display will be roughly 24 feet wide and 16 feet high. Furthermore, our display will contain over one million individual LEDs, because 720 * 480 = 345,600 pixels, and the LEDs per pixel results in 1,036,800 LEDs.

Controlling every LED using a single digital circuit would require millions of output pins and miles of wire to connect all of the LEDs. Instead, as depicted in Figure 7.44, an LED video display is constructed of smaller and smaller components. The LED display consists of an array of smaller components called *panels*, shown in Figure 7.44(a). The panels are large display components typically designed in a modular fashion such that display manufacturers can easily create custom-size video displays and repair broken components within a display simply by replacing individual panels. The LED display panels are further divided into LED *modules* that control the physical LEDs, shown in Figure 7.44(b). An LED module is the basic display component and, depending on the design of the module, can control anywhere from a few hundred to a couple thousand LEDs. For example, in designing a 720x480 pixel display, we may want to use an array of 6x6 panels, where each panel consists of an array of 5x5 LED modules. Each LED module would then need to control an array of 24x16 pixels, where each pixel is composed of three LEDs.

The LED video display functions by dividing the incoming video stream into separate streams for each panel. The panels further process the video stream by dividing the incoming video stream into even smaller streams for the LED modules. Finally, the LEDs modules display the video frames by controlling the LEDs to output the correct colors for each pixel, or LED cluster.

LED Module

The LED module controls the individual LEDs within the video display by turning the LEDs *on* and *off* at the proper times to create the final color images. Because each LED module can consist of thousands of LEDs, directly controlling each LED would require too many wires. Instead, as shown on Figure 7.45, the LEDs within the LED module are connected in a matrix with a single control wire for each row and three control wires for each column (one wire for each colored LED within the LED clusters). In the figure, the LED module controller controls an array of 2x3 pixels, where each pixel consists of three individual LEDs, for a total of 18 LEDs. But as shown, the controller uses only 9 wires to control those 18 LEDs. The wire saving using this row and column approach becomes even more significant for more pixels. An LED module with 24x16 pixels and three LEDs per pixel would have 24*16*3 = 1152 LEDs, but the controller would require only 16 wires (one per row) plus 24*3 wires (three per column), for a total of only 88 wires.

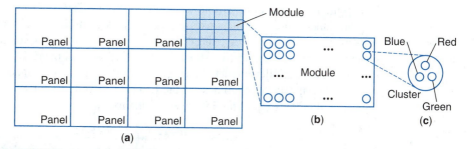

Figure 7.44 LED video displays are designed hierarchically: (a) the LED display consists of several larger panels, which can be composed to create different sized displays, and which can be individually replaced to repair broken panels, (b) each panel consists of several smaller LED modules, responsible for controlling the individual pixels, and (c) each pixel consists of a cluster of red, green, and blue LEDs.

The LED module controller displays a video image by sequentially scanning, or enabling, each row and displaying the pixel values for each column within the video image. Using this technique, only one row of LEDs is illuminated at any given time. However, the LED module scans the rows fast enough such that the human eye perceives all rows as being illuminated.

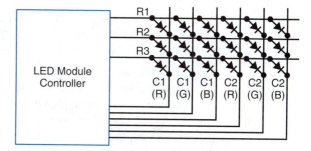

Figure 7.45 LED module circuit consisting of a matrix of red (R), green (G), and blue (B) LEDs controlled by the LED module controller. R1/R2/R3 are rows 1 through 3, and C1/C2 are columns 1 and 2—thus the matrix shown is 2x3 pixels, or 6 pixels total, with 18 LEDs total (3 LEDs per pixel).

The LED module must control the LEDs to create the desired color for each pixel. Each pixel within a video frame is typically represented using an RGB color space. An RGB (red/green/blue) color space is a method to create any color of light by adding specific intensities, or brightnesses, of red, green, and blue colors. Each pixel within a video frame may be represented as three 8-bit binary numbers, where each 8-bit number specifies the intensity of the red, green, or blue colors. Thus, for each color, the LED module must be able to provide 256 distinct brightness levels. However, an LED by itself only supports two values: *on* and *off*, or full intensity and no intensity.

To support 256 brightness levels, the LED module controller uses pulse width modulation. In **pulse width modulation** (also known as **PWM**), a controller drives a wire with a 1 value for a specific percentage of a time period—the signal being 1 is known as a pulse, the duration of the 1 is known as the pulse's width, and the percentage of the period spent at 1 is known as the *duty cycle*. When that pulse drives an LED, a wider pulse causes the LED to appear brighter to the human eye. Figure 7.46 illustrates how the LED module controller uses pulse width modulation to support various brightness levels for the LEDs. To illuminate an LED at full brightness, the controller simply drives the

The largest LED display in 2004 was 135 feet wide by 26 feet tall, built using 10 large FPGAs, 323 moderate-size FPGAs, 333 flash memories, and 3800 PLDs. (Source: Xcell Journal, Winter 2004).

LED with 1 for the entire period, as shown in Figure 7.46(a). To illuminate the LED at half brightness, the controller uses a pulse with a 50% duty cycle, as shown in Figure 7.46(b). For 25% brightness, the controller sets the pulse to 1 for 25% of the period, meaning a 25% duty cycle, as shown in Figure 7.46(c). For an LED video display, the LED module controller divides the length of time each row is scanned into 255 time segments, and controls the brightness of the LEDs by turning each LED *on* for 0 to 255 time segments, thereby supporting 256 levels of intensity.

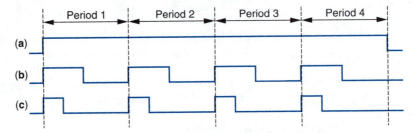

Figure 7.46 Pulse width modulation can be used to create various LED brightness levels: (a) for full brightness, the LED is always on, (b) for half brightness, the LED is turned on 50% of the time, and (c) for quarter brightness, the LED is turned on 25% of the time.

Because an LED module controller must provide precisely timed signals at a fast rate, custom processors are commonly used rather than just microprocessors. FPGAs are a common choice for implementing those custom processor circuits in LED video displays, due to several reasons. First, FPGAs are fast enough to support the required scan rates. Second, the circuit on the FPGAs can be easily changed, making it possible for the display manufacturer to fix bugs in the circuit, and even upgrade the circuit, without requiring the high cost of creating a new ASIC. Third, the displays themselves are fairly large, expensive, and consume much power, and therefore the larger size, higher cost, and more power consumption of FPGAs compared to ASICs do not impact the overall display's size, cost, and power too significantly.

▶ 7.7 CHAPTER SUMMARY

In this chapter, we discussed (Section 7.1) the idea that we must map our circuits to a physical implementation so that those circuits can be inserted into a real system. We introduced (Section 7.2) some technologies that require that a new chip be fabricated to implement our circuit. Full-custom technology gives the most optimized implementation, but is expensive and time-consuming to design. Semicustom technologies give very good implementations while costing less and taking less time to design, through the predesigning of the gates or cells that will be used on the IC. We described (Section 7.3) the increasingly popular technology of FPGAs, and showed how a circuit could be mapped onto a set of programmable lookup tables and switch matrices. We highlighted (Section 7.4) several other technologies, including off-the-shelf SSI/MSI ICs, and programmable logic devices. We gave some data (Section 7.5) showing the relative popularity of the technologies described in the chapter.

An interesting trend in physical implementation is the trend toward programmable ICs (FPGAs in particular). Implementing functionality on an FPGA involves the task of downloading a bitstream into the FPGA IC device. One might notice the similarity of that task with the task of implementing functionality on a microprocessor, which also involves downloading bits into an IC device. Thus, the difference between software on a microprocessor and custom digital circuits continues to be blurred—especially when one considers that modern FPGAs can also include one or several microprocessors within the same IC. For more information on the blurring, see "The Softening of Hardware," F. Vahid, *IEEE Computer*, April 2003.

▶ 7.8 EXERCISES

SECTION 7.2: MANUFACTURED IC TECHNOLOGIES

7.1 Explain why gate array IC technology has a shorter production time than full-custom IC technology.

7.2 Explain why the use of NAND or NOR gates in a CMOS gate array circuit implementation is typically preferred over an AND/OR/NOT implementation of a circuit.

7.3 Draw a gate array IC having three rows, the first row having four 2-input AND gates, the second row having four 2-input OR gates, and the third row having four NOT gates. Show how to instantiate wires to the gate array to implement the function $F(a,b,c)$ = abc + a'b'c'.

7.4 Assume a standard cell library has a 2-input AND gate, a 2-input OR gate, and a NOT gate. Use a drawing to show how to instantiate and place standard cells on an IC and wire them together to implement the function in Exercise 7.3. Draw your cells the same size as the gates in Exercise 7.3, and be sure your rows are of equal size.

7.5 Draw a gate array IC having three rows, the first row having four 2-input AND gates, the second row having four 2-input OR gates, and the third row having four NOT gates. Show how to instantiate wires to the gate array to implement the equation $F(a,b,c,d)$ = a'b + cd + c'.

7.6 Assume a standard cell library has a 2-input AND gate, a 2-input OR gate, and a NOT gate. Use a drawing to show how to instantiate and place standard cells on an IC and wire them together to implement the function in Exercise 7.5. Be sure to draw your cells the same size as the gates in Exercise 7.5, and be sure your rows are of equal size.

7.7 Consider the implementations of a half-adder with a gate array in Figure 7.4 and with standard cells in Figure 7.6. Assume each gate or cell (including inverters) has a delay of 1 ns. Also assume that every inch of wire (for each inch in your drawing, not on an actual IC) has a delay of 3 ns (wires are relatively slow in the era of tiny fast transistors). Estimate the delay of the gate array and the standard cell circuits.

7.8 For your solutions to Exercises 7.3 and 7.4, assume that each gate and cell has a delay of 1 ns, and that every inch of wire (for each inch in your drawing, not on an actual IC) corresponds to a delay of 3 ns. Estimate the delays of the gate array and standard cell circuits.

7.9 Draw a circuit using AND, OR, and NOT gates for the following equation: $F(a,b,c)$ = a'bc + abc'. Place inversion bubbles on that circuit to convert the circuit to:
(a) NAND gates only,
(b) NOR gates only.

7.10 Draw a circuit using AND, OR, and NOT gates for the following equation: $F(a,b,c)$ = abc + a' + b' + c'. Place inversion bubbles on that circuit to convert the circuit to:
(a) NAND gates only,
(b) NOR gates only.

7.11 Draw a circuit using AND, OR, and NOT gates for the following equation: $F(a,b,c)$ = $(ab + c)(a' + d) + c'$. Convert the circuit to a circuit using:

(a) NAND gates only,

(b) NOR gates only.

7.12 Draw a circuit using AND, OR, and NOT gates for the following equation: $F(w,x,y,z)$ = $(w + x)(y + z) + wy + xz$. Convert the circuit to a circuit using:

(a) NAND gates only,

(b) NOR gates only.

7.13 Draw a circuit using AND, OR, and NOT gates for the following equation: $F(a,b,c,d)$ = $(ab)(b' + c) + (a'd + c')$. Convert the circuit to a circuit using:

(a) NAND gates only,

(b) NOR gates only.

7.14 Create a template for converting a 3-input AND gate to a circuit using only 3-input NAND gates.

7.15 Create a template for converting a 3-input OR gate to a circuit using only 3-input NAND gates.

7.16 Create a template for converting a NOT gate to a circuit using only 3-input NAND gates.

7.17 Assume a standard cell library consisting of 2-input and 3-input NAND gates with a delay of 1 ns each, 2-input and 3-input AND and OR gates with a delay of 1.8 ns each, and a NOT gate with a delay of 1 ns. Compare the number of transistors and the delay of an implementation using only AND/OR/NOT gates with an implementation using only NAND gates for the function: $F(a,b,c)=ab'c + a'b$. For calculating the size of an implementation, assume each gate input requires two transistors.

7.18 Assume a standard cell library consisting of 2-input AND and OR gates with a delay of 1 ns each, 3-input AND and OR gates with a delay of 1.5 ns each, and a NOT gate with a delay of 1 ns. Compare the number of transistors and the delay of an implementation using only 2-input AND/OR gates and NOT gates with an implementation using only 3-input AND/OR gates and NOT gates for the function: $F(a,b,c)= abc + a'b'c + a'b'c'$. For calculating the size of an implementation, assume each gate input requires two transistors.

7.19 Assume a standard cell library consisting of 2-input NAND and NOR gates with a delay of 1 ns each, and 3-input NAND and NOR gates with a delay of 1.5 ns each. Compare the number of transistors and the delay of an implementation using only 2-input NAND/NOR gates with an implementation using only 3-input NAND/NOR gates for the function: $F(a,b,c)= a'bc + ab'c + abc'$. For calculating the size of an implementation, assume each gate input requires two transistors.

SECTION 7.3: PROGRAMMABLE IC TECHNOLOGY—FPGA

7.20 Show how to implement on a 3-input 2-output lookup table the function $F(a,b,c)$ = $a + bc$.

7.21 Show how to implement on two 3-input 2-output lookup tables the function $F(a,b,c,d)$ = $ab + cd$. Assume you can connect the lookup tables in a custom manner (i.e., do not use a switch matrix, just directly connect your wires).

7.22 Show how to implement on two 3-input 2-output lookup tables the following function: $F(a,b,c,d)$ = $a'bd$ + $b'cd'$. Assume the two lookup tables are connected in the manner shown in Figure 7.47. You may not need to use every lookup table output.

7.23 Show how to implement on two 3-input 2-output lookup tables the following functions: $F(x,y,z)$ = $x'y$ + xyz' and $G(w,x,y,z)$ = $w'x'y$ + $w'xyz'$. Assume the two lookup tables are connected in the manner shown in Figure 7.47.

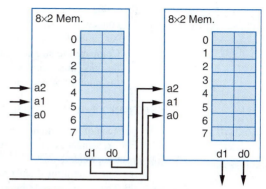

Figure 7.47 Two 3-input 2-output lookup tables implemented using 8x2 memory.

7.24 Show how to implement on two 3-input 2-ouput lookup tables the following functions: $F(a,b,c,d)$ = abc + d and G = a'. You must implement both F and G with only two lookup tables connected in the manner shown in Figure 7.47.

7.25 Implement a 2-bit comparator that compares two 2-bit numbers and has three outputs indicating greater-than, less-than, and equal-to, using any number of 3-input 2-output lookup tables and custom connections among the lookup tables.

7.26 Show how to implement a 4-bit carry-ripple adder using any number of 3-input 2-input lookup tables and custom connections among the lookup tables. Hint: map one full-adder to each lookup table.

7.27 Show how to implement a 4-bit carry-ripple adder using any number of 4-input 1-output lookup tables and custom connections among the lookup tables.

7.28 Show how to implement a comparator that compares two 8-bit numbers and has a single equal-to output, using any number of 4-input 1-output lookup tables and custom connections among the lookup tables.

7.29 Show the bit file necessary to program the FPGA fabric in Figure 7.29 to implement the function $F(a,b,c,d)$ = ab + cd, where a, b, c, and d are external inputs.

7.30 Show the bit file necessary to program the FPGA fabric in Figure 7.29 to implement the function $F(a,b,c,d)$ = $abcd$, where a, b, c, and d are external inputs.

7.31 Show the bit file necessary to program the FPGA fabric in Figure 7.29 to implement the function $F(a,b,c,d)$ = $a'b'$ + $c'd$, where a, b, c, and d are external inputs.

SECTION 7.4: OTHER TECHNOLOGIES

7.32 Use any combination of 7400 ICs listed in Table 7.1 to implement the function $F(a,b,c,d)$ = ab + cd.

7.33 Use any combination of 7400 ICs listed in Table 7.1 to implement the function $F(a,b,c,d)$ = abc + $ab'c$ + $a'bd$ + $a'b'd'$.

7.34 By drawing Xs on the circuit, program the PLD of Figure 7.38(a) to implement a full-adder.

7.35 By drawing Xs on the circuit, program the PLD of Figure 7.38(a) to implement a 2-bit equality comparator. Assume the PLD has an additional I4 input.

7.36 *(a)Design a PLD device capable of supporting a 2-bit carry-ripple adder. By drawing Xs on your PLD circuit, program the PLD to implement the 2-bit carry-ripple adder.

(b) Using a CPLD device consisting of several PLDs from Figure 7.38 and assuming you can connect the PLDs in a custom manner, implement the 2-bit carry-ripple adder by drawing Xs on the PLDs.

(c) Compare the size of your PLD and the CPLD by determining the gates required for both designs (make sure you compare the number of gates within the PLD and CPLD and not the number of gates used for your implementation).

SECTION 7.5: IC TECHNOLOGY COMPARISONS

7.37 For each of the system constraints below, choose the most appropriate technology from among FPGA, standard cell, and full-custom IC technologies for implementing a given circuit. Justify your answers.

(a) The system must exist as a physical prototype by next week.

(b) The system should be as small and low-power as possible. Short design time and low cost are *not* priorities.

(c) The system should be reprogrammable even after the final product has been produced.

(d) The system should be as fast as possible and should consume as little power as possible, subject to being completely implemented in just a few months.

(e) Only five copies of the system will be produced and we have no more than $1000 to spend on all the ICs.

7.38 Which of the following implementations are *not* possible? (1) A custom processor on an FPGA. (2) A custom processor on an ASIC. (3) A custom processor on a full-custom IC. (4) A programmable processor on an FPGA. (5) A programmable processor on an ASIC. (6) A programmable processor on a full-custom IC. Explain your answer.

CHAPTER **8**

Programmable Processors

▶ 8.1 INTRODUCTION

Digital circuits designed to perform a single processing task, such as a seat belt warning light, a pacemaker, or an FIR filter, are indeed a very common class of digital circuits. We might refer to a circuit performing a single processing task as a ***single-purpose processor***. Single-purpose processors represent a class of digital circuits enabling tremendously fast or power-efficient computation. However, another class of digital circuits, known as programmable processors, is also extremely popular, as well as being more widely known. The programmable processor is largely responsible for the computing revolution that has taken place in the past several decades, leading to what many call the information age. A ***programmable processor***, also known as a ***general-purpose processor***, is a digital circuit whose particular processing task is stored in a memory, rather than being built into the circuit itself. The representation of that processing task in the memory is known as a ***program***. Figure 8.1 illustrates single-purpose versus general-purpose processors. We could create a custom digital circuit for a seat belt warning light system (Chapter 2) or an FIR filter system (Chapter 5), or instead we could program a general-purpose processor circuit to implement those systems.

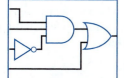

Seat belt warning light single-purpose processor

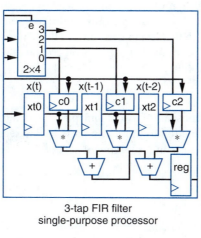

3-tap FIR filter single-purpose processor

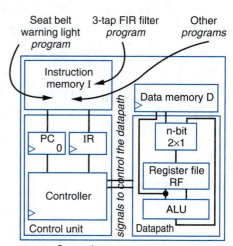

General-purpose processor

Figure 8.1 Single-purpose versus general-purpose processors.

421

Some programmable processors, like the well-known Intel Pentium processor or Sun's Sparc processor, are intended for use in desktop computers. Other programmable processors, like ARM, MIPS, 8051, and PIC processors (which are widely known in the design community but less known by the general public), are intended for embedded systems, like cellular telephones, automobiles, video games, or even tennis shoes with blinking lights. Some programmable processors, like the PowerPC, are intended for both desktop and embedded domains.

A benefit of a programmable processor is that its circuit can be mass-produced and then programmed to do almost anything. Thus, the same programmable desktop processor can run Windows 98, Windows XP, Linux, or whatever new operating system program comes about. Likewise, that same processor can run application programs like word processors, spreadsheets, video games, web browsers, etc. Furthermore, the same programmable embedded processor can be used in a cell phone, automobile, video game, or tennis shoe by programming the processor for the desired processing task. Mass-production results in low costs due to amortization of design costs (see "Why such cheap calculators?" in Chapter 4 for a discussion of amortization).

Of course, because programmable processors are mass-produced and then used for a wide variety of applications, there aren't as many unique programmable processor designs as there are single-purpose processor designs. It follows then that there are far fewer programmable processor *designers* than there are single-purpose processor designers. Nevertheless, even though you may never design a programmable processor as part of your job, it is interesting and enlightening to understand how such a programmable processor works. Some people argue that people who understand how a processor works are even better software programmers. And technology trends have led to the situation of designers being able to create semicustom processors ("application-specific" processors) that have just the right architecture for one or a small number of applications, making knowledge of programmable processor designs important. Finally, there are indeed people who do design programmable processor architectures, and you never know if you might end up being one of them.

In this chapter, we show how to design a simple programmable processor using our previously-described digital design methods. Our purpose is mainly to demystify these devices and to provide an intuition of how programmable processors work. We point out that real mass-produced processors are designed using different methods, and their designs can be much more complex than the design described in this chapter—learning about those processors' designs is the subject of many textbooks on computer architecture.

▶ 8.2 BASIC ARCHITECTURE

A programmable processor consists of two main parts: a datapath and a control unit. We'll provide a general introduction to those two parts in this section, then we'll provide a more detailed look at those parts in a subsequent section.

Basic Datapath

We can view processing generally as:

- *Loading* data, meaning reading the data on which we wish to work from some input locations,

- *Transforming* that data, meaning performing some computations with that data that result in new data, and

- *Storing* the new data, meaning writing the new data to some output locations.

For example, a seat belt warning system reads bit data from sensors representing whether a seat belt is fastened and whether a person is sitting in a seat, transforms that data by computing a new bit indicating whether to turn on a warning light, and writes that new data to a warning light. An FIR filter reads data representing the most recent set of input signal samples, transforms that data by performing multiplies and adds, and writes new data to an output representing the filtered signal.

A ***data memory*** holds all the data that a programmable processor can access, as input data or output data—for now, assume the words in that data memory are somehow connected to the outside world (e.g., to the seat belt sensors or to the FIR input and output signals). To process that data, a programmable processor needs to be able to *load* data from data memory into one of several registers (typically a register file) within the processor, needs to be able to feed data from some subset of registers through functional units that can perform all possible *transformation* operations (typically an ALU) we might consider with results stored back into a register, and needs to be able to *store* data from a register back into data memory. Therefore, we see the need for a programmable processor to include the basic circuit shown in Figure 8.2, showing a data memory, register file, and ALU. That circuit is known as the programmable processor's ***datapath***. The basic datapath shown in Figure 8.2 can perform the following possible ***datapath operations*** in a given clock cycle:

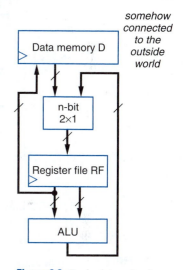

Figure 8.2 Basic datapath of a programmable processor.

- ***Load operation:*** This operation loads (reads) data from any location in the data memory into any register in the register file. A load operation is illustrated in Figure 8.3(a).

- ***ALU operation:*** This operation transforms register data by passing any two registers through the ALU configured for any of the ALU's supported operations, and back into any register of the register file. An ALU operation is illustrated in Figure 8.3(b). Typical ALU operations include addition, subtraction, logical AND, logical OR, etc.

- ***Store operation:*** This operation stores (writes) data from any register in the register file to any data memory location. A store operation is illustrated in Figure 8.3(c).

These possible datapath operations are illustrated in Figure 8.3. Each such operation requires the appropriate setting of the control inputs of the data memory, mux, register file, and ALU—those control inputs will be shown shortly. For now, just familiarize yourself with the basic datapath's abilities. Notice that the datapath in Figure 8.2 cannot directly operate on data memory locations with the ALU in one clock cycle, because the data must first be read into the register file, which itself requires a clock cycle, before the data can be operated on by the ALU. A datapath that requires all data to first pass through the register file before that data can be transformed by the ALU is known as a *load-store architecture*.

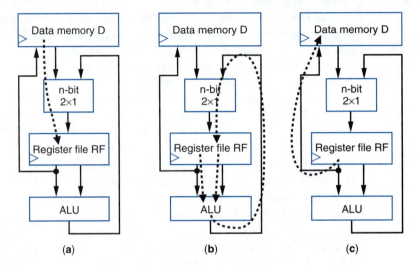

Figure 8.3 Basic datapath operations: (a) load (read), (b) ALU operation (transform), and (c) store (write).

▶ **EXAMPLE 8.1** Understanding datapath operations

Which of the following are valid single-clock-cycle datapath operations for the datapath of Figure 8.2?

1. Copy data from a data memory location into a register file location.

2. Read data from two data memory locations into two register file locations.

3. Add data from two data memory locations and store the result in a register file location.

4. Copy data from one register file location to another register file location.

5. Subtract data in a register file location from a data memory location, storing the result in a register file location.

(1) is a valid operation, known as a load operation. (2) is *not* a valid operation. We cannot read more than one data memory location during a datapath operation (for this datapath), and we cannot write to more than one register file location during an operation. (3) is *not* a valid operation. Not only can we not read from two data memory locations during one operation, but we cannot feed the read values directly into the ALU to perform the add—we must first perform operations that read the data items into register file locations. (4) is a valid operation. We can configure the ALU operation to simply pass one of its inputs through to the output (perhaps by adding 0) and store the result in the register file. (5) is *not* a valid operation. We cannot feed a read data memory location directly to the ALU—there is no such connection in the datapath. Values read from data memory must be loaded into the register file first. ◀

Basic Control Unit

Suppose we want to use the basic datapath of Figure 8.2 to perform the simple processing task of adding data memory locations 0 and 1 together, and writing the result in data memory location 9—in other words, we want to compute $D[9] = D[0] + D[1]$. We can achieve this processing task by "instructing" the datapath to perform the following operations:

- *load* datapath memory location 0 to register file register $R0$ (i.e., $RF[0] = D[0]$),
- *load* datapath memory location 1 to register file register $R1$ (i.e., $RF[1] = D[1]$),
- perform an *ALU* operation that adds $R0$ and $R1$ and writes the result back into $R2$ (i.e., $RF[2] = RF[0] + RF[1]$), and
- *store* $R2$ into data memory location 9 (i.e., $D[9] = RF[2]$).

Note that we could have used any registers in the register file, rather than $R0$, $R1$, and $R2$.

If $D[0]$ contained the value 99 (in binary, of course), and $D[1]$ contained the value 102, then after carrying out the above operations, $D[9]$ would contain 201.

You might think that having to instruct the datapath to perform four distinct operations is a rather cumbersome way of adding two data items. If you could build your own custom digital circuit to implement $D[9] = D[0] + D[1]$, you would likely just feed $D[0]$ and $D[1]$ through an adder whose output you would connect to $D[9]$, thus avoiding the four operations involving the register file and ALU. We see the basic tradeoff of single-purpose versus programmable processors—programmable processors have the drawback of computation overhead because they have to be general, but they provide the benefits of a mass-produced processor that can be programmed to do almost anything.

Somehow we need to describe the sequence of operations—$RF[0] = D[0]$, then $RF[1]=D[1]$, then $RF[2] = RF[0] + RF[1]$, then $D[9] = RF[2]$—that we desire to execute on the datapath. Such a description of desired processor operations are known as ***instructions***, and a collection of instructions is known as a ***program***. We will store the desired program as words in another memory, called the ***instruction memory***. We'll describe how to represent those instructions later. For now, assume that the four instructions are somehow stored in locations 0, 1, 2, and 3 of the instruction memory I, as shown in Figure 8.4.

Now is where the control unit plays a role. The ***control unit*** reads each instruction from instruction memory, and then executes that instruction on the datapath. To execute our simple program, the control unit would begin by performing the following tasks, known as ***stages***, to carry out the first instruction:

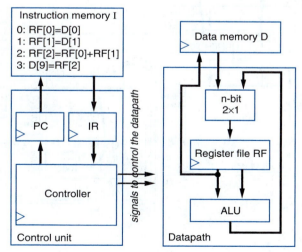

Figure 8.4 The control unit in a programmable processor.

1. ***Fetch***: The control unit would start by reading *I[0]* into a local register, a task known as ***fetching***. This stage requires one clock cycle.

2. ***Decode***: The control unit would then determine what operation this instruction is requesting, a task known as ***decoding***. This stage also requires one clock cycle.

3. ***Execute***: Seeing that this instruction requests the datapath operation *RF[0] = D[0]*, the control unit would set the control lines of the datapath to read *D[0]*, pass the read data through the 2x1 mux in front of the register file, and write that data into *R[0]*. The task of carrying out the operation is known as ***executing***. Most operations are datapath operations (such as a load operation, ALU operation, or store operation), but not all operations require the datapath (an example is the jump instruction to be discussed later). This stage requires one clock cycle.

Thus, the basic stages the control unit carries out for that first instruction are: *fetch, decode,* and *execute*, requiring three clock cycles to complete just that first instruction.

The local register in which the control unit stores the fetched instruction is known as the ***instruction register***, or ***IR***, as shown in Figure 8.4. Notice that the control unit needs to keep track of the location in instruction memory from which to fetch the next instruction. Since the instruction locations are usually in sequence, we can use a simple up-counter to keep track of the current program instruction—such a counter is known as a ***program counter***, or ***PC*** for short. The processor starts with *PC=0*, so the instruction in *I[0]* represents the first instruction of the program.

Figure 8.5 illustrates the three stages of executing the instruction *RF[0] = D[0]* stored in *I[0]*. Assuming PC was previously initialized to 0, Figure 8.5(a) shows the first

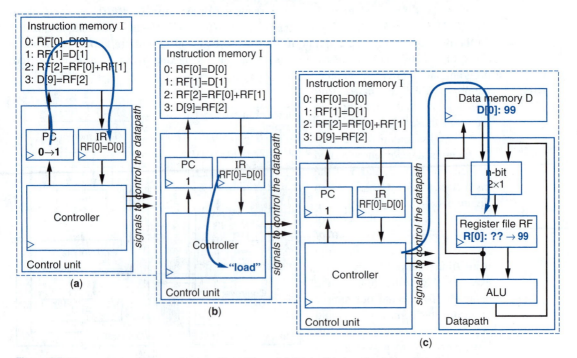

Figure 8.5 Three stages of processing *one* instruction: (a) fetch, (b) decode, (c) execute.

stage fetching *I[0]*'s contents, the instruction *RF[0]=D[0]*, into *IR*. Figure 8.5(b) shows the second state decoding the instruction and thus determining that the instruction is a load instruction. Figure 8.5(c) shows the controller executing the instruction by configuring the datapath to read the value of *D[0]* and storing that value into *RF[0]*. If *D[0]* contained 99, then *R[0]* will contain 99 after completion of the execute stage.

After processing the instruction in *I[0]*, the control unit would fetch the instruction that is in *I[1]*, decode that instruction, and execute that instruction (thus executing *RF[1]* = *D[1]*), requiring another three cycles. Next, the control unit would fetch the instruction that is in *I[2]*, decode that instruction, and execute that instruction (thus executing *RF[2]* = *RF[0]* + *RF[1]*), requiring another three cycles. Finally, the control unit would fetch the instruction that is in *I[3]*, decode that instruction, and execute that instruction (thus executing *D[9]* = *RF[2]*), requiring another three cycles. The four instructions would require 4*3 = 12 cycles to run to completion on the programmable processor.

The control unit will require a controller, like those described in Chapter 3, that in this case repeatedly performs the fetch, decode, and execute steps (after having initialized *PC* to 0)—note that a controller appears inside the control unit in Figure 8.4. An FSM for that controller appears in Figure 8.6. The controller increments the program counter after fetching each instruction in state *Fetch*, so that the next fetch state will fetch the next instruction (notice that *PC* gets incremented at the end of the fetch stage in Figure 8.5(a)). We'll describe the actions of the *Decode* and *Execute* states later.

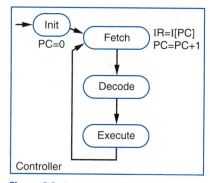

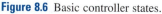

Figure 8.6 Basic controller states.

Thus, the basic parts of the control unit include the program counter *PC*, the instruction register *IR*, and a controller, as illustrated in Figure 8.4. In previous chapters, our nonprogrammable processors consisted only of a controller and a datapath. Notice that the programmable processor instead contains a control unit, which itself consists of some registers and a controller.

To summarize, the control unit processes each instruction in three stages:

1. first *fetching* the instruction by loading the current instruction into *IR* and incrementing the *PC* for the next fetch,

2. next *decoding* the instruction to determine its operation, and

3. finally *executing* the operation by setting the appropriate control lines for the datapath, if applicable. If the operation is a datapath operation, the operation may be one of three possible types:

   (a) *loading* a data memory location into a register file location,

   (b) transforming data using an *ALU* operation on register file locations and writing results back to a register file location, or

   (c) *storing* a register file location into a data memory location.

▶ **EXAMPLE 8.2**   Creating a simple sequence of instructions

Create a set of instructions for the processor in Figure 8.4 to compute $D[3] = D[0] + D[1] + D[2]$. Each instruction must represent a valid single-clock-cycle datapath operation.

We might start with three operations that read the data memory locations into register file locations:

    0. $R[3] = D[0]$

    1. $R[4] = D[1]$

    2. $R[2] = D[2]$

Note that we intentionally chose arbitrary register locations, to make clear that we can use any registers.

Next, we need to add the three values and store the result in a register file location, say $R[1]$. In other words, we want to perform the following operation: $R[1] = R[2] + R[3] + R[4]$. However, the datapath of Figure 8.4 cannot add three register file locations in a single operation, but rather can only add two locations. Instead, we can describe the desired addition computation by dividing the computation into two datapath operations:

    3. $R[1] = R[2] + R[3]$

    4. $R[1] = R[1] + R[4]$

Finally, we write the result into $D[3]$:

    5. $D[3] = R[1]$

Thus, our program consists of the six instructions appearing above, which we might store in instruction memory locations 0 through 5.   ◀

▶ **EXAMPLE 8.3**   Evaluating the time to carry out a program

Determine the number of clock cycles required for the processor of Figure 8.4 to execute the six-instruction program of Example 8.2.

The processor requires 3 cycles to process each instruction: 1 cycle to fetch the instruction, 1 to decode the fetched instruction, and 1 to execute the instruction. At 3 cycles per instruction, the total cycles for 6 instructions is: 6 instr * 3 cycles/instr = 18 cycles.   ◀

▶ 8.3 A THREE-INSTRUCTION PROGRAMMABLE PROCESSOR

A First Instruction Set with Three Instructions

The way we represent instructions in the instruction memory, and the list of allowable instructions, are known as a programmable processor's ***instruction set***. Let's assume that a processor uses 16-bit instructions, and that the instruction memory *I* is 16-bits wide. Instruction sets typically reserve a certain number of bits in the instruction to denote what operation to perform. The remaining bits specify any additional information needed to perform the operation, such as the source or destination registers. We define a simple, three-instruction set, with the most significant (meaning leftmost) 4 bits identifying the appropriate operation and the least significant 12 bits containing register file and data memory addresses, as follows:

- ***Load*** instruction—**0000 $r_3r_2r_1r_0$ $d_7d_6d_5d_4d_3d_2d_1d_0$**: This instruction specifies a move of data from the data memory location whose address is specified by the bits $d_7d_6d_5d_4d_3d_2d_1d_0$ into the register file register whose location is specified by the bits $r_3r_2r_1r_0$. For example, the instruction "0000 0000 00000000" specifies a move of data memory location 0, or *D[0]*, into register file location 0, or *RF[0]*—in other words, that instruction represents the operation *RF[0]=D[0]*. Likewise, "0000 0001 00101010" specifies *RF[1]=D[42]*. We've inserted spaces between some bits for ease of reading by you the reader—those spaces have no other significance and would not exist in the instruction memory.

- **Store** instruction—**0001 $r_3r_2r_1r_0$ $d_7d_6d_5d_4d_3d_2d_1d_0$**: This instruction specifies a move of data in the opposite direction as the instruction above, meaning a move from the register file to the data memory. So "0001 0000 00001001" specifies *D[9]=RF[0]*.

- **Add** instruction—**0010 $ra_3ra_2ra_1ra_0$ $rb_3rb_2rb_1rb_0$ $rc_3rc_2rc_1rc_0$**: This instruction specifies an addition of two register file registers specified by $rb_3rb_2rb_1rb_0$ and $rc_3rc_2rc_1rc_0$, with the result stored in the register file register specified by $ra_3ra_2ra_1ra_0$. For example, "0010 0010 0000 0001" specifies the instruction *RF[2]=RF[0]+RF[1]*. Note that *add* is an ALU operation.

None of these instructions modifies the contents of the instructions' source operands. In other words, the *load* instruction copies the contents of the data memory location to the specified register, but leaves the data memory location itself unchanged. Likewise, the *store* instruction copies the specified register to data memory, but leaves the register's contents unchanged. The *add* instruction reads its *b* and *c* registers without changing them.

Using this instruction set, we would describe our earlier program that computes *D[9]=D[0]+D[1]* as shown in Figure 8.7.

Notice that the first four bits of each instruction are a binary code that indicates the instruction's operation. Those bits are known as the instruction's *operation code*, or **opcode** for short. "0000" means a move from data memory to register file, "0001" means a move from register file to data memory, and "0010" means an add of two registers, based on the instruction set defined in the bulleted list above. The remaining bits of the instruction represent *operands*, which indicate what data to operate on.

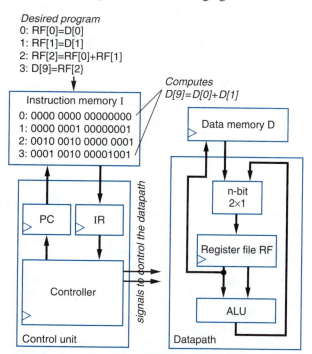

Figure 8.7 A program that computes D[9]=D[0]+D[1], using a given instruction set. We've inserted spaces between the instruction memory's bits for readability only—those spaces don't exist in the memory.

We could write a different program using the same three-instruction instruction set. For example, we could write a program that computes $D[5] = D[5] + D[6] + D[7]$. We must perform that computation using instructions chosen from the three-instruction instruction set. We might write the program as shown in Figure 8.8. The number before the colon represents the instruction's address in the instruction memory I. The text following the two forward slashes (//) represent comments, and are not part of the instructions.

```
0: 0000 0000 00000101  // RF[0] = D[5]
1: 0000 0001 00000110  // RF[1] = D[6]
2: 0000 0010 00000111  // RF[2] = D[7]
3: 0010 0000 0000 0001  // RF[0] = RF[0] + RF[1]
                        // which is D[5]+D[6]
4: 0010 0000 0000 0010  // RF[0] = RF[0] + RF[2]
                        // now D[5]+D[6]+D[7]
5: 0001 0000 00000101  // D[5] = RF[0]
```

Figure 8.8 A program to compute $D[5]=D[5]+D[6]+D[7]$ using the three-instruction instruction set.

Note how that program ultimately computes the desired sum. This might be the first time that you have had to think of computations in terms of low-level programmable processor instructions. Thinking in terms of such register-level operations can be difficult at first, but becomes easier as you see and develop more programs at that level.

Machine Code versus Assembly Code

As you have seen, the instructions of a program exist in instruction memory as 0s and 1s. A program represented as 0s and 1s is known as *machine code*. Writing and reading programs represented as 0s and 1s are tasks that humans are not particularly good at. We humans can't understand those 0s and 1s easily, and thus will likely make plenty of mistakes when writing such programs. Thus, early computer programmers developed a tool, known as an *assembler* (which itself is just another program), to help humans write other programs. An assembler allows us to write instructions using *mnemonics*, or symbols, that the assembler automatically translates to machine code. Thus, an assembler may tell us that we can write instructions from our three-instruction instruction set using the following mnemonics:

* *Load* instruction—**MOV Ra, d**: specifies the operation $RF[a]=D[d]$. a must be 0, 1, ..., or 15—so *R0* means *RF[0]*, *R1* means *RF[1]*, etc. d must be 0, 1, ..., 255.

* *Store* instruction—**MOV d, Ra**: specifies the operation $D[d]=RF[a]$.

* *Add* instruction—**ADD Ra, Rb, Rc**: specifies the operation $RF[a]=RF[b]+RF[c]$.

▶ COMPUTERS WITH BLINKING LIGHTS.

Big computers shown in the movies often have many rows of small blinking lights. In the early days of computing, computer programmers programmed using machine code, and they entered that code into the instruction memory by flipping switches up and down to represent 0s and 1s. To enable debugging of the program, as well as to show the computed data, those early computers used rows of lights—on lights meant 1s, off lights meant 0s. Today, nobody in their right mind would try writing or debugging a program by using machine code. So computers today look like big boxes—with no rows of lights. But big plain boxes don't make for interesting backgrounds in movies, so movie makers continue to use movie props with lots of blinking lights to represent computers—lights that are useless, but entertaining.

▶ **"BOOTING" A COMPUTER.**

Turning on a personal computer causes the operating system to load, a process known as "booting" the computer. The computer executes instructions beginning at address 0, which usually has an instruction that jumps to a built-in small program that loads the operating system (the small program is often called the basic input/output system, or BIOS). Most computing dictionaries state that the term "boot" originates from the popular expression "to pull oneself up by one's bootstraps," which means to pick yourself up without any help, though obviously you can't do this by grabbing onto your own bootstraps and pulling—hence the cleverness of the expression. Since the computer loads its own operating system, the computer is in a sense picking itself up without any help. The term bootstrap eventually got shortened to boot. A colleague of mine who has been around

computing a long time claims a different origin. One way of loading a program into the instruction memory of early computers was to create a ribbon with rows of holes. Each row might have enough room for say 16 holes, thus each row would represent a 16-bit machine instruction—a hole meant a 0, no hole a 1 (or vice versa). A programmer would punch holes in the ribbon to store the program on the ribbon (using a special hole-punching machine), and then feed the ribbon into a computer's ribbon reader, which would read the rows of 0s and 1s and load those 0s and 1s into the computer's instruction memory. Those ribbons might have been several feet long, and looked a lot like the straps of a boot, hence the term bootstrap, shortened to boot. Whichever is the actual origin, we can be fairly sure the term "boot" comes from the bootstraps on the boots we wear on our feet.

Using those mnemonics, we could rewrite the program $D[9]=D[0]+D[1]$ as follows:

0: MOV R0, 0

1: MOV R1, 1

2: ADD R2, R0, R1

3: MOV 9, R2

That program is much easier to understand than the 0s and 1s in Figure 8.7. A program written using mnemonics that will be translated to machine code by an assembler is known as **_assembly code_**. Hardly anybody writes machine code directly these days. An assembler would automatically translate the above assembly program to the machine code shown in Figure 8.7.

You might be wondering how the assembler can distinguish between the load and store instructions above, when the mnemonic for both instructions is the same—"MOV." The assembler distinguishes those two types of instructions by looking at the first character after the mnemonic "MOV"—if the first character is an "R," then that operand is a register, and thus that instruction must be a load instruction.

Control Unit and Datapath for the Three-Instruction Processor

From the definition of the three-instruction instruction set and an understanding of the basic control unit and datapath architecture of a programmable processor as shown in Figure 8.4, we can design a complete digital circuit for a three-instruction programmable processor. The design process is actually very similar to the RTL design process of Chapter 5.

We begin with a high-level state machine description of the system, shown in Figure 8.9. Assume that *op* is shorthand for *IR[15..12]*, meaning the leftmost four bits of the instruction register. Likewise, assume that *ra* is shorthand for *IR[11..8]*, *rb* is shorthand for *IR[7..4]*, *rc* is shorthand for *IR[3..0]*, and *d* is shorthand for *IR[7..0]*.

Recall that the next step in the RTL design process was to create the datapath. We already created the datapath in Figure

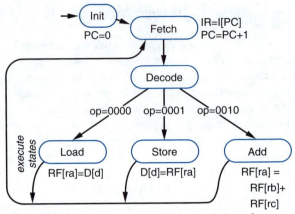

Figure 8.9 High-level state machine description of a three-instruction programmable processor.

8.4, which we refine to show every control signal from the controller, as shown in Figure 8.10. The refined datapath has control signals for each read and write port of the register file (see Chapter 4 for information on register files). The register file has 16 registers because the instructions have only 4 bits with which to address registers. The datapath has a control signal to the ALU called `alu_s0`—we'll assume the simple ALU adds its inputs when `alu_s0=1`, and just passes input *A* when `alu_s0=0`. The datapath has a select line for the

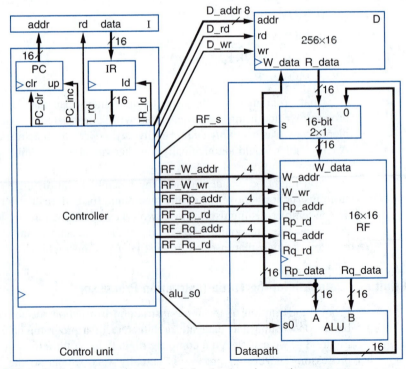

Figure 8.10 Refined datapath and control unit for the three-instruction processor.

2x1 mux in front of the register file's write data port. Finally, we have also included the control signals for the data memory, which we assume has a single address port, and can thus support only a read or a write, but not both simultaneously. The data memory has 256 words, since the instruction only has 8 bits with which to address the data memory.

The datapath is now able to carry out all of the load/store operations and arithmetic operations that we need for the high-level state machine from Figure 8.9. Thus, we can proceed to the third step of the RTL design process of connecting the datapath with a controller. Figure 8.10 shows those connections, as well as the connections of the controller to the *PC* and *IR* registers in the control unit, and to the instruction memory *I*.

The last step of the RTL design process is to derive the controller's FSM. We can do this straightforwardly by replacing the high-level actions of the state machine in Figure 8.9 by Boolean operations on the controller's input and output lines, as shown in Figure 8.11. (Remember that *op*, *d*, *ra*, *rb*, and *rc* are shorthand notations for *IR[15..12]*, *IR[7..0]*, *IR[11..8]*, *IR[7..4]*, and *IR[3..0]*, respectively.) We could then finish the controller's design by converting the FSM to a state register and combinational logic, using the methods from Chapter 3.

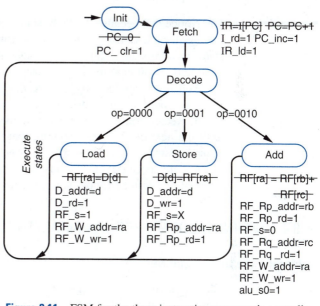

Figure 8.11 FSM for the three-instruction processor's controller.

We would have thus designed a programmable processor.

Let's trace through the controller's FSM behavior to see how a program would execute on the three-instruction processor. As a reminder, remember that we follow the FSM conventions that all transitions are implicitly ANDed with a rising clock edge, and that any control signal not explicitly assigned a value in a state is implicitly assigned a 0.

- The FSM initially starts in state *Init*, which sets PC_clr=1, causing the *PC* register to be cleared to 0.

- The FSM on the next clock cycle enters the *Fetch* state, in which the FSM reads the instruction memory at address 0 (because *PC* is 0) and loads the read value into *IR*—that read value will be the instruction that was stored in *I[0]*. At the same time, the FSM increments the *PC*'s value.

- The FSM on the next clock cycle enters the *Decode* state, which has no actions but which branches on the next clock cycle to one of three states, *Load*, *Store*, or *Add*, depending on the values of the highest four bits of the *IR* register (the current instruction's opcode).

- In the *Load* state, the FSM sets the data memory address lines to the low eight bits of the *IR* and sets the data memory read enable to 1, sets the 2x1 mux's select line to pass the data memory output to the register file, and sets the register file write address to *IR[11..8]* and the write enable to 1, causing whatever gets read from the data memory to be loaded into the appropriate register in the register file.

- Likewise, the *Store* and *Add* states set the control lines as needed for the store and add operations.

- Finally, the FSM returns to the *Fetch* state, and begins fetching the next instruction.

Notice that because the *Store* state does not write to the register file, then the value of the register file's mux select lines don't matter, so we've assigned signal RF_s=X in that state, meaning the signal's value does not matter. Using such don't care values (see Section 6.2) can help us to minimize logic in the controller.

You may wonder why the *Decode* state is necessary when that state contains no actions—could we not have just had *Decode*'s transitions originate instead from state *Fetch*? Recall from Section 5.3 that register updates listed in a state do not actually occur until the next clock edge, meaning that transitions originating from a state use the previous register values. Thus, we could not have originated *Decode*'s transitions from the *Fetch* state, because those transitions would have been using the old opcode in the instruction register *IR*, not the new value read during the *Fetch* state.

► 8.4 A SIX-INSTRUCTION PROGRAMMABLE PROCESSOR

Extending the Instruction Set

Clearly, having only a three-instruction instruction set limits the behavior of the programs that we can write. All we can do with those instructions is add numbers. A real programmable processor will support many more instructions, perhaps 100 or more, so that a wider variety of programs can be written.

Let's extend our programmable processor's instruction set with a few more instructions, in order to give you a slightly better idea of how a programmable processor with a full instruction set would look.

We'll begin by introducing an instruction able to load a constant value into a register file register. For example, suppose we wanted to compute *RF[0] = RF[1] + 5*. The 5 is a constant. A ***constant*** is a value that is part of our program, not something to be found in data memory. We need an instruction that allows us to load a constant into a register, after which we could add that register to *RF[1]* using the ADD instruction. Thus, we introduce a new instruction with the following machine and assembly code representations:

- ***Load-constant*** instruction—**0011** $r_3 r_2 r_1 r_0$ $c_7 c_6 c_5 c_4 c_3 c_2 c_1 c_0$: specifies that the binary number represented by the bits $c_7 c_6 c_5 c_4 c_3 c_2 c_1 c_0$ should be loaded into the register specified by $r_3 r_2 r_1 r_0$. The binary number being loaded is known as a *constant*. The mnemonic for this instruction is:

  MOV Ra, #c—specifies the operation *RF[a]=c*

a can be 0, 1, ..., or 15. Assuming two's complement representation (see Section 4.8), *c* can be −128, −127, ..., 0, ..., 126, 127. The "#" enables the assembler to distinguish this instruction from a regular load instruction.

We continue by introducing an instruction for performing subtraction of two registers, similar to addition of two registers, having the following machine and assembly code representations:

- *Subtract* instruction—**0100 ra$_3$ra$_2$ra$_1$ra$_0$ rb$_3$rb$_2$rb$_1$rb$_0$ rc$_3$rc$_2$rc$_1$rc$_0$**: specifies subtraction of two register file registers specified by rb$_3$rb$_2$rb$_1$rb$_0$ and rc$_3$rc$_2$rc$_1$rc$_0$, with the result stored in the register file register specified by ra$_3$ra$_2$ra$_1$ra$_0$. For example, "0100 0010 0000 0001" specifies the instruction *RF[2]=RF[0] − RF[1]*. The mnemonic for this instruction is:

    SUB Ra, Rb, Rc—specifies the operation *RF[a]=RF[b] − RF[c]*

Let's also introduce an instruction that allows us to jump to other parts of a program:

- *Jump-if-zero* instruction—**0101 ra$_3$ra$_2$ra$_1$ra$_0$ o$_7$o$_6$o$_5$o$_4$o$_3$o$_2$o$_1$o$_0$**: specifies that if the contents of the register specified by ra$_3$ra$_2$ra$_1$ra$_0$ is 0, we should load the *PC* with the current value of *PC* plus o$_7$o$_6$o$_5$o$_4$o$_3$o$_2$o$_1$o$_0$, which is an 8-bit number in two's complement form representing a positive or negative offset amount. The mnemonic is:

    JMPZ Ra, offset—specifies the operation *PC = PC + offset* if *RF[a]* is 0.

By using two's complement for the jump offset, which allows representation of positive or negative numbers, the program can jump backwards in the program, thus implementing a loop. With an 8-bit offset, the instruction can specify a jump forward by 127 addresses, or backward by 128 addresses (-128 to +127).

Table 8.1 summarizes the six-instruction instruction set. A programmable processor typically comes with a databook that lists the processor's instructions, and the meaning of each instruction, using a format similar to the format of Table 8.1. Typical programmable processors have dozens, even hundreds, of instructions.

TABLE 8.1 Six-instruction instruction set..

Instruction	Meaning
MOV Ra, d	RF[a] = D[d]
MOV d, Ra	D[d] = RF[a]
ADD Ra, Rb, Rc	RF[a] = RF[b]+RF[c]
MOV Ra, #C	RF[a] = C
SUB Ra, Rb, Rc	RF[a] = RF[b]-RF[c]
JMPZ Ra, offset	PC=PC+offset if RF[a]=0

Extending the Control Unit and Datapath

The three new instructions require some extensions to our control unit and datapath of Figure 8.10, with those extensions shown in Figure 8.12. First, the *load constant* instruction requires that the register file be able to load data from *IR[7..0]*, in addition to data from data memory or the ALU output. Thus, we widen the register file's multiplexer from 2x1 to 3x1, add another mux control signal, and also create a new signal coming from the controller labeled *RF_W_data*, which will connect with *IR[7..0]*—these changes are highlighted by the dashed circle labeled "*1*" in Figure 8.12. Second, the subtract

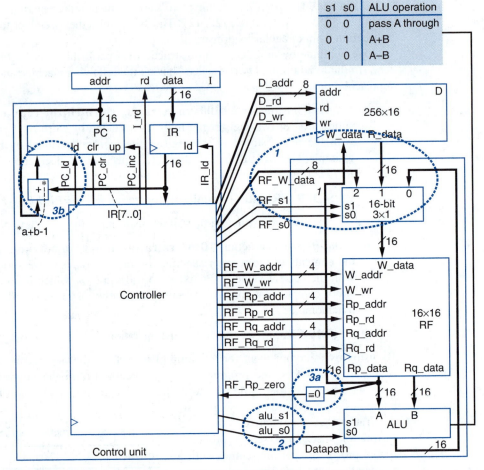

Figure 8.12 Control unit and datapath for the six-instruction processor.

instruction requires that we use an ALU capable of subtraction, so we add another ALU control signal—highlighted by the dashed circle labeled "*2*" in the figure. Third, the jump-if-zero instruction requires that we be able to detect if a register is zero, and that we be able to add $IR[7..0]$ to the *PC*. Thus, we insert a datapath component to detect if the register file's *Rp* read port is all zeros (that component would just be a NOR gate), labeled as dashed-circle "*3a*" in the figure. We also upgrade the *PC* register so it can be loaded with *PC* plus $IR[7..0]$, labeled as "*3b*" in the figure. The adder used for this also subtracts 1 from the sum, to compensate for the fact that the *Fetch* state already added 1 to the *PC*.

We also need to extend the FSM for the controller within the control unit to handle the three additional instructions. Figure 8.13 shows the extended FSM. The *Init* and *Fetch* states stay the same. We added three new transitions from the *Decode* state for the three new instruction opcodes. We made a minor revision to the *Load*, *Store*, and *Add* states' actions (the new actions are italicized) since the register file mux has a mux with two select lines instead of just one. Likewise, we revised the *Add* state actions to configure the ALU with two control lines instead of one. We added four new states, *Load-constant*, *Subtract*,

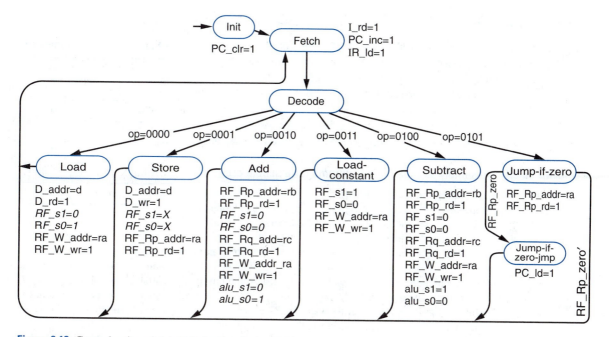

Figure 8.13 Control unit and datapath for the six-instruction processor.

Jump-if-zero, and *Jump-if-zero-jmp*, for the three new instructions. The new instruction states perform the following functions on the datapath:

- In the *Load-constant* state, we configure the register file mux to pass the RF_W_data signal, and we configure the register file to write to the address specified by *ra* (which is *IR[11..8]*).

- In the *Subtract* state, we perform the same actions as in the *Add* state, except that we configure the ALU for subtraction instead of addition.

- In the *Jump-if-zero* state, we configure the register file to read the register specified by *ra* onto read port *Rp*. If the value of the read register *Rp* is all 0s, RF_Rp_zero will become 1 (and 0 otherwise). Thus, we include two transitions from the *Jump-if-zero* state. One transition will be taken if RF_Rp_zero is 0, meaning the read register was not all 0s—that transition takes the FSM back to the *Fetch* state, meaning no actual jump occurs. The other transition will be taken if RF_Rp_zero is 1, meaning the read register was all 0s. That transition goes to another state, *Jump-if-zero-jmp*, which should actually carry out the jump. That state carries out the jump simply by setting the load line of the *PC*.

Notice that with the addition of a *Jump-if-zero* instruction, the processor may take up to four cycles to complete an instruction. Namely, when the *ra* register of a *Jump-if-zero* instruction is all 0s, then an extra state is needed to load the *PC* with the address of the instruction to which to jump.

▶ 8.5 EXAMPLE ASSEMBLY AND MACHINE PROGRAMS

Using the six-instruction instruction set of the previous section, we now provide an example of assembly-language programming using the six-instruction processor to perform a particular task, and we show how the assembly code would be converted to machine code by an assembler. An assembler would make use of the table shown in Table 8.2, which maps instructions to opcodes.

TABLE 8.2 Instruction opcodes.

Instruction	Opcode
MOV Ra, d	0000
MOV d, Ra	0001
ADD Ra, Rb, Rc	0010
MOV Ra, #C	0011
SUB Ra, Rb, Rc	0100
JMPZ Ra, offset	0101

▶ **EXAMPLE 8.4**   Assembly and machine programs for a simple program

Write a program that counts the number of words that are not equal to 0 in data memory locations 4 and 5, and that stores the result in data memory location 9. Thus, the possible results that would be stored in location 9 are zero, one, or two.

Using the instruction set of Table 8.2, we can write an assembly program as shown in Figure 8.14(a). The program maintains the count in register $R0$, which the program initializes to 0. The program may need to add 1 to this register later, so the program loads the value 1 into register $R1$. The program next loads data memory location 4 into register $R2$. The program then jumps to the instruction labeled as "lab1" if the value of $R2$ is zero. If $R2$ is not zero, the program will execute an add instruction that adds one to register $R0$, and will then proceed to the instruction labeled "lab1" since that instruction is the next instruction. The instruction labeled "lab1" loads data

MOV R0, #0; // initialize result to 0	0011 0000 00000000
MOV R1, #1; // constant 1 for incrementing result	0011 0001 00000001
MOV R2, 4; // got data memory location 4	0000 0010 00000100
JMPZ R2, lab1; // if zero, skip next instruction	0101 0010 00000010
ADD R0, R0, R1; // not zero, so increment result	0010 0000 0000 0001
lab1:MOV R2, 5; // get data memory location 5	0000 0010 00000101
JMPZ R2, lab2; // if zero, skip next instruction	0101 0010 00000010
ADD R0, R0, R1; //not zero, so increment result	0010 0000 0000 0001
lab2:MOV 9, R0; // store result in data memory location 9	0001 0000 00001001

(a)   (b)

Figure 8.14 A program to count the number of nonzero numbers in $D[4]$ and $D[5]$, storing the result in $D[9]$: (a) assembly code, and (b) corresponding machine code generated by an assembler. The spaces in the machine code's 16-bit instructions are there for your convenience as you read this book; actual machine code has no such spaces.

memory location 5 into register $R2$. The program jumps to the instruction labeled "lab2" if $R2$ is zero. If $R2$ is not zero, the program executes an add instruction that adds one to register $R0$, and then proceeds to the next instruction, which is the instruction labeled "lab2." That instruction stores the contents of register $R0$ to data memory location 9.

In writing the assembly program, we arbitrarily chose the registers that we used to store the result, the constant 1, and the data memory location copy. We could have used any registers for those purposes. For example, we could have used register $R7$ to hold the result, meaning all occurrences of $R0$ in the code would instead have been $R7$. Furthermore, in writing the assembly program, we arbitrarily chose the labels "lab1" and "lab2." We could have picked other names for those labels, such as "skip1" and "done," or "Fred" and "George." It's best, though, to use descriptive labels that help people reading the assembly code to understand the program.

An assembler would automatically convert the assembly code to the machine code shown in Figure 8.14(b). For each assembly instruction, the assembler determines the specific instruction type by looking at the mnemonic as well as the operands if necessary, and then outputs the appropriate opcode bits (four bits) for that instruction type, as defined in Table 8.2. For example, the assembler would look at the first instruction "MOV R0, #0" and thus know from the first three letters "MOV" that this is one of the data movement instructions; the assembler would look at the operands, and seeing "R0" would know this is either a regular load or a load-constant instruction; finally, the assembler would see the "#" and conclude this is a load-constant instruction, thus outputting the opcode "0011" for a load-constant instruction, as shown in the first machine instruction of the figure.

The assembler converts the operands to bits also, converting "R0" of the first instruction to "0000," and "#0" to "00000000," as shown in the first machine instruction of the figure.

The JMPZ instruction requires some extra handling. The assembler recognizes this as a *Jump-if-zero* instruction and thus outputs the opcode "0101." The assembler converts the first operand, "R2," to "0010." The assembler then reaches the second operand, "lab1," and does not know what bits to output, since the assembler doesn't yet know the address of the instruction labeled "lab1," as the assembler hasn't reached that instruction yet in the program. To solve this problem, many assemblers actually make *two passes* over the assembly code: during the first pass, the assembler creates a table of all labels and their addresses, and then on the second pass the assembler outputs machine code. Such an assembler would therefore know during the second pass that the instruction labeled "lab1" is at an address two addresses beyond the first JMPZ instruction—specifically, that the "lab1" instruction is at address 5, while the JMPZ instruction is at address 3 (assuming that the first instruction is at address 0, not 1). Thus, the assembler would output an offset of 2 to jump forward 2 addresses. Notice that the labels "lab1" and "lab2" do not appear in the machine code—they are merely a convenience construct that the assembler provides for the assembly-language programmer. ◄

► 8.6 FURTHER EXTENSIONS TO THE PROGRAMMABLE PROCESSOR

Instruction Set Extensions

Extending the instruction set with further instructions would require similar types of extensions and modifications to the control unit, datapath, and FSM. A programmable processor might contain dozens more ***data movement instructions***, which move data between data memory and the register file, or between registers. For example, a processor might have instructions for copying the contents of one register to another (e.g., MOV R0, R1, which would copy *R1*'s contents into *R0*), and would carry out that instruction using a state that reads the source register, passes the read value through the ALU unchanged, and writes the ALU output to the destination register. As another example, a processor might have instructions that would use the contents of a register as the address from which to read data memory, known as *indirect* addressing.

A programmable processor would also contain dozens of ***arithmetic/logic instructions***, which perform arithmetic and logic operations on registers in the register file. For example, a processor might include not just add and subtract instructions, but also increment, complement, decrement, AND, OR, XOR, shift left, shift right, and other instructions that could be carried out by an ALU.

A programmable processor would furthermore contain several *flow-of-control instructions*, which determine the next value of the *PC*. For example, a processor might include not just a jump-if-zero instruction, but also a jump-if-not-zero, an unconditional jump, an indirect jump, and perhaps even jump-if-negative and similar such instructions. Furthermore, a processor may include instructions that can jump farther than just a small offset from the current *PC*, and perhaps even to an absolute address rather than an offset address.

Input/Output Extensions

Section 1.3 introduced a basic microprocessor having eight inputs *I0*, *I1*, ..., *I7*, and eight outputs *P0*, *P1*, ..., *P7*. We can extend the basic programmable processor of Figure 8.12 to implement such external inputs and outputs. One method for such an extension would utilize a specially designed data memory. In that data memory, we might replace the last 16 words of the memory by direct connections to the input and output pins, as illustrated in Figure 8.15. The data memory stores locations 0 through 239 in a normal RAM. Location 240, however, is actually a special word whose high 15 bits are all 0s, and whose lowest bit comes from a flip-flop loaded every cycle with the value on external input pin *I0*. Thus, reading location 240 will result in either 00...01 (integer 1), or

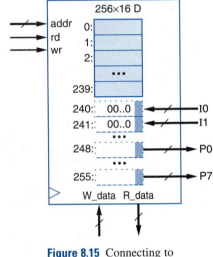

Figure 8.15 Connecting to external pins.

00...00 (integer 0), depending on the value appearing at *I0*. Likewise, location 241 is connected to pin *I1*, location 242 to *I2*, and so on, with location 247 connected to *I7*. Locations 248 through 255 are connected to pins *P0* through *P7*, except the pins are connected to those locations' flip-flop output. rather than inputs. For example, writing to location 255 writes the flip-flop with either 0 or 1 (only the low-order bit matters during the write), and that flip-flop drives external output pin *P7*.

Thus, an assembly-language programmer can read or write a microprocessor's external data pins simply by reading or writing particular data memory locations.

▶ **EXAMPLE 8.5** Motion-in-the-dark detector in assembly language

Section 1.3 included an example, illustrated in Figure 1.13, that utilized a microprocessor to implement a motion-in-the-dark detector. That section utilized C code to compute the expression P0 = I0 && !I1. In this example, we show the underlying assembly code that would implement that C expression. Assuming that the microprocessor's external pins *I0..I7* and *P0..P7* are mapped to data memory locations as in Figure 8.15, we can program the expression in assembly as follows:

```
0: MOV R0, 240        // move D[240], which is the value at pin I0, into R0
1: MOV R1, 241        // move D[241], which is that value at pin I1, into R1
2: NOT R1, R1         // compute !I1, assuming existence of a complement instruction
3: AND R0, R0, R1     // compute I0 && !I1, assuming an AND instruction
4: MOV 248, R0        // move result to D[248], which is pin P0
```
◀

Performance Extensions

One difference between real processors and the basic processor architecture in this chapter is that many real processors are pipelined (see Section 6.5 for an introduction to pipelining). The basic, three-instruction architecture utilized a controller with three stages: *fetch*, *decode*, and *execute*. By inserting appropriate pipeline registers throughout the design and modifying the controller appropriately, we could pipeline the fetch, decode, and execute stages. In other words, as the control unit decodes instruction 1, the control unit could be simultaneously fetching instruction 2. Next, as the control unit executes instruction 1, the control unit could be decoding instruction 2, and fetching instruction 3. Thus, rather than processing one instruction every 3 cycles, the control unit could be processing one instruction every cycle. Each instruction still takes 3 cycles to process (3 cycle latency), but the pipelining results in single cycle throughput. The net result would be that programs would execute three times faster.

Another extension involves creating deeper pipelines. Thus, rather than just three stages (fetch, decode, execute), we might break the stages down to stages of even finer granularity (e.g., fetch, decode, read operands, execute, store results). Creating finer grained stages may shorten the longest register-to-register delay, which enables a faster clock frequency. The net result would again be faster program execution.

Another extension involves having multiple ALUs in the datapath. The control unit may then perform multiple ALU operations simultaneously in the datapath. One form of this extension involves a processor whose instruction set uses instructions with multiple opcodes and associated operands in a single instruction, known as a ***Very Large Instruction Word (VLIW)*** processor. Another form uses a processor with a control unit that reads in multiple instructions simultaneously and then assigns those instructions to execute simultaneously on available ALUs, known as a ***superscalar*** processor. A high-end desktop processor may support perhaps 5 simultaneous instructions, with perhaps 10 stages of pipelining. Thus, at any moment, such a processor may be in the middle of processing $5*10 = 50$ different instructions. Needless to say, modern processor architectures can become quite complex.

This chapter described the basic idea of how a programmable processor's design works and how the design could be extended to support a fuller instruction set. We leave the role of describing a complete processor, as well as modern processor design techniques for improved performance (such as pipelining, caching, etc.), to textbooks on computer architecture.

► 8.7 CHAPTER SUMMARY

In this chapter, we stated (Section 8.1) that programmable processors are widely used for implementing a system's desired functionality, due in part to their easy availability and short design time (namely, writing software). We provided (Section 8.2) the basic architecture of a programmable processor, consisting of a general-purpose datapath having a register file and ALU; a control unit having a controller, *PC*, and *IR*; and memories for storing the program and the data. The control unit would fetch the next instruction from program memory, decode the instruction, and then execute the instruction by configuring the datapath to carry out the instruction's specified operation. We then designed (Section

8.3) a simple three-instruction programmable processor, and showed how a program would be represented as 0s and 1s (machine code) in the processor's program memory. We went further to design (Section 8.4) a six-instruction processor, and discussed how further extensions could be made to add more instructions and hence achieve a more reasonable processor architecture. We provided (Section 8.5) an example of assembly and machine code for the six-instruction processor. We discussed a few extensions to the programmable processor architecture (Section 8.6).

Programmable processors are typically produced in huge quantities (numbering in the tens of millions, or even billions), and so tremendous attention is given to their design. Readers should realize that the programmable processor designs in this chapter are extremely simplistic and used for illustration purposes only. Yet, seeing even the simplistic designs, you hopefully now have an understanding of the principle of how a programmable processor works. Modern commercial processors are based on the same principles—instructions are stored as machine code in program memory, control units fetch, decode, and execute the instructions, and datapaths support the operations of the instructions using register files and ALUs. Modern processors just do a much better job, using concurrency, pipelining, and many other techniques to obtain high clock frequencies and fast program execution.

▶ 8.8 EXERCISES

SECTION 8.2: BASIC ARCHITECTURE

8.1 If a processor's program counter is 20-bits wide, up to how many words can the processor's instruction memory hold (ignoring any special tricks to expand the instruction memory size)?

8.2 Which of the following are legal single-cycle datapath operations for the datapath in Figure 8.2? Explain your answer.
(a) Copy data from a memory location into another memory location.
(b) Copy two register locations into two memory locations.
(c) Add data from a register file location and a memory location, storing the result in a memory location.

8.3 Which of the following are legal single-cycle datapath operations for the datapath in Figure 8.2? Explain your answer.
(a) Copy data from a register file location into a memory location.
(b) Subtract data from two memory locations and store the result in another memory location.
(c) Add data from a register file location and a memory location, storing the result in the same memory location.

8.4 Assume we are using a dual-port memory from which we can read two locations simultaneously. Modify the datapath of the programmable processor of Figure 8.2 to support an instruction that performs an ALU operation on any two memory locations and stores the result in a register file location. Trace through the execution of this operation, as illustrated in Figure 8.3.

8.5 Determine the operations required to instruct the datapath of Figure 8.2 to perform the operation: $D[8] = (D[4] + D[5]) - D[7]$, where D represents the data memory.

SECTION 8.3: A THREE-INSTRUCTION PROGRAMMABLE PROCESSOR

8.6 If a processor's instruction has 4 bits for the opcode, how many possible instructions can the processor support?

8.7 What does the following assembly program, which uses the three-instruction instruction set of this chapter, compute? MOV R5, 19; ADD R5, R5, R5; MOV 20, R5.

8.8 What does the following assembly program, which uses the three-instruction instruction set of this chapter, compute? MOV R4, 20; MOV R9, 18; ADD R4, R4, R9; MOV R5, 30; ADD R9, R4, R5; MOV 20, R9.

8.9 Using the three-instruction instruction set of this chapter, write an assembly program that updates the data memory D as follows: D[0] = D[0] + D[1].

8.10 Using the three-instruction instruction set of this chapter, write an assembly program that updates the data memory D as follows: D[4] = D[1]*2 + D[2].

8.11 Convert the following assembly program to machine code based on the three-instruction instruction set of this chapter: MOV R5, 19; ADD R5, R5, R5; MOV 20, R5.

8.12 List the basic register/memory transfers and operations that occur during each clock cycle for the following program, based on the three-instruction instruction set of this chapter: MOV R0, 1; MOV R1, 9; ADD R0, R0, R1.

SECTION 8.4: A SIX-INSTRUCTION PROGRAMMABLE PROCESSOR

8.13 List the basic register/memory transfers and operations that occur during each clock cycle for the following program, based on the six-instruction instruction set of this chapter, assuming that the content of D[9] is 0: MOV R6, #1; MOV R5, 9; JMPZ R5, label1; ADD R5, R5, R6; label1: ADD R5, R5, R6. What is the value in R5 after the program completes?

8.14 Add a new instruction to the six-instruction instruction set of this chapter that performs a bitwise AND of two registers and stores the result in a third register. Extend the datapath, control unit, and the controller's FSM as needed.

8.15 Add a new instruction to the six-instruction instruction set of this chapter that performs an unconditional jump (jumps always) to a location specified by a 12-bit offset. Extend the datapath, control unit, and the controller's FSM as needed.

8.16 Add a new instruction to the six-instruction instruction set of this chapter that performs a jump if two registers are equal, to a location specified by a 12-bit offset. Extend the datapath, control unit, and the controller's FSM as needed.

8.17 Using the six-instruction instruction set of this chapter, write an assembly program for the following C code, which computes the sum of the first N numbers, where N is another name for D[9]. *Hint:* Use a register to first store N.

```
i=1;
sum=0;
while (i!=N) {
    sum = sum + i;
    i = i + 1;
}
```

8.18 Using the extended instruction set you designed in Exercise 8.16, write an assembly program for the C code in Exercise 8.17.

SECTION 8.5: EXAMPLE ASSEMBLY AND MACHINE PROGRAMS

8.19 Define two new data movement instructions for the six-instruction instruction set of this chapter. Extend the datapath, control unit, and the controller's FSM as needed.

8.20 Define two new arithmetic/logic instructions for the six-instruction instruction set of this chapter. Extend the datapath, control unit, and the controller's FSM as needed.

8.21 Define two new flow-of-control instructions for the six-instruction instruction set of this chapter. Extend the datapath, control unit, and the controller's FSM as needed.

8.22 Assuming that the microprocessor's external pins $I0..I7$ and $P0..P7$ are mapped to data memory locations as in Figure 8.15 and an AND instruction has been added to the six-instruction instruction set of this chapter, create an assembly program that will output 0 on $P4$ if all eight inputs $I0..I7$ are 1s.

▶ DESIGNER PROFILE

Carole grew up in a country where the best students went to engineering school, as engineering was highly respected. "I was good in school, so engineering seemed like a natural option. I was also very interested in building things, and very curious about how one builds new things—so I was attracted to engineering at an early age, around 10 years of age."

Carole has worked at Intel for 15 years. She was one of the original architects of the popular MMX (Multimedia Extension of the Intel Architecture) part of Pentium processors. "It was fascinating to learn the algorithms used to compress video and audio, and to invent new instructions for the Intel Architecture to run these applications efficiently. It is not always easy for processor architects to quantify the benefits of new features, and to motivate the expense in silicon area (or chip die size) for new instructions. In the case of multimedia applications, the benefits are well understood: running a video clip at a few frames per second, or running it in real time (about 30 frames per second) makes a huge, visible difference to everyone." As is the case with so many engineers, she is very proud of what she accomplished: "When the first Pentium processor with MMX came up, it was really rewarding to think that a small piece of my mind was in all of these machines running video real time popping up everywhere."

Carole was also one of the architects on the Intel / Hewlett-Packard team that defined the Itanium computer architecture. "This was a unique opportunity to define a processor 'from scratch.' Technically this was a very challenging project, and working with so many top notch architects was very enriching. But I also learned what it takes to build something big, involving a very large team, and two large companies. The two companies had different cultures, different methodologies, and reconciling the differences was sometimes more challenging than solving the technical problems. But this is all part of 'building things,' and this was a great lesson in leadership."

What Carole likes most about her career is "the constant change. After 22 years as a computer architect, I am still doing new things every day. Computer science is a work in progress, and it offers new opportunities that one has to grab, and run with. This is where the fun is."

Asked to give some advice to students, Carole suggests two things:

- "Stay at school as long as possible. Get a PhD if you can. To be able to adapt to constant change, you will need a very robust, and theoretical foundation. Only learning how to do things is not enough; it will get you a job for 2 years, but then your skills will be obsolete."

- "Be open for change. It is important to build an in-depth expertise in one area, in my case, it is computer architecture. But one has to be ready to use this expertise in many different projects, with different people, and more and more in different parts of the world. Fifteen years ago multimedia applications were the focus of many computer architects. Today it is bioinformatics and data mining. Change requires a lot of work to learn new domains, but not adapting to change is not an option."

CHAPTER 9

Hardware Description Languages

▶ 9.1 INTRODUCTION[1]

In this book, we have been drawing the circuits that we design. For example, in Chapter 2, we designed an automatic door opener circuit and drew the circuit shown in Figure 9.1. A drawing has more information than is really necessary to describe the circuit. In particular, the drawing gives information about the location of the inputs and outputs: in the drawing of Figure 9.1, the inputs are on the left, the output on the right, and the c input is on the top, the h input in the middle, and the p input on the

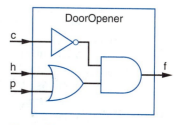

Figure 9.1 Drawn circuit.

bottom. The drawing also gives information about the size and location of the components in the circuit: the inverter is at the top, the OR gate below the inverter, the AND gate on the right, and each component is about a half inch by a half inch. The drawing gives information about the wires too: the wire from the inverter goes to the right, then down, then to the right again, for example. However, all that information about the drawing is really irrelevant, and has nothing to do with how the design will be physically implemented. We had to draw the circuit somehow, so we chose to draw the circuit in the manner shown in the figure. But we could have drawn the circuit many other ways too. A drawing of a circuit is commonly referred to as a circuit *schematic*.

A problem with drawing all our circuits arises when we deal with larger circuits. Does the schematic in Figure 9.2 mean anything to you? That schematic has just a couple dozen components—what if there were a couple thousand components, as is quite common? Drawing a large circuit would require tremendous effort on our part to figure out how to place each component in the drawing, and how to route wires among the components. And if a tool generated the circuit, the tool would have to spend compute time to figure out a visually-appealing way to draw the circuit (rather than a spaghetti-like mess), and such computation is time-consuming and still may not result in a good drawing. Furthermore, the files used to store such schematics would be very large, as those files would contain all that extra information about the precise location and size of every component. All that extra

1 Substantial content of this chapter was contributed by Roman Lysecky.

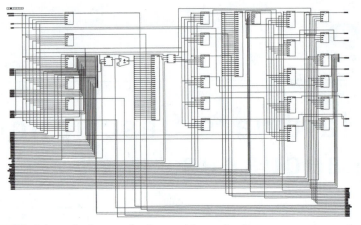

Figure 9.2 Schematics become hard to read beyond a dozen or so components—the graphical information becomes a nuisance rather than an aid.

effort, file size, and time, would be needed for something that is really not very useful—humans can't comprehend circuit drawings of more than perhaps a hundred or so gates, so what's the point of drawing such circuits? What we really want is a way to just describe the circuit itself—what are the inputs and outputs, what components exist, and what are the connections? Ideally, we would do this description in a textual language, so that we humans could type such descriptions with a computer keyboard, just like we type email messages and C programs.

We could therefore describe the circuit in Figure 9.3(a) using the textual language of English as shown in Figure 9.3(b). We've given names to each gate in the circuit and to the internal wires in Figure 9.3(a).

(a)

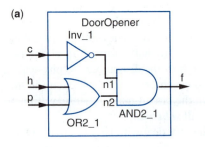

Figure 9.3 Describing a circuit using a textual language rather than a graphical drawing: (a) schematic, (b) textual description in the English language.

(b) We'll now describe a circuit whose name is DoorOpener.
   The external inputs are c, h and p, which are bits.
   The external output is f, which is a bit.

We assume you know the behavior of these components:
   An inverter, which has a bit input x, and bit output F.
   A 2-input OR gate, which has inputs x and y, and bit output F.
   A 2-input AND gate, which has bit inputs x and y, and bit output F.

The circuit has internal wires n1 and n2, both bits.
The DoorOpener circuit internally consists of:
   An inverter named Inv_1, whose input x connects to
      external input c, and whose output connects to n1.
   A 2-input OR gate named OR2_1, whose inputs connect to external
      inputs h and p, and whose output connects to n2.
   A 2-input AND gate named AND2_1, whose inputs connect to n1
      and n2, and whose output connects to external output f.
That's all.

Of course, English is not a good language if you want to use a computer tool to read in the description—a computer tool requires a language with a precise syntax and precise meaning for every language construct. Computer-readable languages thus evolved in the 1970s and 1980s for describing hardware circuits. Such languages became known as **_hardware description languages_**, or **_HDLs_**. Hardware description languages not only enable us to describe the structural interconnections of components, but also include methods for us to describe the behavior of components themselves. Modern digital design relies heavily on the use of HDLs at all stages of design.

We'll provide a brief introduction to the most popular hardware description languages—VHDL, Verilog, and SystemC—in this chapter, but to really learn each language, one may want to consult textbooks specifically dedicated to each language. Each section of this chapter can be covered immediately after corresponding earlier chapters (Section 9.2 after Chapter 2, Section 9.3 after Chapter 3, Section 9.4 after Chapter 4, and Section 9.5 after Chapter 5)—or these sections may be covered all at once after completing those earlier chapters. Furthermmore, each section has three parts, one for VHDL, one for Verilog, and one for SystemC. Each of those parts is independent of the other parts of the section, so a reader interested only in one of the HDLs, say Verilog, can read only the Verilog parts of each section, skipping the VHDL or SystemC parts.

A reader interested in comparing the three HDLs may read the sections of all three HDLs. In doing so, you may notice that the HDLs have similar capabilities, differing primarily in their syntax. Thus, after learning one HDL thoroughly, a designer can likely learn other HDLs quickly.

► 9.2 COMBINATIONAL LOGIC DESCRIPTION USING HARDWARE DESCRIPTION LANGUAGES

Structure

This chapter's introduction sought to describe a circuit using a textual language. We now show how some different HDLs describe a circuit. The term ***structure*** is sometimes used to refer to a circuit, with structure meaning an interconnection of component.

VHDL

Figure 9.4(c) shows a VHDL description of the *DoorOpener* circuit of Figure 9.4(a). For convenience, we've also shown the English description in Figure 9.4(b), and the correspondence between the English description and the VHDL description.

The description begins with an ***entity*** declaration, which defines the design's name and the design's inputs and outputs, known as ***ports***. An entity declaration says nothing about the internals of the design—just the design's name and interface. The description lists the port names and defines their type, which in this case is type `std_logic`. That type essentially means a bit, but isn't built into VHDL (the predefined *bit* type in VHDL is too limited, for reasons beyond our scope here). To use `std_logic`, we actually must include the statements: "`library ieee; use ieee.std_logic_1164.all;`" at the top of the file.

The description continues with an ***architecture*** definition, which describes the internals of the design. We named the architecture *Circuit*, but we could have named it anything we wanted: *DoorOpenerCircuit*, *DoorOpenerStructure*, *Structure*, or even *Fred*, although we want a name that is helpful in understanding the architecture. The architecture starts by declaring what components the design will be using—those components must be defined elsewhere, perhaps earlier in the description's file, or perhaps in another file. We'll discuss those components' definitions later—for now, assume they are somehow already defined. Each component declaration must define the inputs and outputs of each component, and those inputs and outputs must match the component's entity declaration (found elsewhere) exactly.

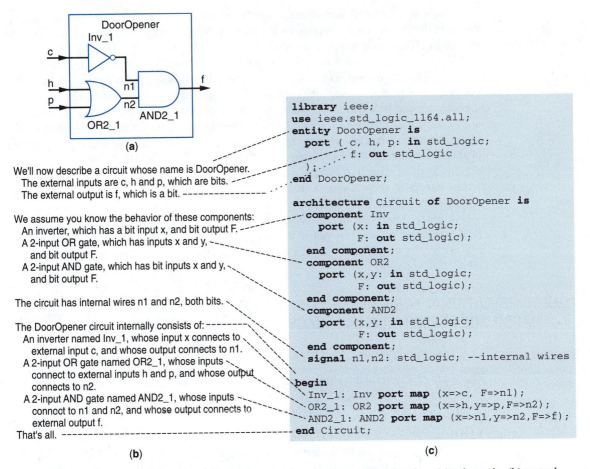

Figure 9.4 Describing a circuit using a textual language rather than a graphical drawing: (a) schematic, (b) textual description in the English language, (c) textual description in the VHDL language. Bolded words are reserved words in VHDL.

The description then includes a declaration of the design's internal *signals*, which are essentially internal wires. Next to that declaration, the description includes an example of a VHDL comment: "`-- internal wires`". Comments start with "`--`" followed by any text we want on the rest of the line. That text is ignored by VHDL tools, but is useful to us humans who must read the descriptions.

Finally, the description instantiates the circuit's components and defines those components' connections. For example, the description instantiates a component named *Inv_1*, which is a component of type *Inv* (which we declared earlier in the VHDL description), and indicates that *Inv_1*'s input *x* connects to *c*, which is an external input. An alternate, more concise port map notation omits the port names. Using this notation, we could instantiate our inverter by writing "`Inv_1: Inv port map (c, n1);`". The order of the signals in the port map of *Inv* corresponds to the order of the ports in the component definition of *Inv*. We will use this alternate notation in subsequent examples.

The bold words in the description represent reserved words, also known as keywords, in VHDL. We cannot use reserved words for names of entities, architectures, signals, instantiated components, etc., as those words have special meaning that guide VHDL tools to understand our descriptions.

Summarizing, the VHDL structural description has an entity that describes the design's name, inputs, and outputs; a declaration of what components will be used; a declaration of internal signals; and finally, an instantiation of all components, along with their interconnections.

The entity that we've just defined could then be used as a component in another entity.

Verilog

Figure 9.5(c) shows a Verilog description of the *DoorOpener* circuit of Figure 9.5(a). For convenience, we've also shown the English description in Figure 9.5(b), and the correspondence between the English description and the Verilog description.

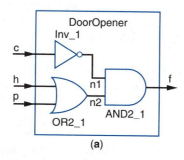

(a)

We'll now describe a circuit whose name is DoorOpener.
  The external inputs are c, h and p, which are bits.
  The external output is f, which is a bit.

We assume you know the behavior of these components:
  An inverter, which has a bit input x, and bit output F.
  A 2-input OR gate, which has inputs x and y,
    and bit output F.
  A 2-input AND gate, which has bit inputs x and y,
    and bit output F.

The circuit has internal wires n1 and n2, both bits.

The DoorOpener circuit internally consists of:
  An inverter named Inv_1, whose input x connects to
    external input c, and whose output connects to n1.
  A 2-input OR gate named OR2_1, whose inputs
    connect to external inputs h and p, and whose output
    connects to n2.
  A 2-input AND gate named AND2_1, whose inputs
    connect to n1 and n2, and whose output connects to
    external output f.
That's all. --

(b)

```verilog
module Inv(x, F);
  input x;
  output F;
  // details not shown
endmodule
module OR2(x, y, F);
  input x, y;
  output F;
  // details not shown
endmodule
module AND2(x, y, F);
  input x, y;
  output F;
  // details not shown
endmodule

module DoorOpener(c, h, p, f);
  input c, h, p;
  output f;
  wire n1, n2;
  Inv Inv_1(c, n1);
  OR2 OR2_1(h, p, n2);
  AND2 AND2_1(n1, n2, f);
endmodule
```

(c)

Figure 9.5 Describing a circuit using a textual language rather than a graphical drawing:
(a) schematic, (b) textual description in the English language, (c) textual description in the Verilog language. Bold words are reserved words in Verilog.

The description begins by defining modules for an inverter *Inv*, a 2-input OR gate *OR2,* and a 2-input AND gate *AND2*. We'll skip discussion of those modules, and begin our discussion with the definition of the fourth module *DoorOpener*.

The description declares a ***module*** named *DoorOpener*. The module declaration defines a design's name and the names of that design's inputs and outputs, known as ports. The module declaration says nothing about the internals of the design or the ports—just the design's name and interface.

The description then defines the type of each port, assigning the types ***input*** and ***output*** in this example.

The description then includes a declaration of the design's internal ***wires***, named *n1* and *n2*.

Finally, the description instantiates the circuit's components and defines those components' connections. In the *DoorOpener* module, the description instantiates a component named *Inv_1*, which is a component of type *Inv*. The connections to the inputs and outputs of the instantiated components are specified in the order in which the component's modules declare the inputs and outputs. In the instantiation of *Inv_1*, the input *c* is connected to the input *x* of the *Inv* component. In Verilog, the module does not need to specify the interface of a component within the module instantiating the component. For example, the *DoorOpener* module does not include a declaration of which components it will instantiate or any information regarding those components. The components, of course, must be defined elsewhere, perhaps earlier in the same file as shown in Figure 9.5(c), or perhaps in another file. For reference purposes, the example shown here provides incomplete specifications for the *Inv*, *AND2*, and *OR2* components in order to clearly show the ports and interface for these components. In place of specifying the internal behavior of these components, we simply included an example of a Verilog comment. Comments start with "//" and then any text we want on the rest of the line.

The bold words in the description represent reserved words, also known as keywords, in Verilog. We cannot use reserved words for names of modules, ports, wires, instantiated components, etc., as those words have special meaning that guide Verilog tools to understand our descriptions.

Summarizing, the Verilog structural description has a module that describes the design name, lists the module's inputs and outputs, and specifies the type for each input and output; a declaration of internal wires; and finally, an instantiation of all components, along with their interconnections.

SystemC

Figure 9.6(c) shows a SystemC description of the *DoorOpener* circuit of Figure 9.6(a). For convenience, we've also shown the English description in Figure 9.6(b), and the correspondence between the English description and the SystemC description. The SystemC language is built on top of the C++ programming language, but it is not necessary to be an expert C++ programmer to use SystemC. However, it is important to keep in mind that certain restrictions exist as a result, such as not using C++ keywords to name modules, ports, signals, etc.

Before defining the circuit behavior, we must include the statement "`#include "systemc.h"`" at the top of each SystemC file. The description begins with an ***SC_MODULE*** declaration, which defines the design's name, in this case *DoorOpener*. The

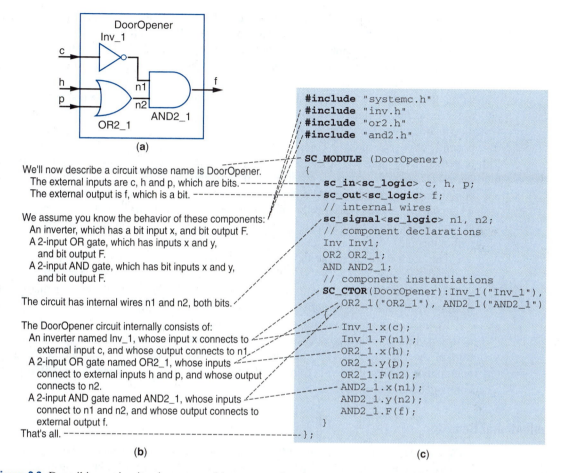

(a)

(b)

We'll now describe a circuit whose name is DoorOpener.
  The external inputs are c, h and p, which are bits.
  The external output is f, which is a bit.

We assume you know the behavior of these components:
  An inverter, which has a bit input x, and bit output F.
  A 2-input OR gate, which has inputs x and y,
    and bit output F.
  A 2-input AND gate, which has bit inputs x and y,
    and bit output F.

The circuit has internal wires n1 and n2, both bits.

The DoorOpener circuit internally consists of:
  An inverter named Inv_1, whose input x connects to
    external input c, and whose output connects to n1.
  A 2-input OR gate named OR2_1, whose inputs
    connect to external inputs h and p, and whose output
    connects to n2.
  A 2-input AND gate named AND2_1, whose inputs
    connect to n1 and n2, and whose output connects to
    external output f.
That's all.

(c)

```
#include "systemc.h"
#include "inv.h"
#include "or2.h"
#include "and2.h"

SC_MODULE (DoorOpener)
{
  sc_in<sc_logic> c, h, p;
  sc_out<sc_logic> f;
  // internal wires
  sc_signal<sc_logic> n1, n2;
  // component declarations
  Inv Inv1;
  OR2 OR2_1;
  AND AND2_1;
  // component instantiations
  SC_CTOR(DoorOpener):Inv_1("Inv_1"),
    OR2_1("OR2_1"), AND2_1("AND2_1")
  {
    Inv_1.x(c);
    Inv_1.F(n1);
    OR2_1.x(h);
    OR2_1.y(p);
    OR2_1.F(n2);
    AND2_1.x(n1);
    AND2_1.y(n2);
    AND2_1.F(f);
  }
};
```

Figure 9.6 Describing a circuit using a textual language rather than a graphical drawing: (a) schematic, (b) textual description in the English language, (c) textual description in the SystemC language. Bold words are reserved words in SystemC.

module declaration says nothing about the internals of the design—just the design's name. Within the module description, the input and output ports of the design are specified, using the *sc_in<>* and *sc_out<>* statements respectively. The description lists the port names and defines their types, which in this case is type sc_logic, which specifies a single bit.

The description then includes a declaration of the design's internal signals, specified as *sc_signal,* which are essentially internal wires. Next to that declaration, the description includes an example of a SystemC comment: "$// \ internal \ wires$". Comments start with "$//$" and then consist of any text we want on the rest of the line.

The module then declares what components the design will be using. The SystemC module does not need to specify the interface of the components, but rather just the type of component as well as a unique name for each component within the design.

The module defines a constructor function *SC_CTOR* that is responsible for instantiating and connecting the components within our SystemC design. The constructor function takes as an argument the name of the current SystemC module, which is in this case *Door-Opener*. Following the **SC_CTOR** statement after the colon is a list of component instantiations. The SystemC module's instantiations are used to call the constructor functions of each component being instantiated. However, we point out that the connections between the individual components are not specified at this point. Instead, the statements within the constructor finally define the connections between the components. For example, the inverter *Inv_1's* input *x* is connected to *c*, which is an external input. In SystemC, the module does not need to specify the interface of a component within the module. The components, of course, must be completely defined elsewhere, perhaps earlier in the same file, or perhaps in another file. In our SystemC *DoorOpener* description, the descriptions for the *Inv, AND2,* and *OR2* components are specified in other SystemC files. In order to use those components, we must include a statement at the beginning of the current file indicating where we can find this description. For example, our *DoorOpener* description includes the statement "#include "inv.h"", and the description of the component *Inv* can be found within this file.

The bolded words in the description represent reserved words, also known as keywords, in SystemC and C++. We cannot use reserved words for names of modules, ports, signals, instantiated components, etc., as those words have special meaning that guide SystemC and C++ tools to understand our descriptions.

Summarizing, the SystemC structural description has: a module that defines the design name; a list of inputs and outputs of the module specifying their types, a declaration of internal signals; a declaration of components providing the name for each component, a constructor function instantiating the module's components, and finally, the components' interconnections.

Combinational Behavior

HDLs typically support the ability to describe the internals of a design as behavior rather than as a circuit. This ability enables us to describe the bottom-level building-block components that we use in a design, such as the behavior of an AND gate or OR gate.

VHDL

Figure 9.7 contains a behavioral description of a 2-input OR gate, which you'll recall we used as a component in Figure 9.4(c). The description begins with the declarations necessary to use std_logic. It then declares the entity with the name *OR2* as having two input ports *x* and *y*, and having output port *F*, all of type std_logic, which means bit. The description then defines an architecture named *behavior* for *OR2*. That architecture consists of a ***process***, which is the VHDL construct that describes behavior. The process declaration here is

```
library ieee;
use ieee.std_logic_1164.all;

entity OR2 is
  port (x, y: in std_logic;
            F: out std_logic
  );
end OR2;

architecture behavior of OR2 is
begin
  process (x, y)
  begin
    F <= x or y;
  end process;
end behavior;
```

Figure 9.7 Behavioral VHDL description of an OR gate.

"process(x,y)", which means the process should execute from beginning to end whenever there's a change on *x* or *y*—in other words, the process is *sensitive* to x and y. A process body (the part between the process's begin and end) can contain sequential statements, just like sequential statements in C, but with a different syntax. The process shown has only one such statement, assigning the value of "x or y" to *F*. "or" happens to be a built-in operator in VHDL, making the internal description of the OR gate simple.

As another example of a behavioral description, let's revisit our *DoorOpener* example from Figure 9.4(c), for which we created an architecture having a structural description. We can alternatively create an architecture having a behavioral description—a VHDL entity may have multiple architecture descriptions for that same entity. Assuming the same entity declaration as in Figure 9.4(c), we show an alternative architecture definition in Figure 9.8. The behavior consists of a process that is sensitive to inputs *c*, *h*, and *p*. When the process executes (which is whenever *c*, *h*, or *p* changes), then the process executes its one statement, which updates the value of *f*.

In designing the *DoorOpener* circuit, we might start with the behavioral description, and run a simulation to verify correct behavior. We might then create a structural description, and run simulation again to verify that the circuit has the same functionality as the behavior. In fact, tools exist that automatically convert such behavior to a circuit.

```
architecture beh of DoorOpener is
begin
   process(c, h, p)
   begin
      f <= not(c) and (h or p);
   end process;
end beh;
```

Figure 9.8 Behavioral VHDL description of the *DoorOpener* design.

When writing a VHDL process describing a combinational circuit's behavior, care must be taken to include all the circuit's inputs in the process's sensitivity list. Omitting an input is not a VHDL error, but such omission results in different behavior than combinational behavior—with an input omitted, the output does not change when that input changes, meaning there must be some storage in the circuit.

Verilog

Figure 9.9 contains a behavioral description of a 2-input OR gate, which you'll recall we used as a component in Figure 9.5. The description begins by declaring the module named *OR2* and specifying that the module has three ports named *x*, *y*, and *F*. The description then defines that the ports *x* and *y* are both inputs and the port *F* is an output. The description then defines the output *F* to be a *reg* output. In Verilog, all ports are by default assumed to be a *wires*, which do not store values. Instead, wires can only create connec-

```
module OR2(x,y,F);
   input x, y;
   output F;
   reg F;

   always @(x or y)
   begin
      F <= x | y;
   end
endmodule
```

Figure 9.9 Behavioral Verilog description of an OR gate.

tions between components. If we want to assign a value to an output port, we must define the port to be a *reg*, which indicates the output port stores the values we assign to the port. The Verilog code for our design continues with an *always* procedure that defines a block of code that will be repeatedly executed whenever a change occurs on an input in the block's input list. The always procedure declaration is "always @(x or y)", which means the procedure should execute from beginning to end whenever there is a change on *x* or *y*—in other words, the procedure is *sensitive* to x and y. The always procedure's statements (the part between the procedure's *begin* and *end* statement) can contain sequential statements, just like sequential statements in C, but with a different syntax. The block shown has only one such statement, assigning the value of "x | y" to *F*, where | is a built-in Verilog operation to compute an OR.

As another example of a behavioral description, let's revisit our *DoorOpener* example from Figure 9.5(c), for which we created a structural Verilog description. We can alternatively create a behavioral description. Figure 9.10 presents a behavioral Verilog description of the *DoorOpener* circuit. The module declaration is similar to the structural description of Figure 9.5(c), but in the behavioral description we need to declare the output *f* as a **reg**. The behavior consists of an always procedure sensitive to inputs *c*, *h*, and *p*. When the procedure executes (which is whenever *c*,

```
module DoorOpener(c,h,p,f);
   input c, h, p;
   output f;
   reg f;

   always @(c or h or p)
   begin
      f <= (~c) & (h | p);
   end
endmodule
```

Figure 9.10 Behavioral Verilog description of the DoorOpener design.

h, or *p* changes), then the procedure executes a single statement that updates the value of *f*, by assigning the value "(~c) & (h | p)", where ~ , &, and | perform the invert, AND, and OR operations, respectively.

In designing the *DoorOpener* circuit, we might start with the behavioral description, and run a simulation to verify correct behavior. We might then create a structural description, and run a simulation again to verify that the circuit has the same functionality as the behavior. In fact, tools exist that automatically convert such behavior to a circuit.

SystemC

Figure 9.11 contains a SystemC behavioral description of a 2-input OR gate, which you'll recall we used as a component in Figure 9.6(c). The SystemC description declares the module with the name *OR2* and has two input ports *x* and *y* and one output port *F*, all of type sc_logic, indicating each input and output is an individual bit. The module defines the constructor function **SC_CTOR** that consists of a single process named *comblogic* defined as a **SC_METHOD**. **SC_METHOD** is one SystemC construct that describes behavior. The process declaration here is "SC_METHOD (comblogic); sensitive << x << y;", which means the

```
#include "systemc.h"

SC_MODULE(OR2)
{
   sc_in<sc_logic> x, y;
   sc_out<sc_logic> F;

   SC_CTOR(OR2)
   {
      SC_METHOD(comblogic);
      sensitive << x << y;
   }

   void comblogic()
   {
      F.write(x.read() | y.read());
   }
};
```

Figure 9.11 Behavioral SystemC description of an OR gate.

process will execute the circuit behavior described in the function *comblogic* whenever there is a change on *x* or *y*. In other words, the process is **sensitive** to x and y. The process body is defined in the function *comblogic* and is declared as "void comblogic()". The process function (the part between the open brace "{" and close brace "}") can contain sequential statements, just like sequential statements in C or C++, but sometimes requires different syntax. The process shown has only one such statement, writing the value of "x.read() | y.read()" to *F*, where | executes an OR operation. In SystemC, one can read the current value of an input port using the **read()** function and can write a value to an output port using the **write()** function. While we can use other methods of accessing the input and output ports, the **read()** and **write()** functions are recommended.

As another example of a behavioral description, let's revisit our *Door-Opener* example from Figure 9.6(c), for which we created a structural SystemC description. We can alternatively create a behavioral description. Figure 9.12 presents a behavioral SystemC description of the *DoorOpener* circuit. The module declaration is the same as the structural description of Figure 9.6(c). The behavior consists of a single process, named *comblogic*, that is sensitive to inputs *c*, *h*, and *p*. When the process executes (which is whenever *c*, *h*, or *p* changes), then the process executes its one statement, which updates the value of *f* by assigning the value "(~c.read()) & (h.read() | p.read())", where ~ performs an invert operation, & performs an AND operation, and | performs an OR operation.

```
#include "systemc.h"

SC_MODULE(DoorOpener)
{
  sc_in<sc_logic> c, h, p;
  sc_out<sc_logic> f;

  SC_CTOR(DoorOpener)
  {
    SC_METHOD(comblogic);
    sensitive << c << h << p;
  }

  void comblogic()
  {
    f.write((~c.read()) & (h.read() |
            p.read()));
  }
};
```

Figure 9.12 Behavioral SystemC description of the *DoorOpener* design.

In designing the *DoorOpener* circuit, we might start with the behavioral description, and run a simulation to verify correct behavior. We might then create a structural description, and run simulation again to verify that the circuit has the same functionality as the behavior. In fact, tools exist that automatically convert such behavior to a circuit.

Testbenches

One of the main uses of an HDL is that of simulating a new design to ensure that the design is correct. To simulate a design, we need to set the design's inputs to certain values, and then check that the design's output values are what we expect them to be. A system that sets input values and checks output values is known as a **testbench**. We now show how to create an HDL testbench to test our *DoorOpener* circuit.

VHDL

Figure 9.13 shows a VHDL testbench for the *DoorOpener* design of Figure 9.4(c). Notice that the entity, named *Testbench*, has no ports—the entity is self-contained, requiring no inputs and generating no outputs. The architecture declares the component that we plan to test—namely, the *DoorOpener* component. The architecture instantiates one instance of the *DoorOpener* component, which we named *DoorOpener1*. A single process in the architecture sets the inputs of the component and checks for correct output. This testbench tries all possible cases of the three inputs, of which there are eight cases. Many components have too many inputs to try all possible cases—in that situation, we might try border cases (e.g., all 0s, all 1s) and then some random cases.

Each case sets the three inputs of the component to a particular input combination, and waits for those values to

```
library ieee;
use ieee.std_logic_1164.all;

entity Testbench is
end Testbench;

architecture behavior of Testbench is
   component DoorOpener
      port ( c, h, p: in std_logic;
                f: out std_logic
      );
   end component;
   signal c, h, p, f: std_logic;
begin
   DoorOpener1: DoorOpener port map (c,h,p,f);

   process
   begin
      -- case 0
      c <= '0'; h <= '0'; p <= '0';
      wait for 1 ns;
      assert (f='0') report "Case 0 failed";

      -- case 1
      c <= '0'; h <= '0'; p <= '1';
      wait for 1 ns;
      assert (f='1') report "Case 1 failed";
      -- (cases 2-6 omitted from figure)
      -- case 7
      c <= '1'; h <= '1'; p <= '1';
      wait for 1 ns;
      assert (f='0') report "Case 7 failed";

      wait; -- process does not wake up again
   end process;
end behavior;
```

Figure 9.13 Behavioral VHDL description of *DoorOpener* testbench.

propagate through the component—we arbitrarily wait for 1 ns of simulated time, but could have picked any time, since we didn't actually create a time delay within the component. But we do have to wait for some time, as VHDL simulation is defined such that no signal is updated instantaneously, but rather after an infinitely small period of simulated time. After waiting, each case checks for the correct value on the output *f*, using an *assert* statement. If the condition of the assert statement evaluates to true, simulation proceeds to the next statement. But if the condition evaluates to false, the corresponding error message will be reported and the simulation will terminate.

Verilog

Figure 9.14 shows a Verilog test-bench for the *DoorOpener* design of Figure 9.5(c). Notice that the module, named *Testbench*, has no ports—the module is self-contained, requiring no inputs and generating no outputs. The module first declares three registered signals *c*, *h*, and *p* and a single wire *f*. The signals *c*, *h*, and *p* are declared as *reg* because we must assign values to the signals that will be connected to the inputs of the design we are testing. However, because we do not need to assign a value to the output we are monitoring, the signal *f* is declared as a *wire*. The testbench then instantiates one instance of the *DoorOpener* compo-

```verilog
module Testbench;
  reg c, h, p;
  wire f;

  DoorOpener DoorOpener1(c, h, p, f);

  initial
  begin
    // case 0
    c <= 0; h <= 0; p <= 0;
    #1 $display("f = %b", f);
    // case 1
    c <= 0; h <= 0; p <= 1;
    #1 $display("f = %b", f);
    // (cases 2-6 omitted from figure)
    // case 7
    c <= 1; h <= 1; p <= 1;
    #1 $display("f = %b", f);
  end
endmodule
```

Figure 9.14 Behavioral Verilog description of *DoorOpener* testbench.

nent, named *DoorOpener1,* and connects the inputs and outputs of the component to our internal signals. The testbench then contains an *initial* procedure that defines a block of code that will be executed only once when execution of the testbench begins. The initial procedure sets the inputs of the *DoorOpener* component and displays the resulting value of the component's output. This testbench tries all possible cases of the three inputs, of which there are eight cases. Many components have too many inputs to try all possible cases—in that situation, we might try border cases (e.g., all 0s, all 1s) and then some random cases.

Each case sets the three inputs of the component to a particular input combination, and waits for those values to propagate through the component—we arbitrarily wait for 1 unit of simulated time using the delay control statement "#1", but we could have picked any length of time, since we didn't actually create a time delay within the component. The Verilog language does not define standard time units, such as nanoseconds, but instead simply defines time in terms of time units, which a designer can use within a simulation environment. We do have to wait for some time, as the assignments within the testbench are nonblocking statements that are not updated until the current simulation time completes. After waiting, each case outputs the value of the output *f* using a *$display* statement. The statement "$display("f = %b", f)" outputs the value of *f* in binary. For example, if the value of *f* is 1, then the display statement will output "f = 1". The display statement consists of a format string followed by a comma-separated list of wires, registers, or ports. Within the format string of our display statement, the *%b* indicates that the value of the signal specified after the format string will be displayed in binary. After simulation has completed, we can compare the values output during simulation to the expected values, to determine if our circuit is working correctly.

SystemC

Figure 9.15 shows a SystemC testbench for the *DoorOpener* design of Figure 9.6(c). Notice that the module, named *Testbench*, has three output ports, *c_t*, *h_t*, and *p_t*, and one input port *f_t*. In SystemC, we design the testbench circuit as a separate module that connects to the design we are testing. Therefore, for every input port on the circuit we are testing, our testbench will have a corresponding output port. Likewise, for every output port on the circuit we are testing, our testbench will have a corresponding input port. The testbench module defines a single process named *testbench_proc*. The testbench process is defined as an **SC_THREAD**, which is similar to an **SC_METHOD** process except that the **SC_THREAD** allows us to use the **wait()** function within the process body to control the timing behavior of the process. In contrast, SystemC does not allow us to use the **wait()** function within an **SC_METHOD** process. The testbench process controls the inputs of the circuit we are testing and checks for correct output. This testbench tries all possible cases of the *DoorOpener's* three inputs, of which there are eight cases. Many

```
#include "systemc.h"

SC_MODULE(Testbench)
{
  sc_out<sc_logic> c_t, h_t, p_t;
  sc_in<sc_logic> f_t;

  SC_CTOR(Testbench)
  {
    SC_THREAD(testbench_proc);
  }

  void testbench_proc()
  {
    // case 0
    c_t.write(SC_LOGIC_0);
    h_t.write(SC_LOGIC_0);
    p_t.write(SC_LOGIC_0);
    wait(1, SC_NS);
    assert( f_t.read() == SC_LOGIC_0 );

    // case 1
    c_t.write(SC_LOGIC_0);
    h_t.write(SC_LOGIC_0);
    p_t.write(SC_LOGIC_1);
    wait(1, SC_NS);
    assert( f_t.read() == SC_LOGIC_1 );

    // (cases 2-6 omitted from figure)
    // case 7
    c_t.write(SC_LOGIC_1);
    h_t.write(SC_LOGIC_1);
    p_t.write(SC_LOGIC_1);
    wait(1, SC_NS);
    assert( f_t.read() == SC_LOGIC_0 );

    sc_stop();
  }
};
```

Figure 9.15 Behavioral SystemC description of *DoorOpener* testbench.

components have too many inputs to try all possible cases—in that situation, we might try border cases (e.g., all 0s, all 1s) and then some random cases.

Each case sets the three inputs of the *DoorOpener* circuit to a particular input combination, and waits for those values to propagate through the component—we arbitrarily wait for 1 ns of simulated time, but could have picked any time, since we didn't actually create a time delay within the component. But we do have to wait for some time, as SystemC simulation is defined such that no signal or port is updated instantaneously, but rather after an infinitely small period of simulated time. After waiting, each case checks for the correct output by reading the port *f_t* using an **assert** statement. If the condition of the assert statement evaluates to true, simulation proceeds to the next statement. But if the condition evaluates to false, simulation will stop and the corresponding error message will be reported.

In SystemC, values such as 0 and 1 are integer values and not logic values. Instead, SystemC defines the values *SC_LOGIC_0* and *SC_LOGIC_1* that correspond to the logic values of 0 and 1, respectively, which we used in the description.

▶ 9.3 SEQUENTIAL LOGIC DESCRIPTION USING HARDWARE DESCRIPTION LANGUAGES

Register

The most basic component in sequential logic is a register. We now show how to model a basic register in HDLs.

VHDL

Figure 9.16 shows a basic 4-bit register in VHDL. The register is identical to that described in Figure 3.30. The entity defines the data input *I* and the data output *Q*, as well as the clock input *clk*. The input *I* and output *Q* of this design correspond to 4-bit values. Instead of using eight individual *std_logic* inputs and outputs, the entity's *I* and *Q* ports are defined as *std_logic_vector*. A *std_logic_vector* is a vector, or array, of multiple *std_logic* elements. For example, the

```
library ieee;
use ieee.std_logic_1164.all;

entity Reg4 is
    port ( I: in std_logic_vector(3 downto 0);
           Q: out std_logic_vector(3 downto 0);
           clk: in std_logic
    );
end Reg4;

architecture behavior of Reg4 is
begin
    process(clk)
    begin
        if (clk='1' and clk'event) then
          Q <= I;
        end if;
    end process;
end behavior;
```

Figure 9.16 Behavioral VHDL description of a 4-bit register.

type declaration "std_logic_vector(3 downto 0)" defines a 4-bit vector of *std_logic* elements, where the bit positions within the vector are numbered from 3 to 0. The ***downto*** statement defines the ordering of the elements within the vector, indicating that element 3 is located in the leftmost position. The statement "I<="1000"" would thus assign the value '1' to position 3 of the vector I and the value '0' to the remaining three positions. When assigning a value to a *std_logic_vector*, the vector's value must be specified within double quotations. For example, the decimal value 5 would be specified as a 4-bit *std_logic_vector* as "0101".

The architecture describes the register behaviorally, using a process statement. The process is sensitive to its *clk* input only—because the process should only update its output during a rising clock edge, the process need not execute if input I changes. If *clk* changes, the process begins executing its statements. The first statement checks if the process began executing due to a rising clock edge (0 to 1), as opposed to a falling clock edge (1 to 0). The statement checks for a rising edge by checking if the *clk* input just changed (clk'event) and that change was to a 1 (clk='1'). If the process began executing due to a rising clock edge, then the process updates the register's contents using the statement "Q <= I". For a falling clock edge, the process will begin executing, check the *if* statement condition, and then reach the end of the process and hence stop executing, without updating *Q*. Ideally, VHDL would have a way to begin executing a process only on a rising clock edge, but VHDL has no such feature.

In VHDL, output ports are a type of signal, and signals have memory in simulation. Thus, assigning *I* to *Q* causes *Q* to retain the new value, even when the process stops executing, thus implementing the storage part of the register.

Verilog

Figure 9.17 shows a basic 4-bit register in Verilog. The register is identical to that described in Figure 3.30. The module defines the data input *I* and the data output *Q*, as well as the clock input *clk*. The input *I* and output *Q* of this design correspond to a 4-bit value. Instead of using eight individual inputs and outputs, the module's *I* and *Q* ports are defined as vectors. For example, the type declaration "input [3:0] I" defines a 4-bit input vector where the bit positions within the vector are numbered from 3 to 0. The [3:0] defines the ordering of the elements within the vector, indicating that element 3 is located in the leftmost position. The statement "I<=4'b1000" would thus assign the value

```
module Reg4(I, Q, clk);
   input [3:0] I;
   input clk;
   output [3:0] Q;
   reg [3:0] Q;

   always @(posedge clk)
   begin
      Q <= I;
   end
endmodule
```

Figure 9.17 Behavioral Verilog description of a 4-bit register.

1 to position 3 of the vector *I* and the value 0 to the remaining three positions. When assigning a value to vector, we must specify the number of bits within the value we are assigning, the base in which we are specifying the value, and the value itself. For example, the decimal value 5 would be specified as 4-bit binary value *4'b0101*.

The module describes the register behaviorally, using an *always* procedure. The procedure block is sensitive to the positive edge of the *clk* input, specified using the *posedge* keyword—because the module should only update its output during a rising clock edge, the always procedure need not execute if *I* changes. On the positive edge of the clock, the procedure updates the register's contents using the statement "Q <= I". Because we defined the output *Q* as a *reg*, assigning *I* to *Q* causes *Q* to retain the new value, even when the procedure is done executing, thus implementing the storage part of the register.

SystemC

Figure 9.18 shows a basic 4-bit register in SystemC. The register is identical to that described in Figure 3.30. The module defines the data input *I* and the data output *Q*, as well as the clock input *clk*. The input *I* and output *Q* of this design correspond to a 4-bit value. Instead of using eight individual *sc_logic* inputs and outputs, the module's *I* and *Q* ports are defined as *sc_lv* logic vector. An *sc_lv* is a vector of multiple *sc_logic* elements. For example, the type declaration "sc_lv<4>" defines a 4-bit vector of *sc_logic* elements where the bit positions within the vector are numbered from 3 to 0. In SystemC, the ordering of the elements within the vector is defined such that the leftmost position is the most significant bit. For example, the statement "I<="1000"" would thus assign the value 1 to position 3 of the vector *I* and the value 0 to the remaining three positions. When assigning a value to an *sc_lv*, the vector's value must be specified within double quotations. For example, the decimal value 5 would be specified as a 4-bit *sc_lv* as *"0101"*. Notice that in defining the input port for *I*, we included a space between the two closing angle brackets, >, the space being required in SystemC.

The module consists of a single process, named *seq_logic*, that is sensitive to the positive edge of the *clk* input, specified using the *sensitive_pos* statement for defining the sensitivity list—because the module should only update its output during a rising clock edge, the *seq_logic* process need not wake up if I changes. On the positive edge of the clock, the register updates the register's contents using the statement "Q.write(I.read())".

In SystemC, output ports are a type of signal, and signals have memory. Thus, assigning *I* to *Q* causes *Q* to retain the new value, even when the process is done executing, thus implementing the storage part of the register.

```
#include "systemc.h"

SC_MODULE(Reg4)
{
  sc_in<sc_lv<4> > I;
  sc_out<sc_lv<4> > Q;
  sc_in<sc_logic> clk;

  SC_CTOR(Reg4)
  {
    SC_METHOD(seq_logic);
    sensitive_pos << clk;
  }

  void seq_logic()
  {
    Q.write(I.read());
  }
};
```

Figure 9.18 Behavioral SystemC description of a 4-bit register.

Oscillator

VHDL

The register presented in Figure 9.16 has a clock input. We thus need to define an oscillator component that generates a clock signal. Figure 9.19 illustrates an oscillator described in VHDL. The entity defines one output, *clk*. The architecture consists of a process, but notice that process does not have a sensitivity list. By default, such a process executes its statements as if they were enclosed in an infinite loop. So the process sets the clock to 0, sleeps until 10 ns of simulated time passes, sets the clock to 1, sleeps another 10 ns of simulated time, goes back to the first statement in the process that sets the clock to 0, and so on. The output waveform for such an oscillator will be identical to the waveform shown in Figure 3.17.

The *wait for* statement in VHDL tells the simulator the amount of simulated time that the process should not execute. A process *without* a sensitivity list *must* have at least one wait statement, otherwise the simulator will never finish simulating that process (because the process is in an implicit infinite loop), and thus the simulator will never get a chance to update outputs or to simulate other processes. On the other hand, a process *with* a sensitivity list *cannot* include wait statements, because by definition, the sensitivity list defines when the process should execute.

```
library ieee;
use ieee.std_logic_1164.all;

entity Osc is
  port ( clk: out std_logic );
end Osc;

architecture behavior of Osc is
begin
  process
  begin
    clk <= '0';
    wait for 10 ns;
    clk <= '1';
    wait for 10 ns;
  end process;
end behavior;
```

Figure 9.19 VHDL oscillator description.

Verilog

The register presented in Figure 9.17 has a clock input. We thus need to define an oscillator component that generates a clock signal. Figure 9.20 illustrates an oscillator described in Verilog. The module defines one output, *clk*. The module consists of an *always* procedure, but notice that the always procedure does not have a sensitivity list. By default, such a procedure executes its statements as if they were enclosed in an infinite loop. Assuming we are using a time scale of nanoseconds, the always procedure sets the clock to 0, delays for 10 ns of simulated time, sets the clock to 1, delays for another 10 ns of simulated time, goes back to the first statement in the procedure that sets the clock to 0, and so on. The output waveform for such an oscillator will be identical to the waveform shown in Figure 3.17.

```
module Osc(clk);
  output clk;
  reg clk;

  always
  begin
    clk <= 0;
    #10;
    clk <= 1;
    #10;
  end
endmodule
```

Figure 9.20 Verilog oscillator description.

The delay control statement, specified with the **#** character, tells the simulator the amount of simulated time that the procedure should not execute. A procedure *without* a sensitivity list *must* have at least one delay control statement, otherwise the simulator will never finish simulating that procedure (because the procedure is in an implicit infinite loop), and thus the simulator will never get the chance to update outputs or to simulate other procedures. On the other hand, a procedure *with* a sensitivity list *cannot* include delay control statements, because by definition the sensitivity list defines when the procedure should awake.

SystemC

The register presented in Figure 9.18 has a clock input. We thus need to define an oscillator component that generates a clock signal. Figure 9.21 illustrates an oscillator described in SystemC. The module defines one output, *clk*. The module consist of a single process, named *seq_logic*, implemented as an **SC_THREAD**. By default, an **SC_THREAD** process is only executed once. In order to ensure the process executes continuously, we enclose the statements within the process in an infinite loop, implemented using the statement "while(true)". Thus, the loop will execute the statement included within the braces forever. During execution, the process sets the clock to 0, suspends execution for 10 ns of simulated time, sets the clock to 1, sleeps another 10 ns of simulated time, sets the clock to 0, and so on. The output waveform for such an oscillator will be identical to the waveform in Figure 3.17.

```
#include "systemc.h"

SC_MODULE(Osc)
{
  sc_out<sc_logic> clk;

  SC_CTOR(Osc)
  {
    SC_THREAD(seq_logic);
  }

  void seq_logic()
  {
    while(true) {
      clk.write(SC_LOGIC_0);
      wait(10, SC_NS);
      clk.write(SC_LOGIC_1);
      wait(10, SC_NS);
    }
  }
};
```

Figure 9.21 SystemC oscillator description.

The **wait()** function in SystemC tells the simulator the amount of simulated time that the process should not execute. For example, the statement "wait(10, SC_NS);" will suspend the execution of the process for 10 ns. An **SC_THREAD** process explicitly implementing an infinite loop *must* have at least one wait statement, otherwise the simulator will never finish simulating that process (because the process is in an infinite loop), and thus the simulator cannot update outputs or simulate other processes.

Controllers

Recall that a common type of sequential circuit is a controller, which implements a finite-state machine. The controller consists of a state register and combinational logic.

VHDL

Figure 9.22 shows one way to model a controller in VHDL. The controller modeled is described by the FSM shown in Figures 3.38 and 3.39. The VHDL entity, named *LaserTimer*, defines the controller's inputs and outputs.

The VHDL architecture describes the behavior of the entity. The architecture consists of two processes, one modeling the state register, the other modeling the combinational logic, that form the standard controller architecture from Figure 3.47.

The first process describes the controller's state register. That process, named *statereg*, is sensitive to inputs *clk* and *rst*. If the *rst* input is enabled, then the process asynchronously sets the *currentstate* signal to the FSM's initial state, *S_Off*. Otherwise, if the clock is rising, the process updates the state register with the next state.

```vhdl
library ieee;
use ieee.std_logic_1164.all

entity LaserTimer is
   port (b: in std_logic;
         x: out std_logic;
         clk, rst: in std logic
   );
end LaserTimer;

architecture behavior of LaserTimer is
   type statetype is
      (S_Off, S_On1, S_On2, S_On3);
   signal currentstate, nextstate:
      statetype;
begin
   statereg: process(clk, rst)
   begin
      if (rst='1') then -- intial state
         currentstate <= S_Off;
      elsif (clk='1' and clk'event) then
         currentstate <= nextstate;
      end if;
   end process;

   comblogic: process (currentstate, b)
   begin
      case currentstate is
         when S_Off =>
            x <= '0'; -- laser off
            if (b='0') then
               nextstate <= S_Off;
            else
               nextstate <= S_On1;
            end if;
         when S_On1 =>
            x <= '1'; -- laser on
            nextstate <= S_On2;
         when S_On2 =>
            x <= '1'; -- laser still on
            nextstate <= S_On3;
         when S_On3 =>
            x <= '1'; -- laser still on
            nextstate <= S_Off;
      end case;
   end process;
end behavior;
```

Figure 9.22 Behavioral VHDL description of the *LaserTimer* controller.

The *currentstate* and *nextstate* signals are defined as a user-defined type, named *statetype*. The statetype is defined by the **type** statement and specifies the possible values a signal of that type can represent. In specifying *statetype*, which represents the states of an FSM, the **type** declaration consists of the names of all the states in our controller, specifically *S_Off, S_On1, S_On2*, and *S_On3*.

The second process describes the controller's combinational logic. That process, named *comblogic*, is sensitive to the inputs to the combinational logic of Figure 3.47, namely, the external inputs (in this case, *b*), and the state register outputs (*currentstate*). When either of those items change, the process sets the FSM's outputs, in this case *x*, with the appropriate value for the current state. The process also determines what the next state should be, based on the current state and the values of inputs (i.e., the conditions on the FSM transitions). The next state will be loaded into the state register by the state register process on the next rising clock edge.

Notice that the architecture declares two signals, *currentstate* and *nextstate*. Signals are visible across all processes in an architecture. The *currentstate* signal represents the actual storage of the state register. The *nextstate* signal represents the value coming from the combinational logic and going to the state register. Notice also that the architecture declares those signals as type *statetype*, defined in the architecture as a type whose value can be either *S_Off*, *S_On1*, *S_On2*, or *S_On3*.

Verilog

Figure 9.23 shows one way to model a controller in Verilog. The controller modeled is described by the FSM shown in Figures 3.38 and 3.39. The Verilog module, named *LaserTimer*, defines the controller's inputs and outputs.

The module consists of two procedures, one modeling the state register, the other modeling the combinational logic, that together form the standard controller architecture from Figure 3.47.

The state register procedure is sensitive to the positive edge of the *rst* input and the positive edge of the *clk* input. The state register has an asynchronous reset signal and in order to model the asynchronous reset, the state register procedure must be sensitive to the positive

```verilog
module LaserTimer(b, x, clk, rst);
   input b, clk, rst;
   output x;
   reg x;

   parameter S_Off = 2'b00,
             S_On1 = 2'b01,
             S_On2 = 2'b10,
             S_On3 = 2'b11;

   reg [1:0] currentstate;
   reg [1:0] nextstate;
   // state register procedure
   always @(posedge rst or posedge clk)
   begin
      if (rst==1) // initial state
         currentstate <= S_Off;
      else
         currentstate <= nextstate;
   end
   // combinational logic procedure
   always @(currentstate or b)
   begin
      case (currentstate)
         S_Off: begin
            x <= 0; // laser off
            if (b==0)
               nextstate <= S_Off;
            else
               nextstate <= S_On1;
         end
         S_On1: begin
            x <= 1; // laser on
            nextstate <= S_On2;
         end
         S_On2: begin
            x <= 1; // laser still on
            nextstate <= S_On3;
         end
         S_On3: begin
            x <= 1; // laser still on
            nextstate <= S_Off;
         end
      endcase
   end
endmodule
```

Figure 9.23 Behavioral Verilog description of the *LaserTimer* controller.

edge of the *rst* input. On the positive edge of the *rst* input, the procedure will wake asynchronously and sets the *currentstate* signal to the FSM's initial state, *S_Off*. On the rising edge of the clock input, *clk*, if the reset input is not enabled, the procedure updates the state register with the *nextstate* value determined by the combinational logic procedure.

In Verilog, we must explicitly specify the size of the state registers as well as define the values associated with each state within the FSM. Within the *LaserTimer* module we declare four parameter values, namely, *S_Off*, *S_On1*, *S_On2*, and *S_On3*, which specify the values assigned to each state within the FSM. For example, "`S_Off = 2'b00`" defines the state name *S_Off* and assigns the 2-bit value "`00`" to this state. We can then refer to this state throughout the module using *S_Off* instead of using specific bit values. While not required to define a state machine, using parameters increases the readability of our design and makes revisions to the FSM much easier. As the *LaserTimer*'s FSM has four states, we need a 2-bit state register, and we therefore declare the *currentstate* and *nextstate* signals as 2-bit registers.

The second procedure is the combinational procedure implementing the control logic of the FSM. That procedure is sensitive to the inputs to the combinational logic of Figure 3.47, namely, the external inputs (in this case, *b*), and the state register outputs (*currentstate*). When either of those items change, the procedure sets the FSM's outputs, in this case *x*, with the appropriate value for the current state. The procedure also determines what the next state should be, based on the current state and the values of inputs (i.e., the conditions on the FSM transitions). The next state will be loaded into the state register by the state register procedure on the next positive clock edge.

Notice that the module declares two signals, *currentstate* and *nextstate*. Signals are visible across all procedures in a module. The *currentstate* signal represents the actual storage of the state register. The *nextstate* signal represents the value coming from the combinational logic and going to the state register.

SystemC

Figure 9.24 shows one way to model a controller in SystemC. The controller modeled is described by the FSM shown in Figure 3.38 and Figure 3.39. The module, named *LaserTimer*, defines the controller's inputs and outputs.

The module consists of two processes, one modeling the state register named *statereg*, the other process modeling the combinational logic named *comblogic*, that together form the standard controller architecture from Figure 3.47.

The state register process is sensitive to the positive edge of the *rst* input and the positive edge of the *clk* input. The state register has an asynchronous reset signal. In order to model the asynchronous reset, the state register process is sensitive to the positive edge of the *rst* input. On the positive edge of the *rst* input, the process will wake asynchronously and sets the *currentstate* signal to the FSM's initial state, *S_Off*. On the rising edge of the clock input, *clk*, if the reset input is not enabled, the process updates the state register with the *nextstate* value determined by the combinational logic process.

The *currentstate* and *nextstate* signals are defined as a user-defined type, named *statetype*. *statetype* is defined by the **enum** statement and specifying the possible values a signal of that type can represent. In specifying *statetype*, which represents the states of an FSM, the **enum** declaration consists of the names of all the states in our controller, specifically *S_Off*, *S_On1*, *S_On2*, and *S_On3*.

The second process, named *comblogic*, is sensitive to the inputs to the combinational logic of Figure 3.47, namely, the external inputs, and the state register outputs. When either of those items change, the process sets the FSM's outputs, in this case *x*, with the appropriate value for the current state. The process also determines what the next state should be, based on the current state and the values of inputs (i.e., the conditions on the FSM transitions). The next state will be loaded into the state register by the state register process on the next rising clock edge. Within the first state, we determine the next state depending on the value of input *b* by performing the comparison "b.read() == SC_ LOGIC_0". Note that the comparison for equality uses the syntax "==". Instead, if we accidentally used the syntax "=", which is a valid statement, our design would function incorrectly.

Notice that the module declares two *sc_signals*, *currentstate* and *nextstate*. Signals are visible across all processes in a module. The *currentstate* signal represents the actual storage of the state register. The *nextstate* signal represents the value coming from the combinational logic and going to the state register. Notice also that the architecture declares those signals as a type *statetype*, defined in the architecture as a type whose value can be either *S_Off*, *S_On1*, *S_On2*, or *S_On3*.

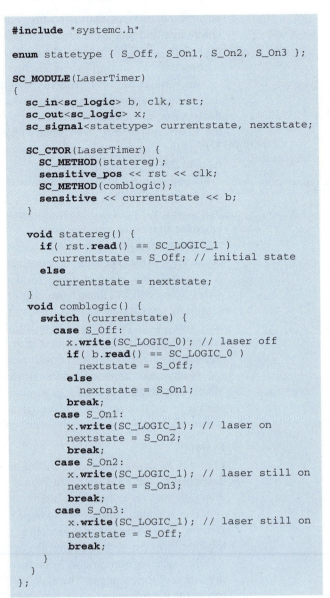

```
#include "systemc.h"

enum statetype { S_Off, S_On1, S_On2, S_On3 };

SC_MODULE(LaserTimer)
{
  sc_in<sc_logic> b, clk, rst;
  sc_out<sc_logic> x;
  sc_signal<statetype> currentstate, nextstate;

  SC_CTOR(LaserTimer) {
    SC_METHOD(statereg);
    sensitive_pos << rst << clk;
    SC_METHOD(comblogic);
    sensitive << currentstate << b;
  }

  void statereg() {
    if( rst.read() == SC_LOGIC_1 )
      currentstate = S_Off; // initial state
    else
      currentstate = nextstate;
  }
  void comblogic() {
    switch (currentstate) {
      case S_Off:
        x.write(SC_LOGIC_0); // laser off
        if( b.read() == SC_LOGIC_0 )
          nextstate = S_Off;
        else
          nextstate = S_On1;
        break;
      case S_On1:
        x.write(SC_LOGIC_1); // laser on
        nextstate = S_On2;
        break;
      case S_On2:
        x.write(SC_LOGIC_1); // laser still on
        nextstate = S_On3;
        break;
      case S_On3:
        x.write(SC_LOGIC_1); // laser still on
        nextstate = S_Off;
        break;
    }
  }
};
```

Figure 9.24 Behavioral SystemC description of the *LaserTimer* controller.

▶ 9.4 DATAPATH COMPONENT DESCRIPTION USING HARDWARE DESCRIPTION LANGUAGES

Full-Adders

Recall that a full-adder is a combinational circuit that adds three bits (a, b, and ci) and generates a sum (s) and a carry-out (co) bit. This section shows how to describe a full-adder behaviorally in an HDL.

VHDL

Figure 9.25 shows a full-adder described behaviorally in VHDL. The full-adder design corresponds to the full-adder described in Figure 4.31. The VHDL entity, named *FullAdder*, defines the full-adder's three inputs *a*, *b*, and *ci* and two outputs *s* and *co*.

The architecture describes the behavior of the full-adder. The architecture consists of a single process describing

```vhdl
library ieee;
use ieee.std_logic_1164.all;

entity FullAdder is
    port ( a, b, ci: in std_logic;
              s, co: out std_logic
    );
end FullAdder;

architecture behavior of FullAdder is
begin
    process (a, b, ci)
    begin
        s <= a xor b xor ci;
        co <= (b and ci) or (a and ci) or (a and b);
    end process;
end behavior;
```

Figure 9.25 Behavioral VHDL description of a full-adder.

the combinational behavior of the full-adder. The process is sensitive to all three inputs (*a*, *b*, and *ci*) of the full-adder. When any of the inputs change, the process executes its two statements updating the values for the sum (*s*) and carry-out (*co*).

Verilog

Figure 9.26 shows a full-adder described behaviorally in Verilog. The full-adder design corresponds to the full-adder described in Figure 4.31. The Verilog module, named *FullAdder*, defines the full-adder's three inputs *a*, *b*, and *ci* and two outputs *s* and *co*.

The module describes the behavior of the full-adder and consists of a single always procedure describing the combinational behavior of the full-adder. The pro-

```verilog
module FullAdder(a, b, ci, s, co);
    input a, b, ci;
    output s, co;
    reg s, co;

    always @(a or b or ci)
    begin
        s <= a ^ b ^ ci;
        co <= (b & ci) | (a & ci) | (a & b);
    end
endmodule
```

Figure 9.26 Behavioral Verilog description of a full-adder.

cedure is sensitive to all three inputs (*a*, *b*, or *ci*) of the full-adder. When any of the inputs change, the procedure executes its two statements updating the values for the sum (*s*) and carry-out (*co*).

SystemC

Figure 9.27 shows a full-adder described behaviorally in SystemC. The full-adder design corresponds to the full-adder described in Figure 4.31. The SystemC module, named *Full-Adder*, defines the full-adder's three inputs *a*, *b*, and *ci* and two outputs *s* and *co*.

The module describes the behavior of the full-adder and consists of a single process, named *comblogic*, describing the combinational behavior of the full-adder. The process is sensitive to all three inputs (*a*, *b*, or *ci*) of the full-adder. When any of the inputs change, the process executes its two statements updating the values for the sum (*s*) and carry-out (*co*).

```
#include "systemc.h"

SC_MODULE(FullAdder)
{
  sc_in<sc_logic> a, b, ci;
  sc_out<sc_logic> s, co;

  SC_CTOR(FullAdder)
  {
    SC_METHOD(comblogic);
    sensitive << a << b << ci;
  }

  void comblogic()
  {
    s.write(a.read() ^ b.read() ^ ci.read());
    co.write((b.read() & ci.read()) |
             (a.read() & ci.read()) |
             (a.read() & b.read()));
  }
};
```

Figure 9.27 Behavioral SystemC description of a full-adder.

Carry-Ripple Adders

We now show how to structurally describe a 4-bit carry-ripple adder using the full-adder we designed in the previous section.

VHDL

Figure 9.28 is a VHDL description of a 4-bit carry-ripple adder with a carry-in, as appeared in Figure 4.33. The VHDL entity, named *CarryRippleAdder4*, has two 4-bit inputs, *a* and *b*, and a carry-in input, *ci*. The carry-ripple adder outputs a 4-bit sum, *s*, and a final carry-out *co*.

The architecture structurally describes the carry-ripple adder composed of four full-adders. The architecture begins by declaring the component *FullAdder*,

```
library ieee;
use ieee.std_logic_1164.all;

entity CarryRippleAdder4 is
  port ( a:  in std_logic_vector(3 downto 0);
         b:  in std_logic_vector(3 downto 0);
         ci: in std_logic;
         s:  out std_logic_vector(3 downto 0);
         co: out std_logic
  );
end CarryRippleAdder4;

architecture structure of CarryRippleAdder4 is
  component FullAdder
    port ( a, b, ci: in std_logic;
           s, co: out std_logic
    );
  end component;
  signal co1, co2, co3: std_logic;
begin
  FullAdder1: FullAdder
    port map (a(0), b(0), ci, s(0), co1);
  FullAdder2: FullAdder
    port map (a(1), b(1), co1, s(1), co2);
  FullAdder3: FullAdder
    port map (a(2), b(2), co2, s(2), co3);
  FullAdder4: FullAdder
    port map (a(3), b(3), co3, s(3), co);
end structure;
```

Figure 9.28 Structural VHDL description of a 4-bit carry-ripple adder.

which was described in the previous section. The design has three internal signals, *co1*, *co2*, and *co3*, that are used for internal connection between the full-adders. The architecture then instantiates four *FullAdder* components. In VHDL, each instantiated component must have a unique name. The four *FullAdder* components in this design are uniquely-identified by the names *FullAdder1*, *FullAdder2*, *FullAdder3*, and *FullAdder4*.

In VHDL, the *std_logic_vector* type provides a convenient method of specifying ports or signals consisting of multiple bits. However, a design may need to access the individual bits of these vectors. The individual bits of a *std_logic_vector* can be accessed by specifying the desired bit position within parentheses after the vector's name. For example, to access bit 0 of the 4-bit input *a* of this design, one would use the syntax "a(0)". In defining the connections to the instantiated components in the carry-ripple adder, individual bits of the inputs *a* and *b* and output *s* are accessed using this syntax. The first full-adder, *FullAdder1*, connects bit 0 of the inputs *a* and *b* as well as the carry-ripple adder's carry-in, *ci*, to the full-adder's three inputs. The *s* output of *FullAdder1* is connected to bit 0 of the 4-bit adder's sum output, *s*, represented as *s(0)*. The design then connects the carry-out bit of *FullAdder1* to the internal signal *co1*, which is subsequently connected to the carry-in input of the next full-adder, *FullAdder2*. The component connections of the remaining three full-adders are connected in a similar fashion, with the exception of the last full-adder in the carry-ripple chain. The carry-out from that last full-adder, *FullAdder4*, is connected to the carry-out output (*co*) of the carry-ripple adder.

Verilog

Figure 9.29 is a Verilog description of a 4-bit carry-ripple adder with a carry-in, as appeared in Figure 4.33. The Verilog module, named *CarryRippleAdder4*, has two 4-bit inputs, *a* and *b*, and a carry-in input, *ci*. The carry-ripple adder outputs a 4-bit sum, *s*, and a final carry-out *co*.

The module structurally describes the carry-ripple adder composed of four full-adders. The design has three internal wires, *co1*, *co2*, and *co3*, that are used for internal connection between the full-adders. The

```verilog
module CarryRippleAdder4(a, b, ci, s, co);
  input [3:0] a;
  input [3:0] b;
  input ci;
  output [3:0] s;
  output co;

  wire co1, co2, co3;

  FullAdder FullAdder1(a[0], b[0], ci,
                       s[0], co1);
  FullAdder FullAdder2(a[1], b[1], co1,
                       s[1], co2);
  FullAdder FullAdder3(a[2], b[2], co2,
                       s[2], co3);
  FullAdder FullAdder4(a[3], b[3], co3,
                       s[3], co);
endmodule
```

Figure 9.29 Structural Verilog description of a 4-bit carry-ripple adder.

module instantiates four *FullAdder* components. In Verilog, each instantiated component must have a unique name. The four *FullAdder* components in this design are uniquely-identified by the names *FullAdder1*, *FullAdder2*, *FullAdder3*, and *FullAdder4*.

In Verilog, vectors provide a convenient method of specifying ports or signals consisting of multiple bits. However, a design may need to access the individual bits of these vectors. The individual bits of a vector can be accessed by specifying the desired bit position within brackets after the vector's name. For example, to access bit 0 of the 4-bit input *a* of this design, one would use the syntax "a[0]". In defining the connections to the instantiated components in the carry-ripple adder, individual bits of the inputs *a* and *b* and output *s* are accessed using this syntax. The first full-adder, *FullAdder1*, connects bit 0 of the inputs *a* and *b* as well as the carry-ripple adder's carry-in, *ci*, to the full-adder's three inputs. The *s* output of *FullAdder1* is connected to bit 0 of the 4-bit adder's sum output, *s*, represented as *s[0]*. The design then connects the carry-out bit of *FullAdder1* to the internal signal *co1*, which is subsequently connected to the carry-in input of the next full-adder, *FullAdder2*. The component connections of the remaining three full-adders are connected in a similar fashion, with the exception of the last full-adder in the carry-ripple chain. The carry-out from the last full-adder, *FullAdder4*, is connected to the carry-out output (*co*) of the carry-ripple adder.

SystemC

Figure 9.30 is a SystemC description of a 4-bit carry-ripple adder with a carry-in, as appeared in Figure 4.33. The SystemC module, named *CarryRippleAdder4*, has two 4-bit inputs, *a* and *b*, and a carry-in input, *ci*. The carry-ripple adder outputs a 4-bit sum, *s*, and a final carry-out *co*.

```
#include "systemc.h"
#include "fulladder.h"

SC_MODULE(CarryRippleAdder4)
{
    sc_in<sc_logic> a[4];
    sc_in<sc_logic> b[4];
    sc_in<sc_logic> ci;
    sc_out<sc_logic> s[4];
    sc_out<sc_logic> co;

    sc_signal<sc_logic> co1, co2, co3;

    FullAdder FullAdder_1;
    FullAdder FullAdder_2;
    FullAdder FullAdder_3;
    FullAdder FullAdder_4;

    SC_CTOR(CarryRipple4):
        FullAdder_1("FullAdder_1"),
        FullAdder_2("FullAdder_2"),
        FullAdder_3("FullAdder_3"),
        FullAdder_4("FullAdder_4")
    {
        FullAdder_1.a(a[0]); FullAdder_1.b(b[0]);
        FullAdder_1.ci(ci); FullAdder_1.s(s[0]);
        FullAdder_1.co(co1);

        FullAdder_2.a(a[1]); FullAdder_2.b(b[1]);
        FullAdder_2.ci(co1); FullAdder_2.s(s[1]);
        FullAdder_2.co(co2);

        FullAdder_3.a(a[2]); FullAdder_3.b(b[2]);
        FullAdder_3.ci(co2); FullAdder_3.s(s[2]);
        FullAdder_3.co(co3);

        FullAdder_4.a(a[3]); FullAdder_4.b(b[3]);
        FullAdder_4.ci(co3); FullAdder_4.s(s[3]);
        FullAdder_4.co(co);
    }
};
```

Figure 9.30 Structural SystemC description of a 4-bit carry-ripple adder.

The module structurally describes the carry-ripple adder composed of four full-adders. The design has three internal signals, *co1*, *co2*, and *co3*, that are used for internal connection between the full-adders. The module first instantiates four *FullAdder* components. In SystemC, each instantiated component must have a unique name. The four *FullAdder* components in this design are uniquely identified by the names *FullAdder_1*, *FullAdder_2*, *FullAdder_3*, and *FullAdder_4*.

Previously, we defined multiple-bit inputs as an input vector using the *sc_lv* type. However, SystemC does not support connecting individual bits within a signal or port of type *sc_lv* in a structural description. In our *CarryRippleAdder4* design, we instead defined the inputs and outputs, *a*, *b*, and *s*, as arrays of *sc_logic* with four elements each, rather than using type *sc_lv*. The individual bits of the array can be accessed by specifying the desired bit position within brackets after the array's name. For example, to access bit 0 of the 4-element input array *a* of this design, one would use the syntax "a[0]". In defining the connections to the instantiated components in the carry-ripple adder, individual bits of the inputs *a* and *b* and output *s* are accessed using this syntax. The first full-adder, *FullAdder_1*, connects bit 0 of the inputs *a* and *b* as well as the carry-ripple adder's carry-in, *ci*, to the full-adder's three inputs. The *s* output of *FullAdder_1* is connected to bit 0 of the 4-bit adder's sum output, *s*, represented as *s[0]*. The design then connects the carry-out bit of *FullAdder_1* to the internal signal *co1* that is subsequently connected to the carry-in input of the next full-adder, *FullAdder_2*. The component connections of the remaining three full-adders are connected in a similar fashion, with the exception of the last full-adder in the carry-ripple chain. The carry-out from the last full-adder, *FullAdder_4*, is connected to the carry-out output (*co*) of the carry-ripple adder.

Up-Counter

VHDL

Figure 9.31 is a VHDL description of a 4-bit up-counter, as appeared in Figure 4.48. The VHDL entity, name *UpCounter*, defines the counter's inputs and outputs, consisting of a clock input *clk*, a count enable control input *cnt*, the 4-bit count value *C*, and a terminal count output *tc*.

The *UpCounter's* architecture structurally describes the design consisting of three components, namely *Reg4*, *Inc4*, and *AND4*. *Reg4* is a 4-bit parallel load register with a load control input *ld*. *Inc4* is a 4-bit incrementer. *AND4* is a four-input AND gate that will output 1 if and only if all four inputs are 1. The architectures further specifies two signals, *tempC* and *incC*, used as internal wires within the structural description.

```vhdl
library ieee;
use ieee.std_logic_1164.all;

entity UpCounter is
    port ( clk: in std_logic;
           cnt: in std_logic;
           C: out std_logic_vector(3 downto 0);
           tc: out std_logic
    );
end UpCounter;

architecture structure of UpCounter is
    component Reg4
        port ( I: in std_logic_vector(3 downto 0);
               Q: out std_logic_vector(3 downto 0);
               clk, ld: in std_logic
        );
    end component;
    component Inc4
        port ( a: in std_logic_vector(3 downto 0);
               s: out std_logic_vector(3 downto 0)
        );
    end component;
    component AND4
        port ( w,x,y,z: in std_logic;
               F: out std_logic
        );
    end component;
    signal tempC: std_logic_vector(3 downto 0);
    signal incC: std_logic_vector(3 downto 0);
begin
    Reg4_1: Reg4 port map(incC, tempC, clk, cnt);
    Inc4_1: Inc4 port map(tempC, incC);
    AND4_1: AND4 port map(tempC(3), tempC(2),
                          tempC(1), tempC(0), tc);

    outputC: process(tempC)
    begin
        C <= tempC;
    end process;
end structure;
```

Figure 9.31 Structural VHDL description of 4-bit up-counter.

The architecture instantiates each of the three components and specifies the connections between them. *Reg4* is the only sequential component within the up-counter and thus the *clk* input only needs to be connected to the clock input of the register. We control the up-counter's counting by connecting the count enable input, *cnt*, to the load enable, *ld*, of the register. The output *Q* of *Reg4_1* is connected to the internal signal *tempC*, which connects the register's output to both the *Inc4_1* and *AND4_1* components. *Inc4_1* receives the current count from the *tempC* connection and outputs the incremented count on its output *s*, which is connected to the other internal signal *incC*. The *incC* signal connects the incremented count from *Inc4_1* to the parallel load input *I* of *Reg4_1*. The current count is also connected to the four inputs of the *AND4_1* component. The *AND4_1*'s output *F* is then connected to the counter's terminal count output *tc*.

In the *UpCounter* design, we need to connect the output of the 4-bit register to the incrementer, the AND gate, and the counter's output port *C*. VHDL does not allow us to connect multiple signals or ports within the *port map* of an instantiated component. Therefore, the architecture uses the *tempC* signal to connect *Reg4_1*'s output to both the *AND4_1* and *Inc4_1* components. We still need to connect the register's output to the output port *C*. The architecture makes this connection by specifying a process, named *outputC*, that is used to connect the output of the register to the output port *C*. The *outputC* process is sensitive to the signal *tempC*, previously used as an internal wire between the three components. Whenever *tempC* changes, which corresponds to a change in the up-counter's stored count, the *outputC* process assigns the new count to the output port *C*.

Verilog

Figure 9.32 is a Verilog description of a 4-bit up-counter, as appeared in Figure 4.48. The Verilog module, named *UpCounter*, defines the counter's inputs and outputs, consisting of a clock input *clk*, a count enable control input *cnt*, the 4-bit count value *C*, and a terminal count output *tc*.

The *UpCounter*'s module structurally describes the design consisting of three components, namely *Reg4*, *Inc4*, and *AND4*. *Reg4* is a 4-bit parallel load register with a load control input *ld*. *Inc4* is a 4-bit incrementer. *AND4* is a four-input AND gate that will output 1 if and only if all four inputs are 1. The module further specifies two 4-bit wires, *tempC* and *incC*, used as internal wires within the structural description.

The module instantiates each of the three components and specifies the connections between them. *Reg4* is the only sequential component within the up-counter and thus the *clk* input only needs to be connected to the clock input of the register. We control the up-counter's counting by connecting the count enable input, *cnt*, to the load enable, *ld*, of the register. The output *Q* of *Reg4_1* is

```verilog
module Reg4(I, Q, clk, ld);
   input [3:0] I;
   input clk, ld;
   output [3:0] Q;
   // details not shown
endmodule

module Inc4(a, s);
   input [3:0] a;
   output [3:0] s;
   // details not shown
endmodule

module AND4(w,x,y,z,F);
   input w, x, y, z;
   output F;
   // details not shown
endmodule

module UpCounter(clk, cnt, C, tc);
   input clk, cnt;
   output [3:0] C;
   reg [3:0] C;
   output tc;

   wire [3:0] tempC;
   wire [3:0] incC;

   Reg4 Reg4_1(incC, tempC, clk, cnt);
   Inc4 Inc4_1(tempC, incC);
   AND4 AND4_1(tempC[3], tempC[2],
               tempC[1], tempC[0], tc);

   always @(tempC)
   begin
      C <= tempC;
   end
endmodule
```

Figure 9.32 Structural Verilog description of 4-bit up-counter.

connected to the internal signal *tempC*, which connects the register's output to both the *Inc4_1* and *AND4_1* components. *Inc4_1* receives the current count from the *tempC* connection and outputs the incremented count on its output *s* which is connected to the other internal signal *incC*. The *incC* signal connects the incremented count from *Inc4_1* to the parallel load input *I* of *Reg4_1*. The current count is also connected to the four inputs of the *AND4_1* component. The *AND4_1*'s output *F* is then connected to the counter's terminal count output *tc*.

In the *UpCounter* design, we need to connect the output of the 4-bit register to the incrementer, the AND gate, and the counter's output port *C*. Therefore, the module uses the *tempC* signal to connect *Reg4_1*'s output to both the *AND4_1* and *Inc4_1* components. We still need to connect the register's output to the output port *C*. The module makes this connection by specifying a procedure that is used to connect the output of the register to the output port *C*. The procedure is sensitive to the signal *tempC*, previously used as an internal wire between the three components. Whenever *tempC* changes, which corresponds to a change in the up-counter's stored count, the procedure assigns the new count to the output port *C*.

SystemC

Figure 9.33 is a SystemC description of a 4-bit up-counter, as appeared in Figure 4.48. The SystemC module, named *UpCounter*, defines the counter's inputs and outputs, consisting of a clock input *clk*, a count enable control input *cnt*, the 4-bit count value *C*, and a terminal count output *tc*.

The *UpCounter's* module structurally describes the design consisting of three components, namely, *Reg4*, *Inc4*, and *AND4*. *Reg4* is a

```
#include "systemc.h"
#include "reg4.h"
#include "inc4.h"
#include "and4.h"

SC_MODULE(UpCounter)
{
  sc_in<sc_logic> clk, cnt;
  sc_out<sc_lv<4> > C;
  sc_out<sc_logic> tc;

  sc_signal<sc_lv<4> > tempC, incC;
  sc_signal<sc_logic> tempC_b[4];

  Reg4 Reg4_1;
  Inc4 Inc4_1;
  AND4 AND4_1;

  SC_CTOR(UpCounter) : Reg4_1("Reg4_1"),
                       Inc4_1("Inc4_1"),
                       AND4_1("AND4_1")
  {
   Reg4_1.I(incC); Reg4_1.Q(tempC);
   Reg4_1.clk(clk); Reg4_1.ld(cnt);

   Inc4_1.a(tempC); Inc4_1.s(incC);

   AND4_1.w(tempC_b[0]); AND4_1.x(tempC_b[1]);
   AND4_1.y(tempC_b[2]); AND4_1.z(tempC_b[3]);
   AND4_1.F(tc);

   SC_METHOD(comblogic);
   sensitive << tempC;
  }

  void comblogic()
  {
   tempC_b[0] = tempC.read()[0];
   tempC_b[1] = tempC.read()[1];
   tempC_b[2] = tempC.read()[2];
   tempC_b[3] = tempC.read()[3];
   C.write(tempC);
  }
};
```

Figure 9.33 Structural SystemC description of 4-bit up-counter.

4-bit parallel load register with a load control input *ld*. *Inc4* is a 4-bit incrementer. *AND4* is a four-input AND gate that will output 1 if and only if all four inputs are 1. The module further specifies two 4-bit signals, *tempC* and *incC*, used as internal wires within the structural description. Additionally, the module defines a four-element array of *sc_logic* signals, named *tempC_b*, used to access the individual bits within the 4-bit vector *tempC*.

The module first instantiates each of the three components and then specifies the connections between them. *Reg4* is the only sequential component within the up-counter and thus the *clk* input only needs to be connected to the clock input of the register. We control the up-counter's counting by connecting the count enable input, *cnt*, to the load enable, *ld*, of the register. The output *Q* of *Reg4_1* is connected to the internal signal *tempC*, which connects the register's output to *Inc4_1*. *Inc4_1* receives the current count from the *tempC* connection and outputs the incremented count on its output *s* which is connected to the internal signal *incC*. The *incC* signal connects the incremented count from *Inc4_1* to the parallel load input *I* of *Reg4_1*. The current count is also connected to the four inputs of the *AND4_1* component using the *tempC_b* array to access the individual bits. The *AND4_1*'s output *F* is then connected to the counter's terminal count output *tc*.

In the *UpCounter* design, we need to connect the output of the 4-bit register to the incrementer, the AND gate, and the counter's output port *C*. Therefore, the module uses the *tempC* signal to connect *Reg4_1*'s output to the *Inc4_1* component and uses the *tempC_b* array to connect *Reg4_1*'s output to the *AND4_1* component. Thus, we still need to connect the register's output to the output port *C* and assign the individual bits of the register's output to the *tempC_b* array. The module makes these connections by defining a process, named *comblogic*, that is sensitive to the signal *tempC*. Whenever *tempC* changes, which corresponds to a change in the up-counter's stored count, the *comblogic* process assigns the new count to the output port *C*. Additionally, the process assigns the bits within vector *tempC* to the individual *sc_logic* signals within the *tempC_b* array. In order to access the individual bits of the vector signal *tempC*, we use the syntax, "tempC.read()[0]".

▶ 9.5 RTL DESIGN USING HARDWARE DESCRIPTION LANGUAGES

We now show how to create RTL descriptions using HDLs. We will show HDL descriptions of the starting point of RTL design, namely, high-level state machines, and of the ending point of RTL design, namely, connected controllers and datapaths. RTL designers will commonly create a testbench to test the high-level state machine description, and then use that same testbench for the controller/datapath description, thus helping to verify that the designer created a correct controller/datapath implemention.

High-Level State Machine of the Laser-Based Distance Measurer

VHDL

Figures 9.34 and 9.35 present a VHDL description of a high-level state machine for the laser-based distance measurer shown in Figure 5.15. The entity, named *LaserDistMeasurer*, defines the inputs and outputs, including a user-pressed button input *B*, a laser sensor input *S*, a laser control output *L*, and a 16-bit output *D* for the distance measured.

```
library ieee;
use ieee.std_logic_1164.all;
use ieee.std_logic_arith.all;

entity LaserDistMeasurer is
  port ( clk, rst: in std_logic;
    B, S: in std_logic;
    L: out std_logic;
    D: out unsigned(15 downto 0)
  );
end LaserDistMeasurer;

architecture behavior of LaserDistMeasurer is
  type statetype is (S0, S1, S2, S3, S4);

  signal state : statetype;
  signal Dctr : unsigned(15 downto 0);

  constant U_ZERO :
    unsigned (15 downto 0) := "0000000000000000";
  constant U_ONE : unsigned(0 downto 0) := "1";
begin
  statemachine: process(clk, rst)
  begin
    if (rst='1') then
      L <= '0';
      D <= U_ZERO;
      Dctr <= U_ZERO;
      state <= S0;                    -- initial state
    elsif (clk='1' and clk'event) then
      case state is
        when S0 =>
          L <= '0';                   -- laser off
          D <= U_ZERO;                -- clear D
          state <= S1
```
(continued in Figure 9.35)

Figure 9.34 Behavioral VHDL description of a high-level state machine of the laser-based distance measurer.

Instead of using a 16-bit *std_logic_vector*, we defined the output *D* as *unsigned*. For logic operations, an *unsigned* behaves the same as a *std_logic_vector*. However, we can also perform arithmetic operations on *unsigned* values. Whenever using *unsigned*, we must include the statement "use ieee.std_logic_arith.all;" at the top of our VHDL description. The ***use*** statement specifies which packages we will use within our design. The package *ieee.std_logic_arith* defines the *unsigned* type as well as a set of operations and functions we can perform on *unsigned* values.

The entity also defines a clock input *clk* and reset input *rst*. We assume that the clock input is 300 MHz, as was assumed in the laser-based distance measurer design shown in Figure 5.19. We omit details of generating the 300 MHz clock (see Section 9.3 for an example of describing an oscillator).

The VHDL architecture describes the behavior of the entity. Instead of using two processes as shown in Figure 9.22, the architecture consists of a single process describing the behavior of our high-level state machine. The high-level state machine process, named *statemachine*, is sensitive to inputs *clk* and *rst*. If the *rst* is 1, then the process asynchronously sets the *state* signal to the state machine's initial state, *S0*, and initializes

```
(continued from Figure 9.34)
            when S1 =>
                Dctr <= U_ZERO;              -- reset count
                if (B='1') then
                    state <= S2;
                else
                    state <= S1;
                end if;
            when S2 =>
                L <= '1';                    -- laser on
                state <= S3;
            when S3 =>
                L <= '0';                    -- laser off
                Dctr <= Dctr + 1;
                if (S='1') then
                    state <= S4;
                else
                    state <= S3;
                end if;
            when S4 =>
                D <= SHR(Dctr, U_ONE); -- calculate D
                state <= S1;
          end case;
        end if;
      end process;
end behavior;
```

Figure 9.35 Behavioral VHDL description of a high-level state machine of the laser-based distance measurer *(continued)*.

the outputs, *L* and *D*, and the internal counter signal, *Dctr*, to their default values. The default values should correspond to the values assigned to the signals within the initial state of our high-level state machine. Notice that we defined a constant, named *U_ZERO*, corresponding to the 16-bit *unsigned* value of zero. When the *rst* is not enabled, on the rising clock, the process evaluates the current state, assigns the appropriate outputs for the current state, determines the next state, and updates the state register signal, *state*. In our high-level state machine description, we only need a single state register signal to model the behavior of our state machine, instead of the two signals *currentstate* and *nextstate* we previously used in the controller design shown in Figure 9.22.

The high-level state machine for the laser-based distance measurer performs two arithmetic operations, addition and shifting. By using the *unsigned* type, to increment the counter signal *Dctr* in state *S3*, we use the syntax, "Dctr <= Dctr + 1;". This statement will add one to the current value of *Dctr* and store the result in *Dctr*. In state *S4*, we calculate the distance, *D*, by dividing the value of *Dctr* by 2. However, we perform this division using a right-shift-by-one operation. To perform the shift and assign the value to the output *D*, we use the statement "D <= SHR(Dctr, U_ONE);". The function **SHR()**, defined within the `ieee.std_logic_arith` package, shifts the first parameter, *Dctr*, by the amount specified by the second parameter, *U_ONE*, where *U_ONE* is a constant we defined earlier in the architecture.

Verilog

Figures 9.36 and 9.37 present a Verilog description of a high-level state machine for the laser-based distance measurer shown in Figure 5.15. The module, named *Laser-DistMeasurer*, defines the inputs and outputs, including a user-pressed button input *B*, a laser sensor input S, a laser control output L, and a 16-bit output D for the distance measured.

The module also defines a clock input *clk* and reset input *rst*. We assume that the clock input is 300 MHz, as was assumed in the laser-based distance measurer design shown in Figure 5.19. We omit details of generating the 300 MHz clock (see Section 9.3 for an example of describing an oscillator).

The Verilog module behaviorally describes the *LaserDistMeasurer's* high-level state machine. Instead of using two procedures as shown in Figure 9.23, the module consists of a single procedure describing the behavior of our high-level state machine. The high-level state machine procedure is sensitive to the positive edge of the reset input, *rst*, and the positive edge of the clock input, *clk*. If the *rst* is enabled, then the procedure asynchronously sets the state register, *state*, to the state machine's initial state, *S0*, and initializes the outputs,

```verilog
module LaserDistMeasurer(clk, rst, B, S, L, D);
  input clk, rst, B, S;
  output L;
  output [15:0] D;
  reg L;
  reg [15:0] D;

  parameter S0 = 3'b000,
            S1 = 3'b001,
            S2 = 3'b010,
            S3 = 3'b011,
            S4 = 3'b100;

  reg [2:0] state;
  reg [16:0] Dctr;

  always @(posedge rst or posedge clk)
  begin
    if (rst==1) begin
      L <= 0;
      D <= 0;
      Dctr <= 0;
      state <= S0; // initial state
    end
    else begin
      case (state)
        S0: begin
          L <= 0;            // laser off
          D <= 0;            // clear D
          state <= S1;
        end
        S1: begin
          Dctr <= 0;         // reset count
          if (B==1)
            state <= S2;
          else
            state <= S1;
        end
        S2: begin
          L <= 1;            // laser on
          state <= S3;
        end
```

(continued in Figure 9.37)

Figure 9.36 Behavioral VHDL description of a high-level state machine of the laser-based distance measurer.

L and D, and the internal counter register, *Dctr*, to their default values. The default values should correspond to the values assigned to the signals within the initial state of our high-level state machine. When the *rst* is not enabled, on the rising clock, the procedure evaluates the current state, assigns the appropriate outputs for the current state, determines the next state, and updates the state register. In our high-level state machine description, we only need a single state register signal to model the behavior of our state machine, instead of the two register signals *currentstate* and *nextstate* we previously used in the controller design shown in Figure 9.23.

The high-level state machine for the laser-based distance measurer performs two arithmetic operations, addition and shifting. To increment the counter *Dctr* in state *S3*, we use the syntax, "Dctr <= Dctr + 1;". This statement will add one to the current value of *Dctr* and store the result in *Dctr*. In state *S4*, we calculate the distance, *D*, by dividing the value of *Dctr* by 2. However, we perform this division using a right shift by one operation. To perform the shift and assign the value to the output *D*, we use the statement "D <= Dctr >> 1;", where >> performs a right shift operation.

SystemC

Figures 9.38 and 9.39 present a SystemC description of a high-level state machine for the laser-based distance measurer shown in Figure 5.15. The module, named *Laser-DistMeasurer*, defines the inputs and outputs, including a user-pressed button input *B*, a laser sensor input *S*, a laser control output *L*, and a 16-bit output *D* for the distance measured.

The module also defines a clock input *clk* and reset input *rst*. We assume that the clock input is 300 MHz, as was assumed in the laser-based distance measurer design shown in Figure 5.19. We omit details of generating the 300 MHz clock (see Section 9.3 for an example of describing an oscillator).

```verilog
(continued from Figure 9.36)
        S3: begin
          L <= 0;              // laser off
          Dctr <= Dctr + 1;
          if (S==1)
            state <= S4;
          else
            state <= S3;
        end
        S4: begin
          D <= Dctr >> 1; // calculate D
          state <= S1;
        end
      endcase
    end
  end
endmodule
```

Figure 9.37 Behavioral Verilog description of a high-level state machine of the laser-based distance measurer *(continued)*.

```cpp
#include "systemc.h"

enum statetype { S0, S1, S2, S3, S4 };

SC_MODULE(LaserDistMeasurer)
{
  sc_in<sc_logic> clk, rst;
  sc_in<sc_logic> B, S;
  sc_out<sc_logic> L;
  sc_out<sc_lv<16> > D;

  sc_signal<statetype> state;
  sc_signal<sc_uint<16> > Dctr;

  SC_CTOR(LaserDistMeasurer)
  {
    SC_METHOD(statemachine);
    sensitive_pos << rst << clk;
  }

  void statemachine()
  {
    if( rst.read() == SC_LOGIC_1 ) {
      L.write(SC_LOGIC_0);
      D.write(0);
      Dctr = 0;
      state = S0; // initial state
    }
    else {
      switch (state) {
        case S0:
          L.write(SC_LOGIC_0);      // laser off
          D.write(0);               // clear D
          state = S1;
          break;
        case S1:
          Dctr = 0;                 // clear count
          if (B.read() == SC_LOGIC_1)
            state = S2;
(continued in Figure 9.39)
```

Figure 9.38 Behavioral SystemC description of a high-level state machine of the laser-based distance measurer.

The SystemC module behaviorally describes the *LaserDistMeasurer's* high-level state machine. Instead of using two processes as shown in Figure 9.24, the module consists of a single process describing the behavior of our high-level state machine. The high-level state machine process, named *statemachine*, is sensitive to the positive edge of the reset input, *rst*, and the positive edge of the clock input, *clk*. If the *rst* is enabled, then the process asynchronously sets the *state* signal to the state machine's initial state, *S0*, and initializes the outputs,

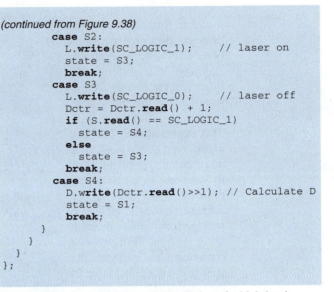

```
(continued from Figure 9.38)
        case S2:
          L.write(SC_LOGIC_1);    // laser on
          state = S3;
          break;
        case S3
          L.write(SC_LOGIC_0);    // laser off
          Dctr = Dctr.read() + 1;
          if (S.read() == SC_LOGIC_1)
            state = S4;
          else
            state = S3;
          break;
        case S4:
          D.write(Dctr.read()>>1); // Calculate D
          state = S1;
          break;
      }
    }
  }
};
```

Figure 9.39 Behavioral SystemC description of a high-level state machine of the laser-based distance measurer *(continued)*.

L and *D*, and the internal counter signal, *Dctr*, to their default values. The default values should correspond to the values assigned to the signals within the initial state of our high-level state machine. When the *rst* is not enabled, on the rising clock, the process evaluates the current state, assigns the appropriate outputs for the current state, determines the next state, and updates the state register signal, *state*. In our high-level state machine description, we only need a single state register signal to model the behavior of our state machine, instead of the two signals *currentstate* and *nextstate* we previously used in the controller design shown in Figure 9.24.

The high-level state machine for the laser-based distance measurer performs two arithmetic operations, addition and shifting. To increment the counter *Dctr* in state *S3*, we use the syntax, "`Dctr = Dctr.read() + 1;`". This statement will add one to the current value of *Dctr* and store the result in *Dctr*. In state *S4*, we calculate the distance, *D*, by dividing the value of *Dctr* by 2. However, we perform this division using a right shift by one operation. To perform the shift and assign the value to the output *D*, we use the statement "`D.write(Dctr.read()>>1);`", where >> performs a right shift operation.

Controller and Datapath of the Laser-Based Distance Measurer

VHDL

Figure 9.40 is a VHDL description of the laser-based distance measurer shown in Figure 5.19. The entity, named *LaserDistMeasurer*, defines the inputs and outputs, including a user-pressed button input *B*, a laser sensor input *S*, a laser control output *L*, and a 16-bit output *D* for the distance measured. The entity also defines a 300 MHz clock input *clk* and reset input *rst* for the design's controller.

```vhdl
library ieee;
use ieee.std_logic_1164.all;

entity LaserDistMeasurer is
   port ( clk, rst: in std_logic;
          B, S: in std_logic;
          L: out std_logic;
          D: out std_logic_vector(15 downto 0)
   );
end LaserDistMeasurer;

architecture structure of LaserDistMeasurer is
   component LDM_Controller
      port ( clk, rst: in std_logic;
             B, S: in std_logic;
             L: out std_logic;
             Dreg_clr, Dreg_ld: out std_logic;
             Dctr_clr, Dctr_cnt: out std_logic
      );
   end component;
   component LDM_Datapath
      port ( clk: in std_logic;
             Dreg_clr, Dreg_ld: in std_logic;
             Dctr_clr, Dctr_cnt: in std_logic;
             D: out std_logic_vector(15 downto 0)
      );
   end component;
   signal Dreg_clr, Dreg_ld: std_logic;
   signal Dctr_clr, Dctr_cnt: std_logic;
begin
   LDM_Controller_1: LDM_Controller
      port map (clk, rst, B, S, L,
                Dreg_clr, Dreg_ld, Dctr_clr,
                Dctr_cnt);
   LDM_Datapath_1: LDM_Datapath
      port map (clk, Dreg_clr, Dreg_ld,
                Dctr_clr, Dctr_cnt, D);
end structure;
```

Figure 9.40 Structural description of top-level VHDL description of laser-based distance measurer.

The *LaserDistMeasurer*'s architecture structurally describes the connections of the controller and datapath components. The architecture instantiates two components. *LDM_Controller_1* is the controller for the laser-based distance measurer and *LDM_Datapath_1* is the datapath for this design. The architecture connects the entity's *clk*, *rst*, *B*, and *S* inputs to the inputs of *LDM_Controller_1* and connects the controller's laser control output to the corresponding output port *L*. Additionally, the four signals, *Dreg_clr*, *Dreg_ld*, *Dctr_clr*, and *Dctr_cnt*, connect the controller's four control signals to the four inputs of *LDM_Datapath_1*. The *LaserDistMeasurer* datapath has a single output *D*, providing the distance measured, that is connected to the output port *D* of the entity.

Figure 9.41 is a VHDL description of the *LaserDistMeasurer's* datapath component shown in Figure 5.17. The entity, named *LDM_Datapath*, defines a clock input *clk*, four control inputs *Dreg_clr*, *Dreg_ld*, *Dctr_clr*, and *Dctr_cnt,* and a 16-bit distance output *D*.

The architecture defines three components, a 16-bit up-counter, a 16-bit register, and a 16-bit right shifter that shifts right by one position. *UpCounter16* is a 16-bit up-counter with a count control input *cnt* and a count clear input *clr*. *Reg16* is a 16-bit

```vhdl
library ieee;
use ieee.std_logic_1164.all;

entity LDM_Datapath is
   port ( clk: in std_logic;
          Dreg_clr, Dreg_ld: in std_logic;
          Dctr_clr, Dctr_cnt: in std_logic;
          D: out std_logic_vector(15 downto 0)
   );
end LDM_Datapath;

architecture structure of LDM_Datapath is
   component UpCounter16
      port ( clk: in stdlogic;
             clr, cnt: in std_logic;
             C: out std_logic_vector(15 downto 0)
      );
   end component;
   component Reg16
      port ( I: in std_logic_vector(15 downto 0);
             Q: out std_logic_vector(15 downto 0);
             clk, clr, ld: in std_logic
      );
   end component;
   component ShiftRightOne16
      port ( I: in std_logic_vector(15 downto 0);
             S: out std_logic_vector(15 downto 0)
      );
   end component;
   signal tempC : std_logic_vector(15 downto 0);
   signal shiftC : std_logic_vector(15 downto 0);
begin
   Dctr: UpCounter16
      port map (clk, Dctr_clr, Dctr_cnt, tempC);
   ShiftRight: ShiftRightOne16
      port map (tempC, shiftC);
   Dreg: Reg16
      port map (shiftC, D, clk, Dreg_clr, Dreg_ld);
end structure;
```

Figure 9.41 Structural VHDL description of the laser-based distance measurer's datapath.

parallel load register with a register load control signal *ld* and a register clear signal *clr*. *ShiftRightOne16* is a 16-bit right shifter that shifts the input *I* right by one position and assigns the shifted value to the output *S*. The architecture instantiates an *UpCounter16* component named *Dctr*, a *Reg16* component named *Dreg*, and a *ShiftRightOne16* component named *ShiftRight*. *Dctr*'s instantiation connects the datapath's *Dctr_clr* and *Dctr_cnt* inputs to *Dctr*'s clear and count control inputs. *Dctr*'s count output *C* is then connected to the architecture's internal signal *tempC* that connects the count value to the *ShiftRight* shifter's input. The shifted count is then connected to the input of the *Dreg* register using the internal signal *shiftC*. The instantiation of the *Dreg* register connects the register's clear and load control inputs to the datapath's *Dreg_clr* and *Dreg_ld* input ports. Finally, the register's data output *Q* is connected to *LDM_datapath*'s measured distance output *D*.

Figure 9.42 and Figure 9.43 are the VHDL description of the laser-based distance measurer's FSM controller described in Figure 5.21. The entity, named *LDM_Controller*, defines a clock input *clk*, a reset signal *rst*, a user-pressed button input *B*, a laser sensor input *S*, and five output control signals, *L, Dreg_clr, Dreg_ld, Dctr_clr,* and *Dctr_cnt*. The output *L* is used to turn the laser on and off, where if *L* is 1, the laser is on. The four other output signals are used to control the RTL design's data-path components.

The VHDL architecture describes the behavior of the entity. Similar to the controller design shown in Figure 9.22, the architecture consists of two processes, one modeling the state register, the other modeling the combinational logic. The state register process, named *statereg*, is sensitive to inputs *clk* and *rst*. If the *rst* is enabled, then the process asynchronously sets the *currentstate* signal to the FSM's initial state, *S0*. Otherwise, if the clock is rising, the process updates the state register with the next state.

The second process, named *comblogic*, is sensitive

```vhdl
library ieee;
use ieee.std_logic_1164.all;

entity LDM_Controller is
    port ( clk, rst: in std_logic;
           B, S: in std_logic;
           L: out std_logic;
           Dreg_clr, Dreg_ld: out std_logic;
           Dctr_clr, Dctr_cnt: out std_logic
);
end LDM_Controller;

architecture behavior of LDM_Controller is
    type statetype is (S0, S1, S2, S3, S4);
    signal currentstate, nextstate: statetype;
begin
    statereg: process(clk, rst)
    begin
        if (rst='1') then
            currentstate <= S0; -- initial state
        elsif (clk='1' and clk'event) then
            currentstate <= nextstate;
        end if;
    end process;

    comblogic: process(currentstate, B, S)
    begin
        L <= '0';
        Dreg_clr <= '0';
        Dreg_ld <= '0';
        Dctr_clr <= '0';
        Dctr_cnt <= '0';
        case currentstate is
            when S0 =>
                L <= '0';              -- laser off
                Dreg_clr <= '1';   -- clear Dreg
                nextstate <= S1;
            when S1 =>
                Dctr_clr <= '1'     -- clear count
                if (B='1') then
                    nextstate <= S2;
                else
                    nextstate <= S1;
                end if;
```

(continued in Figure 9.43)

Figure 9.42 Behavioral VHDL description of laser-based distance measurer's controller.

to the inputs to the combinational logic of Figure 5.21, namely, the external inputs *B* and *S*, and the state register output *currentstate*. When either of those items change, the process sets the FSM's outputs, in this case *L, Dreg_clr, Dreg_ld, Dctr_clr,* and *Dctr_cnt*, with the appropriate value for the current state. In the controller example of Figure 9.22, the FSM's output *x* was defined within the case statement for all possible states. With five outputs that must be defined in the *LDM_Controller* and five possible states, assigning the values to all outputs in each state would be cumbersome. Furthermore, finding a mistake and making corrections or modifications to the controller would become very difficult in a larger FSM consisting of more states and having many more outputs. The *comblogic* process uses a different approach in which a default value for the outputs is first assigned and only the deviations from the defaults are assigned later. The *comblogic* process first assigns a default value of 0 to all five outputs. The process then evaluates the current state and assigns the values to the outputs only when the output should be 1. The process also assigns the value 0 to several signals within the **when** statements, however, these assignments are included only to clearly indicate the behavior of the controller (they are redundant, but help make the description easier to understand).

```
(continued from Figure 9.42)
      when S2 =>
        L <= '1';               -- laser on
        nextstate <= S3;
      when S3 =>
        L <= '0';               -- laser off
        Dctr_cnt <= '1';  -- count up
        if (S='1') then
            nextstate <= S4;
        else
            nextstate <= S3;
        end if;
      when S4 =>
        Dreg_ld  <= '1'; -- load Dreg
        Dctr_cnt <= '0'; -- stop counting
        nextstate <= S1;
    end case;
  end process;
end behavior;
```

Figure 9.43 Behavioral VHDL description of laser-based distance measurer's controller *(continued)*.

The process also determines what the next state should be, based on the current state and the values of inputs *B* and *S*. The next state will be loaded into the state register by the state register process on the next rising clock edge.

Verilog

Figure 9.44 is a Verilog description of the laser-based distance measurer shown in Figure 5.19. The module, named *LaserDistMeasurer*, defines the inputs and outputs, including a user-pressed button input *B*, a laser sensor input *S*, a laser control output *L*, and a 16-bit output *D* for the distance measured. The module also defines a 300 MHz clock input *clk* and reset input *rst* for the design's controller.

```
module LaserDistMeasurer(clk, rst, B, S, L, D);
  input clk, rst, B, S;
  output L;
  output [15:0] D;

  wire Dreg_clr, Dreg_ld;
  wire Dctr_clr, Dctr_cnt;

  LDM_Controller
    LDM_Controller_1(clk, rst, B, S, L,
                     Dreg_clr, Dreg_ld,
                     Dctr_clr, Dctr_cnt);
  LDM_Datapath
    LDM_Datapath_1(clk, Dreg_clr, Dreg_ld,
                     Dctr_clr, Dctr_cnt, D);
endmodule
```

Figure 9.44 Structural description of top-level Verilog description of laser-based distance measurer.

The *LaserDistMeasurer* structurally describes the connections of the controller and datapath components. The module instantiates two components. *LDM_Controller_1* is the controller for the laser-based distance measurer and *LDM_Datapath_1* is the datapath for this design. The architecture connects the module's *clk*, *rst*, *B*, and *S* inputs to the inputs of *LDM_Controller_1* and connects the controller's laser control output to the corresponding output port *L*. Additionally, the four internal wires, *Dreg_clr*, *Dreg_ld*, *Dctr_clr*, and *Dctr_cnt*, connect the controller's four control signals to the four inputs of *LDM_Datapath_1*. The *LaserDistMeasurer* datapath has a single output *D*, providing the distance measured, that is connected to the output port *D* of the module.

Figure 9.45 is a Verilog description of the *LaserDistMeasurer*'s datapath component shown in Figure 5.17. The module, named *LDM_Datapath*, defines a clock input *clk*, four control inputs *Dreg_clr*, *Dreg_ld*, *Dctr_clr*, and *Dctr_cnt*, and a 16-bit distance output *D*.

The datapath consists of three components, a 16-bit up-counter, a 16-bit register, and a 16-bit right shifter that shifts right by one position. *UpCounter-16* is a 16-bit up-counter with a count control input *cnt* and a count clear input *clr*. *Reg16* is a 16-bit parallel load register with a register load control signal *ld* and a register clear signal *clr*. *ShiftRightOne-16* is a 16-bit right shifter that shifts the input *I* right by one position and assigns the shifted value to the output *S*. The data-

```
module UpCounter16(clk, clr, cnt, C);
  input clk, clr, cnt;
  output [15:0] C;
  // details not shown
endmodule

module Reg16(I, Q, clk, clr, ld);
  input [15:0] I;
  input clk, clr, ld;
  output [15:0] Q;
  // details not shown
endmodule

module ShiftRightOne16(I, S);
  input [15:0] I;
  output [15:0] S;
  // details not shown
endmodule

module LDM_Datapath(clk, Dreg_clr, Dreg_ld,
                    Dctr_clr, Dctr_cnt, D);
  input clk;
  input Dreg_clr, Dreg_ld;
  input Dctr_clr, Dctr_cnt;
  output [15:0] D;

  wire [15:0] tempC, shiftC;

  UpCounter16 Dctr(clk, Dctr_clr, Dctr_cnt,
                   tempC);
  ShiftRightOne16 ShiftRight(tempC, shiftC);
  Reg16 Dreg(shiftC, D, clk, Dreg_clr, Dreg_ld);
endmodule
```

Figure 9.45 Structural Verilog description of the laser-based distance measurer's datapath.

path module instantiates an *UpCounter16* component named *Dctr*, a *Reg16* component named *Dreg*, and a *ShiftRightOne16* component named *ShiftRight*. The module connects the datapath's *Dctr_clr* and *Dctr_cnt* inputs to *Dctr*'s clear and count control inputs, respectively. The counter's count output *C* is then connected to the 16-bit internal wire *tempC* that connects the count value to the *ShiftRight* shifter's input. The shifted count is then connected to the input of the *Dreg* register using the internal 16-bit wire *shiftC*. The module connects the *Dreg* register's clear and load control inputs to the datapath's *Dreg_clr* and *Dreg_ld* input ports. Finally, the register's data output *Q* is connected to *LDM_datapath*'s measured distance output *D*.

Figures 9.46 and 9.47 are the Verilog description of the laser-based distance measurer's FSM controller described in Figure 5.21. The module, named *LDM_Controller*, defines a clock input *clk*, a reset signal *rst*, a user-pressed button input *B*, a laser sensor input *S*, and five output control signals, *L, Dreg_clr, Dreg_ld, Dctr_clr,* and *Dctr_cnt*. The output *L* is used to turn the laser on and off, where if *L* is 1, the laser is on. The four other output signals are used to control the RTL design's datapath components.

```verilog
module LDM_Controller(clk, rst, B, S, L, Dreg_clk,
                        Dreg_ld, Dctr_clr,
                        Dctr_cnt);
  input clk, rst, B, S;
  output L;
  output Dreg_clk, Dreg_ld;
  output Dctr_clr, Dctr_cnt;
  reg L;
  reg Dreg_clr, Dreg_ld;
  reg Dctr_clr, Dctr_cnt;

  parameter S0 = 3'b000,
            S1 = 3'b001,
            S2 = 3'b010,
            S3 = 3'b011,
            S4 = 3'b100;

  reg [2:0] currentstate;
  reg [2:0] nextstate;

  always @(posedge rst or posedge clk)
  begin
    if (rst==1)
       currentstate <= S0; // initial state
    else
       currentstate <= nextstate;
  end

  always @(currentstate or B or S)
  begin
    L <= 0;
    Dreg_clr <= 0;
    Dreg_ld <= 0;
    Dctr_clr <= 0;
    Dctr_cnt <= 0;
    case (currentstate)
      S0: begin
        L <= 0;             // laser off
        Dreg_clr <= 1;      // clear Dreg
        nextstate <= S1;
      end
```
(continued in Figure 9.47)

Figure 9.46 Behavioral Verilog description of laser-based distance measurer's controller.

The Verilog module behaviorally describes the *LaserDistMeasurer*'s FSM. Similar to the controller design shown in Figure 9.23, the module consists of two procedures, one modeling the state register, the other modeling the FSM's control logic. The state register procedure is sensitive to the positive edge of the reset input, *rst*, and the positive edge of the clock input, *clk*. If the *rst* input is enabled, then the procedure asynchronously sets the *currentstate* signal to the FSM's initial state, *S0*. Otherwise, on the rising edge of the clock, the procedure updates the state register with the next state.

The second procedure is sensitive to the inputs to the combinational logic of Figure 5.21, namely, the external inputs *B* and *S*, and the state register output *currentstate*. When either of those items change, the procedure sets the FSM's outputs, in this case *L, Dreg_clr, Dreg_ld, Dctr_clr,* and *Dctr_cnt*, with the appropriate value for the current state. In the controller example of Figure 9.22, the FSM's output *x* was defined within the case statement for all possible states. With five outputs that must be defined in the *LDM_Controller* and five possible states, assigning the values to all outputs in each state would be cumbersome. Furthermore, finding a mistake and making corrections or modifications to the controller would become very difficult in a larger FSM consisting of more states and having many more outputs. Instead, the procedure uses a different approach in which a default value for all the outputs is first assigned and only the deviations from the defaults are assigned later. The procedure first assigns a default value of 0 to all five outputs. The procedure then evaluates the current state and assigns the values to the outputs only when the output should be 1. The procedure also assigns the value 0 to several signals within the ***case*** statements, however, these assignments are included only to clearly indicate the behavior of the controller (they are redundant, but help make the description easier to understand).

The procedure also determines what the next state should be, based on the current state and the values of inputs *B* and *S*. The next state will be loaded into the state register by the state register procedure on the next positive clock edge.

```
(continued from Figure 9.46)
      S1: begin
        Dctr_clr <= 1;        // clear count
        if (B==1)
          nextstate <= S2;
        else
          nextstate <= S1;
      end
      S2: begin
        L <= 1;               // laser on
        nextstate <= S3;
      end
      S3: begin
        L <= 0;               // laser off
        Dctr_cnt <= 1;        // count up
        if (S==1)
          nextstate <= S4;
        else
          nextstate <= S3;
      end
      S4: begin
        Dreg_ld <= 1;         // load Dreg
        Dctr_cnt <= 0;        // stop counting
        nextstate <= S1;
      end
    endcase
  end
endmodule
```

Figure 9.47 Behavioral Verilog description of laser-based distance measurer's controller *(continued)*.

SystemC

Figure 9.48 is a SystemC description of the laser-based distance measurer shown in Figure 5.19. The module, named *LaserDistMeasurer*, defines the inputs and outputs, including a user-pressed button input *B*, a laser sensor input *S*, a laser control output *L*, and a 16-bit output *D* for the distance measured. The module also defines a 300 MHz clock input *clk* and reset input *rst* for the design's controller.

The *LaserDistMeasurer* structurally describes the connections of the controller and datapath components. The architecture instantiates two components. *LDM_Controller_1* is the controller for the laser-based distance measurer and *LDM_Datapath_1* is the datapath for this design. The module connects the module's *clk*, *rst*, *B*, and *S* inputs to the inputs of *LDM_Controller_1* and connects the controller's laser control output to the corresponding output port *L*. Additionally, the four internal wires, *Dreg_clr*, *Dreg_ld*, *Dctr_clr*, and *Dctr_cnt*, connect the controller's four control signals to the four inputs of *LDM_Data-path_1*. The *LaserDistMeasurer* datapath has a single output *D*, providing the distance measured, that is connected to the output port *D* of the module.

```
#include "systemc.h"
#include "LDM_Controller.h"
#include "LDM_Datapath.h"

SC_MODULE(LaserDistMeasurer)
{
  sc_in<sc_logic> clk, rst;
  sc_in<sc_logic> B, S;
  sc_out<sc_logic> L;
  sc_out<sc_lv<16> > D;

  sc_signal<sc_logic> Dreg_clr, Dreg_ld;
  sc_signal<sc_logic> Dctr_clr, Dctr_cnt;

  LDM_Controller LDM_Controller_1;
  LDM_Datapath LDM_Datapath_1;

  SC_CTOR(LaserDistMeasurer) :
    LDM_Controller_1("LDM_Controller_1"),
    LDM_Datapath_1("LDM_Datapath_1")
  {
    LDM_Controller_1.clk(clk);
    LDM_Controller_1.rst(rst);
    LDM_Controller_1.B(B);
    LDM_Controller_1.S(S);
    LDM_Controller_1.Dreg_clr(Dreg_clr);
    LDM_Controller_1.Dreg_ld(Dreg_ld);
    LDM_Controller_1.Dctr_clr(Dctr_clr);
    LDM_Controller_1.Dctr_cnt(Dctr_cnt);

    LDM_Datapath_1.clk(clk);
    LDM_Datapath_1.Dreg_clr(Dreg_clr);
    LDM_Datapath_1.Dreg_ld(Dreg_ld);
    LDM_Datapath_1.Dctr_clr(Dctr_clr);
    LDM_Datapath_1.Dctr_cnt(Dctr_cnt);
    LDM_Datapath_1.D(D);
  }
};
```

Figure 9.48 Structural description of top-level SystemC description of laser-based distance measurer.

Figure 9.49 is a SystemC description of the *LaserDistMeasurer's* datapath component shown in Figure 5.17. The module, named *LDM_Datapath*, defines a clock input *clk*, four control inputs *Dreg_clr*, *Dreg_ld*, *Dctr_clr*, and *Dctr_cnt,* and a 16-bit distance output *D*.

The datapath consists of two components, a 16-bit up-counter, a 16-bit register, and a 16-bit right shifter that shifts right by one position. *UpCounter16* is a 16-bit up-counter with a count control input *cnt* and a count clear input *clr*. *Reg16* is a 16-bit parallel load register with a register load control signal *ld* and a register clear signal *clr*. *ShiftRight One16* is a 16-bit right shifter that shifts the input *I* right by one position and assigns the shifted value to the output *S*. The datapath module instantiates an *UpCounter16* component named *Dctr*, a *Reg16* component named *Dreg,* and a *ShiftRightOne16* component named *ShiftRight*. The module connects the datapath's *Dctr_clr* and *Dctr_cnt* inputs to *Dctr*'s clear and count control inputs, respectively. The counter's count output *C* is then connected to the 16-bit internal signal *tempC* that connects the count value

```
#include "systemc.h"
#include "upcounter16.h"
#include "reg16.h"
#include "shiftrightone16.h"

SC_MODULE(LDM_Datapath)
{
  sc_in<sc_logic> clk;
  sc_in<sc_logic> Dreg_clr, Dreg_ld;
  sc_in<sc_logic> Dctr_clr, Dctr_cnt;
  sc_out<sc_lv<16> > D;

  sc_signal<sc_lv<16> > tempC;
  sc_signal<sc_lv<16> > shiftC;

  UpCounter16 Dctr;
  Reg16 Dreg;
  ShiftRightOne16 ShiftRight;

  SC_CTOR(LDM_Datapath) :
    Dctr("Dctr"), Dreg("Dreg"),
    ShiftRight("ShiftRight")
  {
    Dctr.clk(clk);
    Dctr.clr(Dctr_clr);
    Dctr.cnt(Dctr_cnt);
    Dctr.C(tempC);

    ShiftRight.I(tempC);
    ShiftRight.S(shiftC);

    Dreg.I(shiftC);
    Dreg.Q(D);
    Dreg.clk(clk);
    Dreg.clr(Dreg_clr);
    Dreg.ld(Dreg_ld);
  }
};
```

Figure 9.49 Structural SystemC description of the laser-based distance measurer's datapath.

to the *ShiftRight* shifter's input. The shifted count value is then connected to the input of the *Dreg* register using the internal signal *shiftC*. The module connects the *Dreg* register's clear and load control inputs to the datapath's *Dreg_clr* and *Dreg_ld* input ports. Finally, the register's data output *Q* is connected to *LDM_datapath*'s measured distance output *D*.

Figures 9.50 and 9.51 are the SystemC description of the laser-based distance measurer's FSM controller described in Figure 5.21. The module, named *LDM_Controller*, has a clock input *clk*, a reset signal *rst*, a user-pressed button input *B*, a laser sensor input *S*, and five output control signals, *L, Dreg_clr, Dreg_ld, Dctr_clr,* and *Dctr_cnt*. The output *L* is used to turn the laser on and off; where is *L* is 1, the laser is on. The four other output signals are used to control the RTL design's datapath components.

```cpp
#include "system.h"

enum statetype { S0, S1, S2, S3, S4 };

SC_MODULE(LDM_Controller)
{
  sc_in<sc_logic> clk, rst, B, S;
  sc_out<sc_logic> L;
  sc_out<sc_logic> Dreg_clr, Dreg_ld;
  sc_out<sc_logic> Dctr_clr, Dctr_cnt;

  sc_signal<statetype> currentstate, nextstate;

  SC_CTOR(LDM_Controller)
  {
    SC_METHOD(statereg);
    sensitive_pos << rst << clk;
    SC_METHOD(comblogic);
    sensitive << currentstate << B << S;
  }

  void statereg() {
    if ( rst.read() == SC_LOGIC_1 )
      currentstate = S0; // initial state
    else
      currentstate = nextstate;
  }

  void comblogic() {
    L.write(SC_LOGIC_0);
    Dreg_clr.write(SC_LOGIC_0);
    Dreg_ld.write(SC_LOGIC_0);
    Dctr_clr.write(SC_LOGIC_0);
    Dctr_cnt.write(SC_LOGIC_0);

    switch (currentstate) {
      case S0:
        L.write(SC_LOGIC_0);        // laser off
        Dreg_clr.write(SC_LOGIC_0); // clear Dreg
        nextstate = S1;
        break;
```

(continued in Figure 9.51)

Figure 9.50 Behavioral SystemC description of laser-based distance measurer's controller.

The SystemC module behaviorally describes the *LaserDistMeasurer's* FSM. Similar to the controller design shown in Figure 9.24, the module consists of two processes, one modeling the state register, the other modeling the FSM's control logic. The state register process, named *statereg*, is sensitive to the positive edge of the reset input, *rst*, and the positive edge of the clock input, *clk*. If the *rst* is enabled, then the process asynchronously sets the *currentstate* to the FSM's initial state, *S0*. Otherwise, on the rising edge of the clock, the process updates the state register with the *nextstate*.

The second process, named *comblogic*, is sensitive to the inputs to the combinational logic of Figure 5.21, namely, the external inputs *B* and *S*, and the state register output *currentstate*. When either of those signals change, the process sets the FSM's outputs, in this case *L, Dreg_clr, Dreg_ld, Dctr_clr,* and *Dctr_cnt*, with the appropriate value for the current state. In the controller example of Figure 9.24, the FSM's output *x* was defined within the case statement for all possible states. With five outputs that we must define in the *LDM_Controller* and five possible states, assigning the values to all outputs in each state would be cumbersome. Furthermore, finding a mistake and making corrections or modification to the controller would become very difficult in a larger FSM consisting of more states and having many more outputs. Instead, the process uses a different approach in which a default value for the all outputs is first assigned and only the deviations from the defaults are assigned later. The process first assigns a default value of 0 to all five outputs. The process then evaluates the current state and assigns the values to the outputs only when the output should be 1. The process also assigns the value 0 to several signals within the **case** statements; however, these assignments are included only to clearly indicate the behavior of the controller (they are redundant, but help make the description easier to understand).

Figure 9.51 Behavioral SystemC description of laser-based distance measurer's controller *(continued)*.

```
(continued from Figure 9.50)

          case S1
            Dctr_clr.write(SC_LOGIC_1);    // clear count
            if (B.read() == SC_LOGIC_1)
              nextstate = S2;
            else
              nextstate = S1;
            break;
          case S2:
            L.write(SC_LOGIC_1);           // laser on
            nextstate = S3;
            break;
          case S3:
            L.write(SC_LOGIC_0);           // laser off
            Dctr_cnt.write(SC_LOGIC_1);    // count up
            if (S.read() == SC_LOGIC_1)
              nextstate = S4;
            else
              nextstate = S3;
            break;
          case S4:
            Dreg_ld.write(SC_LOGIC_1);     // load Dreg
            Dctr_cnt.write(SC_LOGIC_0);    // stop counting
            nextstate = S1;
            break;}
    }
};
```

The process also determines what the next state should be, based on the current state and the values of inputs *B* and *S*. The next state will be loaded into the state register by the state register process on the next positive clock edge.

▶ 9.6 CHAPTER SUMMARY

In this chapter, we stated that hardware description languages (HDLs) are widely used in modern digital design. We provided brief introductions to several widely used HDLs, namely, VHDL, Verilog and SystemC. We introduced those HDLs primarily through the use of examples, illustrating how each HDL might be used to describe combinational logic, sequential logic, datapath components, as well as RTL behavior and structure. To become proficient at the use of HDLs, a more thorough study of a particular HDL might be helpful. This chapter also illustrates the point that different HDLs have several commononalities.

▶ 9.7 EXERCISES

The following exercises can be completed using any of the HDLs described in this chapter.

SECTION 9.2: COMBINATIONAL LOGIC DESCRIPTION USING HARDWARE DESCRIPTION LANGUAGES

9.1 Create a structural HDL description of the binary number to seven-segment display described in Example 2.23, consisting of the simple logic gates, *Inv, AND2*, and *OR2*. Be sure to include combinational behavioral descriptions of the simple logic gates.

9.2 Create combinational behavioral HDL descriptions for each of the following two-input logic gates, where each logic gate has two inputs, *a* and *b*, and a single output *F*:
(a) NAND2,
(b) NOR2,
(c) XOR2,
(d) XNOR2.

9.3 (a) Create a combinational behavioral HDL description of the three 1s pattern detector of Example 2.24.
(b) Create a testbench that checks that your description works properly.

9.4 (a) Create a combinational behavioral HDL description of the Number-of-1s counter shown in Figure 2.41, by describing the combinational behavior of both outputs *x* and *y* in sum-of-minterms form.
(b) Create a testbench that checks that your description works properly.

9.5 Create an HDL description of the 2x4 decoder shown in Figure 2.50, as:
(a) combinational behavior,
(b) structure.
(c) Create a testbench to test either description (the same testbench can test either description).

9.6 Create an HDL description of the 4x1 multiplexer described in Figure 2.55, as:
(a) combinational behavior,
(b) structure.
(c) Create a testbench to test either description (the same testbench can test either description).

9.7 Create a behavioral HDL description of a 2x1 multiplexor described in Figure 2.54. Then, create a structural HDL description that combines three 2x1 multiplexors to create a 4x1 multiplexor as shown in Figure 9.52.

9.8 Create a combinational behavioral HDL description of an 8-bit 4x1 multiplexor. Be sure to specify the design input and output ports using a multiple bit data type.

9.9 Clearly explain the difference between a structural HDL description and a behavioral HDL description. Explain the benefits of using both kinds of descriptions.

9.10 Explain why a combinational behavioral HDL description must include all the combinational circuit's inputs in a sensitivity list. In particular, explain why omitting an input actually describes a sequential circuit.

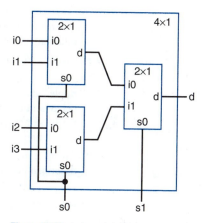

Figure 9.52 4x1 multiplexor composed of three 2x1 multiplexors.

9.11 Create a behavioral HDL description of a 16x4 priority encoder. The priority encoder has 16 inputs, *d15, d14, ..., d1, d0*, and four outputs *e3, e2, e1, e0*. The priority encoder outputs a 4-bit binary number indicating which of the 16 inputs is a 1. If more than one input is a 1, the priority encoder will output the binary number for the highest numbered input.

SECTION 9.3: SEQUENTIAL LOGIC DESCRIPTION USING HARDWARE DESCRIPTION LANGUAGES

9.12 (a) Create a behavioral HDL description of a 32-bit parallel load register.
(b) Create a testbench to test the description.

9.13 (a) Create behavioral HDL description of the FSM controller for the improved code detector described in Figure 3.46.
(b) Create a testbench to test the description.

9.14 (a) Create a behavioral HDL description of the button press synchronizer described in Figure 3.53.
(b) Create a testbench to test the description.

9.15 (a) Create a behaviroal HDL description of the secure car key controller described in Figures 3.57 and 3.58.
(b) Create a testbench to test the description.

SECTION 9.4: DATAPATH COMPONENT DESCRIPTION USING HARDWARE DESCRIPTION LANGUAGES

9.16 (a) Create behavioral HDL description of an 8-bit parallel load register with register clear input *clr*.
(b) Create a testbench to test the description.

9.17 (a) Create a behavioral HDL description of an 8-bit parallel load register with a clear low input *clr_l* and a set high input *set_h*. When the *clr_l* input is 1, the register contents should be cleared to "00000000". When the *set_h* inputs is 1, the register's contents should be set to "11111111". If both inputs are 1, the clear low input has priority.
(b) Create a testbench to test the description.

9.18 Create a behavioral HDL description of an 8-bit register with two control inputs *s0* and *s1* with the following control behavior described in Figure 9.53.

9.19 Create a structural HDL description of a half-adder.

9.20 Create a structural HDL description of a 4-bit carry-ripple adder without a carry input. First create a behavioral description of a full-adder, and then use the full-adder component in your carry-ripple adder description.

s1	s0	Operation
0	0	Maintain present value
0	1	Parallel load
1	0	Shift right
1	1	Rotate right

Figure 9.53 Operation table of the 8-bit register for Exercise 9.18.

9.21 Create a behavioral HDL description of the approximate Celsius-to-Fahrenheit converter described in Figure 4.40.

9.22 Create a behavioral HDL description of an approximate Fahrenheit-to-Celsius converter using the following approximation for the conversion: $C = (F - 32)/2$.

9.23 (a) Create a behavioral HDL description of a 1-bit comparator.
(b) Create a structural description of a 4-bit comparator, using the 1-bit comparators.

9.24 Create a behavioral HDL description of a 32-bit equality comparator with three 8-bit inputs *a*, *b*, and *c*.

9.25 Create a structural HDL description of the up-down-counter circuit described in Figure 4.55. Be sure to first create a behavioral HDL description of each component used in your structural HDL design.

9.26 Create a structural HDL description of a 4-bit down-counter with parallel load. Be sure to first create a behavioral HDL description of each component used in your structural HDL design.

9.27 Create a structural HDL description of the RGB to CMYK converter described in Figure 4.68. Be sure to first create a behavioral HDL description of each component used in your structural HDL design.

9.28 Create a structural HDL description of a CMYK to RGB converter. Hint: Use the information presented in Example 4.20 describing the RGB to CMYK converter to assist in designing the CMYK to RGB converter.

9.29 Create a structural HDL description of a 4-bit adder/subtractor circuit. Be sure to first create a behavioral HDL description of each component used in your structural HDL design.

SECTION 9.5: RTL DESIGN USING HARDWARE DESCRIPTION LANGUAGES

9.30 Create a behavioral HDL description of the high-level state machine for the simple bus interface shown in Figure 5.24.

9.31 Create a structural HDL description of the controller/datapath for simple bus interface shown in Figure 5.26.

9.32 Create a behavioral HDL description of the high-level state machine for the sum-of-absolute-differences component shown in Figure 5.29.

9.33 Create a structural HDL description of the controller/datapath design of the sum-of-absolute-differences component shown in Figure 5.30.

9.34 Create an RTL design of a reaction timer circuit that measures the time elapsed between the illumination of a light, and the pressing of a button by the user. The reaction timer has three inputs, a clock input *clk*, a reset input *rst*, and a button input *B*, and three outputs, a light enable output *len*, a 10-bit reaction time output *rtime,* and a *slow* output indicating the user was not fast enough. The reaction timer works as follows. On reset, the reaction timer waits for 2 seconds before illuminating the light by setting *len* to 1. The reaction timer then measures the length of time in milliseconds before the user presses the button *B*, outputting the time as a 10-bit binary number on *rtime*. If the user did not press the button within 1 second (1000 milliseconds), the reaction timer will set the output *slow* to 1 and output 1000 on *rtime*. Assume a clock frequency of 1 KHz. (a) Start by capturing the design using a high-level state machine in an HDL. (b) Convert the high-level state machine to a controller/datapath description in an HDL.

9.35 Starting from the C description shown in Figure 9.54, create an RTL design of a Greatest Common Divisor (GCD) calculator that takes as input two 16-bit inputs *a* and *b*, an enable input *go*, and a 16-bit output *D*. When the *go* is '1', the GCD calculator will compute the greatest common divisor and output the GCD on the output *D*. Start with a high-level state machine in an HDL, and then create an HDL implementation with a datapath, controller, and all their internal components.

```
uint GCD(uint a, uint b)  // not quite C syntax
{
    while ( a ! = b ) {
        if( a > b ) {
            a = a - b;
        } else {
            b = b - a;
        }
    }
    return(a);
}
```

Figure 9.54 C program description of a greatest common divisor calculator.

A

Boolean Algebras

This appendix is reproduced with permission from the textbook "Introduction to Digital Systems" by Ercegovac, Lang, and Moreno, ISBN 0-471-52799-8, John Wiley and Sons publishers, 1999.

Boolean algebras is an important class of algebras that has been studied and used extensively for many purposes (see Section A.5). The **switching algebra**, used in the description of switching expressions discussed in Section 2.4, is an instance (an element) of the class of Boolean algebras. Consequently, theorems developed for Boolean algebras are also applicable to switching algebra, so they can be used for the transformation of switching expressions. Moreover, certain identities from Boolean algebra are the basis for the graphical and tabular techniques used for the minimization of switching expressions.

In this appendix, we present the definition of Boolean algebras as well as theorems that are useful for the transformation of Boolean expressions. We also show the relationship among Boolean and switching algebras; in particular, we show that the switching algebra satisfies the postulates of a Boolean algebra. We also sketch other examples of Boolean algebras, which are helpful to further understand the properties of this class of algebras.

▶ A.1 BOOLEAN ALGEBRA

A **Boolean algebra** is a tuple $\{B, +, \bullet\}$, where

- B is a set of elements;
- $+$ and $\bullet$ are binary operations applied over the elements of B,

satisfying the following postulates:

P1: If $a, b \in B$, then

    (i) $a + b = b + a$

    (ii) $a \cdot b = b \cdot a$

That is, $+$ and $\bullet$ are commutative.

P2: If $a, b, c \in B$, then

(i) $a + (b \cdot c) = (a + b) \cdot (a + c)$

(ii) $a \cdot (b + c) = (a \cdot b) + (a \cdot c)$

P3: The set B has two distinct **identity elements**, denoted as 0 and 1, such that for every element in B

(i) $0 + a = a + 0 = a$

(ii) $1 \cdot a = a \cdot 1 = a$

The elements 0 and 1 are called the **additive identity element** and the **multiplicative identity element**, respectively. (These elements should not be confused with the integers 0 and 1.)

P4: For every element $a \in B$ there exists an element a', called the **complement** of a, such that

(i) $a + a' = 1$

(ii) $a \cdot a' = 0$

The symbols + and • should not be confused with the arithmetic addition and multiplication symbols. However, for convenience + and • are often called "plus" and "times," and the expressions $a + b$ and $a \cdot b$ are called "sum" and "product," respectively. Moreover, + and • are also called "OR" and "AND," respectively.

The elements of the set B are called **constants**. Symbols representing arbitrary elements of B are **variables**. The symbols a, b, and c in the postulates above are variables, whereas 0 and 1 are constants.

A precedence ordering is defined on the operators: • has precedence over +. Therefore, parentheses can be eliminated from products. Moreover, whenever single symbols are used for variables, the symbol • can be eliminated in products. For example,

$$a + (b \cdot c) \text{ can be written as } a + bc$$

▶ A.2 SWITCHING ALGEBRA

Switching algebra is an algebraic system used to describe switching functions by means of switching expressions. In this sense, a switching algebra serves the same role for switching functions as the ordinary algebra does for arithmetic functions.

The switching algebra of the set of two elements $B = \{0, 1\}$, and two operations AND and OR defined as follows:

AND	0	1
0	0	0
1	0	1

OR	0	1
0	0	1
1	1	1

These operations are used to evaluate switching expressions, as indicated in Section 2.4.

Theorem 1
The switching algebra is a Boolean algebra.
Proof We show that the switching algebra satisfies the postulates of a Boolean algebra.

P1: **Commutativity** of (+), (•). This is shown by inspection of the operation tables. The commutativity property holds if a table is symmetric about the main diagonal.

P2: **Distributivity** of (+) and (•). Shown by **perfect induction**, that is, by considering all possible values for the elements a, b, and c. Consider the following table:

abc	$a + bc$	$(a + b)(a + c)$
000	0	0
001	0	0
010	0	0
011	1	1
100	1	1
101	1	1
110	1	1
111	1	1

Because $a + bc = (a + b)(b + c)$ for all cases, P2(i) is satisfied. A similar proof shows that P2(ii) is also satisfied.

P3: **Existence of additive and multiplicative identity element**. From the operation tables

$$0 + 1 = 1 + 0 = 1$$

Therefore, 0 is the additive identity. Similarly

$$0 \cdot 1 = 1 \cdot 0 = 0$$

so that 1 is the multiplicative identity.

P4: **Existence of the complement**. By perfect induction:

a	a'	$a + a'$	$a \cdot a'$
1	0	1	0
0	1	1	0

Consequently, 1 is the complement of 0 and 0 is the complement of 1.

Because all postulates are satisfied, the switching algebra is a Boolean algebra. As a result, all theorems true for Boolean algebras are also true for the switching algebra.

▶ A.3 IMPORTANT THEOREMS IN BOOLEAN ALGEBRA

We now present some important theorems in Boolean algebra; these theorems can be applied to the transformation of switching expressions.

Theorem 2 Principle of Duality

Every algebraic identity deducible from the postulates of a Boolean algebra remains valid if

- the operations + and • are interchanged throughout; and
- the identity elements 0 and 1 are also interchanged throughout

Proof   The proof follows at once from the fact that for each of the postulates there is another one (the dual) that is obtained by interchanging + and • as well as 0 and 1.

This theorem is useful because it reduces the number of different theorems that must be proven: every theorem has its dual.

Theorem 3

Every element in B has a **unique** complement.

Proof   Let $a \in B$; let us assume that a'_1 and a'_2 are both complements of a. Then, using the postulates we can perform the following transformations:

$$
\begin{aligned}
a'_1 &= a'_1 \cdot 1 && \text{by P3(ii)} && \text{(identity)} \\
&= a'_1 \cdot (a + a'_2) && \text{by hypothesis} && (a'_2 \text{ is the complement of } a) \\
&= a'_1 \cdot a + a'_1 \cdot a'_2 && \text{by P2(ii)} && \text{(distributivity)} \\
&= a \cdot a'_1 + a'_1 \cdot a'_2 && \text{by P1(ii)} && \text{(commutativity)} \\
&= 0 + a'_1 \cdot a'_2 && \text{by hypothesis} && (a'_1 \text{ is the complement of } a) \\
&= a'_1 \cdot a'_2 && \text{by P3(i)} && \text{(identity)}
\end{aligned}
$$

Changing the index 1 for 2 and vice versa, and repeating all steps for a'_2, we get

$$
\begin{aligned}
a'_2 &= a'_2 \cdot a'_1 \\
&= a'_1 \cdot a'_2 \text{ by P1(ii)}
\end{aligned}
$$

and therefore $a'_2 = a'_1$.

The uniqueness of the complement of an element allows considering $'$ as a unary operation called **complementation**.

Theorem 4

For any $a \in B$:

1. $a + 1 = 1$
2. $a \cdot 0 = 0$

Proof   Using the postulates, we can perform the following transformations:

Case (1):

$$a + 1 = 1 \cdot (a + 1) \qquad \text{P3(ii)}$$
$$= (a + a') \cdot (a + 1) \qquad \text{P4(i)}$$
$$= a + (a' \cdot 1) \qquad \text{P2(i)}$$
$$= a + a' \qquad \text{P3(ii)}$$
$$= 1 \qquad \text{P4(i)}$$

Case (2):

$$a \cdot 0 = 0 + (a \cdot 0) \qquad \text{P3(i)}$$
$$= (a \cdot a') + (a \cdot 0) \qquad \text{P4(ii)}$$
$$= a \cdot (a' + 0) \qquad \text{P2(ii)}$$
$$= a \cdot a' \qquad \text{P3(i)}$$
$$= 0 \qquad \text{P4(ii)}$$

Case (2) can also be proven by means of Case (1) and the principle of duality.

Theorem 5

The complement of the element 1 is 0, and vice versa. That is,

1. $0' = 1$
2. $1' = 0$

Proof By Theorem 4,

$$0 + 1 = 1 \quad \text{and}$$
$$0 \cdot 1 = 0$$

Because, by Theorem 3, the complement of an element is unique, Theorem 5 follows.

Theorem 6 Idempotent Law

For every $a \in B$

1. $a + a = a$
2. $a \cdot a = a$

Proof

(1):

$$a + a = (a + a) \cdot 1 \qquad \text{P3(ii)}$$
$$= (a + a) \cdot (a + a') \qquad \text{P4(i)}$$
$$= (a + (a \cdot a')) \qquad \text{P2(i)}$$
$$= a + 0 \qquad \text{P4(ii)}$$
$$= a \qquad \text{P3(i)}$$

(2): duality

Theorem 7 Involution Law

For every $a \in B$,

$$(a')' = a$$

Proof From the definition of complement $(a')'$ and a are both complements of a'. But, by Theorem 3, the complement of an element is unique, which proves the theorem.

Theorem 8 Absorption Law

For every pair of elements $a, b \in B$,

1. $a + a \cdot b = a$
2. $a \cdot (a + b) = a$

Proof

(1):

			by
$a + ab$	$=$	$a \cdot 1 + ab$	P3(ii)
	$=$	$a(1 + b)$	P2(ii)
	$=$	$a(b + 1)$	P1(i)
	$=$	$a \cdot 1$	Theorem 4 (1)
	$=$	a	P3(ii)

(2): duality

Theorem 9

For every pair of elements $a, b \in B$,

1. $a + a'b = a + b$
2. $a(a' + b) = ab$

Proof

(1):

			by
$a + a'b$	$=$	$(a + a')(a + b)$	P2(i)
	$=$	$1 \cdot (a + b)$	P4(i)
	$=$	$a + b$	P3(ii)

(2): duality

Theorem 10

In a Boolean algebra, each of the binary operations ($+$) and ($\cdot$) is associative. That is, for every $a, b, c \in B$,

1. $a + (b + c) = (a + b) + c$
2. $a(bc) = (ab)c$

The proof of this theorem is quite lengthy. The interested reader should consult the further readings suggested at the end of this appendix.

Corollary I

1. The order in applying the + operator among n elements does not matter. For example,

$$a + \{b + [c + (d + e)]\} = \{[(a + b) + c] + d\} + e$$
$$= \{a + [(b + c) + d]\} + e$$
$$= a + b + c + d + e$$

2. The order in applying the • operator among n elements does not matter.

Theorem 11 DeMorgan's Law

For every pair of elements $a, b \in B$:

1. $(a + b)' = a'b'$
2. $(ab)' = a' + b'$

Proof

We first prove that $(a + b)$ is the complement of $a'b'$. By the definition of the complement (P4) and its uniqueness (Theorem 3), this corresponds to showing that $(a + b) + a'b' = 1$ and $(a + b)a'b' = 0$. We do this proof by the following transformations:

		by
$(a + b) + a'b'$	$= [(a + b) + a'][(a + b) + b']$	P2(i)
	$= [(b + a) + a'][(a + b) + b']$	P1(i)
	$= [b + (a + a')][a + (b + b')]$	associativity
	$= (b + 1)(a + 1)$	P4(i)
	$= 1 \cdot 1$	Theorem 3 (1)
	$= 1$	idempotency

		by
$(a + b)(a'b')$	$= (a'b')(a + b)$	commutativity
	$= (a'b')a + (a'b')b$	distributivity
	$= (b'a')a + (a'b')b$	commutativity
	$= b'(a'a) + a'(b'b)$	associativity
	$= b'(aa') + a'(bb')$	commutativity
	$= b' \cdot 0 + a' \cdot 0$	P4(ii)
	$= 0 + 0$	Theorem 3 (2)
	$= 0$	Theorem 5 (1)

By duality, $(a \cdot b)' = a' + b'$

Theorem 12 Generalized DeMorgan's Law

Let $\{a, b, ..., c, d\}$ be a set of elements in a Boolean algebra. Then, the following identities hold:

    1. $(a + b ... + c + d)' = a'b'...c'd'$

    2. $(ab...cd)' = a' + b' + ... + c' + d'$

Proof   By the method of **finite induction**. The basis is provided by Theorem 11, which corresponds to the case with two elements.

Inductive step: Let us assume that DeMorgan's Law is true for n elements, and show that it is true for $n + 1$ elements. Let $a, b, ..., c$ be the n elements, and d be the $(n + 1)$st element. Then, by associativity and the basis,

$$(a + b + ... + c + d)' = [(a + b + ... + c) + d]'$$

$$= (a + b + ... + c)'d'$$

By the induction hypothesis

$$(a + b + ...c)' = a'b'...c'$$

Thus

$$(a + b + ...c + d)' = a'b'...c'd'$$

DeMorgan's theorems are useful in manipulating switching expressions. For example, finding the complement of a switching expression containing parentheses is achieved by applying DeMorgan's Law and the Involution Law repeatedly to bring all $(')$ inside the parentheses. That is,

$$[(a + b')(c' + d') + (f' + g)']' = [(a + b')(c' + d')]'[(f' + g)']'$$

$$= [(a + b')' + (c' + d')']'(f' + g)$$

$$= (a'b + cd)(f' + g)$$

The symbols $a, b, c, ...$ appearing in theorems and postulates are **generic variables**. That is, they can be substituted by complemented variables or expressions (formulas) without changing the meaning of these theorems. For example, DeMorgan's Law can read as

$$(a' + b')' = ab$$

or

$$[(a + b)' + c']' = (a + b)c$$

We have described a general mathematical system, called Boolean algebra, and established a basic set of algebraic identities, true for any Boolean algebra, without actually specifying the nature of the two binary operations, $(+)$ and $(\bullet)$. In Chapter 2, we presented an algebra useful for the representation of switching functions by switching expressions.

▶ A.4 OTHER EXAMPLES OF BOOLEAN ALGEBRAS

There are other algebras that are also instances of Boolean algebras. We now summarize the two most commonly used ones.

Algebra of Sets. The elements of B are all subsets of a set S (the set of all subsets of S is denoted by $P(S)$), and the operations are set-union ($\cup$) and set-intersection ($\cap$). That is,

$$M = (P((S), (\cup, \cap)))$$

The additive identity is the empty set, denoted by ϕ, and the multiplicative identity is the set S. The set $P(S)$ has $2^{|S|}$ elements, where $|S|$ is the number of elements of S.

It can be shown that every Boolean algebra has 2^n elements for some value $n > 0$.

Venn diagrams are used to represent sets as well as the operations of union and intersection. Consequently, since the algebra of sets is a Boolean algebra, Venn diagrams can be used to illustrate the theorems of a Boolean algebra.

Algebra of Logic (Propositional Calculus). In this algebra, the elements are T and F (true and false), and the operations are LOGICAL AND and LOGICAL OR. It is used to evaluate logical propositions. This algebra is isomorphic with the switching algebra.

▶ A.5 FURTHER READINGS

The topic of Boolean algebras has been extensively studied, and many good books on the subject exist. The following is a partial list, in which the reader can obtain additional material that goes significantly beyond the limited treatment of this appendix: *Boolean Reasoning: The Logic of Boolean Equations* by F. M. Brown, Kluwer Academic Publishers, Boston, MA, 1990; *Introduction to Switching and Automata Theory* by M. A. Harrison, McGraw-Hill, New York, 1965; *Switching and Automata Theory* by Z. Kohavi, 2nd. ed., McGraw-Hill, New York, 1978; *Switching Theory* by R. E. Miller, Vols. 1 and 2. Wiley, New York, 1965; *Introduction to Discrete Structures* by F. Preparata and R. Yeh, Addison-Wesley, Reading, MA, 1973; and *Discrete Mathematical Structures* by H. S. Stone, Science Research Associates, Chicago, IL, 1973.

Additional Topics in Binary Number Systems

▶ B.1 INTRODUCTION

In Chapter 1, we introduced the concept of *binary* or base two numbers. We showed how one could convert a decimal integer to binary through the *subtraction method* or the *divide-by-two method*. However, numbers we use in digital design may not always be represented as whole numbers.

Consider a doctor who uses an in-ear digital thermometer that works in Celsius units to check if a patient's body temperature is normal. We know that a human's normal body temperature is 37 degrees C (98.6 degrees F). If the thermometer's temperature sensor outputs integer values, then a readout of 37 C corresponds to an actual temperature anywhere between 36.5 C and 37.4 C, assuming the temperature sensor rounds its output to the nearest integer. Clearly, a thermometer working in this fashion would be of little use to a doctor, as a more precise temperature readout is necessary to tell if a patient's temperature is abnormal. A readout of 37 C may mean that the patient has a normal body temperature or it may mean that the patient is close to having a fever. In order to be useful, we need the thermometer to output fractional components of the temperature so that the doctor can differentiate between 37.0 C and 37.9 C, for example.

In this appendix, we will discuss how real numbers are represented in binary, and discuss methods that modern digital designs use to work with real numbers.

▶ B.2 REAL NUMBER REPRESENTATION

Just as we looked closely at how integers are represented in decimal before moving on to binary numbers, understanding how real numbers are represented in decimal can illuminate how real numbers are represented in binary.

We saw in Chapter 1 that each digit in a number had a certain weight that was a power of 10. The ones place had a weight equal to $10^0 = 1$, the tens place had a weight equal to $10^1 = 10$, the hundreds place had a weight equal to $10^2 = 100$, and so on. If a decimal number had an 8 in the hundred's place, a 6 in the ten's place, and a 0 in the one's place, we could calculate the value of the number by multiplying each digit by their weight and adding them together: $8*10^2 + 6*10^1 + 0*10^0 = 860$. This calculation is trivial to us since we manipulate decimal numbers all the time.

The same concept of weights for each digit can be extended to the fractional components of the number. Consider the decimal number "923.501." We refer to the dot in the middle of the digits as the **decimal point**. The decimal point separates the fractional component of the number from the whole part. While the weights of each digit in the whole part of the number are increasing powers of 10, the weights of the fractional digits are decreasing powers of 10, giving the digits fractional weights (e.g., $10^{-1} = 0.1$ and $10^{-2} = 0.01$). Therefore, the digits "923.501" represent $9*10^2 + 2*10^1 + 3*10^0 + 5*10^{-1} + 0*10^{-2} + 1*10^{-3}$, as shown in Figure B.1.

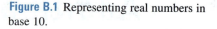

9	2	3 .	5	0	1
10^3	10^2	10^1 10^0	10^{-1}	10^{-2}	10^{-3} 10^{-4}

Figure B.1 Representing real numbers in base 10.

*Generally, the point used to separate the whole part of the number from the fractional part is called a **radix point**, a term applicable to any base.*

We can represent real numbers in binary in a similar manner. Instead of a decimal point, real binary numbers feature a **binary point**. Digits to the right of the binary point are weighted with negative powers of 2. For example, the binary number 10.1101 equals $1*2^1 + 0*2^0 + 1*2^{-1} + 1*2^{-2} + 0*2^{-3} + 1*2^{-4}$, or 2.8125 in decimal, as shown in Figure B.2.

1	0 .	1	1	0	1
2^2	2^1 2^0	2^{-1}	2^{-2}	2^{-3}	2^{-4} 2^{-5}

Figure B.2 Representing real numbers in base 2.

By now, you may be comfortable with counting up powers of two (1, 2, 4, 8, 16, 32, etc.). Counting down powers of two may be difficult to memorize, but the numbers can be easily derived by dividing by 2: 1, 0.5, 0.25, and so on. Table B.1 illustrates this pattern.

The subtraction method we used in Chapter 1 to convert decimal integers to binary is also a suitable method for converting real numbers, requiring no modifications other than needing to work with negative powers of two.

TABLE B.1 Powers of two.

Power	Value
2^2	4
2^1	2
2^0	1
2^{-1}	0.5
2^{-2}	0.25
2^{-3}	0.125
2^{-4}	0.0625
2^{-5}	0.03125

▶ **EXAMPLE B.1** Converting real numbers from decimal to binary with the subtraction method

Convert the number 5.75 to binary using the subtraction method.

To perform this conversion, we follow the two-step process discussed in Section 1.2. The conversion is detailed in Figure B.3.

	Decimal	Binary

1. Put 1 in highest place
Place 8 too big, but 4 works 5.75

1	0	0 . 0	0	*(current value: 4)*
4	2	1 0.5	0.25	

2. Update decimal number
Decimal not zero, return to Step 1

5.75
− 4
1.75

1. Put 1 in highest place
Next place is 2, too big (2>1.75)
1 works (1<1.75) 1.75

1	0	1 . 0	0	*(current value: 5)*
4	2	1 0.5	0.25	

2. Update decimal number
Decimal not zero, return to Step 1

− 1
0.75

1. Put 1 in highest place
Next place is 0.5, works (0.5<0.75) 0.75

1	0	1 . 1	0	*(current value: 5.5)*
4	2	1 0.5	0.25	

2. Update decimal number
Decimal not zero, return to Step 1

− .5
0.25

1. Put 1 highest place
Next place is 1, works (0.25=0.25) 0.25

1	0	1 . 1	1	*(current value: 5.75)*
4	2	1 0.5	0.25	

2. Update decimal number
Decimal number is zero, done

− 0.25
0

Figure B.3 Converting the decimal number 5.75 to binary using the subtraction method. ◀

The alternative method in Chapter 1 for converting a decimal number to a binary number, namely, the divide-by-2 method, can be adapted to work with decimal numbers. We first separate the whole part of the number from the fractional part, and perform the divide-by-2 method on the whole part by itself. Second, we take the fractional part of the number and *multiply* it by 2. After multiplying the fractional part by two, we append the digit in the one's place of the product after the binary point in the converted number. We continue multiplying the fractional part of the product and appending one's place digits until the fractional part of the product is 0.

For example, let's convert the decimal number 9.8125 to binary using the divide-by-2 method variant. First, we convert 9 to binary, which we know is 1001. Next, we take the fractional part of the number, 0.8125, and multiply by 2: 0.8125*2 = 1.625. The one's digit is a 1, therefore we write a 1 after the binary point of the converted number: 1001.1. Since the fractional part of the product is not 0, we continue multiplying the fractional part of the product by 2: 0.625*2 = 1.25. We append a 1 to the end of our converted number, giving us 1001.11, and we continue multiplying by 2: 0.25*2 = 0.5. Now we append a 0 to the end of our converted number, yielding 1001.110. We multiply by 2 once more: 0.5*2 = 1.0. After appending the 1 to our converted number, we are left with 1001.1101. Since the fractional part of the last product is 0, we are finished converting the number and can declare $9.8125_{10} = 1001.1101_2$.

A decimal real number can often require a very long sequence of bits after the binary point to represent the number in binary. In digital design, we are typically constrained to a finite number of bits available to store a number. As a result, the binary number may need to be truncated and the binary number becomes an approximation.

▶ B.3 FIXED POINT ARITHMETIC

If we fix the binary point of a real number in a certain position in the number (e.g., after the 4th bit), we can add or subtract binary real numbers by treating the numbers as integers and adding or subtracting normally. In the resulting sum or difference, we maintain the binary point's position. For example, assume we are working with 8-bit numbers with half of the bits used to represent the fractional part of the number. If we wanted to add 1001.0010 (9.125) and 0011.1111 (3.9375), we can simply add the two numbers as

```
  1 1 1   1 1
  1 0 0 1 . 0 0 1 0
+ 0 0 1 1 . 1 1 1 1
-------------------
  1 1 0 1 . 0 0 0 1
```

Figure B.4 Adding two fixed point numbers.

if they were integers. The sum, shown in Figure B.4, can be converted back to a real number by maintaining the binary point's position within the sum. Converting the sum to decimal verifies that the calculation was correct: $1*2^3 + 1*2^2 + 0*2^1 + 1*2^0 + 0*2^{-1} + 0*2^{-2} + 0*2^{-3} + 1*2^{-4} = 8 + 4 + 1 + 0.0625 = 13.0625$.

Multiplying binary real numbers is also straightforward and does not require that the binary point be fixed. We first multiply the two numbers as if they were integers. Second, we place a binary point in the product such that the precision of the product is the sum of the precisions of the multiplicand and multiplier (the two numbers being multiplied), just like what is done when we multiply two decimal numbers together. Figure B.5 shows how we might multiply the binary numbers 01.10 (1.5) and 11.01 (3.25) using the partial product method described in Section 4.7. After we calculate the product of the two numbers, we place a binary point in the appropriate loca-

```
        0 1 . 1 0
      × 1 1 . 0 1
      -----------
        0 1 1 0
        0 0 0 0
      0 1 1 0
  +   0 1 1 0
  ---------------
    0 1 0 0 . 1 1 1 0
```

Figure B.5 Multiplying two fixed point numbers.

tion. Both the multiplier and multiplicand feature two bits of precision, therefore the product must have four bits of precision, and we insert a binary point to reflect this. Converting the product to decimal verifies that the calculation was correct: $0*2^3 + 1*2^2 + 0*2^1 + 0*2^0 + 1*2^{-1} + 1*2^{-2} + 1*2^{-3} + 0*2^{-4} = 4 + 0.5 + 0.25 + 0.125 = 4.875$.

The previous example was convenient in that we never had to add four 1s together in a column when we summed up the partial products. To make the calculations simpler and to allow for the partial product summation to be implemented using full-adders, which can only add three 1s at a time, we add the partial products incrementally instead of all at once. For example, let's multiply 1110.1 (14.5) by (0111.1) 7.5. As seen in Figure B.6, we begin by generating partial products as we did earlier. However, we add partial products immediately into partial product sums,

`1 1 1 0 . 1`	*multiplicand*
`× 0 1 1 1 . 1`	*multiplier*
`1 1 1 0 1`	*partial product 1 (pp1)*
`+ 1 1 1 0 1`	*pp2*
`1 0 1 0 1 1 1`	*pps1 = pp1 + pp2*
`+ 1 1 1 0 1`	*pp3*
`1 1 0 0 1 0 1 1`	*pps2 = pps1 + pp3*
`+ 1 1 1 0 1`	*pp4*
`1 1 0 1 1 0 0 1 1`	*pps3 = pps2 + pp4*
`+ 0 0 0 0 0`	*pp5*
`0 1 1 0 1 1 0 0 . 1 1`	*product = pps3 + pp5*

Figure B.6 Multiplying two fixed point numbers using intermediate partial products.

labeled *pps* in the figure. Eventually, we find that the product is 01101100.11, which corresponds to the correct answer, 108.75. You may want to try adding the five partial products together at once instead of using the intermediate partial product sums to see why this method is useful.

Before proceeding to binary real number division, we will introduce binary integer division, which was not discussed in previous chapters.

We can use the familiar process of long division to divide two binary integers. For example, consider the binary division of 101100 (44) by 10 (2). The full calculation is shown in Figure B.7. Notice how the procedure is exactly the same as decimal long division except that the numbers are now in binary.

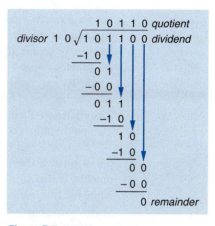

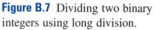

Figure B.7 Dividing two binary integers using long division.

Dividing binary real numbers, like multiplication, also does not require that the binary point be fixed. However, to simplify the calculation, we shift both the dividend and divisor's binary points right until the divisor no longer has a fractional part. For example, consider the division of 1.01_2 (1.25) by 0.1_2 (0.5). The divisor, 0.1_2, has one digit in its fractional part, therefore we shift the dividend and divisor's binary points right by one digit, changing our problem to 10.1_2 divided by 1_2. We now treat the numbers as integers (ignoring the binary point) and can divide them using the long division approach. Trivially, $101_2/1_2$ is 101_2. We then restore the binary point to where it was in the dividend, giving us the answer 10.1_2 or 2.5.

Why does shifting the binary point not change the answer? In general, shifting the radix point right by one digit is the same as multiplying the number by its base. For binary numbers, shifting the binary point right is equivalent to multiplying the number by 2. Dividing two numbers will give you the ratio of the two numbers to each other. Multiplying the two numbers by the same number (by means of shifting the binary point) will not affect that ratio, since doing so is equivalent to multiplying the ratio by 1.

Fixed point numbers are simple to work with, but are limited in the range of numbers that they can represent. For a fixed number of bits, increasing the precision of a number comes at the expense of the range of whole numbers that we can use, and vice versa. Fixed point numbers are suitable for a variety of applications, such as a digital thermometer, but more demanding applications need greater flexibility and range in their real number representations.

▶ B.4 FLOATING POINT REPRESENTATION

When working with decimal numbers, we often represent very large or very small numbers by using scientific notation. Rather than writing a googol as a 1 with a hundred 0s after it, we could write $1.0*10^{100}$. Instead of 299,792,458 m/s, we could write the speed of light as $3.0*10^8$ m/s, as $2.998*10^8$, or even $299.8*10^6$.

If such notation could be translated into binary, we would be able to store a much greater range of numbers than if the binary point were fixed. What features of this notation need to be captured in a binary representation?

First is the whole and fractional part of the number being multiplied by a power of 10, which is called the *mantissa* (or *significand*), as shown in Figure B.8. We do not need to store the whole part of the number if we make sure the number is in a certain form. We call a number written in scientific notation *normalized* if the whole part of the number is greater than 0 but less than the base. In the previous speed of light examples, $3.0*10^8$ and $2.998*10^8$ are normalized since 3 and 2, respectively, are greater than zero but less than 10. The number $299.8*10^6$, on the other hand, is not normalized. If a binary real number is normalized, then the whole part of the mantissa can only be a 1. To save bits, we can assume that the whole part of the significand is 1 and store only the fractional part.

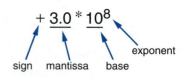

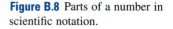

Figure B.8 Parts of a number in scientific notation.

Second is the base (sometimes referred to as the *radix*) and the exponent by which the mantissa is multiplied, shown in Figure B.8. Calling 10 the base is no accident—the number is the same as the base of the entire number. In binary, the base is naturally 2. Knowing this, we do not need to store the 2. We can simply assume that 2 is the base and store the exponent.

Third, we must capture the sign of the number.

The IEEE 754-1985 Standard

The Institute of Electrical and Electronic Engineers (IEEE) 754-1985 standard specifies a way in which the three values described above can be represented in a 32-bit or a 64-bit binary number, referred to as single and double precision, respectively. Though there are other ways to represent real numbers, the IEEE standard is by far the most widely used. We refer to these numbers as *floating point* numbers.

The IEEE standard assigns a certain range of bits for each of the three values. For 32-bit numbers, the first—most significant—bit specifies the sign, followed by 8 bits for the exponent, and the remaining 23 bits are used for the mantissa. This arrangement is pictured in Figure B.9.

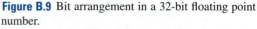

Figure B.9 Bit arrangement in a 32-bit floating point number.

The sign bit is set to 0 if the number is positive, and the bit is set to 1 if the number is negative. The mantissa bits are set to the fractional part of the mantissa in the original number. For example, if the mantissa is `1.1011`, we would store `1011` followed by 19 zeroes in bits 22 to 0. As part of the standard, we add 127 to the exponent we store in the exponent bits. Therefore, if a floating point number's exponent is 3, we would store 130 in the exponent bits. If the exponent was –30, we would store 97 in the exponent bits. The adjusted number is called a *biased* exponent. Exponent bits containing all 0s or all 1s have special meanings and cannot be used. Under these conditions, the range of biased exponents we can write in the exponent bits is 1 to 254, meaning the range of unbiased exponents is –126 to 127. Why don't we simply store the exponent as a signed, two's complement number (discussed in Section 4.8)? Because it turns out that biasing the exponents results in simpler circuitry for comparing the magnitude (absolute value) of two floating point numbers.

The IEEE standard defines certain special values if the contents of the exponent bits are uniform. When the exponent bits are all 0s, two possibilities occur:

1. If the mantissa bits are all 0s, then the entire number evaluates to zero.

2. If the mantissa bits are nonzero, then the number is not normalized. That is, the whole part of the mantissa is a binary zero and not a one (e.g. 0.1011).

When the exponent bits are all 1s, two possibilites occur:

1. If the mantissa bits are all 0s, then the entire number evaluates to + or − infinity, depending on the sign bit.

2. If the mantissa bits are nonzero, then the entire "number" is classified as not a number (NaN).

There are also specific classes of NaNs, beyond the scope of this appendix, that are used in computations involving NaNs.

With this information, we can convert decimal real numbers to floating point numbers. Assuming the decimal number to be converted is not a special value in floating point notation, Table B.2 describes how to perform the conversion.

TABLE B.2 Method for converting real decimal numbers to floating point

	Step	Description
1	*Convert the number from base 10 to base 2.*	Use the method described in Section B.2.
2	*Convert the number to normalized scientific notation.*	Initially multiply the number by 2^0. Adjust the binary point and exponent so that the whole part of the number is 1_2.
3	*Fill in the bit fields.*	Set the sign, *biased* exponent, and mantissa bits appropriately.

▶ **EXAMPLE B.2** Converting decimal real numbers to floating point

Convert the following numbers from decimal to IEEE 754 32-bit floating point: 9.5, infinity, and $-52406.25 * 10^{-2}$.

Let's follow the procedure in Table B.2 to convert 9.5 to floating point. In step 1, we convert 9.5 to binary. Using the subtraction method, we find that 9.5 is 1001.1 in binary. To convert the number to scientific notation per step 2, we multiply the number by 2^0, giving $1001.1 * 2^0$ (for readability purposes, we write the 2^0 part in base 10). To normalize the number, we must shift the binary point left by three digits. In order to not change the value of the number after moving the binary point, we change the 2's exponent to 3. After step 2, our number becomes $1.0011 * 2^3$.

In step 3, we put everything together into the properly formatted sequence of bits. The sign bit is set to 0, indicating a positive number. The exponent bits are set to $3 + 127 = 130$ (we must bias the exponent) in binary, and the mantissa bits are set to 0011_2, which is the fractional part of the mantissa. Remember that the 1 to the left of the binary point is implied since the number is normalized. The properly encoded number is shown in Figure B.10.

Now let's convert infinity to a floating point number. Since infinity is a special value, we cannot employ the method we used to convert 9.5 to floating point. Rather, we fill in the three bit fields with special values indicating that the number is infinity. From the discussion of special values above, we know that the exponent bits should be all 1s and the mantissa bits should be all 0s. The sign bit should be 0 since infinity is positive. Therefore, the equivalent floating point number is 0 11111111 00000000000000000000000.

Converting $-52406.25 * 10^{-2}$ to floating point is straightforward using the method in Table B.2. For step 1, we convert the number to binary. Recall that we represent the

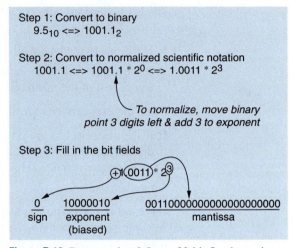

Figure B.10 Representing 9.5 as a 32-bit floating point number, most significant bit first.

sign of the number using a single bit and not using two's complement representation, so we only need to convert $52406.25 * 10^{-2}$ to binary and set the sign bit to indicate that the number is negative. The number $52406.25 * 10^{-2}$ evaluates to 524.0625. Using the subtraction or divide-by-2 method we know that 524 is 1000001100 in binary. The fractional part, 0.0625, is conveniently 2^{-4}. Thus 524.0625 is 1000001100.0001 in binary. In step 2, we write the number in scientific notation: $1000001100.0001 * 2^0$. We must also normalize the number by shifting the binary point left by 9 digits and compensating for this shift in the exponent: $1.0000011000001 * 2^9$. Finally, we combine the sign (1 since the original number is negative), biased exponent ($9 + 127 = 136$), and fractional part of the mantissa into a floating point number: 1 10001000 00000110000010000000000. ◀

▶ **EXAMPLE B.3** Converting floating point numbers to decimal

Convert the number 11001011101010100000000000000000 from IEEE 754 32-bit floating point to decimal.

To perform this conversion, we first split the number into its sign, exponent, and mantissa parts: 1 10010111 01010100000000000000000. We can immediately see from the sign bit that the number is negative.

Next, we convert the 8-bit exponent and 23-bit mantissa from binary to decimal. We find that 10010111 is 151. We unbias the exponent by subtracting 127 from 151, giving an unbiased exponent of 24. Recall that the mantissa in the pattern of bits represents the fractional part of the mantissa and is stored without the leading 1 from the whole part of the mantissa (assuming the original number was normalized). Restoring the 1 and adding a binary point gives us the number 1.01010100000000000000000, which is the same number as 1.010101. By applying weights to each digit, we see that $1.010101 = 1*2^0 + 0*2^{-1} + 1*2^{-2} + 0*2^{-3} + 1*2^{-4} + 0*2^{-5} + 1*2^{-6} = 1.328125$.

With the original sign, exponent, and mantissa extracted, we can combine them into a single number: $-1.327125 * 2^{24}$. We can multiply the number out to $-22,265,462.784$, which is equivalent to $-2.2265462784 * 10^7$. ◀

The format for double precision (64-bit) floating point numbers is similar, with three fields having a defined number of bits. The first, most significant bit represents the sign of the number. The next 11

Figure B.11 Bit arrangement in a 64-bit floating point number.

bits hold the biased exponent and the remaining 52 bits hold the fractional part of the mantissa. Additionally, we add 1023 to the exponent instead of 127 to form the biased exponent. This arrangement is pictured in Figure B.11.

Floating Point Arithmetic

Floating point arithmetic is beyond the scope of this text, but we will provide a brief overview of the concept.

Floating point addition and subtraction must be performed by first *aligning* the two floating point numbers so that their exponents are equal. For example, consider adding the two decimal numbers $2.52*10^2 + 1.44*10^4$. Since the exponents differ, we can change $2.52*10^2$ to $0.0252*10^4$. Adding $0.0252*10^4$ and $1.44*10^4$ gives us the answer $1.4652*10^4$. Similarly, we could have changed $1.44*10^4$ to $144*10^2$. Adding $144*10^2$ and $2.52*10^2$ gives us the sum $146.52*10^2$, which is the same number as our first set of calculations. An analogous situation occurs when we work with floating point numbers. Typically, hardware that performs floating point arithmetic, often referred to as a ***floating point unit***, will adjust the mantissa of the number with the smaller exponent before adding or subtracting the mantissas (with their implied 1s restored) together and preserving the common exponent. Notice that before the addition or subtraction is performed, the exponents of the two numbers are compared. This comparison is facilitated through the use of the sign bit and the biased exponent as opposed to representing the exponent in two's complement form.

Multiplication and division in floating point require no such alignments. Like in decimal multiplication and division of numbers in scientific notation, we multiply or divide the mantissas and add or subtract the two exponents, depending on the operation. When multiplying, we add exponents. For example, let's multiply $6.44*10^7$ by $5.0*10^{-3}$. Instead of trying to multiply 64,400,000 by 0.005, we multiply the two mantissas together and add the exponents. $6.44*5.0$ is 32.2 and $7+(-3)$ is 4. Thus the answer is $32.2*10^4$. When dividing, we subtract the exponent of the divisor from the dividend's exponent. For example, let's divide $31.5*10^{-4}$ (dividend) by $2.0*10^{-12}$ (divisor). Dividing 31.5 by 2.0 gives us 15.75. Subtracting the divisor's exponent from the dividend's gives us $-4-(-12)=8$. Thus the answer is $15.75*10^8$. Floating point division defines results for several boundary cases such as dividing by 0, which evaluates to positive or negative infinity, depending on the sign of the dividend. Dividing a nonzero number by infinity is defined as 0, otherwise dividing by infinity is NaN.

▶ B.5 EXERCISES

SECTION B.2: REAL NUMBER REPRESENTATION

1. Convert the following numbers from decimal to binary:
    (a) 1.5
    (b) 3.125
    (c) 8.25
    (d) 7.75

2. Convert the following numbers from decimal to binary:
    (a) 9.375
    (b) 2.4375
    (c) 5.65625
    (d) 15.5703125

SECTION B.3: FIXED POINT ARITHMETIC

3. Add the following two unsigned binary numbers using binary addition and convert the result to decimal:
    (a) `10111.001 + 1010.110`
    (b) `01101.100 + 10100.101`
    (c) `10110.1 + 110.011`
    (d) `1101.111 + 10011.0111`

SECTION B.4: FLOATING POINT REPRESENTATION

4. Convert the following decimal numbers to 32-bit floating point:
    (a) $-50,208$
    (b) $42.427523 * 10^3$
    (c) $-24,551,152 * 10^{-4}$
    (d) 0

5. Convert the following 32-bit floating point numbers to decimal:
    (a) `01001100010110110101100001011000`
    (b) `01001100010110110101001000000000`
    (c) `01111111111000110000000000000000`
    (d) `01001101000110101000101000000000`

APPENDIX C

Extended RTL Design Example

▶ C.1 INTRODUCTION

In Chapter 5, we performed RTL design of a soda dispenser processor. We started with a high-level state machine, created the datapath's structure, and then described the controller using a finite-state machine. We did not further design the controller to structure, as such design was the subject of Chapter 3, and we did not wish to clutter Chapter 5's RTL design discussion with too many details of previously learned material. In this appendix, we'll complete the RTL design by designing the controller's FSM down to a state register and gates, resulting in a complete custom-processor implementation of a controller and a datapath. We'll then trace through the behavior of the complete implementation. The purpose of demonstrating this complete design is to give the reader a clear understanding of how the controller and datapath work together.

The block symbol for the soda dispenser processor appears in Figure C.1. Recall that the soda dispenser features three inputs, c, s, and a. The 8-bit input s represents the cost of each bottle of soda. The 1-bit input c is 1 for one clock cycle when a coin is inserted. Additionally, the value on 8-bit input a indicates the value of the coin that was inserted. The soda dispenser features one output, d, used to indicate when soda should be dispensed. The 1-bit output d is 1 for one clock cycle after the value of the coins inserted into the soda dispenser is greater than or equal to s. The soda dispenser does not give change.

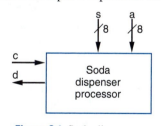

Figure C.1 Soda dispenser block symbol.

In Chapter 5, we developed the high-level state machine seen in Figure C.2. We subsequently decomposed the high-level state machine into a controller (represented behaviorally as an FSM) and datapath, shown in Figure C.3. The datapath supports the data operations necessitated by the high-level state machine, including resetting the value of *tot* (*tot* = 0 in the *Init* state), comparing if *tot* is less than s (for the transitions from the *Wait* state), and adding *tot* and a (in the *Add* state). The controller FSM is similar to the high-level state machine, but is modified to control the datapath and accept status input from the datapath (i.e. tot_lt_s) rather than performing data operations directly. The controller and datapath are shown in Figure C.3.

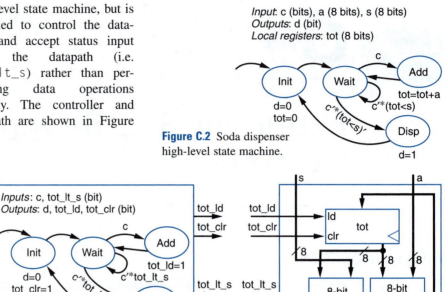

Input: c (bits), a (8 bits), s (8 bits)
Outputs: d (bit)
Local registers: tot (8 bits)

Figure C.2 Soda dispenser high-level state machine.

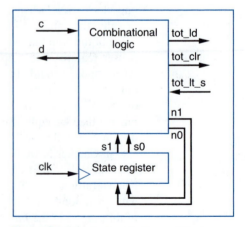

Figure C.3 Soda dispenser: (a) controller (described behaviorally) and (b) datapath (structure).

▶ C.2 DESIGNING THE SODA DISPENSER CONTROLLER

Using the five-step controller design process introduced in Chapter 3, we can complete the design of the controller. The five steps are as follows:

Capture the FSM. The FSM for the soda dispenser's controller was created during step 4 of the RTL design method. The controller's FSM is shown in Figure C.3(a).

Capture the Architecture. As indicated by the controller's FSM, the state machine's architecture requires at least 2 inputs (c and tot_lt_s) and 3 outputs (d, tot_ld, and tot_clr). Additionally, we will use two bits to represent the controller's states, which adds an additional two inputs (the current state s1s0) and two outputs (the next state n1n0) to the controller architecture. The corresponding controller architecture is shown in Figure C.4.

Figure C.4 Standard controller architecture for the soda dispenser.

Encode the States. A straightforward encoding of the soda dispenser's four states is: *Init*: 00, *Wait*: 01, *Add*: 10, and *Disp*: 11.

Create the State Table. From the controller architecture we designed in an earlier step, we know that the state table must account for 4 inputs (c, tot_lt_s, s1, and s0) and 5 outputs (d, tot_ld, tot_clr, n1, and n0). With 4 inputs, the state table will include $2^4 = 16$ rows (Figure C.5).

	Inputs				Outputs				
	s1	s0	c	tot_lt_s	d	tot_ld	tot_clr	n1	n0
Init	0	0	0	0	0	0	1	0	1
	0	0	0	1	0	0	1	0	1
	0	0	1	0	0	0	1	0	1
	0	0	1	1	0	0	1	0	1
Wait	0	1	0	0	0	0	0	1	1
	0	1	0	1	0	0	0	0	1
	0	1	1	0	0	0	0	1	0
	0	1	1	1	0	0	0	1	0
Add	1	0	0	0	0	1	0	0	1
	1	0	0	1	0	1	0	0	1
	1	0	1	0	0	1	0	0	1
	1	0	1	1	0	1	0	0	1
Disp	1	1	0	0	1	0	0	0	0
	1	1	0	1	1	0	0	0	0
	1	1	1	0	1	0	0	0	0
	1	1	1	1	1	0	0	0	0

Figure C.5 The soda dispenser controller's state table.

By examining the outputs specified in the controller FSM, duplicated for convenience in Figure C.6, we fill in the corresponding d, tot_ld, and tot_clr columns in the state table. For example, in Figure C.6, we see that when the controller FSM is in the *Init* state, d=0, tot_clr=1, and tot_ld is implicitly 0. Thus, for rows in the state table that correspond to the *Init* state — namely, the four rows where s1s0=00 since we chose "00" as the encoding for the *Init* state — we set the d column to 0, the tot_clr column to 1, and the tot_ld column to 0.

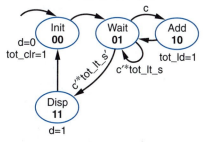

Inputs: c, tot_lt_s (bit)
Outputs: d, tot_ld, tot_clr (bit)

Figure C.6 Soda dispenser controller FSM with state encodings.

We fill in the next state columns, n1 and n0, based on the the transitions specified in the controller FSM and the state encoding we chose in an earlier step. For example, consider the *Wait* state. As indicated in Figure C.6, the FSM transitions to the *Add* state when c=1. Thus, for rows where s1s0c=011 (s1s0=01 corresponds to the *Wait* state), we set the n1 column to 1 and the n0 column to 0 (n1n0=10 corresponds to the *Add* state). When c=0, the FSM transitions to the *Disp* state if tot_lt_s=0 or remains in the *Wait* state of tot_lt_s=1. We represent the transition from *Wait* to *Disp* in the state table by setting n1 to 1 and n0 to 1 (*Disp*) in the row where s1s0=01 (*Wait*), c=0, and tot_lt_s=0. Similarly, we represent the transition from *Wait* back to *Wait* by writing n1n0=01 where s1s0=01, c=0, and tot_lt_s=1. We then examine the remaining transitions in a similar way, filling in the appropriate values for n1 and n0 until all transitions are accounted for. The completed state table is shown in Figure C.5.

Implement the Combinational Logic. For each of the state table's outputs, we write the corresponding Boolean equation. From the state table we obtain the following equations:

```
d = s1s0
tot_ld = s1s0'
tot_clr = s1's0'
n1 = s1's0c'tot_lt_s' + s1's0c

n0 = s1's0' + s1's0c' + s1s0'
n0 = s0' + s1's0c'
```

Note that the first four equations derived from the state table are already minimized. The fifth equation, corresponding to n0, can be minimized to s0' + s1's0c' through algebraic methods, or by using a K-map as shown in Figure C.7. K-maps are discussed in Section 6.2.

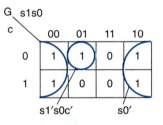

Figure C.7 K-map for the initial equation for n0.

Using techniques discussed in Chapter 2, we convert the above Boolean equations into an equivalent two-level gate-based circuit. This conversion is straightforward since the Boolean equations we are converting are already in sum-of-products form. The final sequential controller circuit and the datapath for the soda dispenser is shown in Figure C.8.

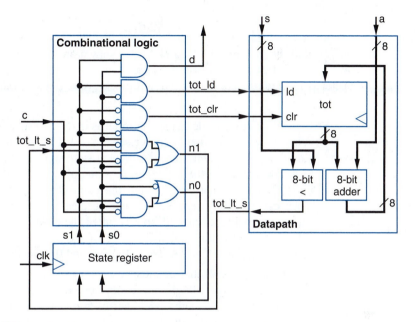

Figure C.8 Final implementation of the soda machine controller Figure C.3(a) with datapath.

▶ C.3 UNDERSTANDING THE BEHAVIOR OF THE SODA DISPENSER CONTROLLER AND DATAPATH

In this section, we will look closely at how the controller and datapath we designed for the soda dispenser interact to form a working implementation of our initial high-level state machine.

Figure C.9 illustrates the behavior of the soda dispenser controller and datapath, including initialization and how the soda dispenser behaves when the user inserts a quarter into the system. The 5 clock cycles shown are labeled 1 through 5 in the figure. We'll assume that the cost of a soda can is 60 cents and that the soda dispenser's controller is in the *Init* state during the first clock cycle. Let's examine what occurs in each clock cycle:

- Initially, in clock cycle 1, the controller is in the *Init* state, shown in Figure C.9(b). When in state *Init*, the controller sets d to 0, tot_ld to 0, and tot_clr to 1. Additionally, the controller sets the next state signals n1n0 to 01, corresponding to the *Wait* state. In the datapath, the value of *tot* and *tot+a* is unknown, denoted by "*??*". Notice that even though the controller set tot_clr to 1 during this clock cycle, the *tot* register will not be cleared immediately (asynchronously). Rather, *tot* will be cleared shortly after the next clock cycle, a synchronous behavior. Finally, notice that the price of the soda, s, is set to 60 cents and the coin input signals, c and a, are initially 0 and 0, respectively.

- Figure C.9(c) shows the soda dispenser in clock cycle 2. The controller is now in the *Wait* state. Accordingly, the controller sets d, tot_ld, and tot_clr to 0. The value of *tot* is cleared, and shortly afterwards, two signals, tot_lt_s and *tot+a*, take a known value. The datapath's comparator sets tot_lt_s to 1 since the total, 0, is less than the price of soda, 60. The datapath's adder sets intermediate signal *tot+a* to 0 since *tot* and a are now known. The next state signals remain set to 01 (*Wait*) since c is 0 and tot_lt_s is 1.

- Figure C.9(d) shows the soda dispenser in clock cycle 3. During the third clock cycle, the user inserts a quarter into the soda dispenser, as indicated by c becoming 1 and a becoming 25. Shortly after a changes, the adder's output *tot+a* changes to 25, the sum of *tot* and a. Since c is 1, the controller sets the next state to 10 (*Add*). The values of d, tot_ld, and tot_clr remain the same since the controller's state has not changed since the previous (2nd) clock cycle.

- In clock cycle 4, shown in Figure C.9(e), the controller is in the *Add* state and sets tot_ld to 1 while keeping d and tot_clr at 0. As was the case with tot_clr during the *Init* state, *tot* will not be updated until the next clock cycle. The controller will unconditionally return to state *Wait*, setting n1n0 to 01 (*Wait*).

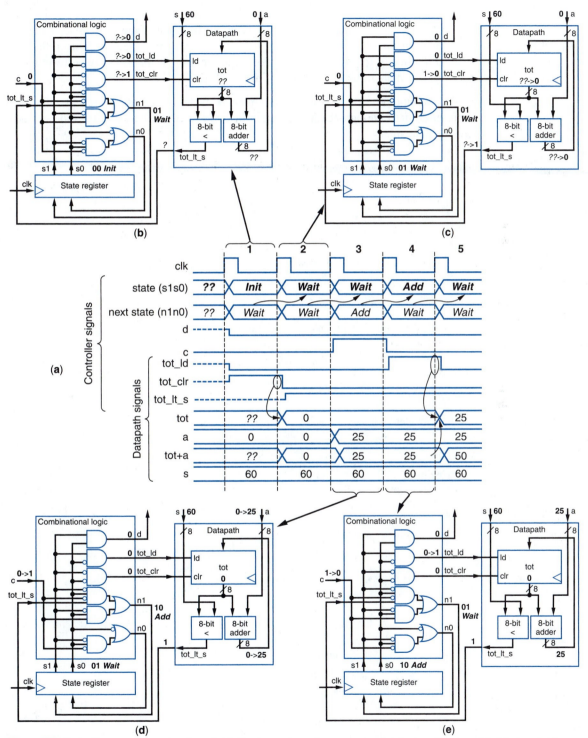

Figure C.9 Soda dispenser operation from initialization to inserting a quarter: (a) timing diagram, (b)–(e) signal values during clock cycles 1–4.

- In clock cycle 5, shown in Figure C.10, the controller sets d, tot_ld, and tot_clr to 0 since the controller is in the *Wait* state. The *tot* register loads the value of *tot+a*, storing 25. Shortly afterwards, *tot+a* changes to 50 to reflect the new value of *tot*, however, 50 is not loaded into *tot* as *tot* will only perform a load synchronous to the rising edge of the clock signal.

The addition procedure demonstrated in clock cycles 3 through 5 is repeated for each coin inserted until enough change has been inserted to cover the cost of a soda, as indicated by input signal s.

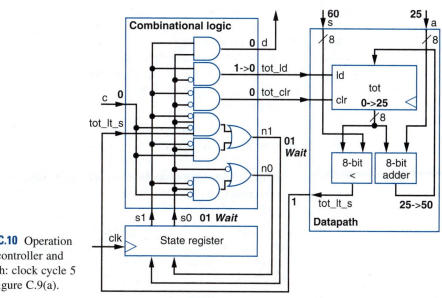

Figure C.10 Operation of the controller and datapath: clock cycle 5 from Figure C.9(a).

Figure C.11 details the behavior of the soda dispenser when the user has inserted enough change into the machine to merit a soda being dispensed. In the timing diagram shown in Figure C.11(a), we duplicate clock cycle 5 from Figure C.9(a) as a point of reference. During the next few dozen clock cycles, we assume that the user has inserted a nickel followed by a quarter. As a result, the register *tot* will contain the value 55 ($25 + 5 + 25$ cents). Let's examine the behavior of the soda dispenser when the user inserts a dime into the machine:

- In Figure C.11(b), corresponding to clock cycle 100, the soda dispenser's controller is in the *Wait* state. Assuming the user inserts a dime into the soda dispenser, the c input will become high for one clock cycle and the a input will change to 10, the value of a dime. Shortly after a changes, the intermediate signal *tot+a* changes to 65 (55+10). With c asserted, the next state signals n1n0 become 10 (*Add*).

- In clock cycle 101, shown in Figure C.11(c), the controller is in the *Add* state and asserts tot_ld. The register *tot* will not load a new total until the rising edge of the next clock cycle. The controller unconditionally sets the next state to 01 (*Wait*).

- Figure C.11(d) shows the status of the soda dispenser in clock cycle 102, where the controller is in the *Wait* state. As indicated by the arrows in Figure C.11(a), tot_ld being asserted on the rising edge of the clock causes *tot* to load the value on its input, which is 65. Shortly after *tot* loads a new value, the comparator's output tot_lt_s changes from 1 to 0 to reflect the fact that *tot* (65) is not less than s (60). Since the controller is in the *Wait* state, and since both c and tot_lt_s are 0, the controller sets the next state signals to 11 (*Disp*). Notice that prior to the next state signals settling on the *Disp* state, the next state was *Wait* for a brief period of time. Depending on the time required for signals to propagate through the datapath and controller, certain signals may initially contain unexpected values, but these signals will eventually settle to their expected values. We can avoid any problems associated with this period of uncertainty by selecting a clock period that is long enough to allow our circuit's intermediate signals to settle into a stable state and stay stable long enough to comply with any setup times required by our circuit's sequential components.

- In Figure C.11(e), the controller is in the *Disp* state. The controller asserts d, indicating to some outside component that a soda should be dispensed. The controller will unconditionally transition to the *Init* state, where the initialization procedure shown in Figure C.9 is repeated (partially shown in clock cycle 104 of Figure C.11(a)).

We see that the controller and datapath work together to implement the behavior of the original high-level state machine.

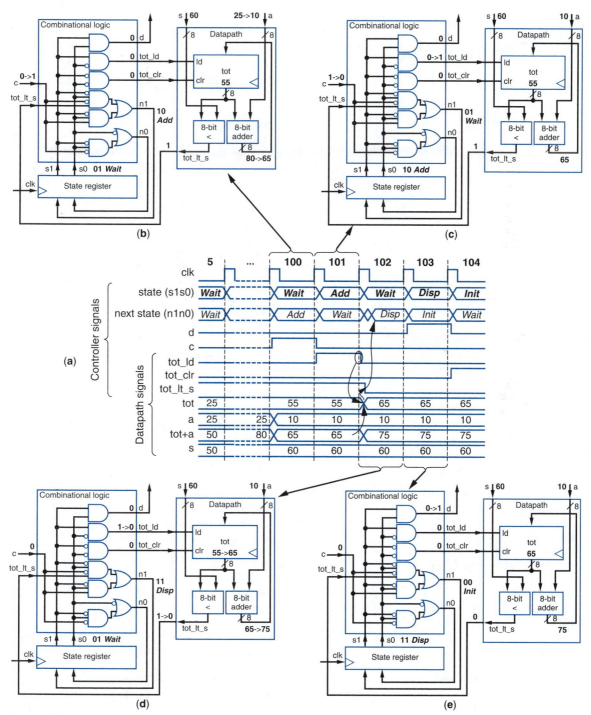

Figure C.11 Soda dispenser operation when sufficient change has been inserted: (a) timing diagram, (b)–(e) signal values during clock cycles 100–103.

Index

=, 241
$display statement, 457
68HC11 microprocessor, 21
74F subseries ICs, 403
74HC subseries ICs, 403
74LS subseries ICs, 403
4000 series ICs, 403
7400 series ICs, 402–404
8051 microprocessor, 21, 422

A

Abext component (AL-extender), 203
Above-mirror display (example):
  with 16 32-bit registers, 204–207
  with 16x32 register file, 208
  with parallel-load registers, 155–156
  with shift registers, 159, 160
  with up-counters, 183
Absorption Law, 501
Abstraction (in RTL design), 276
Access time (RAM), 263
Active-high input, 136
Active-low input, 137
Actuator, 9
Adaptive cruise control, 237
Adder(s), 165–173, 197
  building a subtractor using, 197–200
  carry-lookahead, 334–342
  carry-ripple, 166–173, 339–340, 468–471
  carry-select, 342–343
  creating faster, 333–343
  design examples using, 171–173
  4-bit carry-ripple, 169–171
  full-, 168–169
  half-, 167–168
  N-bit, 165–166
  two-level logic, 334
Adder tree, 215
add instruction, 429–431, 434
Additive identity element, 497
Additive sound, 211
Address (for register), 205
AL-extender, see Arithmetic/logic extender
Algebra(s):

of logic, 504
of sets, 504
switching, 496, 497
Algebraic methods, in two-level logic size optimization, 296–298
Algorithms:
  Espresso tool in, 315
  exact, 308
  selection of, 356–357
  for state reduction, 319
Algorithmic state machines (ASMs), 233
Alternative minimum-bidwidth binary encoding, 323–324
ALUs, see Arithmetic-logic units
always procedure, 453–454
Amperes, 31
Analog circuits, 5
Analog phenomena, encoding of, 9
Analog signals, 4
Analog-to-digital converter, 9
AND gates, 43–44, 404–407
AND operator, 38–40
Application-Specific Integrated Circuits (ASICs), 380–388
  cell arrays, 383
  FPGAs vs., 401
  gate arrays, 381–382
  implementing, using NOR gates, 386–388
  implementing, using only NAND gates, 384–386
  standard cells, 382–383
  structured, 383, 408
Architecture, 447
Arithmetic:
  fixed point, 508–509
  floating point, 513
Arithmetic/logic extender (AL-extender), 202–203
Arithmetic/logic instructions, 439
Arithmetic-logic units (ALUs), 201–203
  multi-function calculator using, 203
  operation, 423–424
ARM microprocessor, 21, 422
Arrays. See also Field programmable gate arrays (FPGAs)
  cell, 383
  gate, 381–382, 389
  programmable logic, 407